55. *The A to Z of the War of 1812* by Robert Malcomson, 2009.
56. *The A to Z of Feminist Philosophy* by Catherine Villanueva Gardner, 2009.
57. *The A to Z of the Early American Republic* by Richard Buel Jr., 2009.
58. *The A to Z of the Russo–Japanese War* by Rotem Kowner, 2009.
59. *The A to Z of Anglicanism* by Colin Buchanan, 2009.
60. *The A to Z of Scandinavian Literature and Theater* by Jan Sjåvik, 2009.
61. *The A to Z of the Peoples of the Southeast Asian Massif* by Jean Michaud, 2009.
62. *The A to Z of Judaism* by Norman Solomon, 2009.
63. *The A to Z of the Berbers (Imazighen)* by Hsain Ilahiane, 2009.
64. *The A to Z of British Radio* by Seán Street, 2009.
65. *The A to Z of The Salvation Army* by Major John G. Merritt, 2009.
66. *The A to Z of the Arab–Israeli Conflict* by P R Kumaraswamy, 2009.
67. *The A to Z of the Jacksonian Era and Manifest Destiny* by Terry Corps, 2009.
68. *The A to Z of Socialism* by Peter Lamb and James C. Docherty, 2009.
69. *The A to Z of Marxism* by David Walker and Daniel Gray, 2009.
70. *The A to Z of the Bahá'í Faith* by Hugh C. Adamson, 2009.
71. *The A to Z of Postmodernist Literature and Theater* by Fran Mason, 2009.
72. *The A to Z of Australian Radio and Television* by Albert Moran and Chris Keating, 2009.
73. *The A to Z of the Lesbian Liberation Movement: Still the Rage* by JoAnne Myers, 2009.
74. *The A to Z of the United States–Mexican War* by Edward H. Moseley and Paul C. Clark Jr., 2009.
75. *The A to Z of World War I* by Ian V. Hogg, 2009.
76. *The A to Z of World War II: The War Against Japan* by Anne Sharp Wells, 2009.
77. *The A to Z of Witchcraft* by Michael D. Bailey, 2009.
78. *The A to Z of British Intelligence* by Nigel West, 2009.
79. *The A to Z of United States Intelligence* by Michael A. Turner, 2009.

The A to Z of Horror Cinema

Peter Hutchings

The A to Z Guide Series, No. 100

The Scarecrow Press, Inc.
Lanham • Toronto • Plymouth, UK
2009

Published by Scarecrow Press, Inc.
A wholly owned subsidiary of
The Rowman & Littlefield Publishing Group, Inc.
4501 Forbes Boulevard, Suite 200, Lanham, Maryland 20706
http://www.scarecrowpress.com

Estover Road, Plymouth PL6 7PY, United Kingdom

British Library Cataloguing in Publication Information Available

Library of Congress Cataloging-in-Publication Data

The hardback version of this book was cataloged by the Library of Congress as follows:

Hutchings, Peter.
    Historical dictionary of horror cinema / Peter Hutchings.
        p. cm. — (Historical dictionaries of literature and the arts ; no. 25)
    Includes bibliographical references.
    1. Horror films—Dictionaries. I. Title
    PN195.9.H6H836 2008
    791.43'616403—dc22   2007043634

ISBN 978-0-8108-6887-8 (pbk. : alk. paper)
ISBN 978-0-8108-7050-5 (ebook)

Printed in the United States of America

Contents

Editor's Foreword

If you rate films by their aesthetic or intellectual content, horror films will certainly not appear at the top of the list. But if you rate films by their popular appeal or their returns at the box office, they will quickly rise to the top—at least some of them. Ever since the cinema has existed, so have horror films. Today there is sure to be at least one showing at a neighborhood theater, as well as a couple on late-night television. So this latest volume in the cinema subseries caters to an extremely large clientele, including many whose passion for this genre is unbounded and who want nothing more than to be frightened out of their wits—by Dracula and Frankenstein, mummies and werewolves, and more sophisticated fare such as *The Omen* and *The Exorcist*. Their tastes have been satisfied and refined by some of the finest (and a few of the worst) actors, directors, and producers in the business.

The A to Z of Horror Cinema takes a close look at the genre, starting with an impressive chronology that ranges from its origins through the present day. This is followed by a broad introduction, while the dictionary details individual actors, directors, producers, authors of horror novels adapted as films, major themes and categories, and notable films. Since local tastes are involved, there are entries on American, British, and Chinese horror, among others. And for fans who want to know more, there is an extensive bibliography.

This volume was written by Peter Hutchings, who is both a specialist on and a fan of horror films. He teaches at Northumbria University and his courses include one on the horror film and others on cinema and television. Over the years, Dr. Hutchings has published a growing series of articles, papers, and books on horror films, on specific subjects such as Hammer Films, Terence Fisher, *Dracula* in the British Film Guide series, and *The Horror Film* in the Inside Cinema series. As an academic he has watched thousands of horror films, and as a fan he has enjoyed the experience even if his judgements on some are less than flattering. This book can both inform and entertain.

Jon Woronoff
Series Editor

Reader's Note

The international character of horror film production and distribution often results in films acquiring more than one title as they move from one market to another. Reissues can also lead to films being retitled yet again. Consequently, some horror films can have five or six titles. In the interests of clarity, this dictionary presents the original film title first and then itemizes significant variants. Where the film in question is not made in English, the original title is followed by the English language titles under which it has been circulated, with the best known of these listed first. In many cases, the English language title will offer a loose translation of the original title. Any significant disparities in translation are discussed in the entries relating to the films in question.

Chronology

1764   Great Britain: Horace Walpole's *The Castle of Otranto* has come to be seen by many literary historians as the first major Gothic novel.

1818   Great Britain: Mary Shelley's *Frankenstein* is published.

1849   United States: Edgar Allan Poe dies. Several of his gothic stories are later adapted for the screen, among them "The Fall of the House of Usher," "Murders in the Rue Morgue," and "The Pit and the Pendulum."

1872   Great Britain: J. Sheridan LeFanu's vampire story *Carmilla* is published. It will provide inspiration for several lesbian vampire films of the 1960s and 1970s.

1886   Great Britain: Robert Louis Stevenson's *The Strange Case of Dr. Jekyll and Mr. Hyde* is published.

1888   Great Britain: The "Jack the Ripper" killings take place in London.

1891   Great Britain: Oscar Wilde's *The Picture of Dorian Gray* is published.

1896   Great Britain: H. G. Wells publishes his prototype "mad scientist" story *The Island of Dr. Moreau*.

1897   Great Britain: Bram Stoker's *Dracula* is published.

1901   Great Britain: Arthur Conan Doyle publishes *The Hound of the Baskervilles*, the most horror-like of all Sherlock Holmes stories.

1910   United States: The earliest known screen adaptation of Mary Shelley's *Frankenstein* is produced.

1915   Germany: An early version of *The Golem* is released.

1919   Germany: Expressionist cinema begins with the release of Robert Wiene's *Das Cabinet des Dr. Caligari* (*The Cabinet of Dr. Caligari*).

1920   Germany: More expressionist cinema comes in the form of Paul Wegener's *Der Golem, wie er in die Welt kam* (*The Golem*) and F. W. Murnau's *Der Januskopf*, an adaptation of *Dr. Jekyll and Mr. Hyde* that features Bela Lugosi in a small role. **United States:** John Barrymore stars in yet another version of *Dr. Jekyll and Mr. Hyde*.

1922   Germany: F. W. Murnau's *Nosferatu: eine Symphonie des Grauens* (*Nosferatu, a Symphony of Terror*) is an unauthorized adaptation of *Dracula*. **Denmark:** The pseudo-documentary *Häxen: Witchcraft through the Ages* is released.

1923   United States: Lon Chaney delivers one of his most celebrated performances as Quasimodo in *The Hunchback of Notre Dame*.

1924   Germany: Robert Wiene's *Orlacs Hände* (*The Hands of Orlac*) and Paul Leni's *Das Wachsfigurenkabinett* (*Waxworks*) continue the Expressionist tradition.

1925   United States: Lon Chaney delivers his most horror-like performance in *The Phantom of the Opera*.

1926   Germany: F. W. Murnau's *Faust* contains some impressive gothic imagery, while Paul Wegener's *Der Student von Prag* (*The Student of Prague*) develops the supernatural doppelganger theme.

1927   Great Britain: Alfred Hitchcock directs the proto-serial killer thriller *The Lodger*. **United States:** The German director Paul Leni combines expressionistic imagery with comedy in *The Cat and the Canary*, an adaptation of a popular Broadway play. Lon Chaney plays a vampire in Tod Browning's *London after Midnight*, now believed to be a lost film.

1928   France: Jean Epstein's experimental adaptation of Edgar Allan Poe's work, *La chute de la maison Usher* (*The Fall of the House of Usher*) is released. **United States:** Paul Leni's gothic-themed melodrama *The Man Who Laughs* is considered by some critics to be his best film.

1929   France: Luis Bunuel and Salvador Dali's surrealist *Un chien andalou* contains some striking horror-like imagery—not least an eye being sliced open—although it has little immediate impact on popular genre cinema.

1931   Germany: Fritz Lang's *M* stars Peter Lorre as a serial child killer. **United States:** The successful release of Universal's *Dracula*, directed by Tod Browning and starring Bela Lugosi, and *Frankenstein*, directed by James Whale and featuring Boris Karloff, kick-starts a boom in horror production. Universal also produces a Spanish-language version of *Dracula*, considered by some critics to be superior to the English language version. Paramount releases Rouben Mamoulian's *Dr. Jekyll and Mr. Hyde*; its star, Fredric March, receives an Academy Award for his performance.

1932   Germany: Danish director Carl Theodor Dreyer's *Vampyr* offers a different, more dream-like take on the vampire story. **United States:** The horror boom begins in earnest. Universal releases Karl Freund's *The Mummy* and James Whale's *The Old Dark House*, both of which star Boris Karloff, and Robert Florey's *Murders in the Rue Morgue*, which stars Bela Lugosi. Michael Curtiz directs *Doctor X* at Warner Brothers, Tod Browning makes the controversial *Freaks* at MGM, Fay Wray features in Ernest B. Schoedsack and Irving Pichel's *The Most Dangerous Game* (*The Hounds of Zaroff*), and Lugosi stars in Victor Halperin's independently produced *White Zombie*.

1933   Great Britain: The Boris Karloff vehicle *The Ghoul* is released. **Mexico:** *La Llorona* (*The Crying Woman*) combines U.S. horror conventions with local superstition. **United States:** James Whale develops his distinctive brand of comedy-horror with *The Invisible Man*. Erle C. Kenton directs *Island of Lost Souls*, a striking adaptation of H. G. Wells' novel *The Island of Dr. Moreau*, while Michael Curtiz directs *Mystery of the Wax Museum*. The classic monster movie *King Kong* is also released, along with *Murders in the Zoo*, *Secret of the Blue Room*, *Supernatural*, and *The Vampire Bat*.

1934   Mexico: *Dos Moinjes* (*Two Monks*) and *El Fantasma del Convento* (*The Phantom of the Convent*) continue a small Mexican cycle of horror films. **United States:** Edgar G. Ulmer's *The Black Cat* turns out to be one of the most stylish of all 1930s Universal horrors. In comparison, the independently produced *Maniac* is a low-budget curiosity.

1935   Great Britain: *The Mystery of the Mary Celeste*, which stars Bela Lugosi, comes from an early version of the Hammer company, a later incarnation of which would become a leading horror specialist in the 1950s. **United States:** This is a key year for the American horror film with the release of James Whale's *Bride of Frankenstein*, Karl Freund's *Mad Love*, and Tod Browning's *Mark of the Vampire*. Other horrors include *The Black Room*, *The Crime of Dr. Crespi*, *The Raven*, and *Werewolf of London*.

1936   France: Julien Duvivier's *Le Golem* (*The Golem*) is a rare French horror production. **Great Britain:** Tod Slaughter stars in two horror-themed melodramas, *The Crimes of Stephen Hawke* and *Sweeney Todd—The Demon Barber of Fleet Street*, while Boris Karloff stars in *The Man Who Changed His Mind*. **United States:** *Dracula's Daughter* is an impressive follow-up to the 1931 *Dracula*. Other horrors include the mad scientist drama *The Invisible Ray*, Tod Browning's *The Devil-Doll*, Victor Halperin's *Revolt of the Zombies*, and Michael Curtiz's final horror film, *The Walking Dead*.

1939   Great Britain: Tod Slaughter returns in *The Face at the Window*, and Bela Lugosi stars in *Dark Eyes of London*. **United States:** Bob Hope stars in a version of *The Cat and the Canary* that increases the comedy element. *The Hound of the Baskervilles* inaugurates a series of occasionally horror-themed Sherlock Holmes stories that feature Basil Rathbone as the great detective. Charles Laughton generates pathos as Quasimodo in *The Hunchback of Notre Dame*, while Boris Karloff is a mad scientist in *The Man They Could Not Hang*. Universal's *Son of Frankenstein* and *Tower of London* represent the company's return to the horror genre after a three year break.

1940   United States: *The Mummy's Hand* starts a cycle of Mummy films. A busy Boris Karloff stars in *The Ape*, *Before I Hang*, and *Black Friday*, and Bela Lugosi stars in *The Devil Bat*. Bob Hope returns to comedy-horror in *Ghost Breakers*, and Karloff, Lugosi and Lorre send themselves up in *You'll Find Out*.

1941   United States: Lon Chaney Jr. becomes a horror star through his role in *The Wolf Man* and also features in *Man Made Monster*. Meanwhile, comedy duo Bud Abbott and Lou Costello make their comedy-horror debut with the haunted house spoof *Hold That Ghost*.

1942   France: *Le loup des Malveneur* (*The Wolf of the Malveneurs*) is an unusual—for French cinema at least—horror-like production. **United States:** Universal's *The Ghost of Frankenstein* and *The Mummy's Tomb* demonstrate the studio's commitment to the production of sequels. By contrast, producer Val Lewton, who is based at RKO, offers a more middlebrow version of horror in *Cat People*. Other horror-themed entertainments include the comedies *The Boogie Man Will Get You* and *I Married a Witch*, as well as the innovative werewolf film *The Undying Monster*.

1943   Denmark: Carl Theodor Dreyer's *Vredens dag* (*Day of Wrath*) is a somber tale of witchcraft. **France:** *La main du diable* (*The Devil's Hand*) is a stylish version of the Faustian pact. **United States:** Universal continues sequel production with *Son of Dracula* and *Frankenstein Meets the Wolf Man*, the first of its multiple monster films. More tasteful is the studio's production of *The Phantom of the Opera*. More ludicrous is *Captive Wild Woman*, in which a mad scientist turns an ape into a woman. Val Lewton develops his artful strain of horror with *The Ghost Ship*, *I Walked with a Zombie*, *The Leopard Man*, and *The Seventh Victim*.

1944   United States: More sequels appear from Universal, namely *House of Frankenstein*, *The Mummy's Ghost* and *The Mummy's Curse*. Val Lewton makes a more upmarket sequel in the form of *The Curse of the Cat People*. Bela Lugosi plays a Dracula-like vampire in *The Return of the Vampire*, while the Sherlock Holmes films *The Pearl of Death*, *The Scarlet Claw*, and *Sherlock Holmes and the Spider Woman* all contain horror-related material. Other horrors include *The Climax* and the ghost story *The Uninvited*.

1945   Great Britain: Ealing Studios produces one of the great horror anthologies, *Dead of Night*. **United States:** Universal's *House of Dracula* is the last of its non-comedy multiple monster films. At RKO, Val Lewton produces the period drama *The Body Snatcher* and the stylish but morbid *Isle of the Dead*. Albert Lewin directs a similarly upmarket adaptation of Oscar Wilde's *The Picture of Dorian Gray*. Robert

Siodmak directs the stylish serial killer drama *The Spiral Staircase*. More prosaically, *Sherlock Holmes and the House of Fear* is another horror-themed adventure for the great detective.

1946   Great Britain: The indefatigable Tod Slaughter performs in another overheated horror melodrama, *The Curse of the Wraydons*, while Vernon Sewell directs *Latin Quarter*, a stylish tale of artistic insanity. **United States:** Insanity is the theme in Robert Florey's *The Beast with Five Fingers* and Val Lewton's final horror film, *Bedlam*. *She-Wolf of London* turns out to be a whodunnit rather than a werewolf film.

1948   Great Britain: Tod Slaughter is back in *The Greed of William Hart*, an everyday tale of body snatching. **United States:** *Abbott and Costello Meet Frankenstein* is the first and best of a series of comedies in which the duo encounter classic monsters, in this case, Frankenstein's monster, Dracula and the Wolf Man (although, oddly, not Frankenstein).

1951   Great Britain: The "X" certificate—denoting films for adults only—is introduced. **United States:** Howard Hawks' production of *The Thing From Another World* successfully combines science fiction conventions with horror material. Many other films of its type are subsequently made during the 1950s, although few are as distinguished.

1952   Great Britain: Bela Lugosi shows how far his career has fallen from grace by appearing in the low-budget comedy-horror *Old Mother Riley Meets the Vampire*. **United States:** Boris Karloff and Lon Chaney return to horror in the unimpressive *The Black Castle*.

1953   United States: Vincent Price stars in *House of Wax*, a color remake of Michael Curtiz's 1933 *Mystery of the Wax Museum*. More alien monsters feature in *Invaders from Mars* and *It Came From Outer Space*.

1954   France: Henri-Georges Clouzot's psychological thriller *Les diaboliques* is released. It will be an inspiration for many later horror filmmakers. **United States:** Jack Arnold's *Creature From The Black Lagoon* and Gordon Douglas's *Them!* are horror-like monster movies.

1955   Great Britain: The science fiction/horror film *The Quatermass Xperiment* (*The Creeping Unknown*) is the first major success for a small company by the name of Hammer.

1956 Great Britain: Hammer follows up its success with *The Quatermass Xperiment* by releasing another SF/horror, *X The Unknown.* **Italy:** Riccardo Freda's *I vampiri* (*The Devil's Commandment*) is the first Italian horror film. It is not commercially successful. **United States:** Horror-themed science fiction production continues with *Invasion of the Body Snatchers* and *It Conquered the World*, while *The Bad Seed* is an early example of the "monstrous child" film. *The Undead* is Roger Corman's first gothic-themed film. Bela Lugosi dies on 16 August.

1957 Great Britain: *The Curse of Frankenstein* is Hammer's first color gothic horror and is directed by Terence Fisher, who will be responsible for many of the later Hammer horrors. The film stars Peter Cushing as Frankenstein and Christopher Lee as the creature and is a substantial commercial success. Hammer also releases the alien invasion fantasy *Quatermass 2* (*Enemy from Space*). *Cat Girl* and *Night of the Demon* (*Curse of the Demon*) are impressive contemporary-set supernatural thrillers. **Mexico:** *La momia Azteca* (*Attack of the Aztec Mummy*), *El Vampiro* (*The Vampire*), and *El Ataud del Vampiro* (*The Vampire's Coffin*), among others, signal the beginning of a new Mexican horror cycle. **United States:** SF/horror films include *The Monster that Challenged the World* and two films from Roger Corman, *Attack of the Crab Monsters* and *Not of This Earth.* A new emphasis on teenage horror is apparent in *Blood of Dracula, I Was a Teenage Frankenstein,* and *I Was a Teenage Werewolf.* American serial killer Ed Gein is arrested in Wisconsin; he will subsequently become an inspiration for such horrors as *Psycho* (1960), *The Texas Chainsaw Massacre* (1974), and *The Silence of the Lambs* (1991), to name but a few.

1958 Argentina: The television horror show *Obras maestras de terror* (*Masterworks of Horror*) is a popular success and runs until 1960. **Great Britain:** Hammer consolidates its position as a horror market leader with *Dracula* (*Horror of Dracula*), which stars Christopher Lee as the vampire; it also releases *The Revenge of Frankenstein.* Other British horrors include *Blood of the Vampire, Corridors of Blood, Grip of the Strangler,* and *The Trollenberg Terror.* **United States:** Teenage horrors include the self-reflexive *How to Make a Monster* along with *Monster on the Campus, The Return of Dracula,* and *Teenage Monster.* Vincent Price stars in *The Fly,* and producer-director William Castle makes his horror debut with *Macabre.* The SF/horror *It! The Terror* *from Beyond Space* is later cited as an influence on *Alien* (1979). Boris Karloff plays Frankenstein for the first time in *Frankenstein—1970* and also hosts the television horror series *The Veil*.

1959   France: Jean Renoir's made-for-television *Le testament du Docteur Cordelier* (*The Testament of Dr. Cordelier*) is an impressive version of the *Dr. Jekyll and Mr. Hyde* story, while Georges Franju's *Les yeux sans visage* (*Eyes without a Face*) is an artful but also gruesome surgical horror. **Germany:** *Die Nackte und der Satan* (*A Head for the Devil*, *The Head*) is a rare German horror production from this period. **Great Britain:** Hammer releases period horrors *The Hound of the Baskervilles*, *The Man Who Could Cheat Death*, and *The Mummy*. Other filmmakers enter the market with *The Flesh and the Fiends*, *Horrors of the Black Museum*, and *Jack the Ripper*. **Philippines:** Gerardo de León's *Terror Is a Man* is an early example of Filipino horror. **United States:** Roger Corman directs *A Bucket of Blood*, one of the best of all comedy-horrors, while William Castle also keeps his tongue in his cheek with the gimmicky *House on Haunted Hill* and *The Tingler*. Ed Wood's cult film *Plan 9 from Outer Space*, which features the last performance from Bela Lugosi, is also released. The sometimes horror-themed television series *The Twilight Zone* begins; it runs until 1964.

1960   France: Roger Vadim's *Et mourir de plaisir* (*Blood and Roses*) is an artful version of Sheridan LeFanu's *Carmilla*. **Germany:** *Der Rächer* (*The Avenger*) is an early entry in a series of Edgar Wallace adaptations that often incorporate horror-like material and imagery. **Great Britain:** Hammer's *The Brides of Dracula* and *The Two Faces of Dr. Jekyll* continue its production of gothic horrors. The non-Hammer contemporary-set *Circus of Horrors* and *Peeping Tom* are gaudier affairs, while the SF/horror *Village of the Damned* develops the theme of monstrous children. *City of the Dead* (*Horror Hotel*) is writer-producer Milton Subotsky's first horror credit; he will subsequently become a significant figure in British horror. **Italy:** Mario Bava's stylish witchcraft film *La maschera del demonio* (*The Mask of Satan*, *Revenge of the Vampire*, *Black Sunday*) begins a cycle of Italian horror and makes a star out of British actor Barbara Steele. *Il mulino delle donne di pietra* (*Mill of the Stone Women*) is an impressive Italian/French co-production. **United States:** A prolific Roger Corman directs *The Wasp Woman* and the comedy-horror *The Little Shop of Horrors*. More significant is his direction of the Edgar Allan Poe adaptation *House of Usher*, which stars Vincent Price and which leads to a cycle of further Poe films. Alfred Hitchcock's *Psycho* is an influential serial killer drama. By contrast, William Castle's *13 Ghosts* offers more gimmicks and a silly story.

1961 Germany: *Die Toten Augen von London* (*The Dead Eyes of London*) is one of the best of the horror-themed Edgar Wallace films. **Great Britain:** Hammer releases what will be its only werewolf film, *The Curse of the Werewolf*, and also begins a cycle of *Psycho*-like thrillers with *Taste of Fear* (*Scream of Fear*). In contrast, Jack Clayton directs *The Innocents*, a classy adaptation of Henry James's ghost story *The Turn of the Screw*. **Italy:** Mario Bava's *Ercole al centro della terra* (*Hercules in the Haunted World*) is one of several musclemen movies that incorporate horror imagery. **Mexico:** *Santo contra los zombies* (*Santo vs. the Zombies*) is the first of many films in which masked wrestlers take on horror monsters, including vampires, werewolves and Frankenstein's monster. **United States:** Roger Corman's second Poe film is *Pit and the Pendulum*, which stars Vincent Price and Barbara Steele. William Castle maintains the jokier tradition in American horror with *Homicidal* and *Mr. Sardonicus*.

1962 Germany: The horror-themed Edgar Wallace cycle continues with *Das Rätsel der roten Orchidee* (*The Secret of the Red Orchid*) and *Die Tür mit den 7 Schlössern* (*The Door with Seven Locks*). **Great Britain:** The commercial failure of Hammer's *The Phantom of the Opera* temporarily slows down the company's gothic horror cycle. From elsewhere, *Night of the Eagle* (*Burn, Witch, Burn!*) is a superior witchcraft film. **Italy:** Riccardo Freda's morbid *L'orribile segreto del Dr. Hichcock* (*The Horrible Dr. Hichcock, The Terrible Secret of Dr. Hichcock*) is one of Barbara Steele's best films. Meanwhile, Mario Bava directs what is often considered to be the first giallo-style psychological horror, *La ragazza che sapeva troppo* (*The Girl Who Knew Too Much, The Evil Eye*). **Spain:** Jesus Franco introduces horror into Spain with the gory surgery-based drama *Gritos en la noche* (*The Awful Dr. Orloff*), although full-scale Spanish horror production does not commence until later in the 1960s. **United States:** Roger Corman adds *The Premature Burial* and *Tales of Terror* to the Poe cycle, while the idiosyncratic *Carnival of Souls* is a ghost story with a final plot twist that will later be re-used by numerous other ghost stories. Bette Davis and Joan Crawford, both in full-on grotesque mode, star in Robert Aldrich's *grand guignol* thriller *What Ever Happened to Baby Jane?*

1963 Great Britain: Hammer delivers Don Sharp's stylish period horror *The Kiss of the Vampire* and continues its psychological thriller cycle with *Maniac* and *Paranoiac*. Robert Wise's ghost story *The Haunting*, shot in Britain for MGM, is also released. **Ireland:** Francis Ford Coppola makes his genre debut with *Dementia 13* (*The Haunted and the Hunted*), shot in Ireland for Roger Corman. **Italy:** It is a good year for Italian horror with Mario Bava's *La frusta et il corpo* (*The Whip and the Body*) and *I tre volti della paura* (*Black Sabbath*), Riccardo Freda's *Lo spettro* (*The Ghost*), and Antonio Margheriti's *La vergine di Norimberga* (*The Virgin of Nuremberg, Horror Castle*) all released. **United States:** Alfred Hitchcock's *The Birds* is an ambitious revenge-of-nature horror. Exploitation specialist Herschell Gordon Lewis introduces an unprecedented level of gore into *Blood Feast*. Roger Corman directs *The Haunted Palace,* which is marketed as a Poe adaptation although it is actually based on a H. P. Lovecraft story, and the charming comedy-horror *The Raven*. More laughs are provided by Jerry Lewis's *The Nutty Professor*, a comedy version of the Jekyll and Hyde story.

1964 Brazil: Director and actor José Mojica Marins begins his controversial career in horror with the confrontational *À meia-noite levarei sua alma* (*At Midnight I Will Take Your Soul*). **Great Britain:** Hammer's gothic output includes the routine *The Curse of the Mummy's Tomb* and *The Evil of Frankenstein*, as well as Terence Fisher's innovative *The Gorgon* and the psychological thriller *Nightmare. Dr. Terror's House of Horrors* is the first of a series of horror anthologies produced by the Amicus company, Hammer's main rival in the British horror market for the next ten years. American director Roger Corman makes two of the best films of his Poe cycle in Britain—*The Masque of the Red Death* and *The Tomb of Ligeia*. **Italy:** Horror specialist Antonio Margheriti directs two of Barbara Steele's finest films, *Danza macabra* (*Castle of Blood*) and *I lunghi capelli della morte* (*The Long Hair of Death*), while Mario Bava is responsible for the seminal giallo thriller *Sei donne per l'assassino* (*Blood and Black Lace*). **Japan:** The upmarket ghost stories *Kaidan* (*Kwaidan*) and *Onibaba* make an international impact. **United States:** Herschell Gordon Lewis offers more extreme gore in

Two Thousand Maniacs, and Robert Aldrich and William Castle more *grand guignol* in, respectively, *Hush... Hush, Sweet Charlotte* and *Strait-Jacket.* Ray Steckler's strikingly titled cult horror *The Incredibly Strange Creatures Who Stopped Living and Became Mixed-Up Zombies* is also released.

1965   Great Britain: Hammer releases two of its best horror-themed psychological thrillers in *Fanatic (Die! Die! My Darling!)* and *The Nanny.* Christopher Lee stars as Fu Manchu in *The Face of Fu Manchu,* the first of a series. Amicus's *The Skull* is a superior contemporary-set horror, while Roman Polanski's *Repulsion,* the director's first English-language film, is a clinical and disturbing study of insanity. On a more escapist note, Sherlock Holmes meets Jack the Ripper for the first time in *A Study in Terror.* **Italy:** Mario Bava's SF/horror *Terrore nello spazio (Planet of the Vampires)* will be yet another influence on Ridley Scott's 1979 film *Alien.*

1966   Great Britain: *Dracula—Prince of Darkness, The Plague of the Zombies,* and *The Reptile* are three of Hammer's best period horrors; other Hammer releases include *Rasputin: The Mad Monk* and *The Witches.* The Amicus psychological thriller *The Psychopath* revisits some of the themes from *Psycho.* **Italy:** Mario Bava's *Operazione paura (Kill, Baby...Kill!)* is an impressive ghost story, while the young British director Michael Reeves makes his debut with *La sorella di satana (Revenge of the Blood Beast, The She Beast).* **Spain:** The television horror series *Historias para no dormir (Stories to Keep You Awake)* is a popular success and runs until 1968. **United States:** Dan Curtis's daytime television soap *Dark Shadows* incorporates horror characters; it runs until 1971. In cinema, *Billy the Kid versus Dracula* provides one of the genre's sillier titles.

1967   Great Britain: It is another impressive year for Hammer period horror with *Frankenstein Created Woman* and the SF/horror *Quatermass and the Pit (Five Million Years to Earth),* although *The Mummy's Shroud* is less successful. Roman Polanski's *Dance of the Vampires (The Fearless Vampire Killers)* is a stylish, and in places disturbing, comedy-horror, while *Carry on Screaming* offers more vulgar horror-themed laughs. Michael Reeves builds on the promise shown in his first film with the London-set *The Sorcerers,* and *Torture Garden* is a superior anthology from Amicus. Other British horrors include the surgery-based *Corruption* and the Lovecraft adaptation *The Shuttered Room*. **United States:** Herschell Gordon Lewis's *The Gruesome Two-some* and Jean Yarbrough's *Hillbillys in a Haunted House* make for an undistinguished year for American horror, although Curtis Harrington's horror-themed psychological thriller *Games* is noteworthy.

1968   France: The cult director Jean Rollin makes his genre debut with *Le viol du vampire* (*The Rape of the Vampire*). **Great Britain:** Terence Fisher's *The Devil Rides Out* and Michael Reeves' third and final film *Witchfinder General* are two of the finest of all British horrors. Less impressive are *Curse of the Crimson Altar* and *Dracula Has Risen from the Grave*. **Philippines:** The mad scientist film *Mad Doctor of Blood Island* demonstrates that older forms of horror still retain popularity. **Spain:** Actor Jacinto Molina, who often works under the name "Paul Naschy," makes his genre debut as werewolf Count Waldemar Daninsky in *La marca del hombre-lobo* (*The Mark of the Werewolf*). He goes on to play the part in several sequels as well as starring in numerous other Spanish horrors. **United States:** This is a key year in the development of modern American horror with the release of George Romero's *Night of the Living Dead*, Roman Polanski's *Rosemary's Baby* and Peter Bogdanovich's *Targets* and the introduction of a film rating system that formally recognizes the possibility of "adult-only" films.

1969   Great Britain: Terence Fisher's *Frankenstein Must Be Destroyed* is an impressive traditional Hammer horror, while Gordon Hessler's *The Oblong Box* and *Scream and Scream Again* confirm the emergence of new youthful talent in British horror. Boris Karloff dies on 2 February. **Italy:** Mario Bava's *Un hacha para la luna de miel* (*Hatchet for the Honeymoon*) innovatively combines a giallo with a ghost story. **Spain:** *La residencia* (*The Finishing School, The House that Screamed*) is a substantial commercial success for Spanish horror.

1970   Germany: Michael Armstrong directs *Hexen bis aufs Blut gequält* (*Mark of the Devil*), a violent and controversial witch hunter drama. **Great Britain:** The youth-friendly *Taste the Blood of Dracula* and the explicit female nudity in *The Vampire Lovers* suggest a change in Hammer's approach, although *The Horror of Frankenstein* and *Scars* *of Dracula* are less successful attempts at innovation. Gordon Hessler's *Cry of the Banshee* is a confident supernatural drama, and Amicus produces another effective horror anthology, *The House That Dripped Blood,* along with a weak Jekyll and Hyde adaptation, *I, Monster.* **Italy:** Dario Argento makes his directorial debut with the giallo *L'uccello dalle piume di cristallo* (*The Bird with the Crystal Plumage, The Gallery Murders*). Initially dubbed the Italian Hitchcock, he will go on to become one of Europe's leading horror directors. **Spain:** Christopher Lee stars as a mustachioed Dracula in Jesus Franco's indifferent *El Conde Dracula* (*Count Dracula*). **United States:** *Count Yorga, Vampire* introduces a Hammer-style vampire into contemporary American settings, and *The Dunwich Horror* is a stylish adaptation of an H. P. Lovecraft story.

1971 Belgium: Harry Kümel's lesbian vampire film *Le rouge aux lèvres* (*Daughters of Darkness*) combines genre conventions with an art-house sensibility. **Great Britain:** New innovations continue to appear in British horror, including Hammer's revisionary *Blood from the Mummy's Tomb, Countess Dracula, Dr. Jekyll and Sister Hyde,* and *Hands of the Ripper* and the more obviously exploitative lesbian vampire films *Lust for a Vampire* and *Twins of Evil.* From other companies come the tongue-in-cheek *The Abominable Dr. Phibes* and *Psychomania,* along with the disturbing rural horror *Blood on Satan's Claw* (*Satan's Skin*) and Ken Russell's controversial witch hunter epic *The Devils.* **Italy:** Some impressive Italian giallo films are released, among them Dario Argento's *Il gatto a nove code* (*The Cat o' Nine Tails*) and *4 mosche di velluto grigio* (*Four Flies on Grey Velvet*), Mario Bava's *Reazione a catena* (*Ecologia del delitto, Twitch of the Death Nerve, Bay of Blood*), and Lucio Fulci's *Una lucertola con la pelle di donna* (*A Lizard in a Woman's Skin*). **Spain:** Amando de Ossorio's *La noche del terror ciego* (*Tombs of the Blind Dead, The Blind Dead*) begins a cycle of four films about undead Knights Templar threatening the modern world. **United States:** Modern vampire stories prove popular, with *Night of Dark Shadows, The Omega Man, The Return of Count Yorga,* and *The Velvet Vampire* all being released. The rural horror *Let's Scare Jessica to Death,* the possession drama *The Mephisto Waltz,* and the rat story *Willard* also make an impression.

1972 Great Britain: The cannibalism film *Death Line (Raw Meat)* imaginatively combines British and American horror themes. Hammer brings Dracula to contemporary London in *Dracula AD 1972* and offers a critique of the family in *Demons of the Mind*, while Amicus comes up with two quality horror anthologies, *Asylum* and *Tales from the Crypt*. **Italy:** Mario Bava, now nearly at the end of his career, directs two impressive horrors, *Gli orrori del castello di Nuremberg (Baron Blood)* and *Lisa e il diavolo (Lisa and the Devil)*, and Lucio Fulci, who is relatively new to the genre, is responsible for the innovative rural giallo *Non si sevizia un paperino (Don't Torture a Duckling)*. **Spain:** Jacinto Molina plays a hunchback in one of his best known films, *El jorobado de la morgue (Hunchback of the Morgue)*, while genre specialist León Klimovsky directs the atmospheric *La orgía nocturna de los vampiros (Vampire's Night Orgy)*. Also released is *La novia ensangrentada (The Blood-Spattered Bride)*, seen by some critics as a powerful critique of machismo values. **United States:** Wes Craven makes his horror debut with the disturbing rape-revenge drama *The Last House on the Left*. More somber horror is provided by *The Other* and *The Possession of Joel Delaney*. *Frogs* is a relatively serious revenge of nature horror while *Night of the Lepus*—about giant rabbits—is a silly one. John Boorman's *Deliverance* is also released; it is not a horror film as such but it provides a template for later rural horrors. Slightly more light-hearted are the blaxploitation production *Blacula* and the zombie film *Children Shouldn't Play with Dead Things*. Meanwhile, the vampire story *The Night Stalker* receives the highest ever ratings for a television film.

1973 Germany: Ulli Lommel's *Die zärtlichkeit der Wölfe (The Tenderness of Wolves)* is a disturbing serial killer film that refers back to Fritz Lang's *M* (1931). **Great Britain:** The period horror cycle is winding down, although *And Now the Screaming Starts!* and *The Creeping Flesh* are creditable late entries. Amicus offers its two final horror anthologies *From Beyond the Grave* and *The Vault of Horror*, Hammer concludes its Dracula cycle with *The Satanic Rites of Dracula,* and British horror sends up its established formats in *Horror Hospital* and *Theater of Blood*. New approaches are also emerging. The ghost story *Don't Look Now*, the pagan-themed thriller *The Wicker Man* and the demonic haunted house drama *The Legend of Hell House* all suggest new ways forward for the British version of the genre. **Italy:** Former Andy Warhol-collaborator Paul Morrissey camps up the Frankenstein story in *Flesh for Frankenstein*. **Spain:** The eerie psychological thriller *La campana del infierno* (*The Bell from Hell*) and the period horror *Pánico en el Transiberiano* (*Horror Express*) are impressive contributions to European horror. **United States:** The main event is the release of the phenomenally successful *The Exorcist*. Other interesting work is done by George Romero (*The Crazies*) and Brian De Palma (*Sisters*). Blaxploitation horror continues with *Blackenstein*, *Ganja & Hess* and *Scream, Blacula, Scream*, and John Landis makes his directorial debut with *Schlock*. Television provides revisionary versions of classic movie monsters in *Dracula* and *Frankenstein: The True Story*. Lon Chaney Jr. dies on 12 July.

1974   Australia: Peter Weir incorporates American horror themes into an Australian landscape in *The Cars That Ate Paris*. **Canada:** Bob Clark directs the proto-slasher film *Black Christmas*. **Great Britain:** Hammer's period horror cycle finally comes to an end with *Captain Kronos —Vampire Hunter*, *Frankenstein and the Monster from Hell* (which is also Terence Fisher's final film) and the kung fu horror *The Legend of the Seven Golden Vampires*. Pete Walker's nihilistic *House of Whipcord* and *Frightmare* and José Larraz's sensual *Vampyres* offer a type of horror more in keeping with the times. **Italy:** Paul Morrissey follows up *Flesh for Frankenstein* (1973) with the equally over-the-top *Blood for Dracula*. *L'anticristo* (*The Antichrist*) and *Chi sei* (*Beyond the Door, The Devil Within Her*) are the first of many attempts to cash in on the success of *The Exorcist* (1973). **Spain:** *Non si deve profanare il sonno dei morti* (*The Living Dead at the Manchester Morgue)* is a striking and gruesome zombie film, shot largely in Britain. **United States:** Larry Cohen's *It's Alive!* and Tobe Hooper's *The Texas Chain Saw Massacre* engage with the family horror theme. *Deranged* is a gory, thinly fictionalized account of Ed Gein, Brian De Palma's *Phantom of the Paradise* is a more playful treatment of horror material, while *Abby* and *Sugar Hill* are blaxploitation projects. Mel Brooks' *Young Frankenstein* is an affectionate, and very funny, tribute to classic horror of the 1930s.

1975   Canada: David Cronenberg makes his horror debut with *The Parasite Murders* (*They Came From Within, Shivers*). **Great Britain:** By this stage the kind of period horror offered by *Legend of the Werewolf* seems anachronistic. Pete Walker's *House of Mortal Sin* (*The Confessional*) is a more convincing expression of the troubled 1970s. *I Don't Want to Be Born* (*The Devil Within Her*) is another *Exorcist*-influenced possession story, while the horror musical *The Rocky Horror Picture Show* is not initially a success but later becomes a significant cult phenomenon. **Italy:** Dario Argento directs *Profondo rosso* (*Deep Red*), which takes his work emphatically into the horror genre. **United States:** Steven Spielberg's *Jaws* draws upon old horror films for inspiration. In comparison, the more conventional horrors *Bug* and *The Devil's Rain* seem tame, although *Race with the Devil* is an effective combination of horror and road movie.

1976   Great Britain: Hammer releases its last horror film (to date at least), *To the Devil a Daughter*. Also released are Norman J. Warren's *Satan's Slave* and Pete Walker's *Schizo*. **Italy:** Pupi Avati's *La casa dalle finestre che ridono* (*The House of the Laughing Windows*) is one of the more unusual giallo films. **United States:** The key horror films are Brian De Palma's adaptation of Stephen King's *Carrie* and the apocalyptic thriller *The Omen*; both are substantial successes. Less spectacular but in their own more modest ways intelligent and worthwhile are *Burnt Offerings*, *Communion* (*Alice Sweet Alice*), *God Told Me To* (*Demon*), and *Squirm*.

1977   Australia: Peter Weir provides a compelling Australian version of apocalyptic horror with *The Last Wave*. **Canada:** *Rabid*, David Cronenberg's second horror film, develops his distinctive vision. **Italy:** Dario Argento's witchcraft drama *Suspiria* is his biggest international commercial success, while Mario Bava directs his last horror film, the ghost story *Schock* (*Shock, Beyond the Door II*). *Holocaust 2000* is a more routine attempt to emulate the success of *The Omen* (1976). **United States:** Wes Craven's *The Hills Have Eyes* proves more audience-friendly than his earlier *Last House on the Left* (1972), while George Romero's *Martin* is one of the most important of all modern-day vampire stories, and Tobe Hooper's *Eaten Alive* (*Death Trap*) is a strange but compelling piece of Southern Gothic. The misconceived *Exorcist II: The Heretic* is a commercial disaster. By contrast, Robert Wise's *Audrey Rose* is a superior possession drama that offers quiet thrills rather than the more customary blood and thunder, and Curtis

Harrington's *Ruby* is also a modest but effective ghost story. *Day of the Animals* and *The Sentinel* are more conventional.

1978   Australia: A mini-cycle of Australian horror continues with the revenge-of-nature drama *The Long Weekend* and the telekinesis thriller *Patrick*. **United States:** George Romero's *Dawn of the Dead* redefines the cinematic zombie and John Carpenter's *Halloween* inaugurates the slasher cycle (as well as making a star out of Jamie Lee Curtis). There is a thoughtful remake of *Invasion of the Body Snatchers* and good sequels to both *It's Alive* (1974) and *The Omen* (1976). Joe Dante makes his horror debut with *Piranha*. The low-budget rape-revenge drama *I Spit On Your Grave* is not much noticed at the time but it will become notorious later as part of the British Video Nasties scare of the early 1980s.

1979   Canada: David Cronenberg creates a horror version of *Kramer versus Kramer* with *The Brood*. **Germany:** Werner Herzog remakes the 1922 *Nosferatu* as *Nosferatu: Phantom der Nacht* (*Nosferatu the Vampyre*). **Great Britain:** Bob Clark turns the Jack the Ripper story into a political conspiracy and throws in Sherlock Holmes for good measure in *Murder by Decree*. **Italy:** Lucio Fulci directs *Zombi 2 (Zombie Flesheaters)*, an unauthorized follow-up to George Romero's *Dawn of the Dead* (1978). Numerous gory zombie films will follow. **United States:** More revisionary vampires feature in *Dracula*, which stars Frank Langella as the Count, *Love at First Bite* and Tobe Hooper's television production of Stephen King's *Salem's Lot*. *The Amityville Horror* is a successful haunted house story, *Alien* combines horror with science fiction, *Phantasm* is a cult oddity, and *When a Stranger Calls* is an early example of urban legend horror.

1980   Great Britain: Hammer, now under new management, produces the television horror series *Hammer House of Horror*. **Italy:** Graphic nastiness of the zombie and cannibal kind features in *Apocalypse domani* (*Cannibal Apocalypse*), *Cannibal Holocaust*, and *Incubo sulla città contaminata* (*Nightmare City*). Lucio Fulci's *Paura nella città dei morti viventi* (*City of the Living Dead*) is just as gory but considerably more stylish. In *Inferno*, Dario Argento offers a sequel of sorts to *Suspiria* (1977). Lamberto Bava, son of Mario, makes his directorial debut with the atmospheric psychological thriller *Macabro* (*Macabre*).

United States: *Friday the 13th* is critically disliked but very popular with teenage audiences; it inaugurates one of the major horror franchises of the 1980s. Other slashers include the Jamie Lee Curtis vehicles *Prom Night* and *Terror Train*. These, along with Brian De Palma's self-consciously Hitchcockian thriller *Dressed to Kill*, inspire a public debate about violence against women in film. John Carpenter's *The Fog* is an atmospheric ghost story, while Stanley Kubrick's monumental *The Shining* confuses many on its initial release but has since come to be considered by many as one of the greatest of all horror films.

1981   Canada: David Cronenberg's *Scanners* turns out to be a more audience-friendly affair than his previous grimmer work in the genre. **Italy:** *L'aldilà* (*The Beyond*) and *Quella villa accanto al cimitero* (*The House by the Cemetery*) are key films from Lucio Fulci, combining gore with an intensely dream-like atmosphere. **United States:** John Landis's *An American Werewolf in London* and Joe Dante's *The Howling* reinvent the cinematic werewolf and together represent a significant step forward in special effects technology. Sam Raimi's *The Evil Dead* joins gory horror with slapstick, while sequels to *Friday the 13th* (1980) and *Halloween* (1978), along with *Hell Night*, keep the slasher cycle going. *The Final Conflict*, the third entry in the *Omen* cycle, is also released, as are interesting films from Tobe Hooper (*The Funhouse*) and Wes Craven (*Deadly Blessing*).

1982   Italy: Dario Argento directs *Tenebre (Tenebrae)*, considered by some to be one of the greatest of all giallo films. **United States:** John Carpenter's impressive *The Thing* is not a commercial success, although it later becomes a cult classic. Tobe Hooper's *Poltergeist* is more popular. Paul Schrader remakes the 1942 version of *Cat People* and George Romero directs Stephen King's comic-influenced *Creepshow*, and there are more sequels to *Friday the 13th* and *Halloween*, along with other slashers, including *The House on Sorority Row* and *The Slumber Party Massacre*. In defiance of market trends, Larry Cohen makes the eccentric *Q—the Winged Serpent*.

1983   Canada: David Cronenberg directs *Videodrome*, one of his more challenging and obscure films. **Great Britain:** Pete Walker, master of grim British horror, directs his last film, the surprisingly gentle and nostalgic *House of the Long Shadows*, which features horror icons

John Carradine, Peter Cushing, Christopher Lee, and Vincent Price. **United States:** Adaptations of Stephen King novels prove particularly popular, with John Carpenter making *Christine*, Lewis Teague directing *Cujo* and David Cronenberg responsible for *The Dead Zone*. Richard Franklin revives the *Psycho* story with *Psycho II*; more sequels will follow.

1984   Great Britain: Neil Jordan's *The Company of Wolves* is an ambitious and innovative werewolf film drawing upon the writings of Angela Carter. **United States:** Wes Craven's *A Nightmare on Elm Street* is the first in what will be the most commercially successful horror cycle of the 1980s; it will generate seven sequels. *Re-animator* combines gore and comedy in a manner akin to that of the *Evil Dead* films, while more family-friendly comedy-horror is offered by *Ghostbusters* and Joe Dante's *Gremlins*.

1985   Italy: Lamberto Bava directs and Dario Argento produces the slick Euro-horror *Demoni* (*Demons*); Argento also directs the innovative giallo *Phenomena*. **United States:** George Romero directs *Day of the Dead*, the third in his Living Dead series, with less serious zombie fare coming from Dan O'Bannon's comedy-horror *The Return of the Living Dead*. More tongue in cheek horror can be found in the vampire film *Fright Night* and Larry Cohen's satirical *The Stuff*.

1986   United States: James Cameron combines action, science fiction and horror in *Aliens*, and David Cronenberg has one of his biggest commercial successes with his remake of the 1950s monster movie *The Fly*. The serial killer also makes an impact in Michael Mann's *Manhunter*, an adaptation of Thomas Harris's novel *Red Dragon* which introduces the character of Hannibal Lecter, and in John Naughton's grim *Henry— Portrait of a Serial Killer*.

1987   Germany: Jörg Buttgereit's *Nekromantik* is a confrontational, necrophilia-themed low-budget horror project. **Great Britain:** Clive Barker makes his directorial debut with *Hellraiser*, a striking horror influenced by sadomasochistic iconography. **Italy:** The talented director Michele Soavi debuts with *Deliria* (*Stagefright, Bloody Bird*), while Dario Argento directs the equally theatrical *Opera* (*Terror at the Opera*). **New Zealand:** The comedy-horror *Bad Taste* is yet another directorial debut, this time from Peter Jackson. **United States:** Idiosyncratic genre fare is provided by Kathryn Bigelow's inventive vampire-western film *Near Dark*, John Carpenter's Lovecraftian *Prince of Darkness* and Joseph Ruben's family horror *The Stepfather*, while a more straightforward action/SF/horror combination is offered by the Arnold Schwarzenegger vehicle *Predator*.

1988 Canada: David Cronenberg continues to develop his own very personal type of cinematic horror with the gynecology themed *Dead Ringers*. **United States:** Two minor horror cycles commence with the release of *Child's Play* and *Maniac Cop*. Wes Craven directs the revisionary voodoo film *The Serpent and the Rainbow*.

1989 Japan: The cyberpunk science fiction/horror *Tetsuo* contains some groundbreaking body horror imagery. **United States:** The satirical cannibalism drama *Parents* and the body-horror epic *Society* provide off-beat genre thrills, while Mary Lambert's *Pet Sematary* is a more straightforward Stephen King adaptation. The anthology television horror show *Tales from the Crypt* begins; it runs until 1996.

1990 Great Britain: *Nightbreed*, Clive Barker's ambitious follow-up to *Hellraiser*, is not a success. **Italy:** Dario Argento and George Romero collaborate on the Poe project *Due occhi diabolici* (*Two Evil Eyes*). **United States:** William Peter Blatty directs *The Exorcist III*, Tom Savini remakes *Night of the Living Dead*, and Roger Corman returns to direction after a long absence with *Frankenstein Unbound*.

1991 United States: *The Silence of the Lambs* is a box-office smash and wins several Academy Awards, including for Jodie Foster, director Jonathan Demme, and for Anthony Hopkins as the cannibalistic psychiatrist Hannibal Lecter. Wes Craven directs the socially critical *The People Under the Stairs*, one of his best films.

1992 New Zealand: Peter Jackson's *Braindead* takes comedy-horror onto a new level of gore. **United States:** *Candyman* explores racial politics from within a horror idiom, *Buffy the Vampire Slayer* relocates vampires within a high school setting, and Francis Ford Coppola directs a blockbusting new version of *Dracula* featuring Gary Oldman as the Count and Anthony Hopkins as Van Helsing. *Alien 3* is the grimmest entry to the *Alien* cycle.

1993 Mexico: Guillermo del Toro makes his directorial debut with *Cronos*, an innovative vampire film. **United States:** Two more Stephen King adaptations appear, *Needful Things* and George Romero's *The Dark Half*. Tim Burton produces the horror-themed animation *The Nightmare Before Christmas*. The horror-influenced television series *The X Files* begins; it runs until 2002 and also generates a cinema film. Vincent Price dies on 25 October.

1994 Great Britain: Peter Cushing dies on 11 August. **Italy:** Michele Soavi directs his best film, the zombie drama *Dellamorte dellamore* (*Cemetery Man*). **United States:** Big-budget horror includes Neil Jordan's adaptation of Anne Rice's *Interview with the Vampire*, a version of *Frankenstein* starring Robert De Niro as the Monster, and the Jack Nicholson werewolf drama *Wolf*. *Ed Wood* is Tim Burton's tribute to the film director and features an Academy Award-winning performance from Martin Landau as Bela Lugosi. Wes Craven returns to the *Nightmare on Elm Street* cycle with the intensely self-reflexive *New Nightmare*. *The Crow*'s offering of morbid gothic is underlined by the accidental death of its star, Brandon Lee, during filming.

1995 Spain: *El día de la bestia* (*Day of the Beast*) is a stylish horror from a national cinema that has produced little horror since the 1970s. **United States:** Dark serial killer films prove popular with the release of *Copycat* and *Seven*. *In the Mouth of Madness* and *Vampire in Brooklyn* are the latest from, respectively, John Carpenter and Wes Craven. *Dracula —Dead and Loving It* is a crude Mel Brooks spoof that seeks to recapture the glory of *Young Frankenstein* (1974), while *Species* combines science fiction and horror in *Alien*-style.

1996 Spain: Alejandro Amenabar's *Tesis*, which deals with snuff movies, is an impressive feature debut. **United States:** Peter Jackson comes to Hollywood to make the comedy-horror *The Frighteners*, Robert Rodriguez combines crime and horror effectively in *From Dusk Till Dawn*, *Mary Reilly* is an upmarket revision of the Jekyll and Hyde story, and John Frankenheimer provides an eccentric version of *The Island of Dr. Moreau* that stars Marlon Brando in the title role. However, the main horror film of note is Wes Craven's *Scream*, which cleverly combines slasher conventions with generic in-jokes. Sequels and other teenage horror films wanting to cash in on its success inevitably follow.

1997   United States: *I Know What You Did Last Summer* is an effective *Scream*-like film, while Wes Craven directs *Scream 2*. Guillermo del Toro makes his American debut with *Mimic*, a giant insect story. *Alien: Resurrection* is the final (to date) film in the *Alien* cycle (although *AVP: Alien versus Predator* shows up in 2004). The horror-themed television series *Buffy the Vampire Slayer* begins; it runs until 2003 and also generates a spin-off series, *Angel*.

1998   Japan: Hideo Nakata's *Ringu* is a breakthrough international success for Japanese horror; it will lead to sequels and remakes and encourage the development of a broader East Asian horror cinema. **United States:** A preoccupation with horror's past becomes apparent. Black horror is triumphantly revived with the urban vampire drama *Blade*, *Halloween H20: 20 Years Later* is a clever sequel that brings Jamie Lee Curtis back to the cycle, and *Gods and Monsters* is a fine biopic dealing with James Whale, director of the 1931 *Frankenstein*. More eccentric is Gus van Sant's remake of *Psycho*. *The Last Broadcast*, a mock documentary about a folk legend, is little noticed at the time, although it does seem to anticipate themes more successfully addressed by the following year's *Blair Witch Project*. Other *Scream*-like horrors include *I Still Know What You Did Last Summer* and *Urban Legend*.

1999   Japan: The development of Japanese horror continues with *Ringu 2* and Takashi Miike's shocking, torture-based *Ôdishon* (*Audition*). **Korea:** The release of *The Ring Virus*, a version of the *Ringu* story, along with the evocative ghost story *Yeogo goedam II* (*Memento Mori*) highlight the development of a distinctive North Korean horror cinema. **United States:** Two supernatural dramas capture the public attention. The mock documentary *The Blair Witch Project* makes highly effective use of internet marketing, while *The Sixth Sense* offers the chills of an old-fashioned ghost story topped by a much-discussed plot twist. Other ghost stories—including remakes of *House on Haunted Hill* (1959) and *The Haunting* (1963)—are less impressive. Arnold Schwarzenegger takes on the Devil in the millennial *End of Days*, Stephen Sommers directs the action-horror *The Mummy*, Antonia Bird is responsible for the cannibalism horror-western *Ravenous*, and Tim Burton's *Sleepy Hollow* is a handsome period horror. Roman Polanski's Spanish-French-American production *The Ninth Gate* offers an altogether more idiosyncratic take on horror themes.

2000   France: *Promenons-nous dans les bois* (*Deep in the Woods*) and the serial killer drama *Les rivières pourpres* (*The Crimson Rivers*) offer a distinctively French take on horror conventions. **Germany:** The surgical horror *Anatomie* does something similar for Germany, cleverly relating its narrative to German history. **United States:** Wes Craven concludes the *Scream* trilogy, *Scary Movie* sends up the *Scream* films, and *Cherry Falls* and *Final Destination* demonstrate that there is still life in the teenage horror formula. Robert Zemeckis's *What Lies Beneath* is an intelligent big budget ghost story, *Lost Souls* a noisy millennial thriller, and *Ed Gein* a disturbing account of the real-life serial killer who inspired several horror films. The international co-production *Shadow of the Vampire* deals with the production of the 1922 *Nosferatu* and speculates that the actor who played the vampire was actually a vampire.

2001   France: *Le pacte des loups* (*The Brotherhood of the Wolf*) successfully combines horror elements with period drama, while *Trouble Every Day* is an artier exploration of the cannibalism theme. **Great Britain:** The Second World War supernatural drama *The Bunker* is an early sign of a revival of the British horror film. **Spain:** The Fantastic Factory company is established to produce English-language horror films in Spain. Early examples of its products are *Dagon* and *Faust*. Guillermo del Toro directs the ghost story *El espinazo del diablo* (*The Devil's Backbone*). *Tuno negro* is a distinctly Spanish version of the *Scream* films. **United States:** Jack the Ripper returns in *From Hell*, Hannibal Lecter returns in *Hannibal*, and *Friday the 13th* killer Jason is sent into outer space in *Jason X*, which, as the title suggests, is the tenth film in the cycle. Alejandro Amenabar's international production *The Others* is a worthy addition to the fast developing ghost story cycle, while *Jeepers Creepers* is an inventive monster movie.

2002   China: The Hong Kong-Singapore production *Gin gwai* (*The Eye*) is another international success for East Asian horror. **Great Britain:** The release of First World War horror *Deathwatch*, werewolf drama *Dog Soldiers*, the psychological thriller *My Little Eye*, the apocalyptic thriller *28 Days Later* and the international co-production *Resident Evil* confirm the renaissance of the British horror film. **Japan:** Hideo Nakata's *Honogurai mizu no soko kara* (*Dark Water*) is another successful example of East Asian horror. **United States:** The influence of East Asian horror is felt, both in the American remake *The Ring* and in the Japan-style internet horror *FeardotCom*. Hannibal Lecter returns for the remake *Red Dragon*, the comedy-horror *Scooby Doo* gets a live-action makeover, and the gruesome low budget *Cabin Fever* suggests that a new toughness has entered American horror. By contrast, *Bubba Ho-tep* is an enjoyably eccentric affair in which Elvis Presley takes on a mummy.

2003   France: Alexandre Aja directs *Haute tension* (*High Tension*, *Switchblade Romance*), a slasher that manages to be stylish, gory and iconoclastic. **Japan:** *Ju-On: The Grudge* is the latest international success to come from Japanese horror. **United States:** *Freddy vs. Jason* is the latest in the *Friday the 13th* and *Halloween* cycles. Rock musician Rob Zombie makes his directorial debut with the 1970s-style horror *House of 1000 Corpses*; more references to the 1970s crop up in the remake of *The Texas Chainsaw Massacre* (1974) and the rural horror *Wrong Turn*.

2004   France: *Calvaire* (*The Ordeal*) is an effective rural horror. **Great Britain:** The revival of British horror continues with the London Underground-based *Creep*. **Korea:** The North Korean production *R-Point* combines an evocative ghost story with an account of Korean involvement in the Vietnam war. **United States:** George Romero's 1978 production of *Dawn of the Dead* is remade, and there is a prequel to *The Exorcist* in *Exorcist: The Beginning* and a remake of the Japanese *Ju-on: The Grudge*. The horror musical *The Phantom of the Opera* and the action blockbuster *Van Helsing* also revive old horror conventions. More original is M. Night Shyamalan's rural horror *The Village*.

2005   Australia: *Wolf Creek* is Australia's disturbing contribution to the new emphasis on torture in horror cinema. **Great Britain:** The subterranean horror *The Descent* and the animated horror *The Curse of the Were-Rabbit*, each in its own way, testify to the new vitality of British horror. **United States:** *The Devil's Rejects* and *Hostel* are America's contribution to the new "nasty" horror. George Romero makes a fourth zombie film, *Land of the Dead*, and Tim Burton returns to animated horror with *Corpse Bride*. Remakes include *Dark Water* (from the Japanese original) and *The Fog* (from John Carpenter's original). *Doom* is a computer-game adaptation while *Dominion: Prequel to the Exorcist* is Paul Schrader's original prequel, temporarily shelved by its producer while another film prequel was produced and released. Japanese director Hideo Nakata makes his first American film, *The Ring Two*. The horror television anthology series *Masters of Horror* showcases the work of many cinema directors.

2006   Great Britain: *Severance* and *Wilderness* lead British horror into rural horror territory. **Spain:** Guillermo del Toro's dark fantasy *El laberinto del fauno* (*Pan's Labyrinth*) is considered by many to be his finest film. **United States:** This year's remakes include *The Hills Have Eyes*, *The Omen* and *Pulse* (the latter from a Japanese original). *Slither* is a throwback to the alien invasion format, while the international production *Silent Hill* is a computer game adaptation and *Stay Alive* is a horror film about a deadly computer game.

2007   Great Britain: *28 Weeks Later* is a successful sequel to *28 Days Later*. **United States:** Remakes of *Halloween* and *The Hitcher* appear. The release of *Captivity*, *Grindhouse*, and *Hostel Part 2* spark a debate about the cinematic use of torture and the extent to which such films offer "torture porn."

Introduction

The horror genre is one of the more provocative and controversial areas of mainstream film production. However, it has also retained a remarkable popularity throughout its history, to the extent that there has been no sustained period since the 1930s when horror films were not being made somewhere in the world. Because of this ubiquity, horror cinema has become a familiar part of our culture. Even if we do not like horror films, we usually have a clear idea of what a horror film actually is and what kind of experience it will offer us. Given this familiarity, it is perhaps predictable that horror has frequently been characterized by its critics—and it has many critics—as a repetitive and formulaic area of mass culture. However, even a superficial overview of its history reveals a range of types of film on offer at any point. In addition, horror's numerous overlaps with other genres, such as science fiction or the thriller, make it yet more difficult to assign definitive limits to the genre or discover some essential core identity to which all horror films can be related.

THE BIRTH OF HORROR

This generic indeterminacy is evident in the origins of horror cinema, which are complex, multi-layered and open to interpretation. The term "horror film" itself did not emerge as a distinctive and recognizable classificatory term until the early 1930s, when it was associated in particular with a series of films from Universal, beginning with *Dracula* (1931) and *Frankenstein* (1931) (although *Dracula* was initially marketed as a macabre thriller rather than as a horror). Before then, one can find an array of narratives that, to modern eyes at least, exhibit horror-like properties but were not presented to their original audiences in those terms. In some instances, it is possible to establish a direct relationship between the pre-horror material and the horror films that followed, although other connections are more indirect or obscure and require some teasing out.

One area of culture often invoked as a source for horror cinema is Gothic literature of the 18th and 19th centuries. It is certainly the case that Gothic novels such as Ann Radcliffe's *The Mysteries of Udolpho* (1794), Matthew Lewis's *The Monk* (1796), and Mary Shelley's *Frankenstein* (1818) introduced imagery and themes that would subsequently be detected in horror films. However, none of the key Gothic novels—with the notable exception of *Frankenstein*, of course—were adapted for the screen during the 1930s (and very few of them since), and Universal's 1931 version of *Frankenstein* had very little to do with Shelley's novel. Much the same could be said of the 1931 film version of *Dracula* that, although ostensibly based on Bram Stoker's 1897 novel, developed its own distinctive storyline. Indeed, it could be argued that horror cinema's renditions of Frankenstein and Dracula have so completely supplanted the literary originals in the public imagination that any contemporary reader of Shelley's or Stoker's work would be surprised at how widely they differ from the common expectations of stories involving the characters of Frankenstein or Dracula.

This does not mean that one should discount entirely the importance of the Gothic to an understanding of the horror film. The Gothic's emphasis on the sensational, for instance, certainly resonates in the later development of horror. In addition, some critical accounts of Gothic have viewed it not just as a historically defined movement but also as a more pervasive cultural mode that incorporates part or all of the horror genre.[1] At the same time, one needs to acknowledge that early horror's relation with the historical Gothic is, at the very least, indirect, and other, more contemporaneous factors exerted a more obvious influence on the genre's early development.

It is worth noting in this respect that the 1931 versions of both *Dracula* and *Frankenstein* were not, strictly speaking, adaptations of the original novels but instead taken from stage versions. The contribution made by the theater to the "birth" of the horror film has often been overlooked in histories of the genre, but it was important in two distinct ways. The numerous stage versions of *Dracula* and *Frankenstein* that appeared, along with similarly themed macabre tales, throughout the

19th and into the 20th century helped to develop elements of visual spectacle—often involving the creation or destruction of the monster— in a manner that readily lent itself to translation into the cinematic medium (more so than did the often very convoluted plots of the original novels).

Just as importantly, such theatrical enterprises demonstrated that there was a commercial market for this kind of entertainment, even if it did not at this point go under the name "horror." From this perspective, the fact that Universal wanted to produce a screen version of *Dracula* in the early 1930s had nothing to do with the intrinsic qualities of Stoker's novel and everything to do with the box-office success enjoyed by the 1927 Broadway stage adaptation of the novel. The popularity of other macabre-themed plays in the 1920s, among them *The Cat and the Canary* and *The Gorilla* (both of which were repeatedly adapted for the cinema) further underlined how much the entertainment industry, especially in the United States, was catering to a public appetite for fictional horror before the term "horror film" ever appeared.

Historians in search of horror's roots have also looked to pre-1930s cinema in both Europe and the United States. Of particular significance in this respect were the German Expressionist films produced in the aftermath of World War I—most notably, *The Cabinet of Dr. Caligari* (1919), *The Golem* (1920), and *Nosferatu* (1922), an unauthorized *Dracula* adaptation—and a series of U.S. productions starring Lon Chaney, the most horror-like of which were *The Hunchback of Notre Dame* (1923), *The Phantom of the Opera* (1925), and *London After Midnight* (1927). Again one can find connections to the horror to come. The expressive style associated with *Caligari* and *Nosferatu* found its way into a number of early 1930s U.S. horrors (not least *Dracula*, which was photographed by Karl Freund, who had first made his mark with his work on some German Expressionist films and who would go on to direct the 1932 version of *The Mummy*), while the lumbering walk of the monsters in *The Golem* and *Caligari* has been seen by many critics as an influence on Boris Karloff's famous performance as the Monster in *Frankenstein*. Similarly, Lon Chaney's distortion of his own facial features and body in order to produce a convincing monster established a template for later horror monsters, while Chaney's main director, Tod Browning, went on to direct some of the key 1930s horrors, including *Dracula* and *Freaks* (1932).

As was the case with Gothic literature and the theater, however, these connections cut across significant differences, here to do with national distinction, cultural location and generic identity, in a way that undermines any sense of there being a straightforward cultural continuity between the films concerned. For example, German Expressionist cinema might have been an influence on horror but it was also more upmarket culturally than the early American horrors of the 1930s, to the extent that it constituted a form of European art cinema, while Chaney's films were more melodramas, often expensive and prestigious ones, than they were monster movies.

It seems from this that the work done by horror filmmakers in the formative period of the 1930s involved, in part at least, a Frankenstein-like stitching together of elements taken from other genres, other media, other nations and other historical periods, with this undertaken in the interests of producing commercially viable popular entertainments for mass audiences. What these filmmakers came up with might eventually have taken on a life of its own as a distinctive cinematic form or forms, but the birthing of horror was a protracted, chaotic and rather messy affair. Early horrors such as Universal's *Dracula* and *Frankenstein* or its *Murders in the Rue Morgue* (1932), or Paramount's *Dr. Jekyll and Mr. Hyde* (1931), or Warner Brothers' *Doctor X* (1932) or the independently produced *White Zombie* (1932) were actually very different from each other in terms of subject, style, theme, tone and production values, and the borders of the early 1930s version of the horror genre proved extremely permeable. Films we do not think of now as horror were marketed as horror while what seem to us to be classic horrors were marketed in other ways. If nothing else, this overturns one overly neat reading of the genesis of the horror film, which views the release of the Universal *Dracula* as marking the explosive beginning of a cinematic category that appeared ready-formed in the market. As is so often the case with the apparently familiar category of horror cinema, the story of the beginnings of the genre reveals instead an area of our culture that is fragmented, constantly negotiable and surprisingly difficult to pin down.

THE LOCATION OF HORROR

Some of the sprawl and fragmentation evident in horror's unruly "birth" has been maintained in the genre's subsequent development. Horror has never really solidified into a unified object but instead has tended to be characterized by dispersal into localized centers of activity that have sometimes connected with each other but have also gone their own distinctive ways. Bearing this in mind, an engagement with the horror genre in terms of the specific sites of its production and reception—whether this is in terms of particular cycles of films or in terms of different national versions of horror—seems a necessary prerequisite to grasping the nature of horror itself.

There was certainly a sprawling quality to horror during the 1930s. Sequels—the feature of the genre that has usually been seen as binding it together more than is the case with other mainstream film genres—were few and far between in this period, numbering only *Bride of Frankenstein* (1935), *Dracula's Daughter* (1936), and *Son of Frankenstein* (1939). Each of the major studios offered its own particular version of horror, while the horror films from Universal, the main genre producer in the first half of the 1930s, were considerably more varied than is sometimes supposed, with the high camp of *Bride of Frankenstein* sitting uneasily alongside the modernist chic of *The Black Cat* (1934) or the somber expressionism that characterized *Son of Frankenstein*.

One quality that did underpin most of 1930s cinematic horror, so far as its production context was concerned, was its Americanness. Throughout the 1930s and the 1940s, the United States was the only significant producer of horror films in the world. There was a minicycle of horrors from Mexico in the 1930s and a few British horrors from the same period, with both of these appropriating Hollywood horror conventions and combining them with local material. However, such productions were few in number and lacking in influence, and it was American horror films that captured the public imagination, not just in the United States but in many other countries as well. Given the international appeal of these films, it was perhaps fitting that non-Americans were involved in their production, sometimes in key roles. James Whale, director of *Frankenstein* and *Bride of Frankenstein*, was British, as was Boris Karloff (and, for that matter, most of the cast of *Bride of Frankenstein*), Bela Lugosi and Michael Curtiz, director of *Doctor X* and *Mystery of the Wax Museum* (1933), were both Hungarian, Robert Florey, director of *Murders in the Rue Morgue*, was French, and cinematographer-director Karl Freund was German (although, ironically, George Melford, the director of Universal's Spanish-language *Dracula*, shot on the same sets as the Lugosi version and considered by some critics to be a better film, was thoroughly American and reportedly could not even speak Spanish). Many of these films were set in Europe and, as noted above, sometimes drew upon European culture for their stories or their visual inspiration. It does not follow that this made the films less American—they were clearly all made with American audiences in mind—but the presence of non-American sensibilities behind the scenes and non-American accents in front of the camera often bestowed a kind of exoticism on the proceedings. If anything could define the generic sprawl of 1930s horror production, it was probably a sense of foreignness, of this being a type of fiction that was both fascinating but also distant from the everyday reality of American lives.

The first wave of American horror production petered out from 1936 onwards, with Universal's 1939 production of *Son of Frankenstein*, which marked Karloff's third and final appearance as the monster, a belated flourish to this period. When horror returned in the 1940s, it came in a form that was both more domesticated and more organized. American settings, often contemporary ones, and American characters were more prominent, and the exoticism associated with 1930s U.S. horror had by this stage been largely dissipated. While Lugosi and Karloff were still working in the genre, the new Universal horror star was Lon Chaney Jr., an altogether more American presence. Meanwhile, the producer Val Lewton was making a series of horror films at RKO that mixed historical subjects such as *The Body Snatcher* (1945) and *Bedlam* (1946) with psychological horrors set in a recognizable modern America, among them *Cat People* (1942), *The Seventh Victim* (1943), and *The Curse of the Cat People* (1944). The undoubted intelligence and stylistic accomplishment of these films has rightly earned critical approval over the years, although in retrospect they seem less important to the subsequent development of the horror genre than less reputable activities taking place elsewhere in the industry.

Universal in particular was busy developing branded cycles of horror films (or what today would be called horror franchises). *The Ghost of Frankenstein* (1942) followed on from *Son of Frankenstein* and was itself quickly followed by *Frankenstein Meets the Wolf Man* (1943), which was also a sequel to the 1941 hit *The Wolf Man*. The later multiple-monster films *House of Frankenstein* (1944) and *House of Dracula* (1945)—both of which brought together Dracula, Frankenstein's monster, and the Wolf Man—confirmed Universal's status as a veritable monster factory committed to sequel production. (By contrast, Lewton's only sequel, *The Curse of the Cat People*, purposefully set out to be as different as possible from the first film, as if disdainful of the commercialism evident in the very idea of the sequel.) Universal also produced a 1940s cycle of mummy films — including *The Mummy's Hand* (1942), *The Mummy's Tomb* (1942), *The Mummy's Ghost* (1944), and *The Mummy's Curse* (1944) — that introduced the mummy into contemporary American settings and displayed a level of ruthlessness in killing off principal characters that would not be seen again in the genre until Alfred Hitchcock's *Psycho* (1960). This commercial activity might have been more downmarket than the middlebrow version of horror purveyed by Lewton, but its reliance on rapid serial production and franchised monsters established a pattern for later horror productions. This kind of serialized production has since acquired a certain critical notoriety for what appears to be its naked exploitativeness, yet at the same time — if one is willing to keep an open mind when judging individual horror films — it has provided a context in which filmmakers have managed to produce lively and innovative work.

This second burst of horror activity came to an end in the late 1940s. Critics and fans have discovered elements of horror in the monster movies that were popular during the 1950s — including the science-fiction themed *The Thing from Another World* (1951) and *Creature from the Black Lagoon* (1954) — but horror was not reformed as a marketable cinematic category in itself until the mid-1950s. At this point, horror production became more internationalized than it had been before, with activity in, among other places, Great Britain, Italy, Spain and Mexico and with horror films continuing to be made in the United States.

A number of factors were involved in this geographical reconfiguration of the horror genre. The breakup of the classical Hollywood studio system in the 1950s led to a partial opening of the American market to foreign producers (with the British company Hammer, which was in many ways a horror market leader in the latter part of the 1950s, particularly benefiting from American finance). A relaxation of censorship, especially in Western Europe, also permitted the development of non-American horror cycles that were often gorier, more violent and more sexually explicit than anything seen before in the genre. This manifested itself in different ways in different places. In Britain, Hammer offered a color gothic reinvention of the Dracula and Frankenstein franchises, while in Italy a more dream-like version of gothic horror prevailed, and in the U.S. Roger Corman directed a series of intensely psychologized period adaptations of Edgar Allan Poe stories. Various versions of contemporary-set psychological horrors were also appearing in the United States, Britain, Italy, and France, among other places, with these exploring, often in explicit detail, sexualized psychopathologies.

From this moment in its history onwards, horror is not only harder to place but also harder to present in terms of an overall cohesion, at least without denying what seems to be an undeniable variety and prolificity in horror production. Again there are sequels and cycles, generic fads and fashions, but the relations between these different aspects of the horror phenomenon tend to be very localized. For example, the connection between Japanese forms of horror and the American horror film from the late-1990s onwards makes for an interesting case study of cultural exchange, with Japanese films such as *Ringu (Ring)* (1998) and *Ju-on: The Grudge* (2003) being remade as American productions, Japanese directors such as Hideo Nakata working in the United States, and there being a more general interchange of ideas and themes between nations. But it is a case study that is very particular in terms of its historical specificity, and it is hard to generalize about the genre on the basis of it.

A key issue arising from this concerns the extent to which post-1950s horror cinema is just the sum total of different national expressions of horror and the extent to which it is more than this, either in terms of some underlying common features or in terms of the sort of cross-national trading apparent, for instance, in the recent Japanese-American horror connections. Again, it is hard to address this for the genre as a whole. Attempts that have been made have often ended up excluding sections of the genre or suppressing what others have seen as important differences between films. As noted above, it is arguably more effective to engage in detail with specific instances of horror production—particular generic formats or particular moments in a generic history—and to consider the complexities of national identity and transnational exchange within circumscribed contexts. Perhaps inevitably, such an approach leads us back to the notion of horror as a genre that is constantly remaking itself within different locations.

THE MEANING OF HORROR

The idea that horror is a low cultural form used to be a problem, at least for those critics who wanted to take it seriously. Some have dealt with this by relating horror to more reputable areas of culture.[2] Others have considered horror in terms suggesting that there is some significance or meaning lurking beneath its vulgar commercial veneer. For example, psychoanalytical critics have explored the ways in which horror films might be seen as addressing repressed fears and anxieties, in effect acting as a kind of therapy for unwitting audiences.[3] The ideology of horror is another recurrent preoccupation in critical writings on the genre. To what extent are horror films, consciously or inadvertently, expressing values and attitudes in support of particular views of the world? Working from this perspective, the influential critic Robin Wood has divided horror into socially progressive and reactionary wings, according to the extent to which the films concerned adhere to or deviate from social norms.[4]

Others have found misogynistic values embedded in particular sectors of horror production—with women characters frequently victimized by male killers or monsters—although yet more critics, sometimes writing about the same films, have identified what they see as a more ambivalent treatment of gender.[5] The end result of such interpretative activity has often been a clearer sense of the ambiguities and tensions within films. To give a specific instance, critics have related Frankenstein's monster in Universal's 1930s horror cycle to, among other things, rampant heterosexuality, gayness, the proletariat and the plight of African Americans. All of these interpretations are supportable with evidence from the films, but at the same time those films are not contained within or completely explained away by any of the interpretations. It could in fact be argued that the fascination of these films, and their capacity to generate so many compelling readings, derives from a kind of persistent ambiguity, as various socially or ideologically meaningful elements are picked up and put down according to the changing demands of the films' narratives. In the case of Frankenstein's monster, the shifting back and forth between menace and pathos invokes different representational strategies that do not necessarily cohere with each other, in ideological terms at least.

Focusing on audiences for horror films, and especially fan-based audiences, rather than on horror films in themselves has in recent years provided an effective grounding for further critical discussion of some of the ways in which horror films have been interpreted. In earlier genre criticism, audiences were often presented in terms of passivity, whether this was the passivity of the mass audience mindlessly soaking up formulaic entertainments or that of the audience not consciously aware of what was being done to it by the genre. If nothing else, looking at horror fans as agents in the construction of meaning reminds us that this particular sector of the audience is defined through its activity, both in its constructing interpretations and in its circulating these within communities of like-minded people. Whether the interpretations thus generated are any more convincing or totalizing than those constructed by professional critics is another matter, but the all-too-obvious presence here of multiple interpretations, debates and disagreements underlines the extent to which the significance and value of horror remains a contested issue.

It could be argued that the ability of the horror genre to regenerate and multiply, constantly adapting itself to different social and historical contexts, has made it difficult to pin it down in critical terms. Nevertheless, some issues arise out of the critical work on horror that, if systematically addressed (and some of them are currently being dealt with), have the potential to further our understanding of this part of our culture. For example, the emphasis on fans in work on horror audiences has certainly been productive, but the marginalization of the rest of the audience for horror—consisting of people who do not think of themselves as dedicated fans but like going to see horror films anyway—potentially limits our awareness of the experiences and interpretations generated by the genre, especially given that its current commercial popularity could only be sustained by its appealing beyond what appears to be a relatively small active fan-base. An associated issue is to do with the critical emphasis on interpretation. To what extent do audiences, however one defines them, interpret what they see in a horror film and to what extent do they experience it? The critical language for discussing horror as a particular kind of experiential and sensual event is currently quite limited, but thinking of the genre in these terms would surely lead us closer to an explanation of why audiences have found and continue to find horror films such enthralling entertainments. Finally, the idea that horror is inevitably a low cultural form needs to be challenged rather more than it has been. The genre has constantly insinuated itself across cultural distinctions and hierarchies. There are upmarket horrors, downmarket horrors and middlebrow horrors, and identifying the relation between these could provide a more nuanced sense of how the genre has spread itself across certain markets.

It seems unlikely that pursuing any of these lines of enquiry will produce a more unified understanding of the horror genre, however. What is more likely to emerge is an enhanced sense of the multiple identities of horror, of patterns of generic fragmentation and coalescence that define a type of cinema which has the power to surprise, shock and delight audiences but which remains, as ever, unpredictable.

NOTES

1. See, for example, David Punter, *The Literature of Terror: Volume 2—The Modern Gothic, 2nd edition*. London: Longman, 1996.

2. For example, see S. S. Prawer, *Caligari's Children: The Film as Tale of Terror*. Oxford: Oxford University Press, 1980.

3. For example, see James B. Twitchell, *Dreadful Pleasures: An Anatomy of Modern Horror*. Oxford: Oxford University Press, 1985.

4. Robin Wood, *Hollywood from Vietnam to Reagan*. New York: Columbia University Press, 1986.

5. For a relevant discussion of the slasher film, see Carol J. Clover, *Men, Women and Chainsaws: Gender in the Modern Horror Film*. London: British Film Institute, 1992.

The Dictionary

– A –

ABBOTT, BUD (1895–1974), AND COSTELLO, LOU (1906–1959). It was the fate of most of **Universal**'s horror monsters of the 1930s and 1940s to end up in the hands of **comedy** performers Bud Abbott and Lou Costello. The duo had already encountered horror material in the haunted house spoof *Hold That Ghost* (1941), and from the late 1940s onwards comedy-horror formed an important part of their output. These films have not been valued highly by horror historians who have tended to view them as the embarrassing last gasp of Universal horror. However, they do contain some inventive scenes and they also underline the undeniable fact that horror and comedy sit very close to each other in the cultural spectrum. The best of them was *Abbott and Costello Meet Frankenstein* (1948). This continued the multiple-monster format established by Universal in the early 1940s by featuring **Dracula**, the Wolf Man, Frankenstein's monster and—in a brief cameo—the Invisible Man (although oddly, given the film's title, Frankenstein himself did not appear). The film is of historic significance inasmuch as it houses final performances from **Bela Lugosi** as Dracula and **Lon Chaney Jr.** as the Wolf Man. But it is also a funny film that plays interesting and clever games with Universal's horror myths, noting their absurdity when placed in a contemporary American setting while also acknowledging their continuing power to fascinate.

Abbott and Costello's subsequent comedy-horrors offered progressively less but they remain essential viewing for horror aficionados. They are *Abbott and Costello Meet the Killer, Boris Karloff* (1949), *Abbott and Costello Meet the Invisible Man* (1951), *Abbott and*

1

Costello Meet **Dr. Jekyll and Mr. Hyde** (1953), and *Abbott and Costello Meet the* **Mummy** (1955). *See also* AMERICAN HORROR.

AJA, ALEXANDRE (1978–). The French director Alexandre Aja made a striking horror debut with his **slasher** film *Haute Tension* (2003), which was released in the United States as *High Tension* and in some other markets under Aja's preferred English language title *Switchblade Romance.* Horror **fans** applauded the stylish but hard-edged treatment of a stock horror situation in which a resourceful young woman, or **Final Girl**, was stalked by an implacable male killer. They were generally less convinced by the film's bizarre conclusion in which it was revealed that much of the narrative has been the extended fantasy of one of the characters in the film, although this development could be seen as an audacious and provocative upturning of our expectations. Aja has expressed his admiration for **American horror**, so it was unsurprising that his next film was the 2006 **remake** of **Wes Craven**'s 1970s classic *The Hills Have Eyes.* The ambivalence about violence evident in the original was replaced in the remake by a survivalist ruthlessness, and Aja handled both the relentless mayhem and the atmospheric desert setting with great skill. *See also* FRENCH HORROR.

ALDRICH, ROBERT (1918–1983). The films of American director Robert Aldrich were often strident and confrontational, and his horror films were no exception. *What Ever Happened to Baby Jane?* (1962) and *Hush . . . Hush, Sweet Charlotte* (1964) were ostensibly **psychological thriller**-whodunnit combinations but the emphasis throughout was on the grotesque, especially as manifested in the form of older women of questionable sanity. In *What Ever Happened to Baby Jane?*, **Bette Davis** and **Joan Crawford** played parodies of their own screen personas; each would go on to make other horror films, with their performances tinged with a "Baby Jane" grotesquerie. *Hush . . . Hush, Sweet Charlotte* was an overheated example of Southern **Gothic** that offered yet another histrionic, scene-stealing turn from Davis. Both films displayed a fascination with the decay of classic Hollywood, its conventions and its performers. It was perhaps no coincidence that they appeared in the wake of **Alfred Hitchcock**'s *Psycho* (1960), a film that introduced an altogether more modern outlook not just into the **American horror** film but into mainstream cinema in general.

ALIEN **(1979). Dan O'Bannon's** screenplay for a **science fiction**/horror hybrid called *Star Beast* was originally intended as a low-budget production. Its eventual transformation into a stylish, expensive and much-imitated Ridley Scott film entitled *Alien* undoubtedly helped to secure both its international success and its lasting cult status. The narrative was simple—an alien monster stalks the hapless crew of a space freighter—and the film drew heavily on stock horror conventions. However, these were wrapped around an imaginative and detailed vision of a dystopian future, and the creature itself, as designed by **H. R. Giger**, was genuinely scary. The alien's method of reproduction—which involved "impregnating" humans through the mouth, with the resulting baby ripping itself out of the victim's stomach—was also memorably unpleasant. In addition, *Alien* helped to introduce the female hero into the horror genre. As played by Sigourney Weaver, the character of Ellen Ripley exhibited much of the courageous behavior also being shown in the late 1970s by the **slasher** film's **Final Girl**, although at the same time Ripley was constantly defined through her biological nature. Indeed, the convoluted sexual politics of the film has attracted the attention of film critics and theorists ever since its release.

Sequels followed, although not as rapidly as was the case elsewhere in horror cinema, and each sequel was markedly different from what had gone before in the series, with this reflecting the strong creative personalities of the directors involved. **James Cameron's** militaristic *Aliens* (1986) increased the number of aliens and turned Ripley into a powerful Amazonian figure who fought the mother alien one-on-one in the film's conclusion. By contrast, David Fincher's *Alien 3* (1992) was a moody drama set in a space prison into which a shaven-headed Ripley crashes. The film had a troubled production and initially was not well-received, although in retrospect its oppressive atmosphere and its relentlessly grim narrative seem more striking. Jean-Pierre Jeunet's *Alien: Resurrection* (1997) was, to date at least, the last Ripley film. As stylish as previous entries, it explored the modish subjects of genetic engineering and cloning and generally seemed more interested in the Ripley character than it was in the increasingly familiar figures of the aliens. **Paul W. S. Anderson**'s *AVP: Alien versus Predator* (2004) was a sidebar to the series rather than another sequel, offering a brand new set of characters taking on alien monsters. It was enthusiastically violent but added little to the *Alien* corpus.

AMENABAR, ALEJANDRO (1972–). The writer-director (and also film composer) Alejandro Amenabar was born in Chile but has worked mainly in Spain. *Tesis* (1996), his feature debut, was a stylish **serial killer** film about the production of **snuff** movies on a university campus which skillfully combined American genre conventions with a European sensibility. After a diversion into **science fiction** with *Abre los ojos* (*Open Your Eyes*) (1997)—which was subsequently remade as the Tom Cruise vehicle *Vanilla Sky* (2001)—he had a notable success with *The Others* (2001). Starring the Australian actor Nicole Kidman, set on the island of Jersey, shot in English but filmed largely in Spain, this was a truly international production that contributed to the cinematic revival of the **ghost** story that took place from the late 1990s onwards. Eschewing the updating process undertaken by films such as *Ringu* (*Ring*) (1998) and *The Sixth Sense* (1999), *The Others* opted for a more traditional, literary-based approach, and its stately pacing made the climactic shocks all the more effective. *See also* SPANISH HORROR.

AMERICAN HORROR. The version of horror cinema produced within the United States of America has proved the most consistently popular and influential of all national horror cinemas. Other types of horror have occasionally challenged its supremacy—**British horror** in the late 1950s, for example—but none of these challenges have been sustained for any length of time.

Some of the roots of American horror cinema as it developed from the 1930s onwards were in European cultural history rather than in American culture, for example in Europe's **gothic** literary tradition (which has arguably been more influential on American horror than America's own gothic literature) or in more recent cultural developments such as **Surrealism** and German **Expressionism**. Indeed, many of the key horror filmmakers in the 1930s, which was horror cinema's first decade as a recognizable generic category, were

European—including **Karl Freund, Boris Karloff, Bela Lugosi, Edgar G. Ulmer,** and **James Whale**. However, developments within American popular culture since World War I also anticipated and helped to form the horror to come. The films of **Lon Chaney,** for example, were made in an American idiom, even when they were set abroad. In addition, haunted house spoofs such as *The Bat* and *The Cat and the Canary* were popular on stage and screen, and helped to establish another distinctly American approach to horrifying events and experiences. The mixing of different traditions and influences entailed in the formation of American horror was very apparent in the film that is usually seen as inaugurating the 1930s horror boom, the **Universal** production of *Dracula* (1931), which was an adaptation of a Broadway adaptation of an English adaptation of a novel written by an Irish author.

During the 1930s, horror became a staple cinematic category for the first time. Universal led the way with its **Frankenstein** and Dracula films, along with a range of other productions set mainly in Europe, but other studios also dabbled in horror and offered different approaches. The presence of **Michael Curtiz**'s horrors for Warner Brothers, **Victor Halperin**'s *White Zombie* (1932), **Tod Browning**'s *Freaks* (1932), and *King Kong* (1933) within the horror market testified to a generic variety that makes it hard to set definitive limits on that horror or to generalize about this period. Having noted this, the emphasis in many of these films was more on fantasy than it was on realism. Some horror historians have seen this as involving a disavowal of the social vicissitudes of the American Depression, although the Depression itself was rarely acknowledged explicitly in 1930s horror cinema.

In any event, horror survived the Depression, albeit without some of its earlier inventiveness and energy. During the 1940s, Universal became increasingly dependent on horror **sequels** featuring not just Frankenstein and Dracula but revised versions of the Wolf Man and the **mummy,** while at RKO producer **Val Lewton** eschewed the monster-centered Universal approach and instead offered a more psychologically complex form of horror in films such as *Cat People* (1942), *I Walked with a Zombie* (1943), and *The Seventh Victim* (1943). Other films also contained horror-like material and imagery —including some of the **Sherlock Holmes** films that featured **Basil**

Rathbone as the great detective, as well as **psychological thrillers** such as John Brahm's *The Lodger* (1944) and **Robert Siodmak**'s *The Spiral Staircase* (1946). However, this wave of activity faded away from the mid-1940s onwards, with the horror parodies featuring comedians **Bud Abbott** and **Lou Costello**—most notably *Abbott and Costello Meet Frankenstein* (1948)—usually seen as marking the end of this phase in American horror history.

There were some isolated horror projects during the first half of the 1950s—for example, *The Black Castle* (1952) or *House of Wax* (1953). But the monsters in this period were based elsewhere, in a series of **science fiction** films that often had horror-like qualities, among them *The Thing From Another World* (1951) and **Jack Arnold**'s *Creature from the Black Lagoon* (1954). It was not until the late 1950s that there was a revival in American horror's fortunes, and this took place in a very different industrial context from that which had housed 1930s horror production.

During the 1950s, the old-fashioned American studio system had been broken up by the U.S. government, and by the late 1950s the film market was more readily open to independent producers. At the same time, audiences were declining, and filmmakers were struggling to tempt people away from **television** and other domestic comforts through offering entertainments that were more spectacular—this was the age of Cinemascope and 3D—or more sensational or exploitative. The producer **Herman Cohen**'s low-budget horrors for the teenage market—*Blood of Dracula* (1957), *I Was a Teenage Werewolf* (1957), and *I Was a Teenage Frankenstein* (1957)—formed one early response to the new entertainment market. However, the international success of period horror films produced by the British company **Hammer** from 1957 onwards, along with a wave of late 1950s **Italian horror**, paved the way for the next major American horror cycle, which this time was not based on any particular monster but rather on a long-dead author. Producer-director **Roger Corman**'s period adaptations of **Edgar Allan Poe** stories, which began with *House of Usher* (1960) and *Pit and the Pendulum* (1961) and which were made for exploitation specialists **American International Pictures,** helped to establish **Vincent Price** as a horror star and also brought a level of ambition to the genre not seen since Lewton's 1940s work. These films showed more interest than Hammer ever did in exploring extreme psychological states, something that was also apparent in the otherwise very different *Psycho* (1960), **Robert Aldrich**'s grotesque *What Ever Happened to Baby Jane?* (1962), and a series of macabre thrillers from producer-director **William Castle**, among them *The House on Haunted Hill* (1959) and *The Tingler* (1959). Meanwhile, at the lower end of the industry, grindhouse specialist **Herschell Gordon Lewis** was pioneering the **gore** or splatter film with the much-censored *Blood Feast* (1963) and *Two Thousand Maniacs* (1964), while an unclassifiable oddity such as the dream-like *Carnival of Souls* (1962) was a reminder that generic variety was again the order of the day.

The sense of an increasing ruthlessness in 1960s American horror was confirmed in 1968 with the release of the big-budget **Roman Polanski** Satanic thriller *Rosemary's Baby* and **George Romero**'s low-budget zombie story *Night of the Living Dead*. Both were self-consciously contemporary as well as relentlessly grim and paranoid, and both decisively rejected any prospect of the affirmation of goodness that had climaxed so many previous horror narratives. However, it was not until the astonishing commercial success experienced by *The Exorcist* (1973) that American filmmakers began seriously to engage with this new type of horror. Low-budget offerings such as **Tobe Hooper**'s *The Texas Chainsaw Massacre* (1974), **Larry Cohen**'s *It's Alive* (1974), **Brian De Palma**'s *Carrie* (1976), and **Wes Craven**'s *The Hills Have Eyes* (1977), among many others, offered a view of American society, and especially the American family, that was both disturbing and, potentially at least, critical, while the bigger-budgeted **apocalyptic horror** *The Omen* (1976) equally managed to convey a sense that the world was doomed. As was the case with 1930s horror and the Depression, horror historians have related the anxiety and distrust of authority evident in 1970s horror to a troubled social context that involved not just the Vietnam war and its aftermath but also civil rights protests and an international oil crisis.

Times changed, however, and the arrival of the **slasher**—starting with **John Carpenter**'s *Halloween* (1978) and **Sean S. Cunningham**'s *Friday the 13th* (1980)—signaled a re-engagement with the teenage audience, as teenage characters were picked off by judgmental **serial killers** in a series of low-budget horrors that ran into the early 1980s. At the time these films were criticized for their violence against women, although more recently their introduction of the feisty female hero, or **Final Girl**, into American horror has been recognized by critics. The slasher also led to a greater reliance on sequels and cycles than had been apparent in the 1950s, 1960s and 1970s. *Halloween* and *Friday the 13th* generated numerous sequels but the major horror cycle—or franchise—of the 1980s was initiated by Wes Craven's *A Nightmare on Elm Street* (1984). This supernatural reworking of the slasher format retained a focus on teenagers but added some striking surreal imagery. Just as sequelized 1940s American horror has been judged inferior to the 1930s version, so 1980s horror has sometimes been accused of "dumbing down" after the achievements of the 1970s. Such a perspective arguably overvalues the 1970s and underestimates the innovation and creativity apparent in the 1980s (although, as is the case with every era of horror production, formulaic films are easy to find).

The 1990s saw a small resurgence in period horror—with **Francis Ford Coppola**'s *Dracula* (1992) and **Neil Jordan**'s *Interview with the Vampire* (1994)—but the emphasis remained on the contemporary with serial killer films such as *The Silence of the Lambs* (1991) and the revival of the slasher format with Craven's *Scream* (1996), the success of which ushered in a new cycle of very self-conscious **teenage horror**. The international success experienced by **Japanese horror** from the late-1990s onwards also exerted an influence on American horror, with this evident not just in **remakes** of films such as **Hideo Nakata**'s *Ringu* (*Ring*) (1998) and **Takashi Shimizu**'s *Ju-On: The Grudge* (2003) but also in other films that drew upon the slow-burn Japanese style. Associated both with this and the success of **M. Night Shyamalan**'s *The Sixth Sense* (1999), **ghost** stories became more of a presence than they had ever been before in American cinema. Meanwhile *The Blair Witch Project* (1999) discovered the marketing power of the **internet** in its playful engagement with American folklore. Horror filmmakers also raided the genre's past, with nostalgic resurrections of classic monsters in **Stephen Sommers**' *The Mummy* (1999) and *Van Helsing* (2004) and remakes of 1970s classics *The Texas Chainsaw Massacre*, *The Hills Have Eyes*, and *Dawn of the Dead* (1978), along with 1970s-style tough films like *Wrong Turn* (2003), **Rob Zombie**'s *The Devil's Rejects* (2005), and **Eli Roth**'s *Cabin Fever* (2002) and *Hostel* (2005).

The closer one gets to the present, the more obviously varied and fractured American horror production becomes. One can detect trends and mini-cycles but there is always something else going on elsewhere, whether this be an isolated but interesting project or some innovative work that will possibly lead to another mini-cycle of films. American horror has been like this since the 1930s, and any attempt to periodize or categorize it too neatly risks losing a sense of the variety that has made it such a distinctive and important sector of the genre.

AMERICAN INTERNATIONAL PICTURES (AIP). The 1950s was one of the most important decades for American exploitation cinema, and, for a while at least, the independent production and distribution company American International Pictures led the field. Formed in 1954 by producers **Samuel Z. Arkoff** and **James Nicholson** as American Releasing Corporation and retitled American International Pictures (or AIP) in 1956, the company specialized in low-budget genre films with lurid titles that were designed primarily for teenage audiences. Representative AIP horrors from the 1950s were **Bert I. Gordon**'s *The Amazing Colossal Man* (1957) and *The Spider* (1958) and **Herbert L. Strock**'s *I Was a Teenage Frankenstein* (1957) and *How to Make a Monster* (1958) but the company's main director was the prolific **Roger Corman**, who worked in a variety of genres, both for AIP and other companies, throughout the 1950s. His AIP horrors *It Conquered the World* (1956) and *The Undead* (1957) were a cut above the average for this type of production. It was Corman's ambition that ultimately led, after some resistance from Arkoff and Nicholson, to AIP embarking on a series of Corman-directed **Edgar Allan Poe** adaptations, which had higher production values than usual and which featured intelligent scripts from the likes of **Richard Matheson** and **Charles Beaumont** and witty performances from **Vincent Price**. The Poe cycle—which included *House of Usher* (1960), *Pit and the Pendulum* (1961), and *The Masque of the Red Death* (1964)—capitalized on the success of the British company **Hammer** in popularizing period horror but maintained its own distinctive style and character.

During the 1960s and into the 1970s, AIP continued to churn out low-budget teenage fare—including a series of *Beach Party* movies—but it retained its interest in horror. Corman directed *X: The Man with X Ray Eyes* (1963), while **Francis Ford Coppola** made his feature directorial debut with AIP's **psychological thriller** *Dementia 13* (*The Haunted and the Hunted*) (1963). There was also involvement in British productions, among these the camp horrors *The Abominable Dr. Phibes* (1971) and its **sequel** *Dr. Phibes Rises Again* (1972) and the **witchcraft** drama *Cry of the Banshee* (1970), as well as collaborations with **Amicus** on *Scream and Scream Again* (1969) and *The Oblong Box* (1968) and with Hammer on the lesbian **vampire** story *The Vampire Lovers* (1970). AIP also made some interesting contributions to 1970s **American horror**, with its productions including the impressive **H. P. Lovecraft** adaptation *The Dunwich Horror* (1970), the **revenge of nature** horror *Frogs* (1972), the blaxploitation classic *Blacula* (1972), a version of *The Island of Dr. Moreau* (1977), and the haunted house drama *The Amityville Horror* (1979), one of the company's most commercially successful titles. As the 1970s progressed, themes and material associated with the exploitation sector entered the mainstream and AIP itself became a less distinctive production setup. The company was taken over by Filmways in 1980 but by then its place in horror history was secure.

AMICUS. Amicus is usually seen as **British horror**'s second company, after **Hammer**. It did not seek to emulate the commercially dominant Hammer product but instead, from the mid-1960s onwards, developed its own distinctive brand of horror. Set up by American producers Max J. Rosenberg and **Milton Subotsky**, Amicus's first films were the pop musicals *It's Trad Dad* (1962) and *Just for Fun* (1963). It switched to horror in 1964 with *Dr. Terror's House of Horrors*, which was directed by frequent Amicus collaborator **Freddie Francis** and written by Subotsky himself. This was a horror **anthology** that brought together stories about **werewolves, vampires**, killer plants and **voodoo**. Hammer never used the anthology format but it became an Amicus speciality. *Dr. Terror* also established the company's preference for contemporary settings. Amicus would only make two period horror films—**I, Monster** (1970) and *And Now the Screaming Starts* (1973)—and these would not come until near the end of the company's existence.

More anthologies followed—Francis's *Torture Garden* (1967), Peter Duffell's *The House that Dripped Blood* (1970), **Roy Ward Baker**'s *Asylum* (1972), Francis's *Tales from the Crypt* (1972), Baker's *Vault of Horror* (1973), and **Kevin Connor**'s *From Beyond the Grave* (1973). Many of these drew upon American sources—with *Torture Garden* and *The House that Dripped Blood* adapted by American writer **Robert Bloch** from his own stories, and *Tales from the Crypt* adapted from E. C. horror **comics**, and they all exhibited an urbane and often cynical sense of humor, something that again rendered them quite distinct from the Hammer product. The twist endings which became an essential feature of the Amicus anthology quickly became predictable—usually the characters narrating the stories within the film were revealed as already dead or as doomed to die—but the quality of some of the individual stories was remarkable.

Amicus was less successful with its single-narrative features. Francis's *The Skull* (1965) and *The Psychopath* (1965) both contained some impressively stylish sequences but lacked overall cohesion. Another Francis film, *The Deadly Bees* (1966) lacked even the stylish sequences, while **Stephen Weeks'** *I, Monster* was a dramatically inert rendition of the **Dr. Jekyll and Mr. Hyde** story. Bill Bain's *What Became of Jack And Jill?* (1971) was an uninspired **psychological thriller**, Jim Clark's *Madhouse* (1974) a laboured attempt at self-reflexive horror and Paul Annett's *The Beast Must Die* (1974) an odd, blaxploitation-influenced werewolf film that was marketed in the United States as *Black Werewolf* and which featured a gimmicky "werewolf break" in which the audience was given the opportunity to guess which character was the werewolf.

Amicus also produced some **science fiction**/horror hybrids. Montgomery Tully's *The Terrornauts* (1967) and Francis's *They Came from Beyond Space* (1967) were both conventional alien invasion fantasies. By contrast, **Gordon Hessler's** *Scream and Scream Again* (1969)—a co-production with **American International Pictures**—was a fascinating, if idiosyncratic and sometimes obscure, tale of super-strong androids. Considerably gentler was Alan Cooke's *The Mind of Mr. Soames* (1969), in which Terence Stamp played a man with the mind of a child, as indeed was Warris Hussein's *A Touch of Love* (1969), an adaptation of Margaret Drabble's novel *The Millstone* that was Amicus's only non-genre project. As the market for

British horror faded away in the mid-1970s, Amicus—in what turned out to be a final burst of activity—also produced a series of Edgar Rice Burroughs' adaptations, *The Land that Time Forgot* (1974), *At the Earth's Core* (1976), and *The People that Time Forgot* (1977), all of which were directed by **Kevin Connor**.

***THE AMITYVILLE HORROR* (1979).** In 1975, George and Kathy Lutz moved into a house on Long Island, New York, a house in which a man had previously murdered six members of his own family. Twenty-eight days after their arrival, the Lutz family left, claiming that the house was haunted. *The Amityville Horror*, a book detailing their experiences, became an international bestseller, and it was adapted into a successful film by director Stuart Rosenberg in 1979. The veracity of the Amityville story has been much debated, but the film version was a straightforward haunted house story slightly hampered by an anticlimactic narrative in which eventually the protagonists just leave the site of danger. The **sequels** that followed compensated for this by abandoning whatever factual basis there had been in the original and replacing it with some standard **ghost** story conventions. *Amityville II: The Possession* (1982), directed by Damiano Damiani, was a stylish prequel that gave some of the house's back story. *Amityville 3-D* (1983), despite being directed by veteran Richard Fleischer, was silly and tiresome. Not all the low budget follow-ups were official sequels but in any event none of them added much of interest to the Amityville cycle; they included *Amityville: The Evil Escapes* (1989), *The Amityville Curse* (1990), *Amityville 1992: It's About Time* (1992), *Amityville: A New Generation* (1993), and *Amityville: Dollhouse* (1996). *The Amityville Horror* (2005), directed by Andrew Douglas, was a **remake** of the 1979 original that added new material about the source of the haunting in order to provide a more dramatic story arc. *See also* AMERICAN HORROR.

ANDERSON, PAUL W. S. (1965–). Paul Anderson is a British-born writer-director based mainly in the United States who has specialized in horror/**science fiction** hybrids. His first major success was *Mortal Kombat* (1995), an adaptation of a popular martial arts **computer game** that contained some horror imagery. *Event Horizon* (1997) was a stylish **ghost** story set on board a spaceship, while *Resident Evil*

(2002), based on another computer game, was a horror-action thriller featuring **zombies**. Anderson's films tend to be slick and fast-paced, with the visuals underpinned by pounding rock **music**. He also directed the SF/**western** hybrid *Soldier* (1998), the supernatural **television** movie *The Sight* (2000), and the ultra-high concept *AVP: Alien versus Predator* (2004), as well as scripting and co-producing *Resident Evil: Apocalypse* (2004) and co-producing *The Dark* (2005).

ANIMATION. Animation within the American commercial mainstream has tended to be directed at **children** and family audiences. Consequently, what horror-like imagery it has contained—and there has been such imagery—has usually been presented in an attenuated form or within an unthreatening context. For example, the witch in Walt Disney's version of *Snow White and the Seven Dwarfs* (1937) might have scared generations of children and possesses some of the qualities of the horror monster but essentially she is a figure from the more positive world of fairy tales. By comparison, Japanese animation, which is often directed at adult audiences, has been more willing to engage in an explicit way with horror material, as is evident in animated **vampire** stories such as *Vampaia hantâ D* (*Vampire Hunter D*) (1985) and *Blood—The Last Vampire* (2000), gruesome monster films such as *Chôjin densetsu Urotsukidôji* (*Legend of the Overfiend*) (1989), and action/horror hybrids like *Yôjû toshi* (*Wicked City*) (1987). From the early 1990s onwards, both American and British animation has also offered a few feature films that have located themselves more confidently in relation to the horror genre, possibly reflecting the growing popularity of horror fiction with younger audiences. **Tim Burton**'s *The Nightmare Before Christmas* (1993) and *Corpse Bride* (2005) both contained some surprisingly unnerving moments, while Nick Park's *The Curse of the Were-Rabbit* (2005) and Robert Zemeckis's production of *Monster House* (2006) managed a more consistently comic treatment of horror themes.

Outside of the commercial mainstream, it is easier to find disturbing and horrifying film animation; one only has to look at the work of the Czech animator Jan Svankmajer or of the American-born, European-based Quay Brothers. However, experimental or avant-garde films of this kind owe as much to **surrealism** as they do to cinematic horror and arguably they do not function in any significant way as part of a horror genre that is overwhelmingly defined by its commercial imperatives.

ANKERS, EVELYN (1918–1985). Evelyn Ankers was the leading lady in numerous 1940s **American horror** films. More graceful and poised than some of the more melodrama-prone "scream queens" of the 1930s such as **Fay Wray,** Ankers was well-suited to the solid and workmanlike B-movie projects that defined much horror production during the following decade. Born in Chile to English parents, she moved to the United States in the early 1940s. An early genre credit was the **Bud Abbott** and **Lou Costello comedy**-horror *Hold That Ghost* (1941). More substantial roles followed alongside **Lon Chaney Jr.** in **Universal's** *The Wolf Man* (1941), *The Ghost of Frankenstein* (1942), and *Son of Dracula* (1943), as well as an uncharacteristically sultry turn in the noir-like *Sherlock Holmes and the Voice of Terror* (1942). Somehow she managed to retain her dignity in *Captive Wild Woman* (1943), in which **mad scientist John Carradine** transformed an **ape** into a woman (with Ankers playing the romantic female lead, not the ape woman), and its equally silly **sequel** *Jungle Woman* (1944). She was reunited with Chaney Jr. in *Weird Woman* (1944) and *The Frozen Ghost* (1945) and also starred in the minor *The Mad Ghoul* (1943) and *The Invisible Man's Revenge* (1944), as well as returning to the Sherlock Holmes series with *The Pearl of Death* (1944). The end of the 1940s low-budget horror boom was also in effect the end of Ankers' cinematic career. She worked mainly on **television** during the 1950s and retired from acting in 1960. She was married to the Hollywood actor Richard Denning.

ANTHOLOGIES. The anthology or portmanteau format—in which a number of shorter films are linked together—has proved sporadically popular in mainstream cinema. For horror filmmakers, it has facilitated the adaptation of **gothic** short stories that would not otherwise lend themselves easily to translation into the feature format. For example, a series of **Edgar Allan Poe**-based anthologies—among them *Unheimliche Geschichten* (*Tales of the Uncanny*) (1932), *Tales of Terror* (1962), and *Histoires extraordinaires* (*Tales of Mystery and Imagination, Spirits of the Dead*) (1968)—proved more faithful (although only slightly in some cases) to the brief literary originals than some feature-length adaptations of Poe's work, while *Twice Told Tales* (1963) tried to do something similar with the writings of Nathaniel Hawthorne. The supernatural drama *Dead of Night* (1945) and **Mario Bava**'s *I tre volti della paura* (*Black Sabbath*) (1963) also took advantage of the anthology format to offer a mixture of different types of story, ranging from the serious to the comic and from period to contemporary, while the more upmarket production *Kaidan* (*Kwaidan*) (1964) showcased the Japanese **ghost** story tradition. The British company **Amicus** produced a series of horror anthologies during the 1960s and 1970s, beginning with *Dr. Terror's House of Horrors* (1964) and including *Torture Garden* (1967) and *Tales from the Crypt* (1972). These displayed both the strengths of the anthology format—an ability to draw upon non-novel length sources, including the short stories of **Robert Bloch** and E.C. horror **comics**—and its weaknesses—notably an unevenness of quality from one segment to another and often feeble linking narratives. Other anthology horrors sharing both these virtues and faults include *The Uncanny* (1977), *Creepshow* (1982), *Twilight Zone: the Movie* (1983), *Cat's Eye* (1985), *After Midnight* (1989), *Due occhi diabolici* (*Two Evil Eyes*) (1990), *Tales from the Darkside: the Movie* (1990), *Necronomicon* (1994), *Quicksilver Highway* (1997), *Bangkok Haunted* (2001), *Cradle of Fear* (2001), and *Saam gaang yi* (*Three . . . Extremes*) (2004).

THE ANTICHRIST. The **American horror** film *The Omen* (1976), and its **sequels**, popularized the idea of the Antichrist, the son of the **Devil**, and in so doing also drew upon apocalyptic prophecies lifted from the Book of Revelations (although the word *antichrist* never actually appears in Revelations). The blasphemous inversion of the story of Jesus Christ, with the "word" of the Devil made flesh on Earth, had first been introduced into horror cinema with **Roman Polanski**'s *Rosemary's Baby* (1968), in which Rosemary (played by **Mia Farrow**) was apparently raped by the Devil and gave birth to his son. While Polanski offered a darkly comic treatment, *The Omen* was both more ponderous and more doom-laden. Its vision of a world in which the rise of the Antichrist is preordained chimed with the cynical mood of the 1970s, and the film was a huge commercial success. The Antichrist returned in *Damien—Omen II* (1978) and *The Final Conflict* (1981) and also featured in *Omen*-clone *Holocaust 2000*

(1977). More recently, the evil one—in the form of Michael York, this time—has sought to bring about the world's destruction in *The Omega Code* (1999) and *Meggido: Omega Code 2* (2001), Ben Chaplin played a potential Antichrist in waiting in *Lost Souls* (2000), and *The Omen* was remade in 2006.

An early comic version of the Antichrist can be found in the Vincente Minnelli-directed musical *Cabin in the Sky* (1943), where he goes under the name of Lucifer Jr.

APES. Apes were stock figures in **American horror** films from the 1920s through to the 1950s. The giant ape in *King Kong* (1933, remade in 1976 and 2005) is the most remembered, but the more typical horror ape usually came in the considerably less impressive form of a man wearing a gorilla suit. The **Edgar Allan Poe** adaptation *Murders in the Rue Morgue* (1932) contained a murderous ape, and the popular murder mystery play *The Gorilla* was filmed three times, in 1927, 1930 and 1939. A fascination with evolutionary progression and regression was evident in *Captive Wild Woman* (1943), in which an ape was transformed into a beautiful woman by a **mad scientist**. Savage gorillas featured in *The Monster and the Girl* (1941) and *Bride of the Gorilla* (1951); *Bela Lugosi Meets a Brooklyn Gorilla* (1952) offered a comic treatment of the theme. In 1961, **British horror** cinema came up with a belated addition to the ape horror cycle with the ludicrous mad scientist film *Konga*, while *Schlock* (1973), **John Landis**'s directorial debut, made fun of the whole ape business.

Since then, modern horror has made little use of the ape-centered horror narrative, and on the few occasions that apes have featured, they have tended to be presented in more realistic terms, with real apes deployed and not a gorilla suit in sight. A razor-wielding chimpanzee showed up in **Dario Argento**'s *Phenomena* (1985) and homicidal monkeys also starred in **Richard Franklin**'s *Link* (1986) and **George Romero**'s *Monkey Shines* (1988).

APOCALYPTIC HORROR. In 1930s and 1940s horror films, the monster was invariably defeated in the end, and there was little or no sense that the threat posed by the monster could escalate to a point where it became unstoppable. From the 1960s onwards, however, notions of the apocalypse, and of scenarios where we are all doomed, have become more prevalent in the horror genre, with this reflecting a greater willingness to question the effectiveness of social authority and to depict the collapse of social institutions. One area where this has been evident is in some **revenge of nature** horrors where nature threatens to supplant mankind entirely, with the most notable examples of this **Alfred Hitchcock**'s *The Birds* (1963), the eco-horror *Frogs* (1972) and **Peter Weir**'s *The Last Wave* (1977). Other apocalyptic horror films have deployed the idea of infection and plague in their depictions of the overthrow of humanity. For example, **George Romero**'s **zombie** films—including *Night of the Living Dead* (1968) and *Dawn of the Dead* (1978)—presented zombiedom as an incurable and fast-spreading infection, with the risen dead gradually taking over the world. *The Omega Man* (1971) did something similar, while **Lamberto Bava**'s *Demoni* (*Demons*) (1985) did a demon-centered version of apocalypse by infection. Grim and pseudo-scientific versions of this end-of-the-world scenario were offered by **David Cronenberg** with *The Parasite Murders* (*They Came From Within*, *Shivers*) (1975) and *Rabid* (1977) and Danny Boyle with *28 Days Later* (2002). By contrast, **John Carpenter** explored the subject in more mystical terms in the **H. P. Lovecraft**-influenced *Prince of Darkness* (1987) and *In the Mouth of Madness* (1995), while the **Internet**-based **Japanese horror** *Kairo* (*Pulse*) (2001) artfully associated the end of the world with social alienation and loneliness. Another key type of apocalyptic horror has drawn upon Biblical and other religious prophecies in its depiction of the human race's apparently preordained passage to Armageddon. For example, *The Omen* (1976) and its **sequels** presented the rise of the **Antichrist** with some conviction, while *Holocaust 2000* (1977) and *The Seventh Sign* (1988) dealt with related material.

ARGENTO, ASIA (1975–). The daughter of noted Italian film director **Dario Argento** and **Italian horror** star **Daria Nicolodi**, the actor Asia Argento has acquired a cult following of her own. Small roles in two films produced by her father—*Demoni 2: L'incubo ritorna* (*Demons 2*) (1986) and *La Chiesa* (*The Church*) (1989)—led to starring roles in three films directed by him—*Trauma* (1993), *La sindrome di Stendhal* (*The Stendhal Syndrome*) (1996), and *Il fantasma dell'opera* (***The Phantom of the Opera***) (1998). As is the case with

Daria Nicolodi's appearances in Dario Argento's work, Asia Argento is repeatedly terrorized in these films and on one occasion—in *La sindrome di Stendhal*—raped as well. However, the strength of her screen persona often belies her apparent helplessness. The same could be said for the no-nonsense character she plays in **George Romero**'s *Land of the Dead* (2005).

In addition to her acting career, Asia Argento has also directed and starred in two non-horror feature films, *Scarlet Diva* (2000) and *The Heart Is Deceitful Above All Things* (2004). Her other genre acting credits include *DeGenerazione* (1994) and *Les morsures de l'aube* (*Love Bites*) (2001).

ARGENTO, DARIO (1940–). As a key European horror auteur, the Italian director Dario Argento's films have not only been commercially successful but have also attracted a substantial cult following. Starting out as a film critic, he quickly graduated to scriptwriting, including a contribution to Sergio Leone's classic **western** *C'era una volta il West* (*Once Upon a Time in the West*) (1968), and as an industry insider—his father, Salvatore, was a film producer—made the transition to film direction more easily than others might have. His first three films as director (all of which he also scripted)—*L'uccello dalle piume di cristallo* (*The Bird with the Crystal Plumage, The Gallery Murders*) (1970), *Il gatto a nove code* (*The **Cat** O' Nine Tails*) (1971), and *4 mosche di velluto grigio* (*Four Flies on Grey Velvet*) (1971)—were **giallo** thrillers, stylish and convoluted psychological dramas built around a series of violent set pieces. At the time, Argento was dubbed "the Italian **Alfred Hitchcock**" but after an unsuccessful foray into **comedy** with *Le cinque giornate* (*Five Days of Milan*) (1973), he emerged as a distinctive filmmaker in his own right.

Profondo Rosso (*Deep Red*) (1975) was another giallo but much more ambitious, thematically and stylistically, than its predecessors. In essence, the film was a reworking of material from Michelangelo Antonioni's *Blow Up* (1966), with the same actor in both (David Hemmings) trying to solve a murder. In place of *Blow Up*'s cerebral meditation on the nature of reality, *Profondo Rosso* offered a visceral assault on the senses, most obviously manifested in the film's scenes of shocking violence—with a hatchet murder, stabbings, a scalding and two decapitations all presented with a loving attention to detail.

Suspiria (1977), Argento's next film, was a supernatural drama in which a student discovers that her ballet school is the front for a witches' coven. "Magic is all around us," says one character, and Argento's stylized approach conveys very powerfully a sense of the witches' elemental powers. Narrative development is minimal and the set pieces more spectacular than before, with the deafening **music** provided by rock group **Goblin** helping to emphasize the film's assaultive qualities. *Suspiria*'s first 15 minutes—depicting the heroine's arrival at the ballet school and an ensuing double murder—remains one of the most brilliant (and most violent) opening sequences in horror history. *Inferno* (1980) was a **sequel** of sorts to *Suspiria*, albeit one that jettisoned that film's shock tactics in favour of a cooler but still very stylish invocation of an alchemical worldview. *Tenebre* (*Tenebrae*, 1982), by contrast, marked a return to the giallo format, with a decidedly perverse narrative in which the detective turns out to be the killer and where the rationality usually associated with the detective story is comprehensively overthrown.

Seen together, *Profondo rosso*, *Suspiria*, *Inferno*, and *Tenebre* comprise one of the most remarkable directorial runs in horror. Perhaps inevitably, Argento's subsequent films have not always matched the extraordinarily high standard of this, his best work. *Phenomena* (1985) is a weird thriller in which **insects** communicate telepathically with the heroine while *Opera* (*Terror at the Opera*) (1987) is an uneven giallo that contains one of Argento's most unsettling images—a closeup of the heroine's **eyes** with needles placed under the eyelids so that she is compelled to watch scenes of extreme violence (an image seized upon by some theorists to illustrate the paradoxes of horror spectatorship). Similarly, Argento's contribution to *Due occhi diabolici* (*Two Evil Eyes*) (1990)—co-directed with **George Romero**—as well as his giallo films *Trauma* (1993), *La sindrome di Stendhal* (*The Stendhal Syndrome*) (1996), and *Nonhosonno* (*Sleepless*) (2001) contain impressive moments and sequences interspersed with less successfully realized material.

Argento supervised the Italian release of Romero's *Dawn of the Dead* (1978) and has produced (and sometimes scripted) horror films for other directors, *Demoni* (*Demons*) (1985) and *Demoni 2: L'incubo ritorna* (*Demons 2*) (1986) for **Lamberto Bava** and *La Chiesa* (*The Church*) (1989) and *La Setta* (*The Sect*) (1991) for **Michele**

Soavi. He also oversaw the production of *Maschera di cera* (*Wax Mask*) (1997).

Other credits include *Il fantasma dell'opera* (*The Phantom of the Opera*) (1998), *Il cartaio* (*The Card Player*) (2004), and contributions to the **television** series *La porta sul buio* (*Door into Darkness*) (1973) and *Masters of Horror* (2005–). *See also* ITALIAN HORROR.

ARKOFF, SAMUEL Z. (1918–2001). The producer Samuel Z. Arkoff was a prolific purveyor of low-budget exploitation and horror films from the 1950s through to the 1970s. With his business partner **James H. Nicholson**, he founded **American International Pictures** (AIP) in the mid-1950s and helped to nurture the career of, among many others, **Roger Corman** and **Jack Nicholson**. After AIP was taken over by Filmways in 1980, Arkoff formed his own company and acted as executive producer on, amongst others, **Brian De Palma**'s *Dressed to Kill* (1980) and **Larry Cohen**'s *Q—the Winged Serpent* (1982).

ARMSTRONG, MICHAEL (1944–). The British writer-director Michael Armstrong has had a checkered career. Trained as an actor at the Royal Academy of Dramatic Art, he moved into filmmaking in his early twenties with the short *The Image* (1967), which featured a then unknown David Bowie in his acting debut. Armstrong went on to direct two striking but uneven horror films, both of which had troubled production histories involving conflict between the director and his producers. *The Haunted House of Horror* (1969), which was originally titled *The Dark* and also known as *Horror House*, was a British psychological horror featuring a largely teenage cast that was, for its time, surprisingly violent. The German-produced period horror *Hexen bis aufs Blut gequält* (*Mark of the Devil*) (1970) took the violence even further in its graphic depiction of witchfinders torturing their victims. This grim film lacked the nuances of **Michael Reeves**' similarly themed *Witchfinder General* (1968) but it was undeniably powerful. Armstrong also scripted the **British horror anthology** *Screamtime* (1983) and **Pete Walker**'s *The House of the Long Shadows* (1983). *See also* GERMAN HORROR.

ARNOLD, JACK (1916–1992). The 1950s work of American director Jack Arnold is usually classified as **science fiction**. However, his eerie use of landscape—especially in *It Came From Outer Space* (1953) and *Creature From The Black Lagoon* (1954)—has influenced later horror films. He also developed the idea of the spider as scary movie monster in *Tarantula* (1955) and, most memorably, in *The Incredible Shrinking Man* (1957).

Other Arnold films of interest to horror aficionados are *Revenge of the Creature* (1955) and *Monster on the Campus* (1958). See also AMERICAN HORROR.

ART CINEMA. "Art cinema" is a loose term encompassing a wide range of approaches and styles. It is rarely associated with the horror genre, probably because the latter is usually seen as a vulgarly commercial enterprise operating lower down the cultural hierarchy than anything going under the name "art." However, these two apparently distinct areas of culture have influenced each other. For example, imagery derived from **expressionism** recurs in later horror films, while some of the prestigious work of canonical directors such as **Carl Theodor Dreyer**, **Ingmar Bergman**, and more recently, Michael Haneke has drawn upon imagery or themes commonly associated with horror cinema. Even an eminent director such as Federico Fellini offers a fine **Mario Bava**-influenced **gothic** study in "Toby Dammit," his contribution to the horror **anthology** *Histoires extraordinares* (*Spirits of the Dead, Tales of Mystery and Imagination*) (1968). Other reputable directors, among them Stanley Kubrick (with *The Shining* in 1980) and **Michael Powell** (with *Peeping Tom* in 1960), have made striking excursions into horror without fully committing themselves to the genre. There are also a number of films that hover, provocatively or uneasily, between the realms of art and of horror. Controversial films such as **Georges Franju**'s *Les yeux sans visage* (*Eyes without a Face*) (1959), Andrzej Zulawski's *Possession* (1981), **Abel Ferrara**'s *The Addiction* (1995) or Claire Denis' *Trouble Every Day* (2001) have sometimes proved too arty for the horror crowd and too gory or disturbing for the arthouse circuit. By contrast, directors such as **Dario Argento** and **Jean Rollin** are more readily located within a horror mainstream, although even the most superficial study of their work reveals conventions and strategies more associated with upmarket art films. It seems from this that the border between art and horror is not always as clear as is sometimes supposed and that exchanges across apparent cultural divides can provide a valuable source of inspiration for all concerned.

ARTISTS. The mad artist has become a stock figure in the horror genre, although he (or more rarely, she) has often been overshadowed by his cousin, the **mad scientist**. Both share a concern to shape reality according to their own self-centered vision, no matter what the consequences for the people around them. In the case of the artist, this usually involves murder as a means to an artistic end or as an artistic strategy in its own right. The classic exemplar of the former was provided by the character played by **Lionel Atwill** in *Mystery of the Wax Museum* (1933), who constructed his **waxworks** around the bodies of his victims, an idea further explored in the 1953 **remake** *House of Wax*, the early **British horror** *Latin Quarter* (1946), the **comedy**-horror *Carry On Screaming* (1966), and the recent *House of Wax* (2005). The Phantom in numerous ***Phantom of the Opera*** films has often been figured as a mad composer, while **Roger Corman**'s *A Bucket of Blood* (1959), **Herschell Gordon Lewis**'s *Color Me Blood Red* (1965) and **Pupi Avati**'s *La casa dalle finestre che ridono* (*The House With Laughing Windows*) (1976) offered representations of artists compelled to murder for inspiration. **Lucio Fulci**'s *L'aldilà* (*The Beyond*) (1981) and **John Carpenter**'s *In the Mouth of Madness* (1995) adopted a different approach in featuring inadvertently disruptive artists or writers whose visionary work has opened up gateways to fearful other dimensions.

Other films have explored the idea of killing itself as a kind of art, with **serial killers** in particular expressing themselves through stylish stagings of violence and **gore**, with this most evident in some **giallo** thrillers as well as in films such as *Peeping Tom* (1960), *The Silence of the Lambs* (1991), *Seven* (1995), and *Scream* (1996). Underpinning this is a clear sense of the artist as a monstrously egotistical and antisocial figure whose art can only be achieved at the expense of human feeling and emotion.

ASHER, JACK (1916–1991). The British cinematographer Jack Asher was largely responsible for the distinctive look of the early **Hammer**

horrors. The garish red of the blood spilled in *The Curse of Frankenstein* (1957) and **Dracula** (*The Horror of Dracula*) (1958) shocked critics and fascinated audiences, but Asher was also capable of producing more atmospheric effects. His lighting helped to make the films appear subtler and more expensive than they actually were. Other Hammer credits included *The Revenge of Frankenstein* (1958), *The Hound of the Baskervilles* (1959), *The Man Who Could Cheat Death* (1959), *The Mummy* (1959), *The Brides of Dracula* (1960), and *The Two Faces of Dr. Jekyll* (1960).

ASHTON, ROY (1909–1995). From the 1980s onwards, horror **makeup** specialists such as **Tom Savini** or **Rob Bottin** acquired star status in their own right. Earlier generations of makeup artists worked in obscurity, however. One such overlooked figure is the Australian-born Roy Ashton, who was a key member of the team that made the **Hammer** horrors. He was responsible for the look of the monster in *The Mummy* (1959), the **werewolf** in *The Curse of the Werewolf* (1961), the unnervingly visceral **zombies** in *The Plague of the Zombies* (1966), and the memorable title creature in *The Reptile* (1966). Other credits are too numerous to list here. Throughout his career he remained a busy but unheralded figure.

ATWILL, LIONEL (1885–1946). The British-born character actor Lionel Atwill appeared in a variety of American films from the end of World War I onwards but he is best remembered for his horror performances, usually in authority roles. His gruff persona could be modulated into the avuncular—in the stylish *Doctor X* (1932), for example—or into villainy in films such as *Mystery of the Wax Museum* (1933) and *Murders in the Zoo* (1933). During the 1930s, he was also a reliable presence in *The Vampire Bat* (1933), *Secret of the Blue Room* (1933), *Mark of the Vampire* (1935), *The Hound of the Baskervilles* (1939), and *The Gorilla* (1939). However, his most striking performance from the decade was as the one-armed police inspector in **Universal**'s *Son of Frankenstein* (1939) who, during a game of darts, absent-mindedly sticks his darts into his wooden arm. In the early 1940s, a Hollywood sex scandal damaged Atwill's career but he continued to show up in low-budget horror productions such as *Man Made Monster* (1941), *The Mad Doctor of Market Street*

(1942), *The Strange Case of Doctor Rx* (1942), *Night Monster* (1942), and *Fog Island* (1945). For Universal, he appeared in quick succession in *The **Ghost** of Frankenstein* (1942), *Frankenstein Meets the Wolf Man* (1943), *House of Frankenstein* (1944), and *House of **Dracula*** (1945), playing different parts each time.

AUSTRALIAN HORROR. There are not many Australian horror films. However, the few that do exist have managed to engage in interesting and critical ways with the experience of being Australian, although this has often involved an appropriation of non-Australian generic conventions. A recurrent preoccupation has been with wild and alienating landscapes into which complacent city-dwellers venture at their peril, with this seeming to reflect anxieties about the relation between modernity and Australian history. Key to this was director **Peter Weir**, whose three horror-themed films—*The Cars That Ate Paris* (1974), *Picnic at Hanging Rock* (1975), and *The Last Wave* (1977)—made a major contribution to the development of Australian cinema during the 1970s, both in their international popularity and in their evocation of a peculiarly Australian sense of the apocalypse. Colin Eggleston's *Long Weekend* (1978) was less well-known internationally but, like Weir's work, it offered a powerful critique of modernity in its depiction of a young couple destroyed by the forces of nature, while Russell Mulcahy's stylish *Razorback* (1984) embodied hostile nature in the form of a large and vicious killer pig. Other Australian horror films have borrowed key ideas from **American horror** cinema but have reinterpreted these in a distinctive manner. *Thirst* (1979) and *Outback **Vampires** (The Wicked)* (1987) presented decidedly weird versions of the movie vampire, and **Richard Franklin**'s psychic thriller *Patrick* (1978) and **serial killer** drama *Roadgames* (1981) also played inventive variations on the formats established by, respectively, **Brian De Palma**'s *Carrie* (1976) and **John Carpenter**'s *Halloween* (1978). Similarly, *Bloodmoon* (1990) was an Australian **slasher** film and *Body Melt* (1993) a striking example of **body horror**. More recently, *Wolf Creek* (2005)—a grueling drama in which some backpackers are tortured to death by a serial killer—has offered an Australian take on the provocative **torture**-based horror associated most of all with American films such as **Eli Roth**'s *Hostel* (2005) and **Rob Zombie**'s *The Devil's Rejects* (2005).

AVATI, PUPI (1938–). The work of the Italian writer-director Pupi Avati has periodically shown a propensity for the **gothic** and for horror. Early directorial efforts such as *Balsamus l'uomo di Satana* (*Blood Relations*) (1970) and *Thomas e gli indemoniati* (*Thomas and the Bewitched*) (1970) contained fantastic elements, but it was Avati's **giallo** *La casa dalle finestre che ridono* (*The House With Laughing Windows*) (1976) that established him as a filmmaker with a distinctive vision. This horror thriller made evocative use of its rural setting and delivered a weird and dream-like story quite distinct from the more aggressive work of giallo specialists **Dario Argento** and **Mario Bava**. Avati's supernatural drama *Zeder* (1983) was comparably offbeat (although mislabeled a **zombie** film in some markets) and *L'Arcan incantatore* (*Arcane Sorcerer, The Mysterious Enchanter*) (1996) was a stylish gothic mystery. Avati also co-wrote the screenplays for **Lucio Fulci**'s **comedy**-horror *Il cavaliere Costante Nicosia demoniaco . . . orrero Dracula in Brianza* (*Young Dracula*) (1975) and **Lamberto Bava**'s **psychological thriller** *Macabro* (*Macabre*) (1980). *See also* ITALIAN HORROR.

– B –

BAKER, RICK (1950–). There has always been a blurring between **makeup** and special effects in horror cinema, but from the 1980s onwards makeup artist Rick Baker has developed this in a way that has won him approval from the industry and attracted a significant **fan** following. Early work included effective contributions to low budget horrors such as **John Landis**'s **comedy**-horror *Schlock* (1973), **Larry Cohen**'s *It's Alive!* (1974), **Jeff Lieberman**'s **revenge of nature** film *Squirm* (1976), the **science fiction**/horror hybrid *The Incredible Melting Man* (1977), and **Tobe Hooper**'s *The Funhouse* (1981). He was also the man in the **ape** suit in the expensive 1976 **remake** of *King Kong* (1976) and worked on *Star Wars* (1977) and **Brian De Palma**'s telekinesis thriller *The Fury* (1978). However, it was his **werewolf** transformation effects in Landis's *An American*

Werewolf in London (1981) that brought him to prominence. Instead of the clumsy fade effects that had been used in older werewolf films, Baker offered a realistic transformation that appeared to take place in real time, with the actor's body experiencing impossible contortions before an astonished audience's **eyes**. It was enough to win Baker the first ever Academy Award for Best Makeup (an award he has won five times since). He went on to devise some equally impressive bodily transformations for **David Cronenberg**'s **body horror** film *Videodrome* (1983) and also designed the horror makeup for Michael Jackson's 1983 "Thriller" video. Since then he has provided a **Rondo Hatton** look-alike villain for the action adventure *The Rocketeer* (1991), turned the actor Martin Landau into **Bela Lugosi** for **Tim Burton**'s biopic *Ed Wood* (1994), created some relatively restrained werewolf effects for the **Jack Nicholson** film *Wolf* (1994) and also fashioned an appropriately frightening monster for **Peter Jackson's** *The Frighteners* (1996). Less scary Baker creations have included aliens in *Men in Black* (1997), fantasy creatures in *How the Grinch Stole Christmas* (2000) and a return to apes in Tim Burton's 2001 remake of *Planet of the Apes*, as well as the comical transformation of Eddie Murphy in *The Nutty Professor* (1996). The rise of computer generated effects might have given filmmakers alternative ways of conjuring up their monsters but Baker remains in demand, most recently designing some unnerving corpses for *The Ring* (2002) and *The Ring Two* (2005) and fantasy creatures for **Guillermo del Toro**'s *Hellboy* (2004) and **Wes Craven**'s werewolf film *Cursed* (2005).

BAKER, ROBERT S. (1916–), AND BERMAN, MONTY (1912–2006). Robert S. Baker and Monty Berman were British producers who occasionally dabbled in film direction. Throughout the 1950s, they specialized in crime thrillers, with **John Gilling** their main director. However, when **British horror** became an eminently marketable category following the commercial success of the early **Hammer** horror films, Baker and Berman co-directed *Jack the Ripper* (1958) and *The Hellfire Club* (1960). Neither of these were especially innovative or accomplished, and *The Hellfire Club*, although drawing upon Hammer-like imagery, was more of a historical melodrama than it was a horror film. However, the fact that they were made at all underlines the way in which the low-budget sector of the British film industry was moving away from crime production to horror production in the late 1950s as a response to changing public tastes. Baker and Berman also produced *Blood of the Vampire* (1958), *The Trollenberg Terror* (1958), *The Flesh and the Fiends* (1959), and the **comedy**-horror *What a Carve Up* (1961). They would both go on to have very successful careers as **television** producers.

BAKER, ROY WARD (1916–). Roy Ward Baker was one of a group of directors—others included **Terence Fisher** and **John Gilling**—who had worked in a range of genres before becoming **British horror** specialists. In Baker's case, the pre-horror career had been a prestigious one that included a stint in Hollywood as well as the direction of the Titanic film *A Night to Remember* (1958). (He was billed as Roy Baker for this work; the Ward came later to distinguish him from a sound editor also called Roy Baker.) If Baker felt any disappointment over his "relegation" to the low-budget horror sector, it did not show in the films he made for leading British horror companies **Hammer** and **Amicus**. His first for Hammer was the **science fiction**/horror hybrid *Quatermass and the Pit* (1967), which was the third in the Quatermass cycle and one of the last of Hammer's more traditional productions before it began to experiment with its horror formula. Thereafter, Baker's solidly professional direction helped to anchor some of the company's more outré projects, including *The Anniversary* (1968), a bizarre and grotesque **comedy** featuring **Bette Davis** at her most histrionic, and *The Vampire Lovers* (1970), Hammer's first lesbian vampire film and a fine adaptation of J. Sheridan LeFanu's story "Carmilla." *Scars of Dracula* (1970) was an uninspiring entry in the Dracula cycle, but *Dr. Jekyll and Sister Hyde* (1971), which involved Jekyll transforming into a woman, was a surprisingly inventive example of late Hammer horror. Subsequently, Baker moved to Amicus where he made two horror **anthologies**—*Asylum* (1972) and *Vault of Horror* (1973)—and an interesting gothic period piece, *And Now The Screaming Starts* (1973). *The Legend of the Seven Golden Vampires* (1974), his final film for Hammer and the company's last period production, was a kung fu/horror hybrid, and it helped to confirm Baker's status as a director of unusual films. One more horror film, *The Monster Club* (1980), followed some years later.

BALDERSTON, JOHN L. (1889–1954). The main claim to horror fame for American playwright and screenwriter John L. Balderston was that he revised Hamilton Deane's theatrical adaptation of *Dracula* for a Broadway production which starred **Bela Lugosi** and which formed the basis for the **Universal** 1931 film. Thereafter he made some contributions to other horrors—most notably *The Mummy* (1932), *The Bride of Frankenstein* (1935), and *Mad Love* (1935)—although he was usually just one writer amongst many and it is hard to detect any distinctive authorial style or theme connecting his work. He also co-wrote the early **British horror** film *The Man Who Changed His Mind* (1936). His time travel fantasy play *Berkeley Square* has been filmed twice, first as *Berkeley Square* (1933) and subsequently as *The House in the Square* (1951).

BAND, ALBERT (1924–2002). The horror career of American writer-director-producer Albert Band began promisingly with the atmospheric low-budget thriller *I Bury the Living* (1958). Unfortunately he did not direct another horror film for 20 years and when he did it was the enjoyable but very silly *Dracula's Dog* (*Zoltan, Hound of Dracula*) (1978). His subsequent directorial credits—which included *Ghoulies 2* (1987) and *Robot Wars* (1993)—were negligible direct-to-video efforts. He produced numerous low budget films, often in association with his son **Charles Band** with whom he also co-directed *Doctor Mordrid* (1992). Another son, Richard Band, is a film composer.

BAND, CHARLES (1951–). The prolific director-producer Charles Band is the son of producer **Albert Band** and shares a similar commitment to low-budget genre cinema. His best film as director is probably the **science fiction** thriller *Trancers* (1985). The horror films he has directed have rarely transcended their budgetary limitations although this is often offset by a weird sense of humor. They include *Parasite* (1982), *The Alchemist* (1984), *Dollman versus Demonic Toys* (1993), *Hideous* (1997), *The Creeps* (1997), *Blood Dolls* (1999), *Dr. Moreau's House of Pain* (2004), *The Gingerdead Man* (2005), *Decadent Evil* (2005), and *Doll Graveyard* (2005). However, Band is more significant as a producer, first with his Empire Pictures company and then with Full Moon Films. Since the 1970s, he has produced or executive produced well over 200 films, the majority of which were for the direct-to-video and subsequently the direct-to-DVD market.

BARKER, CLIVE (1952–). Clive Barker is a British-born writer, director and producer, whose distinctive form of dark fantasy has proved both popular and influential. His breakthrough commercial success came with *The Books of Blood* series of horror stories that began publication in 1984 and which eventually formed six volumes. Before then he had been involved in experimental theater and as one aspect of this activity had made several **gothic**-influenced avant-garde short films—including *Salome* (1972), *Jack O Lant* (1972) and *The Forbidden* (1978). After *The Books of Blood*, Barker wrote the screenplays for two underwhelming **British horror** films, *Underworld* (1985) and *Rawhead Rex* (1986). Unhappy with the results, he made his own directorial debut with *Hellraiser* (1987). In its depiction of demons, this articulate and assured horror film drew upon the provocative imagery associated with sadomasochistic and body-piercing subcultures. At the same time, it also offered a downbeat domestic realism, which made the gory horrors all the more disturbing when they showed up. During post-production, some of the characters in the film were redubbed with American accents to make the film more palatable to the U.S. market but it remained a recognizably British production. *Hellraiser* generated several **sequels**, with Barker himself less involved as each film passed, and the demon Pinhead (played by Barker associate **Doug Bradley**)—a minor presence in the first film—went on to become a significant horror icon in its own right.

Nightbreed (1990), Barker's second film as director, was an ambitious but troubled production that underwent extensive revisions before its release. Barker's key idea—that the monsters should be more positive figures than the forces of normality—turned out to be too radical for film executives, and the resulting compromised film did not do well at the box office, although some of its perverse imagery was as memorable as anything in *Hellraiser*.

In the early 1990s, Barker relocated to the United States where he directed the psychic thriller *Lord of Illusions* (1995). Since then, he has concentrated on novel writing, painting and acting as a film producer—with his most notable producer credit being *Gods and Monsters* (1998), a biopic of horror director **James Whale**. In 1992, one of the stories from Barker's *Books of Blood* was adapted as the successful horror film *Candyman*.

BATES, RALPH (1940–1991). For a brief period in the early 1970s, the British actor Ralph Bates was groomed by **Hammer** as one of its new young horror stars. His first appearance for Hammer was in *Taste the Blood of **Dracula*** (1970), where his saturnine good looks served him well as the evil Lord Courtley. Next he starred as Baron **Frankenstein** in *The Horror of Frankenstein* (1970), Hammer's unsuccessful attempt to update its Frankenstein cycle, and he also took on a character role originally intended for **Peter Cushing** in Hammer's lesbian **vampire** film *Lust for a Vampire* (1971). These films were of variable quality but Bates had undoubted screen presence in them. His best film was *Dr. Jekyll and Sister Hyde* (1971), which, as its title suggested, was Hammer's transsexual rendition of the **Dr. Jekyll and Mr. Hyde** story. As Jekyll, Bates ably conveyed a mixture of horror and fascination as he succumbed to the female side of his character (with the female side played by **Martine Beswick**). Bates appeared in one more Hammer film, the **psychological thriller** *Fear in the Night* (1972) and two non-Hammer horrors, *Persecution* (1974) and the **possession** thriller *I Don't Want to Be Born* (*The Devil Within Her*) (1975). From the mid-1970s onward, Bates worked mainly for **television**, in particular starring in the popular situation **comedy** *Dear John*. He died young of pancreatic cancer.

BATHORY, ELIZABETH (1560–1614). The Hungarian Countess Elizabeth Bathory is reported to have been involved in the murder of several hundred women and to have bathed in their blood in order to retain her youth. The extent to which this story has any historical veracity is unclear, although it does appear that Bathory was accused of serious crimes and spent the last years of her life imprisoned. Whatever the truth of the case, the legend of the "Bloody Countess" has proved an attractive one to horror filmmakers, not just for its intrinsic drama but also for the opportunities it affords for displays of both **gore** and female nudity. Some treatments have turned Bathory into a **vampire**, a female equivalent of Count **Dracula**. The most notable of these was **Harry Kümel**'s eerie modern-day drama *Les lèvres rouges* (*Daughters of Darkness*) (1971). A vampiric countess clearly based on Bathory also took on the **Spanish horror** star **Jacinto Molina** in *La noche de walpurgis* (*Shadow of the Werewolf*) (1970) and *El retorno de walpurgis* (*The Return of Walpurgis, Curse of the Devil*) (1973), and Bathory herself showed up in the Molina film *El retorno del hombre-lobo* (*Night of the Werewolf*) (1980). A more history-based approach was offered by **Hammer**'s *Countess Dracula* (1970), in which, despite the film's title, **Ingrid Pitt** played a non-vampiric murderous Countess based on Bathory, and by **Jorge Grau**'s Spanish horror *Ceremonia sangrienta* (*Blood Castle*) (1973). The Bloody Countess also featured in *Necropolis* (1970), **Walerian Borowczyk**'s *Contes immoraux* (*Immoral Tales*) (1974) and in the modern day thrillers *The Mysterious Death of Nina Chereau* (1988), *Eternal* (2004), and *Tomb of the Werewolf* (2004). A Bathory-like countess appeared in Terry Gilliam's *The Brothers Grimm* (2005) and, most bizarrely, Bathory was a **computer game**-based villain in the **teenage horror** film *Stay Alive* (2006).

BAVA, LAMBERTO (1944–). Lamberto Bava is the son of **Italian horror** maestro **Mario Bava** and began his career as a filmmaker working in minor capacities on some of his father's films, culminating in his co-scripting Mario Bava's final project, *Schock* (*Shock, Beyond the Door II*) (1977). His own directorial debut was the atmospheric **psychological thriller** *Macabro* (*Macabre*) (1980), which told the disturbing tale of a woman who kept her ex-lover's severed head in her refrigerator. During the early 1980s, Bava also acted as assistant director on **Dario Argento**'s *Inferno* (1980) and *Tenebre* (*Tenebrae*) (1982), and Argento would later become a significant influence on his career. *La casa con la scala nel buio* (*A Blade in the Dark*) (1983), Bava's second film as director, was a highly effective **giallo** thriller. By contrast, *Shark rosso nell'oceano* (*Devil Fish, Devouring Waves*) (1984) was a routine *Jaws* clone for which Bava billed himself as John Old Jr. (a backhanded tribute to his father who was sometimes credited as John Old). The supernatural thriller *Demoni* (*Demons*) (1985), in which demons invade a cinema during the screening of a horror film, was Bava's biggest international commercial success. It was produced by Argento and reflected his distinctive themes and style as much as Bava's, but the director did generate an intensely claustrophobic atmosphere. Bava also directed the inferior **sequel** *Demoni 2: L'incubo ritorna* (*Demons 2*) (1986), and a number of his later films were sometimes marketed as further sequels, although none of them had anything to do with the *Demons* films. Since the mid-1980s, Bava has worked mainly for Italian **television**, and his cinematic career has become patchy. *Morirai a mezzanotte* (*The Midnight Killer*) (1986), *Le foto di gioia* (*Delirium*) (1987) and *Body Puzzle* (1991) were effective giallo films, albeit not particularly distinctive, while *Una notte al cimitero* (*Graveyard Disturbance*) (1987) was a routine **zombie** film and *La maschera del demonio* (*Black Sunday*) (1989) a very loose **remake** of his father's classic **witchcraft** film of 1960. Bava has also directed numerous horror and fantasy television films and series, although he recently returned to cinematic horror with *The Torturer* (2005) and **Ghost Son** (2006).

BAVA, MARIO (1914–1980). The great **Italian horror** director and cinematographer Mario Bava specialized in morbidity. The subject matter of his films was varied but the best of them shared a death-ridden mood. He was also a supreme stylist, with the ability to conjure up beautiful but oppressive worlds from very limited resources. His first experience of the horror genre came with **Riccardo Freda**'s *I vampiri* (aka *The Devil's Commandment*) (1956). Initially hired as a cinematographer, he took over as director for a few days of the production. His first solo directorial credit came with *La maschera del demonio* (*The Mask of Satan, Revenge of the Vampire, Black Sunday*) (1960), a **witchcraft** drama that starred **Barbara Steele** in her first major role. Although made to cash in on the international success of **Hammer** horror, the film's stylish black-and-white photography and its brooding atmosphere made it a distinctive experience in its own right, and its commercial success generated a cycle of Italian period horror.

Bava's subsequent career saw him working in various genres but he always seemed to be more engaged by psychologically introspective or fantasy-based scenarios. His **westerns** and **comedies** were conventional affairs, as was *Ercole al centro della terra* (*Hercules in the Haunted World*) (1961), the muscle-man epic he made immediately after *La maschera del demonio*, until its remarkable **gothic** conclusion in which Hercules takes on an army of **zombies**. *La ragazza che sapeva troppo* (*The Girl Who Knew Too Much, The Evil Eye*) (1962), a contemporary-set **psychological thriller** widely considered to be the first Italian **giallo**, was clearly a more amenable project. The whodunnit narrative was silly but, in true giallo style, Bava used it primarily as a pretext for a depiction of disturbed psychologies and exercises in style.

The horror **anthology** *I tre volti della paura* (*Black Sabbath*) (1963) showcased the breadth of Bava's abilities in its combination of a **ghost** story, a crime thriller, and an impressive vampire narrative (the latter featuring **Boris Karloff**). It was followed by *La frusta e il corpo* (*The Whip and the Body*) (1963), a psychological thriller masquerading as a period horror that offered one of Bava's most compelling representations of perverse desire. *Sei donne per l'assassino* (*Blood and Black Lace*) (1964) was another giallo, although this time more brutal in its violence and more stylish in its fashion house setting, while *Terrore nello spazio* (*Planet of the Vampires*) (1965) was a **science fiction**-horror hybrid that some critics have seen as an influence on Ridley Scott's *Alien* (1979). *Operazione paura* (*Kill, Baby . . . Kill!*) (1966) and the Spanish-Italian co-production *Un hacha para la luna de miel* (*Hatchet for the Honeymoon*) (1969) were both ghost stories, with the former a particularly chilling example of the genre. *Cinque bambole per la luna d'agosto* (*Five Dolls for an August Moon*) (1970) was yet another giallo, one in which the Agatha Christie-like narrative was particularly dispensable and the film's almost abstract stylization especially prominent. *Reazione a catena* (*Ecologia del delitto, Twitch of the Death Nerve, Bay of Blood*) (1971) mingled extreme violence with a sardonic sense of humor in its convoluted story about a series of murders, all of them committed by different people (many of whom then become victims themselves). The high body count, the set piece killings and the lakeside setting have led to the film being seen as inspiration for the American **slasher** *Friday the 13th* (1980), although Bava's version is a far more sophisticated and classy rendition of mass murder. The ghost story *Gli orrori del castello di Norimberga* (*Baron Blood*) (1972) was followed by the director's most ambitious project and arguably his masterpiece, *Lisa e il diavolo* (*Lisa and the Devil*) (1972). A daringly experimental narrative eroded distinctions between reality and dreams; the result was enigmatic and extraordinarily haunting. Unfortunately this was not what the producers had in mind; the film was shelved for a while and in 1975, after the phenomenal success of *The Exorcist* (1973), an alternate version was released that removed much of the dream-like atmosphere and replaced it with a clumsy framing narrative in which a priest exorcises the film's heroine. The *House of Exorcism*, as this version was called, was something of an embarrassment in Bava's career, although thankfully his original version was later restored. After the crime thriller *Cani arrabbiati* (*Rabid Dogs*) (1974), Bava's last film as director was *Schock* (*Shock, Beyond the Door 2*) (1977), a slight but elegant mix of psychological drama and ghost story. His son **Lamberto Bava** is also a director of horror films.

BAXTER, LES (1922–1996). Les Baxter was a prolific composer and recording artist, whose film **music** ranged from lush melodies to dissonant sounds. He worked on **William Castle**'s *Macabre* (1958) and on numerous **Roger Corman** films, including *House of Usher* (1960), *Pit and the Pendulum* (1961)—which was arguably his most evocative score—*Tales of Terror* (1962) and *The Raven* (1963). He also wrote new scores for some **Italian horror** films—including **Mario Bava**'s *La maschera del demonio* (*The Mask of Satan, Revenge of the Vampire, Black Sunday*) (1960) and *I tre volti della paura* (*Black Sabbath*) (1963)—in order to make them more palatable for American audiences. Other noteworthy scores include *The Dunwich Horror* (1970) and *Cry of the Banshee* (1970). His complete credits are too numerous to list here.

BEAUMONT, CHARLES (1929–1967). The American writer Charles Beaumont's most distinctive horror and fantasy work was done for literature and **television**. He published many short stories—including the horror classic "Miss Gentilbelle"—and made numerous contributions to the fantasy-based television series *One Step Beyond* (1959–1961), *Thriller* (1960–1962) and *The Twilight Zone* (1959–1964). *Queen of Outer Space* (1958), Beaumont's screen debut, was an undistinguished piece of **science fiction**. Considerably more impressive was the work he did for director **Roger Corman**, co-scripting the **Edgar Allan Poe** adaptations *The Premature Burial* (1962) and *The Masque of the Red Death* (1964) and receiving sole writing credit for the **H. P. Lovecraft** adaptation *The Haunted Palace* (1963). With fellow writer and friend **Richard Matheson**, he also penned the superior British **witchcraft** film *Night of the Eagle* (*Burn, Witch, Burn!*) (1962) and by himself wrote the idiosyncratic fantasy drama *7 Faces of Dr. Lao* (1964). Beaumont died of Alzheimer's disease at the age of 38.

BERGMAN, INGMAR (1918–2007). Of all the great European film directors who appeared after World War II, it was Ingmar Bergman who seemed most attuned to **gothic** and horror themes and imagery. This did not make him a horror artist—although a few overly partisan accounts of the horror genre have claimed him as such—but it does suggest that the boundary between what is thought of as **art cinema** and a popular genre cinema is more permeable than is sometimes supposed. The common understanding of Bergman as a grim filmmaker is unjustified; in a long career he made successful **comedies** and other charming dramas. Nevertheless, his classic *Det sjunde inseglet* (*The Seventh Seal*) (1957) can be seen as an example of **apocalyptic horror**, while the nightmare depicted at the opening of *Smultronstället* (*Wild Strawberries*) (1957) remains one of cinema's most unnerving sequences. By contrast, *Ansiktet* (*The Magician, The Face*) (1958) made more playful use of some horror conventions. Of greater significance to an understanding of this aspect of Berman's art is *Persona* (1966), a dream-like psychological drama featuring vampiric imagery, and *Vargtimmen* (*Hour of the Wolf*) (1968), in which an artist's inner turmoil is externalized in the form of what appear to be supernatural beings. The intended effect of Bergman's treatment of this material is clearly not meant to be the kind of frisson delivered by a good horror film. However, the scene in *Vargtimmen* in which an old woman casually pulls off her own face indicates that this was a director more than aware of the power of shock.

BERMAN, MONTY (1912–2006). *See* BAKER, ROBERT S.

BERNARD, JAMES (1925–2001). The British composer James Bernard's strident and percussive **music** was a distinctive feature of many **Hammer** horror films. Early work for the company included brooding scores for *The Quatermass Xperiment* (*The Creeping Unknown*) (1955), *X the Unknown* (1956), and *The Curse of Frankenstein*

(1957). However, his first outstanding score was for *Dracula* (*Horror of Dracula*) (1958). His three-note theme for this was based on the word *Dracula* itself, and it would subsequently feature in most of Hammer's *Dracula* films. He was also capable of producing a more melodic sound, an example being the delicate main theme for *Taste the Blood of Dracula* (1970). Bernard rarely composed for anyone other than Hammer, although he did write some music for the **Amicus** production *Torture Garden* (1967) and in 1997 recorded a new score for **F. W. Murnau**'s classic **vampire** film *Nosferatu* (1922). His other scores include *Quatermass 2* (*Enemy from Space*) (1957), *The Hound of the Baskervilles* (1959), *The Stranglers of Bombay* (1959), *The Terror of the Tongs* (1961), *The Damned* (*These are the Damned*) (1963), *The Kiss of the Vampire* (1963), *The Gorgon* (1964), *She* (1965), *The Plague of the Zombies* (1966), *Dracula—Prince of Darkness* (1966), *Frankenstein Created Woman* (1967), *The Devil Rides Out* (1968), *Dracula Has Risen from the Grave* (1968), *Frankenstein Must Be Destroyed* (1969), *Scars of Dracula* (1970), *Frankenstein and the Monster from Hell* (1974), *The Legend of the Seven Golden Vampires* (1974), and *Murder Elite* (1985).

BESWICK, MARTINE (1941–). The Jamaican-born actor Martine Beswick first made an impact as a gypsy in the James Bond film *From Russia with Love* (1963) and returned to the series in a different role in *Thunderball* (1965). For **Hammer**, she made decorative appearances in the prehistoric adventures *One Million Years B.C.* (1966) and *Slave Girls* (*Prehistoric Women*) (1967). However, her most striking role was as the female side of **Ralph Bates** in Hammer's transsexual *Dr. Jekyll and Sister Hyde* (1971); here she captured perfectly the character's sensuality and her perverse desire for extreme sensation. She was also impressive as the Queen of Evil in **Oliver Stone**'s **American horror** *Seizure* (1974). Since then she has worked mainly for American **television**, with occasional appearances in low-budget horrors such as *The Offspring* (*From a Whisper to a Scream*) (1987), *Evil Spirits* (1990), and *Night of the Scarecrow* (1995).

BLACK HORROR. The representation of black characters in early horror cinema was far from flattering. Blackness was often associated with a threatening exoticism in films such as *White Zombie* (1932), *King Kong* (1933), *King of the Zombies* (1941), and *I Walked with a Zombie* (1943), and black actors such as Willie Best or **Mantan Moreland** were usually cast as cowardly sidekicks to white protagonists. Some film historians have since detected positive, or at least ambiguous, elements in some of these films. For example, the **Val Lewton-Jacques Tourneur** collaboration *I Walked with a Zombie* certainly seems to offer a critique of its white characters, while the wisecracking Moreland, who frequently received top billing in black theaters, often highlighted the absurdity of the white characters' behavior. Whether these elements registered with audiences of the time, black or white, remains unclear, however.

As the civil rights movement developed in the United States during the 1950s, representations of this kind faded away, and black characters were notable for their absence in much **American horror** of the period. **British horror**, by contrast, retained a fascination with black exoticism as late as the 1960s in films such as the **Amicus** horror **anthology** *Dr. Terror's House of Horrors* (1964) and **Hammer's** post-imperial *The Plague of the Zombies* (1966) and Satanic thriller *The Devil Rides Out* (1968). Within such a context, **George Romero's** now classic American zombie film *Night of the Living Dead* (1968) was strikingly innovative in featuring a personable young black man as its hero. The film's dialogue made no reference to race, although the hero's ultimate fate—shot and burned by a group of redneck law enforcers—connected in a disturbing way with the ongoing civil rights struggle. The challenge offered by this provocative piece of casting was not taken up immediately by filmmakers. However, a 1970s cycle of blaxploitation films included not just crime thrillers like *Shaft* (1971) and *Superfly* (1972) but also horror films, with black characters installed in roles that in the past had been reserved for white performers. *Blacula* (1972), *Blackenstein* (1973), the experimental *Ganja & Hess* (1973), the *Exorcist*-like *Abby* (1974), the **voodoo** drama *Sugar Hill* (1974), and *Dr. Black, Mr. Hyde* (1976) either rendered white characters as villains or marginalized them, although many of these films were made by white directors. The political value of blaxploitation, and the extent to which the values of a dominant white society were challenged by such representations, remains a contentious issue.

The advent of the American **slasher** film in the late 1970s tended to marginalize black characters once again, although there were occasional productions that engaged in interesting ways with issues arising out of racial difference. **Wes Craven**'s voodoo thriller *The Serpent and the Rainbow* (1988) and his **comedy**-horror *Vampire in Brooklyn* (1995) revisited traditional black horror scenarios from a modern, revisionary perspective, while his *The People under the Stairs* (1991) intelligently explored black social exclusion from within a horror idiom. **Bernard Rose**'s equally distinguished *Candyman* (1992) did something similar in its representation of a resurrected ex-slave transformed into an urban legend and was successful enough to generate two **sequels**, *Candyman: Farewell to the Flesh* (1995) and *Candyman: Day of the Dead* (1999). *Def by Temptation* (1990) was an interesting attempt to revive blaxploitation horror, but *Blade* (1998), which starred Wesley Snipes as a heroic vampire hunter who is himself part-vampire, was a more confident and commercially successful treatment of this material; *Blade 2* (2002) and *Blade: Trinity* (2004) followed.

The racist tenor of much early horror has certainly been dissipated over the years, although the extent to which blackness has become normalized in horror production is far from clear, with the majority of the genre's heroes and heroines still noticeably white.

BLAIR, LINDA (1959–). As Regan, the possessed child in *The Exorcist* (1973), Linda Blair gave one of the keynote performances in 1970s **American horror**, and was utterly convincing in what was probably the most difficult screen role a child has ever been asked to play. Like many child actors, she subsequently found it difficult to establish herself as an adult performer. She returned to the part of Regan in the eccentric *Exorcist II: The Heretic* (1977), starred in **Wes Craven**'s effective **television** horror film *Stranger in Our House* (*Summer of Fear*) (1978), and was a spirited **Final Girl** in the **slasher** *Hell Night* (1981). Subsequent genre credits—which included *Grotesque* (1988), *Witchery* (1988), *The Chilling* (1989), and *Sorceress* (1995)—were underwhelming. *Repossessed* (1990), in which she co-starred with Leslie Nielsen, was a belated *Exorcist* spoof, while her cameo role in *Scream* (1996) underlined her status as horror icon.

BLATTY, WILLIAM PETER (1928–). Given his association with one of the most controversial and profitable horror films ever made, it is suprising to discover that William Peter Blatty started out as a **comedy** writer, with one of his early credits being the first *Pink Panther* **sequel**, *A Shot in the Dark* (1964). His bestselling—and overwhelmingly humorless—novel *The Exorcist* changed all that. He wrote and produced the 1973 adaptation (and also made a cameo appearance in it), and much of his subsequent career has been played out in the shadow of that remarkable film. His directorial debut came with the **psychological thriller** *The Ninth Configuration* (1980). Ten years later, he wrote and directed *Exorcist III* (1990), which was adapted from his novel *Legion*. This was a somber, intelligent affair, albeit one that, perhaps inevitably, lacked the impact of the original.

THE BLIND DEAD. The "Blind Dead" cycle of films is an important example of **Spanish horror** and an innovative variant on the **zombie** film. The Blind Dead themselves are the resurrected eyeless corpses of the Knights Templar who can track their victims through sound. The first two films of the cycle—*La noche del terror ciego* (*Tombs of the Blind Dead*, *The Blind Dead*) (1971) and *El ataque de los muertos sin ojos* (*Return of the Blind Dead*) (1973)—offered similar narratives in which cosmopolitan modern characters inadvertently strayed into the realm of the Blind Dead and suffered gruesome fates. Characterizations were minimal, with the films offering instead nightmarish sequences in which the Blind Dead slowly but inexorably advanced upon their victims. That these revenants sometimes rode zombie horses added an unusual twist to the zombie formula.

El buque maldito (*The Ghost Galleon*, *Horror of the Zombies*, *The Blind Dead 3*) (1974), the third film in the cycle, opted for an oceanic setting but, despite some atmospheric moments, was let down badly by clumsy model work for the ghostly zombie galleon. The final Blind Dead film, *La noche de las gaviotas* (*Night of the Seagulls*) (1975) was in many ways the most imaginative of the four and made excellent use of its desolate coastline setting. However, by this stage the galloping blind zombies had become overly familiar figures of threat, and no more films followed.

All four of the Blind Dead films were directed by Amando de Ossorio, whose few other horror credits were negligible. *La cruz del diablo* (*The Devil's Cross*) (1975), directed by **John Gilling**, dealt with similar thematic material but is not part of the cycle.

BLOCH, ROBERT (1917–1994). The American writer Robert Bloch began publishing fantasy-based stories in the 1930s, but it was not until the early 1960s that he received any significant recognition. His success was, in part at least, due to **Alfred Hitchcock**'s *Psycho* (1960), an adaptation of Bloch's 1959 novel of the same title. Bloch had nothing to do with the film itself, but his association with psychological horror subsequently led to several screen-writing credits. He worked on the **serial killer** drama *The Couch* (1962) and the eccentric **remake** *The Cabinet of Caligari* (1962), with both of these making extensive use of psychoanalytical terminology. *Strait-Jacket* (1964) and *The Night Walker* (1964), both for producer-director **William Castle**, were more straightforward mystery thrillers. An association with **British horror** began when the **Amicus** company adapted his short story "The Skull of the Marquis de Sade" into *The Skull* (1965). He went on to write or co-write several screenplays for the company. *The Deadly Bees* (1966) was a mundane monster movie, but *The Psychopath* (1965) was an imaginative reworking of themes first introduced in *Psycho* and arguably the closest British cinema ever came to imitating the Italian **giallo** form of **psychological thriller**. Thereafter Bloch specialized in the horror **anthologies** for which Amicus became well-known, in the process often recycling some of his old short stories. *Torture Garden* (1967), *The House That Dripped Blood* (1970), and *Asylum* (1972) turned out to be three of the best of this type of film, both in the inventiveness of the individual episodes and in the cleverness of the framing narratives (often the weak point in Amicus's productions).

Bloch also wrote extensively for **television**, specializing in horror and crime. His credits include *Alfred Hitchcock Presents* (1955–1962), *Thriller* (1960–1962), *Journey to the Unknown* (1968), and *Night Gallery* (1970). He penned some of the more **gothic** episodes of *Star Trek* (1966–1969), including one featuring **Jack the Ripper**, as well as two interesting television films for director **Curtis Harrington**, *The Cat Creature* (1973), and *The Dead Don't Die* (1975).

BODY HORROR. The term *body horror* has been used by horror critics to describe a type of horror film that first emerged during the 1970s, one which offered graphic and sometimes clinical representations of human bodies that were in some way out of the conscious control of their owners. In a sense, body horror describes the ultimate alienation—alienation from one's own body—but this has often been coupled with a fascination with the possibility of new identities that might emerge from this. The term is most associated with the work of Canadian director **David Cronenberg**, whose early horror films—among them *The Parasite Murders* (*They Came from Within, Shivers*) (1975), *Rabid* (1977), and *The Brood* (1979)—focused on mutation and other physical transformations; *Videodrome* (1983) and *The Fly* (1986) were later body horror examples from his remarkable oeuvre. Other horror films that share a Cronenbergian fascination with fleshy metamorphoses include **Stuart Gordon**'s *Re-animator* (1985), **Clive Barker**'s *Hellraiser* (1987) and Shinya Tsukamoto's *Tetsuo* (1989). Philip Brophy's Australian production *Body Melt* (1993) is another example and contains a quintessential body horror scene in which a man is attacked by an excreted placenta.

BOLL, UWE (1965–). The writer-director Uwe Boll began making films in his native Germany, including the **serial killer** drama *Amoklauf* (1994). He has since become a specialist in English-language horror with the knack of attracting well-known actors to what are usually low-budget, self-financed genre projects. Boll's films have not always been well-received by horror **fans**, and in September 2006 he adopted the novel defensive tactic of challenging his fiercest critics to a boxing bout; he took on four and defeated them all. Boll's horror credits include *House of the Dead* (2003), *Alone in the Dark* (2005), and *BloodRayne* (2005).

BOORMAN, JOHN (1933–). The British director John Boorman is rarely thought of as a horror director, and *Exorcist II: The Heretic* (1977), his one excursion into the genre, was a critical and commercial disaster. However, Boorman's *Deliverance* (1972)—in which a group of complacent urbanites venture into the countryside where they are attacked and violated by the brutal locals—provided a template for later **rural horror** and rape-revenge dramas. Films such as

The Texas Chainsaw Massacre (1974), *The Hills Have Eyes* (1977), *I Spit on Your Grave* (1978), and more recently, *Wrong Turn* (2003), *Calvaire* (*The Ordeal*) (2004), and *Wolf Creek* (2005) owe more than a passing debt to Boorman's unflinching portrayal of human savagery.

BORLAND, CARROLL (1914–1994). Carroll Borland seems to have become a horror icon on the basis of a supporting role in just one film, **Tod Browning**'s *Mark of the Vampire* (1935) (where she is billed as Carol Borland). She played the apparently vampiric Luna, daughter of the equally vampiric Count Mora (played by **Bela Lugosi**), although a final self-reflexive plot twist reveals that they are both actors pretending to be vampires. With her long dark hair, her deathly paleness and her odd but beautiful facial features, Borland is certainly memorable in the role and quite different from the more vapid female leads who populated much of 1930s horror. The fact that this was her only performance of note perhaps added to her allure. Many years later she showed up in small roles in two **Fred Olen Ray** films, *Scalps* (1983) and *Biohazard* (1985).

BOROWCZYK, WALERIAN (1923–2006). The Polish director Walerian Borowczyk worked mainly in France, starting out as an **animation** specialist but switching to live action in the 1960s. His films ranged from art house projects such as *Blanche* (1971) to mildly pornographic fare such as *Contes immoraux* (*Immoral Tales*) (1974), which featured Countess **Elizabeth Bathory**. Borowczyk achieved some notoriety for *La bête* (*The Beast*) (1975), which contained graphic images of bestiality and rape while still retaining some of the conventions of **art cinema**. Other horror-related titles included *Lulu* (1980)—in which **Udo Kier** played **Jack the Ripper**—and *Docteur Jekyll et les femmes* (*Dr. Jekyll and His Women*) (1981), with Kier as Jekyll. Borowczyk might have ended his career ignominiously with the likes of *Emmanuelle V* (1987) but his strange, surreal, sometimes shocking and sometimes boring films have acquired a substantial cult following for what is seen as their provocative transgressiveness.

BOTTIN, ROB (1959–). Like fellow **makeup** artist and mentor **Rick Baker**, Rob Bottin's career-making moment came with a **werewolf**

transformation. With Baker it was *An American Werewolf in London* (1981) while with Bottin it was **Joe Dante**'s *The Howling* (1981). Dante's film had less of a budget but nevertheless Bottin created an impressive onscreen metamorphosis. Earlier he had worked with Dante on *Piranha* (1978) and with **John Carpenter** on *The Fog* (1980), for which he not only created the **ghosts** but played the lead ghost himself. A further collaboration with Carpenter produced what was probably his finest achievement, the shape-shifting alien monster in *The Thing* (1982). In what was one of the last great showcasing of physical effects before the rise of computer generated special effects, Bottin created a surreal, astonishing and disturbingly beautiful array of transformations. Also impressive was Bottin's spectacular makeup for the Lord of Darkness in Ridley Scott's fantasy *Legend* (1985) and his design for the cyborg cop in *Robocop* (1987). Bottin's other horror credits have included *Twilight Zone: The Movie* (1983), *The Witches of Eastwick* (1987), and *Seven* (1995), for which he created some unnervingly realistic dead bodies.

BRADLEY, DOUG (1954–). The British actor Doug Bradley is the demon Pinhead in the *Hellraiser* films. The **makeup** was striking enough, with nails hammered into the character's head, but through the makeup Bradley was also able to instil an impression both of grandeur and of melancholy. In *Hellraiser* (1987), he was only on screen for a few minutes, but his performance was so memorable that he took center stage in the later films, which were *Hellbound: Hellraiser II* (1988), *Hellraiser III: Hell on Earth* (1992), *Hellraiser: Bloodline* (1996), *Hellraiser: Inferno* (2000), *Hellraiser: Hellseeker* (2002), *Hellraiser: Deader* (2005), and *Hellraiser: Hellworld* (2005). In some of these films, he also played Pinhead's human alter ego, an army captain called Eliot Spencer. Earlier in his career he had worked with *Hellraiser* writer-director **Clive Barker** both in the theater and on some experimental short films, and he was reunited with him for a character role in Barker's *Nightbreed* (1990). Other horror roles include *Proteus* (1995), *La lengua asesina* (*The Killer Tongue*) (1996), and *The Prophecy: Uprising* (2005). He is also the author of a thoughtful book on acting in horror, *Sacred Monsters: Behind the Mask of the Horror Actor*.

BRITISH HORROR. Great Britain has a rich tradition of **gothic** literature stretching back to the 18th century. However, horror did not form a significant part of British cinema until the mid-1950s. There was some limited production of American-style horrors during the 1930s—among them the British-born **Boris Karloff** vehicle *The Ghoul* (1933)—as well as a series of lurid melodramas starring the appropriately named **Tod Slaughter** that had some horror-like properties. However, the British censors' disapproval of this kind of material ensured its continued marginality. The outbreak of World War II constrained yet further the possibilities for horror production, and indeed the import of horror films into Britain was banned during the conflict, presumably on the grounds that such films would lower morale. This did not mean that fantasy elements were entirely absent from British film production—one could find them, for example, in some of the films directed by **Michael Powell** or the popular costume melodramas produced by the Gainsborough company—but they often sat awkwardly with more propagandistic imperatives.

The end of war was greeted by Powell's extravagant fantasy *A Matter of Life and Death* (1946) and Ealing Studio's **anthology** of **ghost** stories, *Dead of Night* (1945), but the times were not propitious for the horror genre. The British censors were still disapproving, and the 1940s **American horror** cycle was winding down into **Bud Abbott** and **Lou Costello** parodies. Things had changed by 1957 when a small independent production company called **Hammer** released its first color horror film, *The Curse of Frankenstein*. **Censorship** had relaxed, there was a new adult-only "X" film certificate, and also, as Hammer's success demonstrated, a substantial public appetite for horror fictions. Hammer capitalized on this through producing a series of period horrors, including *Dracula* (*Horror of Dracula*) (1958), *The Mummy* (1959), and *The Curse of Werewolf* (1961), many of which were directed by **Terence Fisher** and starred new horror icons **Peter Cushing** and **Christopher Lee**. Other companies also moved into this market, and directors such as Henry Cass, **Robert Day**, **Freddie Francis**, **John Gilling**, and **Sidney Hayers** turned out a varied diet of horrors, ranging from Hammer-like period dramas to contemporary-set films. Even Michael Powell contributed with his **serial killer** drama *Peeping Tom* (1960), the critical notoriety of which allegedly shortened the director's British career. From the early 1960s onwards, the **Amicus** company became Hammer's main rival, specializing in horror anthologies such as *Dr. Terror's House of Horrors* (1964) and *Torture Garden* (1967).

On their initial release, films like *The Curse of Frankenstein* and *Dracula* had proved controversial with critics. This shock effect had largely worn off by the mid-1960s, and British horror had become an accepted part of the British cinema scene. Things were changing in the horror genre, however. In America, disturbing horrors such as *Night of the Living Dead* (1968) and *Rosemary's Baby* (1968) were beginning to appear, and, in a comparable British shift, a younger generation of filmmakers with more questioning attitudes to social norms and institutions entered horror production. Chief among them was the brilliant writer-director **Michael Reeves**; others included directors **Gordon Hessler, Peter Sasdy, Peter Sykes**, and screenwriter **Christopher Wicking**. Their films often sided with youth and criticized the family unit or patriarchal authority, as well as experimenting with narrative structure. More innovation was taking place elsewhere in the British genre in the first part of the 1970s as filmmakers attempted to update the old period formats for a changing market. Nudity featured with increasing frequency, Hammer dabbled in lesbian **vampire** films as well as a kung fu vampire film, *The Legend of the Seven Golden Vampires* (1974), and a new company called Tyburn bravely set out to make more period horrors at a time when this type of horror was proving unpopular, especially in the crucial American market.

The phenomenal success of the American horror film *The Exorcist* (1973) encouraged the development of horrors with contemporary settings, with period horror now looking decidedly old-fashioned. Although British horror had not been entirely wedded to period settings, nevertheless it struggled to keep up with the American competition. Difficulties in obtaining funding for British films during the 1970s also made life hard for horror producers. Hammer made one more horror film, the contemporary-set Satanic thriller *To the Devil a Daughter* (1976), before ceasing horror production. In the second half of the 1970s, a few directors working in the low-budget exploitation sector—notable among them **Pete Walker** and **Norman J. Warren**—made some tough and violent contemporary horrors that, formally and thematically, had a lot in common with 1970s American horror, but this activity too faded away by the end of the decade.

Given the popularity of British horror, it is surprising how few horror films were made in Britain during the 1980s and 1990s. Heritage films such as *A Room with a View* (1985) or *Howard's End* (1992), as well as gritty state-of-the-nation films like *My Beautiful Laundrette* (1985), caught the attention of critics and achieved some commercial success, but the serial production of popular genres such as horror was no longer a feature of British film production. **Clive Barker**'s *Hellraiser* (1987) and *Nightbreed* (1990) were American-funded while **Neil Jordan**'s *The Company of Wolves* (1984) was an isolated exercise in upmarket fantasy.

However, the early 2000s saw a modest revival in the fortunes of British horror with the likes of *The Bunker* (2001), *Deathwatch* (2002), *My Little Eye* (2002), **Neil Marshall**'s *Dog Soldiers* (2002), *Shaun of the Dead* (2004), *Creep* (2004), and *Severance* (2006), although none of these films showed much interest in returning to traditional Hammer-style formats. It is also, perhaps, a sign of the times that, while made by British directors and deploying British actors, many of the new British horror films are international co-productions shot outside of Britain.

BROOKS, MEL (1926–). The American writer-producer-director-performer Mel Brooks has made two **comedy**-horror films. *Young Frankenstein* (1974) is a nostalgic tribute to **Universal** horror of the 1930s and 1940s that displays a detailed awareness of its source material, reuses some of the original props from the 1931 version of *Frankenstein*, and is shot in beautiful black and white. It is also very funny. *Dracula—Dead and Loving It* (1995), which functions largely as a parody of **Francis Ford Coppola**'s *Dracula* (1992), is a more hit-and-miss affair. However, any Dracula film in which a character assumes that being *nosferatu* means that you are Italian does deserve some recognition. *See also* AMERICAN HORROR.

BROWNING, TOD (1880–1962). The American director Tod Browning—whose real name was Charles Browning—was responsible for **Universal**'s production of *Dracula* (1931), the commercial success of which helped to establish the horror genre as a distinctive presence within 1930s American cinema. However, Browning's critical reputation as a horror pioneer is nowhere near as secure as that of his fellow Universal director, **James Whale**. An oft-repeated criticism of *Dracula* is that its opening sequences are impressive but thereafter it is turgid and theatrical, as opposed to Whale's more consistently cinematic approach in *Frankenstein* (1931). Some have gone so far as to attribute the quality of *Dracula*'s opening to the cinematographer **Karl Freund**, while others have compared the film with the Spanish-language version of *Dracula* that was produced simultaneously on the same sets and have found the Browning version wanting. Whatever the merits and demerits of the 1931 *Dracula*—and it has undoubtedly dated more than the 1931 *Frankenstein*—it should be noted that it was an untypical project for the director, whose artistic sensibilities were more evident in other types of film, both those made before and after the distracting success of *Dracula*.

Browning began as a director in pre-sound American cinema and worked regularly with actor **Lon Chaney**, whose ability to transform his appearance through an often grueling application of makeup became a key feature of his stardom. As a young man, Browning had worked in carnivals and freak shows and he was probably the ideal director for the weird masochistic dramas into which Chaney seemed drawn. Together they made a series of lurid melodramas, a number of which now seem decidedly horror-like—notably *The Unknown* (1927) and *London after Midnight* (1927)—although at the time these were not marketed as horror. *London after Midnight*, all copies of which are now apparently lost, dealt with **vampires**, although—characteristically for Browning who, despite *Dracula*, never seemed that interested in the supernatural—it eventually turned out that these vampires were really actors in disguise. (Browning remade the film in 1935 as *Mark of the Vampire*.) Chaney was the first choice for the part of Dracula but he died of cancer before this could come about, and it was **Bela Lugosi**, with whom Browning had earlier worked on the mystery thriller *The Thirteenth Chair* (1929), who took on the role.

The MGM production *Freaks* (1932), Browning's first major post-*Dracula* film, clearly connected more with his pre-*Dracula* work, but at the same time it was remarkably confrontational, and one wonders how it ever got made at all. Browning used real "freaks," many of them carnival performers, in a circus melodrama of the kind he had once directed with Chaney. The freaks were thoroughly humanized, although the film never shied away from detailing their unconventional bodies. Given the realism that this entailed, it is actually hard to think of *Freaks* as a horror film, such is its difference from the manufactured monstrosities being generated elsewhere in American cinema at the time. Unsurprisingly, it was a much-banned project and it remains today a powerful and disturbing piece of work, and arguably represents Browning's finest achievement as a filmmaker. Browning's subsequent films were more conventional. *Mark of the Vampire* was another Lugosi vehicle, while *The Devil-Doll* (1936) was an oddity about people being shrunk to miniature size. *See also* AMERICAN HORROR.

BUECHLER, JOHN CARL. The filmmaker John Carl Buechler began as a special effects **makeup** artist but has also made occasional forays into film direction, usually working on very low-budget horror projects. These include *Troll* (1986), *Cellar Dweller* (1988), *Friday the 13th Part VII: The New Blood* (1988), *Ghoulies III: Ghoulies Go to College* (1991), *Watchers Reborn* (1998), *Deep Freeze* (2003), *Curse of the Forty-Niner* (2003), and *The Strange Case of Dr. Jekyll and Mr. Hyde* (2006). Makeup credits include *Ghoulies* (1985), *From Beyond* (1986), *Dolls* (1987), *Bride of Re-Animator* (1990), and *Freddy's Dead: The Final Nightmare* (1991).

BURTON, TIM (1958–). The American director Tim Burton has managed throughout his career to preserve an idiosyncratic approach to his subject matter while still attracting large budgets. His work has often showed an affection for classic horror and is also marked visually by the influence of the **gothic** and of German **Expressionism**. He began as an animator with two striking Disney shorts that introduced his key theme—that of the outsider who defines himself through horror-like behavior; in *Vincent* (1982), a little boy wants to be **Vincent Price** (and Price himself provided the narration), while in *Frankenweenie* (1984) another little boy brings his **dog** back to life as a **Frankenstein**-like monster. Burton graduated to live-action direction with the **comedy** *Pee-wee's Big Adventure* (1985) and the comedy-horror **ghost** story *Beetle Juice* (1988), the style of both of which displayed cartoon-like qualities. *Batman* (1989), his first major production, was more impersonal, although it had a distinctive look—which was part-German Expressionist, part film noir—and the emphasis on the tortured outsider was retained from Burton's earlier work. *Edward Scissorhands* (1990) reunited the director with Vincent Price in this story of a scissor-handed "monster" (played by regular Burton collaborator Johnny Depp) trying to fit into normal society. In essence, this was another reworking of the Frankenstein story, with the film firmly identifying with the scientist's creation rather than with the forces of normality. This was followed by *Batman Returns* (1992), which was a more self-consciously playful take on the superhero than the first film, with one of the villains named after **Max Schreck**, the actor who played the **vampire** in **F. W. Murnau**'s classic *Nosferatu* (1922). *Ed Wood* (1994) was a loving biopic of the horror and exploitation director, who was figured here as yet another romanticized Burtonesque outsider. The film also featured an Academy Award-winning performance from Martin Landau as an ageing **Bela Lugosi**. *Mars Attacks!* (1996), a gory but comic alien invasion fantasy based on a series of trading cards, resembled a big-budget version of some of the more exploitative **science fiction**/horror hybrids of the 1950s, while *Sleepy Hollow* (1999) was a beautifully staged period horror film containing a cameo from yet another horror icon, this time **Christopher Lee** (who also showed up in Burton's 2005 production of *Charlie and the Chocolate Factory*).

Burton has retained an interest in **animation**, especially of the darker kind. He produced the animated feature *The Nightmare before Christmas* (1993) as well as co-directing *Corpse Bride* (2005). *See also* AMERICAN HORROR.

BUTTGEREIT, JÖRG (1963–). Even by the often specialized standards of the horror genre, the films of German director Jörg Buttgereit are an acquired taste. Their relentlessly nasty scenarios combine extremely limited production values with convincing representations of violence and atrocity. To his **fans**, Buttgereit's work offers a deeply serious meditation on the darker aspects of life, to others it is pretentious, boring or just unwatchable. The director's best known and most notorious film is *Nekromantik* (1987), in which a necrophile couple steal a corpse and have a sexual threesome with it (with this by no means the film's most disturbing scene). Other credits include *Der Todesking* (*The Death King*) (1990), *Nekromantik 2* (1991), and *Schramm* (1993). *See also* GERMAN HORROR.

– C –

CAMERON, JAMES (1954–). The writer-director James Cameron might now be widely considered as the king of action spectaculars but he started out working in horror. Early production credits include *Galaxy of Terror* (1981), a **Roger Corman**-produced **science fiction**/horror hybrid designed to exploit the success of *Alien* (1979). Cameron's directorial debut was the American/Italian co-production *Piranha II: Flying Killers* (also known as *Piranha II: The Spawning*) (1981), a less than impressive **sequel** to **Joe Dante**'s *Piranha* (1978). *The Terminator* (1984) made Cameron's name as a director of science fiction/action, although some critics have since noted the film's reliance on conventions associated with the **slasher**, namely its representations of an unstoppable killer and a heroic **Final Girl**. *Aliens* (1986), Cameron's next project, offered a masterfully choreographed coming together of science fiction, action, and horror and remains one of the finest films of its kind. Since then Cameron has moved onto to more "uplifting" projects. *See also* AMERICAN HORROR.

CAMPBELL, BRUCE (1958–). The American actor Bruce Campbell shows up in numerous low-budget genre films, but his cult reputation rests largely on his performance as the long-suffering hero Ash in his old high school friend **Sam Raimi**'s *The Evil Dead* (1981), *Evil Dead II* (1987), and *Army of Darkness: Evil Dead 3* (1992). Campbell brought a manic energy to the role fully in keeping with the films' excessive tone and threw himself into some ultra-violent slapstick with complete abandon. By contrast, his performance as an ageing Elvis (or an Elvis impersonator; the film is deliberately vague about this) in **Don Coscarelli**'s horror fantasy *Bubba Ho-tep* (2002) displayed moments of genuine pathos. Campbell also made cameo appearances in Raimi's *Darkman* (1990), *Spiderman* (2002), *Spiderman 2* (2004), and *Spiderman 3* (2007), as well as featuring in, among others, *Maniac Cop* (1988), *Maniac Cop 2* (1990), *Mindwarp* (1990), *Sundown: The Vampire in Retreat* (1991), *Waxwork II: Lost in Time* (1992), *Escape from L.A.* (1996), and *From Dusk till Dawn 2: Texas Blood Money* (1999). He also directed, as well as starred in, the **comedy**-horror *Man with the Screaming Brain* (2005).

CANNIBALISM. The horror genre has always been attracted to socially taboo subjects, so it was perhaps inevitable that at some point it would encounter cannibalism. However, the disturbing nature of the subject ensured that 1930s and 1940s horror hardly ever went anywhere near it—the **mad scientist** film *Doctor X* (1932) offered a rare and brief passing reference—while 1950s horror only invoked it subtly and indirectly, notably in **Hammer**'s *The Revenge of Frankenstein* (1958) when the monster acquired a barely mentioned taste for human flesh. **Herschell Gordon Lewis**'s *Blood Feast* (1963) was more direct and graphic but it was **George Romero**'s *Night of the Living Dead* (1968) that brought cannibalism to the fore through the introduction of flesh-eating **zombies** into the horror genre. A good deal of *Night*'s iconoclastic edginess derived from its unflinching portrayal of the consumption of human flesh, and subsequently other zombie films—including work from Romero and a group of Italian zombie films—explored the gory possibilities of this scenario. Another strain of equally hard-edged cinematic cannibalism that emerged during the 1970s involved the presentation of degraded working class characters as flesh-eaters, in films as various as **Gary Sherman**'s *Death Line* (*Raw Meat*) (1972), **Tobe Hooper**'s *The Texas Chainsaw Massacre* (1974), **Pete Walker**'s *Frightmare* (1974), **Wes Craven**'s *The Hills Have Eyes* (1977), and **Kevin Connor**'s *Motel Hell* (1980). Both Stanley Kubrick's *The Shining* (1980) and Antonia Bird's *Ravenous* (1999) made reference to the Donner party, a real-life incident of 19th century American cannibalism, to underline how civilized behavior can collapse when confronted with the wilderness. At about the same time, **Italian horror** cinema offered a series of mock-anthropological exposés of jungle-based natives indulging in cannibalism, among them **Ruggero Deodato**'s *Ultimo mondo cannibale* (*Cannibal*) (1977) and *Cannibal Holocaust* (1980). These are often categorized as horror although they have more in common, thematically at least, with the Italian *mondo* sensationalist **documentary** tradition.

All these forms of cannibalism share the sense of it as a primitive activity occurring in the context of the decline or absence of modern civilization. Potentially more disturbing are those films in which the cannibals are presented as apparently "normal" individuals making what in effect is a lifestyle choice. Notable here are *Il profumo della signora in nero* (*Perfume of the Lady in Black*) (1974), which depicted a cannibal cult operating in contemporary Italy, *Welcome to Arrow Beach* (1974), the black **comedy**-horror *Eating Raoul* (1982), and *Parents* (1989). Most significant in this respect is master **serial killer** Hannibal Lecter whose cannibalism in **Jonathan Demme**'s *The Silence of the Lambs* (1991) and Ridley Scott's *Hannibal* (2001) has become an expression of a *bon viveur*'s excellent taste.

CARLSON, VERONICA (1944–). The actor Veronica Carlson was a statuesque blonde presence in **British horror** cinema from the late 1960s to the mid-1970s. For **Hammer**, she was the female lead in **Freddie Francis**'s *Dracula Has Risen from the Grave* (1968) and the tragic heroine of **Terence Fisher**'s *Frankenstein Must Be Destroyed* (1969). She was also in *Horror of Frankenstein* (1970), writer-director **Jimmy Sangster**'s unsuccessful attempt to restart Hammer's Frankenstein cycle with a younger cast. Her later genre credits included the **comedy**-horror *Vampira* (1974) and, for the Tyburn company, *The Ghoul* (1974). Two decades later, she showed up in the **American horror** film *Freakshow* (1995).

CARPENTER, JOHN (1948–). John Carpenter has made a significant contribution to **American horror** cinema, not just as a director but also as a screenwriter and a composer. His first two feature films— the **science fiction comedy** *Dark Star* (1974) and the stylish urban thriller *Assault on Precinct 13* (1976)—contained mild horror-like elements but it was his third film that established him as a horror auteur. *Halloween* (1978) is now often seen as the first **slasher** film. Its huge commercial success spawned numerous imitations, although very few of these were as effective as Carpenter's original. *Halloween*'s story was deceptively simple. Three young women are terrorized by a masked killer on Halloween night. However, Carpenter's innovative direction generated both suspense and shock, and his characterizations were more nuanced than is often the case with this type of low-budget horror. He should also receive some of the credit for popularizing the now standard horror convention that the monster makes a sudden reappearance just when everyone thinks it is dead (although the 1967 **psychological thriller** *Wait until Dark* tried this idea out first). Crucial to the film was Carpenter's haunting synthesizer-based score, and the director would go on to write scores for most of his other films.

While 1970s and 1980s American horror films from the likes of **Larry Cohen, Wes Craven, Brian De Palma** and **George Romero** contain elements of social critique, Carpenter's work has tended instead to privilege style and effects (often shock effects). This is certainly the case with *Halloween*, in which the idea that the killer is actually the product of the small town in which the film takes place is gradually supplanted by his presentation as an unstoppable, quasi-supernatural killing machine. It is also the case for Carpenter's directorial follow-up to *Halloween*, the **ghost** story *The Fog* (1980). Here ghosts take revenge on a town that was founded on treasure stolen from them many years before, but again Carpenter is more interested in conjuring up a sinister atmosphere than he is in exploring some of the social ramifications of such a story. *The Thing* (1982), Carpenter's ambitious reworking of Howard Hawks' production *The Thing From Another World* (1951), was a claustrophobic and paranoid drama featuring some impressive special effects from **Rob Bottin**, although its isolated setting also distanced it from any sense of social reality.

So far as Carpenter's other films are concerned, *Christine* (1983) is one of the better adaptations of a **Stephen King** novel, while *Prince of Darkness* (1987, written by Carpenter under the name "Martin Quatermass") and *In the Mouth of Madness* (1994) are good examples of **apocalyptic horror** that also display the influence of American horror writer **H. P. Lovecraft**. Carpenter's more recent work—including *Village of the Damned* (1995), *Vampires* (1998) and *Ghosts of Mars* (2001)—has been uneven but nevertheless has contained noteworthy sequences. Reflecting his association with the horror genre, some of Carpenter's non-horror work has also referenced horror traditions. Notable here are the futuristic thrillers *Escape from New York* (1981) and its **sequel** *Escape from L.A.* (1996), the action film *Big Trouble in Little China* (1986), the alien invasion fantasy *They Live* (1988), and the comedy *Memoirs of an Invisible Man* (1992).

Carpenter also directed for **television** the psychological thriller *Someone's Watching Me* (1978), co-scripted the upmarket slasher *The Eyes of Laura Mars* (1978), co-scripted and produced *Halloween*

II (1981), produced *Halloween III: Season of the Witch* (1982) and directed a segment of the horror **anthology** television movie *Body Bags* (1993) and an episode of the television series *Masters of Horror* (2005–).

CARRADINE, JOHN (1906–1988). The American actor John Carradine had a long but not always distinguished career in horror cinema. He was also a successful stage performer and appeared regularly in other genres but from the late 1950s onwards he became increasingly associated with horror. He had walk-on parts in *The Invisible Man* (1933), *The Black Cat* (1934), and *Bride of Frankenstein* (1935), but starring roles did not come until the 1940s, when he was cast as a **mad scientist** in some low-budget projects. He turned an orangutan into a woman in *Captive Wild Woman* (1943), tried to create pro-Nazi **zombies** in *Revenge of the Zombies* (1943), and sought yet again to resuscitate the dead in *The Face of Marble* (1946). He also acted alongside **Bela Lugosi** in Monogram cheapies *Voodoo Man* (1944) and *Return of the Ape Man* (1944). Roles for **Universal** were more upmarket. He was the **mummy**'s acolyte in *The Mummy's Ghost* (1944), and this was followed by his most memorable 1940s role, that of **Dracula** in *House of Frankenstein* (1944) and *House of Dracula* (1945). Carradine's **vampire** lacked Lugosi's exoticism or the brutality of **Lon Chaney Jr.**'s version in the earlier *Son of Dracula* (1943) but he was infinitely more dapper than either and better suited to the rather decorous world of 1940s Universal horror.

With a few notable exceptions, Carradine's horror work from the 1950s onwards was generally of much lower quality as he insisted on showing up in independently produced films that made Monogram horrors look expensive. His credits in this period are too numerous to list here but titles such as *Hillbillys in a Haunted House* (1967), *The Mummy and the Curse of the Jackals* (1969), and *Vampire Hookers* (1978) are fairly representative. He returned to the role of Dracula on several occasions, for an American **television** drama in 1956 and in more exploitative fashion for *Billy the Kid versus Dracula* (1966), which as its title suggested was a horror **western**, and the **Mexican horror** *Las Vampiras* (1968).

There were a few moments of dignity in the latter part of Carradine's career, however. He cheerfully parodied his mad scientist persona in the horror episode of Woody Allen's *Everything You Always Wanted to Know About Sex But Were Afraid to Ask* (1972), was entertaining as an aged **werewolf** in **Joe Dante**'s *The Howling* (1981), provided able support in the New Zealand horror film *The Scarecrow* (1982), and appeared alongside **Peter Cushing, Christopher Lee,** and **Vincent Price** in *House of the Long Shadows* (1983), **Pete Walker**'s affectionate tribute to classic horror.

Other later credits of interest include *The House of Seven Corpses* (1974), *The Sentinel* (1977), *Shock Waves* (1977), and *The Monster Club* (1980).

CARRERAS, JAMES (1909–1990). Sir James Carreras was the British showman behind **Hammer** horror during the period of its greatest commercial success. The son of Enrique Carreras, one of Hammer's founders, he became managing director of the company in the late 1940s. He oversaw the production of a stream of low-budget thrillers in the first half of the 1950s, and from the late 1950s onwards, after the success of *The Curse of Frankenstein* (1957), guided Hammer's transformation into a horror factory. By all accounts, Carreras showed little interest either in the filmmaking process or in the horror genre but instead concentrated on raising the finance for films, often on the basis of just a title and a poster, and marketing the Hammer product. He was once quoted as saying "We're in the business to make money, not to win Oscars. If the public decided tomorrow that it wanted Strauss waltzes, we'd be in the Strauss waltz business." Fortunately for horror **fans**, the public never made that switch, and Hammer horror has become an indispensable part of horror history. Carreras was knighted in 1970 for his services to charity. He was the father of writer-producer-director **Michael Carreras**. *See also* BRITISH HORROR.

CARRERAS, MICHAEL (1927–1994). Michael Carreras was the son of **Hammer** chief **James Carreras** and ran the company himself for part of the 1970s. He was involved with Hammer from its beginnings and went on to become producer or executive producer on some of its major horror films, including *The Curse of Frankenstein* (1957), *Dracula (Horror of Dracula)* (1958), *The Mummy* (1959), and *The Curse of the Werewolf* (1961). He was also a competent director, who made some of Hammer's more conventional films—notably *Maniac* (1963), one of its **psychological thrillers**, and the period horror *The Curse of the Mummy's Tomb* (1964)—as well as some of its oddest—namely the exotic adventures *Slave Girls* (*Prehistoric Women*) (1967) and *The Lost Continent* (1968). He finished *Blood from the Mummy's Tomb* (1971) when **Seth Holt**, the original director, died a week before the end of production, and directed one of Hammer's last feature films, the thriller *Shatter* (1974). In addition, he wrote screenplays, sometimes under his own name and sometimes under the pseudonyms Henry Younger (*The Curse of the Mummy's Tomb*, *Slave Girls*) and Michael Nash (*The Lost Continent*). He occasionally attempted to lead Hammer away from its reliance on period horror, although the results of this were mixed. The prehistoric fantasy *One Million Years B. C.* (1966), which he wrote and produced, turned out to be one of Hammer's most successful productions, while the **science fiction-western** *Moon Zero Two* (1969) was something of a disaster. *See also* BRITISH HORROR.

CARRIE (1976). *Carrie* is an inventive reworking of the "ugly duckling" theme in which a bullied teenage girl eventually unleashes her awesome telekinetic powers on her tormentors. It is an important **American horror** film for several reasons. It was the first of many screen adaptations of the work of **Stephen King** and, more than most of these, it offered a reasonably accurate rendition of King's distinctive world. It was the most commercially successful horror project from director **Brian De Palma**, whose formal innovations were seamlessly integrated into the narrative. It also made an important contribution to the development of **teenage horror** in its detailed depiction of high school life, although its influence would not be fully evident until the emergence of **slasher** films in the late 1970s. Finally, its now famous shock ending—in which an apparently dead Carrie makes an unexpected reappearance—was a major example of the **startle effect** that would become a key principle in later horrors.

Carrie has also proved a source of fascination for horror critics. In particular, the association of Carrie's telekinetic power with menstruation has provoked debate about the film's sexual politics and the extent to which it might or might not be seen as misogynist. There is no critical consensus about this. One thing is certain, however. Sissy

Spacek's performance as Carrie White renders her one of the most memorable, sympathetic and affecting of all horror's monsters. *Carrie* might seem unusual source material for a stage musical, but nevertheless the musical *Carrie*—with **music** by Michael Gore and lyrics by Dean Pitchford—opened first in Britain and then flopped spectacularly on Broadway in 1988. *The Rage: Carrie 2* (1999) was a belated film **sequel** that, as directed by Katt Shea, depicted the exploits of Carrie's half sister but made little impact at the box office. A **television remake** of the original *Carrie* appeared in 2002.

CASTLE, WILLIAM (1914–1977). The American producer-director William Castle often seemed more interested in the effects his horror films would have on audiences than he was in the content of the films themselves. He was the master of gimmicks during a period when cinema attendance was in decline and showmanship of his kind was required to entice potential customers into film theaters. Already established as a director of low-budget support features, he was apparently inspired by the success in the United States of the French **psychological thriller** *Les diaboliques* (1955) to try his own hand at horror thrillers. His first attempt was *Macabre* (1958). Essentially a crime narrative—in which the protagonist desperately attempts to discover where his daughter has been buried alive—with a *Diaboliques*-like twist ending, it was marketed as a film that was horrifying and fearful. As part of this marketing, Castle insured his audiences with Lloyds of London against dying of fright. (No one did, apparently.) This set the pattern for his subsequent gimmicks, which combined outrageousness with an ingratiating jokiness. It is hard to imagine anyone taking them too seriously but they were an enjoyable augmentation of the horror experience.

Next came *House on Haunted Hill* (1959), starring **Vincent Price**. This was more convincing as a horror film and contained some successful **startle effects**. However, it tends to be remembered now for its gimmick, which was known as Emergo. This involved a skeleton on wires being paraded in front of the screen at a climactic moment in the film. *The Tingler* (1959), which also featured Price, was better yet as a film, dealing this time with a monster that literally feeds on fear. It was filmed in black and white although some prints burst into color during a scene of bloodshed. The major gimmick was much sillier and remains one of Castle's most famous. Percepto entailed wiring buzzers into some cinema seats and using these to give patrons "shocks" during the film. Audiences for *13 Ghosts* (1960) could only see the ghosts if they wore special tinted glasses, the **Psycho**-inspired thriller *Homicidal* (1961) had a fright break in which patrons too scared to see the ending of the film could go to the box office and get their money back, while for *Mr. Sardonicus* (1961) the audience got to vote on which of two endings they were shown—one in which the villain suffered, and another in which he did not. (Apparently audiences nearly always chose the conclusion involving suffering.)

This marked the end of Castle's gimmick period. Subsequent horrors—which included a **remake** of the classic **James Whale** **comedy**-horror *The Old Dark House* (1963) and more Hitchcockian shenanigans in the **Joan Crawford** vehicles *Strait-Jacket* (1964) and *I Saw What You Did* (1965)—were more straightforward. His career took an unexpected turn when, as the owner of the screen rights for the novel **Rosemary's Baby**, he got to produce the successful film adaptation, although he had little creative input into a work that was very much shaped by its director, **Roman Polanski**. The subtle combination of horror and humor in *Rosemary's Baby* (1968) seemed a world apart from Castle's more showman-like approach to the genre. His final horror credit was as producer of *Bug* (1975), a **revenge of nature** film directed by Jeannot Swarzc that dealt with **insects** capable of, in Castle's words, "belching fire from their behinds."

The title of Castle's autobiography sums up his attitude to filmmaking: *Step Right Up! I'm Gonna Scare the Pants Off America—Memoirs of a B-Movie Mogul*. The movie showman featured in **Joe Dante**'s *Matinee* (1993) is, in part at least, a fond recreation of Castle. *See also* AMERICAN HORROR.

CATS. Horror filmmakers have regularly exploited the association of our feline friends with evil and sinister matters. Pathological fear of cats is a plot element in *The Black Cat* (1934) and *Eye of the Cat* (1969), and malign, vengeful or downright murderous cats appear in *The Cat Creeps* (1946), *Shadow of the Cat* (1961), *The Tomb of Ligeia* (1964), *Torture Garden* (1967), *La noche de los mil gatos* (*Night of 1000 Cats*) (1972), *Persecution* (1974), *The Uncanny* (1977), *The Kiss*, (1988) and *Due occhi diabolici* (*Two Evil Eyes*)

(1990), while the cat-like mewling of the **ghost** boy in *Ju-On: The Grudge* (2003) is one of contemporary horror's more unnerving sounds. The cats in *Cat People* (1942, remade in 1982) and *Cat Girl* (1957) turn out to be big jungle cats, however, rather than domestic pussies. Rare representations of heroic cats are offered by *Cat's Eye* (1985) and *Sleepwalkers* (1992), and *Tales from the Darkside: The Movie* (1990) features a cat assassin—or hit-cat—doling out justifiable revenge for crimes against its species. By contrast, Jones, the spaceship cat in *Alien* (1979), is something of a coward.

CENSORSHIP. Given the provocative and extreme nature of much horror imagery, it is perhaps not surprising that conflict with the censors has been a constant theme in the history of the horror genre, although the nature of that conflict has changed over the years. The concern with public morality and the promotion of appropriate social mores that drove censorship during the 1930s has in more recent times been displaced by an effects-based approach to images of sexuality and violence. Thus the attitudes behind the decision to cut the line "Now I know what it's like to be God" from **Universal**'s 1931 version of *Frankenstein*, or the 1930s British censors' attempts to discourage the production of horror films altogether, now seem the product of another age and another cultural mindset. However, British censorship has retained a vaguely paternalistic quality in its decisions about what the general public should see, while the American approach—especially after the introduction of the ratings system in the late 1960s—has, to a limited extent, been less intrusive. In fact, national differences abound in censorship practices, with horror films being passed uncut in one territory only to be banned altogether in another. For example, *Freaks* (1932) and *Island of Lost Souls* (1932) were not shown in Britain for many years after their release in the United States, and other horror classics such as *Les yeux sans visage* (*Eyes without a Face*) (1959), *Peeping Tom* (1960), and *Witchfinder General* (1968) have also experienced censorship difficulties in a number of countries. It usually seems to be the case that censorship becomes an issue when a new type of horror appears or when new ways of viewing horror are made available—notably anxieties about horror on video in the British "video nasties" scare of the 1980s. Ironically, it is the development of new viewing technologies that has recently helped to loosen any national censor's control over what is seen or not seen in any national cinema, with uncut versions from other territories now often available to discerning horror **fans** via **internet** DVD purchasing or downloading.

Censorship has not just had a negative influence on horror, however. Canny filmmakers and distributors have on more than one occasion used the notoriety deriving from their brushes with censorship as a marketing device. For example, **Hammer** titled its **science fiction**/horror hybrid *The Quatermass Xperiment* (1955) in order to exploit the new adults only X certificate that had been introduced in Britain in the early 1950s, while the **British horror** *Creep* (2004) used as its advertising slogan the British Board of Film Classification consumer advice "Contains strong bloody violence." In addition, DVD releases of previously banned horror films often highlight their "forbidden" status. This suggests that disreputability is an integral part of the horror experience and that the censors have had a role to play in this.

CHANEY, LON (1883–1930). The American actor Lon Chaney has often been thought of as one of the first great horror stars. However, this master of disguise, dubbed "the man of a thousand faces," was by no means confined to horror-like dramas but also made an impression in crime films and melodramas. In fact, even those Chaney films now considered as horror—notably *The Hunchback of Notre Dame* (1923), *The Phantom of the Opera* (1925) and *London after Midnight* (1927)—were seen more as romantic melodramas or thrillers at the time of their initial release. Notwithstanding this, the pathos that Chaney was able to endow upon physically repellent creatures such as Quasimodo in *The Hunchback of Notre Dame* and Erik in *The Phantom of the Opera* has set a standard for later horror monsters, notably **Frankenstein**'s monster in **Universal**'s 1930s horror cycle. In addition, the pain he was prepared to inflict upon himself in order to achieve a convincing **makeup** design has also resonated through horror history, with later horror stars such as **Boris Karloff** and **Christopher Lee** similarly suffering for their art, although perhaps not to the extent that Chaney did. One of Chaney's specialties was limbless characters—in films such as *The Penalty* (1920) and *The Unknown* (1927)—and the self-mutilating quality evident in many of his performances arguably spoke to a public fascination with broken and crippled bodies that some historians have traced back to the traumatic experience of World War I.

Chaney frequently collaborated with director **Tod Browning**, whose interest in carnival and the grotesque suited him perfectly to the actor. Their **vampire** story *London after Midnight* (1927) is frequently cited as one of the horror's genre's most significant lost films. Given that Browning went on to direct the Universal *Dracula* (1931), Chaney would have been the obvious choice to play the vampire. Sadly, he died of throat cancer before that could happen, and **Bela Lugosi** became the first horror star of the sound period instead. The image of the legless woman that appears at the end of Browning's *Freaks* (1932) can be seen as a testament to Chaney's perverse but compelling legacy. Decades later, the biopic *The Man of a Thousand Faces* (1957) offered a somewhat romanticized version of Chaney's life story and featured James Cagney as the actor. Chaney's son Creighton went on to become a horror star under the name **Lon Chaney Jr.** See also AMERICAN HORROR.

CHANEY JR., LON (1906–1973). Lon Chaney Jr.'s real first name was Creighton but he changed it to Lon, after his film star father **Lon Chaney**, to help his acting career; some films billed him as Lon Chaney Jr. while others omitted the Jr. His first major role was as the hulking simpleton Lenny in *Of Mice and Men* (1939) and he continued to perform ably in supporting roles in a range of genres (he was in *High Noon*, for example). However, stardom came with his performances in 1940s **American horror** cinema. He was the only actor to play all four of **Universal**'s main monsters—**Dracula**, **Frankenstein**'s monster, the **mummy** and the Wolf Man, but it was the role of **werewolf** Lawrence Talbot that he made his own.

His first horror film was Universal's *Man Made Monster* (1941), in which he was the victim of a **mad scientist**'s experiment. He subsequently developed his ability to generate pathos in *The Wolf Man* (1941). This was Universal's attempt to restart its werewolf cycle after *Werewolf of London* (1935). Chaney played the son of the local squire who gets bitten by what he believes is a wolf and is thereafter doomed to become a werewolf. The actor managed the transitions from complacent self-control to introspection and terror very effectively; his later renditions of this character would lack some of the nuances apparent here.

Chaney next took over from **Boris Karloff** as Frankenstein's monster in *The Ghost of Frankenstein* (1942). Presumably the rationale behind this piece of casting was that the pathos of the Wolf Man would in some way be carried over into the monster, but Chaney looked uncomfortable, with his performance crudely gestural and with none of the subtleties that Karloff brought to the part. Much the same could be said of his turn as the mummy in *The Mummy's Tomb* (1942), with Chaney again giving the impression of being ill at ease in a part where he was completely submerged in heavy **makeup** (unlike Karloff or **Christopher Lee**, both of whom could successfully emote in such circumstances). At least with the wolf man, he remained in human form most of the time. He was back as Talbot in *Frankenstein Meets the Wolf Man* (1943), the first of Universal's multi-monster films. He also offered an interesting, if not entirely successful, performance as Count Dracula in the misleadingly titled *Son of Dracula* (1943), a film in which there is no sign that the **vampire** is anything other than Dracula himself. Chaney played him as a charmless but physically imposing bully rather than the lounge lizard the Count became when **John Carradine** subsequently took over the part.

Chaney's later career was less successful. He was the mummy again in *The Mummy's Ghost* (1944) and *The Mummy's Curse* (1944) and Talbot again in *House of Frankenstein* (1944), *House of Dracula* (1945) and *Abbott and Costello Meet Frankenstein* (1948); he also starred in a series of weird mysteries based on the radio series *Inner Sanctum*—among them the **witchcraft** drama *Weird Woman* (1944). His 1950s horror credits were all minor, including low-budget projects such as *Bride of the Gorilla* (1951), *The Black Sleep* (1956), *The Cyclops* (1957), and *The Alligator People* (1959). He also played Frankenstein's monster again on **television** in 1952 as well as hosting the horror **anthology** series *13 Demon Street* (1959–1960), episodes of which were cut together for the film *The Devil's Messenger* (1961). The 1960s were a little better but not much. He returned to the role of the werewolf in the **Mexican horror** film *La casa del terror* (*The House of Terror*) (1960), parts of which were later cannibalized for *Face of the Screaming Werewolf* (1964). More dignified was his supporting role in **Roger Corman**'s *The Haunted Palace* (1963) and his performance as a menacing warlock in **Don Sharp**'s stylish **British horror** *Witchcraft* (1964). Sadly his final credits were not of this quality. They were *House of the Black Death* (1965), *Dr. Terror's Gallery of Horrors* (1967), *Hillbillys in a Haunted House* (1967), *Spider Baby* (1968), and his last film, *Dracula versus Frankenstein* (1971).

CHILDREN. The first notable appearance of a child in a horror film is probably that of the little girl (played by Marilyn Harris) in *Frankenstein* (1931) who was accidentally drowned by Frankenstein's monster (played by **Boris Karloff**). This fairly conventional representation of the child as a threatened innocent has recurred in later horror films—for example, in **Val Lewton**'s *The Curse of the Cat People* (1944), **Robert Wise**'s *Audrey Rose* (1977), Stanley Kubrick's *The Shining* (1980), **Tobe Hooper**'s *Poltergeist* (1982), **M. Night Shyamalan**'s *The Sixth Sense* (1999), **Guillermo del Toro**'s *El espinazo del diablo* (*The Devil's Backbone*) (2001), and **Alejandro Amenabar**'s *The Others* (2001).

Horror's depiction of children as evil or monstrous has proved more shocking and controversial. There is something to be said for the idea that such representations have articulated anxieties about perceived failings in social authority, particularly as they relate to the family. (*See* FAMILY HORROR.) A first hint that something might be wrong with the family was provided by *The Bad Seed* (1956) in which a blonde, pig-tailed little girl was revealed as a sociopathic murderer. Comparably murderous were the powerful alien children in the **science fiction**/horror hybrid *Village of the Damned* (1960), while **Mario Bava**'s *Operazione Paura* (*Kill, Baby . . . Kill!*) (1966) featured a vengeful **ghost** in the shape of a young girl. However, what might be termed the "golden age" of monstrous and rebellious children was inaugurated in 1968 by **Roman Polanski**'s *Rosemary's Baby*—in which the baby **Antichrist** is born—and **George Romero**'s *Night of the Living Dead*, in which a zombified little girl eats her own father's flesh and stabs her mother to death. A few years later, *The Exorcist* (1973) took this onto another level with its groundbreaking representation of a girl transformed into a foul-mouthed, violent monster. As was the case with *Night of the Living*

Dead, the child in *The Exorcist* was in herself innocent but, like zombification, demonic **possession** afforded an iconoclastic opportunity to depict a young person behaving very badly indeed. By contrast, **The Omen** (1976) featured an irredeemably evil child in Damien, the Antichrist, whose birth signaled the coming end of the world.

Monstrous babies and dangerous children have also appeared in *The House that Dripped Blood* (1970), *The Other* (1972), **Larry Cohen**'s *It's Alive* (1974), **David Cronenberg**'s *The Parasite Murders* (*They Came From Within, Shivers*) (1975) and *The Brood* (1979), *The Child* (1977), **John Carpenter**'s *Halloween* (1978), the **Stephen King** adaptations *Children of the Corn* (1984) and *Pet Sematary* (1989), as well as the **British horror** films *Nothing But The Night* (1972), *I Don't Want to be Born* (*The Devil Within Her*) (1975), and *The Godsend* (1980) and the **Spanish horror** *Quién puede matar a un niño?* (*Island of the Damned, Would You Kill a Child?*) (1976).

CHINESE HORROR. Examples of Chinese horror cinema from the pre-revolutionary era are few and far between. The silent production *Yanzhi* (1925) is sometimes cited as the first Chinese horror film, although it seems to be a lost film. However, the small number of early Chinese horrors that are available suggest a type of genre cinema that sometimes drew upon Western horror conventions but which had a distinctive folkloric character of its own and which relied on **ghosts** in a manner that allied it to other Asian horror traditions. Maxu Weibang's *Ye ban ge sheng* (*Midnight Song*) (1937), a reworking of the **Phantom of the Opera** story, has been seen by some historians as the first major Chinese horror production. The same director made *Gu wu xing shi ji* (*Tales of a Corpse-Ridden Old House*) (1938) and *Ma feng nu* (*Leper Woman*) (1939) as well as *Ye ban ge sheng xu ji* (*Midnight Song II*) (1941) and the Hong Kong production *Qiong lou hen* (*The Haunted House, A Maid's Bitter Story*) (1949). Later Chinese ghost stories, often made in Hong Kong, included *Yan shi huan hun ji* (*Beauty Raised From the Dead*) (1956), *Ching nu yu hun* (*The Enchanting Shadow*) (1960), and King Hu's well-regarded international success *Hsia nu* (*A Touch of Zen*) (1969).

Horror films produced within the Hong Kong film industry from the 1970s onwards have been more widely distributed internationally and are consequently better known in the West. They also make greater use of Western conventions while still retaining an Asian focus on ghosts and demons as the principal threats. Especially popular were knockabout kung fu–**comedy**-horrors such as *Gui da gui* (*Close Encounters of the Spooky Kind, Spooky Encounters*) (1980) and *Ren xia ren* (*The Dead and the Deadly*) (1982), both of which starred portly martial arts comedian Sammo Hung. The similarly themed *Geung si sin sang* (*Mr. Vampire*) (1985), and its **sequels**, featured a hopping cadaver as a source of much slapstick humor. Considerably slicker were the **Tsui Hark**-produced *Chinese Ghost Story* films, beginning with *Sinnui yauwan* (*A Chinese Ghost Story*) (1987). Based on the much filmed writings of Pu Songling (1640–1715), *Sinnui yauwan* was a commercially appealing mix of folkloric material with hi-tech special effects. Underlining the breadth of Hong Kong production, films of this kind mingled both with the more subtle treatment of ghosts found in Stanley Kwan's *Yin ji kau* (*Rouge*) (1987) and with Category III "adult only" films that offered grimmer tales of **serial killers**—for example *Gou yeung yi sang* (*Dr. Lamb*) (1992)—and **cannibalism**—for example, *Baat sin faan dim ji yan yuk cha siu baau* (*The Untold Story*) (1993). A comprehensive history of Chinese horror cinema remains to be written but even a superficial glance at the films that are available reveals a type of genre product that merits further attention.

CLARK, BOB (1941–2007). The 1970s horror films of director Bob Clark (who was occasionally billed as Benjamin Clark) revealed a talented and innovative filmmaker who understood how **American horror** was changing in this period. *Children Shouldn't Play with Dead Things* (1972) was an atmospheric modern **zombie** story. The more ambitious *Dead of Night* (*The Night Walk, Deathdream*) (1974) returned to the idea of dead men walking with a narrative in which a war veteran—implicitly from the Vietnam war—returns home as a blood-drinking monster; the film also explored familial tensions in a manner that made it a prime example of **family horror**. *Black Christmas* (1974) anticipated the **slasher** films of the late 1970s in its sorority-house setting and its extensive use of **point of view** technique, although it possessed a bleak atmosphere all of its own. *Murder by Decree* (1979) set **Sherlock Holmes** against **Jack the Ripper**, as well as drawing upon the political conspiracy theories about the Ripper's identity that became popular during the 1970s. It was a striking period drama that displayed the anti-Establishment attitudes so prevalent elsewhere in the genre at this time.

After his success with the teenage **comedy** *Porky's* (1982), Clark worked in genres other than horror.

CLAYTON, JACK (1921–1995). The British filmmaker Jack Clayton made his name as a director with *Room at the Top* (1959), a realistic study of provincial life that inaugurated a cycle of similarly realistic films known as the British New Wave. However, his other films often possessed a fantastic or **gothic** quality, even if this was only implicit. His Academy Award–winning short film *The Bespoke Overcoat* (1955), was an adaptation of a **ghost** story by Nikolai Gogol, and after the success of *Room at the Top* he returned to the supernatural with *The Innocents* (1961), which was based on the Henry James ghost story "The Turn of the Screw." Both of these offered psychologically complex renditions of hauntings, rendering ambiguous the extent to which the ghosts were real or just projections of the guilt of the living. Later films *The Pumpkin Eater* (1964) and *Our Mother's House* (1967) jettisoned the supernatural but retained a brooding sense of psychological instability. *Something Wicked This Way Comes* (1983) was a stylish version of a Ray Bradbury novel, although Clayton's characteristically dark view of things was softened by the studio in an attempt to make the film more commercial. *See also* BRITISH HORROR.

CLEMENS, BRIAN (1931–). The British writer-producer Brian Clemens is best known for his **television** work (which includes *The Avengers* and the 1970s series *Thriller*). However, he has occasionally strayed into the horror genre. An early effort was his contribution to the **British horror** film *The Tell-Tale Heart* (1960), an expressionistic treatment of an **Edgar Allan Poe** story. *Curse of Simba* (1965), which he co-wrote under the name Tony O'Grady, was a conventional **voodoo** drama. *And Soon the Darkness* (1970) and *Blind Terror* (*See No Evil*) (1971) were effective **serial killer** thrillers, with *Blind Terror* featuring a memorable performance from **Mia Farrow** as a terrorized blind heroine. At a time when **Hammer** was looking for new ideas to refresh its horror formula, Clemens wrote and produced for the company *Dr. Jekyll and Sister Hyde* (1971), a transsexual rendition of the **Dr. Jekyll and Mr. Hyde** story in which the doctor is transformed into a woman. He then wrote, produced and directed another late Hammer horror, *Captain Kronos—Vampire Hunter* (1974), an underrated film that combined period horror conventions with action scenes. He also wrote the Disney-produced horror *The Watcher in the Woods* (1980).

CLIVE, COLIN (1900–1937). The British actor Colin Clive was the original **Frankenstein** in **James Whale**'s **Universal** horror productions *Frankenstein* (1931) and *Bride of Frankenstein* (1935). He had earlier worked with Whale in the theater, and his film performances are defiantly theatrical with a manic edge. To modern audiences, the acting styles on display in horror films of the early 1930s can often seem overwrought, but even by those standards Clive's screen persona was especially histrionic. Biographical accounts suggest that Clive was a deeply troubled individual whose anguish was constantly finding its way onto the screen. His last major genre performance was as a tormented pianist who has a murderer's hands grafted onto him in *Mad Love* (1935). He died as a result of alcoholism not long afterwards. His cry of "It's alive"—from *Frankenstein*—remains one of the horror genre's best known lines.

COHEN, HERMAN (1925–2002). The American writer-producer Herman Cohen had his first brush with the horror genre as associate producer of the **comedy**-horror *Bela Lugosi Meets a Brooklyn Gorilla* (1952). In the late 1950s, he produced (and sometimes wrote or co-wrote as well) a series of **teenage horror** films for exploitation specialists **American International Pictures**. These included the unforgettably titled *I Was a Teenage Werewolf* (1957) and *I Was a Teenage Frankenstein* (1957), both of which were enjoyable horror reworkings of *Rebel without a Cause* (1955), with rebellious teenagers transformed into monsters. *How to Make a Monster* (1958) and *Blood of Dracula* (1957) offered more of the same, although *How to Make a Monster*, which dealt with the exploits of a horror **makeup** artist, was also an interesting example of generic **self-reflexivity**. Subsequently, Cohen was based mainly in Britain, where his credits included *Horrors of the Black Museum* (1959), the very silly giant **ape** film *Konga* (1961), the **Sherlock Holmes** versus **Jack the Ripper** story *A Study in Terror* (1965), and two late **Joan Crawford** vehicles, *Berserk!* (1968) and *Trog* (1970)

Other credits included *The Headless Ghost* (1959), *Black Zoo* (1963), and *Craze* (1973).

COHEN, LARRY (1938–). Of all the directors who made major contributions to the development of **American horror** during the 1970s, Larry Cohen is probably the least known to the general public. While filmmakers such as **John Carpenter, David Cronenberg,** and **Brian De Palma** have gone on to establish significant name recognition for themselves, Cohen has continued to work quietly and largely unheralded in the low-budget sector. This is a shame because his horror films at their best are some of the most intelligent and challenging to be found in the genre.

From the late 1950s onwards, Cohen was mainly a **television** writer, with his numerous credits including the pilots for popular 1960s series *Branded* and *The Invaders*, although he also wrote several screenplays for the cinema. He turned to film direction in the early 1970s, beginning with ambitious blaxploitation thrillers *Bone* (1972), *Black Caesar,* (1973) and *Hell Up in Harlem* (1973). *It's Alive!* (1974), his first horror film, was a remarkable revisionary work that articulated key themes of 1970s horror. The film's title refers to a line spoken by **Frankenstein** in **Universal**'s 1931 version of *Frankenstein* on seeing his creature move for the first time. However, Cohen's contemporary version of the Frankenstein story threw into disarray some of the moral certainties of the earlier work. An ordinary American woman gives birth to a monster that rampages across the city. The father's reaction to his child is unusual for the horror genre at this time. Initially rejecting his offspring, he eventually comes to accept it as his, despite its monstrosity and violence. *It's Alive!* concludes with the child's death and the news that more monstrous babies have been born elsewhere. The contemporary setting, the child as monster, the distrust of social institutions and official authority, the open ending: these elements can be found elsewhere in 1970s American horror, but in *It's Alive* Cohen weaves them with great clarity and conviction into an engaging and ultimately moving narrative. *God Told Me To* (*Demon*) (1976), Cohen's next genre project, was even more daring. Its delirious plot featured a hermaphrodite alien with Christ-like qualities, a sinister conspiracy, and a hero who discovers that he too is an alien. The tone was serious, however, as the film set out a rigorous critique of conventional social and gendered identities.

Cohen's later films have rarely recaptured the intensity and focus of *It's Alive!* and *God Told Me To*, but many of them are distinguished efforts. The **sequel** *It Lives Again* (1978) was a highly effective elaboration on themes from the first film, while *Full Moon High* (1981), *Q—the Winged Serpent* (1982), and *The Stuff* (1985) were enjoyable **comedy**-horrors that also contained some interesting ideas. *It's Alive III: Island of the Alive* (1987) and *A Return to Salem's Lot* (1987) continued the Cohen trait of making normality seem more monstrous than the ostensible monsters. The comedy-horror *Wicked Stepmother* (1989) was a rare complete misfire.

In a busy career that has included work in a variety of film genres, Cohen also wrote and produced **William Lustig**'s *Maniac Cop* (1988–1993) horror trilogy, directed *The Ambulance* (1990) and was credited for the screen story of **Abel Ferrara**'s *Body Snatchers* (1993). More recently, he wrote the screenplay for *Phone Booth* (2002), an urban thriller whose restricted setting and fascination with unstable identities made it appear more than a little Cohenesque, and directed an episode of the television series *Masters of Horror* (2005–). He also co-wrote the controversial **torture**-based film *Captivity* (2007).

He should not be confused with writer-producer Lawrence D. Cohen, who also has some horror credits to his name.

COMBS, JEFFREY (1954–). The American actor Jeffrey Combs has appeared in many horror films, both in the United States and in Europe, and specializes in manic or sinister roles. He was the **mad scientist** Herbert West in **Stuart Gordon**'s *Re-Animator* (1985), a remarkably gory adaptation of an **H. P. Lovecraft** story, and also featured in the **sequels** *Bride of Re-Animator* (1990) and *Beyond Re-Animator* (2003). He has appeared in other Lovecraft adaptations, notably *From Beyond* (1986) and *Lurking Fear* (1994), and played Lovecraft himself in the horror **anthology** *Necronomicon* (1994). He was memorable as a neurotic FBI agent in **Peter Jackson**'s *The Frighteners* (1996) and also offered effective support in *I Still Know What You Did Last Summer* (1998), *House on Haunted Hill* (1999), and *FeardotCom* (2002). His other credits are too numerous to list here.

COMEDY. Horror films have often teetered on the edge of absurdity, with their fantastic and extreme narratives easily transformed into something that is amusing rather than scary. Sometimes this is inadvertent, with an audience mocking a film's unsuccessful attempts to be frightening, and sometimes it has more to with the way in which a horror film is marketed than with the film itself, with humorous advertising gimmicks proving popular at certain moments in the genre's history. In other cases, however, horror filmmakers have chosen to deploy comedic elements. Most commonly, this has to do with providing moments of comic relief within an otherwise serious horror narrative. One thinks here, for example, of witty performances by actors **Mantan Moreland** in some 1940s horrors, **Miles Malleson** in some early **Hammer** horrors or Jamie Kennedy in *Scream* (1996).

There are also films in which the balance is tilted more to comedy than it is to horror, with this often taking the form of parodies of horror stories where any frissons provided by the horror material are safely contained by laughter. Throughout the 19th century there had been numerous **gothic** spoofs and parodies, and from the late 1920s onwards the horror genre continued this tradition, particularly through a series of comedy-horror films set in old and dark and sometimes haunted houses. John Willard's Broadway hit *The Cat and the Canary* was perhaps the best known of these. First filmed by **Paul Leni** in 1927, it was remade in 1939 as a Bob Hope vehicle. Other films of this type included *The Gorilla* (1927), **James Whale**'s *The Old Dark House* (1932), *You'll Find Out* (1940), the British production *What a Carve Up* (1961), and, more recently, the nostalgic *Haunted Honeymoon* (1986).

More knockabout comedy was provided by the likes of ***Ghost Breakers*** (1940), another Bob Hope film, and ***Zombies on Broadway*** (1945), while **Boris Karloff** and **Peter Lorre** sent themselves up in *The Boogie Man Will Get You* (1942). However, it was comedy duo **Bud Abbott** and **Lou Costello** who most helped to establish a type of comedy-horror in which vaudeville performers encountered horror monsters to humorous effect. Beginning with *Abbott and Costello Meet Frankenstein* (1948), they starred in a series of films featuring **Universal**'s horror monsters at a time when the popularity of those monsters as fright figures was fading.

Comedy-horrors of various types continued to be produced sporadically after the Abbott and Costello cycle had finished in the mid-1950s. **Roger Corman**'s *The Raven* (1963) spoofed his own **Edgar Allan Poe** adaptations, while his earlier *A Bucket of Blood* (1959) and *The Little Shop of Horrors* (1960) turned, respectively, murder and monsters into sources of humor. *Carry on Screaming* (1967) parodied Hammer horror in a none-too-subtle manner. Producer-director **Mel Brooks** came up with *Young Frankenstein* (1974), an affectionate send-up of Universal horror, and *Dracula—Dead and Loving It* (1995), a cruder but still amusing parody of **Francis Ford Coppola**'s 1992 version of *Dracula*. The cult favorite *The Rocky Horror Picture Show* (1975) transformed Frankenstein into an extraterrestrial transsexual, while *Love at First Bite* (1979) was another Dracula spoof. *Ghostbusters* (1984) and *Gremlins* (1984) were more original and offered a judicious mixture of comedy, special effects and thrills designed for a family audience. The success of the **slasher** film in the late 1970s and early 1980s encouraged a few quickly forgotten parodies—among them *Student Bodies* (1981) and *Pandemonium* (1982)—but the subsequent *Nightmare on Elm Street* films were so self-consciously humorous that they seemed beyond parody. However, the already tongue-in-cheek *Scream* films did lead to the successful *Scary Movie* (2000) and its **sequels**, which quickly moved on from sending up *Scream* to targeting a range of horror and other popular genre films.

There are other films, fewer in number, that have offered a more unsettling mixture of humor and horror, where comedy seems to accentuate the horror rather than diminish it. For instance, the innuendo and double meaning of some of the dialogue in **Alfred Hitchcock**'s *Psycho* (1960) had a sick comic effect that in no way softened the film's disturbing elements but instead contributed to its nihilism. Something similar occurred in the horror films directed by **Roman Polanski**, from *Dance of the Vampires* (*The Fearless Vampire Killers*) (1967), a spoof of Hammer horror far more unnerving than anything ever produced by Hammer, through to Satanic thrillers *Rosemary's Baby* (1968) and *The Ninth Gate* (1999), where a sense of the absurd only served to underline the helplessness of the films' main protagonists in the face of evil. Operating in a different register was **Tobe Hooper**'s *The Texas Chainsaw Massacre* (1974), in which slapstick moments of physical clumsiness were presented within scenes of extreme terror, cruelty, and violence in a manner that rendered the film even more horrible than it would have been if played straight (as its **remake** was played relatively straight).

Gory slapstick violence played more obviously for laughs can be found in **Sam Raimi**'s *The Evil Dead* (1981), **Stuart Gordon**'s *The Re-Animator* (1985) and **Peter Jackson**'s *Braindead* (1992), along with the rather less distinguished product of the **Troma** company. Disarticulated bodies, reanimated body parts, and bodily organs and fluids presented in unremittingly graphic detail become sources of a sick humor, a quality associated in particular with **body horror**. This was a considerably more specialized and in some instances more adolescent kind of comedy than the decorous humor provided by Bob Hope's *The Cat and the Canary* or Abbott and Costello's films.

It seems from this that the interaction between comedy and horror has been an important one within the horror genre, although the forms of this interaction are varied, ranging from the appreciative laughter over a silly story to tasteless laughter at events and sights that, according to conventional morality at least, should not be even slightly amusing.

COMICS. Horror comics were a popular, if controversial and often censored, form of entertainment during the 1950s. In particular, "EC" Comics—which produced titles such as *Tales from the Crypt, Vault of Horror* and *The Haunt of Fear*—offered an inventively amoral type of horror fiction that in terms of **gore** and general nastiness went way beyond what was available in horror cinema at the time. Some "EC" horror stories were later adapted for film, first by the **British horror** company **Amicus** with *Tales from the Crypt* (1972) and *Vault of Horror* (1973) and subsequently by the American **television** series *Tales from the Crypt* (1989–1996), while the **George Romero-Stephen King** collaboration *Creepshow* (1982) was a nostalgic tribute to such comics.

More recent comic book characters have also provided inspiration to horror filmmakers. **Tim Burton**'s *Batman* (1989) and *Batman Returns* (1992) and Ang Lee's *Hulk* (2003) were comic superhero stories containing some horror-like elements, while two *Swamp Thing* films, **Wes Craven**'s *Swamp Thing* (1982) and *The Return of Swamp Thing* (1989), were more straightforward horror adaptations. Other comic-based films, with varying degrees of horror content, have included *The Crow* (1994), *Spawn* (1997), the **vampire** story *Blade* (1998), *Virus* (1999), the **Jack the Ripper** story *From Hell* (2001), **Guillermo del Toro**'s *Hellboy* (2004), *Constantine* (2005), and *Ghost Rider* (2007). The **science fiction**/horror hybrid *AVP: Alien versus Predator* (2004), by contrast, was inspired by a comic book series that itself was based on the original *Alien* and *Predator* films.

COMPUTER GAMES. Computer games have often drawn upon horror imagery, and occasionally the horror genre has returned the compliment by adapting games for the screen. **Zombie** films *Resident Evil* (2002) and *House of the Dead* (2003) were successful enough to generate **sequels**, while monster movie *Doom* (2005) was a comparably thick-eared action piece. More ambitious was **Christophe Gans'** *Silent Hill* (2006), which transformed one of the leading horror-themed games into a bold concoction of ideas from **Japanese horror** and **Italian horror**. The narrative structures of games and films are sufficiently different for all of these adaptations to be decidedly free and loose, although each film usually seeks to reproduce directly some recognizable aspect of the computer game source. This was most obviously the case with the extended first person shooter scene from *Doom*. The **teenage horror** film *Stay Alive* (2006) took as its subject a computer game that had the ability to kill off its players, while a number of horror films have toyed with the idea of potentially lethal virtual reality games—among them *Brainscan* (1994) and **David Cronenberg**'s *Existenz* (1999).

CONNOR, KEVIN (1937–). Kevin Connor graduated from film editing to direction with *From Beyond the Grave* (1973). This was one of the best of a series of horror **anthologies** produced by the **Amicus** company. Especially impressive was an episode featuring genre stalwart **Donald Pleasence**, which was as fine a study of British social mores as one could find in 1970s British cinema. Connor's remaining British films were more fantasy-oriented and included adaptations of Edgar Rice Burroughs' monster epics *The Land That Time Forgot* (1974) and *At The Earth's Core* (1976). He moved to the United States in the 1980s where he worked mainly for **television**, although for the cinema he also directed *Motel Hell* (1980), a surprisingly cheerful **comedy**-horror about **cannibalism**. *See also* BRITISH HORROR.

CONWAY, TOM (1904–1967). The actor Tom Conway was the Russian-born brother of George Sanders. During the 1940s he was best known as The Falcon in a series of crime thrillers (he took over the role from his brother) but he was also impressive in three of producer **Val Lewton's** horror films. He played the creepy psychiatrist Dr. Judd in *Cat People* (1942), whose unprofessional treatment of his patient led to his own violent death. Next came *I Walked with a* **Zombie** (1943) where his mournfulness contributed to the film's downbeat tone. Finally, Lewton resurrected Conway's Dr. Judd, albeit with a more benign persona, for the stylish Satanic thriller *The Seventh Victim* (1943). Problems with alcohol meant that the latter part of Conway's career was less successful, and he made undignified appearances in low-budget horrors *Bride of the Gorilla* (1951), *The She-Creature* (1956) and **Voodoo** *Woman* (1957).

COOPER, MERIAN C. (1893–1973). Merian C. Cooper's main claim to horror fame is his co-production and co-direction—with **Ernest B. Schoedsack**—of *King Kong* (1933). He started out as a specialist in exotic **documentaries** such as *Grass* (1925) and *Chang* (1927) before moving into the horror-thriller business through producing *The Most Dangerous Game* (*The Hounds of Zaroff*) (1932). His later horror-related credits as producer were *The Monkey's Paw* (1933), *She* (1935), and the **mad scientist** film *Dr. Cyclops* (1940). In the latter part of his career, he became John Ford's producer on a number of classic **westerns**, including *Rio Grande* (1950) and *The Searchers* (1956). *See also* AMERICAN HORROR.

COPPOLA, FRANCIS FORD (1939–). Before becoming one of America's leading directors with, among others, *The Godfather*

(1972) and *Apocalypse Now* (1979), the writer-director Francis Ford Coppola worked occasionally in the horror genre. He was one of many filmmakers who were given early career opportunities by producer-director **Roger Corman**. In Coppola's case, this involved making an uncredited contribution to Corman's *The Terror* (1963) before co-writing and directing *Dementia 13* (*The Haunted and the Hunted*) (1963). This **psychological thriller** was filmed in Ireland, and while its narrative was conventional, the young director conjured up some atmospheric sequences. Thereafter, Coppola worked on more prestigious projects until his return to horror with his big-budget version of *Dracula* (1992), which starred Gary Oldman as Dracula and **Anthony Hopkins** as Van Helsing. Stylistic eclecticism was the order of the day as Coppola borrowed from German **Expressionism** and **Hammer** in his extravagant transformation of the **vampire** story into a doomed romance. He went on to produce Kenneth Branagh's similarly robust reworking of *Frankenstein* (1994), as well as acting as executive producer on **Tim Burton**'s *Sleepy Hollow* (1999) and Victor Salva's *Jeepers Creepers* (2001) and *Jeepers Creepers 2* (2003). *See also* AMERICAN HORROR.

CORMAN, ROGER (1926–). In the world of low budget independent film production, producer-director Roger Corman has become something of a legend. As a director throughout the 1950s and 1960s, he was capable of rapidly churning out films from extremely limited resources. As a producer, he has given early career opportunities to the likes of Peter Bogdanovich, **Francis Ford Coppola, Joe Dante, Jonathan Demme, Jack Nicholson,** and Martin Scorsese and has been responsible for well over 300 films. Not all of these have been very good but, especially so far as his work as a director is concerned, there have been more worthwhile projects than one might have supposed given the hurried circumstances of production.

During the 1950s, he worked mainly for **American International Pictures**, specializing particularly in the **science fiction**/horror monster movies that were popular in this period. His first credit was as the producer of *The Monster from the Ocean Floor* (1954). He switched to direction in the following year and went on to make the nuclear apocalypse drama *Day the World Ended* (1955) (a subject he returned to in 1960 with *Last Woman on Earth*). *It Conquered the World*

(1956) was a cheap and cheerful alien invasion fantasy. A **vampire**-like alien also showed up in the horror-like *Not of This Earth* (1957), while giant telepathic crabs featured in the atmospheric *Attack of the Crab Monsters* (1957). *The Undead* (1957) was an interesting **witchcraft** story and *A Bucket of Blood* (1959) and *The Little Shop of Horrors* (1960) were splendid examples of **comedy**-horror. *The Wasp Woman* (1960) and *Creature from the Haunted Sea* (1961) were more conventional monster movies, although by the time he made them Corman was already moving onto a cycle of **Edgar Allan Poe** adaptations that would prove his most successful work, both financially and critically.

House of Usher (1960), the first of these films, was a noticeable step up in ambition for both Corman and American International Pictures. It was based upon a reputable literary source, had an intelligent screenplay by **Richard Matheson**, higher production values than before, was in color and featured an established star in **Vincent Price**. Although designed to cash in on the success of **Hammer** horror, the film had a more pronounced interest in exploring weird psychologies than did the Hammer product. As would be the case with Corman's subsequent Poe adaptations, a mysterious and sinister house became a representation of the disturbed mind of its owner. *Pit and the Pendulum* (1961), which starred **Barbara Steele** alongside Price, was even better both in its oppressive atmospherics and in conveying the neurosis of its main male character. *The Premature Burial* (1962) was less successful. It was not originally intended as part of the Poe series and drew very little of its narrative from Poe's writings; Price was replaced by Ray Milland, and the film was not as well received as Corman's previous adaptations.

Tales of Terror (1962) connected more obviously to Poe's work. A horror **anthology** film, it contained three episodes—the haunting "Morella," the humorous "Black **Cat**" (which also drew upon "The Cask of Amontillado") and "The Case of Monsieur Valdemar." All three starred Price, who was ably supported by **Peter Lorre** and **Basil Rathbone**. It was followed by the comedy-horror *The Raven* (1963), a delightful send-up of the previous Poe films that boasted excellent performances from Price, Lorre and **Boris Karloff**. Although *The Haunted Palace* (1963) was marketed as part of the Poe series, it was actually an adaptation of **H. P. Lovecraft**'s "The Case of Charles Dexter Ward." It was a fine film in its own right but its departure from Poe, along with the comedy treatments offered by earlier Corman adaptations, suggested that the Poe series might be coming to an end. However, Corman's final two Poe projects proved not just the best in the series but arguably marked the highpoint of the director's whole career.

Both *The Masque of the Red Death* (1964) and *The Tomb of Ligeia* (1964) were filmed in England. As photographed by **Nicolas Roeg**, *The Masque of the Red Death*'s use of color was particularly impressive, while, unusually for the series, *The Tomb of Ligeia* made extensive use of location shooting. Both were richly atmospheric, with fine, nuanced performances from Price, cruel in the former as a despot protecting himself from the plague, obsessed with the memory of his dead wife in the latter. *The Masque of the Red Death* has been accused of pretentiousness, and certainly its references to **Ingmar Bergman**'s *Det sjunde inseglet* (*The Seventh Seal*) (1957) are all-too-obvious, but both it and *Ligeia* exhibited a level of both ambition and achievement that was rare in the horror cinema of this period.

Corman retired from film direction in the early 1970s and has since concentrated on film production, first for New World and subsequently for New Horizons and Concorde. He made a brief comeback as director with *Frankenstein Unbound* (1990), an interesting revisionary account of the Frankenstein story, albeit one that lacked the distinctive style of his best work. He has also made some cameo appearances in films directed by some of his protégés, including Joe Dante's *The Howling* (1981) and Jonathan Demme's *The Silence of the Lambs* (1991).

Corman's other directorial horror credits include *Tower of London* (1962) and *The Terror* (1963). *See also* AMERICAN HORROR.

COSCARELLI, DON (1954–). The Libyan-born writer-director Don Coscarelli is most associated with the *Phantasm* horror cycle. At a time when **American horror** was switching over to teenager-centered **slasher** films, *Phantasm* (1979) went in its own idiosyncratic direction, with a weird narrative involving aliens, grave-robbing, monstrous dwarves and a homicidal floating metal ball. The film had a pleasingly surreal quality to it, although—with the exception of the Coscarelli-directed **sequels** *Phantasm II* (1988),

Phantasm III: Lord of the Dead (1994) and *Phantasm IV: Oblivion* (1998)—it has had little influence on other horror films. Coscarelli changed direction again with *Bubba Ho-tep* (2002), the unlikely story of which involved Elvis Presley (played by genre regular **Bruce Campbell**) fighting a **mummy** in an old people's home. Perhaps surprisingly given this scenario, the film managed to be both refreshingly original and in places rather moving. Coscarelli also directed the fantasy adventure *The Beastmaster* (1982) and contributed an episode to the **television** series *Masters of Horror* (2005–).

COSTELLO, LOU. *See* ABBOTT, BUD.

COURT, HAZEL (1926–). The horror career of the British actor Hazel Court demonstrates what a difference a director can make to a screen persona. Court was a pretty but bland female lead in **Vernon Sewell**'s *Ghost Ship* (1952) and **Terence Fisher**'s *The Curse of Frankenstein* (1957) and *The Man Who Could Cheat Death* (1959) and made similar appearances in *Devil Girl From Mars* (1954) and *Dr. Blood's Coffin* (1961). However, the three horror films she did for American director **Roger Corman**—*The Premature Burial* (1962), *The Raven* (1963), and *The Masque of the Red Death* (1964)—presented her as an altogether more assertive sexual presence. In *The Masque of the Red Death* in particular, she offered a compelling portrayal of jealousy and corruption. Much of Court's later career was spent working on American **television**.

COZZI, LUIGI (1947–). The films of Italian writer-director Luigi Cozzi—who is sometimes billed as Lewis Coates—tend at their best to be lively and derivative and at their worst dull and derivative. Early in his career, he worked for **Italian horror** maestro **Dario Argento**, gaining story credits on Argento's *4 mosche di velluto grigio* (*Four Flies on Grey Velvet*) (1971) and *Le cinque giornate* (*Five Days of Milan*) (1973) as well as contributing to the Argento-produced **television** series *Porta sul buio* (*Doors into Darkness*) (1973). His first horror film as director was the effective **giallo** *L'assassino è costretto ad uccidere ancora* (*The Dark Is Death's Friend*) (1975) and his subsequent rather uneven directorial career included *Contamination* (1980), *Il Gatto Nero* (*The Black Cat*) (1989), and *Paganini Horror*

(1989). He was second unit director on two more Argento films, *Due occhi diabolici* (*Two Evil Eyes*) (1990) and *La sindrome di Stendhal* (*The Stendhal Syndrome*) (1996) and also directed two **documentaries** about Argento's films.

CRABTREE, ARTHUR (1900–1975). Formerly a cinematographer, the British filmmaker Arthur Crabtree made his directorial debut with the overwrought Gainsborough melodrama *Madonna of the Seven Moons* (1945). A sense of the lurid combined with a solid professionalism was also apparent in Crabtree's *Caravan* (1946) and *Dear Murderer* (1947), although much of his 1950s work was more low-key. However, towards the end of that decade he, like many other jobbing filmmakers, was drawn into the commercially vibrant **British horror** movement and seemed to rediscover his taste for excess. *Fiend without a Face* (1958), which despite its Canadian setting was a British production, featured a standard **science fiction**/horror hybrid plot about an experiment gone wrong but was distinguished by some extraordinarily surreal and gory sequences in which disembodied brains attack their victims. The well-known opening sequence of Crabtree's *Horrors of the Black Museum* (1959) showed a woman being blinded by spikes that emerged from the binoculars through which she was looking, and the rest of the film offered a series of equally sadistic murders. *Horrors of the Black Museum* might have been overshadowed by **Michael Powell**'s similarly themed *Peeping Tom* (1960) but for all its crudeness it had an energy that made it memorable. Crabtree retired from filmmaking shortly after its release.

CRAVEN, WES (1939–). Wes Craven was a college teacher before he became a key director of **American horror**. This is an unusual background for someone so firmly associated with the horror genre. However, Craven's films often display a distinctive self-consciousness, intelligence and ambition that, amidst the violence and **gore**, could be seen as bestowing a scholarly quality on them. This was apparent in his directorial debut, the controversial rape-revenge drama *The Last House on the Left* (1972), which, uniquely for a horror film, was a reworking of an **Ingmar Bergman** film, *The Virgin Spring* (1959). The message of Craven's grueling **remake** was clear: we all have within us the capacity for extreme violence. Two young women are raped, tortured and murdered by a gang of low-lifes. Subsequently the well-to-do parents of one of the girls discover the crime and carry out an appalling revenge on the miscreants (involving throat slashing and death by chainsaw), with the narrative's escalating, unstoppable violence leading eventually to the collapse of normality. As Craven himself has indicated, it is the kind of film that would have had a particular resonance in the era of the Vietnam war and the social unrest that this conflict brought about.

The Hills Have Eyes (1977), Craven's next film, was thematically very similar but also slicker and more palatable for a mainstream audience. An example of 1970s **family horror**, it pitted two families against each other. One of these families was normal in a middle-class and slightly complacent sort of way, and the other was made up of lower-class predatory cannibals. While, unsurprisingly, we initially identify with the normal family, their gradual surrender to violence as they take on the cannibals becomes increasingly disturbing, with the culminating in another open, disturbing conclusion.

At this point, Craven's career seemed temporarily to lose direction. *Deadly Blessing* (1981) was an effective thriller about a religious sect (the supernatural conclusion of which was removed from some prints, presumably to make it appear less like a horror film) but *Swamp Thing* (1982) was an uninspired **comic**-book adaptation. Then came *A Nightmare on Elm Street* (1984). As written and directed by Craven, this was a genuinely innovative variant on the **slasher** film that initiated one of the major horror cycles of the 1980s. It also continued the director's preoccupation with proletariat assaults upon a complacent middle class, with the undead janitor Freddy Krueger revenging himself upon the teenage **children** of his murderers. As was the case with Craven's best work in general, it was constructed around and played variations on a concept—here the idea that whatever happens to you in your dreams also happens to you in waking reality.

In the aftermath of *Elm Street*, Craven struggled to find interesting projects. *The Hills Have Eyes Part II* (1985) and *Deadly Friend* (1986) were professionally done but impersonal. *The Serpent and the Rainbow* (1988) was an ambitious attempt to update the **voodoo** film through an exploration of voodoo's anthropological roots, although ultimately it descended into conventional melodrama. *Shocker* (1989) was more along the lines of *A Nightmare on Elm Street* in its depiction of a vengeful **ghost** who attacks his victims, not through their dreams this time but instead through their **television** sets. The film's playful games with the medium of television anticipated the **self-reflexivity** that would characterize much of Craven's work in the 1990s, a period that would be more productive for him than the latter half of the 1980s.

The People Under the Stairs (1991) was Craven's most cohesive film since *A Nightmare on Elm Street*. A social parable about the rich exploiting the poor (and the poor turning the tables on them), it was done with wit and intelligence, with Craven siding more emphatically with the underprivileged characters than he had done in his earlier films. This is one of the few 1990s horror films that can reasonably be described as both politicized and left-wing. It was followed by *New Nightmare* (1994) (sometimes known as *Wes Craven's New Nightmare*), the seventh film in the *Elm Street* cycle. Craven had steered clear of *Elm Street* since his inaugural film but now he turned the established formula on its head in an boldly self-reflexive project in which actors and other crew members (including Craven) played themselves. Like *Shocker*, it was a sign of things to come, but first there was *Vampire in Brooklyn* (1995), an underrated vampire vehicle for Eddie Murphy that struggled to make its **comedy** and horror elements gel with each other.

No such problem was evident in the highly successful *Scream* (1996). Working from a screenplay by **Kevin Williamson**, Craven returned to the world of the slasher film and **teenage horror**, refashioning the self-reflexivity of his earlier films into a knowingness about horror history. He also showed that he was more than capable of delivering shocks and startles at a time when such standard generic devices were starting to look very tired. Craven went on to direct *Scream 2* (1997) and *Scream 3* (2000) as well as *Cursed* (2005), a Williamson-scripted attempt to do for **werewolves** what *Scream* had done for the slasher film.

The sheer length of Craven's career in horror makes him worthy of note, as does his ability to innovate within the genre. To a certain extent, he has now become a recognizable genre brand name, with the label "Wes Craven Presents" used as part of the marketing for horror films directed by others, for example *Carnival of Souls* (1998) and *Dracula 2000* (2000). He was also one of the producers of the 2006 remake of his own *The Hills Have Eyes*.

His television credits include *Stranger in Our House* (*Summer of Fear*) (1978), *Invitation to Hell* (1984), *Chiller* (1985), and *Night Visions* (1990).

CRAWFORD, JOAN (1904–1977). Much like her fellow Hollywood star **Bette Davis**, Joan Crawford turned to horror in the latter part of her career. She starred alongside Davis in **Robert Aldrich**'s *What Ever Happened to Baby Jane?* (1962), a film that rendered in grotesque terms the alleged real-life rivalry between the two women. While in some of her later films, Davis seemed to have embraced this grotesque identity, Crawford opted for more conventional parts. She was originally cast with Davis in Aldrich's follow-up to *Baby Jane*, *Hush . . . Hush, Sweet Charlotte* (1964) but withdrew from the production (her part was eventually played by Olivia de Havilland). Subsequently she played effectively in two **William Castle** productions, *Strait-Jacket* (1964) and *I Saw What You Did* (1965) and then made rather undignified appearances in the **British horror** films *Berserk!* (1968) and the irredeemably ridiculous *Trog* (1970). She also starred in the 1969 pilot film for the **television** horror **anthology** series *Night Gallery*; her segment was directed by **Steven Spielberg**, who was making his professional debut.

CRONENBERG, DAVID (1943–). The horror films directed by Canadian filmmaker David Cronenberg have a reputation for being visceral and unsparingly gruesome, and yet he is also one of the more cerebral talents to have worked within the genre. Unusually for a horror director, his background was in avant-garde cinema. Some of his early films—notably *Stereo* (1969) and *Crimes of the Future* (1970)—exhibited a fascination with alienating institutions and dangerously misguided scientific experiments that would be developed further in his horror work, although the films themselves remained obscure and hermetic. A desire to connect with a broader public led to Cronenberg writing a script for a low-budget horror called *Orgy of the Blood Parasites*. Produced, like most of his other horror films, in his native Canada, the resulting film was retitled *The Parasite Mur-*

ders (1975) for the Canadian market, *They Came From Within* for the United States, and *Shivers* everywhere else. It depicted the spread of an experimental slug-like organism—described in the film as a cross between a parasite and a venereal **disease**—through a modern housing complex, transforming the inhabitants into ravening sex maniacs as it went. An updated **Frankenstein** narrative and an example of biological or **body horror**, *The Parasite Murders* established Cronenberg as an exciting and innovative new talent in the genre, although the fact that the production of this most disturbing of horror films had been supported by the tax-funded Canadian Film Development Corporation caused some controversy on the film's release in Canada.

Cronenberg's next two horror films (he also directed *Fast Company*, a racing drama in this period) elaborated on material introduced in *The Parasite Murders*. *Rabid* (1977) was another infection story in which a radical surgical technique transforms a woman into a plague carrier, while *The Brood* (1979) focused on a woman with the ability to externalize her rage in the form of spontaneously generated monstrous **children**. The relentlessly grim atmosphere of both was coupled with a dispassionate examination of bodies caught up in a process of physiological change and transformation. The telekinesis drama *Scanners* (1981) also contained moments of body horror, this time associated with the male body, although it was also more action-based and less unsettling than the director's previous horrors. The controversial *Videodrome* (1983) was not so much of an audience-pleaser but it did offer a bold investigation of the interaction between consciousness and technology in a manner reminiscent of Cronenberg's earlier avant-garde work.

The most commercial part of Cronenberg's career began with *The Dead Zone* (1983) and ended with *The Fly* (1986). At the time of *The Dead Zone*'s release, this adaptation of a **Stephen King** novel seemed untypical of the director's sophisticated and cosmopolitan approach, with its rural settings and naturalistic style (although Cronenberg's 2005 film *A History of Violence* adopted a comparable approach). *The Fly* was more obviously Cronenbergian in its depiction of a scientist's slow and messy mutation into a human/fly hybrid, but at the same time it was Cronenberg at his most straightforward and accessible.

Since *The Fly*, the director has moved away from the horror genre and transformed himself into a critically respected international auteur, although a concern with the body and a reliance on horror-like imagery continue to inform his films, including *Dead Ringers* (1988), *Naked Lunch* (1991), *Crash* (1996), *eXistenZ* (1999), *Spider* (2002), and *A History of Violence*. Cronenberg has also made some appearances in films. He was an insane psychiatrist in **Clive Barker's** *Nightbreed* (1990), a hitman in *To Die For* (1995), and, less expectedly, also showed up in the *Friday the 13th* film *Jason X* (2001) (although he had earlier directed an episode for the *Friday the 13th* **television** series).

CUNNINGHAM, SEAN S. (1941–). The producer-director Sean S. Cunningham first made an impression as a producer of **Wes Craven's** controversial horror film *The Last House on the Left* (1972). Subsequently he directed the horror-themed sex **comedy** *Case of the Full Moon Murders* (1974), but his most significant film as a director came with *Friday the 13th* (1980), a **slasher** designed to exploit the success of **John Carpenter's** *Halloween* (1978). Cunningham's treatment of his subject—teenagers being slaughtered by an unseen assailant while at summer camp—lacked Carpenter's style and assurance but it was efficient enough to make the film a substantial box-office hit that generated numerous **sequels**. Cunningham's later credits are patchy. He directed horror projects *Someone is Watching* (1982) and *Deep Star Six* (1989) and produced some of the later *Friday the 13th* sequels along with the haunted house film *House* (1986) and some of its sequels. *See also* AMERICAN HORROR.

CURTIS, DAN (1928–2006). During the 1960s and 1970s, the American writer-producer-director Dan Curtis made a significant contribution to the development of horror on **television**, often by placing horror elements within familiar televisual formats. For example, his daytime soap *Dark Shadows* (1966–1971) contained **vampire** and **werewolf** characters and was successful enough to generate two Curtis-directed cinema films, *House of Dark Shadows* (1970) and *Night of Dark Shadows* (1971). He also produced and sometimes directed television adaptations of classic **gothic** novels, including *The Strange Case of Dr. Jekyll and Mr. Hyde* (1968), *Frankenstein* (1973), *Dracula* (1973), *The Picture of Dorian Gray* (1973), and *The Turn of the*

Screw (1974). Of these, *Dracula* was probably the most influential in its exploration of the arch-vampire as a historical personage, something that would be taken up in more detail in later Dracula films. However, Curtis's original television horror films, many of which were scripted by **Richard Matheson**, were also striking and effective. The best known of these, and in its time the highest rated television film ever, was *The Night Stalker* (1972), which was directed by **John Llewellyn Moxey**. This innovative modern-day vampire story introduced the character of journalist Carl Kolchak (who later acquired his own television series) and was an influence on *The X-Files* (1993–2002). Curtis himself directed its **sequel** *The Night Strangler* (1973) along with *The Norliss Tapes* (1973), *Scream of the Wolf* (1974), and the horror **anthology** *Trilogy of Terror* (1975). His cinema horror film *Burnt Offerings* (1976) contained some effective moments but in both its pacing and content seemed more suited to television. Two more television horror films followed, the anthology *Dead of Night* (1977) and *Curse of the Black Widow* (1977). Thereafter Curtis moved away from horror and produced the blockbusting mini-series *The Winds of War* (1983) and its sequel *War and Remembrance* (1988). In the 1990s, he returned to the genre with a short-lived revival of *Dark Shadows* (1990) and another horror anthology, *Trilogy of Terror II* (1996). *See also* AMERICAN HORROR.

CURTIS, JAMIE LEE (1958–). Jamie Lee Curtis might be said to have horror cinema in her blood. The daughter of Tony Curtis and **Janet Leigh**, she first attracted attention in **John Carpenter**'s groundbreaking **slasher** *Halloween* (1978), a film in which one of the main characters is named after a character in *Psycho* (1960), one of Janet Leigh's most famous films. Curtis quickly established an attractive screen personality of her own and for a brief period became one of horror's most bankable stars. As Laurie Strode, the terrorized babysitter in *Halloween*, she combined vulnerability and strength as she battled an apparently unstoppable **serial killer**. She embodied the **Final Girl**, the energetic female hero of the slasher film, and her performance was much copied although never really equaled. Curtis went on to play similar characters in *Prom Night* (1980) and *Terror Train* (1980) and more sexually knowing variants in John Carpenter's **ghost** story *The Fog* (1980) and the **Australian horror** thriller

Roadgames (1981). However, by the time she reprised the role of Laurie Strode in *Halloween II* (1981), she was visibly too old to play a schoolgirl babysitter.

Curtis subsequently developed her career away from horror with notable performances in the drama *Love Letters* (1984), the **comedy** *A Fish Called Wanda* (1988) and **James Cameron**'s action blockbuster *True Lies* (1994). Her role as a rookie cop in the urban thriller *Blue Steel* (1990) drew upon horror iconography as she took on another implacable serial killer, and she played a villain for the first time in the **psychological thriller** *Mother's Boys* (1994), as well as starring in the **science fiction**/horror film *Virus* (1999). Twenty years after the success of *Halloween*, Curtis became Laurie Strode yet again in the unsurprisingly titled *Halloween H20: 20 Years Later* (1998). In many ways this was a standard teens-in-danger film but Curtis brought considerable maturity and class to the proceedings as she fought and defeated the same serial killer who had tormented her in 1978 (and who, it was revealed in *Halloween II*, was actually Laurie's brother). She played Strode one more time in *Halloween: Resurrection* (2002), albeit to less effect.

In 1996, as a result of her husband, the actor-director Christopher Guest, inheriting a British barony, Curtis became Lady Haden-Guest of Saling; this was a rare distinction for a horror star.

CURTIZ, MICHAEL (1886–1962). The Hungarian-born director Michael Curtiz—whose real name was Manó Kertész Kaminer—is most associated with the lush Hollywood escapism of Warner Brothers productions such as *The Adventures of Robin Hood* (1938) or *Casablanca* (1942). However, in the 1930s he also directed some Warner Brothers horror films, instilling in them the same kind of punchy urban energy evident in the studio's musicals and gangster dramas. *Doctor X* (1932) was for the time an unusually grisly **serial killer** story that starred **Lionel Atwill** and **Fay Wray**. The same actors were reunited for *Mystery of the Wax Museum* (1933), although on this occasion Atwill got to play the villain. Unlike 1930s **Universal** horror, Curtiz's films were set in contemporary America and full of recognizable urban types, although they did share with Universal their expressive visuals. Later in the 1930s, Curtiz also directed the **Boris Karloff** vehicle *The Walking Dead* (1936), which in true Warners style managed to combine horror with a gangster narrative as an undead Karloff sought revenge on the criminal gang who framed him. *See also* AMERICAN HORROR.

CUSHING, PETER (1913–1994). A major contributor to **British horror** cinema from the 1950s through to the 1970s, the actor Peter Cushing brought artistry and dignity to a genre not always associated with such qualities. His early acting career included a short and not very successful stint in Hollywood (where he worked with renowned horror director **James Whale** on the 1939 version of *The Man in the Iron Mask*). However, by the time he made his first horror film in 1957, he had become an established star in British **television** drama, with his most notable role that of Winston Smith in a controversial BBC production of George Orwell's *1984* (1954). It was Cushing himself who sought out the role of Baron **Frankenstein** when he heard that **Hammer** Films was planning a new version of the story. The resulting film, *The Curse of Frankenstein* (1957), was a major international success that inaugurated a boom in British horror production. While **Colin Clive**'s performance of Frankenstein in **Universal**'s *Frankenstein* (1931) and *Bride of Frankenstein* (1935) had been manic and highly emotional, Cushing played the Baron instead as a ruthless dandy with a sardonic sense of humor. It was a performance that helped to set the tone for the many Hammer horrors to follow. In the following year, Cushing secured his status as genre icon through his memorable rendition of Van Helsing as a stern but kind authority figure in Hammer's *Dracula* (*Horror of Dracula*) (1958). As was the case with many of his films, Cushing was not content here just to deliver his lines but also offered suggestions for new dialogue or new dramatic business. The film's famous conclusion—in which Van Helsing leaps athletically off a table to pull down curtains and allow in the light that will destroy the **vampire**—arose as a result of one of these suggestions.

Cushing would play Frankenstein five more times and Van Helsing four more times for Hammer, but his versatility as an actor ranged well beyond these two signature roles. In Hammer horror's early days, he was an impressive **Sherlock Holmes** in *The Hound of the Baskervilles* (1959), a role he later played on television, an appealing hero in *The Mummy* (1959) and an obsessive villain in *The Gorgon* (1964). He also offered a kindlier version of the errant scientist in the non-Hammer production *The Flesh and the Fiends* (1959), which dramatized the story of Dr. Knox and graverobbers Burke and Hare. From the mid-1960s onwards, Cushing demonstrated that he was just as capable of playing in horror films with contemporary settings as he was in period roles. For the **Amicus** company, he was the sinister Dr. Schreck in *Dr. Terror's House of Horrors* (1964) and appeared in more sympathetic roles in *The Skull* (1965) and *Torture Garden* (1967). He was Dr. Who in two films aimed at the family audience and, back in the world of horror, he also brought some much-needed gravitas to Hammer's lesbian vampire films *The Vampire Lovers* (1970) and *Twins of Evil* (1971), as well as providing an entertaining portrait of English idiosyncrasy for the Spanish/British co-production *Pánico en el Transiberiano* (*Horror Express*) (1973). His casting as the evil Moff Tarkin in George Lucas's *Star Wars* (1977) introduced his work to a new generation of filmgoers and confirmed his status as one of the screen's great villains. His final horror film was **Pete Walker**'s nostalgic *House of the Long Shadows* (1983), where he appeared alongside fellow horror icons **John Carradine**, **Christopher Lee**, and **Vincent Price**.

Cushing's other horror or horror-related credits are *The Abominable Snowman* (1957), *The Revenge of Frankenstein* (1958), *The Hellfire Club* (1960), *The Brides of Dracula* (1960), *Captain Clegg* (1962), *The Evil of Frankenstein* (1964), *Dr. Who and the Daleks* (1965), *She* (1965), *Island of Terror* (1966), *Daleks' Invasion Earth: 2150 A.D.* (1966), *Night of the Big Heat* (1967), *Corruption* (1967), *Frankenstein Created Woman* (1967), *The Blood Beast Terror* (1968), *Scream and Scream Again* (1969), *Frankenstein Must Be Destroyed* (1969), *The House That Dripped Blood* (1970), *One More Time* (1970), *I, Monster* (1970), *Incense for the Damned* (*Bloodsuckers*) (1970), *Nothing But the Night* (1972), *Tales from the Crypt* (1972), *Fear in the Night* (1972), *Dr. Phibes Rises Again* (1972), *Asylum* (1972), *Dracula AD 1972* (1972), *From Beyond the Grave* (1973), *The Creeping Flesh* (1973), *And Now the Screaming Starts!* (1973), *The Satanic Rites of Dracula* (1973), *Madhouse* (1974), *The Beast Must Die* (1974), *Frankenstein and the Monster from Hell* (1974), *Tendre Dracula* (1974), *The Legend of the Seven Golden Vampires* (1974), *The Ghoul* (1974), *Legend of the **Werewolf*** (1975), *The **Devil**'s Men* (1976), *Shock Waves* (1977), and *The Uncanny* (1977).

– D –

D'AMATO, JOE. *See* MASSACCESI, ARISTIDE.

DANTE, JOE (1946–). Joe Dante was a film **fan** before he was a director, and his own films are informed by his enthusiasm for and knowledge of cinema history. Starting out by editing trailers for **Roger Corman**, his directorial debut—which was co-directed with Allan Arkush—was the ultra low budget spoof *Hollywood Boulevard* (1976). This was followed by *Piranha* (1978), which drew upon both *Jaws* (1975) and 1950s monster movies for inspiration in its depiction of killer piranha attacking the United States but which displayed a liveliness and level of invention that set it apart from other more grim horrors of the period. The **werewolf** drama *The Howling* (1981) was even better. Although overshadowed by **John Landis**'s bigger-budgeted *An American Werewolf in London* (1981), Dante's film had a distinctive cinephile character all of its own. Fond, if ironic, references to horror's past mingled with some suspenseful sequences and impressive werewolf transformation effects provided by **Rob Bottin**. This fascination with American popular-cultural history continued with his direction of a segment for *Twilight Zone: The Movie* (1983). More successful was *Gremlins* (1984), a **Steven Spielberg**-produced small-town drama with a manic edge. The anarchic antics of the gremlins displayed the influence of the cartoons of Chuck Jones, a key influence on Dante, and the film, although a family drama, offered more disturbing scenes than one might have expected. After an excursion into **science fiction** family drama with *Explorers* (1985), he returned to **comedy**-horror with the underrated *The `Burbs* (1989). This Tom Hanks vehicle introduced horror iconography into an apparently peaceful setting in a *Gremlins*-like manner but did not manage the transitions between the comedy and the horror as skillfully as *Gremlins* had. *Gremlins 2: The New Batch* (1990) upped the manic energy of the first film, and also included an appearance by horror icon **Christopher Lee**, but it too struggled to recapture the perfectly judged tone of its predecessor. *Matinee* (1993) was a return to form, however. The setting of the Cuban Missile crisis was juxtaposed with the gimmicks devised by a flamboyant **William Castle**-like movie promoter to sell his genre product. Nostalgia for a type of cinema long since passed was combined with a telling sense of the ways in which films can transform real social fears into an entertaining experience. Some characteristically knowing references to old horror films also showed up in Dante's fantasy adventure *Small Soldiers* (1998).

Dante has also contributed episodes to fantasy/horror **television** series *The Twilight Zone* (1985–1989), *Amazing Stories* (1985–1987), *Eerie, Indiana* (1991–1992), *Night Visions* (2001), and *Masters of Horror* (2005–). *See also* AMERICAN HORROR.

DAVIS, BETTE (1908–1989). One of the greatest of all Hollywood stars steered well clear of the horror genre while in her prime. However, in her latter years, Bette Davis did stray into some upmarket horror-related products. **Robert Aldrich**'s **psychological thriller** *What Ever Happened to Baby Jane?* (1962) set the tone for what was to come. Here Davis's advanced years were transformed via her considerable performance skills into a grotesque mask. Comparable grotesquerie was on show in Aldrich's follow-up, *Hush . . . Hush, Sweet Charlotte* (1964) and in two films Davis did for **Hammer**, *The Nanny* (1965) and *The Anniversary* (1968), as well as in the **television** horror miniseries *The Dark Secret of Harvest Home* (1978). She also featured in **Dan Curtis**'s *Burnt Offerings* (1976), *The Watcher in the Woods* (1980) and in the best-forgotten *Wicked Stepmother* (1989).

DAY, ROBERT (1922–). The British director Robert Day is one of a number of filmmakers who passed through the commercially popular **British horror** genre in the 1950s and 1960s and left some interesting films behind but did not become horror specialists. In Day's case, he worked his way up through the industry and made his debut with the black **comedy** *The Green Man* (1956). His 1950s horror films were efficient but lacked the personality evident in the work of directors such as **Terence Fisher** or **John Gilling**. *Grip of the Strangler* (1958), which starred **Boris Karloff**, was an enjoyably lurid example of period horror. Day's other Karloff vehicle, *Corridors of Blood* (1958), was more somber in its treatment of a story about the development of surgical anesthetic and perhaps because of this was not released until the early 1960s. By contrast, Day's *First Man Into*

Space (1959) was an example of **science fiction**/horror. Day returned to fantasy in the mid-1960s with a decorous version of *She* (1965) for **Hammer** but concentrated in this period on comedies and a series of Tarzan films. From the 1970s onwards, he worked mainly for American **television**.

DE LEÓN, GERARDO (1913–1981). The first part of the career of Filipino director Gerardo de León was apparently distinguished and reputable, although his non-horror films from this period have not circulated widely outside of the Philippines. By contrast, the latter part of his career was mainly spent making thoroughly disreputable low-budget horrors, with many of these receiving international distribution. He began with the garish but atmospheric *Terror is a Man* (1959), a loose reworking of H. G. Wells' *The Island of Dr. Moreau*, and, after a hiatus, returned to the genre with the **vampire** story *Kulay dugo ang gabi (The Blood Drinkers)* (1966). Subsequently, he co-directed two horrors with his protégé **Eddie Romero**, *Mad Doctor of Blood Island* (1968) and *Brides of Blood* (1968), and was solely responsible for *Dugo ng vampira (Blood of the Vampires, Curse of the Vampires)* (1971). These films were often better made than other low-budget horrors, but they never demonstrated the mastery of the cinematic medium associated with the director's earlier works. *See also* FILIPINO HORROR.

DE NIRO, ROBERT (1943–). Robert De Niro's formidable screen career has been built out of intense and edgy performances in films such as *Taxi Driver* (1976) and *Raging Bull* (1980). He is not particularly associated with the horror genre, but enjoyably overblown villainous turns as the **Devil** in the **voodoo** thriller *Angel Heart* (1987) and as a vengeful psychopathic ex-convict in Martin Scorsese's *Cape Fear* (1991) have proved memorable. He seemed less comfortable in the role of the Monster in Kenneth Branagh's adaptation of *Frankenstein* (1994), and he has also given workmanlike, if rather muted, performances in the psychological horror thrillers *The Godsend* (2004) and *Hide and Seek* (2005).

DE PALMA, BRIAN (1940–). Of all the young directors who helped to transform American cinema in the late 1960s and 1970s, Brian De

Palma is probably the most formally inventive and yet also the most enigmatic. This is a director whose work has sometimes been labeled "feminist" by critics but whose films have also been accused of misogyny. De Palma's taciturn public persona—he is notoriously unrevealing in interviews—has not always helped to clarify what his aims are in making the films he does. What is clear is that throughout much of the 1970s and into the 1980s, De Palma's work focused on horror or horror-related themes. One reason for this could be that horror was fashionable in the market at the time. However, the intelligence with which the director engaged with this material suggests that it was appealing to him, at least at this stage of his career.

De Palma's early films, which included *Greetings* (1968) and *Hi Mom!* (1970), were experimental, countercultural pieces that played games with film form while also offering socially critical elements. While the formal games continued in the later horror films and thrillers, attempts to engage with contemporary society were less noticeable. However, an intermittent, albeit sometimes cryptic, exploration of sexual politics was apparent. *Sisters* (1973), his first truly mainstream project, was an extraordinarily stylish **psychological thriller** that in its treatment of voyeurism and its **Bernard Herrmann** score showed the influence, like other De Palma films, of **Alfred Hitchcock**. Some of the film's disturbing dream-like imagery secured its status as a horror-like project and, like much of 1970s **American horror**, it depicted male authority as both monstrous and ineffectual. By contrast, *Phantom of the Paradise* (1974) was a dark **comedy**-horror reworking of *The Phantom of the Opera* story, with pop-musical interludes that resurrected some of the countercultural playfulness of De Palma's earlier work at a time when that type of cinematic game was not popular. The film was clever and beautifully made but it struggled to find an audience. The overblown psychological thriller *Obsession* (1976) was a return to a Hitchcockian world, although what was fresh in *Sisters* was starting to look like pastiche.

Carrie (1976) followed. This was one of the biggest commercial successes of De Palma's career and one of the best adaptations of a **Stephen King** novel. Its high school and prom settings and its teenage characterizations anticipated the **slasher** films that would follow a few years later. However, what was most striking about the film was its presentation of the "monster." The telekinetic Carrie

White (played by Sissy Spacek) managed to be both extremely sympathetic and utterly destructive, and it was this ambiguity that enabled De Palma to create a social world that audiences could either take as normal or interpret as oppressive (and, perhaps unsurprisingly, *Carrie* is one of those films that has been accused of misogyny and praised for its insights into female oppression). The film also contained one of horror cinema's greatest shock endings.

Although *Carrie* was full of slow-motion and split-screen devices, these were usually subordinated to the demands of narrative and atmosphere. *The Fury* (1978), another telekinesis film, was much more extravagant in its formal pyrotechnics and considerably less interested in the human dynamics of the story, to the point where some sections became almost abstract. Extensive slow-motion chases punctuated this conspiracy thriller narrative, with the climax provided by a remarkable **Rick Baker**-designed scene in which the villain—played by John Cassavetes—was telekinetically exploded.

Emphasizing form over content got De Palma into trouble with his next genre project, *Dressed to Kill* (1980). This horror-thriller appeared in the middle of the slasher boom (although it was clearly not a slasher film, at least not in the **teenage horror** sense of that term) and was caught up in public protests over what was perceived as the increasing amount of screen violence directed against women. This led to screenings of the film being picketed by activists, although subsequently—and perhaps predictably—pro-De Palma critics made the case for the film as a progressive exploration of gender issues. So far as the plot of *Dressed to Kill* is concerned, however, one could argue that the negative criticisms had a point. Women are persistently threatened and violated in the film, and the killer's transvestism—which clearly refers back to Hitchcock's *Psycho* (1960)—suggests that it is the feminine side of his character that is responsible for the violence. Having said this, one could argue that the plot is perhaps not that important and that, as in some of his previous work, De Palma is more interested in formal matters, in the movement of the camera and the felicitous juxtaposition of shots. Most notable in this respect is a lengthy wordless scene in an art gallery (and the inevitable Hitchcock reference here is to *Vertigo*) where Angie Dickinson and an unknown male follow and spy on each other. Clearly there is a sexual politics of looking at play here, with Dickinson's gaze constantly thwarted, but at the same time there is also considerable pleasure to be had in what is a bravura display of filmmaking technique. How one values the latter experience is, of course, up to the spectator, and the extent to which a dubious representation of women is designed to provoke remains, as it so often does with De Palma, unclear.

As if saying goodbye to horror, the political thriller *Blow Out* (1981) and the psychological thriller *Body Double* (1984) both made comedic references to, respectively, the slasher film and the **vampire** film. Since then, De Palma has worked mainly in the crime and action genres, although *Raising Cain* (1992) and *Femme Fatale* (2002) were minor throwbacks to the type of film he was making in the 1970s.

DEKKER, FRED (1959–). During the 1980s, the writer-director Fred Dekker was responsible for two lively and engaging **comedy**-horrors. *Night of the Creeps* (1986) combined extraterrestrials with **zombies,** while *The Monster Squad* (1987) pitted **children** against traditional horror monsters such as **Dracula, Frankenstein**'s monster, the Wolf Man and the **mummy.** Dekker also came up with the original story for the haunted house horror-comedy *House* (1986). He went on to direct and co-write *Robocop 3* (1993) and wrote and directed for the **television** horror series *Tales from the Crypt* (1989–1996). *See also* AMERICAN HORROR.

DEL TORO, GUILLERMO (1964–). The innovative films of Mexican writer-director Guillermo del Toro often possess a visionary quality as well as reflecting his fascination with the state of childhood. Since the early 1990s, he has pursued an international career that has marked him out as one of the most exciting talents currently working in the horror genre. Del Toro started out in the Mexican film industry as a **makeup** and special effects artist, working for a while with the leading American makeup artist **Dick Smith.** *Cronos* (1993), his directorial debut, was an imaginative reinvention of the **vampire** story that showed as much interest in the relationships between characters as it did in the conventional horror elements. Like many of Del Toro's later projects, it managed to be both moving and frightening, adult and child-like. *Mimic* (1997), his first American film, was a more straightforward monster movie about giant **insects** living under New York, although Del Toro still managed in places to convey his distinctive vision, notably in scenes involving a mentally handicapped child who witnesses the monstrous actions of the insects in the same dispassionate manner in which the little girl in *Cronos* watches as her beloved grandfather is gradually transformed into a monster. A move to Spain led to *El espinazo del diablo* (*The Devil's Backbone*) (2001), another child-centered project, this time a quietly disturbing **ghost** story set in the context of the Spanish Civil War. As he had done with *Cronos*, Del Toro successfully combined what might be termed arthouse conventions with a passionate commitment to the horror genre. Next came two more mainstream projects, **comic** book adaptations *Blade 2* (2002) and *Hellboy* (2004), although, more than he had been able to do with *Mimic*, Del Toro made something personal of both, endowing what could have been simplistic action based dramas with character nuance and a rich visual style. *El laberinto del fauno* (*Pan's Labyrinth*) (2006), his latest film, is Del Toro's most visually sumptuous project to date and returns him yet again to an unsentimentally presented but nevertheless affecting fantasy world of a child.

DEMME, JONATHAN (1944–). Jonathan Demme was an odd choice for director on the **serial killer** drama *The Silence of the Lambs* (1991). Although Demme had begun his career with low-budget exploitation films such as *Caged Heat* (1974) and *Fighting Mad* (1976), he was best known by the late 1980s for character-driven work on the likes of *Melvin and Howard* (1980) and *Something Wild* (1986) and for his concert film *Stop Making Sense* (1984). *The Last Embrace* (1979), his clever Hitchcock pastiche, suggested a director who was comfortable with thriller conventions, but the film had not made much of an impact. However, Demme did a remarkable job with *Silence*, combining Hitchcockian techniques with *grand guignol* elements and also finding a dark humor in **Anthony Hopkins'** performance as master serial killer Hannibal Lecter. The film set the pattern for later serial killer dramas, although Demme himself—who won an Academy Award for *Silence*—has since steered clear of the horror genre. *Beloved* (1998), his ambitious adaptation of a Toni Morrison novel, did contain supernatural imagery, although this sat uneasily with that film's highminded seriousness.

DEODATO, RUGGERO (1939–). The Italian director Ruggero Deodato has worked in a variety of genres, although he is best known for his often extremely violent horror films, and on this basis he has attracted a minor cult following. His most notorious horror was the much banned *Cannibal Holocaust* (1980), which was comprised in part of mock **documentary** footage of **torture, cannibalism** and other forms of human degradation. It offered a grim and misanthropic experience, although some horror critics and **fans** have found transgressive value in its relentlessly extreme imagery. An earlier similarly themed horror, *Ultimo mondo cannibale (Cannibal)* (1977), was restrained in comparison. *La casa sperduta nel parco (The House on the Edge of the Park)* (1980), Deodato's follow-up to *Cannibal Holocaust*, was a violent thriller in the style of **Wes Craven**'s rape-revenge drama *Last House on the Left* (1972), although it lacked the confrontational intelligence of Craven's film. Deodato's other horror films—which include *Camping del terrore (Body Count)* (1987), *Un delitto poco comune (Off Balance)* (1988) and *Minaccia d'amore (Dial Help)* (1988)—are negligible. *See also* ITALIAN HORROR.

THE DEVIL. Although the horror genre repeatedly deploys various notions of evil, it has rarely depicted the Devil himself. Perhaps this is because the Devil is just too monumental a figure to be used regularly. Instead he has featured as an occasional special guest star in horror films rather than as a recurring character. He showed up, albeit briefly, in traditional horned form in the Danish *Häxen: Witchcraft through the Ages* (1922) and **Hammer**'s *The Devil Rides Out* (1968), and Tim Curry's heavily made-up performance as the Lord of Darkness in Ridley Scott's *Legend* (1985) owed more than a passing visual debt to this conception of the arch-villain. More common is the cinematic presentation of the Devil in human form. Sometimes explicitly identified as the Devil and sometimes called Satan or Lucifer (with the theological distinctions between these not seeming to matter much in horror cinema), he is usually figured as a character with a taste for the theatrical and the melodramatic. Emil Jannings took on the role in **F. W. Murnau**'s *Faust* (1926), and the idea of the Faustian pact, of an innocent succumbing to Satanic temptations, has underpinned many subsequent Devil stories in horror cinema. Accordingly, Walter Huston was a charming tempter in William Dieterle's *The Devil and Daniel Webster* (1941), as was Richard Devon in **Roger Corman**'s *The Undead* (1957). More recently, **Robert De Niro** in *Angel Heart* (1987), Al Pacino in *The Devil's Advocate* (1997), Gabriel Byrne in *End of Days* (1999), Viggo Mortensen in *Prophecy* (1995) and Peter Stormare in *Constantine* (2005) have all offered their own grandstanding versions of the Devil, with the tone ranging from the seductive and witty to the petulant and bombastic.

Satanic cults have featured in, amongst others, *The Black Cat* (1934), *The Seventh Victim* (1943), *Rosemary's Baby* (1968), *Psychomania* (1971), *Blood on Satan's Claw* (*Satan's Skin*) (1971), *The Devil's Rain* (1975), *Race with the Devil* (1975), *The Omen* (1976) and its **sequels**, *To the Devil a Daughter* (1976), *Bless the Child* (2000), and *Lost Souls* (2000), with some of these films also exploring the idea of the **Antichrist**, the son of the Devil.

The Devil's cinematic life has not been restricted to horror, however. **Comedy** Devils have included Laird Cregar in *Heaven Can Wait* (1943), **Vincent Price** in *The Story of Mankind* (1957), Peter Cook in *Bedazzled* (1967), **Christopher Lee** in the **television** production *Little Devil* (1973), **Jack Nicholson** in *The Witches of Eastwick* (1987), Elizabeth Hurley as a rare female Devil in the **remake** *Bedazzled* (2000), and both Harvey Keitel and Rodney Dangerfield (as Satan and Lucifer respectively) in *Little Nicky* (2000). The Devil has also guested in two gangster films, played by **Claude Rains** in *Angel on my Shoulder* (1946) and by Ray Milland in *Alias Nick Beal* (1949), and was a cartoon character in the animated feature *South Park: Bigger, Longer & Uncut* (1999).

The Devil, it seems, has many faces.

DIFFRING, ANTON (1918–1989). The German actor Anton Diffring was frequently cast as a Nazi officer in British and American war films of the 1950s and 1960s, but he also showed up, usually in villainous roles, in some horror films as well. He was Baron **Frankenstein** in the **Kurt Siodmak**-directed pilot for *Tales of Frankenstein* (1958), a planned but never-made American **television** series produced under the auspices of the British **Hammer** company. Diffring went on to star as a **mad scientist** in Hammer's *The Man Who Could Cheat Death* (1959), one of the company's lesser **gothic** productions, and featured in **Sidney Hayers'** garish **British horror** *Circus of Horrors* (1960). He returned to horror in the 1970s with some minor continental European productions, including two **giallo** thrillers, **Riccardo Freda**'s *L'Iguana dalla lingua di fuoco* (*The Iguana with the Tongue of Fire*) (1971) and **Antonio Margheriti**'s *La morte negli occhi del gatto* (*Seven Deaths in the Cat's Eye*) (1973), as well as the unpleasant *Hexen geschändet und zu Tode gequält* (*Mark of the Devil 2*) (1973). Sillier but more palatable was the British **werewolf**-whodunnit *The Beast Must Die* (1974). One of his last appearances was in **Jesus Franco**'s horror *Faceless* (1988).

DISEASE. Horror's treatment of disease has often involved situations in which control—personal or social—is threatened or lost. However, early horror films usually shied away from the theme of disease, perhaps because it offered a less containable threat than that posed by traditional monsters such as **vampires** or **werewolves**. Val **Lewton**'s production *Isle of the Dead* (1945) was a notable exception in its doom-laden treatment of a plague story. A sense of vampirism as a kind of infection was also apparent in the German production *Nosferatu* (1922), although this idea was marginalized in the 1931 **Universal** *Dracula* as well as in many of the vampire films that followed in the 1940s and 1950s.

From the 1960s onwards, disease-based scenarios have been more evident in a horror cinema more willing to entertain notions of physical and social collapse. *The Last Man on Earth* (1964), an adaptation of **Richard Matheson**'s classic vampire novel *I Am Legend*, dealt with the idea of vampirism as a species-threatening infection, while **Roger Corman**'s *The Masque of the Red Death* (1964) offered a period-set treatment of an unstoppable plague. **George Romero**'s *Night of the Living Dead* (1968) featured zombieism as an infection that victims can catch from a **zombie** bite (something that has since become an established convention not just in zombie films but in other films such as the 1995 **Italian horror** *Demoni*, in which the bite of a demon transforms you into a demon). Romero's *The Crazies* (1973) also dealt with a plague-like infection spreading inexorably through a small town. The Canadian director **David Cronenberg** has made a specialty of stories about disease, with *They Came From Within* (*The Parasite Murders*, *Shivers*) (1975) and *Rabid* (1977) depicting a social collapse brought about by infection, while his more intimate *The Brood* (1979) and *The Fly* (1986) drew upon imagery associated with cancer in their representation of bodies rebelling against their owners. *The Omega Man* (1971), a second version of *I Am Legend*, emphasized the infection-based elements in the story more forcefully than *The Last Man on Earth*, and even the late **Hammer** horror *The Satanic Rites of Dracula* (1973) showed Dracula about to unleash a plague on the world.

More recently, the thriller *Outbreak* (1995) articulated comparable anxieties in its depiction of a foreign disease taking hold in the United States, while the **British horror** *28 Days Later* (2002) offered eerie scenes of London depopulated by the onset of a highly infectious disease. Some horror critics have also perceived what they term a "post-AIDS" concern with notions of infection by blood—most self-consciously in **Francis Ford Coppola**'s version of *Dracula* (1992)—although the extent to which this represents a radical new development in horror, or merely a new inflection of something already present, is unclear. In any event, a contemporary concern with the strategic threat posed by biological weapons currently seems to be shifting anxieties about disease into the action thriller genre, which potentially offers a more reassuring outcome than that associated with the horror film.

DISEMBODIED HANDS. Disembodied hands are unlikely horror monsters. However, their sporadic appearances in horror cinema have connected in interesting ways with anxieties about bodily control and integrity. The first film to explore this was **Robert Florey**'s *The Beast with Five Fingers* (1946), in which the animated hand turned out to be the product of **Peter Lorre**'s demented imagination as he sought to disavow his own murderous acts. The severed hand in **Oliver Stone**'s *The Hand* (1981) was similarly connected with the tortured consciousness of the main male protagonist. In comparison, the severed hands in two **British horror** films from the **Amicus** company, *Dr. Terror's House of Horrors* (1964) and *And Now the Screaming Starts!* (1973), along with the American film *The Crawling Hand* (1963), were hell-bent on revenge on the people who had wronged their original owners. "The Body Politic" segment of the **television** horror **anthology** film *Quicksilver Highway* (1997), adapted from a **Clive Barker** story, took this further through its depiction of a massed rebellion of hands intent on liberating themselves from the bodies to which they were attached. Comedic disembodied hands featured in *The Addams Family* (1991) and in **Sam Raimi**'s *The Evil Dead II* (1987), where, in an unforgettable moment, the hand gives its ex-owner the finger.

Horror's other use for disembodied hands has been to attach them to a human, invariably with disastrous consequences. Maurice Reynard's 1920 novel *Les mains d'Orlac* (*The Hands of Orlac*)—in which a murderer's hands are grafted onto an injured pianist and begin to take him over—was filmed as **Robert Wiene**'s *Orlacs Hände* (*The Hands of Orlac*) (1924), **Karl Freund**'s *Mad Love* (1935), Edmond T. Greville's *The Hands of Orlac* (1961) and Newton Arnold's *Hands of a Stranger* (1962).

DR. JEKYLL AND MR. HYDE. Robert Louis Stevenson's 1886 novel *The Strange Case of Dr. Jekyll and Mr. Hyde* has been repeatedly adapted for stage, screen and **television**. However, as has also been the case with Mary Shelley's **Frankenstein** and Bram Stoker's **Dracula**, these adaptations have tended to be loose and selective. In large part, this has something to do with the structure of Stevenson's novel, which, like *Frankenstein* and *Dracula*, is comprised of a series of episodes told in the first person by different characters. An episodic collage of this kind is ill-suited to direct translation into film or, for that matter, other dramatic media. From early stage adaptations onwards, the emphasis has been laid instead on the spectacle of the civilized Jekyll's transformation into the animalistic and sensual Hyde, and sexual themes only implicit in the original novel have also become increasingly foregrounded. It was particularly resonant in this respect that the major 1888 London stage production of *Dr. Jekyll and Mr. Hyde* coincided with the **Jack the Ripper** killings, with Stevenson's conceptualization of male duality clearly informing the way in which the Ripper's activities were discussed, both at the time and since. In fact, the idea of male sexuality as a Hyde-like uncontrollable and dangerous force has proved one of the more fascinating and potentially most pernicious aspects of the Jekyll/Hyde cultural legacy.

There were numerous silent film adaptations of *Dr. Jekyll and Mr. Hyde*, including *Der Januskopf* (1920), a now lost film directed by German master **F. W. Murnau**. The best-known silent version, however, was the 1920 American production directed by John S. Robertson. This starred John Barrymore, whose bravura performance of the transformation scene—without the aid of special effects or special **makeup** until near the end of the transformation—demonstrated the possibilities the role of Jekyll/Hyde offered for a grandstanding style of acting. **Fredric March** relied more on effects and makeup in his rendition of the role in the 1931 version directed by Rouben Mamoulian but nevertheless won an Academy Award for his efforts. Mamoulian's film took advantage of the relatively relaxed **censorship** of the early 1930s to explore with a surprising degree of openness the socio-sexual repression that Hyde sought to evade. By contrast, the 1941 version starring Spencer Tracy and directed by Victor Fleming was more decorous, although it still retained a stately power.

Later versions of Jekyll/Hyde divorced the character even more decisively from his original literary context. Jean Renoir's television film *Le testament du Docteur Cordelier* (*The Testament of Dr. Cordelier*) (1959) was a quietly serious treatment of the subject. In comparison, **Hammer** adopted a gimmicky approach for *The Two Faces of Dr. Jekyll* (1960) by making Hyde a more physically attractive figure than the hirsute Jekyll and entrapping him in a gaudily melodramatic plot that had nothing to do with Stevenson's novel. In the early 1970s, Hammer took this inventiveness yet further through having Jekyll transformed into a woman in *Dr. Jekyll and Sister Hyde* (1971), which, despite its weird premise, turned out to be one of the company's best later films. Even more bizarre was the **Spanish horror** *Dr. Jekyll y el hombre lobo* (*Dr. Jekyll and the* **Werewolf**) (1971) in which a Dr. Jekyll transforms a werewolf into Mr. Hyde. 1970s blaxploitation horror offered *Dr. Black, Mr. Hyde* (1976), while **Walerian Borowczyk's** *Docteur Jekyll et les femmes* (*Dr. Jekyll and his women*) (1981) and the **Anthony Perkins'** vehicle *Edge of Sanity* (1989) helped to keep the character alive, if only in exploitative form. *Mary Reilly* (1996), which recounted the Jekyll story as told by Jekyll's maid, was a more serious treatment of the subject that returned to Stevenson's original narrative but from a revisionary perspective. *The League of Extraordinary Gentlemen* (2003), by contrast, used Jekyll/Hyde as an excuse for some expensive special effects.

Comedy versions of Jekyll and Hyde have included the Tom and Jerry cartoon *Dr. Jekyll and Mr. Mouse* (1947), *Abbott and Costello Meet Dr. Jekyll and Mr. Hyde* (1953), Hammer's *The Ugly Duckling* (1959), *The Nutty Professor* (1963, remade in 1996), *Dr. Heckyl and Mr. Hype* (1980), and *Dr. Jekyll and Ms. Hyde* (1995). There have also been numerous television Jekylls, notably **Jack Palance** in *The Strange Case of Dr. Jekyll and Mr. Hyde* (1968) and Michael Caine in *Jekyll and Hyde* (1990). The British television series *Jekyll* (2007) offered an interesting revisionary account of the story.

DOCUMENTARY. Horror films have occasionally taken the form of mock documentaries as a way of making their dramas seem more real (although audiences are invariably aware that what they are watching is fictional). The most controversial example of this is probably **Ruggero Deodato**'s Italian **zombie** film *Cannibal Holocaust* (1980), which purported to be comprised of footage of a disastrous jungle expedition. *The Blair Witch Project* (1999) adopted a comparable approach in its depiction of an ill-fated student trip out into the woods, although the end result was more commercially successful than Deodato's gruelling and deeply unpleasant film. Other horror "mockumentaries" have included the Belgian **serial killer** film *C'est arrivé près de chez vous* (*Man Bites Dog*) (1992) and the **American horror** *The Last Broadcast* (1998), while, in a related development, *My Little Eye* (2002) was assembled from what appeared to be video surveillance footage. Such enterprises tend to be isolated experiments, however, as the restrictions of the documentary form seem to limit or hinder the traditional emotive and identification-based pleasures of horror.

A few horror films have explored a more transgressive form of factual cinema, namely the **snuff** movie in which people are really murdered, among them **Michael Powell**'s *Peeping Tom* (1960) and **David Cronenberg**'s *Videodrome* (1983), along with dark thrillers such as *Mute Witness* (1994), *Tesis* (1996), *8MM* (1999) and *15 Minutes* (2001).

DOGS. Horror's treatment of man's best friend has been less nuanced than its treatment of **cats**. Usually they are presented as the epitome of savagery in films such as *The Omen* (1976), *The Pack* (1977), *Dogs of Hell* (1982), *Cujo* (1983), *Man's Best Friend* (1993), *Rottweiler* (2004), and *The Breed* (2006) and, most of all, in the numerous horror-inflected versions of the **Sherlock Holmes** story *The Hound of the Baskervilles*. **Dario Argento**'s *Suspiria* (1977) also offers a memorable scene in which a blind man is slaughtered by his own guide dog. A remarkably silly **vampire** dog stars in *Dracula's Dog* (*Zoltan—Hound of Dracula*) (1978), while a more effectively scary talking dog is featured in Spike Lee's **serial killer** drama *Summer of Sam* (1999). By contrast, in both the 1977 and 2006 versions of *The Hills Have Eyes* a dutiful dog by the name of Beast deploys its savagery against the bad guys in order to protect its owners. On a more fantastic level, dogs with human heads appear, mercifully briefly, in both *The Mephisto Waltz* (1971) and the 1978 version of *Invasion of the Body Snatchers*.

DOLLS. Horror often renders the inanimate as animate, and the genre's representation of dolls is a good example of this. Threatening **children**'s dolls show up in *Dolls* (1987), *Poltergeist* (1982) and most of all in *Child's Play* (1988) and its **sequels**, where the doll in question is possessed by the spirit of a **serial killer**. Murderous puppets are the stars of *Puppet Master* (1989) and its sequels, animated murderous toys feature in *Asylum* (1972), while ventriloquist dolls that might or might not be alive appear in *Dead of Night* (1945) and *Magic* (1978). An affection for dolls has also been used by filmmakers to identify adult characters who are in various ways still dangerously caught up in childhood fears and anxieties, for example in the **psychological thrillers** *Bunny Lake Is Missing* (1965) and *The Psychopath* (1965) and the **giallo** *Profondo Rosso* (*Deep Red*) (1975).

DOUGLAS, MELVYN (1901–1981). The American actor Melvyn Douglas had brushes with the horror genre both near the beginning and near the end of a long and distinguished career that included two Academy Awards. His down-to-earth skepticism in **James Whale**'s **comedy**-horror *The Old Dark House* (1932) and the independently produced *The Vampire Bat* (1933) helped ground the over-the-top dramas. Four decades later, he did duty as a character actor, in a sinister role in **Roman Polanski**'s *Le locataire* (*The Tenant*) (1976) and in more benign parts in *The Changeling* (1980) and *Ghost Story* (1981), the latter of which had the distinction of being Fred Astaire's only horror film.

DOURIF, BRAD (1950–). The American character actor Brad Dourif has appeared in supporting roles in numerous horror films, including **Tobe Hooper**'s *Spontaneous Combustion* (1990), **William Peter Blatty**'s *The Exorcist III* (1990), the horror-**western** *Grim Prairie Tales* (1990), **Dario Argento**'s *Trauma* (1993), *Alien: Resurrection* (1997) and *Urban Legend* (1998), to name but a few. However, his main contribution to the horror genre is as the voice of Chucky, the demonic **doll** in the *Child's Play* films, beginning with *Child's Play* (1988). Initially appearing in the cycle as a **serial killer** whose soul is transferred into Chucky, Dourif successfully combined menace and humor through his voice alone.

DRACULA. Vlad Tepes, a 15th-century Romanian warrior prince, used to sign himself as "Dracula" (which meant "Son of the Dragon"). Four hundred years later, the author Bram Stoker borrowed both the name and Vlad's association with copious bloodletting on the battlefield for his famous **vampire** novel *Dracula* (1897). Since then, Dracula has appeared not just in horror films but also in **television** shows, advertisements, stage plays, **comic** books, ballets, musicals, and novels. However, for all his pervasiveness, he is an oddly protean figure who, since his 1897 literary debut, has been constantly revised and reinterpreted, and his enduring popularity is undoubtedly connected with this ability to adapt to the changing shape of our fears and desires.

Although an obscure 1920 Hungarian film was the first to be called *Dracula*, the best-known early screen adaptation of the novel is German director **F. W. Murnau**'s *Nosferatu: eine Symphonie des Grauens* (*Nosferatu: a symphony of terror*) (1922). In this, the vampire was played by **Max Schreck** (whose surname just happens to be the German word for terror) as a truly repulsive and animalistic figure with protruding rat-like incisor fangs. Unfortunately, Murnau's film was an unauthorized adaptation, and simply changing the names of its principal characters—with Count Dracula, for example, becoming Graf Orlok—did not protect the production company from being sued by Bram Stoker's widow. In any event, the film's vision of a bald, grotesque vampiric parasite has not proved very influential on later representations of either Dracula or the vampire in general (although Nosferatu-like characteristics were displayed by the main vampire villain in **Tobe Hooper**'s 1979 television film *Salem's Lot*, as well as featuring in Werner Herzog's 1979 **remake** of Murnau's film).

The version of Dracula that established the norm against which later Draculas defined themselves was the 1931 **Universal** production directed by **Tod Browning** and starring **Bela Lugosi** as the evil Count. Here Dracula was presented in an altogether more attractive and civilized form than he was in *Nosferatu*, for Lugosi's vampire was at home in polite social circles, comfortable in a tuxedo, and also had a seductive power over women. The film was adapted from a successful Broadway play that itself had been adapted—by **John L. Balderston**—from an English stage version written by actor-manager Hamilton Deane. Despite a picturesque opening sequence in Transylvania (present in Stoker's original novel but removed from the stage plays for budgetary reasons), the film never really transcended its theatrical source and it has not dated well. By contrast, the Spanish-language version of *Dracula* shot by Universal at the same time as the Browning film and starring Carlos Villarias as Dracula displayed considerably more visual flair but lacked the charismatically exotic Lugosi, whose Hungarian-accented performance was key to his film's considerable commercial success and its continuing cult status.

Despite this success, **sequels** to *Dracula* were slow to follow. The Count himself was briefly glimpsed as a corpse in Universal's first sequel to *Dracula*, *Dracula's Daughter* (1936), but it was not until the 1940s that he was fully resurrected for the stylish but misleadingly titled *Son of Dracula* (1943), in which Dracula—not, so far as one can tell, his son—was played by **Lon Chaney Jr.**, an altogether more American actor than Lugosi at a time when the foreign exoticism popular in the 1930s had gone out of fashion. The film itself was set in contemporary America, and while the spectacle it offered of Dracula driving around in a motor car might seem odd, this did maintain the emphasis on the contemporary in Universal's previous Dracula films; in an early screenplay for the 1931

Dracula, the Count had fled England in a plane, an escape method that was adopted by his daughter five years later. The gaunt and sinister **John Carradine** donned the vampire cloak for Universal's multiple-monster films *House of Frankenstein* (1944) and *House of Dracula* (1945), while Lugosi himself returned to the role for the second and final time in the **comedy**-horror *Abbott and Costello Meet Frankenstein* (1948).

As if exhausted by this activity, Dracula disappeared from cinema screens for the next 10 years, although old Dracula films found a new popularity on American television during the 1950s. In 1958, however, two new Dracula films appeared in the cinema, one American, the other British. *The Return of Dracula* (1958), a low-budget American production, continued the Lugosi tradition by having a foreign-accented vampire—played by Czech actor Francis Lederer—and adopted the contemporary small-town setting earlier explored by *Son of Dracula*; it made little impression at the box office. The British production was more significant. *Dracula* (*The Horror of Dracula*) (1958) was **Hammer**'s follow-up to *The Curse of Frankenstein* (1957). Directed by **Terence Fisher** and starring **Christopher Lee** in his first major role with **Peter Cushing** as Van Helsing, the film was the first adaptation of Stoker's novel since the 1931 *Dracula*; it was also the first color *Dracula* film and the first since *Nosferatu* to show vampire fangs (although Lee's fangs were elegant canine affairs). The emphasis on the vampire's sensuality was more explicit than ever before, reflecting a relaxation in film **censorship**, and the lurid red blood flowed freely. The film was a notable success and confirmed Hammer's status as a leading horror producer. Although initially hesitant about repeating the role, Lee eventually went on to star in six more Dracula films of variable quality for the company—*Dracula—Prince of Darkness* (1966), *Dracula Has Risen From the Grave* (1968), *Taste The Blood of Dracula* (1970), *Scars of Dracula* (1970), *Dracula AD 1972* (1972), and *The Satanic Rites of Dracula* (1973), with the latter two bringing the vampire to contemporary London. Hammer also found other ways of exploiting Dracula; *The Brides of Dracula* (1960) bore his name although the Count himself was absent, and Dracula later featured in a small role in *The Legend of the Seven Golden Vampires* (1974), where he was played by John Forbes-Robertson.

Hammer's success led to other filmmakers offering their own versions of Dracula. The results ranged from the silly—*Billy the Kid versus Dracula* (1966), for example, in which John Carradine returned to the role of Dracula after 20 years, or **Paul Morrissey**'s enjoyably over-the-top *Blood for Dracula* (1974)—to the somber—with examples here including two further adaptations of Stoker's novel, **Jesus Franco**'s Spanish production *El Conde Dracula* (*Count Dracula*) (1970), featuring Christopher Lee as a mustachioed Count, and **Dan Curtis**'s *Dracula* (1973), an American television film that achieved a limited theatrical release and which innovatively explored the idea of Dracula as historical figure.

Three films released in 1979 suggested that representations of Dracula were becoming increasingly self-conscious about the tradition to which they belonged. The **comedy** *Love at First Bite* (1979), which depicted a bewildered Count trying to come to terms with modern America, affectionately mocked the anachronistic Lugosi version, while Werner Herzog's *Nosferatu: Phantom der Nacht* (*Nosferatu the Vampyre*) (1979), a remake of *Nosferatu*, displayed considerably less faith in the power of good over evil than had Murnau's film. John Badham's *Dracula*, which starred Frank Langella as Dracula and Laurence Olivier as Van Helsing, also returned to an earlier source, in this case the Hamilton Deane/John L. Balderston theatrical adaptation which had provided the source material for the 1931 *Dracula*. Reflecting the anti-authority attitudes found in much 1970s horror, Badham's film had little confidence in the power of Van Helsing (who, in a novel twist, ends up being staked to death by Dracula), and its ambiguous conclusion suggested that Dracula lived on despite all the attempts of the forces of good to destroy him.

At this point, there was another hiatus, and, as he had done before, Dracula went underground, reemerging spectacularly in 1992 with **Francis Ford Coppola**'s *Dracula*, the final—at the time of writing, at least—cinematic adaptation of the Stoker novel. This was a bravura piece of filmmaking that accentuated the self-consciousness of the previous wave of Dracula films to a point where it was hard to find any element of the film that was not referring in some way to an earlier Dracula film. The prologue showing Dracula as a historical warrior could be traced back to the Dan Curtis version, the stress on Dracula as a romantic figure seems to relate to the Badham version,

Gary Oldman's performance as Dracula owed more than a little to Lugosi, and Coppola's style was full of homages to *Nosferatu* and German **Expressionism** in general. In the years since Coppola's film, Dracula has been relegated to guest villain status—in *Blade: Trinity* (2004) and *Van Helsing* (2004) and an episode of the television series *Buffy The Vampire Slayer*—or reworked to such an extent that any connection with previous representations is attenuated or broken by the extremity of the innovation—for example, *Dracula 2000* (2000) in which it is revealed that Dracula is "really" Judas Iscariot.

It is hard to say whether Dracula's current marginal status in horror cinema is a sign that his power to fascinate us is finally waning. The cinematic history of this figure contains several comparably quiet periods interrupted by radical new revisions that have brought him back to life. We might be in one of those quiet periods now. Only the future will tell, but if the past tells us anything, it is that Dracula returns.

DREYER, CARL THEODOR (1889–1968). The Danish director Carl Theodor Dreyer is renowned for a series of austere character-based dramas such as *La Passion de Jeanne d'Arc* (*The Passion of Joan of Arc*) (1928) and *Gertrud* (1964), but he also worked effectively with **gothic** material. *Vampyr—Der Traum des Allan Grey* (*Vampyr*) (1932) was an elliptical study of vampirism that avoided the horror conventions associated with **Dracula** and instead offered an unnerving dream-like atmosphere. Its claustrophobic depiction of someone being buried alive remains powerful even today. *Blade af Satans bog* (*Leaves Out of the Book of Satan*) (1921), an earlier Dreyer film, dealt more prosaically with the activities of the **Devil** as he tempted people from different historical periods. By contrast, the later *Vredens dag* (*Day of Wrath*) (1943) was an intense study of the psychology of witch-hunting.

– E –

ENGLUND, ROBERT (1949–). The American actor Robert Englund found horror fame as the child-killing Freddy Krueger in the *Nightmare on Elm Street* films. In the first film in the cycle, *A Nightmare*

on *Elm Street* (1984), Krueger was a genuinely nasty and cruel figure haunting the dreams of various hapless teenagers. However, in
the seven **sequels** that followed, Englund played him as a prankster,
exuding manic energy and offering a series of wisecracks as he
slaughtered his teenage victims. Perversely, it was Englund/Krueger
who became the hero of these films rather than the anodyne protagonists who represented the forces of good. Englund, in the guise of
Krueger, also hosted the **television** series *Freddy's Nightmares*
(1988–1990).

Englund's other genre credits include *Eaten Alive* (*Death Trap*)
(1977), *Dead & Buried* (1981), *Galaxy of Terror* (1981), *C.H.U.D.
II—Bud the Chud* (1989), **The Phantom of the Opera** (1989), *Dance
Macabre* (1991), *Night Terrors* (1993), *The Mangler* (1995), *The
Vampyre Wars* (1996), *The Killer Tongue* (1996), *Wishmaster* (1997),
Urban Legend (1998), *Strangeland* (1998), *Python* (2000), and *2001
Maniacs* (2005). He also directed the horror film *976-Evil* (1989).

THE EXORCIST (1973). Films such as **Alfred Hitchcock**'s *Psycho*
(1960), **George Romero**'s *Night of the Living Dead* (1968), and **Roman Polanski**'s *Rosemary's Baby* (1968) had suggested that changes
were taking place in **American horror**. However, it was the massive
commercial success of *The Exorcist* (1973) that encouraged a boom
in horror production and established some of the key themes of 1970s
horror—notably the contemporary American setting, the monstrous
child, and the inadequacy of social institutions. As adapted from the
bestselling novel by **William Peter Blatty** (who was also the film's
producer), the film spared no detail in its depiction of a girl's **possession** by a demon. Vomiting, urination, profanity and masturbation
were all present to an extent never seen before in a mainstream Hollywood production, and during the film's initial release there were reports of members of the audience passing out in screenings. The director was **William Friedkin**, who had just won an Academy Award
for *The French Connection* (1971) and who brought a graphic realism and a high level of technical expertise to the proceedings, and the
cast included **Max von Sydow**, Ellen Burstyn, Lee J. Cobb, Jason
Miller, and as the possessed girl, **Linda Blair**.

The tone of *The Exorcist* was unusually somber for horror. The
casting of von Sydow as the main exorcist alluded to the bleak work

of **Ingmar Bergman** (with whom the actor was a regular collaborator), and the film had a loose and in places ambiguous narrative structure that, like many Hollywood films of this period, drew upon European **art cinema** for some of its inspiration. To a certain extent, the film's authorship was split between Blatty, for whom it was clearly a work with religious significance, and Friedkin, who seemed more concerned with fashioning an extremely well-crafted rollercoaster ride. The overall result was provocative and powerful. Numerous Academy Award nominations resulted, with Blatty winning for his screenplay and another awarded for best sound.

The Exorcist II: The Heretic (1977), which was directed by **John Boorman**, was one of the most eccentric **sequels** in horror history. Linda Blair co-starred with Richard Burton in a convoluted narrative that sought to be different from the original but which proved too obscure to connect with a mass audience. It was a critical and commercial flop that temporarily ended the series, although it did contain some interesting sequences and featured a fine score by **Ennio Morricone**. Blatty returned for *The Exorcist III* (1990), which he adapted from his novel *Legion* and also directed. Perhaps wisely, the film ignored the events of the previous sequel and referred directly back to *The Exorcist* itself, with the Jason Miller character—who had apparently died in the original—returning in possessed form. The film was stylish and had some impressive scenes of suspense, but ultimately it was overwhelmed by its own seriousness and lacked Friedkin's ability to move the story along.

Over a decade passed before thoughts turned to the possibility of an *Exorcist* prequel. *Exorcist II* had already dealt in flashback with the early years of the von Sydow character. Now **Paul Schrader** was hired to direct *Dominion*, the official prequel (replacing the original director **John Frankenheimer**). The resulting film was considered too tame by the producers who promptly shelved it and, in an unprecedented maneuver, hired another director, **Renny Harlin**, to make a new prequel, reusing some of the same cast but with a substantially revised story and considerably more **gore** and violence. Harlins' *Exorcist: The Beginning* (2004) was certainly a lively affair but it lacked the measured and ominous approach of Blatty and Friedkin's original. Schrader's version, which was eventually released as *Dominion: Prequel to the Exorcist* (2005), was more thoughtful but perhaps too restrained for its own good. If nothing else, both prequels underlined how effective Blatty and Friedkin had been in balancing ambitious subject matter with the demands of popular entertainment.

EXPRESSIONISM. The artistic movement that came to be called German Expressionism was firmly established in German art and literature before the outbreak of World War I. However, its impact upon cinema was not fully felt until the postwar period. The first, and most extreme, example of Expressionism in cinema was **Robert Wiene**'s *Das Cabinet des Dr. Caligari* (*The Cabinet of Dr. Caligari*) (1919), which self-consciously emulated a painterly look through an extensive use of painted backdrops. Tilted angles and painted shadows, along with a gestural form of acting, gave a powerful sense of an unstable social order and tortured individual psychologies, with this arguably reflecting broader social anxieties evident in the Weimar period. However, *Caligari*'s distinctive look was also part of an attempt to acquire a high cultural status, with the film marketed more as a work of art than as a proto-horror project. Wiene tried unsuccessfully to repeat the success of *Caligari* with the similarly styled *Genuine* (1920). Other films now usually thought of as examples of Expressionism were more restrained in their use of distortion and chiaroscuro lighting—among them Paul Wegener's *Der Golem, wie er in die Welt kam* (*The Golem*) (1920), **F. W. Murnau**'s *Nosferatu, eine Symphonie des Grauens* (*Nosferatu: a Symphony of Terror*) (1922) and **Paul Leni**'s *Das Wachsfigurenkabinett* (**Waxworks**) (1924). Other German directors from the Weimar period also displayed the stylistic influence of Expressionism—notably Fritz Lang, who had contributed to *Caligari*'s screenplay—in their use of claustrophobic framings or tilted camera angles.

The contribution of Expressionism to the development of 1930s **American horror** has been noted by a number of horror historians. Some of the German filmmakers associated with Expressionism subsequently worked in Hollywood on horror films, notable amongst them **Karl Freund** and Paul Leni, while the influence of performances by **Conrad Veidt** in *The Cabinet of Dr. Caligari* and Wegener in *The Golem* has been detected in **Boris Karloff**'s shambling walk as the monster in **Universal**'s *Frankenstein* (1931). A more general propensity for strange camera angles and stylized lighting was also apparent in a wide range of American horror films from the period, while **Robert Florey**'s *Murders in the Rue Morgue* (1932) lifted many of its plot elements from *Caligari*. Similar stylistic devices would later characterize 1940s film noir, although by that time, with a few exceptions, the horror genre had opted for a more solidly realist approach, which has been largely maintained through to the present day. Stylistic echoes of Expressionism can still be found, however, in **Roger Corman**'s **Edgar Allan Poe** adaptations of the early 1960s, for example, or in some of the Italian work of **Dario Argento**, **Mario Bava** or **Lucio Fulci**.

EYES. In many ways the eye is the principal human organ for horror cinema. Directors will frequently use close-ups of the eyes of victims, wide and helpless, and monster, narrowed and aggressive, to accentuate the genre's sado-masochistic thrills. In addition, injuries to eyes have contributed to some of the more assaultive moments in horror, invoking as they do an audience's sense of vulnerability about this softest and most exposed of organs. The eye being cut open by a straight razor at the beginning of the surrealist film *Un chien andalou* (1928) is an early non-horror example of the emotive power of the eye injury, and horror filmmakers have been reproducing that moment ever since. Eyes are slashed, stabbed or mutilated in, among others, *Horrors of the Black Museum* (1959), *La maschera del demonio* (*The Mask of Satan, Black Sunday, The Revenge of the* **Vampire**) (1960), *The Birds* (1963), *Witchfinder General* (1968), *Hands of the Ripper* (1971), *Satan's Slave* (1976), *Zombi 2* (**Zombie**, *Zombie Flesh Eaters*) (1979), *The Fog* (1980), *L'aldilà* (*The Beyond*) (1981), *Dead and Buried* (1981), *Opera* (*Terror at the Opera*) (1987) and *Ôdishon* (*Audition*) (1999).

– F –

FAMILY HORROR. The term *family horror* is often used by horror's critics and historians to describe a type of horror film in which the monster originates from an ostensibly normal family or where the family itself is monstrous. There is not much of this in 1930s and 1940s horror, but from the 1950s onwards there is an increasing sense in the genre of the monster being closer to home than before, with this most clearly manifested through its familial nature. The murderous child in *The Bad Seed* (1956) provided a hint at what was to come, but it was *Psycho* (1960) that crystallized this theme through its representation of an apparently dutiful son who turned out to be a transvestite **serial killer.** More murderous **children** showed up in, amongst others, *Night of the Living Dead* (1968), *The Exorcist* (1973), *It's Alive* (1974), *The Omen* (1976), and *Halloween* (1978), while dangerous parents (or occasionally step-parents) featured, for example, in **British horrors** *Hands of the Ripper* (1971), *Countess Dracula* (1971), *Demons of the Mind* (1972), *The Creeping Flesh* (1973), and *Frightmare* (1974), and **American horrors** *Carrie* (1976), *The Shining* (1980), *The Stepfather* (1987), *Parents* (1989), *Society* (1989), and *The People Under the Stairs* (1991). Monstrous families have been a particular feature of **rural horror** films such as *The Texas Chainsaw Massacre* (1974, remade in 2003), *The Hills Have Eyes* (1977, remade in 2006) and *House of 1000 Corpses* (2003), where they also often represent a degraded version of the working class. Dysfunctional families of a gentler, usually more middle class, kind can also be found in abundance from the 1970s onwards, with weak parents and rebellious children a recurrent feature in **slasher** films and other forms of **teenage horror.**

FANS. The stereotypical horror fan is someone who is immature, inarticulate, socially awkward and none too bright. The reality of horror fandom is more complex, of course, and involves an extraordinarily diverse range of people from different backgrounds. The horror genre has over the years attracted a significant cult following, possibly because of its low cultural status and its potentially transgressive qualities, and horror filmmakers have become increasingly aware of how knowledgeable and demanding horror fans can be and how much they need to cater to them. The fan magazine *Famous Monsters of Filmland*, which first appeared in 1958, encouraged the development of a horror fan culture. Other publications followed, including professionally produced magazines and privately produced fanzines. Fans got to meet each other at horror conventions, while other fans—among them **John Carpenter** and **Joe Dante**—went on to become horror film directors themselves and brought a fan-based knowledge back into cinema. The advent of the **internet** offered new opportunities for horror fans, and a cursory search today will quickly find numerous horror-based sites where fans record and reflect upon their enthusiasms and debate new releases. Such enterprises underline the extent to which horror fans are often active and creative viewers who respond in critical ways to the material about which they care so much. An awareness of fan activity of this kind is a necessary antidote against those approaches to horror that assume that the horror experience is essentially undemanding and repetitive and that it requires little of its audience by way of intelligent reaction.

FANTASTIC FACTORY. The Fantastic Factory production setup was formed by Julio Fernandez and American writer-director **Brian Yuzna** under the auspices of the Spanish company Filmax. Beginning with *Faust: Love of the Damned* (2001), it has specialized in English language horror films shot largely by Spanish crew for the international market. The results have been variable. **Stuart Gordon**'s *Dagon* (2001) was an atmospheric adaptation of an **H. P. Lovecraft** story, while Francisco Plaza's *Romasanta* (2004) was an impressive reinvention of the **werewolf** story. *Arachnid* (2001), *Beyond Re-Animator* (2003), *Rottweiler* (2004), *La Monja* (*The Nun*) (2005) and *Beneath Still Waters* (2005) were more conventional genre projects, however.

FARROW, MIA (1945–). Mia Farrow knows how to suffer. She suffered magnificently in **Roman Polanski**'s *Rosemary's Baby* (1968), where her character's physical frailty and neurotic intensity were indispensable to the film's disturbing representation of pregnancy. She suffered again as a blind woman terrorized by a **serial killer** in the British-set *Blind Terror* (*See No Evil*) (1971) and as a grieving mother haunted by a dead child in the **ghost** story *Full Circle* (1977). Finally, in a canny piece of casting, it was her turn to dish out some suffering as the evil nanny in the **remake** of *The Omen* (2006).

FERRARA, ABEL (1951–). The iconoclastic director Abel Ferrara specializes in edgy urban dramas, and his occasional horror films often reflect this. *The Driller Killer* (1979) is a disturbing and graphic representation of urban alienation; its title combined with a lurid video box cover made the film one of the most notorious of British "video nasties" during the early 1980s. *Ms 45* (1981) is an equally unforgiving rape-revenge story. *Body Snatchers* (1993), an effective third version of the alien invasion fantasy *Invasion of the Body Snatchers* story, abandoned Ferrara's customary urban setting for a military base out in the countryside. The modern **vampire** film *The Addiction* (1995) returned to more familiar territory, with a weird and unsettling mix of urban bloodletting and dense philosophizing that some found pretentious and others compelling. *See also* AMERICAN HORROR.

FERRINI, FRANCO (1944–). Franco Ferrini is an Italian screenwriter who has collaborated regularly with writer-producer-director **Dario Argento** on films such as *Phenomena* (1985), *Demoni* (*Demons*) (1985) *Demoni 2: L'incubo ritorna* (*Demons 2*) (1986), *Opera* (*Terror at the Opera*) (1987), *La Chiesa* (*The Church*) (1989), *Due occhi diabolici* (*Two Evil Eyes*) (1990), *Trauma* (1993), *La sindrome di Stendhal* (*The Stendhal Syndrome*) (1996), *Nonhosonno* (*Sleepless*) (2001), *Il cartaio* (*The Card Player*) (2004), and *Ti piace Hitchcock?* (*Do You Like Hitchcock?*) (2005). He has worked on **giallo** thrillers for other directors, notably *Enigma rosso* (1978), *Sotto il vestito niente* (*Nothing underneath*) (1985) and *Occhi di cristallo* (*Eyes of Crystal*) (2004) and also wrote and directed his own giallo, *Caramelle da uno sconosciuto* (*Sweets from a Stranger*) (1987).

FILIPINO HORROR. The Philippines has a tradition of supernatural cinema running back to the silent period. Films about witches and **ghosts** were a significant feature, although up until the 1950s these rarely circulated outside the Philippines. However, the success of *Terror is a Man* (*Creature from Blood Island*) (1959), an unofficial adaptation of H. G. Wells' *The Island of Dr. Moreau*, brought a degree of international visibility to Filipino horror. There followed a procession of low-budget productions of variable quality featuring **vampires** and **zombies** alongside the more traditional witch films. Some directors became genre specialists—notably **Gerardo de León** and **Eddie Romero**—and, at their best, the horror films had energy and inventiveness that belied their limited production values. More recently, a new generation of filmmakers has continued the Filipino horror tradition with films such as the supernatural drama *Aswang* (1992) and the *Shake, Rattle & Roll* comedy-horror **anthologies** (which at the time of writing have reached Part Eight). It is regrettable that little of this work is known internationally.

FINAL GIRL. The term *Final Girl* was coined by academic Carol J. Clover to describe the female hero of the **slasher** film. Prior to the advent of the slasher, it was very rare to find a female protagonist in a horror film who did not need rescuing by a male. The Final Girl was different, however. She was usually distinguished from her teenage compatriots through her watchfulness and her aggression, and she often had some masculine qualities as well—either a male-sounding name or abilities or types of knowledge conventionally associated with men. Most of all, she could not rely on a male hero to save her but was routinely placed in a situation where she had to save herself. A key Final Girl was Laurie Strode (played by **Jamie Lee Curtis**) in **John Carpenter**'s *Halloween* (1978), but her equivalent can be found in most slashers of the late 1970s and early 1980s; she can also arguably be found in *Alien* (1979), a **science fiction**/horror film that owed more than a little to the slasher in its representation of Ripley (played by Sigourney Weaver). As the 1980s progressed, Final Girls became ever more aggressive and violent, especially in the *Nightmare on Elm Street* films, where they sometimes displayed martial arts abilities, and in *The Texas Chainsaw Massacre 2* (1986) where it was the female protagonist who ultimately got to wield the chainsaw. The fact that it is now commonplace in **American horror** films to have a central female character more than capable of looking after herself suggests that the figure of the Final Girl has become thoroughly institutionalized, a convention that we all take for granted. It is worth remembering that it was not always like this.

FISHER, TERENCE (1904–1980). Terence Fisher was the main director at **Hammer** Films from the mid-1950s to the early 1960s, a period in which the company established itself as a leading purveyor of **British horror** cinema. He included among his credits most of the classic Hammer horrors—including *The Curse of Frankenstein* (1957), *Dracula* (*The Horror of Dracula*, 1958), *The Hound of the Baskervilles* (1959), *The Mummy* (1959), *The Brides of Dracula*

(1960), and *The Curse of the Werewolf* (1961). A common critical perception of Fisher is that his films tend to be both formally traditional and morally conservative. While there is some truth to this view, it does nevertheless obscure the range of Fisher's filmmaking activities.

By the time he made his first horror film—*The Curse of Frankenstein* —Fisher was already an established figure in the industry. He had worked as an editor from the mid-1930s onwards and had been directing films in a variety of genres since the late 1940s. Many of these pre-horror efforts were low-budget crime dramas for Hammer, which before its turn to horror specialized in such B-movie fare (although Fisher also made two **science fiction** films for Hammer at this time—*Four-Sided Triangle* and *Spaceways*, both in 1953). Thanks to this experience, Fisher was by the mid-1950s fully conversant with the demands of low-budget production and had also become a prominent member of a Hammer production team that subsequently made the horror films for which Hammer became famous. While Fisher had little to do with the occasionally moralistic scripting of these horrors, he was largely responsible for what at its best was a precise and balanced visual style perfectly suited to Hammer's dramas of bourgeois morality challenged by sexual passion and violence. Memorable moments from this early stage in Fisher's horror career tended to involve monstrous interventions into an ordered world of social normality. One thinks, for example, of the **vampire**'s first appearance in *Dracula* or the eerie emergence of the undead Kharis from an English swamp in *The Mummy*.

After the box-office flop of *The Phantom of the Opera* (1962), Fisher worked less frequently for Hammer. The German-produced *Sherlock Holmes und das Halsband des Todes (Sherlock Holmes and the Necklace of Death)* (1962) and the **comedy**-horror *The Horror of It All* (1964) were sufficiently uninspiring to suggest that Fisher needed the stable production context provided by Hammer to flourish. More successful were three low-budget alien invasion films— *The Earth Dies Screaming* (1964), *Island of Terror* (1966), and *Night of the Big Heat* (1967). None of these transcended their budgetary constraints but in all of them Fisher managed to convey a sinister rural atmosphere.

However, Fisher's best work continued to be done for Hammer. Unusually for the company, *The Gorgon* (1964) focused on a female monster and, although let down by some poor special effects, contained some haunting sequences, while *Dracula—Prince of Darkness* (1966), *Frankenstein Created Woman* (1967), and *Frankenstein Must Be Destroyed* (1969) were all handsomely mounted and stylish additions to Hammer's Dracula and Frankenstein cycles. Best of all from this later stage in Fisher's career was another Hammer project, *The Devil Rides Out* (1968), an adaptation of a **Dennis Wheatley** novel that benefited from **Richard Matheson**'s excellent screenplay and a career-best performance from **Christopher Lee**. Here Fisher took a conventional battle between absolute good and absolute evil and choreographed it into a series of symmetrical visual patterns and compositions. Good might win through in the end, as it always does with Fisher, but one was left with a sense of the ways in which good and evil balanced each other out and remained inextricably linked.

Fisher's other genre credits include *The Revenge of Frankenstein* (1958), *The Man Who Could Cheat Death* (1959), *The Stranglers of Bombay* (1959), *The Two Faces of Dr. Jekyll* (1960), and *Frankenstein and the Monster from Hell* (1974).

FLOREY, ROBERT (1900–1979). The French director Robert Florey spent most of his filmmaking career in Hollywood. His first encounter with the horror genre came when he was hired by **Universal** to make its film version of *Frankenstein* (1931). Although he worked on a screenplay and shot test footage of **Bela Lugosi** made up as the Monster, both he and Lugosi eventually withdrew from the project, to be replaced by director **James Whale** and actor **Boris Karloff**. However, Florey and Lugosi were quickly reunited for Universal's *Murders in the Rue Morgue* (1932). Although ostensibly an adaptation of an **Edgar Allan Poe** story, the film also borrowed ideas and imagery from the German Expressionist film *Das Cabinet Des Dr. Caligari* (*The Cabinet of Dr. Caligari*) (1919), as well as featuring a **mad scientist** narrative in which the Lugosi character attempted to "cross" humans with gorillas.

Florey's other two genre credits were very different, less lurid and more interested in exploring character psychology. The subject matter of *The Face Behind the Mask* (1941)—a disfigured criminal seeks revenge on those who betrayed him—makes it sound like standard horror fare, but Florey instead offered a sympathetic portrayal of the central character, an immigrant (played by **Peter Lorre**) constantly at odds with American society. Because of its relative gentleness, the film is often not classified as horror, although its final scenes of revenge remain chilling. *The Beast With Five Fingers* (1946) was different again. The **disembodied hand** of the title turned out to be the figment of a murderer's imagination (with Lorre featuring again in a more disturbed role), and Florey provided some suitably unnerving fantasy sequences in which the hand came to life. However, the film as a whole was more conventional than his previous efforts in the genre.

In the 1950s and 1960s, Florey worked mainly for American **television**, including episodes for horror-themed series *The Twilight Zone* (1959–1964), *Thriller* (1960–1962), and *The Outer Limits* (1963–1965). *See also* AMERICAN HORROR.

FRANCIS, FREDDIE (1917–2007). The British filmmaker Freddie Francis had two cinematic careers. He was an eminent cinematographer who won Academy Awards for *Sons and Lovers* (1960) and *Glory* (1989) and was responsible for the visual style of **Jack Clayton**'s **ghost** story *The Innocents* (1961) and David Lynch's Victorian melodrama *The Elephant Man* (1980). But from the early 1960s onwards, Francis was also a director of low-budget **British horror** films, a number of which have since acquired a cult following. After some uncredited work on *The Day of the Triffids* (1962) and adapting **Kurt Siodmak**'s much filmed novel *Donovan's Brain* as *Vengeance* (*The Brain*) (1962), he directed regularly for **Hammer** and **Amicus**, the two leading purveyors of British horror during the 1960s and early 1970s. His films for Hammer proved less distinguished than those he did for Amicus, however. He was the only director, other than **Terence Fisher**, to work on Hammer's **Frankenstein** and **Dracula** cycles but his entries for each cycle—*The Evil of Frankenstein* (1964) and *Dracula Has Risen from the Grave* (1968)—were slackly plotted affairs enlivened only by the occasional directorial flourish. Similarly, *Paranoiac* (1963), *Nightmare* (1964), and *Hysteria* (1965) were slick, if fairly anonymous, contributions to the **psychological thriller** cycle produced by Hammer alongside its **gothic** horrors.

One only has to compare any of these thrillers with the memorably stylish and bizarre psychological thriller *The Psychopath* (1966), directed by Francis for Amicus, to see how the director benefited from Amicus's less regimented production setup. Francis made three of Amicus's best horror **anthologies**—*Dr. Terror's House of Horrors* (1964), *Torture Garden* (1967), and *Tales from the Crypt* (1972)— and successfully brought together traditional horror effects with the mordant wit that characterized this material and which distinguished it from the more somber Hammer product. *The Skull* (1965), another Amicus film, contained a surreal and unnerving dream sequence that in itself rates as one of Francis's finest achievements as director, while the independent production *The Creeping Flesh* (1973) was an unusually thoughtful gothic horror.

Francis's directorial career proved considerably more uneven than his career as a cinematographer, combining as it did significant genre achievements with eccentricities—such as the German-produced **vampire comedy** *Gebissen wird nur nachts* (*The Vampire Happening*) (1971) or the rarely seen cult thriller *Mumsy, Nanny, Sonny and Girly* (1969)—and low-grade embarrassments such as the Amicus production *The Deadly Bees* (1966) and the **Joan Crawford** vehicle *Trog* (1970).

Francis stopped directing in the mid-1970s but later returned with *The Doctor and the Devils* (1985), a treatment of the Burke and Hare story that was based on a screenplay by Dylan Thomas. His other horror or fantasy films include *They Came From Beyond Space* (1967), *Craze* (1973), *Tales That Witness Madness* (1973), *Son of Dracula* (1974), *Legend of the Werewolf* (1975), *The Ghoul* (1975), and *Dark Tower* (1987) (as Ken Barnett).

FRANCO, JESUS (1930–). The films of Spanish director Jesus Franco have brought new meaning, complexity, and nuance to the term *uneven*. Franco has been credited with at least 150 films (figures vary according to which source is being used) made all over Western Europe and occasionally further afield. The majority are low-budget exploitation projects—period and contemporary horror, exotic and sometimes camp thrillers, women-in-prison films, pornography (softcore and hardcore) plus a smattering of hard-to-classify dramas that draw as much upon the conventions of **art cinema** as they do on popular genres. Over the years he has acquired a substantial cult following, although even the most ardent Franco **fan** will acknowledge that some of his films are very bad indeed. Franco's position in the horror genre is far from clear. He has constantly returned to the genre throughout his career but he is an idiosyncratic figure who has rarely fitted into broader generic patterns or trends. In addition, much of his working method has been based on improvisation rather than planned in any detail. This can result in an experimental genre-bending approach but it can also lead to scenes of extraordinary tedium, and most Franco films manage to combine the two in varying proportions.

It was in the early part of his directing career that Franco came closest to being a conventional filmmaker. His Spanish film *Gritos en la noche* (*The Awful Dr. Orloff*) (1962) was a stylish example of the **surgical horror** made popular a few years before by, among others, **Hammer**'s *The Curse of Frankenstein* (1957). The inevitable **sequel**, *El secreto del Dr. Orloff* (*The Secret of Dr. Orloff, The Mistresses of Dr. Jekyll, Dr. Jekyll's Mistresses*) (1964), offered more of the same while *Miss Muerte* (*The Diabolical Dr. Z*) (1966) was a superior revenge melodrama featuring death by poisoned fingernails. Then came *Necronomicon* (*Succubus*) (1968), an obscurely plotted dream-like drama which seemed to have something to do with sado-masochistic fantasies and which contained some striking and beautiful scenes but which did not make any obvious sense, at least not in terms of the horror genre. *Necronomicon* has often been classified as horror although this tends to be an approximate designation given the oddness of the film.

Of Franco's subsequent work, *The Blood of Fu Manchu* (1968), *The Castle of Fu Manchu* (1969), *El Conde **Dracula*** (*Count Dracula*) (1970), *Il trono di fuoco* (*Night of the Blood Monster, The Bloody Judge*) (1970), *Drácula contra Frankenstein* (*Dracula vs. Frankenstein*) (1972), and **Jack the Ripper** (1976) were stolid treatments of familiar genre fare. By contrast, *Paroxismus* (*Venus in Furs*) (1969), *Vampyros lesbos* (*Lesbian **vampires***) (1971), and *Sie tötete in Ekstase* (*She Killed in Ecstasy*) (1971) operated more in the experimental manner of *Necronomicon*, while *Female Vampire* (1973), which starred Franco regular Lina Romay, was an impressive example of erotic horror. Other films—and there are many others as Franco went into overdrive during the 1970s and 1980s, directing four or five films a year—are considerably more negligible. However, *Faceless* (1988), which returned Franco to some of the material he had first covered in *Gritos en la Noche*, was seen by many Franco fans as a welcome return to form.

Other Franco horror or horror-related films include *Les cauchemars naissent la nuit* (*Nightmares Come at Night*) (1970), *Der todesrächer von Soho* (*The Corpse Packs His Bags*) (1972), *Les Démons* (*The Sex Demons*) (1972), *Les expériences érotiques de Frankenstein* (*The Erotic Rites of Frankenstein*) (1972), *La fille de Dracula* (*Daughter of Dracula*) (1972), *Los ojos siniestros del doctor Orloff* (The Sinister Eyes of Doctor Orloff) (1973), *Christina, princesse de l'érotisme* (*A Virgin Among the Living Dead*) (1973), *L'éventreur de Notre-Dame* (*Demoniac*) (1979), *Die Säge des Todes* (*Bloody Moon*) (1981), *El siniestro doctor Orloff* (*The Sinister Dr. Orloff*) (1984), *Sola ante el terror* (*Alone Against Terror*) (1986), and *Killer Barbys* (1996). This is by no means a complete list of Franco's horrors, and there have been many films in other genres as well. As befits a filmmaker who is hard to pin down, Franco has been billed under a variety of pseudonyms, among them Clifford Brown, A.M. Frank, Jess Frank, Frank Hollman, James P. Johnson, and Franco Manera.

FRANJU, GEORGES (1912–1987). The French director Georges Franju merits inclusion in this book for one film, the extraordinary *Les yeux sans visage* (*Eyes without a Face*) (1959), which is a major example of **surgical horror**, albeit one that is so artful that it is sometimes not classified as horror at all. It featured a conventional **mad scientist** narrative of the sort that might show up in **American horror** of the 1930s or 1940s—a surgeon kidnaps young women so that he can transplant their faces onto the disfigured face of his daughter. However, the film's treatment of this story was both serious and poetic, and the unflinching clinical realism of the scenes of surgery was unprecedented in the genre and still has the power to shock today. Amid all the **gore**, the image of the daughter wearing a mask to cover her disfigurement, with only her eyes visible, remains one of horror's most haunting images. *Le sang des bêtes* (Blood of Beasts) (1949), an earlier Franju **documentary** detailing the workings of a slaughterhouse, provides a comparably horrifying experience, albeit one firmly rooted in reality. *See also* FRENCH HORROR.

FRANKENHEIMER, JOHN (1930–2002). The American director John Frankenheimer was best known for his thrillers and action films– including *The Manchurian Candidate* (1962), *Seven Days in May* (1964), and *Grand Prix* (1966). However, he did occasionally dabble in more macabre projects. *Seconds* (1966), a claustrophobic **science fiction** drama about a man changing his identity, featured a truly horrifying conclusion in which the hero is put to death by surgical means. *Prophecy* (1979) was more straightforward horror fare, a well-made but standard **revenge of nature** film about a mutant bear. Frankenheimer took over direction of *The Island of Dr. Moreau* (1996) after its original director, **Richard Stanley**, had been fired. Frankenheimer's version of the tale was overwrought but the film remains an interesting adaptation of its literary source. At the time of his death, Frankenheimer was preparing to direct the prequel to *The Exorcist* (1973), a project eventually taken over by **Paul Schrader**. See also AMERICAN HORROR.

FRANKENSTEIN. The Frankenstein story has proved to be one of the most enduring of all horror's stories. Mary Shelley's novel *Frankenstein, or the Modern Prometheus* (1818) is the only novel from the original **gothic** period in literary history to have been adapted repeatedly for stage, screen, radio and **television** and still to retain a significant hold on our imagination. In comparison, its vampiric counterpart, Bram Stoker's *Dracula*, did not appear until 1897. However, much like *Dracula*, the post-publication history of *Frankenstein* has been one of constant revision, with elements of the original novel discarded and replaced, then subsequently rediscovered, as is deemed necessary to sustain the interest of the intended audience. To the contemporary spectator, who will almost certainly be more familiar with film versions of *Frankenstein* than they are with Shelley's novel, the fact that in the original version there is minimal description of the process by which the creature is created or of its appearance will be surprising, as will the creature's verbal articulacy, so accustomed have we become to cinematic scenes of spectacular mad science and dumb, menacing monsters. It follows that judging any Frankenstein film in terms of its adherence to the novel is a futile activity. The films exist instead in relation to a series of cultural transformations of various fragments of the Frankenstein story.

Theatrical adaptations of Shelley's *Frankenstein* appeared within a few years of its publication and continued to appear throughout the

19th and into the 20th century, with Peggy Webling's 1930 stage version providing the basis for the famous 1931 **Universal** film adaptation. These all tended to emphasize spectacle and action over the convoluted narrative structure and philosophical monologues of the novel, perhaps necessarily so given the differing demands of theater and literature. *Frankenstein* (1910) and *Life Without Soul* (1915), two American pre-sound film versions of the tale were similarly structured around the scenes of the creature's creation and destruction.

The 1931 Universal version of *Frankenstein*, the studio's follow-up to its successful version of *Dracula* (1931) was originally to be directed by **Robert Florey** with **Bela Lugosi** as Frankenstein's creation. For reasons that are still not entirely clear—although some reports indicate that Lugosi balked at playing a part without dialogue—Lugosi and Florey left the project and were replaced by British director **James Whale** and an unknown British actor by the name of **Boris Karloff**. The resulting film was stylish, confident and considerably more sustained than the uneven *Dracula*. Importantly, it formed the character of Frankenstein into the **mad scientist**, who would become a stock figure in 1930s and 1940s horror cinema. It also established an image of the monster that would supplant all previous theatrical, and indeed literary, versions and become the norm against which later representations of the monster would be judged. This was the famous square-headed, bolt-necked creation designed by **makeup** artist **Jack Pierce**. Mute and murderous (thanks to its abnormal brain, an innovation particularly disliked by Shelley purists) but also victimized and sympathetic: this monster was a mass of contradictions, and arguably it was this quality that rendered it such a fascinating figure.

Bride of Frankenstein (1935) was Whale's extravagant follow-up. The film still offered spectacular scenes of creation and destruction and it also brought back Karloff's apparently indestructible monster (who here briefly acquired some rudimentary verbal abilities). At the same time, *Bride of Frankenstein*'s tongue remained firmly in its cheek as it exhibited a type of humor that, to contemporary audiences at least, can seem decidedly camp. Playfulness of this kind would generally be absent from later Universal **sequels**, although it would resurface in other film versions. Such differences in tone are arguably as important to an understanding of the progress of Frankenstein and his various creations through film history as is an awareness of the more repetitive and formulaic qualities associated with the films. The sequels that followed maintained, for the most part, a loose chronology, but the key element that bound them together into a cycle was the Monster himself, with narratives often turning on his resurrection and leading inevitably to his destruction. This was increasingly accompanied by an augmentation of the monster's brutality and an attenuation of the pathos associated with him, especially after Karloff ceased playing the role. *Son of Frankenstein* (1939) was next, directed in somber style by **Rowland Lee**, with **Basil Rathbone** as Frankenstein's son, Lugosi as the broken-necked Ygor, and, for the last time, Karloff as the monster. Then came *The **Ghost** of Frankenstein* (1942), which was directed by **Erle C. Kenton** and which, like most of Universal's 1940s horrors, was lower-budgeted than the likes of *Son of Frankenstein*. Ygor returned, taking the Monster (in a crude performance by **Lon Chaney Jr.**) to meet another of Frankenstein's sons, played by Cedric Hardwicke. The film concluded with Ygor's brain transplanted into the Monster, who for the second and final time in the Universal Frankenstein cycle spoke, albeit with Ygor's voice. *Frankenstein Meets the Wolf Man* (1943), directed by **Roy William Neill**, was the first of Universal's multiple monster films, with Chaney as the Wolf Man and, logically given the events of the previous film, Lugosi as the Monster, a part he had turned down 12 years previously. Baroness Elsa Frankenstein provided the Frankenstein name, although she took no part in the narrative's medical experiments. *House of Frankenstein* (1944) and *House of Dracula* (1945), both directed by Kenton, featured no character bearing the name of Frankenstein, apparently content that all that was now needed was the Monster itself, played this time by Glenn Strange, although in neither film did the Monster have much to do. The final flourish of the Universal Frankenstein, if that is the appropriate term, came with *Abbott and Costello Meet Frankenstein* (1948), which yet again featured Strange as the Monster and from which any character named Frankenstein was conspicuously absent.

The **science fiction**/horror hybrids popular throughout the 1950s featured their share of mad or misguided scientists. However, Frankenstein and his creation were not revived until 1957, when the British company **Hammer** released *The Curse of Frankenstein*, which, like the 1931 version, only drew in a limited way on the original novel. This color production, which was directed by **Terence Fisher**, starred **Peter Cushing** as Frankenstein and a then unknown actor called **Christopher Lee** as a savage and animalistic Creature entirely lacking the pathos apparent in Karloff's earlier performances. Hammer's Frankenstein was far from being a mad scientist. Although capable of great cruelty and ruthlessness, he was also supremely cool and rational, an appropriate embodiment of science in a nuclear age. Unlike the Universal films, the Hammer sequels focused on the scientist himself rather than his creations, who changed from one film to another. The emphasis was always on Frankenstein's schemes. These were often bold and ambitious, involving activities such as brain or soul transplants, but which usually ended up compromised or thwarted by his questionable methods and by the shortsightedness of the society within which he had to work. Fisher's *The Revenge of Frankenstein* (1958) was followed by **Freddie Francis**'s *The Evil of Frankenstein* (1964), with Fisher returning to the cycle with *Frankenstein Created Woman* (1967) and *Frankenstein Must Be Destroyed* (1969). Cushing was replaced by **Ralph Bates** in *The Horror of Frankenstein* (1970), Hammer's unsuccessful attempt to produce a more youthful version of the Frankenstein story, but it was business as usual for *Frankenstein and the Monster from Hell* (1974), the final film in the Hammer cycle, with Cushing starring and Fisher directing.

Two American Frankenstein films were released shortly after the success of *The Curse of Frankenstein*. *I Was a Teenage Frankenstein* (1957), which was part of a late 1950s cycle of **teenage horror**, transplanted the Frankenstein story to a contemporary university setting, while the main noteworthy feature of *Frankenstein—1970* (1958) was that it starred Karloff as the scientist rather than as the Monster. Neither of these seriously challenged Hammer's dominance, however, and it was not until the early 1970s, when Hammer's cycle was visibly running down, that a significant number of alternate Frankenstein films appeared. Some of these were negligible, among them *La figlia di Frankenstein* (*Lady Frankenstein*) (1971), *Dracula versus Frankenstein* (1971) and the blaxploitation film *Blackenstein* (1973). Others did offer an interesting reinterpretation of the Frankenstein story, among them *Frankenstein: The True Story*

(1973), an intelligent television film that achieved a theatrical release in some territories, **Paul Morrissey**'s camp *Flesh for Frankenstein* (1973), **Mel Brooks'** loving homage to Universal horror, *Young Frankenstein* (1974), and the cult favorite *The Rocky Horror Picture Show* (1975).

However, these were all isolated projects, and the increasing emphasis in horror on teenage audiences seemed to lead the genre away from some of its more traditional monsters. Irresponsible scientists still showed up, and were occasionally described in Frankenstein-like terms (for example, in **George Romero**'s 1985 **zombie** film *Day of the Dead*), but Frankenstein himself was generally absent. *Frankenweenie* (1984), **Tim Burton**'s charming animated short about a boy who transforms his dead **dog** into a Frankenstein-like monster, exuded nostalgia for the old horror myths, while **Roger Corman**'s *Frankenstein Unbound* (1990) tried to revise the original Frankenstein story but failed to register with audiences. *Mary Shelley's Frankenstein* (1994), which was made in the wake of the success of **Francis Ford Coppola**'s *Dracula* (1992) and which featured **Robert De Niro** as the monster, offered itself as a return to origins, although anyone expecting a faithful rendition of Shelley's novel would have been disappointed. As directed by Kenneth Branagh, the film invented and revised just as much as any previous Frankenstein film, but its heritage-style high production values did make it stand out to a certain extent in a field dominated by more exploitative fare. Frankenstein and his creation were also guest monsters, alongside Dracula and some **werewolves**, in **Stephen Sommers'** free-wheeling horror fantasy *Van Helsing* (2004), which at least did not claim any kind of adherence to literary sources.

The current marginality of the Frankenstein story in horror is perhaps surprising, given that we live in a world characterized by apparently ceaseless scientific and technological changes. Horror certainly engages with these changes; technophobia of various kinds informs many contemporary horror films. However, this tends not to be done in the name of Frankenstein, who is increasingly seen as a figure from the past, not just a literary past but now a cinematic past as well. This does not mean that Frankenstein has lost his significance for us but—for the present, at least—he remains a distant figure.

FRANKLIN, RICHARD (1948–2007). The Australian director Richard Franklin's first two horror films offered a distinctly Australian take on American formats. *Patrick* (1978) was a telekinesis drama made in the wake of **Brian De Palma**'s *Carrie* (1976) that also sought to emulate that film's shock ending, while *Roadgames* (1981) was an inventive and self-consciously Hitchcockian thriller that starred horror icon **Jamie Lee Curtis**. At the time, the idea of making a **sequel** to **Hitchcock**'s *Psycho* (1960) seemed to some like cinematic heresy. However, Franklin made a good job of it with his American debut, *Psycho II* (1983), successfully turning **serial killer** Norman Bates into the main protagonist and delivering a compelling mystery narrative. Franklin also directed *Link* (1986), a horror film featuring humans threatened by **apes**. In the latter part of his career, he worked mainly for **television**. *See also* AUSTRALIAN HORROR.

FREAKS. Forms of physical abnormality or deformity have frequently been deployed in horror films to denote monstrousness. However, this is usually achieved via **makeup** and special effects rather than through the introduction of real-life deformity, and the term *freak*— once widely associated with extreme deformity—is rarely used at all, unless it is seen to be spoken by an ignorant character. It seems from this that the effectiveness of horror's monsters as scare figures is dependent on our knowing that they are not real, that a recognizable human being lurks under the makeup. Horror films that do feature genuine deformity are disturbing not just ethically—we worry that these people are being exploited by the filmmakers—but also because they challenge horror's status as fiction. The best-known example of this is **Tod Browning**'s *Freaks* (1932), which presented real "freaks" both in sympathetic terms and, in places, as scary, vengeful figures. The film is too challenging ever to have received a widespread release, and watching it remains an uncomfortable experience. More obviously exploitative was the case of actor **Rondo Hatton**, sufferer of the disfiguring **disease** acromegaly, who featured as the monster in several 1940s horror films and thrillers. Since then, the use of real-life deformity in horror has generally been perceived as being in extremely poor taste, and the few examples where it has occurred— notably in the **British horror** film *The Mutations* (*The Freakmaker*) (1974) and the satanic thriller *The Sentinel* (1977)—are often criticized on this count. The one partial exception appears to be dwarfs, with diminutive actors Michael Dunn and Skip Martin regularly appearing in horror films of the 1960s and 1970s.

FREDA, RICCARDO (1909–1999). Throughout the 1950s, the Egyptian-born Italian director Riccardo Freda specialized in historical melodramas and adventure films. However, he was also responsible for what is often seen as the first **Italian horror** film, *I Vampiri* (*The Devil's Commandment*) (1956). Unfortunately, this beautifully made contemporary **vampire** story did not fare well at the box office. However, the international commercial success of **Hammer**'s *The Curse of Frankenstein* (1957) encouraged Freda to return to the genre. First came the stylish monster movie *Caltiki—il mostro immortale* (*Caltiki the Undying Monster, Caltiki, the Immortal Monster*) (1959) and the **gothic**-themed muscleman epic *Maciste all'inferno* (*Maciste in Hell, The Witch's Curse*) (1962). These were followed by the two films upon which Freda's reputation as a horror director has largely rested ever since, *L'orribile segreto del Dr. Hichcock* (*The Horrible Dr. Hichcock, The Terrible Secret of Dr. Hichcock*) (1962), and *Lo spettro* (*The Ghost*) (1963). These period-set mysteries both starred **Barbara Steele** and generated a remarkably morbid atmosphere, with this most evident in *L'orribile segreto del Dr. Hichcock*, which took as its main plot device the subject of necrophilia. In comparison, Freda's later genre films were uneven. They included the **giallo** thrillers *L'iguana dalla lingua di fuoco* (*The Iguana with the Tongue of Fire*) (1971), *Estratto dagli archivi segreti della polizia di una capitale europea* (*Tragic Ceremony*) (1972), and *Follia omicida*, (*Delirium, Murder Syndrome*) (1981). To a certain extent, Freda's contribution to Italian horror has been overshadowed by the more sustained commitment to the genre displayed by his sometimes collaborator **Mario Bava** (who directed sections of some of Freda's early horror films) but he remains a distinctive talent in his own right.

FRENCH HORROR. It is perhaps surprising that a country with the rich cinematic history of France should have contributed so little to the development of the European horror film. However, French horror films are few and far between. The French-produced surrealist film *Un chien andalou* (1928), which contains some horrifying imagery, has become a canonical cinematic text, but Jean Epstein's **gothic**-themed and equally experimental project *La chute de la maison Usher* (*The Fall of the House of Usher*) (1928) is rarely seen today. Throughout the 1930s and 1940s, when American cinema dominated the market, only a few French filmmakers worked on horror-like projects, notably Julien Duvivier with the French/Czech co-production *Le Golem* (*The Golem*) (1936), Guillaume Radot with *Le loup des Malveneur* (*The Wolf of the Malveneurs*) (1942), and Maurice Tourneur with the Faustian drama *Le main du diable* (*The Devil's Hand*) (1943). When European horror became internationally popular during the late 1950s and 1960s, it was Britain, Italy and Spain that churned out a stream of lurid horrors and achieved dominance, while French cinema continued to produce isolated genre works that were usually upmarket and sometimes very distinguished. **Georges Franju**'s controversial and graphic *Les yeux sans visage* (*Eyes without a Face*) (1959) has become a classic example of **surgical horror** and Jean Renoir's *Le testament du Docteur Cordelier* (*The Testament of Dr. Cordelier*) (1959), which was made for **television**, was an interesting treatment of the **Dr. Jekyll and Mr. Hyde** story. **Roger Vadim** directed *Et mourir de plaisir* (*Blood and Roses*) (1960), a decorous adaptation of J. Sheridan LeFanu's **vampire** story "Carmilla" and also, along with fellow French director Louis Malle, contributed an episode to the **Edgar Allan Poe** horror **anthology** *Histoires extraordinaires* (*Tales of Mystery, Spirits of the Dead*) (1968). There were also a few co-productions with other countries—for example, the French/Italian *Il mulino delle donne di pietra* (*Mill of the Stone Women*) (1960)—although these tended to show little connection with French cultural traditions. More successful as an expression of something that might reasonably be described as French horror was a series of erotic vampire films directed by **Jean Rollin** from the late 1960s onwards, beginning with *Le viol du vampire* (*The Rape of the Vampire*) (1967). These combined surreal imagery with copious nudity and some violence and have since acquired a significant cult following.

More recently, horror has become more of a presence in French cinema, albeit still a marginal one. Popular genre films such as *Promenons-nous dans les bois* (*Deep in the Woods*) (2000), *Un jeu d'enfants* (2001), and *Maléfique* (2002) have been joined by slicker and more ambitious projects such as **Christophe Gans'** period horror drama *Le pacte des loups* (*The Brotherhood of the Wolf*) (2001) and **Alexandre Aja's slasher** film *Haute tension* (*High Tension, Switchblade Romance*) (2003), both of which were clearly made with an eye on the international market. Mathieu Kassovitz's **serial killer** film *Les rivières pourpres* (*The Crimson Rivers*) (2000) was similarly international and, like Gans and Aja, Kassovitz has gone on to work on American genre projects. A number of highly controversial French films—among them Claire Denis's *Trouble Every Day* (2001) and Gaspar Noé's *Irréversible* (2002)—have also offered images of violence and mutilation that have been deemed by many to be horrifying, although the extent to which these self-consciously provocative films should be seen as belonging to the horror genre, as opposed to just appropriating its imagery, is far from clear.

FREUND, KARL (1890–1969). The cinematographer Karl Freund's early career in German cinema included distinguished work on **F. W. Murnau's Dr. Jekyll and Mr. Hyde** adaptation *Der Januskopf* (1920) and his *Der Letzte Mann* (*The Last Laugh*) (1924), which was renowned for its use of mobile camera, as well as Paul Wegener's *Der **Golem**, wie er in die Welt kam* (*The Golem*) (1920) and Fritz Lang's *Metropolis* (1927). He moved to Hollywood in the early 1930s, where he photographed **Tod Browning's** *Dracula* (1931) and **Robert Florey's** *Murders in the Rue Morgue* (1932), both of which exhibited the expressionistic visual qualities that would help to define **Universal** horror of the period. Freund also directed the similarly stylized Universal production *The **Mummy*** (1932) and, for MGM, *Mad Love* (1935). After serving in a variety of genres as cinematographer, he concluded his career working on the 1950s **television comedy** show *I Love Lucy*.

***FRIDAY THE 13TH* (1980).** There are eleven *Friday the 13th* films to date, and two of them have the word *Final* in their titles. However, such has been the commercial resilience of this particular horror cycle that it has survived all attempts to kill it off. *Friday the 13th* (1980), which was directed by **Sean S. Cunningham**, appeared in the wake of **John Carpenter's** *Halloween* (1978) and was generally seen by critics as a crude variant on the formula established by Carpenter's film. A group of teenagers visit Camp Crystal Lake and are killed off by a mysterious assailant, who is eventually revealed to be the crazed mother of a boy who drowned there some years before. It is an archetypal **slasher** plot—with teenage victims murdered as they indulge in pre-marital sexual activity, a dark secret from the past, extensive use of **point of view** and **startle effects**, and a **Final Girl** who ultimately defeats the killer.

Although not liked by critics, *Friday the 13th* was very popular with audiences and the inevitable **sequels** soon followed. In an innovation that would define the rest of the cycle, *Friday the 13th Part 2* (1981) resurrected the drowned boy—who went by the name of Jason Voorhees—from the first film and transformed him into a hulking brute intent on homicide. Not much else changed, initially at least. Teenagers continued to visit Crystal Lake and continued to die in inventively horrible ways before Jason's climactic demise. As the cycle progressed, the formula was tweaked slightly through an increased emphasis on supernatural themes and a greater willingness to switch locations, but the cozy familiarity of Jason's world was retained.

Friday the 13th Part III (1982) was followed by *Friday the 13th: The Final Chapter* (1984), which led to *Friday the 13th: A New Beginning* (1985), *Friday the 13th Part VI: Jason Lives* (1986), *Friday the 13th Part VII: The New Blood* (1988), *Friday the 13th Part VIII: Jason Takes Manhattan* (1989), and *Jason Goes to Hell: The Final Friday* (1993). *Jason X* (2001) took Jason into outer space while *Freddy vs. Jason* (2003) brought him back to earth with a brutal fight to the death with Freddy Krueger from the **Nightmare on Elm Street** films. Whether this is the end of Jason, or Freddy, remains to be seen.

The **television** series *Friday the 13th* (1987–1990) had a completely different storyline from the *Friday the 13th* film cycle.

FRIEDKIN, WILLIAM (1935–). The director William Friedkin's principal horror credit is **The Exorcist** (1973). This could so easily have become a schlock-horror piece, but Friedkin—along with producer-writer **William Peter Blatty**—took the whole thing very seriously, and in so doing introduced an unprecedented level of realism into the horror genre. He also managed with great skill the film's shifts from art house-like enigma, most evident in the obscure opening sequence, to barnstorming scenes of **gore** and violence. None of the **sequels** to *The Exorcist* were able to recapture the qualities he instilled in the material, although Friedkin himself has since sometimes struggled to find equally promising subjects. *Cruising* (1980), his controversial gay **serial killer** film, retained the urban grittiness of *The Exorcist* and his earlier success *The French Connection* (1971), but his supernatural thriller *The Guardian* (1990) took him into a rural setting. The story—which dealt with human sacrifices being made to an animate tree—was fanciful, yet the film, while lacking the resonance of *The Exorcist*, contained some extremely well-executed sequences. Friedkin also contributed episodes to the **television** horror series *The Twilight Zone* (1985–1989) and *Tales from the Crypt* (1989–1996). *See also* AMERICAN HORROR.

FRIZZI, FABIO (1951–). The Italian composer Fabio Frizzi made an important contribution to the horror films directed by **Lucio Fulci**. His haunting score for Fulci's *Zombi 2* (***Zombie**, Zombie Flesheaters*) (1979), which operated largely in counterpoint to the film's gory violence, offered one of the most effective uses of a synthesizer in horror **music**. He was also responsible for Fulci's *Sette note in nero* (*The Psychic*) (1977), *Paura nella città dei morti viventi* (*City of the Living Dead*) (1980), *L'aldilà* (*The Beyond*) (1981), *Manhattan Baby* (***Eye of the Evil Dead***) (1982), and *Un gatto nel cervello* (*A **Cat** in the Brain*) (1990).

FRYE, DWIGHT (1899–1943). Dwight Frye was a versatile and accomplished stage actor, but his film career was defined, and indeed constrained, by his appearances in two key early **American horror** films. He was Renfield in the **Universal** *Dracula* (1931). In Bram Stoker's novel, it was Jonathan Harker who traveled to Transylvania to meet Dracula, but in the Universal version Renfield made that journey and had the first historic encounter with the **vampire**. Frye's Renfield was a dapper and somewhat ridiculous figure who was blithely unaware of the dangers that awaited him. His transformation into a raving madman was rapid and histrionic, and accompanied by one of the most unsettling maniacal laughs in horror history. Frye followed this up with the part of Fritz, **Frankenstein**'s hunchbacked assistant, in **James Whale**'s *Frankenstein* (1931). As he had with the mad Renfield, Frye contorted his body and played every line with a manic intensity. Even within the context of American horror films of the early 1930s, which often featured extreme performances—for example, **Colin Clive** as Frankenstein—Frye's expressive and highly physical renditions of insanity stood out. He reprised his cackling madman role in *The Vampire Bat* (1933), *Bride of Frankenstein* (1935), and *The Crime of Dr. Crespi* (1935), although there was also a rare straight performance, albeit in a small uncredited role, in Whale's *The Invisible Man* (1933). By the time he returned to horror in the 1940s, this type of acting was out of fashion, and his brief appearances in *The Ghost of Frankenstein* (1942) and *Frankenstein Meets the Wolf Man* (1943) were suitably restrained. However, the poverty row shocker *Dead Men Walk* (1943) saw him back in hunchback mode for the last time.

FUEST, ROBERT (1927–). The British director—and also production designer—Robert Fuest worked on the highly stylized **television** show *The Avengers* during the 1960s. However, his first few films for the cinema, which included the **serial killer** drama *And Soon The Darkness* (1970), opted for a more downbeat realism. By contrast, *The Abominable Dr. Phibes* (1971) and its **sequel** *Dr. Phibes Rises Again* (1972) were extravagantly over the top in their plotting, design and in **Vincent Price**'s melodramatic performance as the disfigured and vengeful Phibes. Even within the context of 1970s **British horror**, where there was a great deal of experimentation and innovation, these films stood out as distinctive. Next came *The Final Programme* (1973), an idiosyncratic **science fiction** film, and *The Devil's Rain* (1975), an American-produced Satanic thriller that featured John Travolta in a minor role. Thereafter Fuest worked mainly for television.

FULCI, LUCIO (1927–1996). The **Italian horror** film director Lucio Fulci has a considerable following among horror **fans** but his films have never attracted the sort of critical respect afforded fellow Italian genre specialists **Mario Bava** and **Dario Argento**. This might have something to do with the unevenness of his work. Even his admirers will acknowledge that some of his later films are disappointing, and some of his most accomplished projects, for all their brilliant moments, will occasionally lapse into crudity and crassness.

Fulci began directing in 1959, and for the first part of his career specialized mainly in broad comedy. In the late 1960s, he switched to the then popular **giallo** thriller with *Una sull'altra* (*One on Top of the Other*) (1969), *Una lucertola con la pelle di donna* (*A Lizard in a Woman's Skin*) (1971), and *Non si sevizia un paperino* (*Don't **Torture** a Duckling*) (1972). Although this change in career direction coincided with the suicide of Fulci's wife, it is by no means clear that this was anything other than a commercially minded filmmaker latching onto a new market trend. In any event, Fulci was clearly comfortable with the convoluted plotting, emphasis on deviant sexualities, and the foregrounding of extreme style that characterized the giallo. He was also willing to innovate within the format. This was most clearly demonstrated by *Non si sevizia un paperino* which, unusually for a giallo, had a rural setting. Here Fulci offered a thoughtful exploration of the conflict between traditional and modern Italian social mores, took a swipe at the Catholic Church (the killer turns out to be a priest) and also provided one of his keynote set pieces with a graphic, unsparing sequence in which a woman is beaten to death with heavy chains. As one might expect, the sequence is repulsively violent but it is also—through its inventive staging and editing—disturbingly beautiful. It is a provocative moment in what is probably Fulci's best and most challenging film. Later Fulci projects would often be arresting but would also lack the discipline and structure of this particular giallo.

Fulci returned to farce with the **comedy**-horror *Il cavaliere Costante Nicosia demoniaco . . . orrero **Dracula** in Brianza* (1975)—which literally translates as *The Demonic Womanizer Costante Nicosia—or Dracula in Brianza*, although the film's international title was the more manageable *Young Dracula*—and also directed the effective supernatural thriller *Sette note in nero* (*The Psychic*) (1977). However, it was *Zombi 2* (1979) that determined the shape of the latter part of his career. **George Romero**'s **zombie** spectacular *Dawn of the Dead* (1978) had been marketed in Italy as *Zombi*, and *Zombi 2* was so titled to cash in on its success, although outside of Italy it was known as either *Zombie* or *Zombie Flesheaters*. The film combined eerie sequences with narrative longeurs and crude **gore** effects, notably an unpleasant scene in which a woman has a large wooden splinter pushed into one of her **eyes**.

Comparable nasty scenes, which become something of a Fulci trademark, also featured in the three films upon which Fulci's reputation as a horror artist (such as it is) largely rests—*Paura nella città dei morti viventi* (*City of the Living Dead*) (1980), *L'aldilà* (*The Beyond*) (1981), and *Quella villa accanto al cimitero* (*The House by the Cemetery*) (1981). However, here they contributed to a much more developed lurid, visionary quality. The films' narratives, which dealt with gateways being opened to hell or to other dimensions, did not make a great deal of sense. Despite (or perhaps because of) this, Fulci managed to produce not just a series of remarkable set pieces but also an extraordinarily oppressive atmosphere. By contrast, *Black Cat* (1981) and *Manhattan Baby* (*Eye of the Evil Dead*) (1982), which lacked the extreme gore, were bland, and the relentlessly downbeat *Lo squartatore di New York* (*The New York Ripper*) (1982), which contained the gore and little else, was just repellent.

The remainder of Fulci's horror films were made at a time when the boom in Italian horror production was coming to an end, and they ran the gamut from mildly interesting to negligible. They included *Murderock—Uccide a passo di danza* (*Murder Rock—Dancing Death*) (1984), *Aenigma* (1987), *Zombi 3* (on which Fulci was replaced by Bruno Mattei) (1988), *Quando Alice ruppe lo specchio* (*Touch of Death*) (1988), *Il fantasma di Sodoma* (*The Ghosts of Sodom*) (1988), *Demonia* (1990), *Un gatto nel cervello* (*A Cat in the Brain, Nightmare Concert*) (1990), *Urla dal profondo* (*Voices from Beyond*) (1991), and *Le porte del silenzio* (*Door to Silence*) (1991), as well as two **television** films, *La dolce casa degli orrori* (*The Sweet House of Horrors*) (1989) and *La casa del tempo* (*The House of Clocks*) (1989).

– G –

GANS, CHRISTOPHE (1960–). The director Christophe Gans is French, but his work often has an international character and he has been responsible for some of the most stylish horror films of recent years. He directed one of the segments in the **H. P. Lovecraft anthology** *Necronomicon* (1994), and subsequently made *Crying Freeman* (1995), an English-language thriller based on a Japanese **comic**

book series. *Le pacte des loups* (*The Brotherhood of the Wolf*) (2001) turned out to be his biggest commercial success to date. It offered an unusual but exciting combination of French period drama, martial arts fights, and horror imagery in its depiction of a monster terrorizing pre-revolutionary France. Gans' next project was *Silent Hill* (2006), an English-language adaptation of a **computer game** that featured **ghosts** in the manner of **Japanese horror**, but which drew some of its iconography from **Italian horror**, and especially from the work of **Lucio Fulci**. *See also* FRENCH HORROR.

GARRIS, MICK (1951–). The writer-producer-director Mick Garris specializes in horror for **television** and is a regular collaborator with **Stephen King**. His directorial credits for the cinema include the **sequel** *Critters 2: The Main Course* (1988), the King-scripted *Sleepwalkers* (1992), and *Riding the Bullet* (2004), which was adapted by Garris himself from a King story. He directed the television films *Psycho IV: The Beginning* (1990) and *Quicksilver Highway* (1997), as well as the television miniseries adaptations of King's *The Stand* (1994), *The Shining* (1997), and *Desperation* (2006), and he has also contributed episodes to *Amazing Stories* (1985–1987), *Freddy's Nightmares* (1988–1990), *Tales from the Crypt* (1989–1996), and *The Others* (2000). In 2005, he created and produced the television series *Masters of Horror*. *See also* AMERICAN HORROR.

GATES, TUDOR (1930–2007). The writer Tudor Gates' pedigree in upmarket fantasy films was considerable. He worked on the screenplays for both **Mario Bava's** *Diabolik* (1968) and **Roger Vadim's** *Barbarella* (1968) and subsequently introduced some continental exoticism into **Hammer** horror by scripting all three of its lesbian **vampire** films, *The Vampire Lovers* (1970), *Lust for a Vampire* (1971), and *Twins of Evil* (1971). He also wrote the **British horror** *Fright* (1971), an early example of the babysitter-in-peril story.

GEIN, ED (1906–1984). The Wisconsin-based **serial killer** Ed Gein has provided considerable inspiration for horror filmmakers and has become a template for a distinctly American version of the psychopath. Gein was a mother-fixated loner who seemed to have gone over the edge when his mother died. His exploits included murder, digging up corpses that he thought resembled his mother, decorating his house with and making furniture out of body parts, and fashioning for himself a "suit" made out of female skin. He was arrested in 1957 and spent the rest of his life in a mental institution. His crimes were widely reported and became the focus of considerable public shock and also fascination.

The writer **Robert Bloch** loosely based the character of Norman Bates, the killer in his novel *Psycho*, on Gein. Originally Bates was presented as middle-aged and overweight. The casting of young and handsome **Anthony Perkins** in the role in **Alfred Hitchcock**'s version of *Psycho* (1960) distanced him from the unprepossessing Gein, although the mother fixation and sexually aberrant behavior were still apparent. *Deranged* (1974), which was directed by **Alan Ormsby** and Jeff Gillen, was a fictionalized and exceptionally gruesome version of the Gein story, while **William Girdler**'s *Three on a Meathook* (1972) and **Tobe Hooper**'s *The Texas Chainsaw Massacre* (1974) drew some of their details from Gein's activities. The "skin suit" worn by Buffalo Bill, one of the serial killers in *The Silence of the Lambs* (1991), clearly owes something to Gein, and a biopic, *Ed Gein*, finally appeared in 2000.

GELLAR, SARAH MICHELLE (1977–). As Buffy Summers, the likeable heroine of the **television** series *Buffy the Vampire Slayer* (1997–2003), Sarah Michelle Gellar regularly took on and defeated vampires, demons and other supernatural nasties. However, she was considerably more vulnerable in her early horror film appearances. She put up a good fight against **serial killers** in her supporting roles in *I Know What You Did Last Summer* (1997) and *Scream 2* (1997) but ended up dead in both. She did get to survive in **Takashi Shimizu**'s post-*Buffy* **ghost** story *The Grudge* (2004), although the ghosts finally got her in *The Grudge 2* (2006). She was perfectly cast as the glamorous Daphne in horror spoofs *Scooby Doo* (2002) and *Scooby Doo 2: Monsters Unleashed* (2004) and also starred in the supernatural thriller *The Return* (2006).

GERMAN HORROR. The noted film historian Lotte Eisner once suggested that the German soul instinctively preferred twilight. Whether or not this is actually the case, German cinema of the post-World War I years certainly contained a strong horror-like section, much of which has subsequently been labeled **Expressionism**. Films such as *Das Cabinet des Dr. Caligari* (*The Cabinet of Dr. Caligari*) (1919), *Der Golem, wie er in die Welt kam* (*The Golem*) (1920), *Nosferatu, eine Symphonie des Grauens* (*Nosferatu: a Symphony of Terror*) (1922) and *Das Wachsfigurenkabinett* (***Waxworks***) (1924) provided stylistic and thematic inspiration to **American horror** films of the 1930s. In addition, German filmmakers also went on to work on horror-related projects outside of Germany, among them **Karl Freund, Paul Leni, Conrad Veidt** and Paul Wegener. However, the rise of the Nazis to power in the early 1930s brought to an abrupt end the development of a horror cinema within Germany. Neither did Germany play any significant part in the revival of European horror that took place in the late 1950s. A popular 1960s series of adaptations of Edgar Wallace stories sometimes contained horror themes and imagery, notable among these *Der Rächer* (*The Avenger*) (1960) and *Die Toten Augen von London* (*The Dead Eyes of London*) (1961). There were occasional horror productions as well, including *Die Nackte und der Satan* (*A Head for the Devil, The Head*) (1959), *Der Fluch der grünen Augen* (*Night of the Vampires, Cave of the Living Dead*) (1964), *Im Schloß der blutigen Begierde* (*Castle of Bloody Lust*) (1968), *Die Schlangengrube und das Pendel* (*The Snake Pit and the Pendulum, Castle of the Walking Dead*) (1967), and the controversial and gory witchhunter drama *Hexen bis aufs Blut gequält* (*Mark of the Devil*) (1970), but this activity never cohered into a distinctive horror cycle in the manner of Britain and Italy in the same period. During the 1970s, a few experimental genre projects also appeared, among them the vampire story *Jonathan* (1970), the **serial killer** drama *Die zärtlichkeit der Wölfe* (*The Tenderness of Wolves*) (1973), and *Nosferatu: Phantom der Nacht* (*Nosferatu—the Vampyre*) (1979), Werner Herzog's **remake** of the 1922 *Nosferatu*. Subsequent German horror production has remained sporadic. The confrontational low-budget work done by **Jörg Buttgereit** in the 1980s and 1990s—including *Nekromantik* (1987)—has attracted a cult following, while the more commercial **surgical horror** film *Anatomie* (2000) and serial killer drama *Tattoo* (2002) drew upon German history for their subject matter but also relied heavily on American horror conventions.

GHOSTS. Given the preponderance of ghost stories in contemporary horror cinema, it is perhaps surprising how infrequently ghosts featured in horror's formative years. Although ghost stories are a long established literary genre, and the 1920s haunted house spoof was in certain respects a precursor of **American horror** cinema, the key horror monsters of the 1930s and 1940s were not ghosts but instead more corporeal creations such as **vampires, werewolves**, the **mummy** and **Frankenstein**'s monster. There were a few scary cinematic ghost stories in this period, the most distinguished being *The Uninvited* (1944) and **Val Lewton**'s *The Curse of the Cat People* (1944), as well as the **British horror anthology** *Dead of Night* (1945). However, the emphasis tended to be more on comic ghosts, with the likes of *Topper* (1937) and *The Ghost and Mrs Muir* (1947), and, from Great Britain, *Don't Take It To Heart* (1944) and *The Ghosts of Berkeley Square* (1947). So far as American and British cinema were concerned, horror-like ghost stories continued to appear sporadically up until the 1990s. Some were distinguished examples of subtle and suggestive filmmaking, for example, **Jack Clayton**'s *The Innocents* (1961), **Robert Wise**'s *The Haunting* (1963), **Roger Corman**'s *Tomb of Ligeia* (1964), **Curtis Harrington**'s *Ruby* (1977), and Frank LaLoggia's *Lady in White* (1988). Others, such as **William Castle**'s *13 Ghosts* (1960), **John Hough**'s *The Legend of Hell House* (1973), and **John Carpenter**'s *The Fog* (1980), were more robustly populist affairs, while **comedy**-horror ghosts featured in the likes of **Ivan Reitman**'s *Ghostbusters* (1984) and **Peter Jackson**'s *The Frighteners* (1996).

Ghosts were more common in **Italian horror** cinema of the 1960s and 1970s. The leading director **Mario Bava** made *Operazione paura (Kill, Baby . . . Kill!)* (1966), the **giallo**-ghost combination *Un hacha para la luna de miel (Hatchet for the Honeymoon)* (1970) and *Schock (Shock, Beyond the Door II)* (1977), and Italian horror star **Barbara Steele** showed up in a number of ghost stories, including *Danza macabra (Castle of Blood)* (1964) and *I lunghi capelli della morte (The Long Hair of Death)* (1964), both of which were directed by genre specialist **Antonio Margheriti**. *Kaidan eiga*, or period ghost stories, were also popular in Japanese cinema in the post-World War II period, although only the most prestigious of these secured an international release, among them Kineto Shindo's *Onibaba* (1964) and Masaki Kobayashi's epic *Kaidan* (*Kwaidan*) (1964). (*See also* JAPANESE HORROR.)

The popularity of **zombies**, cannibals and **serial killers** as horror monsters during the 1980s and 1990s helped to keep the ghost on the margins of the genre (although supernatural serial killer Freddy Krueger from the *Nightmare on Elm Street* films possessed some ghost-like qualities), and it was not until the late 1990s that ghost stories became a significant presence. Key to this was the success of **Hideo Nakata**'s Japanese ghost story *Ringu* (*Ring*) (1998), which cleverly combined traditional *kaidan eiga* subject matter, particularly the vengeful long-haired female ghost, with Western horror conventions and located this within a modern world, with the ghost manifesting itself through technology. Other similarly themed Asian horror films followed—notably **Takashi Shimizu**'s *Ju-On: The Grudge* (2003)—with some of these remade as American horror films. At the same time, the impact made by **M. Night Shyamalan**'s American ghost story *The Sixth Sense* (1999) encouraged the production of ghost dramas more obviously in a Western tradition. These included *Stir of Echoes* (1999), *What Lies Beneath* (2000), and *The Others* (2001), while *The Blair Witch Project* (1999) offered a ghost rooted firmly in American folklore. Since then, ghost-based films such as *House on Haunted Hill* (1999), *Below* (2002), *Ghost Ship* (2002), *FeardotCom* (2002), *Darkness Falls* (2003), *Gothika* (2003), *An American Haunting* (2005), a 2005 **remake** of *The Fog*, *Stay Alive* (2006), and *Silent Hill* (2006) have firmly established the ghost in all of its manifestations in horror's repertoire of monsters.

GIALLO. Crime novels used to be published in Italy with yellow covers. Consequently, the word *giallo*—which is the Italian for yellow—has become an Italian shorthand reference for crime fiction. From the 1960s onwards, it has also acquired a more specialized cinematic usage, referring to a type of Italian **psychological thriller** that has often ended up being classified as horror. In part, this classification derives from the way in which this kind of giallo film usually privileges style and spectacle over its murder mystery plot, with the rationality associated with the traditional detective story either marginalized or swept aside entirely. This is especially so when it comes to scenes of violence that are normally presented in a lingering, fetishistic manner that far exceeds any possible narrative motivation. The fact that some of the key giallo directors, notably **Mario Bava** and **Dario Argento**, also directed supernatural horrors further underlines the closeness of this type of film to the horror genre.

The giallo film is usually seen as beginning with two Bava films, *La ragazza che sapeva troppo* (*The Girl Who Knew Too Much, The Evil Eye*) (1962) and *Sei donne per l'assassino* (*Blood and Black Lace*) (1964). However, the boom in giallo production did not take place until the 1970s, a decade in which, according to some accounts, over one hundred such films were made. Many of these were international co-productions involving Germany, France or Spain that featured stars little known outside of continental Europe—including from Uruguay George Hilton (real name Jorge Hill Acosta y Lara), from France Edwige Fenech and from Spain Susan Scott (real name Nieves Navarro). Thematically, they were a disparate group of films but certain features recurred. Urban settings predominated, although there were a few distinguished rural gialli, among them **Lucio Fulci**'s *Non si sevizia un paperino* (*Don't **Torture** a Duckling*) (1972) and **Pupi Avati**'s *La casa dalle finestre che ridono* (*The House with Laughing Windows*) (1976). There was also a predilection—possibly influenced by Argento's work—for featuring black-gloved killers and having ornate titles that were often shortened for international distribution. For example, *Perché quelle strane gocce di sangue sul corpo di Jennifer?* (1972)—which translates as "Why are those strange drops of blood on Jennifer's body?"—became the more mundane *The Case of the Bloody Iris*, while *I corpi presentano tracce di violenza carnale* (1973), which means "The bodies show signs of sexual violence," became *Torso*. **Music** was also important, with obtrusive scores by the likes of **Ennio Morricone**, Riz Ortolani and the rock group **Goblin** helping to augment the films' visual spectacle.

Giallo production as a significant feature of the Italian film industry faded away during the 1980s, although some directors have continued to make them, notably Argento with films such as *Opera* (*Terror at the Opera*) (1987) and *Nonhosonno* (*Sleepless*) (2001). The 1970s giallo has sometimes been as anticipating or influencing the American **slasher** film of the late 1970s, although the slasher's preference for rural or suburban settings and teenage characters tends to separate it out from the more cosmopolitan and adult-centered giallo.

Directors associated with the giallo, other than those listed above, include **Lamberto Bava, Franco Ferrini,** Aldo Lado, **Umberto Lenzi, Antonio Margheriti, Sergio Martino,** and **Michele Soavi.** *See also* ITALIAN HORROR.

GIBSON, ALAN (1938–1987). The director Alan Gibson worked mainly for British **television,** but he also directed three films for **Hammer** during the 1970s. *Crescendo* (1970), which had originally been intended as a project for **Michael Reeves,** was one of the company's better **psychological thrillers.** *Dracula AD 1972* (1972) and *The Satanic Rites of Dracula* (1973), the last two films in Hammer's Dracula cycle, were less successful in their updating of the Dracula story to contemporary London. The portrayal of youth culture in each was particularly unconvincing, as indeed it was in Gibson's non-Hammer psychological thriller *Goodbye Gemini* (1970). Gibson also contributed episodes to Hammer's television series *Journey to the Unknown* (1968) and *Hammer House of Horror* (1980). *See also* BRITISH HORROR.

GIGER, H. R. (1940–). The Swiss artist Hans Rudi Giger's lasting claim to horror fame is his designs for *Alien* (1979). He was responsible both for the alien spaceship—which featured some none too subtle references to female anatomy—and for the alien monster itself. The monster design was retained for all the **sequels** and remains one of the scariest genre creations in its angularity, its reptilian/insect-like qualities and, most of all, in its ferocious teeth. Unusually for a horror monster, it is just as disturbing in the light of day as it is lurking in the shadows. Giger's monster design for *Species* (1995), another **science fiction**/horror hybrid, was effective but lacked the impact of his earlier work.

GILLING, JOHN (1912–1984). Throughout the 1950s, the British screenwriter and director John Gilling specialized mainly in crime thrillers. However, he also had some early encounters with horror through his screenplays for **Tod Slaughter's** *The Greed of William Hart* (1948) and **Hammer's Jack the Ripper** thriller *Room to Let* (1950) and his direction of the horror **comedy** *Mother Riley Meets the Vampire* (1952), which starred **Bela Lugosi.** After the success of

Hammer horror in the late 1950s, horror became an important part of British film production, and Gilling, like many commercially minded directors of the day, moved more decisively into the genre. His first major horror project was the handsomely mounted *The Flesh and the Fiends* (1959), which told the story of graverobbers Burke and Hare and featured a dignified performance by **Peter Cushing**. *Shadow of the Cat* (1961) was an eerie thriller that, while not technically a Hammer production, utilized many Hammer personnel. Gilling never seemed particularly comfortable working for Hammer, but he did some of his best work for the company during the 1960s. He wrote the screenplay for **Terence Fisher**'s unusual horror film *The Gorgon* (1964) and went on to direct what are sometimes known as Hammer's Cornish horrors—*The Plague of the Zombies* (1966) and *The Reptile* (1966). Shot back to back, these were stylish and atmospheric tales that undermined many of the moral certainties often associated with Hammer horror and which anticipated the anti-authoritarian attitudes that would appear in **British horror** from the late 1960s onwards. *The Mummy's Shroud* (1967), Gilling's next Hammer horror, was more conventional, however. *La cruz del diablo* (*The Devil's Cross*) (1975), Gilling's final film, was made in Spain, where the director spent his latter years.

His other genre credits include the **science fiction**-horror films *The Gamma People* (1956) and *The Night Caller* (1965).

GIRDLER, WILLIAM (1947–1978). The films made by American director William Girdler were often openly derivative but at their best they were also lively and entertaining affairs. Early horror work included *Asylum of Satan* (1972) and the memorably titled *Three on a Meathook* (1972). More mainstream was the blaxploitation film *Abby* (1974), sometimes described as a black version of *The Exorcist* (1973). *Grizzly* (1976) looked to *Jaws* (1975) for its inspiration, while *Day of the Animals* (1977) was a by-the-numbers **revenge of nature** story. Girdler's final film, *The Manitou* (1978), was described by the director himself as a cross between *The Exorcist* and *Star Wars* (1977). It wasn't, but it was fast-moving enough to satisfy as exploitation fare. Girdler died in a helicopter crash before the film was released. *See also* AMERICAN HORROR.

GOBLIN. The Italian rock group Goblin has been responsible for some distinctive horror **music**, especially for director **Dario Argento**. The group was founded in the 1970s by Claudio Simonetti and Massimo Morante, although the overall lineup has changed several times over the years. The group's fondness for repetitive themes conjoined with weird sounds was apparent in their debut score for Argento's **giallo** *Profondo rosso* (*Deep Red*) (1975), where it perfectly illustrated the fixated world of an obsessed **serial killer**, and in their nerve-jangling music (written under the name The Goblins) for Argento's **witchcraft** film *Suspiria* (1977), where it very effectively conveyed a sense of being trapped in a world full of magic. Billed either as Goblin or under the names of individual members of the group, they went on to produce music for Argento's *Tenebre* (*Tenebrae*) (1982), *Phenomena* (1985), *La Chiesa* (*The Church*) (1989), and *Nonhosonno* (*Sleepless*) (2001). Other Goblin horror scores include *Buio Omega* (*Beyond the Darkness*) (1979), *Contamination* (1980), and *Night of the Zombies* (1981), and the group also provided alternative scores for the Italian releases of **George Romero**'s *Martin* (1977) and *Dawn of the Dead* (1978) as well as the **Australian horror** *Patrick* (1978).

GOLDSMITH, JERRY (1929–2004). Jerry Goldsmith was one of the leading film composers of his generation. He worked successfully in all major genres but his interest in experimental and atonal **music** particularly suited him to fantasy-based films. His best-known horror score was for *The Omen* (1976), for which he deservedly won an Academy Award. The Gregorian-style chanting he utilized there powerfully conveyed the offscreen presence of the **Devil**. Goldsmith developed his score further in **sequels** *Damien—Omen 2* (1978) and *The Final Conflict* (1981), and subsequently the use of choral music in horror became something of a cliché. Dissonance was mixed with more lyrical passages in his highly effective music for *Alien* (1979), *Poltergeist* (1982), and *Psycho 2* (1983).

Goldsmith's other horror or horror-related scores include *The Mephisto Waltz* (1971), *The Other* (1972), *The Reincarnation of Peter Proud* (1975), *Magic* (1978), *Twilight Zone: The Movie* (1983), *Gremlins* (1984), *Poltergeist II: The Other Side* (1986), *The `Burbs* (1989), *Leviathan* (1989), *Warlock* (1989), *Gremlins 2: The New*

Batch (1990), *Deep Rising* (1998), *The **Mummy*** (1999), and *The Haunting* (1999).
When sections of his *Omen* score showed up in the 2006 **remake**, it felt like an old friend returning.

THE GOLEM. The figure of the Golem, who is fashioned from clay and then magically brought to life, came originally from Jewish folklore. So far as his cinematic existence was concerned, he first appeared in the German production *Der Golem* (1915). Paul Wegener co-directed this now lost film (along with Henrik Galeen) and also starred as the Golem. Wegener returned to the role in the **comedy** *Der Golem und die Tänzerin* (*The Golem and the Dancing Girl*) (1917), although his character was here only pretending to be the monster. Considerably more serious was *Der Golem, wie er in die Welt kam* (*The Golem: How He Came Into The World*) (1920), with Wegener again starring and also co-directing, this time with Carl Boese. This version has come to be seen as a classic example of **Expressionism**, and its depiction of an oversized, lumbering monster also seems to have been an influence on **James Whale's** *Frankenstein* (1931). Julien Duvivier directed a French version, *Le Golem*, in 1936, *Císaruv pekar a pekaruv císar* (*The Emperor's Baker and the Golem*) (1951) was a Czech comic version, and the Golem also showed up in the **British horror** film *It* (1966).

GORDON, BERT I. (1922–). The American director Bert I. Gordon specialized in cheap and cheerful horror movies and was a major contributor to the lurid exploitation scene of the 1950s. His films often featured enlarged or magnified monsters, to the extent that this became a kind of authorial signature; as horror **fans** have pointed out, even his initials spell out the word *Big*. *The Cyclops* (1957), *The Amazing Colossal Man* (1957), and its **sequel** *War of the Colossal Beast* (1958) dealt with the transformation of humans into menacing giants, *Beginning of the End* (1957) offered giant grasshoppers and *Earth vs. The Spider* (*The Spider*) (1958) a giant spider, while *Attack of the Puppet People* (1958) went in another direction by engineering the miniaturization of some of its human characters. Gordon's treatment of this material was not particularly original and the special effects—which were often done by Gordon himself—were basic. However, these films sometimes have a B-movie energy and, in retrospect, possess a kind of period innocence that can make them appealing if one is feeling indulgent. In the latter part of his career, Gordon maintained his interest in magnification and miniaturization with two fantasy projects, *The Magic Sword* (1962) and *Village of the Giants* (1965), and the horror films *Empire of the Ants* (1977) and *The Food of the Gods* (1976), both of which were extremely loose adaptations of stories by H. G. Wells. He also directed, with varying degrees of success, **psychological thrillers**, namely *Tormented* (1960) and *Picture Mommy Dead* (1966), and the **witchcraft** dramas *Necromancy* (1972), *Burned at the Stake* (1981), and *Satan's Princess* (1990). Some of Gordon's films have featured on, and been sent up in, the cult **television** series *Mystery Science Theater 3000* (1988–1999). *See also* AMERICAN HORROR.

GORDON, STUART (1947–). The writer-director Stuart Gordon had an auspicious start to his career in horror with the **H. P. Lovecraft** adaptations *Re-Animator* (1985) and *From Beyond* (1986). Lovecraft's stories are often humorless but Gordon successfully introduced humor and a substantial amount of **gore** without sacrificing a Lovecraftian distinctiveness. From the atmospheric *Dolls* (1987) onwards, he has worked mainly in Europe, where he shot *The Pit and the Pendulum* (1990), the **television** film *Daughter of Darkness* (1990), and *Castle Freak* (1995). *Dagon* (2001), which was made in Spain for the **Fantastic Factory** company, marked his return to Lovecraft. It had a powerful sense of place and some impressive sequences although it lacked the overall cohesion of Gordon's previous Lovecraft films. His other genre directorial credits include the dark **psychological thriller** *King of the Ants* (2003) and episodes for the television series *Masters of Horror* (2005). He also contributed to the screenplays for **Abel Ferrara**'s *Body Snatchers* (1993) and for frequent collaborator **Brian Yuzna**'s *The Dentist* (1996) as well as, perhaps surprisingly, working on the story for family film *Honey, I Shrunk the Kids* (1989).

GORE. The horror genre's reliance on gore—or "splatter," to use a term often deployed in horror criticism—has proved one of its more disreputable features. For some, the graphic display of bodily fluids, mutilation and evisceration involves an appeal to degraded and base elements in the human character. For horror theorists and critics, however, the genre's gore effects relate more to a fascination with the body and its workings, a fascination that is marginalized or suppressed in other, more decorous areas of our culture. In addition, horror **fans** often seem more interested in appreciating the **makeup** techniques that produce the gore effects than they are in just witnessing moments of nastiness; for these fans at least there is an aesthetic of gore at work in horror cinema.

American horror films of the 1930s and 1940s were restrained so far as gore was concerned, with barely a glimpse of blood, let alone any more disturbing fluid or body part. However, the general relaxation of **censorship** that took place during the 1950s permitted the **British horror** company **Hammer** to introduce considerable amounts of blood, woundings and mutilation into its product, with the effectiveness of such elements underlined by the fact that the films were being made in color; in particular, the company's **Frankenstein** films contributed to the development of **surgical horror**, which would become a significant feature of European horror and a key location for gore effects. Although controversial on their initial release, Hammer films seem fairly tame now. By contrast, the ultra-low-budget 1960s work of American director **Herschell Gordon Lewis**—sometimes dubbed the "Master of Gore" or the "Father of Gore"—was both cruder and more confrontational than the conventional Hammer output. Films such as *Blood Feast* (1963) or *Two Thousand Maniacs* (1964) offered, respectively, the spectacle of a tongue torn from someone's mouth or a scene in which someone is placed in a barrel of spikes that is then rolled down a hill. The special effects were mercifully unconvincing but the sense of having seen something transgressive lingered.

Lewis worked on the margins of commercial cinema, but the gore with which he had become associated entered the mainstream of horror from the late 1960s onwards, reflecting a tougher and more cynical mood within the genre. *Night of the Living Dead* (1968) and *Dawn of the Dead* (1978) depicted the eating of flesh, *Deranged* (1974) had very explicit and protracted mutilation scenes, *The Exorcist* (1973) made imaginative use of urine and vomit, and **Italian horror** films of the 1970s and 1980s offered a panoply of unnerving eye injuries and eviscerations. Meanwhile the innovative Canadian horror films directed by **David Cronenberg**—among them *The Parasite Murders* (*They Came From Within, Shivers*) (1975) and *The Brood* (1979)—helped to inaugurate what came to be known as **body horror**, a type of horror in which the spectacle of bodies that are out of control, cancerous or mutating becomes a source of macabre fascination. The American **slasher** films of the late 1970s and early 1980s also contained less cerebral but nevertheless inventive variations on slashing, stabbing and bludgeoning.

Since the 1980s, the horror genre has certainly remained gory, with its gore effects ever more realistic. However, the shock value of such imagery appears largely to have worn off. Recent American productions such as *Wrong Turn* (2003) or the 2003 **remake** of *The Texas Chainsaw Massacre* are, scene for scene, probably gorier, and more convincingly gory, than many of their 1970s counterparts but the way the gore is represented has become more familiar and conventionalized. It is now only the occasional horror that breaches the conventional and takes us by surprise. **Takashi Miike's** *Ôdishon* (*Audition*) (1999) is one such film with its unexpected climactic transformation into an extreme experience of **torture**, while a new wave of hard-edged horror in the early 2000s—including *The Devil's Rejects* (2005), *Hostel* (2005) and *Wolf Creek* (2005)—signaled its difference from the glossy **teenage horror** popular in the 1990s by foregrounding a particularly visceral form of gore. It seems from this that gore has become one of the many resources from which horror filmmakers can draw, and, like all the other resources, it can be deployed with greater or less effectiveness and imagination.

GOTHIC. The term *gothic* has several meanings, although these all tend to involve notions of wildness, excess and transgression. Gothic can denote a particular architectural style. It is also a period in literary history, usually defined as running from the 1760s through to the 1820s (although some literary historians see it as beginning earlier and ending later), a period in which the trappings of later horror films—notably castles, dungeons and sinister aristocrats—are first established. Mary Shelley's famous 1818 novel *Frankenstein* is a gothic novel in this sense. However, *Frankenstein* can potentially be thought of as gothic in a generic sense as well inasmuch as it seems to belong to a cultural category that in various forms runs through to the present day and which incorporates much, if not all, of horror cinema. From this perspective, gothic becomes a pervasive cultural mode, one that offers a space within which conventional notions of realism can be undermined or critiqued.

Gothic has more specialized usages too. Gothic horror usually refers to horror narratives set in the past, with **Hammer** horror a good example of this. More recently, gothic shortened to "goth" has described a subculture involving fashion, literature, **music**, art and film.

It is hard to make all these usages cohere together, and harder still to relate them in any straightforward way to the horror film. While some horror films seem devoid of influences that might be described as gothic, others—and not just the period-set ones—do draw upon recognizably gothic conventions. For example, the figure of Hannibal Lecter in *The Silence of the Lambs* (1991) can be traced back to the sinister but charming villains found in the gothic novels of Ann Radcliffe. Equally, some horror films might be seen as undermining our sense of the real in a gothic manner, but by no means all. Matters are complicated yet further by the fact that the term *gothic* has over the years acquired some decidedly upmarket connotations (although it was originally a rather vulgar term) while the term *horror*—which, in the context of popular fiction production, does not appear as a generic label until the 1930s—retains a certain vulgarity.

It follows that attempts to subsume horror into a broader gothic category or genre are problematic inasmuch as they can end up oversimplifying both gothic and horror. At the same time, horror cinema clearly has a relation or, more particularly, relations, with gothic in most of its definitions. One can argue that the usefulness of concepts of the gothic to an understanding of horror cinema depends ultimately on the precision of their use and the contexts within which they are deployed.

GOUGH, MICHAEL (1917–). For **Hammer** horror, the British character actor Michael Gough played pompous characters in *Dracula* (*Horror of Dracula*) (1958) and *The Phantom of the Opera* (1962). Elsewhere, he often showed up as an outright villain and delivered his performances with some relish. He was a mad writer in *Horrors of the Black Museum* (1959), a mad zookeeper in *Black Zoo* (1963), and a **mad scientist** in *Konga* (1961) and *Horror Hospital* (1973). He also had the unusual distinction, for an established actor at least, of playing a corpse in *The Legend of Hell House* (1973), an interesting challenge for someone whose work often possessed a manic intensity. In the latter part of his career, he worked with **Tim Burton**; he was manservant Alfred in *Batman* (1989) and also featured in Burton's homage to classic horror *Sleepy Hollow* (1999).

Other horror credits include *What a Carve Up* (1961), *Dr. Terror's House of Horrors* (1964), *The Skull* (1965), *Curse of the Crimson Altar* (1968), *Berserk!* (1968), *The Corpse* (1970), *Trog* (1970), *Satan's Slave* (1976), and *The Serpent and the Rainbow* (1988).

GRANT, ARTHUR (1915–1972). Although he worked in a variety of genres, the British cinematographer Arthur Grant was most significant as a contributor to **Hammer** horror. While **Jack Asher** photographed most of the classic early Hammer horror productions, Grant did effective black-and-white work on *The Abominable Snowman* (1957), *The Stranglers of Bombay* (1959), *Paranoiac* (1963), and *The Damned* (*These are the Damned*) (1963). He was also responsible for some of the more stylish and visually pleasing Hammers of the 1960s and 1970s, among them *The Curse of the Werewolf* (1961), *The Plague of the Zombies* (1966), *The Reptile* (1966), *Frankenstein Created Woman* (1967), *Quatermass and the Pit* (*Five Million Years to Earth*) (1967), *The Devil Rides Out* (1968), *Dracula Has Risen from the Grave* (1968), *Frankenstein Must Be Destroyed* (1969), *Taste the Blood of Dracula* (1970), and *Blood from the Mummy's Tomb* (1971). In addition, he photographed **Roger Corman**'s outstanding **Edgar Allan Poe** adaptation, *The Tomb of Ligeia* (1964).

GRAU, JORGE (1930–). Throughout the 1960s, the Spanish director Jorge Grau specialized in **documentaries** and dramas, although his best-known films, internationally at least, are the two horrors he made in the early 1970s. Interviews with Grau suggest that he is not entirely comfortable with being classified as a horror director, but he did bring something distinctive to the genre. *Ceremonia sangrienta* (*Blood Castle*) (1973) was a thoughtful and atmospheric version of the story of the notorious medieval **serial killer** Countess **Elizabeth Bathory**. *Non si deve profanare il sonno dei morti* (*The Living Dead* *at the Manchester Morgue*) (1974)—which was filmed in England—was a weird **zombie** film, full of the requisite **gore** but also containing moments of surreal dislocation. *See also* SPANISH HORROR.

GRIFFITH, CHARLES B. (1930–2007). During the 1950s, the screenwriter Charles B. Griffith worked regularly with producer-director **Roger Corman** on low-budget projects such as *Not of This Earth* (1957), *Attack of the Crab Monsters* (1957), and *The Undead* (1957). He displayed a flair for humor in Corman's **comedy**-horrors *A Bucket of Blood* (1959), *The Little Shop of Horrors* (1960), and *Creature from the Haunted Sea* (1961) and also wrote Monte Hellman's *Beast from Haunted Cave* (1959). In the mid-1970s, he co-wrote the Corman-produced black comedy *Death Race 2000* (1975) and made his directorial horror debut with yet another comedy-horror, *Dr. Heckyl and Mr. Hype* (1980).

– H –

HALLER, DANIEL (1926–). During the late 1950s and first half of the 1960s, Daniel Haller was an art director and/or production designer working mainly for **Roger Corman**. Early horror credits included the Corman-directed *A Bucket of Blood* (1959), *The Little Shop of Horrors* (1960), and *The Wasp Woman* (1960) and the Corman-produced *Night of the Blood Beast* (1958) and *Attack of the Giant Leeches* (1959). Corman's bigger-budgeted adaptations of **Edgar Allan Poe**'s writings afforded Haller more of an opportunity to come up with some striking designs, which accordingly he did for *House of Usher* (1960), *Pit and the Pendulum* (1961), *The Premature Burial* (1962), *Tales of Terror* (1962), *The Raven* (1963), *The Haunted Palace* (1963), and *The Masque of the Red Death* (1964). He also designed Corman's *Tower of London* (1962), *X: The Man with X-Ray Eyes* (1963), and *The Terror* (1963), as well as **Reginald LeBorg**'s *Diary of a Madman* (1963).

Haller switched to film direction in the mid-1960s. *Die, Monster, Die!* (1965), his debut, was a stylish adaptation of a story by **H. P. Lovecraft**. He later returned to the genre with a more uneven Lovecraft film, *The Dunwich Horror* (1970). Thereafter he worked mainly for **television**.

HALLOWEEN (1978). *Halloween* helped to establish the **slasher** film as an important format in **American horror** cinema and also made **Jamie Lee Curtis** a horror star. However, the **sequels** it generated did not always capitalize on its reputation and its achievements. Director **John Carpenter**'s original was innovative and atmospheric in its depiction of killer Michael Myers returning to his hometown and causing mayhem. *Halloween II* (1981), which was co-scripted and co-produced by Carpenter but directed by Rick Rosenthal, appeared at a time when many of the conventions introduced by Carpenter—the emphasis on **startle effects**, the killer coming back to life just when everyone thinks he is dead—were fast becoming clichés, and consequently the film did not stand out from its fellow slashers. A Carpenter-devised plot twist revealing that the Curtis character was the killer's sister was potentially interesting but this idea was not developed until later in the cycle. In any event, Curtis looked too old by this stage to play a hapless babysitter (although the film was meant to take place on the same night as its predecessor).

Halloween III: Season of the Witch (1982) was an unusual followup in that it abandoned completely the storyline and characters established in the first two films and dealt instead with an evil toymaker planning to murder **children** on Halloween night. Based on a story by an uncredited **Nigel Kneale**, the film was quirky but not particularly successful, and Michael Myers (along with his nemesis, the psychiatrist played by **Donald Pleasence**) was resurrected for *Halloween 4: The Return of Michael Myers* (1988), *Halloween 5* (1989) and *Halloween: The Curse of Michael Myers* (1995). By this stage, Carpenter was not involved—although the distinctive theme music he had composed for the first film was retained—and these films, in common with the concurrent *Friday the 13th* cycle, developed the supernatural aspects of the monster, aspects that had only been hinted at in *Halloween*. The success of *Scream* (1996) encouraged a further revisioning of the cycle in the light of the new **teenage horror**. Consequently, *Halloween H20: 20 Years Later* (1998) ignored the storyline of Parts 3–6 and refocused on some *Scream*-like teenagers. More interestingly, it also brought the Curtis character back and explored her relationship with her murderous brother. *Halloween: Resurrection* (2002) followed.

In 2007, **Rob Zombie**'s **remake** of the original *Halloween* was released.

HALPERIN, VICTOR (1895–1983). The director Victor Halperin made the extraordinary, independently produced horror film *White Zombie* (1932). Starring **Bela Lugosi** as principal villain, this was stylish, atmospheric, and moody, and it remains one of the great zombie films. The narrative was engaging, the performances effective, and the film also featured an innovative use of spirituals on its soundtrack. It is all the more surprising then that Halperin's subsequent horror films were so indifferent. The **possession** drama *Supernatural* (1933) was effective enough, with a starring role for Carole Lombard, but it lacked the brilliance of *White Zombie*, while *Revolt of the Zombies* (1936) and *Torture Ship* (1939) were lackluster productions that failed to make any impact. *See also* AMERICAN HORROR.

HAMMER. The Hammer company was the main producer of **British horror** films from the late 1950s through to the mid-1970s. Hammer was initially set up in 1934 by William Hinds, a part-time **music** hall performer whose stage persona of "Will Hammer" gave the company its name. In partnership with Enrique Carreras, he produced a few films—including a **Bela Lugosi** vehicle, *The Mystery of the Mary Celeste* (1935)—before the company closed down in the late 1930s.

Hammer was re-established as a production arm of Exclusive, a Hinds-Carreras owned distribution company, in 1949. **James Carreras**, Enrique's son, was the managing director while **Anthony Hinds**, William's son, became its main producer (and **Michael Carreras**, James Carreras's son, also took on some production duties). Initially, Hammer was a distinctly parochial outfit that specialized in cheap and cheerful adaptations of popular British radio series such as *Dick Barton* and *The Adventures of PC 49*. As a result of a distribution deal struck with American producer Robert Lippert in the early 1950s, the company subsequently switched to more cosmopolitan, although still low-budget, thrillers, with many of these featuring fading or minor American stars. In 1951, it also based itself at Bray Studios, a converted country house in Windsor, which would be its production home for the next 15 years.

During the first half of the 1950s, Hammer had half-heartedly dabbled in **science fiction**, with *Four Sided Triangle* (1953) and *Spaceways* (1953). However, the substantial success enjoyed by its science fiction/horror hybrid *The Quatermass Xperiment* (*The Creeping Unknown*) (1955) seems to have taken the company by surprise. Adapted, like so many Hammer projects, from a pre-existing source—in this case **Nigel Kneale**'s groundbreaking **television** series for the British Broadcasting Corporation—the film offered higher production values than usual and was slickly directed by Val Guest. Hammer would subsequently make two *Quatermass* **sequels**, as well as another SF/horror, *X—the Unknown* (1956).

The idea for a color **remake** of the **Frankenstein** story actually came from the American writer-producer **Milton Subotsky** (who later would set up his own British horror company, **Amicus**), although Subotsky took no active part in the production of *The Curse of Frankenstein* (1957). As directed by **Terence Fisher**, who would become Hammer's main horror director, the resulting film was graphic, shocking and quite unlike anything seen before either in British cinema or in horror cinema. Its huge international success encouraged Hammer to develop more color period horrors, starting with *Dracula* (*Horror of Dracula*) (1958), a film that confirmed **Peter Cushing**'s stardom after his performance in *The Curse of Frankenstein* and made an international star out of **Christopher Lee**. Other producers, in Britain, Italy and Spain, also sought to cash in on Hammer's success, to the extent that Hammer can be seen as partly responsible for the boom in European horror production that took place from the late 1950s onwards.

For the next few years, Hammer worked hard to consolidate its horror formula, which usually involved charismatic male authority figures, buxom women and scenarios charged with sensuality and violence. Its rapid serial production was aided by the fact that much of the Hammer team—which included, alongside Fisher, writer **Jimmy Sangster**, cinematographers **Jack Asher** and **Arthur Grant**, production designer **Bernard Robinson**, editor James Needs and composer **James Bernard**—was already established before the company's turn to horror. In this period, Hammer produced its first Frankenstein and Dracula sequels with *The Revenge of Frankenstein* (1958) and *The Brides of Dracula* (1960) (although Dracula himself did not appear in this). It also revived the **werewolf** in *The Curse of the Werewolf* (1961) and **Dr. Jekyll and Mr. Hyde** in *The Two Faces of Dr. Jekyll* (1960), as well as offering new versions of *The Mummy* (1959) and *The Hound of the Baskervilles* (1959) and the **mad scientist** drama *The Man Who Could Cheat Death* (1959). As if this were not enough, it also initiated a series of **psychological thrillers**, beginning with **Seth Holt**'s *Taste of Fear* (*Scream of Fear*) (1961).

The box-office disappointment of *The Phantom of the Opera* (1962) brought this frenetic period to an end. For the remainder of the 1960s, Hammer continued to churn out the horrors, and some of its films were inventive and accomplished—for example **Don Sharp**'s *The Kiss of the Vampire* (1962), Fisher's *The Gorgon* (1964), **John Gilling**'s *The Plague of the Zombies* (1966) and his *The Reptile* (1966), and Fisher's *The Devil Rides Out* (1968). The Dracula, Frankenstein and Mummy films that appeared were more hit and miss, although good work was still being done here, especially by Fisher. Much the same could be said of Hammer's psychological thrillers, which mixed the routine with the worthwhile (with Holt's 1965 film *The Nanny* a particularly outstanding piece of work in this area). The company also diversified in this period, successfully with an exotic adventure *She* (1965) and the dinosaur film *One Million Years B.C.* (1966), and disastrously with the science fiction/**western** *Moon Zero Two* (1969). In 1968 Hammer produced the **television** horror series *Journey to the Unknown* and also received the Queen's Award for Industry.

By the 1970s, Hammer's period horror format was starting to look very tired, and the company's attempts to regenerate itself through increasing the sex, violence and general sensationalism in its films were not uniformly successful. The lesbian vampire film *The Vampire Lovers* (1970) did well at the box office and generated two sequels, *Lust for a Vampire* (1971) and *Twins of Evil* (1971). Other innovative projects such as *Dr. Jekyll and Sister Hyde* (1971) and *Captain Kronos—Vampire Hunter* (1972) and, most of all, the kung fu/horror hybrid *The Legend of the Seven Golden Vampires* (1974) smacked of desperation and did not catch the public's imagination. Good work, if not necessarily commercially successful work, was being done in this period, mainly by the younger directors who had been moving into British horror since the late 1960s. Three films from **Peter Sasdy**,

Taste the Blood of Dracula (1970) (the last good Hammer Dracula film), *Countess Dracula* (1971), and *Hands of the Ripper* (1971), along with Robert Young's *Vampire Circus* (1972) and **Peter Sykes'** *Demons of the Mind* (1972), offered incisive critiques of those authority figures who had been so prominent in the initial cycle of Hammer production back in the late 1950s. Hammer's final horror film, Sykes' Satanic thriller *To the Devil a Daughter* (1976), continued this theme, as well as attempting to harness itself to the success of the **American horror** film *The Exorcist* (1973). Unfortunately, it was not enough, and Hammer ceased horror production.

Under a different management regime, Hammer subsequently produced two more television series, *Hammer House of Horror* (1980) and *Hammer House of Mystery and Suspense* (1984).

HARDY, ROBIN (1939–). The British director Robin Hardy's reputation rests almost entirely on one formidable horror film, which also happened to mark his cinematic directorial debut—*The Wicker Man* (1973). This study of the survival of pagan beliefs on a remote Scottish island was both disturbing and richly textured. The film was not widely appreciated on its initial release and was cut by its distributor, but a restored version was issued in 2001 and *The Wicker Man* is now considered a cult classic. It was remade by Neil LaBute in 2006. Hardy's second—and to date only other—film was *The Fantasist* (1986), an account of a **serial killer** at work in Dublin that was ambitious but which lacked the resonances of *The Wicker Man*. *See also* BRITISH HORROR.

HARK, TSUI (1950–). The Vietnamese-born producer-director Tsui Hark works mainly in Hong Kong, where he has established a distinctive, much-imitated style based on rapid editing of action scenes. He specializes in martial arts thrillers but has occasionally introduced into his films elements of supernatural horror drawn from Chinese mythology. *Die ban* (*The Butterfly Murders*) (1979), his directorial debut, combined horror with martial arts, while his second film, *Diyu wu men* (*Hell Has no Gates, Kung Fu Cannibals*) (1980) added **comedy** to the generic mix. The director's international breakthrough came with *Suk san: Sun Suk san geen hap* (*Zu Warriors, Warriors from the Magic Mountain*) (1983), a delirious fantasy featuring martial arts and demons. More success came with *Sinnui yauwan* (*A Chinese Ghost Story*) (1987), which was directed by Siu-Tung Ching and produced by Hark for his Film Workshop company. Another period supernatural fantasy, this contained one of horror's more unnerving images, that of a monster's astonishingly large tongue enveloping its victims. Hark went on to produce the first **sequel** *Sinnui yauwan II* (*A Chinese Ghost Story Part II*) (1990) and co-directed the second, *Sinnui yauwan III: Do do do* (*A Chinese Ghost Story III*) (1991). Other horror-related credits have included *Shu shan zheng zhuan* (*Zu Warriors*) (2001), a **remake** of Hark's own *Suk san: Sun Suk san geen hap* and his production *The Era of Vampires* (*Tsui Hark's Vampire Hunters*) (2002). *See also* CHINESE HORROR.

HARLIN, RENNY (1959–). The Finnish director Renny Harlin has worked mainly in the United States, where he has alternated action spectaculars such as *Die Hard 2* (1990) and *Cliffhanger* (1993) with horror films. His American debut was *Prison* (1988), a low budget **ghost** story that combined a formulaic narrative with an impressive sense of atmosphere. Harlin followed this with the bigger-budgeted *A Nightmare on Elm Street 4: The Dream Master* (1988), one of the more stylish entries to this popular cycle. Having subsequently established himself as a director of blockbusters, he returned to horror with *Deep Blue Sea* (1999), an effective horror-action hybrid about genetically engineered sharks, and the **serial killer** drama *Mindhunters* (2004). When **Paul Schrader**'s version of the *Exorcist* prequel was shelved by its producers, Harlin was hired to direct a different version of the prequel. Unfortunately *Exorcist: The Beginning* (2004) was not well received. Harlin has also directed the supernatural thriller *The Covenant* (2006). *See also* AMERICAN HORROR.

HARRINGTON, CURTIS (1926–2007). The director Curtis Harrington began his career making experimental short films, including an adaptation of **Edgar Allan Poe**'s *The Fall of the House of Usher*. He moved into more mainstream production with *Night Tide* (1961), an eerie **Val Lewton**-influenced low-budget drama in which a sailor (played by Dennis Hopper) becomes obsessed with a mermaid-impersonator in a sideshow. Harrington's next feature was *Queen of Blood* (1966), a cult **science fiction**/horror hybrid in which astronauts encountered an extraterrestrial female **vampire**. A move upmarket followed with the disturbing **psychological thriller** *Games* (1967), which starred Simone Signoret and contained early performances from James Caan and Katharine Ross; it also inaugurated the director's fondness for casting older women in major roles. Harrington stayed with psychological horror for his next few films. *How Awful About Allan* (1970), which starred **Anthony Perkins**, was made for American **television**, while *Whoever Slew Auntie Roo?* (1971), a perverse retelling of the Hansel and Gretel story in which the **children** turn out to be far from innocent, was produced in Britain. The enjoyably over-the-top *What's the Matter with Helen?* (1971) was clearly intended to repeat the success of **Robert Aldrich**'s *What Ever Happened to Baby Jane?* (1962) in its casting of two ageing Hollywood female stars, in this case Shelley Winters and Debbie Reynolds, but it was more compassionate than Aldrich's somewhat cruel film. Harrington subsequently made some of the best 1970s television horror films, notably *The Cat Creature* (1973), *Killer Bees* (1974), *The Dead Don't Die* (1975), and *Devil Dog—The Hound of Hell* (1978). His experience of directing the supernatural **possession** thriller *Ruby* (1977) was less happy, however. Piper Laurie was the ageing star this time, and Harrington created some suitably creepy atmospherics around the drive-in cinema that was the film's main setting. Unfortunately, he was replaced by Stephanie Rothman before shooting concluded. Subsequently Harrington has worked mainly for television, although in 2002 he directed and starred in the short film *Usher*, his second adaptation of Poe's *The Fall of the House of Usher*. *See also* AMERICAN HORROR.

HARTFORD-DAVIS, ROBERT (1923–1977). The British director Robert Hartford-Davis was an idiosyncratic talent who worked largely in the low-budget exploitation sector and who made some interestingly perverse **British horror** films. The period horror drama *The Black Torment* (1964) was one of his more conventional projects. An obvious attempt to cash in on the success of **Hammer** horror, it lacked Hammer's panache and turned out to be a rather dull affair. Hartford-Davis returned more profitably to the genre in the 1970s, a period in which iconoclastic directors such as **Pete Walker** and **Norman J. Warren** were redefining British horror through a new emphasis on contemporary subjects and a questioning of social authority. Such elements were evident in Hartford-Davis's *The Fiend* (1971), an intensely claustrophobic but compelling film in which religious repression was associated with psychopathic violence. *Incense for the Damned* (1970) was an ambitious modern **vampire** story that also offered a critique of the social establishment. However, the film was re-edited by its producers (and retitled *Bloodsuckers* for some markets) and Hartford-Davis removed his name from the credits and was billed instead as Michael Burrowes. He ended up making blaxploitation films in the United States.

HATTON, RONDO (1894–1946). The actor Rondo Hatton appeared regularly in small roles in American cinema from 1930 onwards, but it was his performance as the murderous Creeper in the **Sherlock Holmes** film *The Pearl of Death* (1944) that brought him to public attention. Subsequently he was a villainous henchman in *The Jungle Captive* (1945) and *The Spider Woman Strikes Back* (1946) and went on to play a horribly deformed villain called the Creeper—albeit not the Creeper from *Pearl of Death*—in *House of Horrors* (*Joan Medford Is Missing*) (1946) and *The Brute Man* (1946). Unfortunately for Hatton, the disfigured facial features that so suited him to screen villainy were not the product of **makeup** but instead the result of a progressive medical condition called acromegaly. To modern viewers, this smacks of exploitation, and watching these films in the knowledge of Hatton's problems can be a discomforting experience. Whether this was how they were perceived at the time of their release is not clear, although the fact that they were in the main commercially successful suggests that there was either a greater public tolerance of or indifference towards this kind of thing back in the 1940s. In any event, Hatton's career offers an extreme case of how far some filmmakers were prepared to go in order to achieve their effects.

HAYERS, SIDNEY (1921–2000). Like a number of other British directors, Sidney Hayers serviced the boom in **British horror** production in the late 1950s and early 1960s without displaying any longterm commitment to the genre. His two main horror films turned out to be accomplished and striking, although the fact that they were so different from each other stylistically and thematically suggested that here was a director who was not particularly interested in imposing his own personality on his work. *Circus of Horrors* (1960) was a gaudy horror melodrama in which an unscrupulous surgeon carries out his illicit trade under the cover of a circus and ruthlessly murders anyone who threatens him. It was from the same company that produced **Michael Powell**'s similarly gaudy *Peeping Tom* (1960) and, while lacking that film's intelligence, it was energetic and inventive (especially in its murder scenes). *Night of the Eagle (Burn, Witch, Burn!)* (1962) was more restrained but arguably more effective in its depiction of **witchcraft** in a university setting. Thereafter, Hayers worked in other genres, although he briefly became a specialist in dark **psychological thrillers** with *Assault* (1971), *Revenge* (1971), and *Deadly Strangers* (1974) before moving to the United States where he spent the last part of his career directing for **television**.

HENENLOTTER, FRANK (1950–). *Basket Case* (1982), writer-director Frank Henenlotter's feature debut, made most other low-budget horror films look expensive. Despite its miniscule budget, the film was sufficiently inventive in its rendition of the story of separated conjoined twins, one of which is horribly deformed, to win the attention and approval of horror **fans**. *Basket Case 2* (1990) and *Basket Case 3: The Progeny* (1992) maintained the inventiveness, while *Brain Damage* (1988) managed to be simultaneously silly and disturbing and is often considered to be Henenlotter's best film. Henenlotter also directed the memorably titled but morally dubious *Frankenhooker* (1990), in which the hero attempts to reconstruct his dead girlfriend using body parts obtained from prostitutes. *See also* AMERICAN HORROR.

HERRMANN, BERNARD (1911–1975). The screeching violins that accompanied the shower murder in **Alfred Hitchcock**'s *Psycho* (1960) have echoed through horror **music** ever since, with *Psycho*-like orchestrations becoming something of a convention. The man responsible was distinguished composer Bernard Herrmann. Early in his career, he had written music suitable for the **Devil** in *The Devil and Daniel Webster* (1941) and had entered the world of a madman in *Hangover Square* (1945). His previous work for Hitchcock—which had included *Vertigo* (1958) and *North by Northwest* (1959)—had utilized the full resources of the orchestra, which made his strings-only score for *Psycho* all the more surprising; the composer later claimed that it was black and white music for a black and white film. He also wrote the orchestral score for the dark **psychological thriller** *Cape Fear* (1962)—which was reused for Martin Scorsese's 1991 **remake**—and was sound consultant for Hitchcock's music-less *The Birds* (1963). For much of the 1960s, Herrmann's type of film music was perceived as old-fashioned and he was not much in demand, for American films at least. Instead he worked for François Truffaut on two films and also wrote the music for the British psychological thriller *Twisted Nerve* (1968). During the 1970s, a new generation of filmmakers, who were more appreciative of the expressive potential of Herrmann's music, hired him for their films. **Brian De Palma** used him for *Sisters* (1973) and *Obsession* (1976), and **Larry Cohen** managed to get a particularly discordant score for his "monstrous baby on the loose" drama *It's Alive!* (1974). Herrmann's final score was for Scorsese's *Taxi Driver* (1976), which, in its shocking violence, was also a kind of horror film.

HESSLER, GORDON (1930–). The German-born director Gordon Hessler contributed to the modernization of **British horror** that took place from the late 1960s onwards. Unlike other filmmakers who at this time were offering new ideas and approaches—among them directors **Michael Reeves** and **Peter Sasdy** and writer **Christopher Wicking**—Hessler had already been in the industry for some years before turning to horror. He had worked in the United States on the **television** show *Alfred Hitchcock Presents* and had also directed two British thrillers, *Catacombs* (1964) and *The Last Shot You Hear* (1968). *The Oblong Box* (1969), his first horror film, had originally been intended as a Michael Reeves project. Like all of Hessler's British horror films, it starred **Vincent Price** and was made for **American International Pictures (AIP)**, which was involved in several co-productions with British companies in this period. While *The Oblong Box* was not distinctive thematically, it did show off a busy visual style—with numerous apparently unmotivated camera movements—quite different from the more stately approach adopted by the classic **Hammer** horrors of the late 1950s and early 1960s. This style evolved further in Hessler's next two horrors, the **science fiction**/horror hybrid *Scream and Scream Again* (1969) and the period horror *Cry of the Banshee* (1970), both of which had fragmented narratives and displayed what for the time was a fashionable identification with youth and a disregard for authority figures. *Murders in the Rue Morgue* (1971) was another AIP production, although shot in Spain and subject to some re-editing by producers as a result of Hessler's increasingly experimental approach to narrative structure. Hessler next made the thriller *Embassy* (1972) and the fantasy adventure *The Golden Voyage of Sinbad* (1973) before returning to the United States, where he specialized in television direction.

HICKOX, ANTHONY (1964–). The British-born son of director Douglas Hickox and award-winning editor Anne V. Coates, Anthony Hickox has himself directed some effective, if sometimes derivative, low-budget horror films alongside thrillers and action films. His genre debut was *Waxwork* (1988), which was followed by *Sundown: The Vampire in Retreat* (1991) and *Waxwork 2: Lost in Time* (1992). *Hellraiser III: Hell on Earth* (1992) was his most ambitious film to date and successfully managed the transition of the *Hellraiser* series from British to American settings, while *Warlock: The Armageddon* (1993) was another effective **sequel**. Since then, Hickox has worked away from horror, although he returned for the Dolph Lundgren **serial killer** drama *Jill Rips* (2000).

HINDS, ANTHONY (1922–). Anthony Hinds was one of the main producers and writers for **Hammer** Films. The son of the company's cofounder Willliam Hinds, he was a key figure in the formation of the distinctive Hammer horror formula, which combined a sensuous style with a fairly rigid moral framework. He produced many Hammer horrors, including *The Curse of Frankenstein* (1957) and *Dracula* (*Horror of Dracula*) (1958), and also wrote screenplays under the name "John Elder" for, among others, *The Curse of the Werewolf* (1961), *Kiss of the Vampire* (1962) and *The Evil of Frankenstein* (1964). He worked less often as producer after the mid-1960s but continued his writing with Hammer's *Frankenstein and the Monster from Hell* (1974) and Tyburn's *The Ghoul* (1974) and *Legend of the Werewolf* (1975).

HITCHCOCK, ALFRED (1899–1980). Only two of British-born director Alfred Hitchcock's 53 feature films are usually thought of as horrors, namely *Psycho* (1960) and *The Birds* (1963). Yet he remains an influential figure within the horror genre. In part this has to do with his contribution to the development of the **psychological thriller**, a format that often has horror-like qualities. *The Lodger* (1927) is an early example of a **serial killer** film, and Hitchcock would elaborate further on the figure of the serial killer in *Shadow of a Doubt* (1943), *Frenzy* (1972), and, not least, in *Psycho* where the killer was based loosely on real-life murderer **Ed Gein**. Even by Hitchcock's innovative standards, *Psycho* was a daring film, in its stark black-and-white appearance, its screeching musical score (provided by **Bernard Herrmann**), its relative openness about the representation of deviant sexuality, and its ruthless killing off of its heroine long before the film's conclusion. In many ways, it inaugurated the modern **American horror** film, although its full influence was not felt for several years. Hitchcock's follow-up, *The Birds*, was a fine example of open-ended **apocalyptic horror**, with the attacking birds pointedly left undefeated at the film's conclusion. Hitchcock himself suggested that *The Birds* offered an attack on the complacency of its characters, and this idea of the complacent getting their come-uppance has subsequently become an important feature of modern horror.

Hitchcock's long-running **television** show *Alfred Hitchcock Presents* (1955–1962) mixed crime stories with horror stories, suggesting that Hitchcock's persona encompassed both genres.

HOLLAND, TOM (1943–). The writer-director Tom Holland started out in horror through scripting the **television** horror film *The Initiation of Sarah* (1978), and followed this up with screenplays for the cult horror *The Beast Within* (1982) and the inventive **sequel** *Psycho II* (1983). He then got his chance to direct with the contemporary **vampire** thriller *Fright Night* (1985). This was a witty **teenage horror** film made in the wake of **Wes Craven**'s *A Nightmare on Elm Street* (1984) and sharing a similar playfulness. *Child's Play* (1988), which centered on a **doll** possessed by a **serial killer**'s soul, was genuinely suspenseful, although its impact has since been eroded by a series of increasingly jokey sequels. Subsequently, Holland has directed two **Stephen King** adaptations, *The Langoliers* (1995) for television and *Thinner* (1996) for the cinema. He has also contributed episodes to the television series *Tales from the Crypt* (1989–1996) and *Masters of Horror* (2005–). *See also* AMERICAN HORROR.

HOLT, SETH (1923–1971). The British filmmaker Seth Holt started out as an editor at Ealing Studios and also worked in this capacity on the realist classic *Saturday Night and Sunday Morning* (1960). Although he only directed six films, he has come to be considered as a significant talent whose promise was never realized. Half of his directorial output was for **Hammer**. *Taste of Fear* (*Scream of Fear*) (1961) was the first, and best, of a series of **psychological thrillers**, designed to complement the company's period horror productions. The elaborate, twist-ridden narrative was not very credible but Holt created an effective brooding atmosphere. In terms of its plot, the thriller *The Nanny* (1965) was more straightforward, but it was one of **Bette Davis**'s best later films and also offered a sharp and unsettling exploration of middle-class social mores. Holt died a week before the end of production on Hammer's *Blood from the Mummy's Tomb* (1971) and the film was completed by **Michael Carreras**. This loose adaptation of Bram Stoker's novel *Jewel of the Seven Stars* was a daring reinvention of the mummy story, and, like all of Holt's previous films, was clearly informed by a cinematic sensibility. One only has to compare it with some of the more literal-minded **British horror** films of the period to realize why Holt is so highly valued by critics.

HOMOSEXUALITY. The relation between homosexuality and horror cinema is an ambiguous one. When gay characters are featured in horror films (and they do not feature very often), they tend to be associated with the abnormal and the monstrous in a manner that might be construed as homophobic. A good case study here, in all its ambiguities, is the lesbian **vampire**. The connection made by horror between lesbianism and predatory vampirism in films such as *Dracula's Daughter* (1936), *The Vampire Lovers* (1970), *Les lèvres rouges* (*Daughters of Darkness*) (1971), or *Vampyres* (1974) can be seen as an expression both of male anxieties about female independence and of an equally masculine voyeurism regarding lesbianism. At the same time, however, some renditions of the lesbian vampire have been praised by critics for offering challenging images of powerful women. The association of male gayness with serial killing in *No Way To Treat a Lady* (1968), *Cruising* (1980), and *The Silence of the Lambs* (1991) has proved more contentious, although even here these figures tend to be located within worlds characterized by a broader breakdown in sexual identities.

To complicate matters yet further, some of the key artists involved in the development of the horror genre were themselves gay, with this arguably manifesting, usually implicitly, in their work. The most notable examples of this are **F. W. Murnau**, whose *Nosferatu* (1922) placed greater emphasis on homosocial relationships than most other versions of the Dracula story, and **James Whale**, whose *Bride of Frankenstein* (1935) has come to be regarded as a classic example of the camp aesthetic. Some critics have also detected homoerotic elements in apparently "straight" horror films, in the homosociality of many Frankenstein films, for example, or in the obscure desires of many of the genre's villains. Interestingly, the horror musical *The Rocky Horror Picture Show* (1975) has become a major cult success on the strength of its foregrounding of gayness. The invitation issued by the *Rocky Horror* phenomenon to its (presumably mainly straight) audience to dress up and participate in a cross-gendered experience might be seen in this respect as suggesting something about the horror experience more generally, namely that gender and sexuality within the genre are considerably less fixed than is sometimes supposed, and that the genre's representations of gayness are themselves caught up in, and need to be viewed in terms of, this broader uncertainty.

HOOPER, TOBE (1943–). For a film with a reputation for being wild and uncontrolled, *The Texas Chainsaw Massacre* (1974), turns out to be a remarkably disciplined piece of work. In large part this is due to the input of its director, Tobe Hooper (who also co-scripted and co-produced the film). His handling of the slow, measured transition from mildly disturbing scenes to the climactic terrorization of the film's **Final Girl** was confident and effective, his camerawork unobtrusively stylish, and he also managed to inject humor into the most appalling scenes in a manner that accentuated the terror rather than dispelling it. It is a testament to his skill that the film appeared far more violent and gory than it actually was, and it is now deservedly considered to be a major work of cinematic horror.

The notoriety of *The Texas Chainsaw Massacre* led to Hooper, who up until then had been a little-known Texas-based independent filmmaker, being typecast as a horror artist, and his subsequent career has combined significant achievements in the genre with some disappointing projects. *Eaten Alive* (*Death Trap*) (1977) was, like *Chainsaw*, a prime example of Southern **Gothic**. Its overwrought narrative, in which a demented hotelier feeds various guests to his pet crocodile, might not have been to everyone's taste, and the film lacked the scary intensity of *Chainsaw*. However, its bizarre atmosphere, which made it quite unlike any other 1970s **American horror**, underlined the originality of Hooper's approach; the film also featured an early appearance from horror star-to-be **Robert Englund**. Hooper subsequently directed the **television** miniseries adaptation of **Stephen King**'s **vampire** novel *Salem's Lot* (1979), which, although more conventional than his earlier work, still contained some genuinely unnerving and frightening moments. *The Funhouse* (1981) was Hooper's typically idiosyncratic contribution to the then popular **slasher** horror.

At this point in his career. Hooper moved onto bigger-budgeted films, but the results were not always successful. *Poltergeist* (1982) did very well at the box office, although many critics saw its loving rendition of the nuclear family under threat from malevolent supernatural forces as being more typical of its producer, **Steven Spielberg**, than it was of Hooper. Next came three films for the Cannon company. *Lifeforce* (1985) was a **science fiction**/horror in which a naked female alien-vampire threatens London; some saw the influence in it of *Quatermass* writer **Nigel Kneale**, although Kneale would probably not have produced anything quite so silly. However, *Lifeforce* was more enjoyable than either *Invaders from Mars* (1986) or *The Texas Chainsaw Massacre 2* (1986), both of which were unbalanced by clumsy moments of humor.

Throughout the 1990s, Hooper worked on some undistinguished low-budget projects, including *Spontaneous Combustion* (1990), *Night Terrors* (1993), *The Mangler* (1995), and *Crocodile* (2000). 2004 saw a welcome return to form with *Toolbox Murders*, an impressive reworking of a not-very-good 1970s horror film which demonstrated that Hooper had not lost the ability to generate claustrophobic scenes of discomfort and terror.

From the mid-1980s onwards, Hooper also directed some films for television—notably a segment of the horror **anthology** *Body Bags* (1993) and *I'm Dangerous Tonight* (1990)—and contributed to some television series, including *Amazing Stories* (1985–1987), *Freddy's Nightmares* (1988–1990), *Tales from the Crypt* (1989–1996), *Dark Skies* (1996–1997), *Perversions of Science* (1997), *The Others* (2000), *Night Visions* (2001), *Taken* (2002), and, appropriately for someone with his status in the horror genre, *Masters of Horror* (2005–). He also co-produced the 2003 **remake** of his own *The Texas Chainsaw Massacre*.

HOPKINS, ANTHONY (1937–). One role can define an actor's screen persona. In the case of the Welsh actor Anthony Hopkins, that role was master **serial killer** Hannibal Lecter in *The Silence of the Lambs* (1991). He was not the first to play Lecter—that honor went to Brian Cox in *Manhunter* (1986)—but it was Hopkins' remarkable performance, combining menace, articulacy and hints of campness, that caught the public's imagination and helped to establish the serial killer as a significant presence in horror films and thrillers. It also won him an Academy Award. Before Lecter, Hopkins was an accomplished stage actor with a sporadically successful cinema career. He was an anguished father in search of his dead daughter's spirit in **Robert Wise's** reincarnation drama *Audrey Rose* (1977) and a psychologically disturbed ventriloquist in *Magic* (1978), but other than this he had no real presence within the horror genre. After Lecter, his performances often had a larger-than-life quality, as if having to live up to his iconic status, and he was cast more frequently in horror-related projects, albeit upmarket ones. He was an enthusiastic Van Helsing in **Francis Ford Coppola's** version of *Dracula* (1992) and returned to the part of Lecter, to less effect, in *Hannibal* (2001) and *Red Dragon* (2002). He confronted Death personified in *Meet Joe Black* (1998), starred in an adaptation of **Shakespeare's** goriest play *Titus* (1999), met the **Devil** in *The Devil and Daniel Webster* (2001), and was a mysterious stranger in the **Stephen King** adaptation *Hearts in Atlantis* (2001). In 1993, he was awarded a knighthood.

HOSTS. The horror host first came to prominence on American **television** during the 1950s and 1960s, when his or her function was to introduce screenings of old horror films. Key hosts included "Vampira," "Zacherley" and "Ghoulardi." Their humorous introductions arguably helped to ease the genre's passage into a domestic setting for which it had never been intended. Elsewhere, the hosts found in 1950s "EC" horror **comics**—most notoriously the Crypt Keeper—served a similar function, while also helping to set a sardonic tone for the amoral horror tales in which "EC" specialized. From the late 1950s onwards, horror-themed television series, including *The Veil* (1958) and *The Twilight Zone* (1959–1964), integrated the host into the program format, again with the figure acting as a bridge between the domestic reality of the audience and the fantasy worlds offered on screen.

The horror host has been less of a feature of the horror scene since then. Attenuated versions of horror hosts show up in some of the **Amicus** horror **anthologies** of the 1960s and 1970s—including two adaptations of "EC" horror stories, *Tales from the Crypt* (1972) and *Vault of Horror* (1973)—while anthology television series such as *Night Gallery* (1970–1973), *Freddy's Nightmares* (1988–1990), and *Tales from the Crypt* (1989–1996) still relied on introductions addressed direct to camera. Meanwhile, Elvira, a Vampira-like figure, made an impact on American television during the 1980s by introducing old horror films in the traditional horror host fashion, "Dr. Terror" did something similar on British television during the 1990s, and the film *Fright Night* (1985) offered a fond representation of a horror host who has to take on a real **vampire**.

HOUGH, JOHN (1941–). John Hough is a British-born director who has worked in a variety of genres in Great Britain and in the United States and who has occasionally strayed into the horror genre. His films are often stylish affairs, although they lack an overall cohesion, suggesting a director with ability but with no strong affinity with horror. *Twins of Evil* (1971) was the final part of **Hammer**'s lesbian **vampire** trilogy. It lacked the dreamy languor of the earlier *The Vampire Lovers* (1970) and *Lust for a Vampire* (1971) and marginalized the lesbianism, but it was a well-paced account of intolerance that owed something thematically to **Michael Reeves'** *Witchfinder General* (1968). *The Legend of Hell House* (1973), adapted from a novel by **Richard Matheson** and filmed in Britain, was an impressive haunted house film. *The Watcher in the Woods* (1980), also filmed in Britain, was an unlikely foray by the Disney company into horror. The need to retain the family audience led to an uneasy and much reshot end-product, albeit one that was still interesting. By contrast, *The Incubus* (1981)—which took as its subject demonic rape and murder in an American town—was strictly for adults only.

Hough's other genre credits include *Howling IV: The Original Nightmare* (1988), *American* **Gothic** (1988) and *Bad Karma* (2002). He also contributed to the British **television** series *Hammer House of Mystery and Suspense* (1984).

THE HUNCHBACK OF NOTRE DAME. Film versions of *The Hunchback of Notre Dame*—adapted, usually very loosely, from Victor Hugo's 1831 novel *Notre Dame de Paris*—are comparable with **Phantom of the Opera** films in that they share horror-like themes and imagery but tend to be located on the margins of the horror genre. Arguably this is because the beauty-and-the-beast scenarios offered by each lend themselves more to tragic romance than they do to straight horror. The first major adaptation was the silent *The Hunchback of Notre Dame* (1923), starring **Lon Chaney** as the hideously deformed hunchback Quasimodo. Although Chaney is now widely regarded as a horror star, his films are often more melodramas than they are horrors, and his version of *Hunchback* is no exception, with its lavish sets and emotive, pathos-ridden narrative. Next came **Charles Laughton**'s Quasimodo in a 1939 version directed by William Dieterle, which again offered itself as a high quality historical melodrama with little or no connection to the horror films that were popular at the time. Much the same can be said for the French production *Notre Dame de Paris* (*The Hunchback of Notre Dame*) (1956), which starred Anthony Quinn as the hunchback. There have also been numerous **television** adaptations—including a 1982 production that featured a pre-Hannibal Lecter **Anthony Hopkins** as Quasimodo—and a Disney cartoon version in 1996.

Notre Dame does not have a monopoly on hunchbacks, however, and horror films have in the past occasionally deployed this particular bodily deformity to generate grotesquerie and sometimes pathos as well. **Dwight Frye** was **Frankenstein**'s deranged hunchbacked assistant in **Universal**'s *Frankenstein* (1931) while a more sympathetic hunchbacked female nurse showed up in *House of Dracula* (1945). The Spanish actor **Jacinto Molina**—in the guise of "Paul Naschy"—offered a mix of the horrible and the mildly sympathetic in *El jorobado de la morgue* (*Hunchback of the Morgue*) (1972), while **Mel Brooks**' horror spoof *Young Frankenstein* (1974) contained a **comedy** hunchback in the form of actor Marty Feldman, whose hunch moved from one shoulder to another and who, when asked about this, replied "What hunch?"

– I –

INDIAN HORROR. In terms of its sheer volume of production, Indian cinema is the biggest cinema in the world. Horror is not a major part of it, however, nor does horror or the **gothic** feature more widely in Indian culture (although India does possess a rich tradition of fantasy). A few Indian horrors appeared during the 1970s, largely as a response to the huge international success experienced by *The Exorcist* (1973), among them *Nagina* (1976) and *Jadu Tona* (1977). More significant were the activities of brothers Tulsi and Shyam Ramsay, who were the closest thing to horror specialists that Indian cinema ever had. They began with *Do Gaz Zameen Ke Neeche* (1972) and subsequently churned out a series of low-budget horrors, among them *Darwaza* (1978), the **disembodied hand** thriller *Guest House* (1980), *Ghunghroo Ki Awaaz* (1981), and the **ghost** story *Hotel* (1981). Their biggest success came with *Purana Mandir* (1984), which dealt with a family curse and which encouraged other producers to enter the genre. Like most other Indian films, the Ramsay productions usually inserted songs and dance numbers into stories that drew upon both Indian mythology and Western horror conventions. Thus, ghosts, curses, witches and **vampires** manifested themselves in relation to familiar Indian settings and characterizations. Horror aficionados have also noted liftings in these films both from the older horror of **Hammer** and **Mario Bava** and from the more contemporary **American horror** represented by, for example, the *Nightmare on Elm Street* films.

The Ramsays' vampire drama *Bandh Darwaza* (1989) is often seen as their best horror film, although its modest performance at the box office marked the end of the Indian horror boom. The association of horror with productions of low cultural status, which had largely been established by the Ramsays, has meant that subsequent attempts to move the genre upmarket or to broaden its appeal have not done well—for example, the **possession** drama *Raat* (1992), which excluded songs and dances. Neither has Indian cinema managed to produce an internationally palatable mixture of Western and non-Western horror conventions in the manner, say, of some recent **Japanese horror** films. For the time being at least, it seems that the Indian experiment with horror is over.

INSECTS. The horror genre has long been in the habit of using insects both for general atmospheric purposes and as monsters in their own right. Spiders in particular have scuttled through many a sinister castle or dungeon from the **Universal** *Dracula* (1931) onwards, while the **Italian horror** *La maschera del demonio* (*The Mask of Satan, Revenge of the Vampire, Black Sunday*) (1960) offered the unnerving spectacle of scorpions crawling out of the **eye** sockets of a dead witch. The American **science fiction**/horror monster movies of the 1950s introduced the practice of enlarging insects (or in a few cases making humans small so that the insects appear large), with this often connecting with nuclear anxieties and an associated sense that nature was out of control. Giant ants featured in *Them!* (1954), giant spiders in *Tarantula* (1955), *The Incredible Shrinking Man* (1957), and *Earth vs. The Spider* (*The Spider*) (1958), giant locusts in *Beginning of the End* (1957), a giant preying mantis in *The Deadly Mantis* (1957) and a range of magnified insects in *The Black Scorpion* (1957). Since the 1950s, giant insects have made only occasional appearances, notably in the 1970s with *The Giant Spider Invasion* (1975) and *Empire of the Ants* (1977). Many of these films were let down by some unconvincing model work, but more recently state of the art special effects have produced some convincing giant spiders in *Eight Legged Freaks* (2002) and, most of all, in horror-like sequences in fantasy films *Harry Potter and the Chamber of Secrets* (2002) and **Peter Jackson**'s *The Lord of the Rings: The Return of the King* (2003). Jackson's 2005 **remake** of *King Kong* also contained its fair share of large ferocious insects, as did Paul Verhoeven's earlier *Starship Troopers* (1997), while **Guillermo del Toro**'s *Mimic* (1997) featured giant insects that can imitate human beings.

Horror's other way of transforming insects into something that is menacing is to show large numbers of them massing and swarming, with this usually announcing a **revenge of nature** theme. Normal-sized ants threatened humans in *The Naked Jungle* (1954), *Phase IV* (1973), *Kingdom of the Spiders* (1977), and *Arachnophobia* (1990) while bees did the same in *The Deadly Bees* (1966) and *The Swarm* (1978). Thousands of worms rose to the surface in *Squirm* (1976) and a new breed of fire-starting cockroach attacked a small town in *Bug* (1975). The horror genre has also occasionally explored the transformation of humans into insects, most notably in *The Fly* (1958), which generated two **sequels** and a 1986 remake by **David Cronenberg** that itself spawned another sequel. *The Wasp Woman* (1960) and *The Blood Beast Terror* (1968) offered low-budget treatments of comparable stories.

THE INTERNET. Given the ubiquity of the internet, it is perhaps surprising how little it has featured in contemporary horror films. The visionary **Japanese horror** film *Kairo (Pulse)* (2001) associated the popularity of the internet with social alienation and collapse; it was remade as the **American horror** *Pulse* in 2006. On a more mundane level, the American production *FeardotCom* (2002) featured a vengeful **ghost** haunting the internet, while *My Little Eye* (2002) and *Halloween: Resurrection* (2002) depicted murderous events being broadcast via webcam over the internet.

THE ISLAND OF DR. MOREAU. H. G. Wells' 1896 novel *The Island of Dr. Moreau* is a cautionary tale about scientific research undertaken without moral constraints that still retains much of its significance today. Dr. Moreau's attempts to transform animals into humans might have as their aim the betterment of humanity but the brutal reality of his experiments leads inevitably to violence and death. **Erle C. Kenton**'s *Island of Lost Souls* (1932) was the first film adaptation. This Paramount production featured highly effective **makeup** effects and a flamboyant performance from **Charles Laughton** as Moreau, rendering him more of a 1930s **mad scientist** figure than he had been in Wells' original; it also clearly and disturbingly conveyed the pain involved in the monstrous experiments. The 1977 version of *The Island of Dr. Moreau*, directed by Don Taylor and featuring Burt

Lancaster as Moreau, was a sober affair, with creature designs from John Chambers, who had also been responsible for *Planet of the Apes* (1968). By contrast, the 1996 adaptation, also titled *The Island of Dr. Moreau*, was more chaotic in terms both of production—the original director **Richard Stanley** was replaced by **John Frankenheimer** shortly after production had commenced—and content, with some interesting ideas co-existing with an unevenness in tone. Wells' novel was also the uncredited inspiration for the **Filipino horror** *Terror is a Man* (1959).

ITALIAN HORROR. Italian horror cinema has a well-earned reputation for excess, be this stylistic excess or excessive violence or **gore**. It has also sometimes been accused of being imitative of films produced elsewhere. However, even the most obvious Italian rip-offs of American successes often have a distinctive identity of their own, and at its best Italian horror has made a major contribution to the development of the horror genre. In particular, it has perfected a provocative and assaultive type of horror that has often fallen foul of censors but which has also attracted a devoted **fan** following.

Italian horror is usually seen as beginning with **Riccardo Freda**'s **vampire** film *I Vampiri* (*The Devil's Commandment*) (1956), although this turned out to be something of a false start inasmuch as the film was a commercial failure. It took the international success of the British **Hammer** horror films to demonstrate that there was a market for European horror, and **Mario Bava**'s **witchcraft** drama *La maschera del demonio* (*The Mask of Satan, Revenge of the Vampire, Black Sunday*) (1960) was the first successful Italian entry into this market. Like the Hammer horrors, it had a period setting but it also offered a more dream-like and morbid scenario than that associated with the more solid Hammer product, with hints of necrophilia and a fascination with powerful women; it also featured the British actor **Barbara Steele**, who would become the major star of 1960s Italian horror.

A procession of similarly themed period horrors followed throughout the 1960s, including films from Bava, Freda and more workmanlike directors such as **Antonio Margheriti**. Cast and crew often adopted English-sounding names for international release versions, highlighting the way in which this type of horror sought to associate itself with Hammer. At the same time, there was often a stylistic bravura to these films and an ability to convey extreme emotional states in what might be described as an operatic manner. The 1960s also saw some weird genre hybrids, including horror/peplum combinations such as Bava's *Ercole al centro della terra* (*Hercules and the Haunted World*) (1961) and *Roma contra Roma* (*War of the Zombies*) (1963) (peplum films were period adventure epics, often with Greco-Roman settings and featuring legendary heroes such as Hercules) and Bava's **science fiction**/horror hybrid *Terrore nello spazio* (*Planet of the Vampires*) (1965).

By the 1970s, Italian period horror had faded away, and it was the contemporary **giallo** thriller that was in vogue. This distinctly Italian format had been present during the 1960s, with Bava yet again a significant figure as the director of several early giallo films. During the 1970s, other directors also specialized in this area, most notable among them the brilliant **Dario Argento**, who also directed supernatural films such as *Suspiria* (1977) and *Inferno* (1980). Other cycles were more obviously a response to non-Italian sources. For example, there was a small cycle of films that drew upon the **American horror** film *The Exorcist* (1973) for inspiration, among them *L'anticristo* (*The Antichrist*) (1974), *Chi sei?* (*The Devil within Her*) (1974), and *L'ossessa* (*The Sexorcist*) (1974). Later in the 1970s, **Lucio Fulci**'s *Zombi 2* (*Zombie, Zombie Flesheaters*) (1979) offered itself as an unauthorized **sequel** to **George Romero**'s *Dawn of the Dead* (1978), which had been marketed in Italy with the title *Zombi*, and other Italian zombie films quickly followed. As imitative as these films sought to be, their content and style were often markedly different from the original sources, with a greater emphasis on spectacle and gore and also an evident willingness on the part of the filmmakers to deploy unconventional and sometimes downright confusing narrative structures. There was also a cycle of very graphic **cannibalism** films, the most notorious of which was **Ruggero Deodato**'s *Cannibal Holocaust* (1980). Although cannibalism had been a theme in 1970s American horror, the Italian versions were not imitative of American sources in the manner of the zombie films. Instead the pseudo-anthropological approach they often adopted allied them more with the sensationalist **documentaries**—known as *Mondo* films after the first such production, *Mondo cane* (*A Dog's Life*)

(1961)—popular in Italy throughout the 1960s and 1970s. It could be argued that these were only classified as horror because of the nastiness of their content and that in fact they belonged elsewhere, thematically at least.

Horror ceased to be a significant feature of Italian cinema during the 1990s. Some of the more established directors, among them Argento and Fulci, continued to produce work, while some of the younger and promising directors who had appeared during the 1980s, including **Lamberto Bava** and **Michele Soavi**, moved into **television**. The early 2000s saw a mini-revival of European horror, especially in Britain, France, Germany and Spain, but Italian filmmakers contributed little to this. Nevertheless, the Italian horror film in all of its innovative and exploitative forms remains a key feature of European genre history.

– J –

JACK THE RIPPER. Jack the Ripper's murky historical origins have helped to establish him both as a disturbing cultural icon and as the **serial killer** *par excellence*. No one knows who murdered a series of prostitutes in London in 1888 (although there has been and continues to be much debate as to the Ripper's identity) and there is no definitive agreement as to how many were killed (although the consensus appears to be five victims). It is also not clear where the name "Jack the Ripper" came from, although some historians have suggested that it was devised by an enterprising journalist rather than by the murderer himself (or herself, if you believe some of the theories). In any event, the mystery of the Ripper's identity has encouraged both speculation and exploitation, with artists of all kinds returning repeatedly to the scenes of the Ripper's crimes and extracting a range of stories from them. In many of the ensuing representations, the city itself has acquired a Ripper-like hue as a location that is fascinating but dangerous (especially dangerous for women).

Early cinematic appearances for the Ripper or Ripper-like killers included two German films, **Paul Leni**'s *Das Wachsfigurenkabinett* (*Waxworks*) (1924)—in which the killer was billed as "Springheel Jack" but was presented more as a Ripper figure—and G. W. Pabst's

Die Büchse der Pandora (*Pandora's Box*) (1929), in which it was the Ripper who killed the film's unfortunate heroine. **Alfred Hitchcock's** British production *The Lodger* (1927) was an adaptation of Marie Belloc Lowndes's Ripper novel, although in Hitchcock's version the mysterious lodger, played by Ivor Novello, turned out to be innocent rather than the novel's killer. *The Lodger* was remade three times: *The Lodger* (1932), directed by Maurice Elvey, featured Novello again as the unjustly accused innocent, while both John Brahm's *The Lodger* (1944) and Hugo Fregonese's *Man in the Attic* (1954) restored the lodger's serial killer status, with Laird Cregar and **Jack Palance** respectively playing the Ripper. **Hammer's** *Room to Let* (1950) also dealt with similar material.

1960s **British horror** cinema came up with two Ripper films, both of which rejected the psychologizing of the killer found in the various versions of *The Lodger* and instead offered atmospheric whodunnits that drew upon some of the traditional suspects for the killings (e.g., mad doctors, aristocrats). In *Jack the Ripper* (1958), an American policeman helped to track down the killer, who was revealed to be a doctor avenging the death of his son, while *A Study in Terror* (1965) pitted **Sherlock Holmes** against the Ripper, revealed this time as an aristocrat. In the 1970s, Hammer added to the Ripper canon **Roy Ward Baker's** *Dr. Jekyll and Sister Hyde* (1971), in which the title character turned out to be Jack the Ripper as well. This was not as ridiculous a plot twist as might be imagined; at the time of the original killings, newspapers had made references to **Dr. Jekyll and Mr. Hyde** and an actor playing the role of Jekyll on stage in London had apparently become a Ripper suspect, albeit briefly. (The 1989 **Anthony Perkins'** film *Edge of Sanity* would also make a connection between Jekyll and the Ripper.) More successful was **Peter Sasdy's** Hammer film *Hands of the Ripper* (1971), which dealt with the Ripper's daughter seeking to escape from her father's influence and which was a rare example of a horror film engaging, if only tentatively, with the sexual politics of the Ripper story.

Jesus Franco's German production *Jack the Ripper* (1976) lacked this kind of ambition, but it was stylish in places and also remarkably gory. **Bob Clark's** *Murder by Decree* (1979) was another Holmes versus the Ripper narrative, although in a characteristically 1970s anti-establishment maneuver, the killings were shown as part of a political conspiracy involving the Royal Family (a theory that was becoming increasingly popular with "Ripperologists" at the time). In a more fantastic vein, *Time After Time* (1979) had the Ripper escaping from Victorian London to contemporary America in H. G. Wells' time machine, a plot development that underlined the extent to which the Ripper could be moved from one context to another. The most recent Ripper outing is *From Hell* (2001), which was based on the acclaimed **comic** book series by Alan Moore and Eddie Campbell, starred Johnny Depp as Inspector Abberline and was directed by Albert and Allen Hughes. *From Hell* resurrected the political conspiracy narrative found in *Murder by Decree* and also offered an impressive visualization of Victorian London, although other than this it added little of substance to Ripper cinema. In addition, the Ripper has made cameo appearances in *Waxwork 2: Lost in Time* (1992) and *Deadly Advice* (1993).

The name "Jack the Ripper" has also become a shorthand term denoting serial killings of women, often involving mutilation of the bodies, both in real life (most notoriously, the British serial killer, the Yorkshire Ripper) and in fiction. Films that have referenced the Ripper in this way without actually representing him include the German thriller *Das Ungeheuer von London City* (*The Monster of London City*) (1964), the Spanish production *Jack el destripador de Londres* (*Jack the Mangler of London*) (1971), **Lucio Fulci**'s *Lo squartatore di New York* (*The New York Ripper*) (1982), *Jack's Back* (1988), and the gender-bending *Jill Rips* (2000). In addition, characters who believe that they are the Ripper show up in *The Ruling Class* (1972), *The Ripper* (1985), *Ripper Man* (1994), and *Bad Karma* (2002).

The Ripper has had two **television** films devoted to him, the British-produced *Jack the Ripper* (1988) and the American-produced *The Ripper* (1997), and has also appeared as guest villain (often of the alien or time-traveling sort) in numerous television series, including *The Veil* (1958), *Thriller* (1960–1962), *The Twilight Zone* (1959–1964), *Star Trek* (1966–1969), *Kolchak the Night Stalker* (1974–1975), *Fantasy Island* (1978–1984), and *Babylon 5* (1994–1998).

Given that the Ripper story is almost by definition a story of male violence against women, it is disappointing how rarely this has featured as an issue in any of the films cited above. Instead the emphasis has been either on the tortuous psychology of the killer or on the idea of the Ripper as the epitome of evil. The increasingly tiresome attempts to identify him have also become something of a distraction.

JACKSON, PETER (1961–). The writer-director Peter Jackson began his filmmaking career in his native New Zealand with the **comedy-horror** feature *Bad Taste* (1987), in which he also starred. An over-the-top alien invasion fantasy, this started out as an amateur film but managed to secure a theatrical release and became a cult favorite. After the weird comedy-musical *Meet the Feebles* (1989), Jackson returned to horror with the **zombie** film *Braindead* (1992), which retained the **gore** and humor evident in *Bad Taste* but was also a slicker work that demonstrated the director's growing discipline as a filmmaker. His next project, *Heavenly Creatures* (1994), was a new departure. This beautifully made account of a real-life murder case was an international hit with audiences who were probably unaware of Jackson's less reputable earlier films, although the film's disturbing content and its fantasy scenes demonstrated the director's continuing ability to provide unnerving thrills. Next came a move to Hollywood and the **ghost** story *The Frighteners* (1996), which contained some scary sequences and impressive visuals but did not match its comedy to its horror as effectively as had *Braindead*. The film was not a great commercial success and Jackson was obliged—temporarily at least—to shelve his plans for a **remake** of the 1933 classic *King Kong*. Instead he labored for several years on the epic *Lord of the Rings* trilogy (2001–2003), with his experience in horror very evident in the depiction of various villains and monsters. After the phenomenal box-office returns enjoyed by the trilogy, Jackson finally got to remake *King Kong* in 2005, in a version that again displayed strong horror elements, notably in its graphic depiction of the dangers awaiting humans on Skull Island.

JAPANESE HORROR. For a Western viewer, the world of Japanese horror can sometimes seem an unfamiliar terrain organized around some strange-sounding sub-generic categories such as *bakenoko mono* (**cat ghost** stories) or *diakaiyu eiga* (giant monster films). One of the most consistently popular Japanese horror formats has proved to be *kaidan eiga* or ghost stories, which draw on Japanese literary, theatrical, and religious traditions. Such films are often set in the past and feature vengeful female ghosts. Perhaps the best known example in the West of this type of supernatural period drama is Masaki Kobayashi's *Kaidan* (*Kwaidan*) (1964), although this was not very popular in Japan. Other upmarket ghost stories were provided by Kaneto Shindo with *Onibaba* (1964) and *Yabu no naka no kuroneko* (*Kuroneko*) (1968), while films such as Nobuo Nakagawa's *Tokaido Yotsuya kaidan* (*Ghost Story of Yotsuya*) (1959) and Kazuo Haso's *Kaidan zankoku monogatari* (*Cruel Ghost Legend, Curse of the Blood*) (1968), amongst many others, were more mainstream entertainments.

Also popular from the mid-1950s onwards were a series of giant monster films. The best known of these was Ishiro Honda's *Gojira* (*Godzilla*) (1954), an international success that generated numerous **sequels**. Critics have detected a nuclear subtext in the repeated destruction of Tokyo in these films, although more juvenile **comic**-book elements became increasingly evident as the series progressed. By contrast, *Daimajiin* (*Majiin*) (1966) had a period setting and featured a giant animated statue as its monster; two sequels followed in quick succession.

Japanese horror also has a more challenging and transgressive sector involving films that push back the limits of what is acceptable in cinema entertainment. Explicit representations of **torture** occur in, among others, Teruo Ishii's *Tokugawa onna kaibatsu-shi* (*The Joys of Torture*) (1968) and Akira Inoue's *Hiroku onna ro* (*Secret Report from a Woman's Prison*) (1968). More recently, directors such as **Takashi Miike** with *Ôdishon* (*Audition*) (1999) and Shinya Tsukamoto with *Tetsuo* (1989) and *Tetsuo II: Body Hammer* (1992) have taken the **body horror** film onto a new level of grim spectacle above anything offered by Western mainstream horror.

The relation of Japanese horror cinema to Western genre traditions is complex. Some Japanese genre types—notably the period ghost stories—seem designed primarily for domestic consumption, while others—particularly the Gojira/Godzilla films—seem to have an eye on Western markets as well. Occasionally, Japanese horror has sought to incorporate Western conventions, not always with success. For example, Nakagawa's *Onna kyuketsuki* (*The Woman Vampire*) (1959) and **Michio Yamamoto**'s vampire films from the 1970s struggled to make sense of Western forms of vampirism within a cultural context ill-suited to understanding the Christian ideology underpinning the vampire myth. The cycle of contemporary ghost stories initiated by the international commercial success of **Hideo Nakata**'s *Ringu* (*Ring*) (1998) has offered a more confident mixing of Japanese and Western horror traditions, however. The long-haired female ghost familiar from numerous *kaidan eiga* is here aligned with modern technologies in a Japan clearly in the thrall of Western influence, while references are made to American horrors such as *The Omen* (1976). Nakata's *Ringu 2* (*Ring 2*) (1999) and *Honogurai mizu no soko kara* (*Dark Water*) (2002) and **Takashi Shimizu**'s *Ju-on: The Grudge* (2003) have further helped to establish the international character of Japanese horror, and, perhaps inevitably, American **remakes** have also been released, sometimes by the original Japanese directors. The extent to which the distinctive strangeness of Japanese horror cinema will survive its increased visibility in the West remains unclear at this time.

JORDAN, NEIL (1950–). Neil Jordan is an Irish writer-director who has made films both in his home country and internationally and whose work has sometimes engaged with horror or **gothic** material. His ability to conjure up sequences that are both visually striking and eerie was apparent in *The Company of Wolves* (1984), an upmarket **werewolf** story, and in *Interview with the Vampire* (1994), an adaptation of **Anne Rice**'s bestselling novel that featured Tom Cruise in one of his more challenging roles. *The Butcher Boy* (1997) was a more low-key psychological drama that nevertheless contained some intense and disturbing moments. The American **psychological thriller** *In Dreams* (1999) was more conventional so far as its narrative was concerned but it did offer some haunting set pieces.

– K –

KARLOFF, BORIS (1887–1969). Although one of horror's most enduring stars, Boris Karloff did not appear in a horror film until he was in his mid-forties. His real name was William Henry Pratt and he was born in Camberwell, London. His father and brothers worked in the Indian consular service, but the young William Pratt decided against a diplomatic career and emigrated to Canada in May 1909. Acquiring the stage name "Boris Karloff," he spent the next decade touring both Canada and the United States in stock theatrical companies. From 1919 he also appeared in movies, usually in small parts. His first major film role was also the role that helped to define not just his subsequent career but also the horror genre itself. The director **James Whale** cast him as **Frankenstein**'s monster (a part originally intended for **Bela Lugosi**), mainly because of his gaunt appearance. Despite the handicaps of cumbersome **makeup** and having no dialogue, Karloff's performance in *Frankenstein* (1931) was remarkable, managing to convey the essential humanity of the monster through gesture and facial expression alone. Karloff returned to the role in *Bride of Frankenstein* (1935)—in which the monster temporarily acquired the ability to speak—and *Son of Frankenstein* (1939) and each time added nuance and depth to his characterization. It is a mark of his success that none of the actors—among them Bela Lugosi and **Lon Chaney Jr.**—who later took on the role of the Monster ever matched Karloff's quality.

Karloff was a versatile actor capable of playing a range of types but his sinister physical appearance and his slight lisp suited him particularly well to horror cinema. The 1930s was probably his most successful decade. While some of his horror roles were purely menacing—the mute butler in *The Old Dark House* (1932) and the sadistic villains in *The Mask of Fu Manchu* (1932) and *The Black Cat* (1934)—most of his 1930s performances contained elements of pathos reminiscent of his rendition of Frankenstein's monster. These included the animated corpses he played in *The Mummy* (1932), *The Ghoul* (1933), and *The Walking Dead* (1936), the victimized servant in *The Raven* (1935) and demented scientists in both *The Invisible Ray* (1936) and *The Man They Could Not Hang* (1939). Demonstrating his dramatic range, he also successfully played twin brothers, one good and one evil, in the period piece *The Black Room* (1935). In the 1940s, Karloff reprised several times the role of the mad or misunderstood scientist—notably in *The Man with Nine Lives* (1940), *Before I Hang* (1940), *The Ape* (1940), *The Devil Commands* (1941), and *House of Frankenstein* (1944)—and displayed his comedic ability in horror farces *You'll Find Out* (1940), *The Boogie Man Will Get You* (1942), and *Abbott and*

Costello Meet the Killer, Boris Karloff (1949). However, his finest 1940s work was done for horror producer **Val Lewton**, with disturbing studies of obsession and cruelty in *The Body Snatcher* (1945), *Isle of the Dead* (1945), and *Bedlam* (1946). During the 1950s and early 1960s, the melodramatic style of horror with which Karloff had become associated went out of fashion and he worked less in the genre, although his status as horror icon led to his presenting two horror-themed **television** shows, *The Veil* (1958) and *Thriller* (1960–1962). The last few years of his life did see a revival in his fortunes, however. Although suffering from ill health, he managed a spirited **comedy** turn in director **Roger Corman**'s reworking of *The Raven* (1963), played a particularly sinister **vampire** in **Mario Bava**'s *Il tre volti della paura* (*Black Sabbath*) (1963), and went on to produce two of his best performances since the 1930s in **Michael Reeves'** *The Sorcerers* (1967) and Pete Bogdanovich's *Targets* (1968). In *The Sorcerers* he returned yet again to the role of the misunderstood scientist, while in *Targets* he played an ageing horror star confronted by the modern horror of a motiveless sniper. Both Reeves and Bogdanovich used Karloff's all-too-obvious physical frailty to comment elegaically on the passing of an old horror cinema in a harsh modern world; Karloff conducted himself with great dignity throughout.

Boris Karloff died on 2 February 1969 in Sussex, England. Some **Mexican horror** films in which he appeared were released in the two years following his death. His other horror or horror-related credits are *Behind the Mask* (1932), *Juggernaut* (1936), *The Man Who Changed His Mind* (1936), *Tower of London* (1939), *Black Friday* (1940), *The Climax* (1944), *The Strange Door* (1951), *The Black Castle* (1952), *Abbott and Costello Meet **Dr. Jekyll and Mr. Hyde*** (1953), ***Voodoo Island*** (1957), *Grip of the Strangler* (1958), *Frankenstein—1970* (1958), *Corridors of Blood* (1958), *The Terror* (1963), *The Comedy of Terrors* (1964), *Die, Monster, Die!* (1965), *Ghost in the Invisible Bikini* (1966), *Serenata macabra* (*House of Evil*) (1968), *La camera del terror* (*The Fear Chamber*) (1968), *Curse of the Crimson Altar* (1968), *El coleccionista de cadavere* (*The Corpse Collector, Cauldron of Blood*) (1970), *La muertre viviente* (*Isle of the Snake People*) (1971), and *La invasión siniestra* (*The Incredible Invasion*) (1971).

KEIR, ANDREW (1926–1997). The Scottish actor Andrew Keir played in a variety of genres but he is best known for his performances in two **Hammer** horror films. In **Terence Fisher**'s *Dracula—Prince of Darkness* (1966), he made the monk Father Sandor a more approachable and worldly hero than the ascetic **vampire**-hunter played by **Peter Cushing** in Fisher's previous Dracula films. Similarly, in **Roy Ward Baker**'s *Quatermass and the Pit* (1967), he offered a kinder and more avuncular rendition of the scientist-hero than that offered by Brian Donlevy in Hammer's other Quatermass films (and in 1996 he would play the part of Quatermass again, on radio this time in *The Quatermass Memoirs*). In 1971, he appeared in his third Hammer horror, *Blood from the Mummy's Tomb*, replacing at very short notice Cushing who had withdrawn from the production because of his wife's death.

KEITH, SHEILA (1920–2004). By all accounts, Sheila Keith was a sweet Scottish lady, and most of her roles in film and on **television** reflected this. However, she also played some of the most vile and evil women in British cinema history. This was almost entirely due to the efforts of British director **Pete Walker**, for whom Keith worked regularly during the 1970s. She began in Walker's *House of Whipcord* (1974), where her supporting role as a sadistic prison warder stole the film. *Frightmare* (1974), her next for Walker, was tailored with her in mind. In a ferocious and terrifying performance, she played an apparently innocuous character who was actually addicted to **cannibalism** and was also not averse to attacking her victims with a red-hot poker or a pitchfork. The ecstatic expression on her blood-bespattered face as she drives a power drill into someone's head remains one of British cinema's more unsettling moments. By contrast, her performances in Walker's *House of Mortal Sin* (*The Confessional*) (1975), *The Comeback* (1978), and *House of the Long Shadows* (1983) were quieter, more decorous affairs, although she maintained a sinister aura throughout. Her cameo appearance in the pastiche horror television series *Dr. Terrible's House of Horrible* (2001) underlined her status as a minor icon of **British horror**.

KELLJAN, BOB (1930–1982). The **American horror** films of writer-director Bob Kelljan contributed to the updating of the **vampire** myth that took place in the 1970s. In *Count Yorga, Vampire* (1970) and its sequel *The Return of Count Yorga* (1971), the aristocratic vampire—played by Robert Quarry—moved comfortably among the citizens of modern America, and both films had the open endings that at the time were becoming something of a generic convention. Kelljan also directed *Scream, Blacula, Scream* (1973), a similarly themed vampire story that was the sequel to the blaxploitation hit, *Blacula* (1972).

KENTON, ERLE, C. (1896–1980). Like most of the directors working in **American horror** of the 1930s and 1940s, Erle C. Kenton was not a horror specialist but instead moved between genres. In Kenton's case, he had started out working for **comedy** producer Mack Sennett. However, his first horror film was far from humorous. The Paramount production *Island of Lost Souls* (1932) was an adaptation of H. G. Wells's *The Island of Dr. Moreau*. It starred **Charles Laughton** as Moreau and also featured **Bela Lugosi** in a supporting role. In this early example of **surgical horror**, Kenton conveyed the pain and suffering involved in Moreau's inhuman experiments more effectively than did the decorous surgical goings-on in **Universal**'s production of *Frankenstein* (1931). Kenton's next horror outings were for Universal in the 1940s, when he directed *The Ghost of Frankenstein* (1942) and two of the studio's multiple monster films, *House of Frankenstein* (1944) and *House of Dracula* (1945). These were solidly made but, perhaps inevitably given the source material, they lacked the perverse flair of *Island of Lost Souls*. Kenton also directed *The Cat Creeps* (1946). The latter part of his career was spent mainly in **television**.

KIER, UDO (1944–). The German actor Udo Kier's credits have included work for distinguished directors such as Rainer Werner Fassbinder, Werner Herzog, Gus Van Sant, Lars von Trier and Wim Wenders. However, he has also appeared in numerous horror films, usually in sinister, soft-spoken parts. He had a strong supporting role in the controversial witch hunter drama *Hexen bis aufs Blut gequält* (*Mark of the Devil*) (1970) but came to genre prominence with his performances as **Frankenstein** and **Dracula** in **Paul Morrissey**'s Euro-camp extravaganzas *Flesh for Frankenstein* (1973) and *Blood for Dracula* (1974). He further established his horror credentials by playing **Jack the Ripper** and Doctor Jekyll in two **Walerian Borowczyk** films, *Lulu* (1980) and *Docteur Jekyll et les femmes* (*Dr. Jekyll and his women* (1981). Kier's other European horror credits include a leading role in the British **psychological thriller** *Exposé* (1976), a cameo in **Dario Argento**'s *Suspiria* (1977) and appearances in *Das Deutsche Kettensägen Massaker* (literally *The German Chainsaw Massacre* but sold overseas as *Blackest Heart*) (1991) and *Shadow of the Vampire* (2000). From the late 1990s onwards, he has also appeared with increasing frequency in American films, usually in villainous roles. He showed up in the vampire movie *Blade* (1998), the Satanic thriller *End of Days* (1999), the apocalyptic drama *Revelation* (2001) and the **ghost** story *FeardotCom* (2002), as well as in lower-budgeted productions such as *Headspace* (2005) and *BloodRayne* (2005). Perhaps his most striking genre performance was done for Danish **television**, however. He was the principal villain in Lars von Trier's horror-themed miniseries *Riget* (*The Kingdom*) (1994) and also played a deformed baby in its sequel *Riget 2* (*The Kingdom 2*) (1997).

KING, STEPHEN (1947–). Stephen King is the most commercially successful horror writer ever. His many novels and short stories tend to be located within contemporary America, and his ability to capture the mundane habits and social interactions of ordinary Americans remains one of his fiction's most distinctive features. However, King's association with horror, an often disreputable genre, along with the fact that he has been remarkably prolific, has meant that his work has not always received the critical attention it merits. There have been numerous cinematic and **television** adaptations of King's fictions, with some of these adapted by King himself. These have varied widely in terms both of quality and of their degree of faithfulness to the original stories. In any event, few adaptations, including the ones penned by King, have successfully captured the conversational tone of much of his prose, although their ubiquity has ensured that King's name has remained a powerful presence in the horror market.

Early cinematic adaptations included **Brian De Palma**'s telekinesis drama *Carrie* (1976) and Stanley Kubrick's *The Shining* (1980). Both of these were impressive films in their own right that retained King's perennial interest in dysfunctional families but which also showcased the cinematic sensibilities of their directors. This was particularly the case with *The Shining*, which was not well-received on its initial release but which is now widely considered to be one of the great horror films (although King has expressed his dislike of it, perhaps because its cool approach to the story was so different from King's own emotive approach.) Other adaptations of King's horror novels quickly followed—beginning with **John Carpenter**'s *Christine* (1983) and continuing with **David Cronenberg**'s *The Dead Zone* (1983), *Cujo* (1983), *Firestarter* (1984), the King-scripted *Pet Sematary* (1989), *Misery* (1990), **George Romero**'s *The Dark Half* (1993), *Needful Things* (1993), and *Dreamcatcher* (2003). In addition, **Children** *of the Corn* (1984), *Silver Bullet* (1985), *Graveyard Shift* (1990), **Tobe Hooper**'s *The Mangler* (1995), *The Night Flier* (1997), *Apt Pupil* (1998), *Secret Window* (2004), and *Riding the Bullet* (2004), as well as the horror **anthologies** *Cat's Eye* (1985) and *Tales from the Darkside—The Movie* (1990), were all based on King's short stories or novellas. King adapted his own short stories for Romero's anthology *Creepshow* (1982), while Romero adapted more King stories for the **sequel** *Creepshow 2* (1987). There was also two adaptations of novels written by King under the name Richard Bachman, *The Running Man* (1987)—a very loose translation of King's dystopian fantasy into an Arnold Schwarzenegger action story—and *Thinner* (1996). (The 1992 film *The Lawnmower Man*, although billed as a King adaptation, turned out to have very little to do with the King short story of the same name.) King himself wrote the original screenplay for **Mick Garris**'s *Sleepwalkers* (1992).

King's fiction has occasionally moved away from traditional horror fare and explored other genres and subjects, and some of the more critically successful King adaptations have been based on this work. Most notable here are the coming-of-age drama *Stand by Me* (1986) and the prison drama *The Shawshank Redemption* (1994), both of which were based on short novels. *Dolores Claiborne* (1995), *The Green Mile* (1999), and *Hearts in Atlantis* (2001) have also drawn upon the non-horror King.

The sprawling nature of King's often lengthy novels has lent itself particularly well to adaptation as television miniseries. The best of these was the first, Tobe Hooper's atmospheric and genuinely scary version of the **vampire** story *Salem's Lot* (1979), which was remade as a Rob Lowe vehicle in 2004. Other miniseries of this kind have included *It* (1990), *The Tommyknockers* (1993), *The Langoliers* (1995, adapted from a novella), and King's own adaptations of *The Stand* (1994), *The Shining* (1997), and *Desperation* (2006). King has also written original television scripts. Perhaps the best of these was the miniseries *Storm of the Century* (1999), a disturbing piece in which, unusually both for King and for American television, evil triumphed unequivocally. Other credits include episodes for the series *Tales from the Darkside* (1984–1988) and *The X Files* (1993–2002) and the miniseries *Golden Years* (1991) and *Rose Red* (2002), as well as King's reworking of Lars von Trier's Danish series *Riget* (*Kingdom*) (1994) into the miniseries *Kingdom Hospital* (2004). King's short stories have been adapted by others as the television films *Sometimes They Come Back* (1991), *Quicksilver Highway* (1997), and *Trucks* (1997) and as episodes in the television series *The Twilight Zone* (1985–1989), *Monsters* (1988–1990), *The Outer Limits* (1995–2002), and the miniseries *Nightmares and Dreamscapes* (2006). His novel *The Dead Zone*, already filmed by Cronenberg, inspired the television series *The Dead Zone* (2002–), and *Carrie* was filmed again as a television film in 2002 and also turned into a musical.

As if this were not enough, King also wrote and directed *Maximum Overdrive* (1986), an **apocalyptic horror** film in which machines turn on mankind. It was not very good but the fact that he found time to do it was noteworthy in itself. He has also made numerous cameo appearances in films and television programs, the most significant of which was his performance in Romero's *Creepshow*.

KINSKI, KLAUS (1926–1991). The German actor Klaus Kinski is best known for the films he made with director Werner Herzog. Among these was *Nosferatu: Phantom der Nacht* (*Nosferatu the Vampyre*) (1979), a **remake** of **F. W. Murnau**'s 1922 original, with Kinski taking the role of the **vampire** originally played by **Max Schreck**. This bald-headed and animalistic character was well-suited to Kinski's gestural and often extreme style of acting. Elsewhere, the actor's slightly unnerving appearance had already tended to restrict him to menacing roles. He was a regular sinister presence in a popular 1960s German series of Edgar Wallace adaptations that often contained elements of horror, among them *Der Rächer* (*The Avenger*)

(1960), *Die Toten Augen von London* (*Dead Eyes of London*) (1961), *Das Rätsel der roten Orchidee* (*The Puzzle of the Red Orchid*) (1962), and *Die Tür mit den 7 Schlössern* (*The Door with Seven Locks*) (1962). He also played the insane Renfield in **Jesus Franco**'s lethargic *El Conde Dracula* (*Count Dracula*) (1970). His other genre credits are minor; they include *La Bestia uccide a sangue freddo* (*The Beast Kills in Cold Blood, Slaughter Hotel*) (1971), a performance as **Edgar Allan Poe** in *Nella stretta morsa del ragno* (*In the Grip of the Spider*) (1971), *La morte ha sorriso all'assassino* (*Death Smiles on a Murderer*) (1973), *La mano che nutre la morte* (*The Hand That Feeds the Dead*) (1974), *Le amanti del mostro* (*Lover of the monster*) (1974), *Jack the Ripper* (1976), *Creature* (1985), *Crawlspace* (1986), and the bizarre *Nosferatu in Venice* (1988). To see Kinski at his extravagant best, look to his Herzog films.

KLIMOVSKY, LEÓN (1906–1996). The Argentinian León Klimovsky worked mainly in Spain on a variety of genre productions but specialized in horror, bringing pace and energy to conventional horror plots without ever developing a recognizable personal style. He worked regularly with **Spanish horror** star **Jacinto Molina** (Paul Naschy), with their films together including *La noche de walpurgis* (*Shadow of the Werewolf*) (1970), *Dr. Jekyll y el hombre lobo* (*Doctor Jekyll and the Werewolf*) (1971), *La rebelión de las muertas* (*Vengeance of the Zombies*) (1972), *Una libélula para cada muerto* (*A Dragonfly for Each Corpse, Red Killer*) (1973), *El mariscal del infierno* (*Devil's Possessed*) (1974), and *Tres días de noviembre* (1976). Away from Molina, he directed three atmospheric **vampire** films, *La saga de los Drácula* (*The Dracula Saga*) (1972), *La orgía nocturna de los vampiros* (*Vampire's Night Orgy*) (1972), and *Extraño amor de los vampiros* (*Night of the Walking Dead*) (1975), as well as the **science fiction**/horror hybrids *Odio mi cuerpo* (*I Hate My Body*) (1973) and *Último deseo* (*Planeta Ciego*) (1975). Klimovsky's final genre film was the **giallo**-like thriller *El violación fatal* (*Trauma*) (1977).

KNEALE, NIGEL (1922–2006). The British writer Nigel Kneale worked mainly for **television**, but he also had some film credits, and his innovative and ambitious scripts have been influential on horror artists such as **John Carpenter**, Chris Carter (creator of *The X-Files*), **Stephen King** and **Dan O'Bannon**. Kneale's horror and fantasy stories relied far more on subtle chills than they did on shocks and **gore**, and they often showed an interest in folklore and ritual. He first achieved prominence with the three alien invasion series that he wrote for the BBC during the 1950s, *The Quatermass Experiment* (1953), *Quatermass II* (1955), and *Quatermass and the Pit* (1958–1959). These were later adapted for the big screen by **Hammer**, although Kneale only worked on the screenplays for the second and third, *Quatermass 2 (Enemy from Space)* (1957) and *Quatermass and the Pit (Five Million Years to Earth)* (1967). He also adapted his own 1955 television play *The Creature* into Hammer's *The Abominable Snowman* (1957). This was not entirely successful, although, like the Quatermass films, it was a more intelligent treatment of the monster than was generally apparent in the horror genre at the time. Similarly compromised was Kneale's *The Witches* (1966), a Hammer **witchcraft** drama. Indeed Kneale's best work in the 1960s and 1970s was all done for television, notably the **Peter Sasdy**-directed **ghost** story *The Stone Tape* (1972) and the **anthology** series *Beasts* (1976).

In 1979, Kneale wrote the fourth Quatermass television series, which was entitled simply *Quatermass*; a cut-down version of this was released theatrically in some markets at *The Quatermass Conclusion*. He also worked on the screenplay for *Halloween III: Season of the Witch* (1982), although ultimately he withdrew from the project.

KOMEDA, KRZYSZTOF (1931–1969). The Polish jazz musician and composer Krzysztof Komeda—who was sometimes billed as Christopher Komeda—wrote two of the most haunting of all horror scores, both of them for director **Roman Polanski**. *The Fearless Vampire Killers (Dance of the Vampires)* (1967) was a British-made spoof of vampire films, although Komeda's **music** was far from comic and accentuated the underlying seriousness of the project. He eschewed traditional horror music again with *Rosemary's Baby* (1968) where a simple lullaby—sung by the film's star, **Mia Farrow** —provided an unnerving counterpoint to the film's depiction of the birth of the **Antichrist**. Komeda died young of injuries resulting from an accident.

KOREAN HORROR. Korean horror cinema—or, to be more precise, South Korean horror cinema—is a recent phenomenon that has developed in the wake of the international success of **Japanese horror** films such as *Ringu* (Ring) (1998). Some Korean horrors are decidedly Japanese-like in their focus on vengeful female **ghosts** attacking their victims through modern technology, for example, *The Ring Virus* (1999), an adaptation of the same novel that inspired *Ringu*, and *Pon* (*Phone*) (2002). However, other productions have been more willing to engage with aspects of Korean society and history. Ghost stories *Yeogo goedam* (*Whispering Corridors*) (1998) and *Yeogo goedam II* (*Memento Mori*) (1999) provided a compelling portrayal of Korea's notoriously tough educational system. *R-Point* (2004) also used a ghost story format to explore Korean involvement in the Vietnam war, while the **serial killer** drama *Salinui chueok* (*Memories of Murder*) (2003) and the monster movie *Gwoemul* (*The Host*) (2006), both of which were directed by Joon-Ho Bong, transformed Western generic conventions through playing them out in Korean settings. A comparably fascinating examination of Korean social mores via horror-like imagery can be found in the violent vengeance films directed by Chan-wook Park, namely *Boksuneun naui geot* (*Sympathy for Mr. Vengeance*) (2002), *Oldboy* (2003), and *Chinjeolhan geumjassi* (*Lady Vengeance*) (2005), as well as in the full-blooded horror story he contributed to the horror **anthology** *Saam gaang yi* (*Three Extremes*) (2004).

Surprisingly, the totalitarian North Korean regime has also dabbled, albeit briefly, in horror with the *Godzilla*-like monster movie *Pulgasari* (1985), the director of which had been kidnapped from South Korea in order that his filmmaking expertise might serve North Korean cinema. The film has been circulated in the West but it seems likely that the South Korean brand of insidious ghostly horror will have the more lasting impact.

KÜMEL, HARRY (1940–). The Belgian director Harry Kümel is responsible for one extraordinary horror film, *Les lèvres rouges* (*Daughters of Darkness*) (1971). This modern-day lesbian **vampire** film, which featured a haunting performance from Delphine Seyrig as **Elizabeth Bathory**, successfully combined a slow, dream-like narrative with some more conventional vampiric action. Kümel did not return to the genre again, although his *Malpertuis* (1972), in which figures from Greek mythology move through the contemporary world, contained some horror-like elements.

– L –

LANCHESTER, ELSA (1902–1986). The British actor Elsa Lanchester—who was the wife of **Charles Laughton**—played both Mary Shelley and the female monster in **James Whale's Universal** horror classic *Bride of Frankenstein* (1935). As Shelley, she was witty and self-deprecating, as the monster she was an extraordinary shrouded figure with a Nefertiti-like hairstyle and an unnerving hiss. Although she appears only briefly in this guise at the film's conclusion, the image of Lanchester in full monstrous **makeup** has since acquired iconic status. She was often cast as eccentric characters. Her genre credits include the **comedy** *The Ghost Goes West* (1935), the **psychological thriller** *The Spiral Staircase* (1946), and roles in the more modern horrors *Willard* (1971) and *Terror in the Wax Museum* (1973).

LANDERS, LEW (1901–1962). In a prolific career, the director Lew Landers, who was occasionally billed under his real name of Louis Friedlander, worked in a variety of genres yet managed to make some solidly professional horror films along the way. *The Raven* (1935) was more stylistically restrained than some of the other **Universal** 1930s horrors, but Landers showcased entertaining performances from **Boris Karloff** and **Bela Lugosi** at the height of their horror fame. *The Boogie Man Will Get You* (1942), which reunited Landers with Karloff, was a superior **comedy**-horror, while *The Return of the Vampire* (1944) was an inventive modern-day vampire story featuring Lugosi as a **Dracula**-like villain. Although his horror credits were few, Landers made a sufficient impression to be immortalized as a character name in **Joe Dante's** *The Howling* (1981), in which nearly all the characters are named after horror directors. *See also* AMERICAN HORROR.

LANDIS, JOHN (1950–). The American director John Landis has specialized mainly in **comedy**—his hits include *National Lampoon's*

Animal House (1978), *The Blues Brothers* (1980), and *Trading Places* (1983)—and his occasional excursions into horror have often had humorous content. *Schlock* (1973), his directorial debut, was a rather juvenile horror spoof. By contrast, *An American **Werewolf** in London* (1981) was a superior comedy-horror film that displayed a genuine affection for the horror genre and which also featured some groundbreaking werewolf transformation effects from **Rick Baker**. Landis also directed one of the episodes in the horror **anthology** *Twilight Zone: the Movie* (1983) and unsuccessfully attempted to recapture the magic of *American Werewolf* with the **vampire** film *Innocent Blood* (1992).

However, his best known horror credit is not for the cinema at all. He directed the hugely successful horror-themed video for Michael Jackson's "Thriller" (1983), which featured **zombies**, werewolves and the voice of **Vincent Price**. He also contributed to the **television** series *Masters of Horror* (2005–). *See also* AMERICAN HORROR.

LARRAZ, JOSÉ (1929–). After working as a **comic**-strip writer and a photographer, the Spanish director José Larraz made a series of low-budget horror films characterized by a fascination with perverse sexual behavior, namely *Whirlpool* (*She Died with Her Boots On*) (1969), *Deviation* (1971), *Scream... and Die!* (*The House that Vanished*, **Psycho** *Sex Fiend*) (1973), *La muerte incierta* (1973), and *Emma, puertas oscuras* (1974). The first three of these were filmed wholly or partly in Great Britain, where Larraz remained for the two horrors upon which his reputation as a horror auteur largely rests. *Symptoms* (1974) was an obscure mood piece about a woman's mental breakdown, while the more obviously commercial *Vampyres* (1974) depicted the murderous activities of two lesbian **vampires**. Both made evocative use of their country house settings, and *Vampyres* in particular offered a more sensual (and also more explicit) treatment of vampirism than the lesbian vampire films produced by **Hammer** earlier in the decade. Later in the 1970s, Larraz returned to Spanish cinema, where he made **comedies** and a few horrors, although none as impressive as his British work. They included *Estigma* (*Stigma*) (1982), *Los ritos sexuales del diablo* (*Black Candles*) (1982), *Descanse en piezas* (*Rest in Pieces*) (1987), *Al filo del hacha* (*Edge of the Axe*) (1988), and *Deadly Manor* (1990).

LAUGHTON, CHARLES (1899–1962). In a career that managed to be both distinguished and uneven, the English actor Charles Laughton featured with varying degrees of effectiveness in a number of horror films. He ably mixed gruffness with pathos in his portrayal of the self-made businessman in **James Whale**'s *The Old Dark House* (1932), while his Dr. Moreau in **Erle C. Kenton**'s *Island of Lost Souls* (1932) was a melodramatic rendition of the **mad scientist** figure. His performance under heavy **makeup** as Quasimodo in the glossy, big budget *The Hunchback of Notre Dame* (1939) has turned out to be the most pathos-laden version of this much-played role but he appeared to less effect in the supernatural **comedy** *The Canterville Ghost* (1944) and, alongside **Boris Karloff**, in the low-budget horror *The Strange Door* (1951). *Night of the Hunter* (1955), Laughton's sole directorial credit, was generally overlooked on its initial release but is now considered something of a classic and has its place, albeit a marginal one, in the horror canon. The story of a psychotic preacher, it brilliantly intertwined fairytale-like elements with **gothic** and nightmarish imagery.

LE BORG, REGINALD (1902–1989). The American director Reginald Le Borg made over sixty films, with the few horrors in that group solidly but impersonally done. In the 1940s, he directed three **Lon Chaney Jr.** films, *Calling Dr. Death* (1943), the **witchcraft** drama *Weird Woman* (1944), and *Dead Man's Eyes* (1944), all for the "Inner Sanctum" B-movie series. He was also responsible for *Jungle Woman* (1944), a **sequel** to *Captive Wild Woman* (1943) that dealt with the further exploits of a gorilla who had been transformed into a woman, and *The Mummy's Ghost* (1944), which reunited him with Chaney. During the 1950s, LeBorg made a **Hammer** film, albeit a melodrama—*The Flanagan Boy* (*Bad Blonde*) (1953)—rather than horror, and two weak horror films showcasing ageing horror stars such as **Boris Karloff**, **Bela Lugosi** and Chaney, *The Black Sleep* (1956) and *Voodoo Island* (1957). *Diary of a Madman*, an adaptation of a Guy de Maupassant story that starred **Vincent Price**, was better. LeBorg also directed the **psychological thriller** *So Evil, My Sister* (*Psycho Sisters*) (1974). *See also* AMERICAN HORROR.

LEE, CHRISTOPHER (1922–). Although Christopher Frank Carandini Lee was born and educated in Great Britain, he was descended on his mother's side from Italian nobility. It was therefore fitting that he achieved worldwide fame through his portrayal of an aristocrat, albeit an evil and vampiric one. His early acting career was not particularly distinguished. He appeared in minor roles and to little effect in over 30 British films from the late 1940s onwards, and when his big break finally came, it had more to do with his height—he is 6'5"—than with his acting ability. **Hammer** needed a tall man to play the creature in *The Curse of Frankenstein* (1957), its first color horror film, and Lee was given the part. The Hammer filmmakers were not permitted to use **Universal**'s distinctive monster design so opted instead for **makeup** that made Frankenstein's creation resemble, in Lee's own words, a road accident victim. Lee played the creature as savage and animalistic, eschewing the pathos offered by **Boris Karloff** in his 1930s portrayal of the role, and the film was a considerable international success. It was Lee's next project for Hammer that made him a star. **Peter Cushing** received top billing for *Dracula* (*Horror of Dracula*) (1958), but it was Lee's rendition of Count Dracula as a sensual, charismatic figure that caught the public's imagination. Lee himself remained wary of Dracula, however. He played the part six more times for Hammer in films of varying quality and also starred as the Count in **Jesus Franco**'s Spanish production *El Conde Dracula* (*Count Dracula*) (1970), but at the same time he constantly sought to broaden his range as an actor. For Hammer, he donned monstrous makeup again for the physically demanding role of Kharis in *The Mummy* (1959) and, by way of a contrast, was the young Henry Baskerville in the **Sherlock Holmes** adventure *The Hound of the Baskervilles* (1959). Later he would become the only actor to play both Sherlock Holmes—in *Sherlock Holmes und das Halsband des Todes* (*Sherlock Holmes and the Necklace of Death*) (1962)—and his brother Mycroft—in Billy Wilder's *The Private Life of Sherlock Holmes* (1970). He was Fu Manchu five times, an aged professor in *The Gorgon* (1964) and, in one of Lee's favorite performances, Rasputin in Hammer's *Rasputin—The Mad Monk* (1966). Unlike **Peter Cushing**, his good friend and frequent co-star, Lee often worked abroad, especially in Italy where he made, amongst others, two films for cult genre director **Mario Bava**, *Ercole al centro della terra* (*Hercules in the Haunted World*) (1961) and *La frusta et il corpo* (*The Whip and the Body*) (1963).

There was a solemnity to many of Lee's performances that could manifest itself as pomposity—for example, in the self-importance of the art critic he plays in *Dr. Terror's House of Horrors* (1964)—or, in the case of the many villains he portrayed, as aloof authority. In what are arguably his two most distinguished roles, this quality is inflected in different ways. In Hammer's satanic thriller *The **Devil** Rides Out* (1968) Lee is utterly convincing as the benevolent and wise Duc de Richleau while in the cult favorite *The Wicker Man* (1973) he is equally convincing as the pagan Lord Summerisle who joyously sings "Summer is a coming in" as an innocent victim is sacrificed to the old gods.

Lee's reputation as screen villain might have been formed within the horror genre but was not restricted to it. He was the evil Rochefort in *The Three Musketeers* (1973) and *The Four Musketeers* (1974) and the assassin Scaramanga in the James Bond adventure *The Man with the Golden Gun* (1974). In the early 2000s, at an age when many actors might have considered retirement, Lee achieved the greatest box-office success of his long career with scene-stealing villainous turns in George Lucas's *Star Wars Episode II: Attack of the Clones* (2002) and *Star Wars Episode III: Revenge of the Sith* (2005) and in **Peter Jackson**'s *Lord of the Rings* (2001–2003) trilogy.

Lee's other horror or horror-related credits are: *Corridors of Blood* (1958), *The Man Who Could Cheat Death* (1959), *Tempi duri per I vampiri* (*Hard Times for **Vampires**, Hard Times for Dracula, Uncle was a Vampire*) (1959), *The City of the Dead* (*Horror Hotel*) (1960), *The Two Faces of Dr. Jekyll* (1960), *The Terror of the Tongs* (1961), *The Hands of Orlac* (1961), *Taste of Fear* (*Scream of Fear*) (1961), *La vergine di Norimberga* (*The Virgin of Nuremberg, Horror Castle, The Castle of Terror*) (1963), *La cripta e l'incubo* (*Crypt of Horror, Terror in the Crypt*) (1963), *Katarsis* (1963), *Il castello dei morti vivi* (*Castle of the Living Dead*) (1964), *The Skull* (1965), *The Face of Fu Manchu* (1965), *She* (1965), *Dracula—Prince of Darkness* (1966), *The Brides of Fu Manchu* (1966), *Theatre of Death* (1966), *Five Golden Dragons* (1967), *Night of the Big Heat* (1967), *The Vengeance of Fu Manchu* (1967), *Die Schlangengrube und das Pendel* (*Castle of the Walking Dead, The Snake Pit and the Pendulum*) (1967), *Curse of the Crimson Altar* (1968), *Dracula has Risen from the Grave* (1968), *The Blood of Fu Manchu* (1968), *The Castle* *of Fu Manchu* (1969), *The Oblong Box* (1969), *Scream and Scream Again* (1969), *The Magic Christian* (1969), *Taste the Blood of Dracula* (1970), *Il trono di fuoco* (*The Bloody Judge, Night of the Blood Monster*) (1970), *Scars of Dracula* (1970), *The House That Dripped Blood* (1970), *I, Monster* (1970), *Death Line* (*Raw Meat*) (1972), *Nothing But the Night* (1972), *Dracula AD 1972* (1972), *The Creeping Flesh* (1973), *Pánico en el Transiberiano* (*Horror Express*) (1973), *Dark Places* (1973), *The Satanic Rites of Dracula* (1973), *To the Devil a Daughter* (1976), *The Keeper* (1976), *Dracula père et fils* (1976), *Meatcleaver Massacre* (1977), *House of the Long Shadows* (1983), *Howling 2* (1985), *Gremlins 2—The New Batch* (1990), *Curse III: Blood Sacrifice* (1993), *Funny Man* (1994), *Tale of the Mummy* (*Talos the Mummy*) (1998), and *Sleepy Hollow* (1999).

LEE, ROWLAND (1891–1975). The director Rowland Lee brought a stately quality to *Son of Frankenstein* (1939), the third film in the **Universal** Frankenstein series. **James Whale** had instilled a nervous, expressive energy into the previous two films, *Frankenstein* (1931) and *Bride of Frankenstein* (1935). By contrast, Lee's direction, while still containing expressive moments, was more balanced and controlled. He adopted a similar approach for the historical horror *Tower of London* (1939), which, like *Son of Frankenstein*, starred **Boris Karloff**. Earlier in his career, Lee had directed the proto-horror projects *The Mysterious Dr. Fu Manchu* (1929) and *The Return of Dr. Fu Manchu* (1930). *See also* AMERICAN HORROR.

LEIGH, JANET (1927–2004). Janet Leigh was first terrorized in a motel in Orson Welles' film noir *Touch of Evil* (1959), but it was her visit to the Bates Motel in **Alfred Hitchcock's** *Psycho* (1960) that earned her a place in horror history. As the sacrificial victim of the famous shower murder scene, she became a symbol of the new ruthlessness seeping into horror at the time. Even by contemporary generic standards, the idea of killing off the leading lady long before the film's conclusion still registers as a considerable provocation. Leigh's other horror roles are negligible. She fought giant killer rabbits in the silly *Night of the Lepus* (1972) and acted alongside her daughter **Jamie Lee Curtis** in *The Fog* (1980) and *Halloween H20: 20 Years Later* (1998).

LENI, PAUL (1885–1929). *Das wachsfigurenkabinett (**Waxworks**)* (1924), the first major film from German designer-turned-director Paul Leni, was a prime example of **Expressionism**. This **anthology**, which included **Jack the Ripper** as one of its characters, clearly demonstrated Leni's ability to convey oppressive and claustrophobic moods and atmospheres through inventive visual means. This quality was also evident in Leni's American films where it was often combined with a sense of humor, with both *The Cat and the Canary* (1927) and haunted theater drama *The Last Warning* (1929) successfully walking the difficult line between being scary and being funny. *The Man Who Laughs* (1928) was a more serious historical horror starring fellow German **Conrad Veidt** in the title role, but it was still visually impressive. Leni's premature death from blood poisoning curtailed a very promising career.

LENZI, UMBERTO (1931–). The Italian director Umberto Lenzi began his career in the 1960s with swashbucklers and thrillers before becoming one of the leading makers of **giallo** thrillers from the late 1960s onwards. *Orgasmo* (1969), *Cosi dolce . . . cosi perversa (So Sweet . . . So Perverse)* (1969), and *Paranoia (A Quiet Place to Kill)* (1970), which all starred the American actor Carroll Baker, offered the convoluted plots, colorful locations and violent murders associated with the giallo format. Although never in the **Dario Argento** league of achievement, Lenzi's later giallos clearly demonstrated his understanding of and commitment to this type of thriller. *Un posto ideale per uccidere (Oasis of Fear)* (1971) was followed by *Sette orchidee macchiate di rosso (Seven Blood-Stained Orchids)* (1972), *Il coltello di ghiaccio (Knife of Ice, Silent Horror)* (1972), *Spasmo* (1974), and *Gatti rossi in un labirinto di vetro (Eyeball)* (1975).

Lenzi's later career in horror took him away from the giallo into lower budgeted areas of exploitation horror. He had earlier directed one of the first Italian cannibal films, *Il paese del sesso selvaggio (Deep River Savages, Sacrifice!)* (1972) and returned to this notoriously gory sub-cycle in the 1980s with *Mangiati vivi (Eaten Alive)* (1980) and *Cannibal Ferox* (1981). He also made the silly **zombie** film *Incubo sulla città contaminata (Nightmare City)* (1980), the main innovation of which involved replacing the standard slow-moving zombies with more athletic running ones. Later horror credits have been minor, including *Nightmare Beach* (1988), *La casa 3 (Ghosthouse)* (1988), *Le porte dell'inferno (Gate of Hell)* (1989), *Paura nel buio (Hitcher in the Dark)* (1989) and *Demoni 3 (Black Demons)* (1991), as well as **television** films *La casa del sortilegio (House of Witchcraft)* (1989) and *La casa delle anime erranti (House of Lost Souls)* (1989). *See also* ITALIAN HORROR.

LEWIS, HERSCHELL GORDON (1926–). Before he became a film director, Herschell Gordon Lewis was a college lecturer and worked in advertising. Neither of these activities seems to have influenced the types of films he made, however, for Lewis is now considered to be the father of the **gore** movie. He started out in the early 1960s making nudie/sexploitation films but quickly moved into horror with *Blood Feast* (1963), a low-budget project that set the pattern for what was to come. A lurid story—in this case involving a caterer assembling various body parts for a "blood feast" that will resurrect an ancient goddess— was conveyed via poor acting, minimal production values, a mainly static camera, and, most of all, by gore, with the film's highlight a scene in which a woman's tongue was torn out. While the special effects involved in this were crude to the point of risibility, its relentlessness somehow rendered it disturbing. Lewis followed *Blood Feast* with *Two Thousand Maniacs!* (1964), a horror version of *Brigadoon* in which the ghostly inhabitants of a town in the Deep South terrorize and kill some visiting Northerners. While the film was comparable with *Blood Feast* in terms of its gore scenes, it had slightly higher production values and Lewis's direction was more fluent. It is generally considered to be his best work and is also an important example of **rural horror**.

More Lewis gore films followed—*Color Me Blood Red* (1965), *The Gruesome Twosome* (1967), *The Wizard of Gore* (1970), and *The Gore Gore Girls* (1972). They were all uneven, disgusting and offensive in places, amusing in others, with their principal virtue as a group of films probably their rough-hewn naivety. By contrast, *A Taste of Blood* (1967) was a more conventional **vampire** film and *Something Weird* (1967) a goreless fantasy thriller. Throughout the 1960s, Lewis also continued with the production of other exploitation subjects, among them biker movies and sex melodramas, as well as making an unsuccessful excursion into family entertainment with *Jimmy, the Boy Wonder* (1966).

The market for Lewis's kind of exploitation fare began to disappear in the late 1960s as mainstream cinema itself acquired a new explicitness so far as the representation of sex and violence was concerned. Lewis withdrew from filmmaking and began a successful career in advertising and marketing. He returned to the director's chair for the **sequel** *Blood Feast 2: All U Can Eat* (2002). His *Two Thousand Maniacs!* was later remade by Tim Sullivan as *2001 Maniacs* (2005). *See also* AMERICAN HORROR.

LEWTON, VAL (1904–1951). The Russian-born producer Val Lewton (whose real name was Vladimir Ivan Leventon) has become a critically lauded figure in horror history because of the nine films he produced—and occasionally wrote under the name "Carlos Keith"—at RKO during the 1940s. Before then, he had first been a writer and publicist and then an assistant to producer David O. Selznick on such blockbuster projects as *A Tale of Two Cities* (1935) and *Gone With the Wind* (1939). By contrast, RKO offered him low budgets and often lurid titles in an attempt to cash in on a 1940s **American horror** revival that was largely driven by **Universal**. Lewton's sensibilities as a filmmaker were considerably more ambitious than this, which resulted in some remarkable films but also in tensions with studio executives who sometimes found Lewton's work puzzling or pretentious.

Lewton's distinctive approach was evident in his first RKO horror production, *Cat People* (1942), which was brilliantly directed by regular Lewton collaborator **Jacques Tourneur**. In place of Universal's vulgar but energetic monster melodramas, Lewton offered a somber adult drama set in contemporary America that dealt subtly with a woman who believed that she would transform into a panther if sexually aroused. The film shied away from the by then conventional representations of movie monsters, preferring instead a more ambiguous treatment of its heroine's situation (although the studio insisted than footage of a killer cat was inserted into the finished film). *Cat People* also contained what was probably the horror genre's first **startle effect**, when in an atmospheric night-time sequence a potential female victim of the cat is startled—along with the audience—as a bus unexpectedly pulls into frame; Lewton himself subsequently called this kind of effect a "bus" and included it in a number of his other horror films.

Lewton's next two horrors were *I Walked with a Zombie* (1943) and *The Leopard Man* (1943), both of which were again directed by Tourneur. These confirmed Lewton's status as a generic innovator capable of throwing into disarray some of the moral certainties and platitudes found in other horrors of the period. *I Walked with a Zombie* discarded the traditional zombie scenario and instead found inspiration for its eerie and disturbing story in *Jane Eyre*, while *The Leopard Man* was a stylish and in places intensely suspenseful **serial killer** thriller that, in terms of its subject matter at least, was arguably years ahead of its time.

Lewton's later films were directed by young up-and-coming directors such as **Mark Robson** and **Robert Wise**. The producer's penchant for inserting references to high culture in his films and for exploring decidedly downbeat themes was increasingly evident, with this sometimes weighing down the films themselves. The Satanic thriller *The Seventh Victim* (1943) and the **ghost** story *The Curse of the Cat People* (1944) were highlights, with the oppressive and deathly atmosphere of the former and the child's fantasy gently represented in the latter indicating Lewton's range as a filmmaker. *Isle of the Dead* (1945), one of the three Lewton films that starred **Boris Karloff,** was also an impressive meditation on death, although its sustained seriousness teetered on the edge of absurdity. Of lesser consequence was *The Ghost Ship* (1943), a low-key **psychological thriller**, while Lewton's final two horrors, *The Body Snatcher* (1945) and *Bedlam* (1946), both of which featured Karloff, were well-made but conventional period melodramas lacking the inventiveness and intensity of his earlier work. As the 1940s horror boom faded, Lewton moved on briefly to other genres. Although his **western** *Apache Drums* (1951) contained a horror-like sequence in which Indians besiege a church, none of Lewton's later films proved as distinctive as his horror projects. Long suffering from ill health, he died of a heart attack in 1951.

Lewton's horror films have come to symbolize a type of horror based on suggestion, ambiguity and artistic intelligence. Sometimes they have been used by critics to lambast a more mainstream monster-centered horror, although such an approach unjustly underrates the achievements of filmmakers working within the more explicit horror tradition. So far as later horror production is concerned, Lewton's influence is hard to detect, outside of two rather obvious Lewton-style horrors from directors who had earlier worked with the producer, Jacques Tourneur's *Night of the Demon* (*Curse of the Demon*) (1957) and Robert Wise's *The Haunting* (1963). However, the emphasis in many cinematic ghost stories from the late 1990s onwards on ambiguity and indirection might reasonably be described as "Lewtonesque."

LIEBERMAN, JEFF (1947–). The American director Jeff Lieberman made an impression with his first two horror films, *Squirm* (1976) and *Blue Sunshine* (1977). In terms of its plot, *Squirm* was a straightforward **revenge of nature** film in which thousands of worms invade a small town, but, like Lieberman's later work, it had a winning sense of humor that helped it overcome some of the absurdities of its story. *Blue Sunshine*'s engaging premise was that some people who took an experimental LSD back in the 1960s lose all their hair in the 1970s and are transformed into homicidal maniacs; never has the idea of 1960s values going sour in the 1970s been set out so clearly. Lieberman returned to the genre with the above-average backwoods **slasher** *Just Before Dawn* (1981) and also made the **science fiction**/horror **comedy** *Remote Control* (1987). More recently, he introduced some dark humor into the **serial killer** drama *Satan's Little Helper* (2004). *See also* AMERICAN HORROR.

LITTLE, DWIGHT H. (1947–). The director Dwight H. Little's first horror credit was *Halloween 4: The Return of Michael Myers* (1988). It was hardly a promising genre debut, but Little's treatment of the story was slick and contained some effective *frissons*. He followed this with a serviceable version of *The Phantom of the Opera* (1989) that starred 1980s horror icon **Robert Englund** in the title role. Little's subsequent cinematic credits were mainly in the thriller genre. However, he also contributed episodes to several horror-themed **television** series, including *Freddy's Nightmares* (1988–1990), *The X Files* (1993–2002), *Millennium* (1996–1999), *Wolf Lake* (2001–2002), and he returned to cinematic horror with *Anacondas: The Hunt for the Blood Orchid* (2004). *See also* AMERICAN HORROR.

LOM, HERBERT (1917–). The Czech actor Herbert Lom is best known for his role as the hapless Chief Inspector Dreyfus in several

Pink Panther comedies. However, he has also provided effective support in a number of European horror films, often bringing a cosmopolitan *savoir-faire* to the proceedings. He was a subdued Phantom in **Hammer**'s *The Phantom of the Opera* (1962) and Van Helsing in **Jesus Franco**'s *El Conde Dracula* (*Count Dracula*) (1970), and he provided some much-needed dignity amidst the carnage in the **German horror** *Hexen bis aufs Blut gequält* (*Mark of the Devil*) (1970) and the female nudity in *Dorian Gray* (1970). A group of relatively sedate **British horror** films—that included *Murders in the Rue Morgue* (1971), *Dark Places* (1973), and two **Amicus** productions, *Asylum* (1972) and *And Now the Screaming Starts!* (1973)—concluded this part of his horror career. In the 1980s, he had a small but effective role in **David Cronenberg**'s *The Dead Zone* (1983) and later showed up in an uninspired version of *Masque of the Red Death* (1990) and in **Michele Soavi**'s accomplished supernatural mystery *La Setta* (*The Sect*) (1991).

LOMMEL, ULLI (1944–). The filmmaking career of the German actor-turned-director Ulli Lommel began auspiciously with *Die Zärtlichkeit der Wölfe* (*The Tenderness of Wolves*) (1973), a disturbing account of real-life **serial killer** Fritz Haarmann that also managed to include references to German **Expressionism**. The film was produced by Rainer Werner Fassbinder, for whom Lommel had acted, and displayed his influence in its emphasis on destructive gay sexuality and its awareness of German history. Lommel's later horror films were mainly made in the United States and lacked the resonances of his genre debut. The **ghost** story *The Boogeyman* (1980) was successful enough to generate two **sequels**, but Lommel's other horrors were mainly direct-to-video affairs. They included *Brain Waves* (1983), *The Devonsville Terror* (1983), *Bloodsuckers* (1998), and *Zombie Nation* (2004).

LORRE, PETER (1904–1964). The Hungarian actor Peter Lorre's first starring role was as a **serial killer** of **children** in Fritz Lang's German film *M* (1931). His remarkable performance anticipated later representations of serial killers in **Alfred Hitchcock**'s *Psycho* (1960) and **Michael Powell**'s *Peeping Tom* (1960) in its humanizing of the murderer as someone incapable of resisting their homicidal urges. In

Lorre's case, he managed to convey through bodily contortions his inner struggle and his ultimate surrender to the desire to kill. He left Germany as Hitler came to power, worked with Hitchcock on two of his British films (*The Man Who Knew Too Much* in 1934 and *Secret Agent* in 1936) and eventually ended up in America where, partly because of his association with *M* and partly because of his own unusual appearance, he was usually cast in sinister but charming roles, not least in *The Maltese Falcon* (1941) and *Casablanca* (1942) (although, rather bizarrely, he also played the Japanese detective Mr. Moto in a series of films). He was splendid as the mad doctor in **Karl Freund**'s **American horror** *Mad Love* (1935), was an *M*-like killer in the proto-film noir *Stranger on the Third Floor* (1940), and was both sympathetic and quietly menacing as the disfigured anti-hero in **Robert Florey**'s *The Face Behind the Mask* (1941); he worked with Florey again on the **disembodied hand** thriller *The Beast with Five Fingers* (1946). He also revealed a talent for **comedy** in the comedy-horrors *You'll Find Out* (1940), in which he starred with **Boris Karloff** and **Bela Lugosi**, *The Boogie Man Will Get You* (1942), which again featured Karloff, and Frank Capra's *Arsenic and Old Lace* (1944). Throughout the 1950s, he worked mainly for **television** —including a performance as the villain in an early adaptation of the James Bond story *Casino Royale* in 1954. In the last few years of his life, he returned to comedy-horror and, unlike some other ageing horror stars—including the likes of **Lon Chaney Jr.** and **John Carradine**—retained his dignity with enjoyable performances in **Roger Corman**'s *Tales of Terror* (1962) and *The Raven* (1963) and **Jacques Tourneur**'s *The Comedy of Terrors* (1964), the last two of which reunited him with Karloff.

LOVECRAFT, H. P. (1890–1937). The American writer Howard Phillips Lovecraft—who is better known as H. P. Lovecraft—is an important figure in the development of modern horror literature, with many other key horror writers expressing admiration for his work. His impact on horror cinema has been less significant, however, perhaps because the visionary and allusive quality of his fiction does not lend itself readily to being filmed. Although Lovecraft died in 1937, the first screen adaptations of his work did not appear until the 1960s, with none of them very faithful to their literary originals. **Roger Cor-**

man's *The Haunted Palace* (1963), which was based on "The Strange Case of Charles Dexter Ward," was actually marketed as an **Edgar Allan Poe** adaptation. It was followed by *Die, Monster, Die!* (1965), *The Shuttered Room* (1967), *Curse of the Crimson Altar* (1968), and *The Dunwich Horror* (1970), the latter two of which used psychedelic imagery as a way of conveying Lovecraft's otherworldly themes.

The next wave of Lovecraft adaptations began in the mid-1980s with *Re-animator* (1985) and *From Beyond* (1986), both directed by **Stuart Gordon**, which introduced **gore** and humor into stories that had originally been entirely lacking in such elements. Subsequent adaptations have tended to be low-budget monster movies often released direct onto video or DVD, although a few have proved more substantial, including Gordon's *Castle Freak* (1995) and *Dagon* (2001) and the bizarre **anthology** *Lovecracked* (2006). Further loose adaptations have included *The Unnamable* (1988), **Dan O'Bannon's** *The Resurrected* (1992), *Necronomicon* (1994), and *Bleeders* (1997). Lovecraft himself was played by **Jeffrey Combs** in *Necronomicon* and by Nick Basile in *Lovecracked*.

Other films that seem to have a Lovecraftian quality in their visionary depiction of the old Gods breaking through into our world include **Lucio Fulci's** *Paura nella città dei morti viventi* (*City of the Living Dead*) (1980) and *L'aldilà* (*The Beyond*) (1981), **John Carpenter's** *Prince of Darkness* (1987), and *In the Mouth of Madness* (1994), and perhaps even **Ivan Reitman's** **comedy** *Ghostbusters* (1984).

LUBIN, ARTHUR (1898–1995). Director Arthur Lubin's best-known horror film is the 1943 **Universal** version of *The Phantom of the Opera*, which starred **Claude Rains** in the title role. This was a more upmarket production than most of the other Universal horrors from the period, with Lubin tastefully emphasizing the romantic elements of the story over the more **gothic** ones. Earlier, however, he had directed the considerably more downmarket horror/gangster hybrid *Black Friday* (1940), which starred **Boris Karloff** and **Bela Lugosi**, and the **Bud Abbott** and **Lou Costello** comedy-horror *Hold That Ghost* (1941). His final horror credit was *The Spider Woman Strikes Back* (1946). From the 1950s onwards, he worked for **television** and also made several films featuring Francis, the talking mule. *See also* AMERICAN HORROR.

LUGOSI, BELA (1882–1956). Bela Lugosi's performance as Count **Dracula** in the 1931 **Universal** production of *Dracula* made him an instant horror star, although subsequent typecasting limited his career more than was the case with other actors associated with the genre. Born Bela Blasko in Lugos, Hungary, he later took the stage name of Lugosi from his hometown. From 1902 onwards, he was a theater actor in Hungary and also appeared in supporting roles in Hungarian and German films, most notably as the butler in *Der Januskopf* (1920), **F.W. Murnau**'s version of the *Dr. Jekyll and Mr. Hyde* story. He emigrated to the United States in 1921, where he continued to mix theatrical and film work, including a featured role in **Tod Browning**'s film thriller *The Thirteenth Chair* (1929). (Browning would later direct him in *Dracula.*) His big break came with a starring role in a stage adaptation of *Dracula* that opened on Broadway in 1927 and later toured the country. Lugosi was not the first choice for the film version, with Universal preferring a more established star in the role, but he secured the role in the end. For modern horror audiences, Lugosi's performance as Dracula can seem mannered and archiac, reliant as it is on theatrical gestures and pregnant pauses in the dialogue. However, this was an acceptable performance style in cinema's early sound period, and for cinema audiences of the 1930s, Lugosi's East European **vampire** was a fascinating and exotic figure.

Lugosi was considered for the role of the monster in *Frankenstein* (1931), Universal's follow-up to *Dracula*, but the part eventually went to **Boris Karloff**. (Reportedly Lugosi was unhappy about the role's muteness.) Despite this, the first half of the 1930s turned out to be the most productive and successful period in Lugosi's career. He played charismatic villains in Universal's *Murders in the Rue Morgue* (1932) and *The Raven* (1935) and the independently produced *White Zombie* (1932), was almost unrecognisable under heavy **makeup** in the controversial *Island of Lost Souls* (1932) and assayed a rare heroic role in **Edgar G. Ulmer**'s stylish *The Black Cat* (1934). He was also a Dracula-like vampire in Tod Browning's *Mark of the Vampire* (1935), although here a plot twist revealed that Lugosi's character was only pretending to be one of the undead.

By the late 1930s, the exoticism associated with Lugosi, who never lost his thick Hungarian accent, was out of fashion. When Universal resurrected Dracula in the 1940s, the role was recast in the more obviously American form of **Lon Chaney Jr.** and **John Carradine**, and Lugosi himself was increasingly relegated to low-budget work or to small character parts in bigger films, aside from a star turn as the vampiric Count Tesla in Columbia's *Return of the Vampire* (1944). Some of his supporting roles were impressively done; his Ygor in *Son of Frankenstein* (1939) and *The Ghost of Frankenstein* (1942) was a genuinely touching creation, and he provided effective local color in *The Wolf Man* (1941), and the **Val Lewton**-produced *The Body Snatcher* (1945). He was also willing to parody himself in **comedy**-horrors such as *The Gorilla* (1939), *You'll Find Out* (1940), *Spooks Run Wild* (1941) and *Abbott and Costello Meet Frankenstein* (1948), in which Lugosi appeared on screen as Dracula for the second and final time in his career. He was less comfortable as Frankenstein's monster (a part he had turned down in the early 1930s) in *Frankenstein Meets the Wolf Man* (1943), and the ultra-low-budget tattiness of *The Corpse Vanishes* (1942), one of several films he made for the poverty-row studio Monogram, only served to underline how far Lugosi had fallen from his earlier stardom. An addiction to drugs led to further decline during the 1950s, and Lugosi ended his career making films for cult director **Ed Wood**. His final screen role was a brief appearance in Wood's *Plan 9 From Outer Space* (1959), which was not released until three years after Lugosi's death and which has since been voted "worst film of all time." As a final macabre touch, Lugosi was buried wearing a Dracula-style cloak.

The depressing sadness of Lugosi's latter years—eloquently portrayed in **Tim Burton**'s biopic *Ed Wood* (1994), with Martin Landau delivering an Oscar-winning performance as Lugosi—has sometimes eclipsed his achievements as an actor. In particular, his portrayal of Dracula might be much parodied but it still possesses a kind of power, and one can find echoes of it in more recent versions of the Count, notably performances by Frank Langella in *Dracula* (1979) and Gary Oldman in *Dracula* (1992).

Lugosi's other horror credits include *The Mystery of the Mary Celeste* (1935), *The Invisible Ray* (1936), *The Dark **Eyes** of London* (1940), *Black Friday* (1940), *The **Devil** Bat* (1940), *The Black Cat*

(1941), *The Invisible Ghost* (1941), *Night Monster* (1942), *Bowery at Midnight* (1942), *The Ape Man* (1943), *Ghosts on the Loose* (1943), *Voodoo Man* (1944), *Return of the Ape Man* (1944), *Zombies on Broadway* (1945), *Scared to Death* (1947), *Old Mother Riley Meets the Vampire* (1952), *Bela Lugosi Meets a Brooklyn Gorilla* (1952), *Bride of the Monster* (1955), and *The Black Sleep* (1956). *See also* AMERICAN HORROR.

LUSTIG, WILLIAM (1955–). The American producer-director William Lustig seems to have specialized in making horror films with the word *Maniac* in the title. He began with *Maniac* (1980), a gruesome **serial killer** drama that gave early opportunities to **makeup** experts **Rob Bottin** and **Tom Savini.** Then came the slightly more palatable *Maniac Cop* (1988), the title of which more or less explained the story. Although scripted by **Larry Cohen,** the film lacked the elements of social critique associated with his work and was instead more standard B-movie fare. However, Lustig made the most of the New York settings in his depiction of the activities of the apparently indestructible evil cop, and also made two effective **sequels,** *Maniac Cop 2* (1990) and *Maniac Cop 3: Badge of Silence* (1993). *Uncle Sam* (1997), another collaboration with Cohen about an undead Kuwait war veteran, was less successful. Since then, Lustig has set up Blue Underground, a company specializing in the distribution of cult classics. *See also* AMERICAN HORROR.

– M –

THE MAD SCIENTIST. The mad scientist was a stock figure in 1930s and 1940s horror cinema, most notably in the form of **Frankenstein** and Dr. Jekyll (although earlier cinematic versions of this figure can be found—for example, in Rex Ingram's *The Magician* in 1926 or Fritz Lang's *Metropolis* in 1927). The "**madness**" involved here tended not to be psychological, although deranged behavior was often in evidence (in the 1933 production of *The Invisible Man*, for instance). Instead it related to the intensely antisocial nature of the scientist's activities. Either his objectives were not socially useful—for example, turning **apes** or other animals into humans in *Island of*

Lost Souls (1932) or *Captive Wild Woman* (1943)—or his methods unacceptable—for example, murdering people to obtain body parts in various Frankenstein films or *Doctor X* (1932). Even though there was something potentially heroic about such figures as they sought to break through normality's constraints and obtain "forbidden" knowledge, most 1930s and 1940s horrors exhibited a mild conservatism by siding with the forces of normality against the mad scientist.

Science itself was often shown by these films as a strange practice that was separate from social normality, with a visual emphasis on bizarre pieces of scientific equipment, the precise function of which was rarely explained. However, in this pre-nuclear era, the idea that science itself might be dangerous was not foregrounded. Instead it was usually the scientist who was solely responsible for the trouble, and his death (or occasional rehabilitation) resolved any problems associated with science.

This started to change after World War II, reflecting not just the advent of nuclear power but also the increasing integration of science into the fabric of everyday life. Antisocial scientists still existed, especially in the 1950s and 1960s, in **Hammer**'s Frankenstein films, for example, or in American **teenage horror** films such as *I was a Teenage Frankenstein* (1957) or *Blood of Dracula* (1957). However, the sense of there being a clear framework of social normality against which these renegades could be defined as "mad" was fading. By the 1970s, irresponsible scientists were often not visibly separate from society, with science itself as much of a problem as the individual practising it. In the films of **David Cronenberg**, for example, irresponsible scientists were rarely the outright villains they once were but instead—especially in *Rabid* (1977), *The Brood* (1979), and *The Fly* (1986)—apparently reasonable people who were just unable to see the disastrous consequences of their experiments. Within such a context, the traditional version of the mad scientist has become something of an anachronism, as is evidenced by the humorous treatment of this figure in the likes of *Everything You Wanted to Know About Sex But Were Afraid to Ask* (1972), *Flesh for Frankenstein* (1973), *Young Frankenstein* (1974), *The Man with Two Brains* (1983), and *Re-animator* (1985).

MADNESS. Insanity has been a key theme in the horror genre from the 1960s onwards. Before then, representations of madness showed up sporadically—with asylums featuring, for example, in the proto-horror *Das Cabinet Des Dr. Caligari* (*The Cabinet of Dr. Caligari*) (1919), *Dracula* (1931), and *Bedlam* (1946). **Mad scientists** were also present in the 1930s and 1940s, although their madness usually derived more from their intensely antisocial activities than it did from any clinical form of insanity. **Alfred Hitchcock**'s *Psycho* (1960) changed this through introducing the idea of the monster as psychological case study, with the scariness of the film's **serial killer** Norman Bates residing not in any supernatural quality but rather in his disturbed mind. An increasing focus on the psychological formed part of a broader shift in the genre during the 1960s towards monsters that were much closer to home than the more obviously fantasy-based monsters of the 1930s. In Italy, the **giallo** thriller frequently relied on madness for its killers' motivation, as did some British psychological horrors, including *Paranoiac* (1963) and *The Psychopath* (1965), while in the United States **William Castle** also churned out a series of *Psycho* look-alikes, most notably *Homicidal* (1961). The popularity of the cinematic serial killer from the 1970s onwards yet further demonstrated horror's interest in disturbed psychologies. While **slasher** films such as *Halloween* (1978) and *Friday the 13th* (1980) offered the insane killer as a disturbingly emotionless killing machine, other films explored the realm of the psychological in much more detail, among them **Brian De Palma**'s *Sisters* (1973), *Deranged* (1974), **Pete Walker**'s *Frightmare* (1974), *Santa Sangre* (1989), and *Ed Gein* (2000). Horror's most successful madman, however, remains Hannibal Lecter, also known as Hannibal the Cannibal, who through five films—*Manhunter* (1986), *The Silence of the Lambs* (1991), *Hannibal* (2001), *Red Dragon* (2002), and *Hannibal Rising* (2007)—has combined immense articulacy and charm with deranged violence. That he has become a kind of cult hero suggests that an audience's relation with images of insanity is not just driven by repulsion but by fascination as well.

MAKEUP. The fact that horror is the only area of cinema in which makeup artists have acquired the kudos usually associated with stars and directors underlines the centrality of makeup effects to the genre. Proto-horror star **Lon Chaney** was renowned for creating his own makeup transformations in *The Hunchback of Notre Dame* (1923) and *The Phantom of the Opera* (1925), but subsequently it was full-time makeup artists who assumed responsibility for the creation of monsters. **Jack Pierce** created **Frankenstein**'s monster as well as **werewolves** and **vampires** at **Universal** during the 1930s and 1940s, and in so doing he helped to define the essence of the horror films produced at that studio. Later, Phil Leakey and **Roy Ashton** bestowed a visceral physicality on **Hammer**'s monsters in a way that set the films apart from their competitors. In the 1970s, **Dick Smith** transformed a sweet little girl into a foul-mouthed abject spectacle in *The Exorcist* (1973), while, among others, **Rick Baker, Rob Bottin, Tom Savini,** and **Stan Winston** have acquired cult followings for their ability to produce unnerving bodily transformations, metamorphoses and disarticulations.

Some of the techniques used by horror makeup artists have changed over the years. However, the continued prominence of such figures within the genre reminds us of how horror's monstrous effects have always been centered on the human body itself. If makeup specialists are to be thought of as artists, it is this body that provides their main canvas.

MALLESON, MILES (1888–1969). Miles Malleson was a successful British playwright and screenwriter, but he was also a busy character actor who specialized in bumbling roles, often stealing the scenes in which he appeared. He did a memorable turn as the sinister hearse driver in Ealing Studio's **ghost** story *Dead of Night* (1945). Later he appeared in several **Hammer** horrors—as an undertaker in *Dracula* (*The Horror of Dracula*) (1958), a bishop in *The Hound of the Baskervilles* (1959), a doctor in *The Brides of Dracula* (1960), and a hansom cab driver in *The Phantom of the Opera* (1962). He even brought charm to the rather seedy role of the gentleman purchasing pornographic "views" in **Michael Powell**'s controversial *Peeping Tom* (1960). Malleson's last horror credit was in **Freddie Francis**'s *Vengeance* (*The Brain*) (1962), where, true to form, he played a bumbling doctor.

MALONE, WILLIAM (1953–). The American director William Malone began with two cheap and cheerful monster films, *Scared to Death* (1981) and *Creature* (*Titan Find*) (1985). *House on Haunted*

Hill (1999) was glossier and more stylish, with Malone successfully combining humor and horror in this **remake** of a **William Castle** film. The supernatural thriller *FeardotCom* (2002) was more uneven, however. Owing something to **Japanese horror** in its combination of **ghosts** with modern technologies—in this case the **internet**—it contained effective sequences but struggled to maintain a coherent narrative. Malone has also contributed to the **television** horror series *Freddy's Nightmares* (1988–1990), *Tales from the Crypt* (1989–1996), *The Others* (2000), and *Masters of Horror* (2005–). *See also* AMERICAN HORROR.

MANN, MICHAEL (1943–). The writer-director Michael Mann tends to be associated with cool urban dramas and thrillers such as *Heat* (1995) and *Collateral* (2004). However, he also brought the master **serial killer** Hannibal Lecter to the cinema screen for the first time in *Manhunter* (1986), an adaptation of Thomas Harris's novel *Red Dragon*. While the later *The Silence of the Lambs* (1991), directed by **Jonathan Demme**, adopted a dank, dark look and featured **Anthony Hopkins'** grandstanding performance as Lecter, Mann opted instead for a cool, modernistic style and a more low-key Lecter from actor Brian Cox. The result was not as commercially successful as Demme's version, but it did offer a different, and equally disturbing, way of representing the serial killer as modern monster. Mann had earlier dabbled in horror with *The Keep* (1983). This World War II drama, in which a group of German soldiers confront a powerful supernatural entity, was uneven, but it was also very stylish and featured one of horror cinema's more impressive monster designs.

MANNERS, DAVID (1900–1998). The actor David Manners was the pleasant but bland male romantic lead in **Universal** horror films *Dracula* (1931), *The Mummy* (1932), and *The Black Cat* (1934), as well as featuring in the **gothic**-themed *Mystery of Edwin Drood* (1935). His amiable ordinariness set off the more dramatic performances given by the likes of **Bela Lugosi** and **Boris Karloff**. He also worked with celebrated horror director **James Whale** on the World War I drama *Journey's End* (1930). However, he subsequently showed little interest in his horror films and claimed never to have seen *Dracula*.

MARCH, FREDRIC (1897–1975). Fredric March was the first actor to win an Academy Award for a leading performance in a horror film, in his case for his remarkable rendition of the lead role(s) in *Dr. Jekyll and Mr. Hyde* (1931). This remained the only horror film in a distinguished career, although he did play Death in the romantic **comedy** *Death Takes a Holiday* (1934) and also showed up in the supernatural comedy *I Married a Witch* (1942). The horror genre would have to wait until *The Silence of the Lambs* (1991) before it saw more Oscars for leading performances, in this case for Jodie Foster and **Anthony Hopkins**.

MARGHERITI, ANTONIO (1930–2002). In a career lasting nearly 40 years, the Italian director Antonio Margheriti—who was sometimes billed as Anthony M. Dawson—contributed to most of the formats popular in **Italian horror** cinema, never offering much that was original but often providing interesting variations on established conventions. He brought considerable visual *élan* to his first three **gothic** horrors, *La vergine di Norimberga* (*The Virgin of Nuremberg, Horror Castle, The Castle of Terror*) (1963), *I lunghi capelli della morte* (*The Long Hair of Death*) (1964), and *Danza macabre* (*The Castle of Terror, Castle of Blood*) (1964), with the last two of these representing some of the best work done by horror star **Barbara Steele**. He also showed himself adept at making **giallo** thrillers with *Nude... si muore* (*School Girl Killer*) (1968), *Contronatura* (*Screams in the Night*) (1969), and *La morte negli occhi del gatto* (*Seven Deaths in the Cat's Eye*) (1973). His other horror films were uneven, however. *Nella strata morsa del ragno* (*In the grip of the Spider*) (1971) was a crude **remake** of his own *Danza macabre*, and *Killer Fish* (1979) was a clumsy piranha-on-the-loose story. *Apocalypse domani* (*Cannibal Apocalypse*) (1980), Margheriti's contribution to the Italian **cannibalism** cycle, was more restrained than some of its competitors and consequently more watchable, although his final genre credit, the **science fiction**/horror *Alien degli abissi* (*Alien from the Deep*) (1989), was negligible. He has sometimes been credited with the direction of *Flesh for **Frankenstein*** (1973) and *Blood for **Dracula*** (1974), although his input into both was minimal.

MARINS, JOSÉ MOJICA (1936–). The horror films made by the Brazilian director and actor José Mojica Marins are often provocative and confrontational, relying as they do on misanthropic themes, representations of sexual violence and disturbing hallucinatory imagery. His first major success was *À meia-noite levarei sua alma* (*At Midnight I Will Take Your Soul*) (1964), in which he played the role that would become his alter-ego in several later films, the sadistic gravedigger Zé do Caixão (known in English-language versions as Coffin Joe). This character's hunt for the perfect woman to bear his child led to much violence as well as some casual blasphemy. The **sequel** *Esta noite encarnarei no teu cadáver* (*This Night I Will Possess Your Corpse*) (1967) offered more of the same. Marins next directed an episode of the horror **anthology** *Trilogia de terror* (*Trilogy of Terror*) (1968) and all three episodes of another anthology, *O estranho mundo de Zé do Caixão* (*The Strange World of Coffin Joe*) (1968). *O despertar da besta* (*O ritual dos sádicos, Awakening of the Beast*) (1970) combined horror material with a story about drug addiction but was heavily censored, like Marins' earlier work, by the Brazilian authorities. The full version is rated highly by **fans** of Marins, although to the uninitiated it is a difficult film to get through. Marins' subsequent horror films, while sometimes unpleasant, have lacked the intensity associated with his best work. They include *O exorcismo negro* (*Black Exorcism of Coffin Joe*) (1974), *Inferno carnal* (*Hellish Flesh*) (1977), *Delírios de um anormal* (*Hallucinations of a Deranged Mind*) (1978), and *Estupro* (*Perversion*) (1979).

MARSHALL, NEIL (1970–). The British writer-director Neil Marshall made an auspicious horror debut with ***Dog** Soldiers* (2002), in which some soldiers on a training mission take on a band of **werewolves**. This mixture of suspense, violence, **gore** and humor occasionally lost its way, but the film had an energy and level of invention that separated it out from the rest of the horror pack. Marshall's next film was the even more accomplished *The Descent* (2005), which pitted a group of female potholers against predatory subhuman cave dwellers. Unsparingly violent and generating an intense claustrophobic atmosphere, the film ruthlessly put its deftly characterized protagonists through hell and also demonstrated a confidence in cinematic storytelling not always apparent in the horror genre. With only two feature films to his credit, Marshall has already established himself as one of the leading young talents in contemporary horror. *See also* BRITISH HORROR.

MARTIN, EUGENIO (1925–). Spanish director Eugenio Martin's *Una vela para el diablo* (*A Candle for the Devil, It Happened at Nightmare Inn*) (1970) provided a powerful account of generational difference in Spain with its story of middle-aged innkeepers preying murderously on members of the new "permissive" generation. Martin—who was sometimes billed as Gene Martin—followed this with a **giallo** thriller *La última señora Anderson* (*Death at the Deep End of the Swimming Pool, The Fourth Victim*) (1971) and the period horror *Pánico en el Transiberiano* (*Horror Express*) (1973). The latter, which featured excellent performances from **Peter Cushing** and **Christopher Lee,** effectively combined the best of **British horror** with an ornate Spanish visual style in its story of an alien monster being resurrected within the claustrophobic confines of a train. *Pánico en el Transiberiano* has been overlooked in most histories of 1970s horror, but it was one of the most striking horror films from that decade. Martin's other genre credits have included *Aquella casa en las afueras* (*That House in the Outskirts*) (1980) and *Sobrenatural* (*Supernatural*) (1981). *See also* SPANISH HORROR.

MARTINO, SERGIO (1938–). The writer-director Sergio Martino was responsible for some of the more memorable Italian **giallo** thrillers of the 1970s. He often worked with actors Edwige Fenech and George Hilton, both of whom were stalwarts of this type of film, and usually managed to bring some style, along with a certain amount of idiosyncrasy, to the proceedings. Even by the giallo's outré standards, the plots of Martino's *Lo strano vizio della Signora Wardh* (*Blade of the Ripper*) (1971), *La coda dello scorpione* (*Case of the Scorpion's Tail*) (1971), *Tutti i colori del buio* (*All the Colors of the Dark*) (1972), and *Il tuo vizio è una stanza chiusa e solo io ne ho la chiave* (known variously as *Excite Me*, *Eye of the Black Cat*, *Gently Before She Dies*, and *Your Vice Is a Closed Room and Only I Have the Key*) (1972) were often bizarre and incongruous. His best known giallo, *I corpi presentano tracce di violenza carnale* (1973), was more straightforward, although its enthusiastic depiction of a series of young women being terrorized, slaughtered and mutilated by a mysterious assailant sat uncomfortably with the undeniable beauty of the film's setting and photography. The title translates as "The bodies show signs of carnal violence" but the film was released internationally as *Torso*.

When the giallo market faded, Martino, like a number of other directors, switched to different types of horror. *La montagna del dio cannibale* (*Prisoner of the Cannibal God, Slave of the Cannibal God*) (1978) was his contribution to the Italian **cannibalism** cycle, although it contained more elements of adventure than was usual for this kind of gory horror. *L'isola degli uomini pesce* (*Island of Mutations, Screamers*) (1979) was a stylish reworking of themes from *The Island of Dr. Moreau*, but the equally watery *Il fiume del grande caimano* (*Alligators, Big Alligator River*) (1979) was a weak attempt, one of many in Italian cinema, to emulate the success of *Jaws* (1975). Martino's *Assassinio al cimitero etrusco* (*Murders in an Etruscan Cemetery*) (1982) also contained some horror material within its crime narrative. Since then, he has worked in genres other than horror. *See also* ITALIAN HORROR.

MASSACCESI, ARISTIDE (1936–1999). The Italian producer-director Aristide Massaccesi was a prolific exploitation specialist who often worked under the name Joe D'Amato. As a cinematographer, he photographed the horrors *Cosa avete fatto a Solange?* (*What Have They Done to Solange?*) (1972) and *L'anticristo* (*The Antichrist*) (1974). As a director, he started out making **westerns** but switched to horror with *Le morte ha sorriso all'assassino* (*Death Smiles on a Murderer*) (1973), although he spent most of the 1970s directing sex films, including two porn/horror cross-overs, *Emanuelle e gli ultimi cannibali* (*Emanuelle and the Last Cannibals*) (1977) and *Papaya dei Caraibi* (*Papaya: Love Goddess of the Cannibals*) (1978). Massaccesi returned to "straight" horror with the extremely gory and much-censored *Buio omega* (*Blue Holocaust, Beyond the Darkness*) (1979) and *Anthropophagus* (*Anthropophagous, Grim Reaper*) (1980). The former focused on necrophilia, the latter on **cannibalism**, and both films have since attracted a cult following because of their hard-edged, unforgiving nature. Massaccesi then made *Le notti erotiche dei morti viventi* (*Erotic Nights of the Living*

Dead) (1980), another porn/horror hybrid, and *Rosso sangue* (1981), a follow-up to *Anthropophagus* that was sometimes marketed as *Anthropophagus 2* or *Grim Reaper 2*, before resuming his career as a producer of softcore and hardcore porn films. *Sangue negli abissi* (*Deep Blood*) (1989) and *Contamination .7* (*The Crawlers, Troll 3*) (1990) were the only other horrors he directed; both were undistinguished. However, Massaccesi also produced horror films for other directors, most notably **Michele Soavi**'s auspicious debut *Deliria* (*Stagefright, Bloody Bird*) (1987). *See also* ITALIAN HORROR.

MATHESON, RICHARD (1926–). The American writer Richard Matheson has had a long and distinguished career in horror and fantasy, specializing in contemporary-set stories that explore troubled male psychologies. His classic modern **vampire** novel *I am Legend* (1954) has been filmed twice, as *The Last Man on Earth* (1964) and as the Charlton Heston vehicle *The Omega Man* (1971), with a third version, starring Will Smith, in production at the time of writing. However, neither of the completed film versions captured the disturbing power of the literary original, even though the first was scripted by Matheson himself under the name Logan Swanson. More successful as an adaptation of a Matheson novel was **Jack Arnold**'s *Incredible Shrinking Man* (1957), which again was scripted by Matheson. The haunted house drama *The Legend of Hell House* (1973) and the time travel fantasy *Somewhere in Time* (1980) also involved Matheson adapting his own novels, while other writers did the adaptations for *What Dreams May Come* (1998) and the **ghost** story *Stir of Echoes* (1999).

In addition, Matheson has shown himself adept at adapting the work of other writers. Working with **Charles Beaumont**, he turned Fritz Leiber's **witchcraft** novel *Conjure Wife* into the superior **British horror** film *Night of the Eagle* (*Burn, Witch, Burn!*) (1962). For **Hammer**, he adapted an Anne Blaisdell novel as the **psychological thriller** *Fanatic* (*Die! Die! My Darling!*) and also produced a superb screenplay for the **Dennis Wheatley** Satanic thriller *The Devil Rides Out* (1968), helping to make this one of the company's best films. However, his best known adaptation work was done for **Roger Corman**'s **Edgar Allan Poe** films of the early 1960s, including screenplays for *House of Usher* (1960), *Pit and the Pendulum* (1961), the **comedy**-horror *The Raven* (1963), and the horror **anthology** *Tales of Terror* (1962). Given that the original Poe material did not feature much plot, Matheson's screenplays were adaptations only in the loosest of senses, and they gave him the opportunity to develop his own version of psychological horror and alienation, one that made the films in question, for all their period settings, seem very modern in their outlook.

Given how prolific he has been, it is perhaps surprising how few original screenplays Matheson has written for the big screen. There is **Jacques Tourneur**'s comedy-horror *The Comedy of Terrors* (1964) and a contribution to the less than distinguished *Jaws 3-D* (1983). Even his considerable **television** credits—often in collaboration with producer-director **Dan Curtis**—have frequently involved his adapting his own short stories or the work of others. For Curtis he did an innovative and intelligent adaptation of *Dracula* (1973), as well as the modern vampire story *The Night Stalker* (1972), again from a story by another writer. The latter, along with the Matheson-scripted **sequel** *The Night Strangler* (1973), led to the cult television series *Kolchak—the Night Stalker* (1974–1975). Other television horror credits for Curtis include *Scream of the Wolf* (1974), *Trilogy of Terror* (1975), *Dead of Night* (1977) and *Trilogy of Terror II* (1996). Matheson also wrote **Steven Spielberg**'s breakthrough film *Duel* (1971). Based on his own story, this was a classic Matheson setup involving an everyman figure confronting an alienating modernity in the shape of an implacable truck that for no apparent reason wants to kill the man. Further television film credits were *Ghost Story* (1972), which was directed by *Night Stalker* director **John Llewellyn Moxey**, the **science fiction**/horror story *The Stranger Within* (1974) and **Gordon Hessler**'s *The Strange Possession of Mrs. Oliver* (1977).

Matheson also wrote numerous episodes for the television series *The Twilight Zone*, both in its original 1959–1964 version and in the 1985–1989 version, as well as contributing to the Spielberg-produced film *Twilight Zone: The Movie* (1983). Other television series benefiting from Matheson's input were *Thriller* (1960–1962), *Night Gallery* (1970–1973), *Amazing Stories* (1985–1987), and *The Outer Limits* (1995–2002).

MCGILLIVRAY, DAVID (1947–). The critic-turned-screenwriter David McGillivray was an important contributor to the tough contemporary horror cinema that appeared in Great Britain during the 1970s as the more escapist **Hammer** horror faded away. He wrote producer-director **Pete Walker**'s three best films, *House of Whipcord* (1974), *Frightmare* (1974), and *House of Mortal Sin* (*The Confessional*) (1976), using some sly humor to offset the essential grimness of the narratives. His work on the screenplays for **Norman J. Warren**'s *Satan's Slave* (1976) and for Walker's *Schizo* (1976) lacked that kind of intensity, but *Terror* (1978), for Warren, was an enjoyably self-reflexive affair that did not shy away from the absurdity of its story about a witch's curse. Since the 1970s, McGillivray has worked mainly as a critic. *See also* BRITISH HORROR.

MELFORD, GEORGE (1877–1961). The American director George Melford's main claim to horror fame was that he directed for **Universal** the Spanish language version of *Dracula* (1931) that was shot on the same sets as the **Bela Lugosi-Tod Browning** version. (Melford's best-known credit before this was the Rudolph Valentino vehicle *The Sheik* in 1921.) Although Carlos Villarías's **vampire** lacked Lugosi's charisma, the film itself was arguably much more stylish than its English-language counterpart. In particular, Melford staged Dracula's famous appearance on the castle staircase with considerably more cinematic *élan* than was evident in the more theatrical version offered by Browning. Although he apparently spoke no Spanish, Melford directed several other Hollywood-based Spanish-language productions, most notably *La voluntad del muerto* (1930), which was based on the popular success *The Cat and the Canary*. This practice of shooting alternative versions of films faded away quite quickly, and Melford's later directorial credits are inconsequential. He spent his latter years as an actor appearing in small parts in numerous Hollywood films. *See also* AMERICAN HORROR.

MEXICAN HORROR. During the 1930s, Mexico was one of the few countries other than the United States to develop its own cycle of horror production, albeit a small one. These films, like later Mexican horrors, often idiosyncratically mixed traditional Mexican elements with conventions taken from **American horror**. For example, *El baúl macabro* (*The Macabre Trunk*) (1936) and *La herencia macabra* (*The Macabre Legacy*) (1939) both borrowed their villainous **mad scientists** from U.S. productions, whereas *La llorona* (*The Crying Woman*) (1933) centred on a figure from Mexican folklore, a ghostly woman who weeps for the **children** that she has murdered. Other 1930s Mexican horrors included *Dos moinjes* (*Two Monks*) (1934) and *El fantasma del convento* (*The Phantom of the Convent*) (1934).

Mexican horror production tailed away during the 1940s and early 1950s but there was a significant revival in the late 1950s. At their best, the resulting films were inventive and stylish, although the high volume of production throughout the 1960s and first half of the 1970s meant that their quality was not always consistent. The impressive *El vampiro* (*The **Vampire***) (1957) and its **sequel** *El ataud del Vampiro* (*The Vampire's Coffin*) (1957) introduced vampires into Mexican cinema; they would later become stock villains in numerous Mexican films, among them *El mundo de los vampires* (*World of the Vampires*) (1960), *La invasión de los vampiros* (*The Invasion of the Vampires*) (1961) and *El imperio de **Dracula*** (*The Empire of Dracula*) (1966). More specifically Mexicans were the Aztec mummies that featured in such titles as *La momia azteca* (*Attack of the Aztec **Mummy***) (1957), *La maldición de la momia azteca* (*The Curse of the Aztec Mummy*) (1957), and *Las luchadoras contra la momia* (*The Wrestling Women vs. the Aztec Mummy*) (1964), and also the many other films that pitted traditional horror monsters such as vampires or **werewolves** against Mexican masked wrestlers, of whom the most famous and prolific was **Santo**. La Llorona made a comeback in *La maldición de la llorona* (*The Curse of the Crying Woman*) (1961) and took on Santo in *La venganza de la llorona* (*Vengeance of the Crying Woman*) (1974), while witches featured in *El espejo de la bruja* (*The Witch's Mirror*) (1960) and the Santo vehicle *Atacan las brujas* (*The Witches Attack*) (1965).

This cycle of Mexican horror production faded away in the mid-1970s, and *Cronos* (1993), **Guillermo del Toro**'s impressive vampire film, has been the only Mexican horror of note since then.

MIIKE, TAKASHI (1960–). The iconoclastic Japanese director Takashi Miike is best known for his crime thrillers but his work has often featured horror-like imagery. For example, *Ôdishon* (*Audition*) (1999), a deceptively understated study of relations between men and women in contemporary Japan, concludes with a protracted and very graphic **torture** scene in which a woman pushes needles into a man's eyes and saws off one of his feet. *Bijitâ Q* (*Visitor Q*) (2001), *Koroshiya 1* (*Ichi the Killer*) (2001), and *Katakuri-ke no kôfuku* (*The Happiness of the Katakuris*) (2001) are harder to classify, although all contain disturbing scenes of violence and horror. By contrast, *Chakushin ari* (*One Missed Call*) (2003) is a more conventional Japanese **ghost** story in the manner of **Hideo Nakata**'s *Ringu* (1998). Miike also contributed an episode to the horror **anthology** film *Saam gaang yi* (*Three . . . Extreme*) (2004). See also JAPANESE HORROR.

MIKELS, TED (1929–). Like **Herschell Gordon Lewis, Andy Milligan** and **Ray Steckler**, the director Ted Mikels came out of 1960s American exploitation cinema. The garish titles of his ultra-cheap horror films promised more than the films themselves delivered, although Mikels does offer occasional bursts of self-deprecating humor. His horror films include *The Astro-Zombies* (1968), *The Corpse Grinders* (1972)—in which **cats** acquire a taste for human flesh—and *Blood Orgy of the She Devils* (1972); he also produced *The Worm Eaters* (1977). Mikels returned to horror in the early 2000s with *The Corpse Grinders 2* (2000), *Mark of the Astro-Zombies* (2002), and *Cauldron: Baptism of Blood* (2004).

MILLER, DICK (1928–). The actor Dick Miller was a regular in **Roger Corman**'s films of the 1950s and 1960s, including *It Conquered the World* (1956), *Not of This Earth* (1957), *The Undead* (1957), *The Little Shop of Horrors* (1960), *The Premature Burial* (1962), *The Terror* (1963) and *X: The Man with the X-Ray Eyes* (1963), usually in comic or eccentric roles. His performance as Walter Paisley, a downtrodden **artist**-turned-murderer, in Corman's **comedy**-horror *A Bucket of Blood* (1959) clearly made an impression as he has on several occasions since been cast as a character called Walter Paisley—for example, in three of **Joe Dante**'s films, *Hollywood Boulevard* (1976), *The Howling* (1981), and *Twilight Zone: The Movie* (1983), as well as in Jim Wynorski's *Chopping Mall* (1986). Other horror-related credits include for Dante *Piranha* (1978), *Gremlins* (1984), *The 'Burbs* (1989), *Gremlins 2: The New Batch* (1990), and *Matinee* (1993) and for other directors *Dr. Heckyl and Mr. Hype* (1980), *Night of the Creeps* (1986), *Evil Toons* (1992), *Amityville 1992: It's About Time* (1992), *Demon Knight* (1995), and *Route 666* (2001).

MILLIGAN, ANDY (1929–1991). *The Rats Are Coming! The Werewolves Are Here!* (1972) is one of horror's great titles. Sadly, neither the film it graced nor any of the other horror films directed by American exploitation specialist Andy Milligan lived up to its promise. Milligan made a career of sorts out of the production of films that were cheap to the point of almost being home movies, and he has since acquired the sort of cult following that values films that are "so bad they're good." After churning out titles such as *The Naked Witch* (1964) and *The Ghastly Ones* (1968) in the United States, Milligan moved to Great Britain for a while where his films included *Bloodthirsty Butchers* (1970), *The Body Beneath* (1970), and the aforementioned *The Rats Are Coming!* Other Milligan horror-related titles are *Torture Dungeon* (1970), *Guru the Mad Monk* (1970), *The Man with Two Heads* (1972), *Blood* (1974), *Legacy of Blood* (1978), *Carnage* (1984), *The Weirdo* (1989), *Monstrosity* (1989), and *Surgikill* (1990).

MINER, STEVE (1951–). Steve Miner is the only director to have contributed more than once to the *Friday the 13th* cycle; he did *Friday the 13th Part 2* (1981) and *Friday the 13th Part 3* (1982). He also directed *House* (1986) and *Warlock* (1989), both of which were successful enough to generate **sequels** (albeit not with Miner on board). He subsequently added the superior *Halloween H20: 20 Years Later* (1998) to the *Halloween* cycle, while his *Lake Placid* (1999) was a likeable **comedy**-horror about the discovery of a giant alligator in an American lake. *See also* AMERICAN HORROR.

MIRANDA, SOLEDAD (1943–1970). Soledad Miranda—who sometimes worked under the name Susan Korda—was a Spanish actor of extraordinary and haunting beauty who acquired minor cult status following her tragic death in a car accident. She was associated in particular with the prolific director **Jesus Franco**, with whom she made the horror or horror-related films *Les cauchemars naissent la nuit* (*Nightmares Come at Night*) (1970), *El Conde* **Dracula** (*Count Dracula*) (1970), *Vampyros lesbos* (*Lesbian* **Vampires**) (1971), and *Sie tötete in Ekstase* (*She Killed in Esctasy*) (1971).

MOLINA, JACINTO (1934–). As "Paul Naschy," ex-weightlifter turned actor Jacinto Molina is the major star of **Spanish horror**. His many films—some of which he has written and directed—vary wildly in terms of quality and usually mix scenes of pathos and sentiment with copious violence, **gore** and nudity. They are not to everyone's taste, and some of them have been accused of misogyny in their representation of women as victims. However, the best of them are inventive and atmospheric, with some genuinely eerie moments.

Molina's signature role is the **werewolf** Count Waldemar Daninsky, a part he has played a dozen times, beginning with *La marca del hombre lobo* (1968)—which means *The Mark of the Werewolf*, although the film was misleadingly retitled ***Frankenstein's Bloody Terror*** for its American release. The Daninsky **sequels** *Las noches del hombre lobo* (*The Nights of the Wolf Man*) (1968), *Los monstruous del Terror* (*Assignment Terror*, ***Dracula* versus *Frankenstein***) (1969), *La furia del hombre lobo* (*The Fury of the Wolf Man, The Wolf Man Never Sleeps*) (1970), and *La noche de walpurgis* (*Shadow of the Werewolf*) (1970) followed in quick succession. Later Daninsky films became increasingly outré in their plotting. In *Dr. Jekyll y el hombre lobo* (*Dr. Jekyll versus the Werewolf*) (1971) Daninsky meets Dr. Jekyll and in a weird double transformation becomes the first werewolf to be changed into Mr. Hyde. *El retorno de walpurgis* (*The Return of Walpurgis, The Curse of the Devil*) (1973) was comparatively straightforward, but the werewolf's encounter with the Yeti in *La maldición de la bestia* (*Night of the Howling Beast, The Werewolf and the Yeti*) (1975) took the series to new heights of absurdity. He fought with Countess **Elizabeth Bathory** in *El retorno del hombre lobo* (*Night of the Werewolf*) (1980) before appearing in the Japanese-Spanish co-production *La bestia y la espada mágica* (*The Beast and the Magic Sword*) (1983) as well as in *La aullido del diablo* (*Howl of the Devil*) (1987), *Licántropo: El asesino de la luna llena* (*Lycanthropus: The Moonlight Murders*) (1996), and **Fred Olen Ray**'s American production *Tomb of the Werewolf* (2004).

Away from the world of werewolves, Molina/Naschy's best known role is as the hunchback in *El jorobado de la morgue* (*Hunchback of the Morgue*) (1972), although he also played a burly Dracula in *El gran amor del conde Dracula* (*Count Dracula's Great Love*) (1972) where, uniquely in the Dracula canon, he deliberately drives a stake through himself at the film's conclusion. He was the **mummy** in *La venganza de la momia* (*The Mummy's Revenge, The Vengeance of the Mummy*) (1973), played both the hero and the villain in *El espanto surge de la tumba* (*Horror Rises from the Tomb*) (1972) and encountered **zombies** in *La rebelión de las muertas* (*Vengeance of the Zombies*) (1972) and *La orgía de los muertos* (*Hanging Woman, Terror of the Living Dead*) (1973). His many other credits include both period horrors and contemporary-set **psychological thrillers**.

MORELAND, MANTAN (1902–1973). The **comedy** performances given by black American actor Mantan Moreland during the 1930s and 1940s have come to be seen as potentially demeaning in the apparent support they offer to racist stereotypes of blackness. In the context of the civil rights movement in the United States, this discomfort with Moreland (along with fellow actors Willie Best and Stepin Fetchit) was perfectly understandable. However, Moreland's streetwise performances can also be taken as offering resistance to the white characters' perspectives on the dramas in which he features. This is particularly the case in Moreland's horror films, in which, unlike most of the white characters, he sensibly seeks to remove himself from the site of danger and often seems to understand more clearly than anyone else that he is trapped in a horror narrative. He shows up in *King of the Zombies* (1941), *The Strange Love of Doctor RX* (1942) and *Revenge of the Zombies* (1943), and is considered by many horror **fans** to be the best thing in all of these. He was also a regular in Monogram's Charlie Chan films, which occasionally contained horror-like thrills. After some years in the wilderness, he returned to horror in 1964 with the weird *Spider Baby*, which was not released until 1968. See also BLACK HORROR.

MORRICONE, ENNIO (1928–). The Italian composer Ennio Morricone is most celebrated for the scores he has written for **westerns**. However, he has also made an important contribution to horror **mu-**

sic. His first horror score, for the **Barbara Steele** film *Gli amanti d'oltretomba* (*Nightmare Castle*) (1965), was, by Morricone's standards, unobtrusive. The music he wrote for the **giallo** thrillers that became popular during the 1970s was more striking, combining beautiful melodies with harsh, dissonant sounds in order to illustrate the giallo's exploration of dangerous modernity. The distinctiveness of **Dario Argento**'s first three films—*L'uccello dalle piume di cristallo* (*The Bird with the Crystal Plumage, The Gallery Murders*) (1970), *Il gatto a nove code* (*Cat O'Nine Tails*) (1971), and *4 mosche di velluto grigio* (*Four Flies on Grey Velvet*) (1971)—was significantly enhanced by Morricone's music; the composer would work again with Argento 25 years later on *La sindrome di Stendhal* (*The Stendhal Syndrome*) (1996) and *Il fantasma dell'opera* (***The Phantom of the Opera***) (1998). Other giallo films that benefited from Morricone's input included *Le foto proibite di una signora per bene* (*Forbidden Photos of a Lady Above Suspicion*) (1970), *Gli occhi freddi della paura* (*Cold **Eyes** of Fear*) (1971), *Una lucertola con la pelle di donna* (*A Lizard in a Woman's Skin*) (1971), *La tarantola dal ventre nero* (*Black Belly of the Tarantula*) (1971), *Giornata nera per l'ariete* (*The Fifth Cord*) (1971), *Malastrana* (*Short Night of the Glass **Dolls***) (1971), *Chi l'ha vista morire?* (*Who Saw Her Die?*) (1972), *Mio caro assassino* (*My Dear Killer*) (1972), *Cosa avete fatto a Solange?* (*What Have You Done to Solange?*) (1972), *Spasmo* (1974), and *Macchie solari* (*Autopsy*) (1975). Versatile as well as prolific, Morricone could also do supernatural horror, often using choral sounds to illustrate the presence of unearthly forces in films such as *L'anticristo* (*The **Antichrist***) (1974), ***Exorcist II: The Heretic*** (1977), and *Holocaust 2000* (1977). By contrast, his music for **John Carpenter**'s *The Thing* (1982) was unexpectedly minimalist but all the more effective because of that. Morricone's other horror credits include the obscure *Blood Link* (1982) and the **Jack Nicholson werewolf** drama *Wolf* (1994).

MORRISSEY, PAUL (1938–). Director Paul Morrissey's association with Andy Warhol led to such underground classics as *Flesh* (1968), *Lonesome Cowboys* (1969) and *Trash* (1970). Morrissey subsequently went to Italy to make the eccentric *Flesh for **Frankenstein*** (1973) and *Blood for **Dracula*** (1974), both of which camped up the traditional horror stories to an outrageous extent while also offering what was for the time a surprising amount of **gore**. Morrissey's version of *The Hound of the Baskervilles* (1978), which featured the British **comedy** team of Peter Cook and Dudley Moore, was a less successful attempt at comedy-horror.

MOXEY, JOHN LLEWELLYN (1925–). The career of director John Llewellyn Moxey—who is sometimes billed as just John Moxey—falls in two sections, with horror having a part to play in each. From the mid-1950s through to the end of the 1960s, he worked in British cinema and **television**, specializing in thrillers but with occasional diversions into horror or horror-related projects. In fact, his most remarkable film from this period was a horror film, the **Milton Subotsky**-produced *The City of the Dead* (*Horror Hotel*) (1960). Although this **witchcraft** drama was set in America, it was made in Great Britain with a mainly British cast. The black-and-white expressionistic approach adopted by Moxey was unlike anything else in **British horror**, and the killing off of the heroine long before the conclusion was done just as ruthlessly as in **Alfred Hitchcock**'s *Psycho* (1960), which had been released only a few months before. *Circus of Fear* (1966), another of Moxey's British films, was sometimes marketed as a horror film but it was more of a straightforward crime thriller.

From the 1970 onwards, Moxey has worked mainly for American television, again with occasional horror titles to his credit. Most notably, he directed the contemporary-set **vampire** story *The Night Stalker* (1972), which at the time received the highest ever audience ratings for a television film and which spawned the televison series *Kolchak—the Night Stalker* (1974–1975).

THE MUMMY. The **Universal** production of *The Mummy* (1932), which starred **Boris Karloff** and was directed by **Karl Freund**, was cinema's first major mummy narrative. There had been a few earlier films and literary tales featuring Egyptian mummies, and the discovery of Tutankhamun's tomb in the early 1920s had generated significant public interest in the subject of mummies. However, it was the Universal version that set the pattern for later films, with its invoking of the cloth-wrapped monster (although Karloff was only glimpsed in this guise in the film's opening sequence) and its focusing on the theme of reincarnation.

Universal did not return to the mummy until the 1940s when it produced *The Mummy's Hand* (1940), *The Mummy's Tomb* (1942), *The Mummy's Ghost* (1944), and *The Mummy's Curse* (1944). These dispensed with the subleties of the 1932 version, instead offering a shambling, slow-moving mummy—played by Tom Tyler in the first film and by **Lon Chaney Jr.** in the rest—out to avenge some slight to Egyptian gods. The films displayed a rudimentary level of invention and contained some effective moments, but their repetitive quality limited the cycle's development.

Much the same can be said of the British company **Hammer**'s first three mummy films. **Terence Fisher**'s *The Mummy* (1959), which featured **Christopher Lee** in the title role, was a stately retelling of the by then familiar mummy narrative, but the follow-ups *Curse of the Mummy's Tomb* (1964) and *The Mummy's Shroud* (1967) reduced the mummy to a not particularly threatening automaton. By contrast, Hammer's *Blood from the Mummy's Tomb* (1971), as directed by **Seth Holt**, was an innovative adaptation of Bram Stoker's *Jewel of the Seven Stars* that dispensed almost entirely with the cloth-wrapped monster, focusing instead on the theme of **possession**. It remains one of the most distinguished of all mummy films.

Mexican horror offered its own variant with a series of Aztec mummy films, beginning with *La momia azteca* (*The Aztec Mummy*) (1957) and including *La momia azteca contra el robot humano* (*Aztec Mummy vs. the Human Robot*) (1958), *Las luchadoras contra la momia* (*Wrestling Women vs. the Aztec Mummy*) (1964) and *La venganza de la momia* (***Santo** and the Vengeance of the Mummy*) (1970), while **Jacinto Molina** played the mummy in a **Spanish horror** production also called *La venganza de la momia* (*The Mummy's Revenge*) (1973). Later mummy films were sporadic and isolated affairs; they included *The Awakening* (1980), which was another adaptation of *Jewel of the Seven Stars*, *The Tomb* (1986), the **comedy**-horror *The Monster Squad* (1987), *Tales from the Darkside: The Movie* (1990), and *Tale of the Mummy* (*Talos the Mummy*) (1998). By the end of the 1990s, one might have been forgiven for thinking that the mummy had had its day as a movie monster. However, **Stephen Sommers**' big-budget horror-action extravaganza *The Mummy*

(1999) successfully reinvented the cloth-wrapped fiend for a modern audience; a **sequel**, *The Mummy Returns* (2001), followed.

MURNAU, F. W. (1888–1931). The German director Friedrich Wilhelm Murnau died in a car crash in the same year that saw the release of **Universal**'s *Dracula* (1931) and *Frankenstein* (1931). Murnau himself never made a horror film as such—the term did not emerge until after his death—but some of his films did engage with material that would later be associated with the horror genre (and those films have sometimes been retrospectively reclassified as horror). Most notable here, of course, is the **vampire** film *Nosferatu, eine Symphonie des Grauens* (*Nosferatu, a Symphony of Terror*) (1922), an unofficial adaptation of Bram Stoker's *Dracula* that offered an unnerving version of the vampire as an animalistic creature. Murnau's monumental production of *Faust* (1926) also contained some startling supernatural imagery. *Der Bucklige und die Tänzerin* (*The Hunchback and the Dancer*) (1920) and *Der Januskopf* (*The Janus Head*) (1920), two earlier Murnau films now believed lost, appear to have dealt with horror themes as well, with the latter a version of the **Dr. Jekyll and Mr. Hyde** story that featured **Bela Lugosi** in a supporting role. *See also* GERMAN HORROR.

MUSIC. It is hard to think of horror cinema without music. Early sound horrors such as the **Universal** *Dracula* (1931) often featured snatches of classical music, but it was not long before specially commissioned musical scores became the order of the day. Noted composers who have worked intermittently in horror in the context of distinguished careers generally located in other genres include Max Steiner (who composed the score for *King Kong* in 1933), **Jerry Goldsmith, Bernard Herrmann, Ennio Morricone**, and **John Williams**. Other composers have made a more regular contribution to horror, among them **James Bernard** at **Hammer, John Carpenter** (who is also, of course, a noted director), the Italian rock group **Goblin**, and Roy Webb for **Val Lewton**'s RKO horrors.

Music serves several functions in horror. It can contribute to the creation of a suitable atmosphere, often compensating for the limitations of low-budget set design. More particularly, music can evoke a sense of realms beyond the visible, whether this be the supernatural realms conjured up by, for example, Humphrey Searle's score for *The Haunting* (1963) or Goldsmith's score for *The Omen* (1976), or the off-screen space occupied by the killer that Carpenter's music for *Halloween* (1978) so effectively denotes. Apparently innocent music can also accentuate brooding atmospherics when juxtaposed with sinister images, with the charming **children** choruses used to introduce *The Amityville Horror* (1979) and *Poltergeist* (1982) good examples of this. In addition, music itself has the power to shock, with the nerve-jangling dissonance of Herrmann's all-string score for *Psycho* (1960) or Wayne Bell's experimental music for *The Texas Chainsaw Massacre* (1974) integral to those films' iconoclastic character. From the 1970s onwards, horror filmmakers have also regularly deployed loud crashes of music to emphasize their **startle effects**.

Orchestral music has proved to be the mainstay of horror composition, although composers have also explored possibilities offered by choral, electronic and experimental music. Since the 1980s, rock music of various kinds has become a regular feature in horror films, ranging from the *Nightmare on Elm Street* films to **Dario Argento's** *Phenomena* (1985), with this presumably designed to appeal to the predominantly teenage audience for this type of cinema. Some rock musicians have gone on to compose especially for horror films. An early example of this was Goblin, which during the 1970s and 1980s was responsible for distinctive scores for several Argento films. Since then, Marilyn Manson has worked on the score for *Resident Evil* (2002), while **Rob Zombie** not only wrote the music for *House of 1000 Corpses* (2003) and *The Devil's Rejects* (2005) but scripted and directed them as well.

– N –

NAKATA, HIDEO (1961–). The director Hideo Nakata has been one of the major figures overseeing the translation of **Japanese horror** themes into Westernized formats. Like many Japanese filmmakers, Nakata has specialized in **ghost** stories, but he has developed innovative ways of locating these stories within a recognizable modern world. *Joyû-rei* (*Don't Look Up*) (1996) was such a ghost story, although it was little seen outside of Japan. Nakata's next film made his name internationally, however. *Ringu* (*Ring*) (1998) dealt with a cursed videotape which, if viewed, led to a ghastly death for the viewer. The Japanese tradition of the vengeful female ghost was here intertwined with modern technology in a manner that made the technology itself appear ghostly and alienating. Nakata's approach was to establish a mundane reality, which in the course of the film was gradually, and at first almost imperceptibly, invaded by the supernatural. At the same time, the director did not shy away from shock moments—notably the climactic appearance of the ghost—and *Ringu* also contained some conventions that would have been familiar to Western audiences. For example, the distorted photographs of those doomed to die were comparable with the photographs of doom in the Satanic thriller *The Omen* (1976).

After making the thriller *Kaosu* (*Chaos*) (1999), Nakata returned to the *Ringu* series with the **sequel** *Ringu 2* (1999). The narrative this time was slighter and less suspenseful. The ghostly setpieces were still impressive, however, although they lacked the shock impact of the previous film and operated in a more abstract way. *Honogurai mizu no soko kara* (*Dark Water*) (2002), which like *Ringu* was adapted from a novel by Koji Suzuki, benefited from a tighter narrative structure. As he had done with *Ringu*, Nakata focused on a fatherless family unit, with in both cases the strained relationship between mother and child representing a wider sense of social dislocation. Again the film's build-up was slow, patiently establishing a sense of place and character, but the climax—in which the mother makes a most awful sacrifice—was powerful and bleak, while the coda managed to be both moving and quietly chilling.

Given that both *Ringu* and *Honogurai mizu no soko kara* were successfully remade as American films—as *The Ring* (2002) and *Dark Water* (2005), respectively—it is perhaps not surprising that Nakata was himself invited to the United States and that his American debut should be *The Ring Two* (2005). This stylish sequel was not a **remake** of his own *Ringu 2*, but it did share that film's extensive water imagery and also demonstrated that Nakata could function well within the **American horror** idiom.

NALDER, REGGIE (1907–1991). The actor Reggie Nalder—whose real name was Alfred Reginald Natzler—was something of a mystery. He was born in Vienna either in 1907, 1911 or 1922, and the precise cause of the facial scars that suited him to menacing roles remains unclear. Nalder worked mainly in French cinema in the 1940s and 1950s, although he did gain some international recognition for his performance as a villain in **Alfred Hitchcock**'s *The Man Who Knew Too Much* (1956). His horror debut came with **Dario Argento**'s *L'uccello dalle piume di cristallo* (*The Bird with the Crystal Plumage, The Gallery Murders*) (1970), where, true to type, he played a sinister assassin. More nasty roles followed in the controversial **German horror** films *Hexen bis aufs Blut gequält* (*Mark of the Devil*) (1970) and *Hexen geschändet und zu Tode gequält* (*Mark of the Devil 2*) (1973) and in the tamer *Dracula's Dog* (*Zoltan, Hound of Dracula*) (1978) and the **comedy**-horror *The Devil and Max Devlin* (1981). However, his most memorable horror performance was as a **Max Schreck**-like **vampire** in **Tobe Hooper**'s **television** adaptation of **Stephen King**'s *Salem's Lot* (1979).

NASCHY, PAUL. *See* MOLINA, JACINTO.

NEILL, ROY WILLIAM (1887–1946). The prolific director Roy William Neill made over 100 films, beginning his career in the silent period. Early horror-themed work included the horror-whodunnit *The Ninth Guest* (1934), the **voodoo** drama *Black Moon* (1934), and the **Boris Karloff** period horror *The Black Room* (1935). During the 1940s, Neill directed and produced 11 out of **Universal's** 12 **Sherlock Holmes** films, bringing horror imagery to a number of these, notably *Sherlock Holmes Faces Death* (1943), *The Scarlet Claw* (1944), and *The Pearl of Death* (1944). He was also responsible for *Frankenstein Meets the Wolf Man* (1943), the first occasion on which Universal brought some of its monsters together in one film. *See also* AMERICAN HORROR.

NEWBROOK, PETER (1920–). The cinematographer-producer Peter Newbrook was an associate of British exploitation specialist **Robert Hartford-Davis**, for whom he photographed the period horror *The Black Torment* (1964) and the **surgical horror** *Corruption* (1967). He also produced *Corruption* along with Hartford-Davis's *Incense for the Damned* (*Bloodsuckers*) (1970), as well as photographing and producing Ted Hooker's *Crucible of Terror* (1971). Newbrook only directed one film himself, but it was sufficiently distinctive to cause regret that he did not do more. *The Asphyx* (1973) was a literate period horror which eschewed traditional horror monsters in favor of a drama involving mysterious unseen spirits and the quest for immortality. *See also* BRITISH HORROR.

NICHOLSON, JACK (1937–). Some of the actor Jack Nicholson's earliest screen roles were in horror films directed by **Roger Corman.** He was a masochistic dental patient in the **comedy**-horror *The Little Shop of Horrors* (1960) and a bland juvenile lead in *The Raven* (1963) and *The Terror* (1963). In the late 1970s, after having become one of the leading actors of his generation with films such as *Chinatown* (1974) and *One Flew Over the Cuckoo's Nest* (1975), Nicholson returned to the horror genre with a grandstanding performance in Stanley Kubrick's *The Shining* (1980). His portrayal of a writer losing his mind in a haunted hotel teetered on the edge of parody but was all the more striking because of this. Later appearances in horror films were similarly larger than life and over the top—as the **Devil** in *The Witches of Eastwick* (1987) and as a lyncanthropic publishing executive in *Wolf* (1994).

NICHOLSON, JAMES H. (1916–1972). Along with his business partner **Samuel Z. Arkoff,** James H. Nicholson established **American International Pictures** in the 1950s and went on to produce numerous exploitation and horror titles, most notably **Roger Corman's Edgar Allan Poe** adaptations.

NICOLODI, DARIA (1950–). The Italian actor Daria Nicolodi is a striking presence in a number of **Italian horror** films, especially for the director **Dario Argento** (with whom she had a daughter, the actor **Asia Argento**). As a journalist in the Argento **giallo** *Profondo rosso (Deep Red)* (1975), she was for the time an unusually independent heroine who saved the hero more than he saved her. Her role in **Mario Bava's** *Schock (Shock, Beyond the Door 2)* (1977)—as a widow terrorized by her husband's spirit—was more conventional, although Nicolodi performed it with intensity and conviction. She had a more decorative function in two further Argento films, *Inferno*

(1980) and *Tenebre* (*Tenebrae*) (1982), but was an impressive villain in Argento's *Phenomena* (1985), where she suffered one of horror's most unusual demises—slashed to death by a razor-wielding chimpanzee. She suffered again in Argento's *Opera* (*Terror at the Opera*) (1987) where, in one of that film's many set piece death scenes, she was shot through the **eye**.

Nicolodi's other claim to fame for horror **fans** was that she co-scripted Dario Argento's most successful horror film, the **witchcraft** drama *Suspiria* (1977).

Her other genre credits include *Le foto di gioia (Delirium)* (1987) and *Paganini Horror* (1989).

***NIGHT OF THE LIVING DEAD* (1968).** To all intents and purposes, the Living Dead cycle of **zombie** films belongs to the director **George Romero**, who was responsible for *Night of the Living Dead* (1968), *Dawn of the Dead* (1978), *Day of the Dead* (1985), and *Land of the Dead* (2005), and who developed the socially critical approach for which the cycle is known. Mention should be made, however, of two **remakes**, **Tom Savini**'s *Night of the Living Dead* (1990) and Zack Snyder's *Dawn of the Dead* (2004). Both are interesting variations on the original, with Savini introducing a **Final Girl** figure and Snyder diminishing the social critique in favor of intense action. **Dan O'Bannon**'s comedy-horror *Return of the Living Dead* (1985) had no formal connection with the cycle, but it did make humorous reference to it. *See also* AMERICAN HORROR.

***A NIGHTMARE ON ELM STREET* (1984).** The *Elm Street* films formed one of the major **American horror** cycles of the 1980s. In the first film, *A Nightmare On Elm Street* (1984), writer-director **Wes Craven** updated the by then exhausted "teens-in-peril" **slasher** format by injecting into it supernatural elements. The central idea was simple but compelling. Teenagers dream of an assailant with razors attached to his fingers, and if this assailant succeeds in killing them in their dreams, then the teenagers also die in reality. It turns out that the killer, a long-dead janitor by the name of Freddy Krueger, was a child-murderer who was himself killed by the teenagers' parents and is now seeking revenge from beyond the grave. Thematically, the film looked back to the 1970s—when Craven began working in horror—with its focus on repressive families and a rebellious underclass, but its surreal dream imagery also suggested a movement away from the social engagement that had characterized much 1970s American horror.

Indeed, the seven **sequels**, only one of which was directed by Craven, jettisoned the somber qualities apparent in the first film in favor of a more playful approach. Far from being the fearful monster, Freddy Krueger (as played by **Robert Englund**) became a master of ceremonies wittily presiding over the deaths of numerous teenagers. The extent to which Freddy's enduring popularity with teenage audiences was an expression of their masochism or their sick sense of humor is not clear, but Freddy successfully wisecracked his way through *A Nightmare on Elm Street 2: Freddy's Revenge* (1985, directed by Jack Sholder), *A Nightmare on Elm Street 3: Dream Warriors* (1987, **Chuck Russell**), *A Nightmare on Elm Street 4: The Dream Master* (1988, **Renny Harlin**), and *A Nightmare on Elm Street 5: The Dream Child* (1989, Stephen Hopkins). *Freddy's Dead: The Final Nightmare* (1991, Rachel Talahay), which was partially filmed in 3D, brought the cycle to a temporary halt. However, as was the case with the other key 1980s horror cycle, the *Friday the 13th* films (in which "The Final Chapter" was promptly followed by "A New Beginning"), *Wes Craven's New Nightmare* appeared in 1994. As its title indicated, this marked the return of Craven as director, and the resulting film turned out to be one of the more unusual horror sequels. An intensely self-reflexive affair in which some of the cast and crew of the original film played themselves as they were stalked by the "real" Freddy, *New Nightmare* was perhaps too strange to catch on with audiences, and Craven would have to wait until the *Scream* films before finding a more profitable vein of generic **self-reflexivity**. Nine years passed before the next—and last to date—in the cycle. In a weird throwback to **Universal**'s multiple-monster movies of the 1940s, **Ronny Yu**'s *Freddy vs. Jason* (2003) pitted Freddy against Jason Voorhees from the *Friday the 13th* cycle, with predictably bloody and violent results. *Freddy's Nightmares*, a **television** series hosted by Freddy Krueger, also ran from 1988 to 1990.

– O –

O'BANNON, DAN (1946–). The American writer—and occasional director—Dan O'Bannon co-wrote and acted in **John Carpenter**'s directorial debut *Dark Star* (1974). This was a charming **science fiction-comedy**, a subplot of which involved an alien lurking in a spaceship. O'Bannon would return to this idea for a screenplay originally titled *Star Beast*—developed with his regular collaborator Ronald Shusett—and envisaged as a low-budget science fiction/horror project. However, the budget grew, Ridley Scott was hired as director, and the project became *Alien* (1979), arguably the most successful of all SF/horror hybrids. Like many of O'Bannon's narratives, the overall story of *Alien* was generically conventional, but elements within that narrative—notably the bizarre way in which the alien reproduces itself—were innovative, quirky and distinctive.

Next came co-authorship of the screenplay for **Gary Sherman**'s *Dead & Buried* (1981), a contemporary-set **zombie** film that again offered an original take on a well-established horror theme, and a contribution to the horror-themed animated feature *Heavy Metal* (1981). After writing duties on the futuristic action thriller *Blue Thunder* (1983), O'Bannon made his directorial debut with *The Return of the Living Dead* (1985), which he also scripted. This had no formal connection with **George Romero**'s *Night of the Living Dead* (1968), but instead was a lively comedy-horror about an industrial accident that causes the dead to rise and eat the brains of the living. The film was successful enough to generate four **sequels**. None of these involved O'Bannon, who returned to scriptwriting with two alien invasion films for **Tobe Hooper**, the enjoyable but silly *Lifeforce* (1985) and the jokey *Invaders from Mars* (1986). His other genre credits include two Philip K. Dick adaptations, the big-budget *Total Recall* (1990) and the considerably smaller-budget *Screamers* (1995), as well as two **H. P. Lovecraft** adaptations, *The Resurrected* (1992), which O'Bannon directed but did not write, and *Bleeders* (1997), which he co-wrote but did not direct. *See also* AMERICAN HORROR.

OGILVY, IAN (1943–). The actor Ian Ogilvy was an intense presence in **British horror** cinema of the late 1960s, largely through an association with his friend, the director **Michael Reeves**. He played the deeply troubled main protagonists in all three of Reeves' feature films, the Italian-produced *La sorella di satana* (*Revenge of the Blood Beast, The She Beast*) (1966), and the British-produced *The Sorcerers* (1967) and *Witchfinder General* (1968). Reeves' early death terminated this interesting part of Ogilvy's career, although he subsequently made effective appearances in two further British horrors, *From Beyond the Grave* (1973) and *And Now the Screaming Starts!* (1973). In the late 1970s, he found fame as a **television** star with *The Return of the Saint*. More recently, he has become a novelist. He can be seen in supporting roles in the **comedy**-horror *Death Becomes Her* (1992) and *Puppet Master 5: The Final Chapter* (1994).

THE OMEN (1976). The 1970s **American horror** film *The Omen* (1976), which was directed by Richard Donner, has long been overshadowed by the taboo-breaking *The Exorcist* (1973) and *The Texas Chainsaw Massacre* (1974), perhaps because it is so polished and well-crafted in comparison with the rawer appeal of these other films, perhaps because it is set in Europe rather than America. However, it is arguably just as important to an understanding of the genre in this period. It is a key example of **apocalyptic horror** and, even by the cynical standards of 1970s horror, unusually bleak, with the forces of good left comprehensively defeated. Its deployment of Biblical prophecies, which was unusual within a horror genre that rarely engaged explicitly with Christianity, underlined the extent to which this defeat was preordained and unavoidable. Not even an established star like Gregory Peck was able to save the day. Also striking was the film's portrayal of a child as the monster; this was not an uncommon theme in 1970s horror but here it was done with real conviction. While the girl in *The Exorcist* was only possessed and could be rescued, Damien in *The Omen* was the **Antichrist**, fathered by the **Devil** and born of a jackal, and therefore intrinsically and irredeemably evil.

The film's other key innovation was the spectacular death sequences it offered, including one of horror cinema's most awe-inspiring decapitations. On the one hand, these deaths—which were usually accompanied by **Jerry Goldsmith**'s evocative choral score—demonstrated the power of the Devil (although this figure never appeared), but they were also perversely witty and entertaining in the way they transformed peaceful spaces into merciless killing grounds.

The substantial commercial success enjoyed by *The Omen* inevitably led to a **sequel**, *Damien—Omen II* (1978). Directed by Don Taylor, this shifted the action to America and offered elements of social critique in its depiction of a teenage Damien slowly coming to terms with his destiny in a world of social privilege, wealth and power. The film also increased the number of death sequences (including an extraordinary scene depicting death by lift cable). As before, good—this time in the form of old-time Hollywood star William Holden—was defeated, and evil prevailed.

Damien was finally defeated in *The Final Conflict* (1981) which, as directed by Graham Baker, returned to Great Britain and featured Sam Neill as the adult Antichrist. By this stage, much of the energy of the *Omen* cycle had dissipated. The death scenes were less in number and less inventive, and, considering his awesome power in the first two films, Damien's defeat—he is stabbed—proved something of an anticlimax. *Omen IV: The Awakening* (1991), co-directed by Jorge Montesi and Dominique Othenin-Girard and featuring the exploits of Damien's daughter, was a negligible afterthought to the series and was not widely distributed.

The Omen (2006), a **remake** of the original directed by John Moore, stayed close to its source material. However, it had less impact, perhaps because the elaborate death scenes developed by the earlier *Omen* films had subsequently been taken onto a new level by the *Final Destination* (2000–2006) trilogy and perhaps because the sense of doom that pervaded the original film was less a feature of the culture into which the remake was released.

ORMSBY, ALAN (1944–). Not only did Alan Ormsby do the garish **makeup** effects for **Bob Clark**'s **zombie** film *Children Shouldn't Play with Dead Things* (1972), he also contributed to the film's screenplay and starred as the obnoxious theater director who ill-advisedly raises the dead. Subsequently he wrote and did the makeup effects for Clark's *Dead of Night* (*Night Walk*, *Deathdream*) (1974), a more socially critical zombie film in which an undead war veteran terrorizes his home town. *Deranged* (1974), which Ormsby co-directed with Jeff Gillen, remains his only directorial credit to date. Loosely based on the exploits of real-life **serial killer Ed Gein**, it was a gruesome but inventive horror unfortunately overshadowed by **Tobe Hooper**'s similarly themed *The Texas Chainsaw Massacre* (1974). Ormsby also did makeup effects for *Shock Waves* (1977) and wrote the screenplay for **Paul Schrader**'s remake *Cat People* (1982). He was hired to write and direct the horror *Popcorn* (1991) but left the project during shooting, with the film credited to another director; Ormsby received a screenplay credit under the name Tod Hackett.

– P –

PALANCE, JACK (1919–2006). Although a versatile actor, Jack Palance was best known as a leading screen heavy capable of exuding considerable menace. This aspect of his persona suited him well to starring roles in the **Jack the Ripper** film *Man in the Attic* (1954) and in two **television** horror stories, *The Strange Case of Dr. Jekyll and Mr. Hyde* (1968) and *Dracula* (1973), the latter of which was released theatrically in some countries. As directed by **Dan Curtis**, *Dracula* was an innovative exploration of the historical roots of the **vampire** narrative, and Palance played the part of the vampire-warrior with great presence and dignity. He also did a memorable turn as a neurotic collector of **Edgar Allan Poe** memorabilia in the **British horror anthology** *Torture Garden* (1967). His few other horror credits—which include *Craze* (1973), *Without Warning* (1980), and *Alone in the Dark* (1982)—are minor.

His daughter Holly Palance played the nanny who hanged herself in *The Omen* (1976).

PANG, DANNY AND OXIDE (1965–). The Chinese twin brothers Danny and Oxide Pang usually co-write, co-produce and co-direct their films and often work in Thailand. Their first film together was the thriller *Bangkok Dangerous* (1999), but it was the **ghost** story *Gin gwai (The Eye)* (2002) that brought them significant recognition. This told the story of a woman who has disturbing visions after receiving a cornea transplant and sets out to discover the identity of the cornea donor, and it made an important contribution—along with the likes of **Hideo Nakata**'s *Ringu* (*Ring*) (1998) and **Takashi Shimizu**'s *Ju-on: The Grudge* (2003)—to the international popularity of East Asian horror. Since then, the Pang brothers have made two **sequels**, *Gin gwai 2* (*The Eye 2*) (2004) and *Gin gwai 10* (*The Eye: Infinity*) (2005), as well as the fantasy *Gwai wik* (*Re-cycle*) (2006). In 2007, they released their first **American horror** film, *The Messengers*. Oxide Pang also co-directed the horror **anthology** *Bangkok Haunted* (2001) with Pisut Praesangeam.

PERKINS, ANTHONY (1932–1992). Anthony Perkins' remarkable performance as **serial killer** Norman Bates in **Alfred Hitchcock**'s *Psycho* (1960) both defined and limited his later career. So convincing was his portrayal of Bates as the gauche boy next door and so unnerving his eventual transformation into a smiling murderer that a certain neurotic intensity became permanently imprinted on his screen persona. A number of his pre-*Psycho* appearances had possessed a nervous quality, but after *Psycho* this element was often foregrounded. For much of the 1960s, as if to get away from Norman Bates, Perkins worked mainly in Europe. On his return to the United States, he found himself cast as a mentally disturbed murderer in *Pretty Poison* (1968) and as another disturbed character in **Curtis Harrington**'s **television** film *How Awful About Allan* (1970). Even his non-horror performances in this period had a Norman Bates-like jumpiness to them, notably in *Murder on the Orient Express* (1974) and *Mahogany* (1975).

In 1983, he bowed to the inevitable and returned to the Bates Motel in **Richard Franklin**'s *Psycho II*. He was fine in the film, rendering the part yet more sympathetic than it had been in Hitchcock's hands. He returned again in *Psycho III* (1986)—which he also directed—and, finally, in **Mick Garris**'s television film *Psycho IV: The Beginning*. By contrast, his performance as a mad preacher in **Ken Russell**'s erotic thriller *Crimes of Passion* (1984) was clearly a parody of the Bates character. In the latter part of his career, he also starred in *Edge of Sanity* (1989), a version of the **Dr. Jekyll and Mr. Hyde** story, and featured in some horror-themed television films, among them **Stuart Gordon**'s *Daughter of Darkness* (1990) and **Tobe Hooper**'s *I'm Dangerous Tonight* (1990).

THE PHANTOM OF THE OPERA. Gaston Leroux's novel *Le fantôme de l'opéra* (*The Phantom of the Opera*) was first published in 1910. A dark romance set in the Paris Opera, it has been adapted many times, with varying degrees of faithfulness, for cinema, the stage and **television**, including a Chinese film version in 1937. To a certain extent, the story has always sat on the edge of the horror genre, with the central love story ameliorating the nastiness of the Phantom himself and enabling the adaptation to be marketed to a broader audience than that normally associated with horror.

The first film adaptation of Leroux's novel appears to have been the now lost German production *Das Phantom der Oper* (1916). More significant was the lavish **Universal** production *The Phantom of the Opera* (1925), which featured **Lon Chaney** at the height of his powers as the Phantom. Chaney's skull-like **makeup** is impressive even by the standards of today's sophisticated special effects, and the film had an operatic sweep that later versions would never quite match. Although it has come to be considered a horror classic, the term *horror film* did not exist—at least in the way we understand it now—at the time of its initial release, and the film was perceived then more as a vehicle for Chaney's extraordinary talents. By the time of *Phantom of the Opera* (1943), the next Leroux adapation, horror was an established generic category in American cinema. However, this Universal film—which was directed by **Arthur Lubin** and featured **Claude Rains** as the Phantom—offered itself as more upmarket, both in production values and subject matter, than the lurid horror fare also being produced by Universal during the 1940s (e.g., *Frankenstein Meets the Wolf Man*). It introduced the idea of the Phantom being scarred through an accident (rather than being naturally disfigured), but otherwise it remained a tame affair, with the Phantom's unmasking something of an anti-climax. Much the same could be said of **Hammer**'s *The Phantom of the Opera* (1962), which, as directed by **Terence Fisher**, was intended as a more family-oriented form of horror and therefore suppressed elements of **gore** and violence that had been so prevalent in earlier Hammer horrors. The film's commercial failure brought the first phase of Hammer horror production to an end.

Brian De Palma's musical-**comedy**-horror *Phantom of the Paradise* (1974) was a cheeky mix of the *Phantom of the Opera* narrative with the Faust story, with references to *The Picture of Dorian Gray* thrown in for good measure. It was perhaps too self-consciously clever for its own good, although it remains one of the more unusual Phantom films. By contrast, **Dwight H. Little**'s *The Phantom of the Opera* (1989) and **Dario Argento**'s *Il fantasma dell'opera* (*The Phantom of the Opera*) (1998) were both straightforward attempts to claim the story for the full-blooded horror approach. The Little version featured *Nightmare on Elm Street* star **Robert Englund** as a wisecracking, intensely violent Phantom in a story that took very little from the Leroux original. Unfortunately, Argento's film was one of his lesser efforts. He seems uncomfortable with the period setting, although the idea of the Phantom as someone who was not actually scarred but just full of self-loathing was at least innovative.

However, it was Andrew Lloyd Webber's 1986 musical stage version that caught the public's imagination and went on to become one of the most successful musicals of all time. Here the horror elements became decorative rather than central, and the original novel's tragic romance was returned to the foreground. In 2004, Joel Schumacher directed *The Phantom of the Opera*, an adaptation of Webber's musical that underlined the extent to which the story of the Phantom had been secured for the family audience.

PICHEL, IRVING (1891–1954). Unusually for Hollywood, Irving Pichel managed to combine acting and directing throughout his career. His directorial debut—co-directed with **Ernest B. Schoedsack** —was *The Most Dangerous Game* (*The Hounds of Zaroff*) (1932), which mixed adventure with horror elements in its story of a mad hunter tracking down human prey. He also co-directed—with Lansing C. Holden this time—the fantasy adventure *She* (1935). As an actor, he was the **vampire**'s sidekick in *Dracula's Daughter* (1936) and also showed up in **Victor Halperin**'s *Torture Ship* (1939). *See also* AMERICAN HORROR.

THE PICTURE OF DORIAN GRAY. The Picture of Dorian Gray (1891), Oscar Wilde's only novel, told of a hedonistic young man whose many sins are recorded in a painting of him rather on the sinner himself. Its emphasis on duality linked it thematically with another Victorian horror, Robert Louis Stevenson's *The Strange Case of*

Dr. Jekyll and Mr. Hyde (1886), although it has not had the impact on horror cinema of Stevenson's work. There were several silent film adaptations of Wilde's story, including Vsevolod Meyerhold's *Portret Doryana Greya* (1915) and *Az Élet királya* (1918), a Hungarian version featuring **Bela Lugosi** in a supporting role. However, the main screen version was Albert Lewin's *The Picture of Dorian Gray* (1945), a tastefully mounted black-and-white American adaptation which starred Hurd Hatfield in the title role and which burst into color whenever Gray's portrait was shown. By contrast, *Dorian Gray* (1970), which starred Helmut Berger and had a contemporary setting, was considerably sleazier. **Dan Curtis** produced a **television** version in 1973, while another television production, *The Sins of Dorian Gray* (1983), turned Dorian Gray into a female character. Other versions appeared in 2004 and 2006.

PIERCE, JACK (1889–1968). If any one person could be considered the maker of monsters in **American horror** cinema, that person would probably be **makeup** artist Jack Pierce. He worked for **Universal** throughout its 1930s and 1940s horror cycles, and was a key contributor to the distinctive visuals of its films. It was he who turned **Boris Karloff** into a monster for *Frankenstein* (1931) and its two sequels and into an undead cloth-wrapped corpse for *The Mummy* (1932). He also transformed **Bela Lugosi** into the broken-necked Ygor in *Son of Frankenstein* (1939) and *The Ghost of Frankenstein* (1942) and into Frankenstein's monster for *Frankenstein Meets the Wolf Man* (1943), and made **Lon Chaney Jr.** into a **werewolf** in *The Wolf Man* (1941) and its sequels and into the mummy for *The Mummy's Tomb* (1942), *The Mummy's Ghost* (1944), and *The Mummy's Curse* (1944). In addition to this, he came up with one of the few memorable female monsters from this period, the Nefertiti-like **Elsa Lanchester** in *Bride of Frankenstein* (1935). Pierce's makeup designs have subsequently proved very influential, even if only as a norm from which later filmmakers have attempted to differentiate their own work.

Pierce's later makeup credits, which were mainly for low-budget independent productions, were considerably less distinguished. They included *The Brain from Planet Arous* (1957), *Teenage Monster* (1958), and *The Amazing Transparent Man* (1960).

PITT, INGRID (1937–). Ingrid Pitt was a charismatic presence in 1970s **British horror**. This Polish-born actor had earlier appeared in supporting roles in the **Spanish horror** film *El sonido prehistórico* (*Sounds of a Million Years Ago, Sounds of Horror*) (1964) and the big-budget war thriller *Where Eagles Dare* (1968). **Hammer** cast her as the female lead in its lesbian **vampire** film *The Vampire Lovers* (1970), and she delivered an imposing and sultry performance. More than Hammer's previous female vampires, Pitt was able to convey both the seductiveness and the melancholy of the undead. She was also a suitably imperious villain in Hammer's *Countess Dracula* (1971), where she played a fictionalized version of the real-life mass murderer **Elizabeth Bathory**. Away from Hammer, there were effective supporting roles in the **Amicus** horror **anthology** *The House That Dripped Blood* (1970) and in **Robin Hardy's** cult classic *The Wicker Man* (1973). The shutting down of much British horror production in the mid-1970s regrettably curtailed the development of her horror stardom, although she did feature in the **Clive Barker**-scripted horror *Underworld* (1985) and appears regularly at horror conventions to meet her devoted **fans**.

PIVAR, BEN (1901–1963). The British-born, American-based producer Ben Pivar was responsible for some of **Universal's** more lurid 1940s horror titles, including *Horror Island* (1941), *The Mad Ghoul* (1943), and *Captive Wild Woman* (1943), in the latter of which a gorilla was turned into a young woman by a **mad scientist**. In yet more questionable taste were Pivar's *House of Horrors* (1946) and *The Brute Man* (1946), both of which featured as their monster **Rondo Hatton**, who was deformed in real life. Pivar also produced all four films in Universal's 1940s **mummy** cycle, *The Mummy's Hand* (1940), *The Mummy's Tomb* (1942), *The Mummy's Ghost* (1944), and *The Mummy's Curse* (1944), and worked on the *Inner Sanctum* series of horror-themed B movies, with the **witchcraft** drama *Weird Woman* (1944) his most notable credit here. Pivar's other horror credits were *She-Wolf of London* (1946)—which was more of a murder mystery than it was a **werewolf** film—and *The Creeper* (1948). As a producer of 1940s horror, Pivar has been completely overshadowed by the more ambitious and creative **Val Lewton**. However, Pivar's focus on horror **sequels** and series has arguably proved more influential in the development of **American horror** than anything done by Lewton.

PLEASENCE, DONALD (1919–1995). The British actor Donald Pleasence's association with horror ran from the late 1950s through to his death. He acted in a variety of genres, but there was something about his screen persona—which could switch rapidly from quiet menace to wide-eyed **madness**—that particularly suited him to horror. He provided able support in the **British horror** films *The Flesh and the Fiends* (1959) and *Circus of Horrors* (1960), among others, but came into his own with a leading role in **Gary Sherman**'s **cannibalism** story *Death Line* (*Raw Meat*) (1972). As a policeman investigating mysterious disappearances on the London Underground, he subtly combined truculence with a sense of loneliness, thereby giving the film its emotional center. His supporting role in the **Amicus** horror **anthology** *From Beyond the Grave* (1973) was more caricatural, although this fitted well with Amicus's cynical view of human nature (and it also gave Pleasence the opportunity to act alongside his daughter, Angela Pleasence). Most of his other 1970s credits—which included *The Mutations* (*The Freakmaker*) (1973), *Tales That Witness Madness* (1973), *I Don't Want To Be Born* (*The Devil Within Her*) (1975), and *The Devil's Men* (1976)—were negligible. However, his role in **John Carpenter**'s low-budget American **slasher** film *Halloween* (1978) finally made him a horror star. He played Dr. Sam Loomis (named after a character in **Alfred Hitchcock**'s *Psycho*), a psychiatrist who, contrary to the usual representation of such a figure, carries a gun because he is convinced that an escaped **serial killer** is the embodiment of pure evil and probably not even human. Without overplaying, Pleasence effectively conveyed Loomis's manic and disturbed qualities.

Halloween was a substantial commercial success, and Pleasence went on to reprise the part of Loomis in *Halloween 2* (1981), *Halloween 4: The Return of Michael Myers* (1988), *Halloween 5* (1989), and *Halloween: The Curse of Michael Myers* (1995). None of these were particularly impressive, and generally Pleasence, who always seemed to behave more as a jobbing actor than he did a genre star, showed up in more undistinguished horrors during the 1980s than was perhaps good for his reputation. There were highlights, however. He was memorable as an ineffectual asylum keeper in *Dracula* (1979), played another psychiatrist in the minor but lively maniacs-on-the-loose drama *Alone in the Dark* (1982), worked with **Dario**

Argento on the **giallo** *Phenomena* (1985), and was reunited with Carpenter for the supernatural thriller *Prince of Darkness* (1987), in which he played a priest called Father Loomis.

POE, EDGAR ALLAN (1809–1849). Filmmakers have regularly raided Edgar Allan Poe's **gothic** fiction for ideas and images, although the intense nature of his short stories has never lent itself well to transcription into the feature film format. Accordingly, one tends to find allusions to and quotations from Poe's work in films rather than direct adaptations. There were several such treatments of Poe's stories in the silent period, the most notable of which was Jean Epstein's experimental *La chute de la maison Usher* (*The Fall of the House of Usher*) (1928). **Robert Florey**'s *Murders in the Rue Morgue* (1932) borrowed as much from German **Expressionism** as it did from Poe, while *The Black Cat* (1934) and *The Raven* (1935) took their titles from Poe but little else. Producer-director **Roger Corman**'s 1960s cycle of Poe adaptations—which included *House of Usher* (1960), *Pit and the Pendulum* (1961), *The Premature Burial* (1962), *Tales of Terror* (1962), *The Raven* (1963), *The Masque of the Red Death* (1964), and *The Tomb of Ligeia* (1964)—managed to evoke some of Poe's morbidity, although the storylines usually had little or nothing to do with the stories or poems from which they were allegedly adapted; Corman's *The Haunted Palace* (1963) was marketed as a Poe film although it was actually an adaptation of a **H. P. Lovecraft** story. *Histoires extraordinaires* (*Tales of Mystery and Imagination, Spirits of the Dead*) (1968) was a more upmarket European horror **anthology** based on Poe's stories that gathered together short films from Federico Fellini, Louis Malle and **Roger Vadim**. However, it was equally free with its sources, with Fellini's contribution proving the only one of note. Since then, Poe has been repeatedly credited as a source in films too numerous to list here, although in most cases one struggles to find anything of Poe's original work in them. An undead Poe shows up as a character in the **Amicus** anthology *Torture Garden* (1967) and looks suitably fed up.

POINT OF VIEW. In cinema, point of view shots are those shots designated as offering what a character within the film in question is actually seeing. Such shots are usually preceded or followed by shots of that character in the act of looking, with this confirming that what we have just seen or are about to see is through the character's **eyes**. Point of view shots of this kind are present in a wide range of films, including horror. However, the horror genre also has a more specialized use for point of view.

The widely held belief in film criticism that the point of view technique helps to establish an audience's identification with the character who is looking is thrown into some disarray when confronted with horror's practice of assigning point of view shots to its monsters or killers. This particular deployment of point of view first became apparent during the 1950s, when many **science fiction**/horror movies featured the point of view of the alien or monster as it advanced upon its (usually female) victim. More controversial was the reliance of the American **slasher** film of the late 1970s and early 1980s on showing the killer's point of view as he stalked and assaulted his (again usually female) victim. On their initial release, some critics claimed that these films were inviting audiences—and by implication predominantly male audiences—to identify with the killer's sadism, with the slashers thus rendered an expression of misogyny.

Other critics have since questioned whether the point of view technique in itself can lead to character identification, especially in horror where the villains are often so repellent and ugly. As if to underline the obstacles placed in the way of any simple identification, the point of view of monsters in horror films is itself often made strange or alienating. In 1950s films, distorting lenses were sometimes used to denote the alien identity of the monster, while the slasher's point of view shots frequently deployed an obtrusive shaky camera. The fact that the slasher rarely showed the killer until the end of the film also potentially destabilized any straightforward audience identification with such a figure. The extent to which horror spectators are sometimes invited to enjoy acts of sadistic violence, regardless of who is perpetrating them, remains debatable. However, an influential strand in horror criticism argues that horror offers as much a masochistic experience as it does a sadistic one. In this instance, the killer's point of view provides a good vantage point on the victim, who, in her or his fear and terror, can become the main figure of identification.

POLANSKI, ROMAN (1933–). The films of Polish director Roman Polanski have frequently engaged with horror themes, albeit from an idiosyncratic perspective. He has shown himself adept at the **psychological thriller**, from his Polish feature debut *Nóz w wodzie* (*Knife in the Water*) (1962) to the British-set *Cul-de-sac* (1966) and the more recent *Bitter Moon* (1992) and *Death and the Maiden* (1994). *Repulsion* (1965), his first English-language film, was an intense study of psychological breakdown in which a young French woman (played by Catherine Deneuve) based in London goes mad for no apparent reason. Here Polanski put us inside the distorted subjectivity of this character as she fantasizes about walls splitting open and arms reaching out to grab her. *Dance of the Vampires* (*The Fearless Vampire Killers*) (1967) was ostensibly a more cheerful affair, although in its own way it turned out to be just as dark as *Repulsion*. The film affectionately spoofed **Hammer**-style period horror, while at the same time it contained some chilling sequences, not least the vampire dance itself. The film's conclusion—in which vampirism is let loose upon the world—was one of the darkest to a horror film from this period and anticipated later despairing finishes not just from Polanski but from other directors as well.

Rosemary's Baby (1968), Polanski's first Hollywood production, dealt with a woman discovering that she had apparently been impregnated by the **Devil** and has given birth to the **Antichrist**; the film's ambiguous ending showed Rosemary seeming to accept the baby as her own. Along with **George Romero**'s *Night of the Living Dead* (1968), *Rosemary's Baby* has been seen as inaugurating the modern **American horror** film. However, it was very different in style and tone from Romero's work—glossy and slyly humorous as opposed to *Night*'s relentlessly apocalyptic approach.

More than most directors, Polanski's biography has often been invoked to explain the peculiar character of his work. He certainly suffered traumatic experiences during World War II as a Jewish child in German-occupied Poland. More trauma came after the release of *Rosemary's Baby*, when Sharon Tate, Polanski's pregnant wife, was murdered by followers of Charles Manson. Perhaps unsurprisingly, *The Tragedy of Macbeth* (1971), which marked Polanski's return to direction after this appalling incident, was one of the most despairing cinematic renditions of Shakespeare's tale and brimmed with violent horror imagery. Subsequently, Polanski made what many critics consider to be his masterpiece, the period crime drama *Chinatown* (1974). Shortly thereafter, he was convicted of the statutory rape of an underage girl and fled the United States. The European-based films that followed included well-crafted literary adaptations *Tess* (1979) and *Oliver Twist* (2005) as well as *The Pianist* (2002), an adaptation of a novel about Poland during World War II. However, there were also two effective fantasy films. *Le locataire* (*The Tenant*, 1976) was a fine study of urban alienation that can be linked thematically with *Repulsion* and *Rosemary's Baby* and which featured an excellent performance from Polanski himself (who since childhood has had an intermittent second career as a screen actor). *The Ninth Gate* (1999) was a more playful supernatural thriller, albeit one that lacked some of the more disturbing elements that had characterized much of Polanski's earlier work.

POSSESSION. Possession by demons or spirits has not been a major theme in horror cinema, which has tended to have a preference for more visible and solid monsters. *Orlacs Hände* (*The Hands of Orlac*) (1924), *Supernatural* (1933), *The Innocents* (1961), *Diary of a Madman* (1963) and **Roger Corman**'s *The Haunted Palace* (1963) were isolated examples of horrors that explored fearful scenarios in which characters had their bodies and/or minds taken over by an external force or personality, with the emphasis primarily on the psychological. In the early 1970s, **Hammer** also engaged with the subject from a psychological perspective with the innovative *Blood from the Mummy's Tomb* (1971) and *Hands of the Ripper* (1971), in which **Jack the Ripper**'s daughter found herself possessed by the spirit of her father. The American production *The Mephisto Waltz* (1971) offered a wild narrative involving the transmigration of souls, while the more ambitious *The Possession of Joel Delaney* (1972) deployed elements of social critique in a drama involving rich white people being possessed by a spirit emanating from the ethnic underclass.

The phenomenally successful *The Exorcist* (1973) introduced a new visceral quality into its dramatization of a young girl possessed by a demon and focused more on the business of exorcism than it did on psychological matters. Inevitably, other similarly themed films quickly appeared, including the blaxploitation horror *Abby* (1974), from Italy *L'anticristo* (*The Antichrist*) (1974), *Chi sei* (*Beyond the Door, The Devil Within Her*) (1974), and from Spain *La endemoniada* (*Demon Witch Child, The Possessed*) (1975) and *Exorcismo* (*Exorcism*) (1975). *The Exorcist* itself generated several **sequels**, while **Curtis Harrington**'s *Ruby* (1977) and **Robert Wise**'s *Audrey Rose* (1977) dealt in a quieter, less gory way with stories involving possession by **ghosts**. Since this flurry of activity, possession has receded as a horror theme. Demonic possession has featured in *Prince of Darkness* (1987), *Fallen* (1998), *The Exorcism of Emily Rose* (2005), and *Requiem* (2006), while more comic versions have been offered by **Sam Raimi**'s *Evil Dead* films and *Ghostbusters* (1984).

A significant generic sub-category has been formed by **science fiction**/horror hybrids in which humans are possessed by aliens. Such films have included *Invaders from Mars* (1953), *Quatermass 2* (*Enemy from Space*) (1957), *Quatermass and the Pit* (*Five Million Years to Earth*) (1967), *The Faculty* (1998), and *The Astronaut's Wife* (1999).

POWELL, MICHAEL (1905–1990). There was a rich vein of fantasy running through the 1940s and 1950s films that British director Michael Powell made in collaboration with the writer Emeric Pressburger. The wartime production *A Canterbury Tale* (1944) featured the sinister Glueman, a mysterious figure who sneaked up on women in the dark and poured glue into their hair. His motivation for such behavior turned out to be reasonable, at least within the film's terms, although in retrospect he looked like an early version of the **serial killer** who would show up in a later Powell film. *A Matter of Life and Death* (1946), *Black Narcissus* (1947), and *The Red Shoes* (1948) all contained stylized representations of mental disturbance, while *The Tales of Hoffman* (1951) offered a more playful treatment of fantasy themes. However, it was a film made by Powell without the input of Pressburger that took him unambiguously into horror territory. *Peeping Tom* (1960) was a **psychological thriller** about a serial killer who, with the aid of a combination of camera and mirror, filmed his female victims as they watched themselves die. There are some obvious parallels with **Alfred Hitchcock**'s *Psycho* (1960) inasmuch as the young serial killers in both are presented with a degree of sympathy. But the **self-reflexivity** apparent in Powell's film, with numerous references to cameras and the act of looking, arguably rendered it a more confrontational and provocative experience. In any event, its release in Great Britain was greeted with critical outrage. It is now widely considered by critics to be one of the greatest British films ever made. *See also* BRITISH HORROR.

PRICE, DENNIS (1915–1973). The British actor Dennis Price started out with some impressive credits, including the **ghost** story *A Place of One's Own* (1945), **Michael Powell**'s *A Canterbury Tale* (1944), and the Ealing **comedy** *Kind Hearts and Coronets* (1949), in most cases playing supercilious roles. From the 1950s onwards, however, his career was in gradual decline, with his increasing reliance on supporting appearances in low-budget horror films a sign of this. He worked on two of **Terence Fisher**'s lesser films, the comedy-horror *The Horror of it All* (1964) and the alien invasion fantasy *The Earth Dies Screaming* (1964). He also showed up, in fairly insignificant parts, in the **voodoo** thriller *Curse of Simba* (1965), **Michael Armstrong**'s *The Haunted House of Horror* (1969), two **Hammer** horrors, *The Horror of Frankenstein* (1970) and *Twins of Evil* (1971), and the **rural horror** *Tower of Evil* (1972). *Theater of Blood* (1973) and *Horror Hospital* (1973) gave him the opportunity to ham it up in an enjoyable manner. Less entertaining were the films he made with exploitation specialist **Jesus Franco**, in which he seemed a lost and depressed figure. These included *Vampyros lesbos* (*Lesbian Vampires*) (1971), *Les expériences érotiques de Frankenstein* (*The Erotic Rites of Frankenstein, The Curse of Frankenstein*) (1972), and *Drácula contra Frankenstein* (*Dracula vs. Dr. Frankenstein*) (1972). His final film was **Freddie Francis**'s bizarre horror-musical, *Son of Dracula* (1974).

PRICE, VINCENT (1911–1993). Some horror stars achieve their stardom through a key iconic role (for example, **Boris Karloff** as **Frankenstein**'s monster or **Bela Lugosi** or **Christopher Lee** as **Dracula**) but Vincent Price's association with the horror genre developed more gradually. Early in his screen career, he appeared in the horror-themed historical drama *Tower of London* (1939) and also starred as the Invisible Man in *The Invisible Man Returns* (1940), as well as offering an uncredited cameo in the same role for *Abbott & Costello Meet Franken-*

stein (1948). His first major role in a horror film was as the scarred sculptor in *House of Wax* (1953), but neither this nor a similar part in *The Mad Magician* (1954), nor even an appearance as the **Devil** in *The Story of Mankind* (1957), led to his being typecast as a horror actor, and Price continued to work in a variety of genres. In fact, it was not until the late 1950s that Price became firmly associated with the genre, beginning with *The Fly* (1958) and its **sequel** *Return of the Fly* (1959) and two films for producer-director **William Castle**, *House on Haunted Hill* (1959) and *The Tingler* (1959). Price's performance style, which to modern **eyes** can seem theatrical, arch and sometimes slightly camp, was particularly suited to Castle's jokey, gimmick-ridden horror films, and it also translated well into a series of films the actor then made with director **Roger Corman**, films that would finally secure his status as a horror star.

Price's overwrought performance as the neurotic Roderick Usher in *House of Usher* (1960), Corman's adaptation of the **Edgar Allan Poe** story, perfectly expressed that film's sense of morbid masculine psychology. Subsequent starring roles in further Corman-Poe projects—including *Pit and the Pendulum* (1961), *Tales of Terror* (1962, in which Price played three roles), *The Raven* (1963), *The Haunted Palace* (1963, actually an **H. P. Lovecraft** adaptation with a few references to Poe thrown in for good measure), *The Masque of the Red Death* (1964), and *The Tomb of Ligeia* (1964)—afforded Price opportunities to refine and develop this persona, modulating it into outright **madness** in *Pit and the Pendulum* and into sadistic villainy in *The Masque of the Red Death* while playing it for laughs in the **comedy**-horror *The Raven*. Other Price roles during the first half of the 1960s—for example, his turns in *Confessions of an Opium Eater* (1962), *Tower of London* (1962, a **remake** of the film in which Price himself had appeared in the late 1930s), *Diary of a Madman* (1963), *Twice-Told Tales* (1963), and *The Comedy of Terrors* (1963)—were comparably mannered and occasionally self-parodic. It was not until the late 1960s that Price assayed a more serious role as the witchfinder Matthew Hopkins in director **Michael Reeves'** British production *Witchfinder General* (1968). Apparently there was some tension on set between the young director and his star about how the role was to be played, with Reeves preferring a more realistic performance than Price was accustomed to delivering. Despite Price's reservations, the resulting film is one of his finest and displays his qualities as an actor more than any of his later films would. In these, he tended to revert to the theatrical acting style with which he was clearly more comfortable. His best role of this type was one for which such an approach was wholly appropriate, namely the murderous actor Edward Lionheart in the witty **British horror** *Theater of Blood* (1973). He was also impressive, albeit under heavy **makeup**, as the similarly over-the-top Dr. Phibes in the stylish *The Abominable Dr. Phibes* (1971) and its sequel *Dr. Phibes Rises Again* (1972).

Price's later horror films were undistinguished, although he did find a new youthful audience through his narration of director **Tim Burton**'s animated short *Vincent* (1982), a brief cameo appearance in Burton's *Edward Scissorhands* (1990) and, most of all, through providing a voice-over for the Michael Jackson hit song "Thriller" in 1983.

Price's other credits included *The Bat* (1959), *Master of the World* (1961), *The Last Man on Earth* (1964), *The City Under the Sea* (1965), *Scream and Scream Again* (1969), *The Oblong Box* (1969), *Cry of the Banshee* (1970), *Madhouse* (1974), *The Monster Club* (1980), *House of the Long Shadows* (1983), *Bloodbath at the House of Death* (1984), *The Offspring (From a Whisper to a Scream)* (1987), and *Dead Heat* (1988).

PSYCHO (1960). **Alfred Hitchcock**'s *Psycho* is a key film in the development of modern **American horror**. Its representation of psycho-sexual horror played out within recognizably modern settings would be developed further in numerous American horror films of the 1970s and 1980s. Its now famous killing off of its heroine well before the conclusion also anticipated the genre's later reliance on shock effects (although few filmmakers went as far as Hitchcock). *Psycho* was based on a novel by **Robert Bloch**, which in turn had been inspired by the exploits of real-life **serial killer Ed Gein**. While Bloch's work often had a tongue-in-cheek quality, Hitchcock's *Psycho* offered a more provocative sly humor in its depiction of the transvestite serial killer Norman Bates—played, in a career-defining performance, by **Anthony Perkins**—as well as one of horror's great set pieces in the much-analyzed and much-imitated shower murder. In addition, **Bernard Herrmann**'s innovative strings-only score for the film has also proved influential on subsequent horror **music**.

For all of *Psycho*'s success, a **sequel** was a long time coming, perhaps because Hitchcock's canonical status as "The Master of Suspense" was so intimidating to later filmmakers. When it did finally appear, *Psycho 2* (1983), which was directed by **Richard Franklin**, was a much better film than many critics had predicted. It depicted Norman Bates—still played by Perkins—being released from an asylum and returning to the now notorious Bates Motel. The narrative was full of inventive touches and twists but it also offered a sympathetic portrayal of Bates as someone ill-suited to life outside of a mental institution. Hitchcock's *Psycho* had also presented this character with a degree of sympathy, but *Psycho 2* transformed him into a sensitive, misunderstood hero whose violence became acts of defense against people who were out to get him. *Psycho 3* (1986) contained more of the same, although the direction, this time by Perkins himself, was assured and had some effective Hitchcockian moments.

The next two *Psycho* films were both made for **television**. Richard Rothstein's *Bates Motel* (1987) was a pilot for a never-made series which, as its title indicated, took place in the Bates Motel but did not feature Norman Bates. This was rectified for **Mick Garris**'s *Psycho IV: The Beginning* (1990), a kind of prequel in which Perkins/Bates reminisces about his early days. Odder still was a 1998 **remake** of the original *Psycho* that was directed by Gus Van Sant and which featured Vince Vaughan as Norman Bates and Anne Heche as the shower murder victim Marion Crane. Remaking a "classic" is always fraught with danger, and Van Sant's film—which is not the shot-for-shot copy that some have claimed it to be—was not well received by critics. It also seems to have marked the end, for the time being at least, of the serial killer Norman Bates.

PSYCHOLOGICAL THRILLER. The label "psychological thriller" has been applied, often loosely or vaguely, to different types of film. It usually refers to narratives with domesticated settings in which action is suppressed and where the thrills are provided instead via investigations of the psychologies of principal characters. There is nothing intrinsically horror-like about the psychological thriller. However, post-1950s horror cinema has increasingly deployed psychological concepts and scenarios, and consequently there is a category of psychological thriller that sits, sometimes uncomfortably, between the genres of crime and horror. The extent to which any thriller is one thing or another depends on a number of factors. If there is an emphasis on especially morbid or sick psychologies, or if there is a lot of violence or **gore** in the narrative, or if the intended effect on the audience involves a significant dimension of fear or shock, then the film in question is more likely to be considered as a horror film. The marketing of particular films, and the ways in which they are received by audiences, can also have an effect on generic designations, and sometimes there might not be a consensus about where a film belongs. For example, the **serial killer** drama *The Silence of the Lambs* (1991) was initially marketed more as a dark thriller than as a horror (presumably to differentiate it from the **teenage horror** films that were popular at the time). However, horror **fans** have frequently claimed the film as horror on their websites and in their fanzines.

It was the commercial success of two films in particular that arguably helped to push horror towards the psychological, namely Henri-Georges Clouzot's French thriller *Les diaboliques* (1954) and **Alfred Hitchcock**'s *Psycho* (1960). Both generated an intensely morbid and claustrophobic atmosphere and both also contained supreme moments of shock-horror, namely the apparent resurrection of a corpse in *Les diaboliques* and the shower murder in *Psycho*. Although *Les diaboliques* is rarely thought of as a horror film in its own right, American producer-director **William Castle** was inspired by it to create his own series of psychological thrillers that were insistently marketed as horror, including *Macabre* (1958) and the later *Psycho*-influenced *Homicidal* (1961). Similarly, the British **Hammer** company inaugurated its own series of psychological thrillers that usually had *Psycho*-like titles and twisty *Diaboliques*-style plot and which were designed to complement its period horrors (and which often featured on double bills with those period horrors); these included *A Taste of Fear* (*Scream of Fear*) (1961), *Maniac* (1963), *Paranoiac* (1963), *Hysteria* (1965), and *Fanatic* (*Die! Die! My Darling!*) (1965). The Italian **giallo** horror-thrillers also put great emphasis on the psychological in their convoluted and violent invocations of disturbed minds. Even some 1960s period horrors, notably the adaptations of **Edgar Allan Poe**'s writings by **Roger Corman**, focused more on extreme psychological states than they did on traditional horror monsters, to the extent that they too might be considered as psychological thrillers.

The apocalyptic and socially critical elements prevalent in 1970s **American horror** cinema tended to lead it away from such psychological thrills, although isolated psychological horrors such as *The Other* (1972) and *Communion* (*Alice, Sweet Alice*) (1976) did appear, and giallo films continued to proliferate in Europe. The American **slasher** films of the late 1970s and 1980s did not have much time for the psychological, but later serial killer films—such as *The Silence of the Lambs, Seven* (1995), and *Copycat* (1995)—have powerfully reinstated a sense of psychological dysfunctionality as a source of fear and terror. As noted above, the extent to which such films are viewed as belonging to the horror genre is largely dependent on the person actually viewing them. However, the importance of the psychological to the modern horror film is undeniable.

– R –

RAIMI, SAM (1959–). The American writer-producer-director Sam Raimi's horror debut was the audacious *The Evil Dead* (1981). A classic example of **rural horror**, its narrative featured some young people heading out into the woods, where they inadvertently summon up some demons. Based on *Within the Woods*, a short film shot by Raimi on Super-8, the film combined extreme violence and **gore** with images of demonic **possession** and gross-out slapstick humor; its narrative also included references to the work of horror writer **H. P. Lovecraft**. Inventive camerawork and staging, along with a grandstanding performance from **Bruce Campbell**, helped to disguise the film's ultra-cheapness and separated it out clearly from the more restrained horror being offered elsewhere under the **slasher** label. It might have seemed immature in comparison with some of the ambitious and weighty horrors produced in the United States during the 1970s, but, despite a certain unevenness, *The Evil Dead* was energetic and original. It eventually became a considerable commercial success, although it ran into serious difficulties with British **censorship** authorities during the "Video Nasties" scare of the early 1980s.

Crimewave (1985), Raimi's next film, was a disappointing thriller, but the director bounced back with *Evil Dead II* (1987), which was part a **sequel** to and part a **remake** of the original *Evil Dead*. The set pieces were more spectacular and the humor a more prominent feature this time, and while some of the edginess of the original was lacking, *Evil Dead II* was a confident reworking of the material that successfully maintained the right balance between the **comedy** and the horror. *Darkman* (1990), a horror-themed superhero story, was more effective than *Crimewave* but less effective than either of the *Evil Dead* films, suggesting that Raimi could only really function fully as a director within a narrow range of material. When *Army of Darkness—Evil Dead 3* (1992) turned out to be the weakest film in the *Evil Dead* cycle, it seemed as if Raimi's career might be in trouble.

As if to demonstrate that this was not the case, Raimi spent the next few years working away from the horror genre, with his films including a **western** (*The Quick and the Dead* in 1995), a thriller (*A Simple Plan* in 1998), and a baseball film (*For Love of the Game* in 1999). When he returned to horror with *The Gift* (2000), he had become a very different type of filmmaker, less frantic and more measured in the way he created atmosphere and told a story. The narrative of *The Gift* was not particularly original—a woman with mediumistic powers becomes involved in a murder investigation—but the film was evocative and beautifully made.

Since then, Raimi has acquired A-list status through his direction of *Spiderman* (2002), *Spiderman 2* (2004), and *Spiderman 3* (2007). He has also been active as a producer, with his credits including **Takashi Shimizu**'s *The Grudge* (2004) and *The Boogeyman* (2005), as well as two sequels to *Darkman*. *See also* AMERICAN HORROR.

RAINS, CLAUDE (1889–1967). The British actor Claude Rains' first major screen role was as the title character in **James Whale**'s *The Invisible Man* (1933). Although he was glimpsed at the end of the film, his performance was necessarily conveyed almost entirely through his rich, mellifluous voice. It was the beginning of a distinguished Hollywood career, highlights of which included *Mr. Smith Goes to Washington* (1939), *Now Voyager* (1942), *Casablanca* (1942), and *Notorious* (1946). However, Rains did return occasionally to the genre that had made him a star, albeit usually in its more upmarket version. He was a psychic in the British production *The Clairvoyant* (1934), John Jasper in **Universal**'s **gothic** adaptation of Charles Dickens' *Mystery of Edwin Drood* (1935), and **Lon Chaney Jr.**'s father in *The Wolf Man* (1941). He also played the Phantom in **Arthur Lubin**'s tasteful *Phantom of the Opera* (1943) and the **Devil** in the gangster-horror hybrid *Angel on My Shoulder* (1946). Towards the end of his career, Rains was directed by **Italian horror** specalist **Antonio Margheriti** in the low-budget alien invasion fantasy *Il pianeta degli uomini spenti* (*Battle of the Worlds*) (1961).

RATHBONE, BASIL (1892–1967). The actor Basil Rathbone was often cast as a villain, but he was also cinema's definitive **Sherlock Holmes**. Gaunt and authoritative, he appeared on screen 14 times in the role, and a number of these films utilized horror conventions. Most notable in this respect was Rathbone's debut, *The Hound of the Baskervilles* (1939), along with *The Scarlet Claw* (1944), *The Pearl of Death* (1944), and *Sherlock Holmes and the House of Fear* (1945). Rathbone was also Wolf **Frankenstein** in **Rowland Lee**'s *Son of Frankenstein* (1939), the third film in **Universal**'s Frankenstein cycle, and featured in the historical horror *Tower of London* (1939) for the same director, as well as showing up in the horror spoof *The Black Cat* (1941). Later appearances in horror films were not quite so dignified. In *The Black Sleep* (1956), he was cast alongside horror stalwarts **John Carradine, Lon Chaney Jr.**, and **Bela Lugosi**, but the resulting film was a listless affair. **Roger Corman**'s *Tales of Terror* (1962) and **Jacques Tourneur**'s *The Comedy of Terrors* (1964) were better, with Rathbone delivering a fine comic performance in the latter. He appeared only briefly in **Curtis Harrington**'s **science fiction/** horror oddity *Queen of Blood* (1966). His last three films, the comedy-horror *The Ghost in the Invisible Bikini* (1966), *Hillbillys in a Haunted House* (1967), and the **Mexican horror** film *Autopsia de un fantasma* (*Autopsy of a Ghost*) (1968), are best forgotten.

RAVEN, MIKE (1924–1997). Mike Raven, a British disc jockey turned actor, aspired to horror stardom. He certainly looked sufficiently sinister and had a suitably chilling name (once he had changed it from his real name of Austin Churton Fairman, that is); apparently he even had a real-life interest in occult matters. Sadly he did not have much screen presence. Supporting roles in *I, Monster* (1970) and *Lust for a Vampire* (1971) failed to make an impact. *Crucible of Terror* (1971) and *Disciple of Death* (1972), the two films in which he starred (and which he helped to finance), were not financially successful, and Raven's horror career, such as it was, came to an abrupt end.

RAY, FRED OLEN (1954–). The indefatigable American writer-producer-director Fred Olen Ray is a low-budget exploitation specialist who has dipped regularly into the horror genre. There is a certain inventiveness apparent in some of his titles—*Hollywood Chainsaw Hookers* (1988) is surely a kind of exploitation classic—but the formula is usually predictable, involving scenes of horror combined with female nudity and self-deprecating humor. His directorial credits include *The Brain Leeches* (1977), *Alien Dead* (1980), *Scalps* (1983), *Biohazard* (1985), *The Phantom Empire* (1986), *The Tomb* (1986), *Beverly Hills Vamp* (1988), *Scream Queen Hot Tub Party* (1991), *Spirits* (1991), *Haunting Fear* (1991), *Evil Toons* (1992), *Witch Academy* (1993), *Possessed by the Night* (1994), *Night Shade* (1997), *Sideshow* (2000), *Venomous* (2002), *Haunting Desires* (2004), and *Tomb of the Werewolf* (2004). He has produced numerous others.

REED, OLIVER (1938–1999). It was the **Hammer** company that gave the British actor Oliver Reed some of his earliest screen parts. After a small role in *The Two Faces of Dr. Jekyll* (1960), he was the tormented lycanthrope in *Curse of the Werewolf* (1961) and a menacing thug in *The Damned* (*These are the Damned*) (1963) and *Paranoiac* (1963). Thereafter, he worked less frequently in horror but did return occasionally in films of varying quality. He was back in menacing form in the **H. P. Lovecraft** adaptation *The Shuttered Room* (1967), played a suffering priest in **Ken Russell**'s controversial *The Devils* (1971), was cast against type as an ordinary family man in **Dan Curtis**'s haunted house drama *Burnt Offerings* (1976), and was suitably brooding as a misguided scientist in **David Cronenberg**'s *The Brood* (1979). His later genre credits were less significant, reflecting a career that was in trouble throughout much of the 1980s and 1990s until his triumphant comeback in his final film, Ridley Scott's *Gladiator* (2000). He was jolly in the **comedy**-horror *Dr. Heckyl and Mr.*

Hype (1980), but *Venom* (1981), *Spasms* (1983), *The House of Usher* (1988) and *The Pit and the Pendulum* (1991) did not make great demands of him.

REEVES, MICHAEL (1943–1969). Critical reactions to the horror films directed by the British director Michael Reeves have often been colored by his tragic death at the age of 25 from an accidental drug overdose. In retrospect, his small but remarkably accomplished body of work appears grimmer than it probably did on its first release, and the delight in cinema that seemed to have driven Reeves is not always apparent. While still at school, he made short films—including some featuring the actor **Ian Ogilvy**, who would go on to star in all three of Reeves's feature films—and in the early 1960s worked briefly in Hollywood for one of his cinematic idols, the director Don Siegel. Returning to Britain, he was a runner on a number of films produced by Irving Allen before heading off to Italy where he worked as an assistant on the horror film *Il castello dei morti vivi* (*Castle of the Living Dead*) (1964). Subsequently, he made his own feature directorial debut in Italy with the **witchcraft** drama *La sorella di satana* (*Revenge of the Blood Beast, The She Beast*) (1966), for which he also wrote the screenplay under the name Michael Byron. Although suffering from severe budgetary restrictions, the film contained some striking sequences, notably the killing of the witch Vardella, and featured an appearance from horror icon **Barbara Steele**. Reeves's next two films were both shot in Great Britain. In *The Sorcerers* (1967), a scientist (played by **Boris Karloff**) and his wife hypnotically take over a young man (played by Ian Ogilvy) and experience all his physical sensations. Here Reeves captured perfectly the rootless youth culture of the late 1960s and how a desire for new experiences could escalate into something murderous. A similar descent into **madness** was apparent in *Witchfinder General* (1968), which is often considered to be Reeves's masterpiece. Ostensibly an account of witch-hunting in England during the 17th century, the film was actually a powerful revenge drama that owed more than a little to the American **western** in terms of its narrative and also made remarkably effective use of the English rural landscape. In one of horror cinema's most disturbing conclusions, the film's hero (again played by Ian Ogilvy) beats the witchfinder (played by **Vincent Price**) to death with an axe while the hero's violated and tortured wife screams in the background. There is no sense of justice here but instead an intense portrayal of the destructiveness of violence for both the victim and the victimizer.

Largely ignored by critics while alive, Reeves is now recognized as a key figure in the development of **British horror** in the late 1960s. He introduced a more questioning approach to social authority than had been apparent before in the British horror cycle, while his best work is also imaginative, stylish and alive to all the possibilities of cinema.

REITMAN, IVAN (1946–). The producer-director Ivan Reitman has been a big-budget **comedy** specialist ever since his success with *Ghostbusters* (1984). However, he began his filmmaking career in Canada working on low-budget horror. His directorial debut was *Cannibal Girls* (1973), a horror with strong elements of **comedy**. He then went on to produce two of **David Cronenberg**'s early films, *The Parasite Murders* (*They Came from Within*, *Shivers*) (1975) and *Rabid* (1977), along with the rape revenge drama *Death Weekend* (1976) and the horror-themed animated feature *Heavy Metal* (1981). *Ghostbusters* itself clearly contained horror elements, with some critics detecting in it the influence of **H. P. Lovecraft**. Reitman also directed *Ghostbusters II* (1989) and the **science fiction** comedy *Evolution* (2001).

RELIGION. Horror films have often drawn upon Christian imagery and themes. Note, for example, the use made of the crucifix in numerous **vampire** films, the invoking of Biblical concepts in the likes of *Rosemary's Baby* (1968), *The Exorcist* (1973), or *The Omen* (1976), or the appearance of angels in *The Prophecy* (1995) or *Constantine* (2005). The extent to which this renders these and other films as religious texts is far from clear, however. Horror filmmakers have invested a lot of energy in conjuring up forces antithetical to Christianity. Satanists have figured in, among many others, *The Seventh Victim* (1943), *The Devil Rides Out* (1968), *Race with the Devil* (1975), *End of Days* (1999), *Bless the Child* (2000), and *Lost Souls* (2000), while pagans have gone about their sacrificial business in *Blood on Satan's Claw* (*Satan's Skin*) (1971) and *The Wicker Man*

(1973). Yet the representatives of goodness are usually figured as a secular group, with the priests who do show up—in *The Exorcist, The Amityville Horror* (1979), *Stigmata* (1999), and *The Sin-Eater* (2003)—deeply troubled figures. It might be argued that horror films have tended to play out in a thoroughly secularized world in which religious belief still possesses a residual power but where it is nevertheless marginal. Certainly, the struggle between good and evil in the horror genre has customarily been presented—on the side of good, at least—in thoroughly human terms, with little explicit appeal to Christian beliefs and little or no hope of divine intervention. In fact, on the rare occasion in horror where there is divine intervention—in the third *Omen* film, *The Final Conflict* (1981), for example—it has usually been perceived, by **fans** and critics, as something of a cop-out. It seems that if we are to be saved in horror, we are required to do it ourselves.

Critics writing about the East Asian horror film have often detected references to non-Christian religious belief systems, and in part the strangeness of some of these films to Western **eyes** might well derive from this unfamiliar framework. However, as is the case with Western horror, these Asian horrors have not offered themselves as being explicitly religious.

REMAKES. The development of the horror genre has been more reliant on **sequels** than it has been on remakes (so long as one discounts the various film adaptations of **Dracula, Frankenstein,** and **Dr. Jekyll and Mr. Hyde,** which are more returns to literary originals than they are remakes of previous films). Some silent horrors of the 1920s were remade as sound films in the 1930s—notably *The Unholy Three* (1925) under the same title in 1930, *London after Midnight* (1927) as *Mark of the Vampire* (1935) (with both directed by **Tod Browning,** who also directed the original version of *The Unholy Three*), the horror spoof *The Cat and the Canary* (1927) as *Le voluntad del muerto* (a Hollywood-produced Spanish-language version also known as *The Cat Creeps*) (1930), and *The Cat and the Canary* (1939) (and remade again in 1978), and *The Gorilla* (1927), another horror spoof, remade in 1930 and 1939 with the same title both times. There was also a small cluster of apparent remakes in the early 1960s, although these turned out to have very little to do with their illustrious originals so far as either content or style were concerned. They included *What a Carve Up!* (1961) (from the 1933 **British horror** film *The Ghoul*), *The Cabinet of Caligari* (1962) (from the 1919 masterpiece of **German Expressionism** *Das Cabinet Des Dr. Caligari*), and *The Old Dark House* (1963) (from **James Whale**'s 1932 original).

One has to wait until the late 1970s for a more purposeful set of remakes to appear, remakes that engaged with the originals in a provocative and revisionary manner. Key examples were Werner Herzog's German production *Nosferatu: Phantom der Nacht* (*Nosferatu the Vampyre*) (1979) from **F. W. Murnau**'s *Nosferatu: eine Symphonie des Grauens* (*Nosferatu, a Symphony of Terror*) (1922), **John Carpenter**'s *The Thing* (1982) from Howard Hawks' version of *The Thing from another World* (1951), and **David Cronenberg**'s *The Fly* (1986) from the 1958 original. In all of these, old-fashioned moral certainties were replaced by modern doubts and anxieties, with classic horror myths reworked to such an extent that they threatened to become redundant.

Other contemporary horror remakes, especially in American cinema, have offered more straightforward updatings of original material, often as a way of retelling stories to audiences not old enough to have seen them on their initial cinematic release. **Tom Savini**'s 1990 remake of **George Romero**'s *Night of the Living Dead* (1968) is an early example. Romero's *Dawn of the Dead* (1978) was also remade in 2004, as was **Tobe Hooper**'s *The Texas Chainsaw Massacre* (1974) in 2003, **John Carpenter**'s *The Fog* (1980) in 2005, and **Wes Craven**'s *The Hills Have Eyes* (1977) in 2006. For most of these, the creators of the originals were involved in their production, with this helping to explain the respectful attitude adopted by the remakes to their source material. Production values tended to be higher and the films glossier, with the edginess of the originals sometimes lost in the process of revision. Less respectful were looser remakes of **William Castle**'s *The House on Haunted Hill* (1959) in 1999 and *13 Ghosts* (1960) in 2001, or Tobe Hooper's 2004 retelling of the obscure *The Toolbox Murders* (1978).

The recent acceleration in the number of remakes within the genre suggests that a new generation of filmmakers is appropriating some of the horror films with which they grew up. In a different way, contemporary American remakes of **Japanese horror** films such as

Hideo Nakata's *Ringu* (*Ring*) (1998) as *The Ring* (2002) and *Honogurai mizu no soko kara* (*Dark Water*) (2002) as *Dark Water* (2005), and **Takashi Shimizu**'s *Ju-On: The Grudge* (2003) as *The Grudge* (2004) have appropriated them for Western use, although this process is complicated by the involvement of the original filmmakers in the remakes—with Shimizu directing the remake of his own original and Nakata directing the American sequel *The Ring 2* (2005).

REVENGE OF NATURE. The idea of nature turning on humanity first came to the fore in some 1950s monster movies that combined **science fiction** with horror. Giant radioactive ants threatened in *Them!* (1954) and a giant spider, the result of a misguided experiment, attacked in *Tarantula* (1955), while other giant prehistoric **insects** were accidentally unleashed in the likes of *The Monster that Challenged the World* (1957), *The Deadly Mantis* (1957), and *The Black Scorpion* (1957). **Alfred Hitchcock** stripped away the science fiction elements in his innovative *The Birds* (1963), instead focusing on the complacency of his characters in assuming that they had control over the world in which they lived. This kind of thematic preoccupation fitted well into the fears of social collapse that were apparent during the 1970s, and during that decade a cycle of revenge of nature horrors mixed apocalyptic despair with an emerging environmental awareness. Titles included *Frogs* (1972), *Night of the Lepus* (1972), *Phase IV* (1973), *Bug* (1975), *The Food of the Gods* (1976), *Squirm* (1976), *Day of the Animals* (1977), *Kingdom of the Spiders* (1977), *The Long Weekend* (1978), and *Prophecy* (1979).

RICE, ANNE (1941–). The American novelist Anne Rice has made a major contribution to the cultural reshaping of **vampires** into heroic and sensitive figures through *The Vampire Chronicles*, her bestselling series of novels that began publication in 1976. **Neil Jordan**'s *Interview with the Vampire* (1994) was adapted by Rice herself from the first novel in the series. Unsurprisingly, it was faithful to Rice's original, and even the provocative casting of Tom Cruise as one of the vampires worked to the film's benefit. *Queen of the Damned* (2002), which was directed by Michael Rymer and combined plot elements from the second and third books in *The Vampire Chronicles*, was lively but much less faithful to the dreamy and sensual atmosphere conjured up by Rice's fiction.

***RINGU* (*RING*) (1998).** The **Japanese horror** film *Ringu* (*Ring*) is a **ghost** story in which anyone who watches a mysterious videotape dies shortly thereafter. As directed by **Hideo Nakata**, *Ringu* cleverly combined Asian horror motifs—such as the vengeful long-haired female ghost—with more Western horror themes and visuals, and it proved an international breakthrough hit that inspired a slew of similar productions in both East Asia and the United States. The film was based on a 1991 novel by Koji Suzuki that had already been adapted as the Japanese **television** series *Ringu: Kanzen-ban* (1995), and the subsequent proliferation of *Ringu* films would include further reworkings of the source material.

Joji Iida's *Rasen* (*Spiral*) (1998), which was based on Suzuki's own **sequel** to his novel, was made at about the same time as *Ringu* but proved less popular with audiences, perhaps because its move into **science fiction** themes did not sit well with the emphasis on horror in its predecessor. The response of the producers was to come up with what in effect was a replacement sequel that, as directed by Nakata, followed on directly from *Ringu* and ignored the fact that *Rasen* had ever existed. *Ringu 2* (*Ring 2*) (1999) lacked the clearly defined narrative of *Ringu* but what it lacked in clarity it made up for in atmosphere, and it secured Nakata's reputation as a master of the modern Japanese ghost story.

1999 saw two *Ring*-themed series on Japanese television, *Ringu: Saishûshô* and *Rasen*, the latter based on the same novel that had inspired the "forgotten sequel" of the same title. A third version of Suzuki's original novel also appeared—this time entitled *The Ring Virus* (1999) and directed in South Korea by Dong-bin Kim. Back in Japan, Norio Tsuruta's *Ringu 0: Bâsudei* (*Ring 0*) (2000) was a stylish prequel that depicted the early days of the woman who would go on to become the fearsome and relentless ghost in *Ringu*.

Gore Verbinski's *The Ring* (2002) redeployed the original's Japanese elements in an American context, and was the first major American **remake** of a Japanese horror film. Higher production values, more logical plotting and some slick computer generated special effects separated the film out from the lower-budgeted Japanese version but arguably diminished the story's shock effects. However, the film was a substantial commercial success, and *The Ring Two* (2005) followed. This was not a remake of *Ringu 2* but it did share the same director, with Hideo Nakata making his American debut, and was a similar triumph of style over substance.

After all this activity, one might have expected that the story of the ghost Sadako would have been thoroughly exhausted, especially given her reliance on the now nearly defunct technology of videotape. However, Koji Suzuki has written *Loop* (1998), a third novel in the *Ring* series, and at the time of writing this entry the American production *The Ring Three* has just been announced. In true horror style, it seems that this particular monster could be making a surprise comeback.

RIPPER, MICHAEL (1913–2000). The British actor Michael Ripper appeared in more **Hammer** films than any other performer, specializing in working-class characters, among them pub landlords, army sergeants, police constables, and taxi drivers. These roles were usually small but he was often able to fashion nuanced characterizations out of them. Occasionally he was given the opportunity to do something more than this. For example, his performance as the long-suffering private secretary Longbarrow in *The Mummy's Shroud* (1967) is one of British cinema's finest studies of self-abnegation. Selected **British horror** credits include *X: The Unknown* (1956), *Quatermass 2 (Enemy from Space)* (1957), *The Revenge of Frankenstein* (1958), *The Mummy* (1959), *The Brides of Dracula* (1960), *The Curse of the Werewolf* (1961), *The Phantom of the Opera* (1962), *The Curse of the Mummy's Tomb* (1964), *The Reptile* (1966), *The Plague of the Zombies* (1966), *Dracula Has Risen from the Grave* (1968), *Scars of Dracula* (1970), *Taste the Blood of Dracula* (1970), *The Creeping Flesh* (1973), *Legend of the Werewolf* (1975), and *Revenge of Billy the Kid* (1991).

ROBINSON, BERNARD (1912–1970). The production designer Bernard Robinson was a key member of the team that made the **Hammer** horror films from the late 1950s onwards. His first genre credit was the **science fiction**/horror film *Quatermass 2 (Enemy from Space)* (1957), but he came into his own with the color **gothic**

horrors for which Hammer became famous, among them *The Curse of Frankenstein* (1957), *Dracula* (*Horror of Dracula*) (1958), *Curse of the Werewolf* (1961), and *The Devil Rides Out* (1968). Operating on minimal resources, he designed castles, dungeons, and sitting rooms that had a solidity about them, with this quality becoming one of Hammer's defining visual characteristics. For reasons of economy, he also reused props and sets, carefully disguising this from the casual viewer (although dedicated Hammer **fans** would later take great pleasure from constantly encountering familiar bits and pieces of set design).

ROBINSON, GEORGE (1890–1958). George Robinson was the main cinematographer for **Universal** horror films of the 1930s and 1940s. He began auspiciously with some atmospheric photography for Universal's Spanish-language *Dracula* (1931)—shot on the same sets as the **Bela Lugosi** version but considered by many to be a better film— and *La voluntad del muerto* (1930), a version of *The **Cat** and the Canary*. His most visually striking work after this was on *Dracula's Daughter* (1936), *Son of **Frankenstein*** (1939), and *Son of Dracula* (1943), but he also photographed *The Invisible Ray* (1936), *Tower of London* (1939), *The **Mummy's** Tomb* (1942), *Frankenstein Meets the Wolf Man* (1943), *Captive Wild Woman* (1943), the horror-themed **Sherlock Holmes** mystery *The Scarlet Claw* (1944), *House of Frankenstein* (1944), *House of Dracula* (1945), and *The Cat Creeps* (1946). After the Universal horror boom was over, he brought his genre expertise to the **comedy**-horrors *Abbott and Costello Meet the Invisible Man* (1951), *Abbott and Costello Meet **Dr. Jekyll and Mr. Hyde*** (1953), *Abbott and Costello Meet the Mummy* (1955) and *Francis in the Haunted House* (1956).

ROBSON, MARK (1913–1978). The editor-turned-director Mark Robson was part of horror producer **Val Lewton's** team at RKO during the 1940s. He edited *Cat People* (1942), *I Walked with a **Zombie*** (1943), and *The Leopard Man* (1943), all of which were directed by **Jacques Tourneur.** His own horror films as director were uneven. The Satanic thriller *The Seventh Victim* (1943) was one of Lewton's best and contained a shower sequence that might have been an influence on **Alfred Hitchcock** in preparing *Psycho* (1960). Similarly,

Isle of the Dead (1945), in which various characters are trapped on an island by the spread of a plague, demonstrated a mastery of atmosphere. In comparison, the **psychological thriller** *The Ghost Ship* (1943) was interesting but lacked drama, and the historical horror *Bedlam* (1946) was a well-made but uninvolving affair. After *Bedlam*, Robson left horror behind and never returned. Later films included the solidly commercial *Peyton Place* (1958), *The Inn of Sixth Happiness* (1958), *Von Ryan's Express* (1965), and *Earthquake* (1974). *See also* AMERICAN HORROR.

ROEG, NICOLAS (1928–). The British cinematographer-turned-director Nicolas Roeg had his first brush with horror photographing **Roger Corman**'s stylish **Edgar Allan Poe** adaptation *The Masque of the Red Death* (1964). As a director, Roeg's work has often been characterized by fractured narratives and disturbing themes. His film *Don't Look Now* (1973), which made memorable use of its Venetian settings, is one of cinema's great **ghost** stories. An allusive drama involving grief-stricken parents mourning the loss of their child, it generated an extraordinary doom-laden atmosphere. By contrast, *The Witches* (1990), based on a Roald Dahl story, was family-centered entertainment, albeit of the mildly scary kind.

ROLLIN, JEAN (1938–). The low-budget horror films of French director Jean Rollin combine exploitation staples such as sex, nudity and violence with experimental and surreal elements, often at the expense of narrative coherence. His work can be very striking in visual terms although its weirdness has sometimes precluded commercial success. Rollin began promisingly with the avant-garde *Le viol du vampire* (*Queen of the Vampires, The Rape of the Vampire*) (1968). This disjointed black-and-white piece was expanded from a short (which explains why characters killed off halfway through miraculously returned for the latter part of the film) and performed surprisingly well at the box office. It was followed by a series of what came to be known as "sex vampire" films, namely *La vampire nue* (*The Nude Vampire*) (1969), *Le frisson des vampires* (*Sex and the Vampire*) (1970), and *Requiem pour un vampire* (*Requiem for a Vampire, Caged Virgins*) (1972). These were slightly more conventional than *Le viol du vampire* but still obscure in narrative terms, with in particular *Le* *frisson des vampires* taking an unexpected climactic diversion into **science fiction**. Rollin's later films were increasingly uneven. *Les démoniaques* (*Demoniacs, Curse of the Living Dead*) (1974), *Lèvres de sang* (*Lips of Blood*) (1975), *Fascination* (1979), and *La morte vivante* (*The Living Dead Girl*) (1983) were, for all their flaws, distinctive enough to sustain the view of Rollin as a horror auteur. By contrast, the **zombie** films *Les raisins de la mort* (*The Grapes of Death*) (1978) and *Le lac des morts vivants* (*Zombie Lake, The Lake of the Living Dead*) (1980) were tawdry and uninspired, suggesting that the director needed the sexually alluring figure of the female vampire to stimulate his imagination, while the sex-horror project *Phantasmes* (*Once Upon a Virgin*) (1975) remains little seen. After a period away from the horror genre, Rollin, who has also directed porn films under the names Michel Gentil and Robert Xavier and thrillers under his own name, made *Les deux orphelines vampires* (*Two Orphan Vampires*) (1997) and *La fiancée de* **Dracula** (2002), neither of which has had the impact of some of his earlier work. *See also* FRENCH HORROR.

ROMERO, EDDIE (1924–). The Filipino filmmaker Eddie Romero made his horror debut acting as producer on his friend and mentor **Gerardo de León**'s **mad scientist** drama *Terror is a Man* (1959). He later co-directed with de Leon *Mad Doctor of Blood Island* (1968) and *Brides of Blood* (1968), both of which were garish monster movies. Romero went on to be sole director for the similarly themed and styled *Beast of the Yellow Night* (1971), *Beast of Blood* (1971), *The Twilight People* (1973) and *Beyond Atlantis* (1973). His horror films have acquired a cult following outside of the Philippines, but he is most revered in his homeland for his work in other, more culturally reputable genres. In 2003, he was awarded the prestigious title of "National Artist of the Philippines," although probably not for his horror films. *See also* FILIPINO HORROR.

ROMERO, GEORGE (1940–). The American writer-director George Romero has throughout his career generally avoided involvement with the major studios. One consequence of this is that he has not worked as regularly as he might have, with long gaps between some of his films. Another consequence is that his independently produced films can be daring and innovative in ways that mainstream horrors often are not. His debut film turned out to be one of his most significant projects. *Night of the Living Dead* (1968) reinvented the **zombie** story by relocating it to contemporary America and transforming the zombies into flesh-eating ghouls. Romero was inspired by **Richard Matheson**'s **vampire** novel *I Am Legend*, but the film also shows the influence of **Alfred Hitchcock**'s *The Birds* (1963) in its depiction of characters trapped inside a claustrophobic house by marauding monsters. The ruthless nihilism was provided by Romero, however, as he confounded audience expectations by mercilessly killing off all of his good characters, including the hero. Although the film made no explicit reference to the social unrest taking place in the United States during the late 1960s, a sense of social dysfunctionality was palpable.

There's Always Vanilla (1972) and *Jack's Wife* (1972) took Romero away from horror, although distributors retitled *Jack's Wife* as *Hungry Wives* and *Season of the Witch* in an unsuccessful attempt to lure horror audiences into the cinema. Like *Night of the Living Dead*, *The Crazies* (1973)—in which an entire community goes mad—was an **apocalyptic horror** film, but it lacked the sustained intensity of the earlier film. *Martin* (1977), by contrast, was a hugely impressive updating of the vampire myth and a key work in 1970s horror. Here Romero successfully critiqued traditional horror conventions through the tale of a young man who believes that he is a vampire but has to use a hypodermic syringe to subdue his victims.

Romero's next film is considered by many to be his genre masterpiece. *Dawn of the Dead* (1978) was the first and best of three **sequels** to *Night of the Living Dead*. It boldly drew parallels between the zombies and its living characters, made evocative use of its shopping mall setting and, unlike *Night*, managed to conjure up an affirmative ending. Thanks to **makeup** artist **Tom Savini** (who also worked on *Martin*), the film also introduced some unprecedentedly graphic **gore** into the horror genre.

Knightriders (1981) was another of Romero's experimental nonhorror projects that was not widely seen, while *Creepshow* (1982) was a more conventional, **Stephen King**-scripted recreation of the world of horror **comics**. *Day of the Dead* (1985) returned the director yet again to the world of zombies. Apparently cut down at scripting stage from a much more ambitious project, the film remained a fascinating examination of militarism at a time when other horror films were resolutely avoiding any kind of serious issues.

The **psychological thriller** *Monkey Shines* (1988), a collaboration with **Dario Argento** on the co-directed *Due occhi diabolici* (*Two Evil Eyes*) (1990) and *The Dark Half* (1993) were all slick but anonymous affairs, and one got a sense that during this part of his career Romero was treading water. However, *Land of the Dead* (2005), his fourth and to date final zombie film, was as full of ideas as the previous three instalments. The focus this time was on class division, with the zombies represented as an underclass excluded from the attractive parts of the city by the wealthy. If nothing else, its energy and invention suggested that, for all Romero's attempts to develop in new directions, it is the zombie that has brought out the best in him as a filmmaker.

He also acted as executive producer for the television series *Tales from the Darkside* (1984–1988). *See also* AMERICAN HORROR.

ROSE, BERNARD (1960–). The British writer-director Bernard Rose has worked in a variety of genres but shows a particular affinity for horror-related subjects, which he tends to treat with a seriousness that is unusual in the contemporary horror mainstream. His cinematic debut was *Paperhouse* (1988), in which a young girl enters into a scary dream world. Thematically, the film had a lot in common with the then popular and equally dream-orientated *Nightmare on Elm Street* films, but *Paperhouse* was much less interested in pandering to a teenage audience. After the unsuccessful but interesting thriller *Chicago Joe and the Showgirl* (1990), Rose moved to the United States where he adapted a **Clive Barker** short story into *Candyman* (1992), one of the best **American horror** films of the 1990s. Since then, Rose has steered clear of the horror genre, although he recently returned with *Snuff Movie* (2005).

***ROSEMARY'S BABY* (1968).** Along with **George Romero**'s *Night of the Living Dead* (1968), *Rosemary's Baby* has been seen as inaugurating the modern **American horror** film. Based on a bestselling novel by Ira Levin, its transgressive elements are all too obvious from its narrative. A newly wed couple move into an apartment, where the wife begins to suspect that her neighbors are Satanists. She dreams that she has been raped by a beastly creature and, after falling pregnant, fears that the Satanists have designs on her unborn baby. On giving birth, she discovers that the baby is—or so the Satanists claim—the son of the **Devil**, and the narrative concludes ambiguously with her apparent agreement to act as mother to the child regardless of its parentage. Put another way, this is a film where evil secures a comprehensive victory.

As directed by **Roman Polanski**, the film is certainly disturbing but it is also more playful than the above account of the narrative suggests. Apparently Polanski did not take the supernatural elements in the original novel too seriously (his other supernatural films *The Tenant* and *The Ninth Gate* are similarly tongue-in-cheek), and he has carefully structured *Rosemary's Baby* so that the Satanic conspiracy might in reality be the delusion of a group of sad old people rather than an accomplished supernatural fact. As for the appearance of the Devil, it does take place in a dream, and production stills show that, for some of the shots at least, this figure was played by John Cassavetes, the actor who portrayed Rosemary's husband. While *Night of the Living Dead* purveyed a low-budget gritty realism that made its horrors all too believable, the high-budget gloss of *Rosemary's Baby* offered a cooler approach perfectly suited to the slow-burn narrative. The film's main theme—of an older generation corrupting and destroying the young—would become important in 1970s American horror, and its dark and disturbing ending would also become a model for horrors to come.

The **television** film *Look What's Happened to Rosemary's Baby* (1976) was an unnecessary **sequel** that added nothing to its illustrious predecessor.

ROTH, ELI (1972–). The American writer-director Eli Roth made an impact with his first horror feature, *Cabin Fever* (2002). This low-budget combination of biological horror with **rural horror** was uneven in tone but had a gory ferocity about it that was distinctive. Roth followed it up with *Hostel* (2005), a **torture**-based narrative set in Eastern Europe that maintained the hard-edged qualities of *Cabin Fever* but which was a much more disciplined and focused affair. *Hostel: Part 2* (2007) offered more of the same, although it was slightly more nuanced than its predecessor. All of Roth's films have gloried in their own disreputability, but there is clearly a fast developing directorial talent evident in them.

RURAL HORROR. The idea that something bad happens to you if you leave the city and head off into the countryside has proved a potent one in horror cinema. Sometimes the threat emanates from nature itself. (*See* REVENGE OF NATURE.) More often it comes from rural inhabitants, who tend to be presented in this kind of horror as primitive, inbred, and animalistic, as in short a subhuman projection of nature itself. Notions of social class difference clearly play their part here, with city dwellers in rural horror films often presented as well-off and middle-class, while the country folk are by contrast depicted as a monstrous and degraded underclass. Townies are also frequently depicted as complacent and smug, with the rural assault upon them a kind of punishment for their shortcomings.

There are intimations of rural horror in **James Whale**'s comedy-horror film *The Old Dark House* (1932), in which travelers are stranded with a disturbingly idiosyncratic rural family, and a more developed version can be found in **Alfred Hitchcock**'s *Psycho* (1960), when the townie played by **Janet Leigh** stumbles into the countryside motel from hell. However, it was the 1970s that saw this type of horror beginning to take hold, especially in American cinema. A key film in this respect, albeit one not widely seen as horror, was **John Boorman**'s *Deliverance* (1972), a grueling drama in which a group of urban males come into violent conflict with the locals in backwoods America. More obviously horror-based treatments of this theme were provided by **Tobe Hooper**'s *The Texas Chainsaw Massacre* (1974) and **Wes Craven**'s *The Hills Have Eyes* (1977), both of which presented barbaric families who have resorted to **cannibalism** and who relentlessly terrorize some unsuspecting townies. *Let's Scare Jessica to Death* (1971), the Satanic thriller *Race with the Devil* (1975), Hooper's *Eaten Alive (Death Trap)* (1977), and the controversial rape-revenge dramas *I Spit On Your Grave* (1978) and *Death Weekend* (1976) all fitted this pattern, and many of them shared with *Chainsaw* and *Hills* scenes where the violated townies fight back, often deploying violence as savage as that issuing from the rural dwellers. Going to the countryside, it seemed, enabled you to discover the beast within yourself (so long as you weren't killed and eaten first). Some 1980s American **slashers** also contained elements of rural horror, with arrogant teenagers getting their come-uppance from rural **serial killers** in the likes of the *Friday the 13th* films or *The Burning* (1981) or *Just Before Dawn* (1981), amongst others. More recently, a number of films have sought to recapture the edginess of 1970s **American horror** through revisiting the rural horror format as developed by Hooper and Craven. Most obviously, this includes the **remakes** *The Texas Chainsaw Massacre* (2003) and *The Hills Have Eyes* (2006), but there is also **Eli Roth**'s *Cabin Fever* (2002), *Wrong Turn* (2003), **Rob Zombie**'s *House of 1000 Corpses* (2003), and *House of Wax* (2005). Supernatural versions of rural horror include **Sam Raimi**'s *Evil Dead* films and *The Skeleton Key* (2005), while *The Last Broadcast* (1998), *The Blair Witch Project* (1999), and the period drama *An American Haunting* (2005), as well as numerous episodes of the **television** series *The X Files* (1993–2002) and *Supernatural* (2005–), have explored American folklore within rural settings.

Rural horror is not restricted to American cinema. British cinema, for example, has produced some rural horror films, including **Hammer**'s *The Witches* (1966), the period horror *Blood on Satan's Claw* (*Satan's Skin*) (1971), *Tower of Evil* (1972), **Robin Hardy**'s *The Wicker Man* (1973), and **Neil Marshall**'s *Dog Soldiers* (2002) and *The Descent* (2005). From France, there has been *Calvaire* (*The Ordeal*) (2004), from Australia *Wolf Creek* (2005), and from Spain the **Blind Dead** films and, amongst others, **León Klimovsky**'s *La orgía nocturna de los vampiros* (*The Vampires Night Orgy*) (1973) and **Stuart Gordon**'s *Dagon* (2001). A small number of American films have also depicted town-dwellers coming to grief at the hands of foreign countryfolk, with these including Sam Peckinpah's *Straw Dogs* (1971), **John Landis**'s *An American Werewolf in London* (1981), and Eli Roth's *Hostel* (2005).

The pervasiveness of the rural horror format suggests a widespread and deep distrust of the agrarian and the pre-modern, although this has often been coupled with doubts about the efficacy of the forces of rational modernity, as helpless townies continue to suffer at the hands of those poorer and considerably less sophisticated than themselves.

RUSSELL, CHUCK (1952–). Chuck Russell—who is occasionally billed as Charles Russell—is often associated with big-budget films such as the Jim Carrey **comedy** *The Mask* (1994) or the Arnold Schwarzenegger thriller *Eraser* (1996). However, early in his career he also directed **A** *Nightmare on Elm Street 3: Dream Warriors* (1987), a key film in the *Elm Street* cycle that very much set the narrative and tonal pattern for subsequent **sequels**, and *The Blob* (1988), a **remake** of a very ordinary 1958 monster movie that generated some genuine suspense as well as some inventive plot twists. After his breakthough into "A-List" productions, he returned to horror with *Bless the Child* (2000), a slick Satanic thriller that starred Kim Basinger.

RUSSELL, KEN (1927–). The brash, iconoclastic British director Ken Russell established his reputation through his **television** dramatizations of the lives of the great composers and through cinema films as diverse as *Women in Love* (1969) and *Tommy* (1975). *The Devils* (1971), his controversial study of witch trials in France, contained some horrifying imagery, but ultimately it was more of a political thriller than it was a horror film. The American-produced *Altered States* (1980) and *Crimes of Passion* (1984) also featured some horror-like elements, notably **Anthony Perkins'** mad preacher in the latter. However, it was the British films *Gothic* (1986) and *The Lair of the White Worm* (1988) that finally delivered Russell into horror. *Gothic* was a lively, if sometimes overwrought, heritage piece that explored the circumstances within which Mary Shelley devised the **Frankenstein** story. (**Roger Corman**'s 1990 film *Frankenstein Unbound* would later address the same subject matter.) By contrast, *The Lair of the White Worm*, an adaptation of a Bram Stoker novel, was a bizarre horror parody that featured an early and somewhat bemused performance from Hugh Grant. Russell continued in the horror-parodic vein with the ultra-low-budget *The Fall of the Louse of Usher* (2002). *See also* BRITISH HORROR.

RUSSELL, RAY (1924–1999). During the first half of the 1960s, the screenwriter Ray Russell worked for horror specialists **William Castle** and **Roger Corman**, with his two most memorable credits involving spectacular images of male mutilation. For Castle, he wrote

Mr. Sardonicus (1961), in which the central character spent most of the film with a ghastly, disfiguring smile fixed on his face, and for Corman he came up with *X: The Man with the X-Ray Eyes* (1963), with the hero here gouging out his own troublesome eyes in the film's shocking conclusion. Other Russell credits include the Castle film *Zotz!* (1962), the Corman-directed *The Premature Burial* (1962), **Terence Fisher**'s comedy-horror *The Horror of It All* (1964), and *Chamber of Horrors* (1966). His supernatural novel *The Incubus* was filmed by **John Hough** in 1981.

– S –

SACCHETTI, DARDANO (1944–). The remarkably prolific screenwriter Dardano Sacchetti—who is sometimes billed as David Parker, Jr.—has worked with most major **Italian horror** directors, usually in collaboration with other screenwriters. His very first screen credit was for **Dario Argento**'s *Il gatto a nove code* (*The Cat O'Nine Tails*) (1971), and he has also written for **Mario Bava**—*Reazione a catena* (*Bay of Blood, Twitch of the Death Nerve*) (1971), and *Schock* (*Shock, Beyond the Door II*) (1977)—**Antonio Margheriti**—*Apocalypse domani* (*Cannibal Apocalypse*) (1980)—**Sergio Martino**—*Assassinio al cimitero etrusco* (*Murder in an Etruscan Cemetery*) (1982)—and **Ruggero Deodato**—*Camping del terrore* (*Body Count*) (1987). However, his most sustained working relationships have been first with **Lucio Fulci** and subsequently with **Lamberto Bava**. He contributed to most of the key Fulci horror films, including *Sette note in nero* (*The Psychic*) (1977), *Paura nella città dei morti viventi* (*City of the Living Dead*) (1980), *L'aldilà* (*The Beyond*) (1981), *Quella villa accanto al cimitero* (*The House by the Cemetery*) (1981), *Lo squartatore di New York* (*New York Ripper*) (1982), and *Manhattan Baby* (*Eye of the Evil Dead*) (1982); he also did some uncredited work on Fulci's *Zombi 2* (*Zombie, Zombie Flesh Eaters*) (1979). For Lamberto Bava, his credits have included the **giallo** *La casa con la scala nel buio* (*A Blade in the Dark*) (1983), *Shark rosso nell'oceano* (*Devil Fish, Devouring Waves*) (1984), *Demoni* (*Demons*) (1985), *Morirai a mezzanotte* (*The Midnight Killer*) (1986), and *Demoni 2: L'incubo ritorna* (*Demons 2*) (1986), as well as some of the **television** horror films directed by Bava during the second half of the 1980s. Other Sacchetti horror credits are *Spettri* (*Specters*) (1987), *Quella villa in fondo al parco* (*Ratman, Terror House*) (1988), *Killer Crocodile* (1989), and *Killer Crocodile II* (1990). He continues to write for cinema and for television, although not on horror projects.

SANGSTER, JIMMY (1924–). The title of British writer-producer-director Jimmy Sangster's autobiography—*Do You Want It Good Or Tuesday?*—underlines the no-nonsense professionalism and practicality of someone who has spent most of his career working in the low-budget sector. He joined **Hammer** in the late 1940s and by the mid-1950s had become a production manager there. His screenplay for the Hammer short *A Man on the Beach* (1955) was followed by his first feature credit as writer, the **science fiction**/horror *X—The Unknown* (1956). He went on to write many of Hammer's early period horrors, including *The Curse of **Frankenstein*** (1957), ***Dracula*** (*The Horror of Dracula*) (1958), *The Revenge of Frankenstein* (1958), *The **Mummy*** (1959), and *The Man Who Could Cheat Death* (1959). He also contributed to *The Brides of Dracula* (1960) and, under the name "John Sansom," to *Dracula—Prince of Darkness* (1966), as well as providing scripts for non-Hammer productions *The Trollenberg Terror* (1958), *Blood of the **Vampire*** (1958), ***Jack the Ripper*** (1959), and *The Hellfire Club* (1961). At their best, Sangster's screenplays were brisk and tightly plotted, with *Dracula* probably his most outstanding work from this period.

In the early 1960s, he inaugurated Hammer's cycle of **psychological thrillers** with *Taste of Fear* (*Scream of Fear*) (1961), which he wrote and produced. The film combined a sinister atmosphere with what for the time were genuinely surprising plot twists. Hammer's follow-ups, written and sometimes produced by Sangster, were more hit or miss, with *Paranoiac* (1963), *The Nanny* (1965), and *Crescendo* (1970) standing out from the more ordinary *Maniac* (1963), *Nightmare* (1964), and *Hysteria* (1965). The three films Sangster directed for Hammer in the 1970s were also uneven. *The Horror of Frankenstein* (1970) was an unsuccessful attempt to revive the Frankenstein cycle. The lesbian vampire film *Lust for a Vampire* (1971) was better, although it suffered from the pointless inclusion of a contemporary pop song, while *Fear in the Night* (1972) was another psychological thriller made at a time when the formula was looking very worn. Sangster also wrote and produced one of Hammer's oddest films, the **Bette Davis** vehicle *The Anniversary* (1968) and co-wrote and produced the **Curtis Harrington** horror *Whoever Slew Auntie Roo?* (1971). Throughout the 1970s, he wrote mainly for American **television**, including contributions to the horror series *Kolchak—the Night Stalker* (1974–1975) and the television horror films *Scream, Pretty Peggy* (1973) and *Good Against Evil* (1977). He also worked on the screenplays for the **British horror** film *The Legacy* (1978) and John Huston's psychological thriller *Phobia* (1980).

SANTO (1917–1984). The masked wrestler Santo—real name Rodolfo Guzman Huerta—starred in a series of popular Mexican films from the early 1960s to the early 1980s as a crime-fighting superhero. He regularly took on supernatural foes such as **vampires, werewolves,** witches, and **zombies** as well as figures such as **Dracula** and **Frankenstein**'s monster, either by himself or in collaboration with another masked wrestler, Blue Demon. The films were cheap and crudely made but, at their best, they were also energetic, and they have since acquired a cult following. Indicative horror-related titles from Santo's oeuvre of over 50 films include *Santo contra los zombies (Invasion of the Zombies)* (1961), *Santo contra las mujeres vampiro (Santo Versus the Vampire Women)* (1962), *Santo en el museo de cera (Santo in the Wax Museum)* (1963), *El hacha diabólica (Santo vs. the Diabolical Hatchet)* (1964), *Atacan las brujas (Santo in the Witches Attack)* (1964), *El Barón Brakola (Santo vs. Baron Brakola)* (1965), *Santo en El tesoro de Drácula (Santo and Dracula's Treasure)* (1968), *Santo y Blue Demon contra los monstruos (Santo and Blue Demon vs. the Monsters)* (1969), *La venganza de las mujeres vampiro (The Vengeance of the Vampire Women)* (1970), *La venganza de la momia (Santo and the Vengeance of the Mummy)* (1970), *Las momias de Guanajuato (The Mummies of Guanajuato)* (1970), *Santo vs. la hija de Frankenstein (Santo vs. Frankenstein's Daughter)* (1971), *Santo y Blue Demon contra Drácula y el hombre lobo (Santo and Blue Demon vs. Dracula & the Wolfman)* (1972), *Santo contra la magia negra (Santo vs. Black Magic)* (1972), *Santo vs. las lobas (Santos vs. The She-Wolves)* (1972), *Santo y Blue Demon contra el doctor Frankenstein (Santo and Blue Demon vs. Doctor*

Frankenstein) (1973), *La venganza de la llorona* (*Vengeance of the Crying Woman*) (1974), and *Chanoc y el hijo del Santo contra los vampiros asesinos* (*Chanoc and the son of Santo vs. the Killer Vampires*) (1981). *See also* MEXICAN HORROR.

SASDY, PETER (1935–). The Hungarian-born, British-based director Peter Sasdy was part of a wave of filmmakers who re-energized **British horror** cinema during the late 1960s and early 1970s, often introducing socially critical attitudes into their work. After directing for **Hammer**'s **television** series *Journey to the Unknown* (1968), Sasdy went on to make three feature films for the company. *Taste the Blood of Dracula* (1970) was an accomplished account of repressed youths rebelling against their fathers, although like most of Hammer's Dracula films it struggled to find interesting things for the **vampire** to do. *Countess Dracula* (1971) featured another monstrous parent, a bloodthirsty countess memorably played by **Ingrid Pitt** (and loosely based on the historical figure Countess **Elizabeth Bathory**). Similarly, *Hands of the Ripper* (1971) dealt with **Jack the Ripper**'s daughter struggling to rid herself of her father's malign influence. In all cases, Sasdy sided unequivocally with young against old, although the bleakness of the films suggested that the forces of repression were indeed powerful. Away from Hammer, Sasdy returned to this theme with the contemporary-set horror *Nothing But the Night* (1972), in which older people sought to transplant their identities into the bodies of **children**, although an overly busy plot distracted from the film's theme. *Doomwatch* (1972) was a straightforward adaptation of a popular television series, while the post-*Exorcist I Don't Want to Be Born* (*The Devil Within Her*) (1975) was an undistinguished **possession** drama. Sasdy also directed **Nigel Kneale**'s acclaimed television **ghost** story *The Stone Tape* (1972) and contributed episodes to the television horror series *Supernatural* (1977), *Hammer House of Horror* (1980), and *Hammer House of Mystery and Suspense* (1984).

SAVINI, TOM (1946–). The American **makeup** artist Tom Savini's self-acknowledged key influences were his love for old horror films and his experience as a combat cameraman in the Vietnam war where he saw many dead and mutilated bodies. From the 1970s onwards, he helped to introduce a graphic realism to the horror genre with his exceptionally gory and visceral makeup effects. Early credits included *Deranged* (1974), **Bob Clark**'s *Dead of Night* (*The Night Walk, Deathdream*) (1974), and **George Romero**'s modern-day **vampire** story *Martin* (1977), but his first major work was on Romero's groundbreaking **zombie** epic *Dawn of the Dead* (1978). Walking corpses, spectacular wounds, blood spatter and the eating of human flesh: all were presented in unsparing detail, and the film consequently acquired notoriety as a cutting-edge **gore** film. Savini followed this with work on the **slasher** films *Friday the 13th* (1980) and *The Burning* (1981) and the controversial **serial killer** film *Maniac* (1980), where he expertly conjured up stabbings, slashings, mutilations, and shootings. In so doing, he began to acquire a cult following among horror **fans**, becoming for them as much a star as any of the actors appearing in his films. He continued to work with Romero on projects such as *Day of the Dead* (1985) and *Monkey Shines* (1988) and on the Romero-**Dario Argento** collaboration *Due occhi diabolici* (*Two Evil Eyes*) (1990), as well as providing gore effects for Argento's *Trauma* (1993), amongst many others.

Savini has also proved himself a capable character actor, appearing in small roles in numerous films, including *Martin, Dawn of the Dead* (and its 2004 remake), and *From Dusk Till Dawn* (1996). He has written a book about his craft, *Grand Illusions*, and in 1990 directed an effective **remake** of Romero's 1968 film *Night of the Living Dead*.

SCHOEDSACK, ERNEST B. (1893–1979). Ernest B. Schoedsack started out making ethnographic **documentaries** *Grass* (1925) and *Chang* (1927) before switching to fiction with his direction of *The Four Feathers* (1929). He subsequently teamed up with **Merian C. Cooper**, his collaborator on *Grass* and *Chang*, to make *The Most Dangerous Game* (*The Hounds of Zaroff*) (1932), a jungle horror film that Schoedsack co-directed with **Irving Pichel** and which Cooper produced. This was followed by the classic monster movie *King Kong* (1933), which Schoedsack and Cooper co-directed. Schoedsack directed the **sequel** *Son of Kong* (1933) all by himself but co-directed with Wesley Ruggles the Cooper-produced *The Monkey's Paw* (1933), an adaptation of W. W. Jacobs's well-known horror story that, despite its title, had nothing to do with *King*

Kong. Schoedsack's last horror credit was the **mad scientist** film *Dr. Cyclops* (1940), although he subsequently returned to the world of **apes** with the adventure story *Mighty Joe Young* (1949). *See also* AMERICAN HORROR.

SCHRADER, PAUL (1946–). The distinguished American writer-director Paul Schrader—best known for his work on Martin Scorsese's *Taxi Driver* (1976) and *Raging Bull* (1980)—has had two less than successful encounters with the horror genre. He directed *Cat People* (1982), a **remake** of the **Val Lewton-Jacques Tourneur** 1942 original that replaced that film's subtleties with explicit scenes of sex and violence. Schrader's version contained interesting ideas but was marred by shifts in tone and moments of silliness. *Dominion—Prequel to the Exorcist* (2005) was an intelligent but altogether more somber affair. In fact, it proved too somber for its producers, who shelved the film and hired **Renny Harlin** to direct a new, more gory and horror-like version of the prequel that was released as *Exorcist—the Beginning* (2004). Schrader's version was subsequently released as well. *See also* AMERICAN HORROR.

SCHRECK, MAX (1879–1936). The German actor Max Schreck secured a kind of immortality for himself by starring in **F. W. Murnau**'s *Nosferatu: eine Symphonie des Grauens* (*Nosferatu: a Symphony of Terror*) (1922). He appeared in many other films but his performance as the grotesquely fanged, bald-headed **vampire** Orlok is all that is remembered of him today, mainly because it differs so much from the more presentable and dapper vampire popularized by the likes of **Bela Lugosi** and **Christopher Lee. Klaus Kinski** recreated the animalistic Schreck-vampire look for Werner Herzog's *Nosferatu: Phantom der Nacht* (*Nosferatu the Vampire*) (1979) as did actor **Reggie Nalder** in **Tobe Hooper**'s **television** adaptation of **Stephen King**'s *Salem's Lot* (1979). In a bit of in-joke casting in **Tim Burton**'s **Expressionism**-influenced *Batman Returns* (1992), Christopher Walken played a character called Max Shreck, while Willem Dafoe portrayed Schreck as an actual vampire in *Shadow of the Vampire* (2000). Fortuitously for the actor's reputation as a horror icon, "Schreck" just happens to be the German word for terror.

SCIENCE FICTION. The boundaries between horror and other genres have often proved permeable, with this particularly the case for science fiction. Horror and science fiction certainly share some origins, with Mary Shelley's 1818 novel *Frankenstein, or the modern Prometheus* a key text for both. Later attempts by genre scholars to differentiate the two, often through arguing that horror sets out to frighten and thrill while science fiction focuses on more intellectual matters, have tended to be overly reliant on abstract and ideal notions of each genre. As ever in the realm of popular entertainment, the reality is considerably messier and more compromized than these critical accounts have sometimes suggested, with films marketed as science fiction or horror depending on what was currently popular in the market at the time of their release.

The numerous **mad scientist** films of the 1930s and 1940s—notably the **Universal Frankenstein** series—displayed an anxiety about science, although the over-the-top **gothic** and expressionistic qualities of these movies usually saw them classified fully as horror. By comparison, 1950s monster movies and alien invasion fantasies often evoked a more realistic world, one in which elements associated with science fiction—aliens, new technology, speculations about the future—were harder to separate out from horror's characteristic focus on the fearful and the frightful. Films such as *The Thing from Another World* (1951*), Invaders from Mars* (1953), *Creature from the Black Lagoon* (1954), *Invasion of the Body Snatchers* (1956), *It! The Terror from Beyond Space* (1958), and from Great Britain, *The Quatermass Xperiment* (*The Creeping Unknown*) (1955) generated a nuclear-age atmosphere of paranoia and anxiety, with science itself as much a part of the problem as it was a solution.

Later science fiction/horror hybrids have tended to center on representations of the monstrous, whether this be extraterrestrial or scientific in origin, with this usually resulting in them being marketed as horror. A key film here is *Alien* (1979) and its **sequels**, but to this could be added, among many others, *The Thing* (1982), *Lifeforce* (1985), *Predator* (1987), *Hardware* (1990), *Species* (1995), *Starship Troopers* (1997), *The Astronaut's Wife* (1999), *Virus* (1999), *Doom* (2005), and *Slither* (2006). In comparison, the Canadian director **David Cronenberg** has offered a series of more challenging genre hybrids—among them *Rabid* (1977), *The Brood* (1979), and *Videodrome* (1983)—in which science fiction conceits about technology and consciousness are combined with a full-blooded **body horror**.

SELF-REFLEXIVITY. There are two distinct types of self-reflexivity apparent in horror cinema, each of which has its own functions and effects. *Scream* (1996) is a well-known example of one of these types inasmuch as it is a horror film in which the characters talk incessantly about horror films, especially the **slashers** of which *Scream* itself is an extension. In other words, this is a self-reflexivity that operates in terms of subject matter. Other horror films that in some way or other have taken horror fiction as their subject include *How to Make a Monster* (1958), *The House of Seven Corpses* (1974), *Madhouse* (1974), Wes Craven's *New Nightmare* (1994), **John Carpenter**'s *In the Mouth of Madness* (1994), **Alejandro Amenabar**'s *Tesis* (1996), *Urban Legends: Final Cut* (2000), *Shadow of the Vampire* (2000), and *The Last Horror Movie* (2003). *Scream* is slightly different from some of these in that it does not deal directly with the filmmaking process (although *Scream 3* does get round to this) and seeks rather more to ingratiate itself with audiences through appealing to their knowledge of recent horror history. However, like the other films of this particular self-reflexive type, its narrative structure is conventional. The characters might talk about films—just as characters in some of the other films cited above engage in film production—but that activity does not disrupt the film in which it features (i.e., no character in *Scream* ever turns to the camera to analyse *Scream*, nor do we ever see the crew of *Scream* at work).

There is another type of cinematic self-reflexivity, one that is both more confrontational and potentially more disturbing for audiences. It involves foregrounding some of the techniques deployed by horror filmmakers in such a way that the horror spectator's own position becomes uncomfortable. A key film here is **Michael Powell**'s *Peeping Tom* (1960). As this deals with a **serial killer** who works in a film studio and who uses a movie camera as part of his killing technique, it could be seen as self-reflexive in a *Scream*-like manner. However, Powell seeks to make the spectator aware of his or her voyeuristic complicity in the crimes, especially in the opening sequence where we witness the murder of a prostitute through the killer's camera and where, unnervingly, the victim looks directly out at us as she is murdered. Something similar occurs in **Alfred Hitchcock**'s **apocalyptic horror** film *The Birds* (1963), when someone accusing the female protagonist of causing the bird attacks looks directly at the camera (the shot is the protagonist's point of view), thereby accusing the audience as well. In a different way, the scene in **Dario Argento**'s *Opera* (*Terror at the Opera*) (1987) where a woman has needles taped under her eyelids so that she is unable to close her **eyes** and is then compelled to watch violent murders also has the potential to shock an audience into an awareness of its own gaze at the screen, which this time is a reactive gaze rather than the sadistic gaze invoked by *Peeping Tom* and *The Birds*. Equally uncomfortable is the moment in the grueling serial killer drama *Henry—Portait of a Serial Killer* (1986) when we realize that the murder we are seeing on the screen is actually a video recording of a murder being watched by the killers. As the camera pulls back to reveal this, our own complicity with their murderous spectatorship becomes unavoidable.

It is interesting that those horror films that seek to implicate their spectators in the horrifying events on screen have often experienced difficulties with the critics or the censors and that they have since acquired a reputation for being hard-edged genre products. It seems that the knowing wink offered by *Scream* and its ilk is considerably less disturbing than the unforgiving glares presented by the likes of *Peeping Tom* and *Opera*.

SEQUELS. To a certain extent, the horror genre is bound together by sequels. This is particularly the case for its major monsters, most of whom tend to be deemed as major precisely because they have appeared in more than one film. This reliance on sequels has often led to horror being viewed as a formulaic and repetitive area of culture. However, it can be argued that horror is no more formulaic than other film genres, and that the role of the sequel in horror history is more complex and nuanced than is sometimes supposed.

The first horror sequels took a while to appear. There was a four year gap between **Universal**'s *Frankenstein* (1931) and the first horror sequel, *Bride of Frankenstein* (1935), and another four years passed before *Son of Frankenstein* (1939). Similarly *Dracula* (1931) and *Dracula's Daughter* (1936) were separated by five years. By the 1940s, Universal had switched emphatically to serial B-movie horror production, and "sequelitis" had set in with *The Wolf Man* (1941) and *The **Ghost** of Frankenstein* (1942) leading to a joint sequel, *Frankenstein Meets the Wolf Man* (1943), followed by *House of Frankenstein* (1944) and *House of Dracula* (1945). Universal also produced in quick succession three sequels to *The **Mummy**'s Hand* (1940)—*The Mummy's Tomb* (1942), *The Mummy's Ghost* (1944), and *The Mummy's Curse* (1944). (To complicate matters, *The Mummy's Hand* was neither a sequel to nor a **remake** of Universal's 1932 production *The Mummy* but instead a brand new story, albeit one that recycled footage from the older film.) There was also a Universal series of *Invisible Man* films, and another Dracula film, *Son of Dracula* (1943), with Dracula featuring as well in *House of Frankenstein* and *House of Dracula*. Even the considerably more upmarket **Val Lewton** at RKO made a sequel to his **Cat** *People* (1942) with *The Curse of the Cat People* (1944).

The Universal sequels set a pattern. They were based on monsters rather than on heroes, and, as sequel followed sequel, they gradually formed into series or cycles. However, the relationship between the films could vary considerably. Some sequels followed on directly from preceding films, although there were often odd gaps in the chronology. Other sequels were more loosely connected—or in some instances barely connected at all—to what had gone before. Some might argue that such films were not actually sequels, but horror cinema from Universal onwards has constantly blurred the distinction between sequel and series production. For example, the trajectory of Frankenstein's monster through 1930s and 1940s Universal horror maintained a fairly consistent chronology, but, by contrast, Dracula wandered in and out of his films with little sense of progression from one to the other.

It is worth pointing out that while certain types of scenes recurred in these sequels—a laboratory scene in Frankenstein sequels, for example, or a transformation scene in the Wolf Man films—the films were also noticeably different from each other, constantly revising and refreshing stock narrative situations and placing surprising new twists alongside some of the more established conventions. Much the same could be said for the next major set of horror sequels, which came from the British company **Hammer** between the late 1950s and 1970s. Its Frankenstein and Dracula films (with seven titles in each) were clearly in the Universal mold in their combination of familiar scenes with innovative elements. **Jacinto Molina's Spanish horror werewolf** series, which began with *La marca del hombre lobo* (*The Mark of the Werewolf*) (1968), also fitted this pattern.

1980s **American horror** saw the development of a phenomenon that, perhaps more than anything else, gave the sequel a bad name, and that was the practice of numbering sequels. The naked exploitativeness of titles like *Halloween 2* (1981) or *Friday the 13th Part 2* (1981) or *A Nightmare on Elm Street Part 2* (1985) was only partly ameliorated by the occasional inclusion of a subtitle (e.g., for the second Elm Street, "Freddy's Revenge"), particularly when you got up to Part Six or Part Seven. Since the 1980s, it is a rare successful American horror film that does not generate a sequel or two (or three). However, the belief expressed by some cultural commentators that sequels of this kind merely repeat, with decreasing returns, what was distinctive about the first film does need to be challenged. One can easily find substantial changes in emphasis within cycles—for example, the growing importance of the supernatural in both the *Halloween* and *Friday the 13th* sequels—as well as qualitative distinctions. To put it bluntly, some sequels are more imaginative and a lot better made than others.

It would be hard to understand how horror has developed over time without taking horror sequels seriously. The sequel certainly has an economic function, but it has also offered a site where filmmakers have been able to innovate within and around familiar scenes and situations.

SERIAL KILLERS. The serial killer is a major monster in contemporary horror cinema, having successfully supplanted more traditional horror monsters such as the **vampire** and the **werewolf**. Unlike these fantasy-based creatures, serial killers do exist in reality (although the cinematic versions are often very different from their real-life counterparts), and their popularity can be seen as relating to broad anxieties about human identity in an increasingly atomized and individualistic society. The term *serial killer* was not coined until the 1970s—by the Federal Bureau of Investigation's Behavioral Science unit—but such figures, defined through their repetitive and obsessive homicides, were visible in cinema before then, even if we did not have a neat label for them.

American horror of the 1930s and 1940s foregrounded supernatural or quasi-scientific monsters and villains, and when it did feature human killers, these usually turned out to be **mad scientist**s or their assistants. In this period, villains in the serial killer mold tended to be located more in crime-based narratives, such as **Alfred Hitchcock**'s British production *The Lodger* (1927) (which drew upon a key serial-killer template, namely the **Jack the Ripper** murders of 1888), the **Val Lewton-Jacques Tourneur** film *The Leopard Man* (1943), the 1944 **remake** of *The Lodger*, and **Robert Siodmak**'s *The Spiral Staircase* (1946). In fact, the subsequent development of this figure would take place within, and largely help to define, an increasingly significant overlap between crime fiction and the horror genre.

A more detailed, and recognizably modern, engagement with the psychopathology of obsessive killers was evident in Hitchcock's *Psycho* (1960) and **Michael Powell**'s *Peeping Tom* (1960), with a relaxation in **censorship** permitting a greater emphasis on sexual deviance here than was possible before. This was also apparent in some Jack the Ripper films, including *Jack the Ripper* (1958) and *A Study in Terror* (1965), as well as in Richard Fleischer's realistic accounts of real-life serial killers in *The Boston Strangler* (1968) and *Ten Rillington Place* (1970) and in Jack Smight's more flamboyant *No Way To Treat A Lady* (1968). Meanwhile, **Mario Bava**'s seminal Italian **giallo** *Sei donne per l'assassino* (*Blood and Black Lace*) (1964) opted for a different approach, with his serial killer—or, as it turned out, two killers—presented as an impersonal, blank-faced killing machine (although ultimately these killers were revealed to have rational motives). Throughout the 1970s and the first part of the 1980s, it was this killer-as-bogeyman persona that prevailed in horror, both in numerous giallo films and in the American **slashers** that were popular from the late 1970s onwards. Serial murderers such as Michael Myers in the *Halloween* films or Jason Voorhees in the *Friday the 13th* films were not psychological case studies and possessed only the most rudimentary motivations. Instead they were presented as effective and ruthless killers, with the masks they frequently wore denoting a lack of personality or psychological depth.

In the mid-1980s, two films signalled a change in the fortunes of the serial killer. John McNaughton's *Henry—Portrait of a Serial Killer* (1986) was a grimly realistic case study, albeit one where the killer himself remained enigmatic, while **Michael Mann**'s *Manhunter* (1986) was a stylish adaptation of Thomas Harris's bestselling novel *Red Dragon* that introduced master serial killer Hannibal Lecter to the big screen. Neither was very successful in commercial terms, but they did pave the way for the breakthrough film *The Silence of the Lambs* (1991), which was also based on a Harris novel and featured **Anthony Hopkins** in an Academy-Award winning performance as Lecter. The idea of the serial killer as an articulate and charismatic individual capable of offering disturbing but truthful insights into the human condition was underlined through the fact that Lecter himself was a psychiatrist, and the Lecter films also introduced the idea of the disturbed hero-profiler who in some way has to open him or herself up to the killer-therapist in order to solve the case. The case-study approach embodied by the inarticulate, working-class Henry in *Henry—Portrait of a Serial Killer* was also present in the form of the secondary serial killers—the Tooth Fairy in *Manhunter*, Buffalo Bill in *The Silence of the Lambs*—being hunted by the FBI.

More master serial killers followed in films such as *Seven* (1995), *Copycat* (1995), and *The Bone Collector* (1999), which were usually marketed as thrillers but which offered horror-like levels of violence and **gore**. At the same time, masked serial killers of the psychologically shallow kind were populating a new wave of slashers inaugurated by **Wes Craven**'s *Scream* (1996) and developed by the likes of *I Know What You Did Last Summer* (1997) and *Urban Legend* (1998). Character studies of real-life serial killers also made a modest comeback with *Monster* (2003), based on the story of Aileen Wuornos, and the more downmarket *Ed Gein* (2000) and *Ted Bundy* (2002).

Clearly, the figure of the serial killer has been and continues to be interpreted in different ways at different times, and arguably its proliferation in popular culture is, in part at least, a product of this versatility. Much the same can be said of all long-lived horror monsters who have survived only to the extent that they have periodically been reinvented. Of course, the serial killer is distinctive in that s/he is human. In a post-1960 horror cinema that has increasingly located evil within the psychological rather than in the supernatural, it is this quality that has made this particular monster so compelling and so useful for horror artists.

SEWELL, VERNON (1903–2001). The British director Vernon Sewell directed two low-budget thrillers for **Hammer**—*The Dark Light* (1951) and *The Black Widow* (1951)—but never worked on any of the company's horror films. Instead, amid films made in a range of genres, he specialized in the **ghost** story. The eerie thriller *Latin Quarter* (1946) combined spirtualistic elements with the actions of a murderer who conceals his victims within his sculptural work, a storyline with which Sewell had already engaged in the short film *The Medium* (1934). His later ghost stories *Ghost Ship* (1952) and *House of Mystery* (1961) reworked some of these ideas yet again, although this time with ghosts more obviously present. By contrast, *The Ghosts of Berkeley Square* (1947) was a jovial **comedy** romp. The thriller *The Man in the Back Seat* (1960) did not have any supernatural elements, but its claustrophobic representation of the attempts of two men to get rid of a corpse was for the time sinister and disturbing. Sewell's later horror films were much cruder affairs. *The Blood Beast Terror* (1968), a period horror in which a giant moth stalks the British countryside, contained one of **British horror**'s silliest monsters. *Curse of the Crimson Altar* (1968) was more interesting, both for its cast—which included **Boris Karloff, Christopher Lee**, and **Barbara Steele**—and for its now very dated psychedelic scenes. *Burke and Hare* (1972), Sewell's final film, was one of British cinema's more exploitative treatments of these famous bodysnatchers, and it marked an undignified conclusion to what had been an intermittently impressive career.

SHARP, DON (1922–). The Australian director Don Sharp arrived at **Hammer** at a time when the company was reaching out for new talent and immediately showed himself to be an accomplished stylist. From its remarkable opening sequence onwards, *Kiss of the **Vampire*** (1962), his **British horror** debut, was fresh and dynamic, and it brought to life what on paper was a fairly conventional Hammer story. Sharp also made the pirate film *The **Devil** Ship Pirates* (1964) and *Rasputin—The Mad Monk* (1966) for the company. The Rasputin film contains some felicitous directorial touches and also boasted a fine performance by **Christopher Lee** in the title role, but—perhaps because of budgetary limitations—it was not as sustained as *Kiss of the Vampire*. Away from Hammer, Sharp directed the **Lon Chaney**

Jr. vehicle *Witchcraft* (1964), another triumph of style over content, although his subsequent *Curse of the Fly* (1965) was less successful. For *The Face of Fu Manchu* (1965) and *The Brides of Fu Manchu* (1966), both of which starred Christopher Lee as the villain, Sharp's precise and matter-of-fact direction was the perfect counterpoint to some extravagant and lurid plotting. He also directed the **psychological thriller** *Taste of Excitement* (1969) and the weird and wonderful supernatural horror *Psychomania* (1971), in which a gang of bikers come back from the dead only to be turned to stone. In comparison, the haunted house film *Dark Places* (1973) was a sedate, understated affair. Sharp also contributed to the **television** series *Hammer House of Horror* (1980) and directed *What Waits Below* (1984).

SHELLEY, BARBARA (1933–). Roles for women in **Hammer** horror films of the 1950s and 1960s tended to be limited, but the British actor Barbara Shelley managed to bring depth and subtlety to her Hammer characterizations, perhaps because she was older and more imposing than Hammer's normal ingénues. She had worked for Hammer in its pre-horror days on the **Terence Fisher**-directed thriller *Mantrap* (1953) (where she was billed as Barbara Kowin, her real name). Her initial **British horror** credits were not for Hammer, however. She starred as the tormented protagonist of *Cat Girl* (1957), a stylish reworking of themes from the **Val Lewton** production *Cat People* (1942), and played virtuous female leads in the period horror drama *Blood of the Vampire* (1958) and the contemporary chiller *Shadow of the Cat* (1961), a film that utilized many Hammer personnel. She also had a supporting role in the disturbing alien invasion fantasy *Village of the Damned* (1960). By this time she had appeared in a second Hammer film, the prisoner-of-war drama *The Camp on Blood Island* (1958), but her debut in Hammer horror did not come until *The Gorgon* (1964), in which she played a woman haunted by the thought that she might be possessed by a supernatural entity. This was one of Hammer's bleakest films, and Shelley credibly conveyed the requisite vulnerability and fear. Her next role for the company was probably her best. She played the prissy Helen in *Dracula— Prince of Darkness* (1966), whose transformation into a sensual and animalistic vampire was done with absolute conviction. The scene where a snarling Shelley is held down by a gang of monks and staked to death remains one of Hammer's most memorable sequences. Shelley was also effective in Hammer's *Rasputin—The Mad Monk* (1966) and *Quatermass and the Pit* (*Five Million Years to Earth*) (1967) and had a small role in **Stephen Weeks'** horror film *Ghost Story* (1974).

SHERLOCK HOLMES. Arch-detective Sherlock Holmes, the famous fictional creation of Arthur Conan Doyle, is the embodiment of rationality, but he has on occasion been plunged into **gothic** or horror-like mysteries. This is most notably the case with the story *The Hound of the Baskervilles*, with the 1939 screen adaptation starring **Basil Rathbone** as Holmes and **Hammer's** 1959 version with **Peter Cushing** as the detective both exploiting the possibilities for horrifying thrills before the arrival of a boringly rational conclusion. As directed by **Roy William Neill**, some of Rathbone's later Holmes films also played, in part at least, as horrors, among them *The Scarlet Claw* (1944), *The Pearl of Death* (1944), and *The House of Fear* (1945). Detached completely from his original literary context, Holmes went on to confront **Jack the Ripper** in the full-blooded horror films *A Study in Terror* (1965) and **Bob Clark's** *Murder by Decree* (1979).

SHERMAN, GARY (1945–). The American director Gary Sherman made a stunning genre debut with the **British horror** film *Death Line* (*Raw Meat*) (1972). A **cannibalism** story set on the London Underground, it managed successfully to combine American-style socially critical horror with a strong sense of British social and class mores. His next horror was made in the United States. *Dead & Buried* (1981) was an ambitious, **Dan O'Bannon**-scripted film that attempted to do something new with the idea of the **zombie**. The film was suitably atmospheric, inventive and nasty, but it was not as sustained or as intense as *Death Line*. Subsequently, Sherman directed *Poltergeist III* (1988).

SHIMIZU, TAKASHI (1972–). Like fellow Japanese filmmaker **Hideo Nakata**, the director Takashi Shimizu has specialized in **ghost** stories combining **Japanese horror** traditions with **American horror** conventions. As with Nakata and the *Ringu* films, Shimizu has become associated with a series, in his case a number of films all focusing on a haunted house. The story setup here is simple; anyone who goes into a house where a man earlier murdered his family dies. However, Shimizu complicates matters through adopting convoluted, non-chronological narrative structures and also demonstrates a considerable talent for conjuring terrifying moments out of the most mundane domestic settings. The dysfunctionality of the family unit—apparent in the origin of the haunting itself—is as much a theme for Shimizu as it is for Nakata, suggesting that such a subject has a broader social relevance for Japan.

Shimizu first visited his haunted house in two low-budget productions, the direct-to-video *Ju-On* (2000) and the part-**sequel**, part-**remake** *Ju-On 2* (2000). He was back for more in *Ju-On: The Grudge* (2003), the first of the series to achieve international success, and *Ju-On: The Grudge 2* (2003) followed almost immediately. In 2004, Shimizu directed *The Grudge*, a **Sam Raimi**-produced American remake of *Ju-On: The Grudge*. Instead of relocating its story to America, this took the bold step of bringing American characters—among them *Buffy the Vampire Slayer* star **Sarah Michelle Gellar**—to Japan and generated some interesting culture shocks out of the ensuing drama. The fearful frissons were still effective in themselves, although anyone familiar with earlier entries in the series might have been experiencing a certain *déjà vu* by now. However, the 2006 release of *The Grudge 2*—an original story rather than a remake of *Ju-On: The Grudge 2*—suggested that this series was far from over, and in 2006 Shimizu also announced that he was planning *Ju-On: The Grudge 3*.

His other horror credits include *Tomie: Re-birth* (2001), *Marebito* (2004), and *Rinne* (2005).

THE SHINING (1980). *The Shining* was Stanley Kubrick's monumental horror film. Adapted from **Stephen King**'s second published novel, it told the story of a caretaker in an apparently haunted hotel who gradually loses his sanity and ends up threatening his wife and son with an axe. Kubrick eschewed the traditional trappings of the genre, with many of his film's most unnerving scenes taking place in brightly lit settings rather than in sinister shadow. The director also foregrounded darkly comic elements of the story in a manner that amplified the horror rather than dispelling it. In this, he was aided by remarkable performances from both **Jack Nicholson** and Shelley

Duvall, performances that managed to be simultaneously controlled and completely over the top. Finally, *The Shining* made an impressive use of the Steadicam, which enabled ultra-smooth camera movement, in evoking the eeriness of the hotel.

The Shining was not particularly well received on its first release, and Kubrick subsequently removed about 25 minutes of footage (the original version runs approximately 145 minutes). However, the film's reputation has since risen considerably, and in a recent poll it was voted one of the best horror films of all time.

Stephen King was apparently left unimpressed by Kubrick's decidedly loose adaptation of his novel, and in 1997 he penned a **television** miniseries version that was directed by **Mick Garris**. The resulting work was effective enough in its own terms, but it is Kubick's masterful film that continues to capture the public's imagination.

SHYAMALAN, M. NIGHT (1970–). The success of *The Sixth Sense* (1999) contributed to the burgeoning popularity of **ghost** stories in horror cinema and also established the young Indian-born writer-director M. Night Shyamalan (whose real name is Manoj Nelliyattu Shyamalan) as a talent to watch. The film's brooding and melancholic qualities separated it out from other horror films, and its now famous twist ending became a public talking point. The superhero story *Unbreakable* (2000) and the alien invasion fantasy *Signs* (2002) were followed by another horror-themed project, *The Village* (2004). This was an intriguing and visually stunning account of a village sealed off from the outside world and apparently surrounded by monsters. Its denouement disappointed some, although it was a logical outcome of what seemed to be a desire to retreat from reality. Shyamalan's next film, *Lady in the Water* (2006), moved ever further away from quotidian reality in its story of mysterical, fairytale-like beings. *See also* AMERICAN HORROR.

SIODMAK, KURT (1902–2000). Kurt Siodmak—who was often billed as Curt Siodmak—wrote screenplays on a variety of subjects while in his native Germany. He left after the Nazis came to power and, after working in the French and British film industries, he ended up in Hollywood where he became a horror specialist. His first genre credit was *The Invisible Man Returns* (1940), and he followed this with two **Boris Karloff** vehicles, *Black Friday* (1940) and *The Ape* (1940), and the **comedy** *The Invisible Woman* (1940). His screenplay for *The Wolf Man* (1941) revised **Universal**'s concept of the **werewolf** by emphasizing the victim status of the lycanthrope, a theme he developed further in the **sequel** *Frankenstein Meets the Wolf Man* (1943). He also provided the story for his brother **Robert Siodmak**'s *Son of Dracula* (1943) and, away from Universal, wrote the superior **voodoo** film *I Walked with a Zombie* (1943) for producer **Val Lewton** and director **Jacques Tourneur**. In addition, he wrote *Invisible Agent* (1942) and *The Climax* (1944), as well as producing the story for *House of Frankenstein* (1944). His last unequivocally impressive horror screenplay was **Robert Florey**'s **disembodied hand** thriller *The Beast with Five Fingers* (1946).

In the 1950s, Siodmak directed some less than impressive low-budget monster movies, including *Bride of the Gorilla* (1951), *The Magnetic Monster* (1953), and *Curucu, Beast of the Amazon* (1956) and contributed to the screenplays for *Creature with the Atom Brain* (1955) and *Earth vs. the Flying Saucers* (1956). He also wrote and directed episodes for the obscure **television** horror series *13 Demon Street* (1959–1960)—which featured Wolf Man star **Lon Chaney Jr.**—as well as directing the abortive pilot for the never-made series *Tales of Frankenstein* (1958), which was designed to cash in on the success of **Hammer**'s *The Curse of Frankenstein* (1957). His final significant genre credit was for **Terence Fisher**'s German production *Sherlock Holmes und das Halsband des Todes* (*Sherlock Holmes and the Necklace of Death*) (1962).

Siodmak's 1942 novel *Donovan's Brain*—which dealt with a disembodied brain exerting a malign influence on the people around it—has been filmed several times, as *The Lady and the Monster* (1944), as *Donovan's Brain* (1953), as a television production also entitled *Donovan's Brain* (1955), and as **Freddie Francis**'s *Vengeance* (*The Brain*) (1962), although Siodmak was not involved in any of these.

SIODMAK, ROBERT (1900–1973). Like his brother, the writer **Kurt Siodmak**, the director Robert Siodmak began making films in his native Germany, moved to France after the rise of the Nazis and during the 1940s established himself in Hollywood as a film noir specialist. *Son of Dracula* (1943), his only supernatural horror film, was a distinguished contribution to the **Universal** *Dracula* cycle that brought the vampire to contemporary America for the first time and contained some eerie nighttime sequences. While drawing on noir conventions, his **psychological thriller** *The Spiral Staircase* (1946) also utilized **point of view** techniques in a manner that would feature in later **slasher** and **serial killer** films. A later German film, *Nachts, wenn der Teufel kam* (*Nights When the Devil Came, The Devil Strikes at Night*) (1957), was another serial killer drama.

THE SLASHER. There is some disagreement in horror criticism about the origins of the slasher film. Does it begin with **Alfred Hitchcock**'s *Psycho* (1960)? Or is it influenced by the Italian **giallo** or **Bob Clark**'s striking **serial killer** drama *Black Christmas* (1974) or **Tobe Hooper**'s groundbreaking *The Texas Chainsaw Massacre* (1974)? One thing is clear, however. The term *slasher* emerges in the late 1970s and refers primarily to a cycle of **American horror** films commencing with **John Carpenter**'s *Halloween* (1978) and continuing with the likes of *Friday the 13th* (1980), *Terror Train* (1980), *Happy Birthday to Me* (1980), *Prom Night* (1980), *The Burning* (1981), *Hell Night* (1981), and *The House on Sorority Row* (1982). These films featured teenage protagonists being stalked and killed by psychopathic, and sometimes disfigured, serial killers, with the killings often filmed via the **point of view** of the killer (hence trade magazine *Variety*'s alternative label of "teenie-kill-pic"). The films were also very reliant on **startle effects** that had in the past been used sparingly within horror cinema. Although *Halloween* received some positive reviews, this type of horror was not generally liked by critics who tended to find it crudely formulaic, sadistic, reactionary, and—given the emphasis on the victimization of women—misogynist.

The initial slasher cycle faded away in the early 1980s. However, some of the slasher conventions lived on in the post-1982 *Friday the 13th* and *Halloween* **sequels** and, most of all, in the *Nightmare on Elm Street* films that commenced in 1984. The original slashers had avoided or marginalized supernatural elements, but these later films, while maintaining an emphasis on the teenage experience, were more willing to entertain the idea of their characters returning from the dead. A further twist in the slasher story occurred in the mid-1990s, by which time the supernatural slasher cycle was winding down. **Wes**

Craven's *Scream* (1996) returned to the non-supernatural format, albeit equipped with an acutely self-conscious awareness of horror history and numerous knowing jokes about and references to the original slashers. Many of the films that followed—including *I Know What You Did Last Summer* (1997), *Urban Legend* (1998), *Cherry Falls* (2000), *Valentine* (2001), and in a rare diversion back into the supernatural, *Final Destination* (2000)—lacked that kind of self-consciousness but still deployed victimized teenagers, point of view techniques and startle effects.

For all the disreputability of the original slasher, its legacy is clearly a long-lived and potent one. Perhaps most significant is an innovation that was not widely noticed at the time of the cycle's initial popularity, namely its introduction of the active female hero into the genre. Again and again in these films—and this is a convention maintained in most of the later variations on the slasher formula—it is not a male hero but rather a woman, known by horror historians as the **Final Girl**, who defeats the killer. This does not necessarily make these films progressive, but perhaps it makes them more complex and challenging than has sometimes been supposed.

SLAUGHTER, TOD (1885–1956). The term *barnstorming* seems wholly appropriate for the screen performances of British actor Tod Slaughter (real name Norman Slaughter). He toured Great Britain with lurid stage melodramas from 1905 onwards, and when he turned to cinema in the 1930s—invariably as the villain—his performance style maintained its flamboyant theatricality. Horror production in Britain was generally suppressed by the powerful **censorship** authorities during this period, but Slaughter's films managed to avoid any censorial sanctions, perhaps because of their theatrical origins. In any event, they represented a peculiarly British type of horror, one that combined morality tales about good overcoming evil with lip-smacking portrayals of melodramatic nastiness. Slaughter's most horror-like films included *Sweeney Todd—The Demon Barber of Fleet Street* (1936), *The Crimes of Stephen Hawke* (1936), *The Face at the Window* (1939), *The Curse of the Wraydons* (1946), and *The Greed of William Hart* (1948). *See also* BRITISH HORROR.

SMITH, DICK (1922–). The **makeup** artist Dick Smith is probably most celebrated for his work on *The Exorcist* (1973). His transformation of child actor **Linda Blair** into an abject creature still has the power to startle. Equally impressive, although more understated, was his ageing of **Max von Sydow** in the role of Father Merrin. Smith had previously aged Dustin Hoffman and Marlon Brando in, respectively, *Little Big Man* (1970) and *The Godfather* (1972), but Sydow's makeup—the actor was only 44 when the film was released—was probably the most convincing of these. Other than an early credit for *The Alligator People* (1959) and work on **television** shows *Dark Shadows* (1966–1971) and *The Strange Case of Dr. Jekyll and Mr. Hyde* (1968), Smith had had little to do with horror prior to *The Exorcist*. After *The Exorcist*, he became more of a genre specialist, while still continuing to work in other areas of cinema—for example, he won an Academy Award for *Amadeus* (1984). His horror credits have included work on *The Sentinel* (1977), *Exorcist II: The Heretic* (1977), *Scanners* (1981), *The Fan* (1981), *Ghost Story* (1981), *The Hunger* (1983), *Spasms* (1983), *Poltergeist III* (1988), *Tales from the Darkside—the Movie* (1990), and *House on Haunted Hill* (1999).

SNUFF. A snuff movie is a film in which someone is really killed. If such films actually exist (and this is far from certain), they are so far beyond the bounds of fictional horror that they would not merit inclusion in a reference work of this kind. However, snuff has occasionally featured as a subject within horror, offering a particularly disturbing version of **self-reflexivity**. An early and very controversial example was **Michael Powell**'s *Peeping Tom* (1960), the notoriety of which helped to shorten the director's career in Great Britain (although the film has since been re-valued as one of the finest of all British productions). By comparison, *Snuff* (1976) was a tawdry low-budget piece of work that teased its audiences with the possibility that it might be showing a real murder but very obviously did not. *Cannibal Holocaust* (1980) also presented itself, albeit more effectively, as a faux **documentary** in which people "really" died, as did the more stylized Belgian **serial killer** drama *C'est arrivé près de chez vous* (*Man Bites Dog*) (1992). Other horrors have used the practice of snuff both as a plot device and as a fairly obvious signifier of depravity. As a sign of the times, video and digital technologies now figure just as much as old-fashioned celluloid. Films of note in this respect include *Benny's Video* (1992), *Mute Witness* (1994), *Strange Days* (1995), *Tesis* (1996), *8MM* (1999) and *My Little Eye* (2002).

SOAVI, MICHELE (1957–). The Italian director—and occasional actor—Michele Soavi is often seen as one of **Dario Argento**'s protégés, although Soavi's films are distinctive in their own right. His earliest horror credit was as an actor in **Lucio Fulci**'s *Paura nella città dei morti viventi* (*City of the Living Dead*) (1980). Subsequently he worked as an assistant to Argento on **giallo** thrillers *Tenebre* (*Tenebrae*) (1982) and *Opera* (*Terror at the Opera*) (1987) and also assisted **Lamberto Bava** on his giallo *La casa con la scala nel buio* (*A Blade in the Dark*) (1983) and his supernatural thriller *Demoni* (*Demons*) (1985); in addition, he took small acting roles in all of these. His directorial debut was the low-budget giallo *Deliria* (*Stagefright, Bloody Bird*) (1987). The premise for this was utterly conventional—an escaped lunatic threatens some actors trapped inside a theater—but the director's treatment of such unpromising material was imaginative and displayed a taste for the surreal and odd that would feature in later Soavi films. This was most evident in the presentation of the killer, who spends most of the film dressed as a giant bird. This should have been a ridiculous device, but it turned out instead to be very unsettling, if only because it was so bizarre. *La Chiesa* (*The Church*) (1989) and *La Setta* (*The Sect*) (1991), Soavi's next two films as director, were produced by Argento. *La Chiesa*, which dealt with a haunted church, was efficiently but impersonally made. *La Setta* was more idiosyncratic in its depiction of a heroine menaced by a mysterious group of cultists, and it offered some dream-like imagery more characteristic of Soavi than it was of Argento. *Dellamorte dellamore* (*Cemetery Man*) (1994), not made for Argento, showed Soavi at his best. Ostensibly a story, based on a **comic** strip, of a cemetery caretaker who, for no apparent reason, finds himself combating **zombies**, it mixed dark romance, scenes of violence and **gore**, and slapstick **comedy**, and also featured a weird, cryptic conclusion. Although it was recognizably in the **Italian horror** tradition, it was also an unusually ambitious and challenging horror film. Since *Dellamorte dellamore*, Soavi has worked mainly for **television** on non-horror projects, although in 2005 he was an assistant director on Terry Gilliam's *The Brothers Grimm*.

SOLE, ALFRED (1943–). The writer-director Alfred Sole was responsible for the **American horror** film *Communion* (*Alice Sweet Alice*) (1976). While most American horrors of the 1970s opted for a contemporary setting, *Communion* was set in the early 1960s—in one scene a character walks past a poster advertising the release of *Psycho* (1960)—and was a powerful study of familial and religious repression. In its depiction of a masked killer terrorizing a New Jersey neighborhood, it also had an evocative sense of place and period. Sole's next horror credit, the horror spoof *Pandemonium* (1982), was less successful, and since then he has worked as a production designer, mainly for American **television**.

SOMMER, ELKE (1940–). From the late 1950s onwards, the German actor Elke Sommer appeared regularly in films made in France, Germany and Italy with occasional excursions to Great Britain and the United States. One of her early credits, the Italian musical *Urlatori alla sbarra* (*Howlers of the Dock*) (1960), was directed by **Lucio Fulci**, later an **Italian horror** specialist, but perhaps her best known role was as the female lead in the Pink Panther film *A Shot in the Dark* (1964) (which, incidentally, was co-written by **William Peter Blatty**, who would later write *The Exorcist*). She is included here because of the two horror films she made with Italian director **Mario Bava**. In *Gli orrori del castello di Norimberga* (*Baron Blood*) (1972), she was a decorative European presence who, perhaps because she was older than the usual horror ingénue, added some weight to the material. In the more important *Lisa e il diavolo* (*Lisa and the Devil*) (1972), considered by many to be Bava's masterpiece, she was sympathetic as the tormented Lisa but also projected a cold reserve that was an indispensable feature of the film's dream-like narrative. The nuances of her performance were largely lost in *The House of Exorcism*, a recut version of the film that sought to exploit the success of *The Exorcist* (1973). Thankfully, Bava's original version, and Sommer's performance in it, has since been restored.

SOMMERS, STEPHEN (1962–). The writer-director Stephen Sommers has translated some of **American horror** cinema's classic monsters into villains in blockbusting action spectaculars. His early films—which included *The Adventures of Huck Finn* (1993) and *The*

Jungle Book (1994)—were respectable literary adaptations. However, *Deep Rising* (1998), a nautical horror film featuring some particularly unpleasant sea monsters, was lively exploitation fare and demonstrated Sommers' propensity for joining horror with action. *The Mummy* (1999) and its **sequel** *The Mummy Returns* (2001) took this yet further, with an Indiana Jones-like hero and some impressive state-of-the-art special effects, although Sommers's screenplays also displayed knowledge of and affection for the **Universal** mummy films of the 1930s and 1940s. *Van Helsing* (2004) was even more of an homage to Universal horror. **Dracula, Frankenstein** and his creation, and some **werewolves** were all present, and the film began with a black-and-white recreation of a classic horror scene. Perhaps some of the later spectacle overwhelmed the narrative, but the nostalgia for an older form of genre cinema was palpable.

SPANISH HORROR. Spain has been one of the major contributors to the development of European horror cinema. However, it was a late entrant to the genre. While Britain and Italy were churning out horrors from the late 1950s onwards, Spain did not begin large-scale horror production until much later in the 1960s. Before then, **Jesus Franco** directed some idiosyncratic Spanish horrors, including the **surgical horror** film *Gritos en la noche* (*The Awful Dr. Orloff*) (1962) and its **sequel** *El secreto del Dr. Orloff* (*The Secret of Dr. Orloff, The Mistresses of Dr. Jekyll, Dr. Jekyll's Mistresses*) (1964), but he remained an isolated figure who would later leave Spain and embark on an itinerant filmmaking career. More significant, in commercial terms at least, was the emergence of actor **Jacinto Molina** (working under the name Paul Naschy) as a Spanish horror star with the likes of *La marca del hombre-lobo* (*Mark of the* **Werewolf,** *Frankenstein's Bloody Terror*) (1968) and *La noche de walpurgis* (*Shadow of the Werewolf*) (1970), and the success of the psychological horror film *La residencia* (*The Finishing School, The House that Screamed*) (1969).

The horror boom that followed during the 1970s, and the more fragmented horror production that took place in the 1980s, encompassed both traditional period horrors and contemporary-set **giallo**-like thrillers. Directors who specialized in the genre included **León Klimovsky**, Amando de Ossorio and Narciso Ibáñez Serrador, while other directors—among them Vicente Aranda, Eloy de la Iglesia and Bigas Luna—passed through horror on their way from or to other, often more reputable, types of filmmaking. Because of this unusual mix of directorial talent, some film historians have argued that, in the first half of the 1970s in particular, Spanish horror offered covert critiques of society under General Franco's repressive rule. It is certainly the case that films such as Arenda's *La novia ensangrentada* (*The Blood-Spattered Bride*) (1972) and Claudio Guerín's *La campana del infierno* (*The Bell from Hell*) (1973) seemed to attack codes of machismo behaviour and social conformity, although whether this was how they were perceived, in Spain or elsewhere, is far from clear. Alongside this potentially serious thread in Spanish horror ran the more lunatic charms of Molina's gory but often sentimental werewolf stories, as well as conventionally plotted but atmospheric horrors such as de Ossorio's **Blind Dead** films (1971–1975) or Klimovksy's *La orgía nocturna de los vampiros* (*The **Vampires'** Night Orgy*) (1972).

From the mid-1990s onwards, there has been a revival in the fortunes of Spanish horror, especially with films made explicitly with an international market in mind. These have included Alex de la Iglesia's *El día de la bestia* (*Day of the Beast*) (1995), **Alejandro Amenabar**'s *Tesis* (1996) and *The Others* (2001), the *Scream*-like thriller *Tuno negro* (2001), Jaume Balagueró's *Los sin nombre* (*The Nameless*) (1999) and *Darkness* (2002), and **Guillermo del Toro**'s *El Espinazo del Diablo* (*The **Devil**'s Backbone*) (2001) and *El laberinto del fauno* (*Pan's Labyrinth*) (2006). From 1999 onwards, the **Fantastic Factory** company set up by Julio Fernández and **Brian Yuzna** has also produced a series of horror and fantasy films utilizing Spanish cast and crew but filmed in English to aid international distribution.

SPIELBERG, STEVEN (1946–). Steven Spielberg's most commercially successful films have tended to be escapist fantasies. However, there is a darkness also apparent in some of his work that has occasionally led him into horror themes and imagery. This is apparent in both his *Indiana Jones* and *Jurassic Park* films, with this particularly the case for the graphic scenes of human sacrifice depicted in *Indiana Jones and the Temple of Doom* (1984).

Spielberg's professional debut as director was on the pilot for the **television** horror show *Night Gallery* (1969). The television film *Something Evil* (1972) was a **ghost** story, while *Duel* (1971), also made for television and ostensibly a thriller, had some **rural horror** resonances in its **Richard Matheson**-scripted story of a man being terrorized by a large truck. As a number of critics have pointed out, *Jaws* (1975), Spielberg's breakthrough film, owed more than a little to **Jack Arnold**'s *Creature from the Black Lagoon* (1954). Spielberg went on to direct one of the segments in *Twilight Zone: the Movie* (1983) and produced **Tobe Hooper**'s *Poltergeist* (1982) and **Joe Dante**'s *Gremlins* (1984). He also executive produced the television series *Amazing Stories* (1985–1987), which contained some horror material. *See also* AMERICAN HORROR.

STANLEY, RICHARD (1966–). The director Richard Stanley has had a much-interrupted but still interesting career in horror. He began in the genre with the British production *Hardware* (1990), a **science fiction**/horror hybrid about a killer robot let loose in the heroine's apartment. The plot might have been derivative, but the film was stylish and suitably claustrophobic in a manner that belied its low budget. *Dust Devil* (1992) was both more ambitious and harder to classify. Filmed in part in Stanley's native South Africa, it offered an ambiguous and self-consciously mystical treatment of a story in which a demon stalked the lonely and the unhappy. *Dust Devil* was much cut about by its distributors, although a Stanley-approved version did eventually become available. He was next hired to direct *The Island of Dr. Moreau* (1996), which starred Marlon Brando, but was fired by the producers shortly after filming began and replaced by **John Frankenheimer**. Since then, he has worked mainly in **documentary**.

STARTLE EFFECTS. Sudden noises or unexpected movements can make us jump, and when horror films set out to startle us, they will use that knowledge of human vulnerabilities. The startle effect is probably the crudest sensation that horror can invoke inasmuch as it involves an automatic physiological response from the spectator. However, this has not stopped horror filmmakers from resorting to it with increasing frequency as the genre has developed. Probably the first horror startle can be found in the **Val Lewton**-produced *Cat*

People (1942) where, at the climax of a suspenseful sequence, the heroine—and the audience—jumps as a bus unexpectedly drives into view from the side of the frame. Lewton placed several comparable moments in his later horror films, referring to them as "buses." In the 1960s, **Roger Corman** was not averse to having the occasional bus or startle in his horror work, while **Brian De Palma**'s *Carrie* (1976) concluded with what was probably the most effective startle in horror history. However, it was the **slasher** film of the late 1970s and early 1980s that turned the startle effect into a key horror convention. Repeatedly, characters wandered into dark and dangerous places where, inevitably, someone or something jumped out at them, with this moment often accompanied by a deafening crash of **music**. The extent to which this kind of overuse has diminished the effectiveness of the startle is not clear. **Wes Craven**'s *Scream* films have demonstrated that jaded horror audiences can still be made to jump to order. Other horrors that are less dependent on the startle are still using it, albeit sparingly, with some success—for example the **ghost** stories *The Sixth Sense* (1999) and *The Others* (2001), as well as numerous examples of contemporary **Japanese horror**. As crude as it might be, it seems that the startle will remain in horror's repertoire of devices.

STECKLER, RAY (1939–). An exploitation director is always looking for a memorably lurid title, and Ray Steckler found his with *The Incredibly Strange Creatures Who Stopped Living and Became Mixed-Up Zombies* (1964). The film itself was negligible, although screenings of it were occasionally enlivened by people dressed as zombies lurching through the cinema. Steckler also directed *The Thrill Killers* (*The Maniacs Are Loose*) (1964), although, as was usually the case with Steckler's work, production values were so non-existent that at best the film fell into the "so bad it's good" category. Later Steckler horrors often contained porno elements: these included *Sinthia, the **Devil's Doll*** (1968), *The Mad Love Life of a Hot Vampire* (1971), *The Horny Vampire* (1971), and *Sexorcist Devil* (1974). More straightforward horror fare, albeit of a low-budget and not particularly memorable kind, was provided by *Blood Shack* (1971), *The Hollywood Strangler Meets the Skid Row **Slasher*** (1979), and *Las Vegas **Serial Killer*** (1986). Steckler sometimes appeared in his own films under the name Cash Flagg and also directed under several names, including Sven Christian and Wolfgang Schmidt. His most likeable film is probably the superhero spoof *Rat Pfink a Boo Boo* (1966) where, for once, the ultra low budget seemed to work in the film's favor. See also AMERICAN HORROR.

STEELE, BARBARA (1938–). Birkenhead, England, might seem an unusual point of origin for a major horror icon, but this is where the actor Barbara Steele was born. Although she appeared in minor roles in some British films during the late 1950s, her career in horror began in Italy with **Mario Bava**'s *La maschera del demonio (The Mask of Satan, Revenge of the Vampire, Black Sunday)* (1960). Steele played both the heroine and the villainess in a manner that suggested that the two were not clearly separable. Her unusual large-eyed beauty suited her particularly well to the role of Asa the witch, whose pale, wounded face is one of the horror genre's most haunting images. She next appeared in **Roger Corman**'s **Edgar Allan Poe** adaptation *Pit and the Pendulum* (1961), but it was her subsequent films in Italy that developed her distinctive fetishistic screen persona. The best of these were *L'orribile segreto del Dr. Hichcock (The Horrible Dr. Hichcock, The Terrible Secret of Dr. Hichcock)* (1962) and *Lo spettro (The Ghost)* (1963), both of which were directed by **Riccardo Freda**. Other Steele vehicles tended to be more conventional, although she remained a remarkable presence in them. An appearance in Federico Fellini's *8 ½* (1963) widened her range as a performer, but such opportunities were rare in her career. She temporarily stopped making horror films in the late 1960s, returning to the genre a few years later with **David Cronenberg**'s *The Parasite Murders (They Came From Within, Shivers)* (1975), **Joe Dante**'s *Piranha* (1978), and *Silent Scream* (1980). Throughout the 1980s, she worked as a producer for American **television** before returning yet again to the horror genre with a role in **Dan Curtis**'s revival of his vampire-themed show *Dark Shadows* (1990). She retains a significant cult following among horror **fans**.

Steele's other horror or horror-themed films are *I lunghi capelli della morte (The Long Hair of Death)* (1964), *Danza macabra (Castle of Blood)* (1964), *5 tombe per un medium (Cemetery of the Living Dead)* (1965), *Gli amanti d'oltretomba (Nightmare Castle)* (1965), *La sorella di satana (Revenge of the Blood Beast, The She-Beast)*

(1966), *Un angelo per satana* (*An Angel for Satan*) (1966), and *Curse of the Crimson Altar* (1968). *See also* ITALIAN HORROR.

STEVENSON, ROBERT (1905–1986). It might be hard to believe, but the man who directed the much-loved Disney classics *Mary Poppins* (1964), *The Love Bug* (1968), and *Bedknobs and Broomsticks* (1971) also had one **British horror** film to his credit. In fact, the British director Robert Stevenson worked in a variety of genres before arriving at Disney, and in 1936 came up with *The Man Who Changed His Mind*. This **mad scientist** drama was one of the best American-style horrors to emerge from British cinema during the 1930s. It starred **Boris Karloff** as the scientist, and seasoned **American horror** writer **John L. Balderston** worked on the screenplay. Stevenson's American-produced version of *Jane Eyre* (1944) also has a brooding, **gothic** atmosphere.

STONE, OLIVER (1946–). The American writer-director Oliver Stone is now generally thought of as a director of politicized films such as *Platoon* (1986), *JFK* (1991), and *Natural Born Killers* (1994). However, he started out in horror. *Seizure* (1974) and *The Hand* (1981) offered themselves ostensibly as supernatural dramas, although Stone was clearly more interested in exploring the tortured psychologies of his male protagonists. Thematically they can be related to his later films, but they lack the flair and the energy of his best work. *See also* AMERICAN HORROR.

STROCK, HERBERT L. (1918–2005). Herbert L. Strock was one of a group of American directors—others included **Roger Corman** and **Bert I. Gordon**—who contributed to the 1950s boom in low-budget horror production. After some uncredited work on *The Magnetic Monster* (1953) and credited direction of the **science fiction** drama *Gog* (1954), Strock made three **teenage horror** films in rapid succession—*I Was a Teenage Frankenstein* (1957), *Blood of Dracula* (1957), and *How to Make a Monster* (1958). All of these offered conservative narratives in which troubled teenagers were turned into monsters under the baleful influence of predatory adults. Juvenile delinquency was thus figured as something dangerous that had to be contained for the good of the community. *How to Make a Monster* additionally exhibited self-reflexive elements in its depiction of a horror film **makeup** artist taking revenge on his enemies. Strock also directed some episodes of the **television** horror series *The Veil* (1958) and supervised the assembling of episodes from the series *13 Demon Street* (1959–1960) into the feature film *The Devil's Messenger* (1961). His final significant horror credit was *The Crawling Hand* (1963), a lurid **disembodied hand** science fiction/horror hybrid. His later uncredited work on *Monster* (1979) was undistinguished. *See also* AMERICAN HORROR.

STUART, GLORIA (1910–). A picture of blonde elegance, the actor Gloria Stuart graced two of **James Whale**'s classic horror films, *The Old Dark House* (1932) and *The Invisible Man* (1933), as well as the more obscure *Secret of the Blue Room* (1933), and that was it so far as her horror career was concerned. She is still remembered by horror **fans**, however. Many years later, she showed up as the older version of Kate Winslet's character in **James Cameron**'s *Titanic* (1997).

SUBOTSKY, MILTON (1921–1991). If one man can be credited with initating the **British horror** cycle that began in the late 1950s, that man is the American writer-producer Milton Subotsky. It was he who first approached Associated Artists Productions with the idea of doing an updated **Frankenstein** film. Associated Artists passed the idea to the British company **Hammer**. Subotsky had written a Frankenstein screenplay, but the Hammer producers went with their own version, and the success of *The Curse of Frankenstein* (1957) reshaped the company into an internationally renowned horror factory.

Subotsky moved to Great Britain to produce the horror film *The City of the Dead* (*Horror Hotel*) (1960). With his business partner, Max J. Rosenberg, he subsequently set up **Amicus**, a company that would become Hammer's leading rival in British horror production (although Hammer constantly out-produced it in terms of sheer number of films released). Subotsky's innovations included focusing on contemporary settings, introducing more humor than was apparent in Hammer horror, and popularizing the horror **anthology** format. He wrote the screenplays for *Dr. Terror's House of Horrors* (1965), *The Skull* (1965), *I, Monster* (1970), *Tales from the Crypt* (1972), and

Vault of Horror (1973), but his main contribution was as producer. After Amicus closed down in the mid-1970s, he produced a few more horror-related titles, including *Dominique* (1978) and *The Monster Club* (1980).

SURGICAL HORROR. Horror cinema of the 1930s and 1940s often dealt with medical matters, usually via the **mad scientist** format, but generally this did not involve explicit displays of bodies surgically opened up for our inspection. This changed in the late 1950s when surgical horror became an important generic element, especially in European horror. Although **Hammer's Frankenstein** films—beginning with *The Curse of Frankenstein* (1957) and *The Revenge of Frankenstein* (1958)—might seem tame today, the images they offered of severed body parts and blood-spattered operating gowns were shocking enough at the time and helped to distinguish this new iconoclastic horror from what had gone before in the genre. Yet more explicit was **Georges Franju**'s *Les yeux sans visage* (*Eyes without a Face*) (1959), which featured a unsparingly graphic but also perversely beautiful scene in which a surgeon slowly peeled away the skin from a woman's face. From Spain, **Jesus Franco**'s *Gritos en la noche* (*The Awful Dr. Orloff*) (1962) delivered more of the same, albeit in a less elegant form, and went on to generate several **sequels**, while **British horror** cinema saw the production of more Frankenstein films throughout the 1960s and early 1970s, alongside such surgery-based films as *Corridors of Blood* (1958), *Corruption* (1967), and *Scream and Scream Again* (1969).

However, the fearfulness of the unscrupulous surgeon appeared to have become diminished by the 1970s, possibly because of the way in which highly publicized advances in transplant surgery had helped to demystify surgical procedures. A fascination with the objectification of human bodies within medical contexts has continued—for example, in the work of **David Cronenberg**—but the surgeon himself is less central to this. More recently, the German production *Anatomie* (2000) revived surgical horror themes in its exploration of Germany's fascist past.

SURREALISM. The Surrealist movement emerged during the 1920s and generated a series of experimental film projects, the most notable of which was Luis Bunuel and Salvador Dali's *Un chien andalou* (1928). The film's opening sequence—which showed in a graphic closeup an **eye** being sliced open by a razor—had an assaultive quality that the horror genre would later explore and exploit in various ways. Similarly, the breakdown in narrative logic offered by *Un chien andalou* has also been a strategy adopted by subsequent horror productions as they have sought to construct a nightmarish remodelling of reality. However, it is hard to find many direct connections between these two areas of culture, which rather seem to exist in parallel with each other, often engaging with similar material but within very different contexts. (One might compare this with the more obviously influential German **Expressionism**, where creative personnel and films circulated between Germany and the United States.) Directors such as David Lynch, **Roman Polanski** and Jan Svankmajer can be aligned with the surrealist tradition, but the self-conscious artfulness of their work has tended to elevate them above the horror genre in which they have occasionally found themselves. Most horror filmmakers clearly operate independently of any surrealist ideas or practices, and yet, perhaps paradoxically, horror films often seem surrealistic in their invoking of unconscious states and dream-like worlds.

SUTHERLAND, DONALD (1935–). Some of the Canadian actor Donald Sutherland's earliest screen credits are in European horror films. He played several parts in the low-budget **Italian horror** *Il castello dei morti vivi* (*Castle of the Living Dead*) (1964), including a grotesque witch. In Britain, he was a more straightforward leading man in the **vampire** segment of the **Amicus** horror **anthology** *Dr. Terror's House of Horrors* (1964), but reverted to grotesquerie as the simpleton gardener in **Hammer's psychological thriller** *Fanatic* (*Die! Die! My Darling!*) (1965). Subsequently, he became an international star in films such as *MASH* (1970) and *Klute* (1971), and his return to horror was as the grieving father in **Nicolas Roeg's** ambitious and thought-provoking **ghost** story *Don't Look Now* (1973). He also starred in the 1978 **remake** of *Invasion of the Body Snatchers* and played a Victorian medium in **Bob Clark's Jack the Ripper** film *Murder by Decree* (1979). Sporadic character roles followed. He trained Buffy in *Buffy the Vampire Slayer* (1992), the film that inspired the **television** series of the same name, and also featured in *The Puppet Masters* (1994), *Fallen* (1998), *Virus* (1999), and *An American Haunting* (2005). On television, he was a vampire's acolyte in *Salem's Lot* (2004) and Captain Walton in the miniseries *Frankenstein* (2004).

SYKES, PETER (1939–2006). The Australian-born director Peter Sykes was one of a group of filmmakers—others included **Gordon Hessler, Michael Reeves, Peter Sasdy,** and **Christopher Wicking**— who started working in **British horror** during the late 1960s and early 1970s and who threw into question some of the more conservative attitudes prevalent in the genre at the time. In Sykes's case, he had already made *The Committee* (1968), a countercultural film with a Pink Floyd score, before turning to genre cinema with *Venom* (1971), a dark thriller filmed in Germany. Two horror films followed for **Hammer.** *Demons of the Mind* (1972) was a moody period piece that reproduced some of the countercultural criticisms of the institution of the family that were circulating in this period. *To the **Devil** a Daughter* (1976), Hammer's final horror film (to date), was a more straightforward but still stylish Satanic thriller. Away from Hammer, Sykes also made the **comedy**-horror *The House in Nightmare Park* (1973).

Perhaps surprisingly for someone with this kind of cinematic pedigree, Sykes later worked on the widely seen biopic *Jesus* (1979).

– T –

TEENAGE HORROR. Teenagers have formed a major part of the audience for horror films since the 1950s, but not all post-World War II horrors have featured teenagers. The first wave of teenage horror appeared in the late 1950s, in a series of films in which teenage protagonists were often presented as troubled delinquents in the manner of *Rebel without a Cause* (1955). If teenagers were thus framed as a social problem, identification with them was aided by the way in which they were frequently victimized by predatory adults in unscrupulous experiments. Examples included *I Was a Teenage **Frankenstein*** (1957), *I Was a Teenage **Werewolf*** (1957), *Blood of **Dracula*** (1957),

How to Make a Monster (1958), and *Teenage Zombies* (1959). Something similar, albeit in a more chilling and somber form, was offered by **Hammer**'s *The Damned* (*These are the Damned*) (1963), in which delinquents were paralleled with deadly radioactive **children**.

Subsequently, teenagers did not have much of a part to play in the genre until the late 1960s when the theme of generational division again became significant, with this arguably reflecting broader social tensions of the time. Monstrous pre-pubertal children were the main focus of this in films such as *Night of the Living Dead* (1968), *The Exorcist* (1973), and *The Omen* (1976), but teenagers too suffered at the hands both of adults and their own peers in the likes of *The Texas Chainsaw Massacre* (1974) and *Carrie* (1976). The real and lasting turn to the teenage experience began in the late 1970s with the rise of the American **slasher** film—also dubbed, by trade magazine *Variety*, the teenie-kill-pic. *Halloween* (1978) and *Friday the 13th* (1980), and their many **sequels** and imitators, focused almost entirely on the lives (and violent deaths) of teenage characters, with parents and other adults thoroughly marginalized. It has often been suggested that this type of horror offered a judgmental treatment of teenage sexual mores, with virginity a necessary prerequisite for survival. If this was the case, it is hard to understand why teenagers flocked to the slashers for entertainment. A more likely explanation involves the presence in many slashers of a theme found elsewhere in post-1960 horror, namely an intolerance of complacency and an emphasis on the need to be alert. Sex did not get you killed in the slasher; it was not paying enough attention to what was going on around you.

Since the slasher, the horror genre has maintained and developed its interest in teenagers. The *Nightmare on Elm Street* series presented a veritable parade of troubled teenage heroes and heroines, with the knife-fingered killer Freddy Krueger functioning as a monstrous parent who had to be repeatedly defeated. *Scream* (1996), and its sequels and imitators, introduced yet more elaborate soap-opera dramatics and a self-reflexive awareness of horror history into the teenage-horror formula. In recent years, horror cinema has slightly extended its range of protagonists into their twenties, reflecting no doubt the gradual ageing of the horror audience. Nevertheless, recent films such as *Cabin Fever* (2002), *Cry Wolf* (2005), *Hostel* (2005), *Pulse* (2006), *Stay Alive* (2006), and *Wilderness* (2006) continue to underline a point that the horror genre has been making since the 1950s, namely that bad things happen to you when you are young.

TELEVISION. The association of television with domesticity and family viewing would seem to render it an unsuitable site for horror, which is a type of fiction not often connected with entertainment for the family. Yet from the 1950s onwards, television has, sporadically at least, provided a home for horror stories. This began in the late 1950s when horror films made during the 1930s and 1940s were first shown on American television. These were often presented by horror **hosts**—among them Vampira, Criswell and Tarantula Ghoul—whose jocular prefaces helped to make the films appear non-threatening and thereby rendered them more suitable for domestic viewing. Such screenings introduced these old horrors to new audiences and established that there was still a market for the genre, arguably a factor in the development of new forms of horror in the late 1950s. Some of the **anthology** shows popular on American television in the 1950s and 1960s also offered a few horror-themed episodes, again with these usually framed by a friendly host. The most notable series in this respect were *Alfred Hitchcock Presents* (1955–1962), *The Twilight Zone* (1959–1964), *The Outer Limits* (1963–1965), and most horror-like of all, *One Step Beyond* (1959–1961) and two series hosted by **Boris Karloff**, *The Veil* (1958) and *Thriller* (1960–1962).

During the 1960s, horror themes and images showed up in other family-friendly televisual formats. *The Addams Family* (1964–1966) and *The Munsters* (1964–1966) were situation comedies in which a focus on decidedly **gothic** families inverted some of the standard sitcom conventions to humorous effect, while producer-director **Dan Curtis** introduced a **vampire** and a **werewolf** into the cast of his soap opera *Dark Shadows* (1966–1971). Curtis would later be responsible for a series of television horror films, which together probably represented the most sustained attempt, in the 1970s at least, to emulate cinematic horror. The most successful of these was the modern vampire story *The Night Stalker* (1972, directed by **John Llewellyn Moxey**), which inspired the television horror series *Kolchak—The Night Stalker* (1974–1975). In turn, this series was one of the inspirations for the hugely popular **science fiction**/horror series *The X Files* (1993–2002). Other series would also make occasional diversions into the genre—for example horror monster **Jack the Ripper** featured in the science fiction shows *Star Trek* (1966–1969) and *Babylon Five* (1994–1998)—but very few developed a sustained investment in horror. In fact, this seemed generally the fate of horror on television, constantly to be framed by more televisual formats and conventions but rarely embraced fully for what it was.

Anthology shows have continued to be a key format for horror on television, with, among others, *Night Gallery* (1970–1973), *Darkroom* (1981–1982), *Tales from the Darkside* (1984–1988), *Amazing Stories* (1985–1987), *Freddy's Nightmares* (1988–1990), and *Tales from the Crypt* (1989–1996). The series *Millennium* (1996–1999), *Poltergeist: The Legacy* (1996–1999), *Brimstone* (1998–1999), and *The Others* (2000) were more reliant on cinematic conventions and consequently darker and more disturbing, while miniseries adaptations of **Stephen King's** novels—among them *Salem's Lot* (1979) and *The Stand* (1994)—have formed a horror television sub-genre all of their own. However, the television market for horror during the 1990s became increasingly focused on a teenage demographic. This was evident in the success of shows such as *Buffy the Vampire Slayer* (1997–2003), *Charmed* (1998–2006), *Angel* (1999–2004), and *Supernatural* (2005–), all of which offered a cheerful mix of attractive young leads acting out traditional horror scenarios against a background of modern rock music. It seemed that some of horror's conventions had finally become a normalized part of television entertainment and were no longer relegated to late-night adult-only timeslots. More recently, horror series produced for cable—notably *Carnivale* (2003–2005) and the *Masters of Horror* anthology show (2005–)—have benefited from a more relaxed attitude to **censorship** and have generated images and stories as hard-edged as anything available in horror cinema.

Other countries have also developed their own televisual horror traditions. During the late 1950s and 1960s, both Argentina and Spain had their own popular horror anthology shows with, respectively, *Obras maestras de terror* (*Masterworks of Horror*) (1958–1960) and *Historias para no dormir* (*Stories to Keep You Awake*) (1966–1968), while novelist Koji Suzuki's much-adapted novel **Ringu** was first adapted for Japanese television as *Ringu: Kanzen-Ban* (1995). Perhaps most notable in this respect is Great Britain, where **Nigel**

Kneale's 1950s Quatermass stories proved potent SF/horror hybrids (later filmed by **Hammer**), and the cult **children**'s series *Doctor Who* (1963–1989; 2005–) regularly deployed scary and horrifying story elements. Kneale would go on to write for television the unnerving **ghost** story *The Stone Tape* (1972) and the anthology series *Beasts* (1976). The British horror company Hammer produced three television anthology series, *Journey to the Unknown* (1968), *Hammer House of Horror* (1980), and *Hammer House of Mystery and Suspense* (1984), while the BBC offered anthologies such as *Out of the Unknown* (1965–1971), *Late Night Horror* (1968), and *Supernatural* (1977). In addition, upmarket adaptations of classic ghost stories by Charles Dickens and M. R. James have proved a perennially popular aspect of British television programming, especially at Christmas. In the 1990s, the BBC also came up with the character of Dr. Terror, who introduced in humorous fashion a series of horror films. If nothing else, this belated revival of the horror host suggested that no televisual horror convention was safe from resurrection.

Horror cinema has occasionally found sinister uses for televisions, usually as part of a technophobic agenda. Monsters attack their hapless victims via the television in *Poltergeist* (1982), *Demoni 2* (1986), *A Nightmare on Elm Street 3: Dream Warriors* (1987), *Ringu* (1998) and *The Ring* (2002), while the television in **David Cronenberg**'s *Videodrome* (1983) is an unsettling presence.

THE TEXAS CHAINSAW MASSACRE (1974). **Tobe Hooper**'s *The Texas Chainsaw Massacre* is one of the most important of all 1970s **American horror** films. This is partly because it presented in a particularly clear form characteristic horror themes of the period, especially in its focus on the monstrous family and its general sense of American society being in a state of dysfunction. More significant is its quality as a film, for it manages to be both artful and utterly relentless, thereby setting a tone rarely seen before in horror cinema. In fact, it delivers a genuinely nightmarish **rural horror** experience as its central characters, unsuspecting young people out for a drive in the countryside, are stalked and killed by a degenerate family of ex-slaughterhouse workers, the most memorable of which turns out to be an overweight, mask-wearing, chainsaw-wielding psychopath who goes by the name of Leatherface. The lengthy scene in which the last surviving woman is tormented by the family during a grotesque dinner party is almost unbearably horrible although, like much of the rest of the film, it also contains moments of very dark humor. These qualities gave *The Texas Chainsaw Massacre* a unique character, and to his credit Hooper did not try to recapture this when he made the **sequel** *The Texas Chainsaw Massacre 2* (1986). Instead he opted for a much gorier treatment that combined some disturbing sequences with moments of broad **comedy**. The result was a grotesque curiosity that resembled Hooper's own bizarre *Eaten Alive (Death Trap)* (1977) more than it did his earlier *Chainsaw* film. Jeff Burr's *Leatherface: Texas Chainsaw Massacre 3* (1990) and *The Return of the Texas Chainsaw Massacre* (1994), directed by Kim Henkel who had co-written the original *Chainsaw* film, were more conventional in their depiction of young innocents stumbling into Leatherface's world. Probably their main point of interest was that both featured early appearances from young actors who would go on to star in considerably more reputable projects, namely Viggo Mortensen in *Leatherface* and Matthew McConaughey and Renee Zellwegger in *The Return*.

A **remake** of *The Texas Chainsaw Massacre* appeared in 2003. As directed by Marcus Nispel, it was slick and atmospheric but, perhaps inevitably, it lacked the intensity of the original. *The Texas Chainsaw Massacre: The Beginning* (2006), a prequel to the remake, was directed by Jonathan Liebesman.

THESIGER, ERNEST (1879–1961). The British actor Ernest Thesiger is best known for the roles he played for his friend, director **James Whale**. He was the lugubrious Horace Femm in Whale's **comedy**-horror *The Old Dark House* (1932) and stole every scene in which he appeared in *Bride of Frankenstein* (1935) as the sinister but enjoyably camp Dr. Pretorious, whose toast of "To a world of gods and monsters" remains one of horror's most resonant lines. Thesiger's British credits include *The Ghoul* (1933), the dark **psychological thriller** *They Drive By Night* (1938) and the **ghost** stories *A Place of One's Own* (1945) and *The Ghosts of Berkeley Square* (1947).

TODD, TONY (1954–). The imposing American actor Tony Todd starred in the 1990 **remake** of **George Romero**'s *Night of the Living Dead* and also featured in *The Crow* (1994). However, his most significant horror role is as the undead Daniel Robitaille, also known as Candyman, in three films, beginning with *Candyman* (1992) and followed by *Candyman: Farewell to the Flesh* (1995) and *Candyman: Day of the Dead* (1999). Although the films varied in terms of quality, Todd's performance consistently combined a sense of nobility with menace. As the sinister Bludworth in *Final Destination* (2000) and *Final Destination 2* (2003), he gave hapless teenagers clues as to how they were going to die, and he also made a cameo appearance in *Wishmaster* (1997). In addition, he has featured in numerous direct-to-video horror releases.

TORTURE. There is something especially disturbing about cinematic scenes of torture, given that these can so nakedly invoke sadistic elements. Such scenes were rare in 1930s and 1940s horror, with the most memorable exception being **Edgar G. Ulmer**'s *The Black Cat* (1934), in which **Bela Lugosi** skins **Boris Karloff** alive (albeit offscreen). Other moments of torture showed up in **Lew Landers**'s *The Raven* (1935) and **Karl Freund**'s *Mad Love* (1935). Later torture scenes—for example, in **Roger Corman**'s *Pit and the Pendulum* (1961) and the **Italian horror** *Il boia scarlatto* (*Bloody Pit of Horror*) (1965)—were more lurid, but it was not until the late 1960s that representations of torture began to exhibit a genuinely disturbing intensity. Distinguished examples of this included **Michael Reeves'** **British horror** *Witchfinder General* (1968), an intelligent but unsettling account of a witchfinder as he tormented his innocent victims, and **Wes Craven**'s controversial rape-revenge drama *The Last House on the Left* (1972), which offered a similarly challenging experience played out this time in a contemporary American setting. Unfortunately, other films purveyed an altogether more exploitative treatment of torture, for example in the notoriously violent German witchfinder film *Hexen bis aufs Blut gequält* (*Mark of the Devil*) (1970). Torture scenes appeared periodically in horror films from the 1970s onwards, sometimes attracting the attentions of the censors but not really registering as an issue of specific concern.

More recently, a small number of horror films has foregrounded torture in a manner that has provoked adverse comment. Dubbed by some critics "torture porn," films such as **Takashi Miike**'s *Ôdishon* (*Audition*) (1999), **Rob Zombie**'s *House of 1000 Corpses* (2003) and

The Devil's Rejects (2005), James Wan's *Saw* (2004) and its three sequels, **Eli Roth**'s *Hostel* (2005) and *Hostel Part 2* (2007), and Greg McLean's **Australian horror** *Wolf Creek* (2005) have unflinchingly portrayed scenes of protracted and appalling suffering. While these scenes clearly involve sadism on the part of the torturers, the extent to which they also invoke sadism from the films' audiences—the main source of concern for critics—remains unclear. One might argue that such films tend to elicit as much a masochistic response as they do a sadistic one, with audiences encouraged to identify with the terrorized victims rather than with the repellent torturers. This does not necessarily render these films positive in any way but it does suggest that if, as some critics have maintained, they are "sick," then their sickness is complex, challenging and worthy of a more open-minded discussion than it has so far received.

TOURNEUR, JACQUES (1904–1977). The director Jacques Tourneur—son of another director, Maurice Tourneur—was born in France but spent most of his career based in the United States. His first major directorial credits were at RKO, where he was arguably the best of the directors who worked on a series of upmarket horror films produced by **Val Lewton**. Tourneur's *Cat People* (1942), which inaugurated the series, was a superbly staged noir-like horror that transformed its potentially silly story—a woman fears that she will turn into a panther if sexually aroused—into something that was both stylish and unsettling, with some highly effective scenes of suspense and shock. As became customary for Lewton, the emphasis was on suggestion, with the panther only briefly glimpsed. The **voodoo**-based drama *I Walked with a Zombie* (1943) was, if anything, even better. A very loose reworking of *Jane Eyre*, it offered what for the time was an unusually intelligent exploration of racial difference, and the atmospheric sequence in which the heroine walks through the fields to a voodoo ceremony is now considered by many horror aficionados to be one of the genre's classic scenes. *The Leopard Man* (1943), Tourneur's final film for Lewton, lacked the resonances of his earlier work, but it was an effective **serial killer** narrative that, as before, featured some impressive suspense setpieces.

Throughout the remainder of the 1940s and 1950s, Tourneur worked in a variety of genres—including film noir (namely the 1947 noir classic *Out of the Past*), **westerns**, and swashbucklers. The British-produced supernatural drama *Night of the Demon* (*Curse of the Demon*) (1957), an adaptation of the M. R. James story "The Casting of the Runes," marked his return to horror. As was the case with the films Tourneur made for Lewton, this combined suspense with intelligence and was one of the most distinguished **British horror** films of the 1950s. Initially Tourneur planned to show only glimpses of the demon, in the manner of Lewton, but the producers insisted on greater explicitness, with the demon depicted clearly in the film's opening sequence. The result was not the disaster that some critics have made it out to be, however. The demon is an impressive creation and, in any event, its initial appearance bestowed a sense of dread on the rest of the narrative. Tourneur's final horror credit was the enjoyable but slight **comedy**-horror *The Comedy of Terrors* (1964), which starred genre luminaries **Boris Karloff, Peter Lorre, Vincent Price,** and **Basil Rathbone**. *See also* AMERICAN HORROR.

TOWERS, HARRY ALAN (1920–). The writer-producer Harry Alan Towers—who sometimes used the name Peter Welbeck—worked regularly in British cinema throughout much of the 1950s and 1960s, but he never contributed directly to the **British horror** movement. However, he did produce the period adventure films *The Face of Fu Manchu* (1965), *The Brides of Fu Manchu* (1966), and *The Vengeance of Fu Manchu* (1967), all of which starred **Christopher Lee** and featured horror-like elements. Later in the 1960s, he relocated to continental Europe and made several horror films with **Jesus Franco,** namely the Christopher Lee vehicles *El Conde Dracula* (*Count Dracula*) (1970), *Il trono di fuoco* (*Night of the Blood Monster, The Bloody Judge*) (1970), and two more Fu Manchu films, *The Blood of Fu Manchu* (1968) and *The Castle of Fu Manchu* (1969). Towers' other notable horror credit from this period was an adaptation of *The Picture of Dorian Gray* entitled simply *Dorian Gray* (1970). Since then he has produced *Howling IV: The Original Nightmare* (1988), **Edgar Allan Poe** adaptations *The House of Usher* (1988), *Masque of the Red Death* (1990), and *Buried Alive* (1990), the Jekyll and Hyde film *Edge of Sanity* (1989), a version of *The Phantom of the Opera* (1989) starring **Robert Englund,** *The Mummy Lives* (1993), and two **Tobe Hooper**-directed films, *Night Terrors* (1993) and *The Mangler*

(1995). *Dorian* (2001), Towers' most recent genre credit, was yet another adaptation of *The Picture of Dorian Gray*.

TROMA. The Troma production setup was formed by Lloyd Kaufman and Michael Herz in 1974. Initially it specialized in comedies but switched to horror with *The Toxic Avenger* in 1985. This low-budget effort combined **gore**, violence, over-the-top acting, and self-parodying humor in a manner that seemed designed to win it cult status. Three **sequels** followed, along with the similarly cheap, gory and cheerful *Class of Nuke 'm High* (1986), which also generated two sequels, as well as numerous other exploitation projects combining action with **comedy**. Troma has also distributed films from other sources, among them the Belgian-produced *Les mémés cannibales* (1988), re-titled as the more marketable *Rabid Grannies*, and *Stuff Stephanie in the Incinerator* (1989). The company has acquired a devoted **fan** following, although, as is so often the case with cult attractions, the appeal of its product can seem baffling to the uninitiated.

– U –

ULMER, EDGAR G. (1904–1972). Edgar Ulmer was born in Moravia, but most of his early filmmaking experience was acquired in Germany, where he worked as a production designer for both Fritz Lang and **F. W. Murnau** and also collaborated with **Kurt Siodmak**, **Robert Siodmak**, Billy Wilder, and Fred Zinnemann on the charming semi-**documentary** *Menschen am Sontag* (*People on Sunday*) (1930). His Hollywood career proved less distinguished than this, although since his death some of his American films have attracted a significant cult following. His only mainstream horror film was the extraordinary *The Black Cat* (1934), which was one of the most perverse of all **Universal's** 1930s horrors. The film's intimations of necrophilia, and the scene in which **Boris Karloff** is skinned alive by **Bela Lugosi**, have earned it a certain notoriety, but its striking Bauhaus-influenced visual style, and its mordant sense of humor, also made it distinct from anything else being produced by Universal at the time. Unfortunately it marked the highpoint of a career that—apparently as a result of Ulmer's eloping with the wife of a Universal executive—would subsequently be played out largely in the low-budget exploitation sector. Horror titles *Bluebeard* (1944) and *The Man from Planet X* (1951) contained effective moments, but *Daughter of Dr. Jekyll* (1957) and *The Amazing Transparent Man* (1960) proved less rewarding. Ulmer's reputation, such as it is, seems to rest more on *The Black Cat*, along with the crime drama *Detour* (1945) and the melodrama *Ruthless* (1948), than it does on his other horror work. See also AMERICAN HORROR.

UNIVERSAL. Universal was one of the smaller Hollywood studios, but it was the most important so far as the development of the **American horror** film during the 1930s and 1940s was concerned. The company had achieved some success in the 1920s with the **Lon Chaney** vehicles *The Hunchback of Notre Dame* (1923) and *The Phantom of the Opera* (1925) and the **comedy**-thriller *The Cat and the Canary* (1927), all of which are now usually thought of as horror but which were not marketed as such at the time of their initial release. The cycle of horror production inaugurated by Universal's *Dracula* and *Frankenstein* in 1931 was much more focused on **gothic** thrills and suspense than those earlier silent productions. It helped to establish many of the key themes and conventions for the horrors that were to come, from Universal and from elsewhere, as well as discovering two horror stars, **Bela Lugosi** and **Boris Karloff**. Apparently studio founder Carl Laemmle disliked this type of film, and it was his son Julius Laemmle, also known as Carl Laemmle Jr., who was the driving force behind the stream of horror or horror-themed films that emerged after the commercial success of *Dracula* and *Frankenstein*, among them *The Mummy* (1932), *Murders in the Rue Morgue* (1932), *The Old Dark House* (1932), *The Invisible Man* (1933), *The Black Cat* (1934), *The Raven* (1935), *Werewolf of London* (1935), *Bride of Frankenstein* (1935), and *Dracula's Daughter* (1936). Although these were all marketed as Universal horror, they comprised a diverse group in terms of setting, tone and quality, with **James Whale**'s tongue-in-cheek fantasies *The Old Dark House* and *Bride of Frankenstein* existing alongside **Edgar G. Ulmer**'s modernist-styled *The Black Cat* as well as the more stolid *The Raven* and *Werewolf of London*.

After *Dracula's Daughter*, there was a short hiatus in Universal horror production, broken by the handsomely staged *Son of Frankenstein* (1939). The films that followed tended to be lower-budgeted, and a reliance on **sequels** was also more evident than it had been in the 1930s. Universal was in fact the first studio to perfect what would later be known as the horror franchise, churning out series of films based on a returning character. Frankenstein's monster returned in *The Ghost of Frankenstein* (1942), Dracula was back in *Son of Dracula* (1943), *The Mummy's Hand* (1940) generated three sequels, while *The Wolf Man* (1941) introduced a werewolf who would subsequently confront other Universal horror monsters in *Frankenstein Meets the Wolf Man* (1943), *House of Frankenstein* (1944), and *House of Dracula* (1945); there was also another version of *Phantom of the Opera* (1943). The non-American Lugosi and Karloff had been Universal's main 1930s stars, but it was the solidly American **Lon Chaney Jr.** who filled that role in the 1940s, playing the Wolf Man, Dracula, Frankenstein's monster and the mummy, and the tone of these films also shifted away from the exoticism often apparent in the 1930s work and acquired a more prosaic quality. A certain garishness was also evident, not least in what might seem to contemporary audiences to be the very questionable casting of disfigured actor **Rondo Hatton** as a monster in *House of Horrors* (1946).

The critical reputation of 1930s Universal horror now seems unassailable. It undoubtedly led the way in establishing much of what we now think of as the horror genre. The status of 1940s Universal horror is less clear. It has often been unfavorably compared with the more mature horror work being done by producer **Val Lewton** at RKO, and its sequelized nature has not endeared it with those who associate sequels with a crass commercialism. Matters are not helped by the way in which, from the late 1940s onwards, Universal delivered its monsters into the none-too-respectful hands of **comedy** duo **Bud Abbott** and **Lou Costello** in a series of films, the first and best of which was *Abbott and Costello Meet Frankenstein* (1948). However, these later Universal horrors still possess a degree of inventiveness, and their sheer vulgarity is also sometimes a welcome relief after the more tasteful pleasures offered by the films of Val Lewton.

– V –

VADIM, ROGER (1928–2000). The French director Roger Vadim was best known internationally for *Et Dieu . . . créa la femme* (*And God Created Woman*) (1956) and *Barbarella* (1968) and was not widely regarded as a horror specialist. However, he did have two significant genre credits. The most important of these was *Et mourir de plaisir* (*Blood and Roses*) (1960), a stylish adaptation of J. Sheridan LeFanu's lesbian **vampire** story "Carmilla." Vadim also contributed an episode to the **Edgar Allan Poe anthology** *Histoires extraordinaires* (*Tales of Mystery and Imagination, Spirits of the Dead*) (1968), although his and Louis Malle's stories were overshadowed by Federico Fellini's brilliant "Toby Dammit." *See also* FRENCH HORROR.

VAMPIRES. Folklore and literature have given us many different types of vampire. However, so far as the early history of the horror film is concerned, there was only one, and his name was Count **Dracula**. Bram Stoker's 1897 novel *Dracula* was successfully adapted first on the stage and then in the cinema, with **Universal**'s *Dracula* (1931), and there were only a few challenges to his dominance. Notable among these was **Lon Chaney**'s turn as someone suspected of being a vampire in the now presumed lost film *London After Midnight* (1927), **Carl Theodor Dreyer**'s dream-like *Vampyr* (1931), Universal's lesbian-tinged *Dracula's Daughter* (1936), and the independent productions *The Vampire Bat* (1933) and *Dead Men Walk* (1943). From the early 1930s through to the 1960s, however, vampires other than Dracula often resembled the Count in their superficial charm, their sexual motivations, and their aristocratic demeanor. **Bela Lugosi**, the original screen Dracula, played the Dracula-like vampire Count Mora in *Mark of the Vampire* (1935) and the equally Dracula-like Count Tesla in *The Return of the Vampire* (1944), while the vampiric Count Lavud caused mayhem in the **Mexican horror** *El vampiro* (*The Vampire*) (1957). As for 1960s **British horror**, Baron Meinster stood in for Dracula in *The Brides of Dracula* (1960) and the evil Dr. Ravna took on the role in *Kiss of the Vampire* (1962), both of which were **Hammer** productions, and Count von Krolock was the main vampire in **Roman Polanski**'s **comedy**-horror *Dance of the Vampires* (*The Fearless Vampire Killers*) (1967). Even when contemporary vampire stories were in vogue in the 1970s, aristocratic vampires survived in the form of Count Yorga in *Count Yorga, Vampire* (1970) and Prince Mamuwalde in *Blacula* (1972).

Alternative forms of vampirism began to appear in significant numbers from the 1950s onwards, with this development arguably a reflection of the growing internationalization of horror production in the period. A relaxation in **censorship** also permitted a more explicit and sensational engagement with the sexuality of the vampire. Given this, it was perhaps no coincidence that female vampires, of the clothed and unclothed kind, became more prominent than before in the genre, especially with European filmmakers who drew upon both J. Sheridan LeFanu's novel "Carmilla" and the antics of medieval mass murderer Countess **Elizabeth Bathory** for inspiration. Films included **Riccardo Freda**'s *I vampiri* (*The Devil's Commandment*) (1956), **Mario Bava**'s *La maschera del demonio* (*The Mask of Satan, Revenge of the Vampire, Black Sunday*) (1960), **Roger Vadim**'s *Et mourir de plaisir* (*Blood and Roses*) (1960), **Harry Kümel**'s *Les lèvres rouges* (*Daughters of Darkness*) (1971), and from the United States, Stephanie Rothman's *The Velvet Vampire* (1971). In France, **Jean Rollin** made a series of such films, beginning with *Le viol de vampire* (*Queen of the Vampires*) (1968), while Hammer explored the world of nude lesbian vampires in *The Vampire Lovers* (1970) and *Lust for a Vampire* (1971) and **José Larraz** offered yet more explicitness in *Vampyres* (1974). Meanwhile, vampires of both sexes featured as stock villains in Mexican and **Spanish horror**, the director **Michio Yamamoto** offered an idiosyncratic Japanese take on vampirism with three horrors from the early 1970s, and a series of **Chinese horror** films showcased hopping vampires.

Vampirism as **disease** was explored by the **American horror** *The Vampire* (1957) and by *The Last Man on Earth* (1964), one of three adaptations of **Richard Matheson**'s groundbreaking vampire novel *I am Legend*, although the theme of infection was developed more successfully by **George Romero** in his revisionary **zombie** film *Night of the Living Dead* (1968). Romero was also responsible for the revisionary vampire film *Martin* (1977), which effectively deconstructed the classic vampire myth through its depiction of a boy who believes that he is a vampire but has to resort to using a hypodermic in order to subdue his victims.

The rise of the **slasher** film in the late 1970s temporarily marginalized traditional horror monsters such as the vampire, although *Fright Night* (1985), *Fright Night—Part 2* (1988), and *The Lost Boys* (1987), along with *Buffy the Vampire Slayer* (1992) and the **television** series it generated, reintroduced vampires into the world of **teenage horror**. Other vampire films began to explore vampirism as a kind of lifestyle choice that, in certain respects at least, had some attractive features. Key to this were the vampire novels of **Anne Rice**, adapted for the screen as *Interview with the Vampire* (1994) and *Queen of the Damned* (2002) and the television series *Angel* (1999–2004), which featured a vampire as its hero. Kathryn Bigelow offered *Near Dark* (1987), an innovative horror-**western** about an outlaw vampire family, while the idea of vampires having an alternative but viable society was developed by *Blade* (1998), *Blade 2* (2002), *Blade: Trinity* (2004), *Underworld* (2003), and *Underworld: Evolution* (2006).

The film vampire might once have been a strange, exotic creature, but he or she is now much more familiar—still threatening, perhaps, but also capable of near-normality. The barrier between the monster and us has, in this instance at least, become decidedly permeable.

VAN SLOAN, EDWARD (1881–1964). The American actor Edward Van Sloan first played the role of **vampire**-hunter Dr. Abraham Van Helsing in the 1927 Broadway stage production of *Dracula* that featured **Bela Lugosi** as the vampire. He went on to repeat the part in **Universal**'s *Dracula* (1931) and its **sequel** *Dracula's Daughter* (1936), and also featured as a scientist in *Frankenstein* (1931) and *The Mummy* (1932). Often bespectacled, he projected a quiet and decent authority that contrasted with some of the more histrionic performances apparent in these films. He also appeared in the **Boris Karloff** vehicles *The Black Room* (1935) and *Before I Hang* (1940), in both cases predictably cast as a doctor.

VEIDT, CONRAD (1893–1943). The German actor Conrad Veidt found worldwide fame during the 1930s in a series of starring and supporting roles in American and British cinema, including the villainous Major Strasser in *Casablanca* (1942). However, before he quit Germany in the early 1930s—he was a fervent anti-Nazi—he had appeared in a number of horror-like productions, many of them influenced by German **Expressionism**. The most influential of these was *Das Cabinet des Dr. Caligari* (*The Cabinet of Dr. Caligari*) (1919), in which he played the somnambulist Cesare in an expressive manner that arguably influenced **Boris Karloff**'s performance as the Monster in *Frankenstein* (1931). He also starred in *Der Januskopf* (1920), **F. W. Murnau**'s now presumed lost version of the **Dr. Jekyll and Mr. Hyde** story (which featured an early appearance from **Bela Lugosi**), and the **surgical horror** story *Orlacs Hände* (*The Hands of Orlac*) (1924), which would later be remade as the **Peter Lorre** vehicle *Mad Love* (1935). The disturbing grin fixed permanently on his face in the American production *The Man Who Laughs* (1928), which was directed by fellow German **Paul Leni**, apparently provided the inspiration for the character of the Joker in the Batman **comics**. In addition, he featured in the horror-themed *Unheimliche Geschichten* (*Eerie Tales*) (1919), *Nachtgestalten* (*Figures of the Night*) (1920), *Der Graf von Cagliostro* (*The Count of Cagliostro*) (1921), *Das Wachsfigurenkabinett* (***Waxworks***) (1924), and a **remake** of the 1913 Paul Wegener classic *Der Student von Prag* (*The Student of Prague*) (1926), as well as starring in and directing *Wahnsinn* (***Madness***) (1919).

VERNON, HOWARD (1914–1996). The screen career of Swiss-born actor Howard Vernon—real name Mario Lippert—began auspiciously with appearances in films by such luminaries as Jean-Luc Godard, Fritz Lang and Jean-Pierre Melville. However, his increasing association with low-budget exploitation and horror led to roles that made little of his talents, and he never made the transition to horror stardom. Vernon was a regular in the films of exploitation specialist **Jesus Franco**. He was the villainous Dr. Orloff in *Gritos en la noche* (*The Awful Dr. Orloff*) (1962), a part he would play on several more occasions for other directors. He was an unmemorable **Dracula** in Franco's *Drácula contra Frankenstein* (*Dracula vs. Frankenstein*) (1972) and he also worked with **Jean Rollin**—on the inferior *Le lac des morts vivants* (***Zombie Lake***) (1981)—and **Walerian Borowczyk** on *Docteur Jekyll et les femmes* (*Dr. Jekyll and His Women*) (1981). Other credits are too numerous to list here. Sadly few of them are at all distinguished.

VON SYDOW, MAX (1929–). The distinguished Swedish actor Max von Sydow has received critical plaudits for the films he made with director **Ingmar Bergman**. Some of these dealt with horror-like material—notably *Det sjunde inseglet* (*The Seventh Seal*) (1957), *Ansiktet* (*The Magician, The Face*) (1958), and *Vargtimmen* (*Hour of the Wolf*) (1968)—while the rape revenge drama *Jungfrukällan* (*The Virgin Spring*) (1960) was remade by **Wes Craven** as the **American horror** film *The Last House on the Left* (1972). However, it was von Sydow's performance as Father Merrin in *The Exorcist* (1973) that represents his major contribution to the horror genre. He was only in his mid-forties at the time of production but successfully conveyed both the physical frailty and the moral strength of this aged character. In the midst of the narrative's increasingly lurid and shocking events, he provided some much-needed gravitas. He reprised the role in *Exorcist II—The Heretic* (1977) and later switched sides to play the devilish Leland Gaunt in the **Stephen King** adaptation *Needful Things* (1993). He was also a police inspector in **Dario Argento**'s **giallo** thriller *Nonhosonno* (*Sleepless*) (2001).

VOODOO. Horror cinema has shown little interest in the historical origins of the voodoo **religion**. Instead voodoo in horror is usually associated with **zombies**, although after *Night of the Living Dead* (1968), this association has become less evident, in zombie films at least. Those non-zombie horrors that represent voodoo or voodoo-like practices as a threat emanating from black or minority ethnic communities inevitably flirt with racism, although they can also provide compelling portrayals of white complacency. Such ambiguous films include *Dr. Terror's House of Horrors* (1964), *The Possession of Joel Delaney* (1972), *The Believers* (1987), *Angel Heart* (1987), and *The Skeleton Key* (2005). Some of the trappings of voodoo—for example, voodoo **dolls**—show up in, among others, *Night of the Eagle* (*Burn, Witch, Burn!*) (1962), *The Witches* (1966), *The House that Dripped Blood* (1970), and *Child's Play* (1988), although this tends to be more in the context of stories of **witchcraft** and magic.

– W –

WAGGNER, GEORGE (1894–1984). During the 1940s, the American producer-director George Waggner, who had earlier specialized in **westerns**, made a series of well-crafted horror films for **Universal**. He started by directing *Man Made Monster* (1941)—a **mad scientist** story featuring **Lon Chaney Jr.** in his first horror role—and *Horror Island* (1941). Next came his best-known film, *The Wolf Man* (1941). This was a fresh start for Universal's **werewolf** cycle after *Werewolf of London* (1935), and it established Chaney as the Wolf Man, a part he would repeat on several occasions. Waggner's direction for all of these films was unfussy and generally eschewed the expressionistic devices that had characterized much 1930s **American horror** production. Subsequently he acted as producer on *The Ghost of Frankenstein* (1942), *Phantom of the Opera* (1943), and *Frankenstein Meets the Wolf Man* (1943) before returning to direction with the **Boris Karloff** vehicle *The Climax* (1944). From the 1950s onwards, he worked mainly for **television**, and directed some episodes of the Karloff-hosted series *The Veil* (1958).

WALKER, PETE (1939–). The producer-director Pete Walker was an important figure in 1970s **British horror**. At a time when the escapist fare offered by **Hammer** horror was becoming exhausted, Walker introduced a contemporary edge and a rawness into the genre. With a background in low-budget exploitation cinema (he specialized in sex films before turning to horror), he was well-suited to the more explicit and exploitative sector of horror production. However, his horror films at their best also possessed an inventiveness and an integrity that lifted them above work by other directors from this period.

Walker's *Die Screaming, Marianne* (1971) might have sounded like it was a horror film but was actually a fairly straightforward thriller. *The Flesh and Blood Show* (1972), by contrast, combined a whodunnit structure with sufficient violence, **gore** and grotesquerie for it to be thought of as horror. Its narrative—in which an old, psychotic actor terrorizes some helpless young people—also introduced what would become a key theme in Walker's later horror work, namely the attack on youth culture and lifestyles by an older generation.

The three films for which Walker is best known followed in the mid-1970s. In *House of Whipcord* (1974), young women are kidnapped and confined to a brutal private prison where they are punished for their "sins," in *Frightmare* (1974), a cannibalistic old lady kills the young and eats their flesh, and in *House of Mortal Sin* (*The Confessional*) (1975) a corrupt priest ruthlessly murders anyone who threatens to uncover his crimes. These are all relentlessly gory and grim narratives, and good rarely prevails in them. One of the attractive heroines of *House of Whipcord* is eventually hanged, while in the conclusions of *Frightmare* and *House of Mortal Sin*, the murderers are left free and triumphant.

The nihilism apparent here is comparable with that found in some 1970s **American horror** films and can similarly be seen as a response to the social unrest that characterized this period. At the same time, Walker's films seem very British, in their sense of place, their precise attention to social and class divisions and etiquette, and in a dry sense of humor that occasionally surfaces amidst all the horror.

The **psychological thrillers** *Schizo* (1976) and *The Comeback* (1978) were more conventional and lacked the intense focus of Walker's earlier work (although the presence of middle-of-the-road crooner Jack Jones in *The Comeback* gives it a certain curiosity value). *House of the Long Shadows* (1983), Walker's final film, was different from anything he had done before. A loose adaptation of the hoary 1913 novel *Seven Keys to Baldpate*, this haunted house mystery exuded nostalgia for an older type of horror cinema. The presence in it of august horror stars **Peter Cushing, John Carradine, Christopher Lee,** and **Vincent Price** helped with the marketing, but the film never found an audience, perhaps because it was so out of step with a horror cinema that in the early 1980s was becoming increasingly focused on teenagers.

In the mid-1980s, Walker withdrew from the film industry and became a successful property developer.

WALLACE, TOMMY LEE (1949–). The early part of Tommy Lee Wallace's career in cinema involved his working for **John Carpenter.** He was art director on Carpenter's *Dark Star* (1974) and *Assault on Precinct 13* (1976) and then became production designer and editor for the director's *Halloween* (1978) and *The Fog* (1980). It was perhaps not surprising then that his directorial debut was the Carpenter-produced *Halloween III: Season of the Witch* (1982), for which he also received a screenplay credit (as a result of **Nigel Kneale**, the original writer, having his own name removed from the credits); in the same year he also wrote the screenplay for another **sequel,** *Amityville II: The Possession* (1982). More **sequels** followed, with Wallace writing and directing two

vampire films, *Fright Night Part 2* (1988) and the Carpenter-produced *Vampires: Los Muertos* (2002). Wallace also co-wrote and directed the **Stephen King television** miniseries *It* (1990). Most of his other non-horror credits have been for television. *See also* AMERICAN HORROR.

WALTON, FRED. *When a Stranger Calls* (1979), writer-director Fred Walton's feature debut, is the classic screen rendition of the urban legend in which a babysitter discovers that a series of menacing phonecalls are being made from inside the house in which she is babysitting. Walton handled the suspense well and then took the story in an unexpected direction by exploring the motivations of the killer. His next horror, *April Fool's Day* (1986), was an effective late entry into the **slasher** cycle. Walton's last genre credit to date was the made-for-**television sequel** *When a Stranger Calls Back* (1993). His original version was remade by Simon West in 2006, although the **remake** lacked the impact of the original. *See also* AMERICAN HORROR.

WARREN, NORMAN J. (1942–). Like fellow British filmmaker **Pete Walker**, the director Norman J. Warren began by making sex films before switching to horror in the 1970s. His career was not as sustained as Walker's, however, and his films have not since attracted the substantial cult following generated by Walker's best. *Satan's Slave* (1976), Warren's horror debut, was a brisk but minor Satanic thriller. *Prey* (1977) was better. This bizarre tale of alien invasion and **cannibalism**, which featured a lesbian couple as its main protagonists and a scene in which the male alien cross-dresses, could have easily become a piece of camp nonsense, but Warren treated the material with sustained seriousness and managed to generate a doom-filled atmosphere. *Terror* (1978) offered a comparably slight story, this time dealing with a witch's curse, but here Warren was in a more playful mood, with some effective humor and self-reflexive moments.

Warren's subsequent films are all minor, although the *Alien*-inspired **science fiction**-horror *Inseminoid* (1980) merits a mention, if only because of the way in which it manages to be both very nasty and very silly.

Warren's other credits include *Outer Touch* (1979), *Gunpowder* (1984), and *Bloody New Year* (1986). *See also* BRITISH HORROR.

WAXWORKS. Horror films have regularly exploited the sinister blurring of the animate and inanimate found in waxwork museums. An early example of this was provided by **Paul Leni**'s *Das Wachsfigurenkabinett* (*Waxworks*) (1924), but the most influential wax-horror was *Mystery of the Wax Museum* (1933), in which mad sculptor **Lionel Atwill** constructed his wax statues around the bodies of real people; it was remade as *House of Wax* (1953). Other waxwork-based horror was provided by *The Frozen Ghost* (1945), *La casa del terror* (*House of Terror*) (1960), *Santo en el museo de cera* (*Santo in the Wax Museum*) (1963), *Chamber of Horrors* (1966), *Nightmare in Wax* (1969), *The House that Dripped Blood* (1970), *Terror in the Wax Museum* (1973), *Tourist Trap* (1979), *Waxwork* (1988), and *Maschera di cera* (*Wax Mask*) (1997). The melting of wax figures in *Mystery of the Wax Museum*, with all its disturbing connotations of bodily disfigurement, was given an innovative turn in the recent *House of Wax* (2005), in which the wax museum itself was made of wax and melted spectacularly.

WEEKS, STEPHEN (1948–). The British director Stephen Weeks was one of a number of young filmmakers who came to the fore in **British horror** of the late 1960s and early 1970s. However, Weeks' career never really took flight. *I, Monster* (1970), his feature debut, was a potentially interesting version of the *Dr. Jekyll and Mr. Hyde* story made for **Amicus**, although it was hampered by an unimaginative screenplay and a 3D shooting process that was abandoned during production. Next came the fantasy adventure *Gawain and the Green Knight* (1973), which was followed by the atmospheric period supernatural drama *Ghost Story* (1974). Weeks did not make another film for ten years; the resulting production was an unsuccessful **remake** of his own *Gawain and the Green Knight* entitled *Sword of the Valiant* (1984). Since then, Weeks has worked mainly as a restorer of historic buildings.

WEIR, PETER (1944–). While the Australian director Peter Weir is not generally considered a horror director, some of his early films did draw upon horror-like subjects and imagery in their depiction of an alienating Australian landscape. The narrative of *The Cars That Ate Paris* (1974)—in which the inhabitants of a small town deliberately lure outsiders into staged car crashes—was pure **rural horror**, although Weir's comic treatment softened the disturbing elements. *Picnic at Hanging Rock* (1975), Australian cinema's first major international success, was a haunting study of the disappearance of some adolescent girls while on a school trip. Ostensibly a period drama, its refusal to give any explanation for the disappearance, along with its oneiric atmosphere, bestowed an aura of dark fantasy on the proceedings. *The Last Wave* (1977) was equally doom-laden and a more obvious example of **apocalyptic horror**, as a lawyer investigating a murder discovers ominous signs of a forthcoming natural disaster. As with *Picnic*, Weir blurs distinctions between reality and fantasy and creates an intense and unnerving atmosphere. Since the 1970s, he has worked mainly in the United States. *See also* AUSTRALIAN HORROR.

WEREWOLVES. Unlike **Dracula** or **Frankenstein**, the werewolf in horror cinema lacks any major literary antecedents upon which it can draw. Its roots lie instead primarily in folklore, although, with a few exceptions, horror films have made little use of folkloric beliefs, preferring instead to conjure up their own origins. An American film entitled *The Werewolf* was released in 1913, but the first major cinematic treatment of the werewolf was **Universal**'s *Werewolf of London* (1935), which was directed by Stuart Walker. In effect, this was a reworking of the **Dr. Jekyll and Mr. Hyde** story, with its principal lycanthrope a respectable older man who periodically becomes, in true Jekyll style, a ravening beast (although the sexual dimension of Jekyll is marginalized).

When Universal returned to the werewolf in *The Wolf Man* (1941)—solidly directed by **George Waggner** from a **Kurt Siodmak** script—it opted for an approach that stressed the helplessness and pathos of the lycanthrope. Lawrence Talbot (**Lon Chaney Jr.** in a career-defining role) is bitten by a werewolf and becomes subject to terrifying transformations. His response is one of maudlin despair, and he spends the remainder of the film and the **sequels** *Frankenstein Meets the Wolf Man* (1943) and *House of Frankenstein* (1944) working out how to die. He succeeds in the latter, although miraculously he is back in *House of Dracula* (1945), where, equally miraculously, he is cured in what for him is an unprecedented happy ending. Sadly, however, Talbot/Chaney returns to cursed mode for his final appearance in the **comedy**-horror *Abbott and Costello Meet Frankenstein* (1948). *The Wolf Man*, and its sequels, established a particular image of the werewolf far more successfully than had *Werewolf of London*, to the extent that, like other classic Universal monster designs, it provided a baseline for later revisions of the monster's appearance. **Makeup** artist **Jack Pierce**, who worked on both films, fashioned a hirsute look for Chaney, with hair covering the face, hands and feet, although this version of the monster remained recognizably a man. This look was also adopted for the werewolf in Columbia's *The Return of the Vampire* (1944), and in the 1960s would form the basis for British and Spanish versions of the werewolf. By contrast, non-Universal werewolf projects, Twentieth Century-Fox's *The Undying Monster* (1942) and Columbia's *Cry of the Werewolf* (1944), the latter featuring a female werewolf, tried to differentiate themselves from the Universal approach, while Universal's *She-Wolf of London* (1946) turned out not to be a werewolf film at all. However, it was Chaney's self-pitying hairy monster that caught the public's imagination.

Since the Universal Wolf Man films, there has been only one other substantial werewolf cycle. The actor **Jacinto Molina**, who worked under the name Paul Naschy, starred as the lycanthrope Count Waldemar Daninsky in a series of **Spanish horror** films, beginning with *La marca del hombre-lobo* (*The Mark of the Werewolf*) (1968). Daninsky was very much in the Lon Chaney mold, albeit more brooding and surrounded by much more explicit representations of both sex and violence. Other than these films, werewolf dramas were few and far between from the 1950s through into the 1970s. The American productions *The Werewolf* (1956) and *I Was a Teenage Werewolf* (1957) both featured the werewolf as a victim of a **mad scientist**, while Chaney donned his wolf makeup again for the indifferent **Mexican horror** film *La casa del terror* (*The House of Terror*) (1960). **British horror** also engaged only sporadically with the werewolf in this period. **Hammer**'s *The Curse of the Werewolf* (1961), its sole werewolf film, dealt more explicitly than ever before with the sexual dimension of lycanthropy, with one of the werewolf's transformations taking place in a brothel. **Amicus**, another British horror company, also dabbled in the subject, with a werewolf story in its horror **anthology** *Dr. Terror's House of Horrors* (1964) as well as the feature *The Beast Must Die* (1974), although in both cases the whodunnit-like emphasis was on trying to guess who the werewolf was from a series of possible suspects, while the Tyburn company offered a belated British period horror treatment in *Legend of the Werewolf* (1975). 1970s **American horror** cinema had little use for the werewolf, although a lycanthrope did enter the White House in the comedy-horror *Werewolf of Washington* (1973).

The 1980s saw a modest revival in cinematic lycanthrophy. **John Landis's** *An American Werewolf in London* (1981) and **Joe Dante's** *The Howling* (1981) wittily updated the werewolf story, both through humorous references to classic werewolf films and through groundbreaking transformation scenes engineered by, respectively, **Rick Baker** and **Rob Bottin**. Gone were the obtrusive fades from one stage of makeup to another that had characterized the Chaney films; instead transitions from the human form to something more animalistic than the Wolf Man seemed to take place before our astonished eyes. **Neil Jordan's** *The Company of Wolves* (1984) opted for a more fairytale-like approach in its exploration of connections between lycanthrophy and male sexuality. As had *I Was a Teenage Werewolf* before them, the comedies *Full Moon High* (1981) and *Teen-Wolf* (1985) also discovered resonances between the transformations of lycanthrophy and those of male adolescence.

Since the 1980s, the situation has become yet more fragmented. There have been several sequels to *The Howling* while *An American Werewolf in London* has also generated one rather belated follow-up, *An American Werewolf in Paris* (1997). The Canadian *Ginger Snaps* trilogy (2000–2004) has explored the theme of the female werewolf. The werewolf was also a guest monster in **Stephen Sommers'** *Van Helsing* (2004), and **Wes Craven** has offered a werewolf-based whodunnit in *Cursed* (2005). Perhaps the most original recent version of the werewolf story is the compelling Spanish production *Romasanta* (2004), which, as directed by Francisco Plaza, deals with a **serial killer** who believes that he is a werewolf. Unlike most werewolf fictions, it is based on a true story.

WESTERNS. It is well known that the horror genre shares themes and imagery with both the **science fiction** and crime genres. Its connection with the western is more surprising, given that the western is usually seen as a robustly outdoors-based format in comparison with horror's claustrophobic nature. However, a number of horror films have operated as degraded westerns, exploring places or historical moments where the pioneering ideals embodied in the western have become introverted to the point of insanity. One thinks here of Stanley Kubrick's *The Shining* (1980) and Antonia Bird's *Ravenous* (1999), both of which reference the real-life Donner Party incident from the 1840s, in which a party of American settlers resorted to **cannibalism**. Kathryn Bigelow's *Near Dark* (1987) also used western conventions in its depiction of the modern-day exploits of a **vampire** band of outlaws. More conventional, if bizarre, generic hybridity was provided by *Billy the Kid versus Dracula* (1966) and *Jesse James meets Frankenstein's Daughter* (1966). Vampires also showed up in *Curse of the Undead* (1959) and *Sundown: the Vampire in Retreat* (1991), while *Grim Prairie Tales* (1990) was a western-based horror **anthology**. Operating from within the western idiom, some of Clint Eastwood's films have contained supernatural or **gothic** elements, notably *Beguiled* (1971), *High Plains Drifter* (1973), and *Pale Rider* (1985).

WHALE, JAMES (1889–1957). The director James Whale is often seen as one of the founding fathers of **American horror** cinema, although he only made four films that could be described as horror, and two of those were marginal cases. He was born in England and, after military service in World War I, worked in the British theater. His breakthrough success came in the late 1920s with his direction of the war play *Journey's End*. Subsequently, he brought the play to Broadway and, in 1930, directed the film version in Hollywood for **Universal**, following this with the superior tearjerker *Waterloo Bridge* (1931).

Frankenstein (1931), Universal's follow-up to **Tod Browning**'s *Dracula* (1931), was originally due to be directed by **Robert Florey** and to star **Bela Lugosi**, but both withdrew from the project and Whale took over. As he would with all his horror films, he looked to British actors, casting *Journey's End* star **Colin Clive** as Frankenstein and an obscure bit-part actor by the name of **Boris Karloff** as the Monster. The resulting film was far more consistent than *Dracula* had been and still retains a good deal of its dramatic power today. Like many 1930s American horror films, it drew upon German **Expressionism**, both in its style—especially its shadowy lighting and its tilted camera angles—and its iconography. Its laboratory creation scene owed something to Fritz Lang's **science fiction** masterpiece *Metropolis* (1927), and its conceptualization of the Monster was equally indebted to **Conrad Veidt**'s somnambulist in *Das Cabinet des Dr. Caligari* (*The Cabinet of Dr. Caligari*) (1919) and Paul Wegener's **Golem** in *Der Golem, wie er in die Welt kam* (*The Golem*) (1920). But Whale also made the Monster an intensely sympathetic figure whose monstrous acts—he does kill people in the course of the film—were marginalized, with the emphasis instead on the way in which the society through which the Monster moved misunderstood him. Some horror historians have related this to the 1930s American Depression, arguing that the Monster's powerlessness, along with the fact that he dressed like a hobo, made him a potent identificatory figure for socially disempowered audiences. Other critics have pointed to Whale's gayness as a potential explanation for the focus on the Monster's social exclusion. However, no single explanation seems adequate to the complex and resonant drama fashioned by Whale and his collaborators.

The Old Dark House (1932) and The Invisible Man (1933), Whale's next two genre films, are both often classified as horror, although this seems to have more to do with Whale's association with the genre, Karloff's presence in *The Old Dark House* and the **mad scientist** elements in *The Invisible Man* than it has with the actual content of the films themselves. *The Old Dark House*, adapted from a J. B. Priestley novel and set in Great Britain, saw Whale delighting in the eccentric Femm household, into which some cosmopolitan travellers are driven by a storm. It is in certain respects an early example of **rural horror**, but the stress throughout is on **comedy**, with the few chilling elements —notably Karloff's brooding performance as the mute butler, and the discovery of the homicidal maniac locked away in the house—all the more effective for their isolation. *The Invisible Man*, from H. G. Wells' novel and also set in Britain, also offered humorous encounters with rural eccentrics. The main narrative—a Frankenstein-like affair in which a scientist (played by **Claude Rains**) is driven insane by an unwise experiment—was rather conventional. The joy of the film was in its stylized depiction of British village life, along with what for the time were state of the art special effects.

Although Whale was initially reluctant to return to horror, his final work in the genre is now widely considered to be the greatest of all 1930s American horror films. *Bride of Frankenstein* (1935), the first horror **sequel**, revisited the creation scenes and Monster pathos of the first film but added in the emphasis on eccentricity from *The Old Dark House* and *The Invisible Man*. Its combination of humor and horror was both remarkably inventive and well judged. It cheerfully paralleled the sufferings of the Monster with the sufferings of Jesus Christ and also played up what—to modern eyes at least—seems a potentially homoerotic relationship between Frankenstein and his mentor, the decidedly camp Dr. Pretorious (with critics also detecting similar overtones in the forest idyll that the Monster shares with a blind hermit). Finally, it offered one of the most memorable of all female monsters, in **Elsa Lanchester**'s hissing bride (with, in a canny piece of casting, Lanchester also playing Mary Shelley, author of *Frankenstein*, in the film's prologue).

Whale subsequently had a commercial hit with the musical *Showboat* (1936) but the World War I drama *The Road Back* (1937) was not well received. Of his other non-horror credits, the murder mystery *Remember Last Night* (1935) and the swashbuckler *The Man in the Iron Mask* (1939) are well worth seeing, although Whale never again attained the creative heights of his horror work. He retired from cinema in the 1940s, and by all accounts lived a quiet, private life thereafter. He was found dead in his swimming pool in 1957. His death was for many years considered mysterious, although a long-suppressed suicide note was finally disclosed in the 1980s.

Bill Condon's biopic *Gods and Monsters* (1998) was a loving, partly fictionalized account of Whale's later years, with Ian Mc Kellen in the role of the director.

WHEATLEY, DENNIS (1897–1977). From the 1930s through to the 1970s, the British writer Dennis Wheatley was one of the world's leading horror novelists. He specialized in thrillers and historical romances featuring the occult, and although his work is now deeply unfashionable and largely out of print, **Hammer** did adapt three of his novels for the big screen. *The Lost Continent* (1968) was a bizarre adventure story. *The Devil Rides Out* (1968) remains one of the genre's best Satanic thrillers, however. As directed by **Terence Fisher** and scripted by **Richard Matheson**, it was faithful to Wheatley's plot but removed his somewhat bombastic dialogue and reactionary attitudes. *To the Devil a Daughter* (1976), adapted by **Christopher Wicking** for director **Peter Sykes**, was interesting in its own right but only took a few ideas from Wheatley's original story.

WICKING, CHRISTOPHER (1943–). From the late 1960s onwards, a new generation of filmmakers revived the **British horror** cycle, introducing new ideas and new approaches to the genre. The screenwriter Christopher Wicking was one of those filmmakers. In comparison with the norm provided by **Hammer** horror, his scripts were often provocatively fragmented, critical of those authority figures privileged by earlier Hammer horrors, and firmly on the side of the young. He worked several times with director **Gordon Hessler**, first on the fairly conventional *The Oblong Box* (1969) and subsequently on the considerably more daring *Scream and Scream Again* (1969), *Cry of the Banshee* (1970), and *Murders in the Rue Morgue* (1971). He also wrote for Hammer during its final years as a horror film producer, a period in which the company was also attempting to reinvent itself. *Blood from the Mummy's Tomb* (1971), for maverick director **Seth Holt**, was an inventive and daring reinterpretation of the mummy story, while *Demons of the Mind* (1972), for director **Peter Sykes**, explicitly critiqued paternal authority. Also for Sykes, Wicking co-scripted what would turn out to be Hammer's final horror film (to date, at least), the **Dennis Wheatley** adaptation *To the Devil a Daughter* (1976). Here he successfully translated a decidedly old-fashioned novel into the modern horror idiom. His other genre credits include *Venom* (1971)—for Sykes again—and *Dream Demon* (1988).

WIENE, ROBERT (1873–1938). It is perhaps paradoxical that German director Robert Wiene's best-known credit is the classic example of **Expressionism** *Das Cabinet des Dr. Caligari* (*The Cabinet of Dr. Caligari*) (1919) as this is a film that seemed more dependent for its distinctiveness on the production designers than it did on the director, with the camera largely static throughout. Wiene's *Genuine* (1920) was *Caligari*-like in style, although it lacked that film's impact. *Orlacs Hände* (*The Hands of Orlac*) (1924), the first of several adaptations of Maurice Renard's novel, was more conventional but nevertheless a stylish horror thriller. *See also* GERMAN HORROR.

WILLIAMS, JOHN (1932–). The composer John Williams has written the **music** for some of the most commercially successful films of all time, including the *Star Wars* and *Indiana Jones* series. His horror scores are few and far between—perhaps because low-budget horror films usually cannot afford such a distinguished figure—but they are all impressive. The most famous is, of course, his score for **Steven Spielberg**'s monster movie *Jaws* (1975), the main theme of which has become an instantly recognizable part of contemporary popular culture. Less well known but just as effective are his scores for **Brian De Palma**'s telekinesis thriller *The Fury* (1978) and John Badham's *Dracula* (1979). In both cases, Williams' lush orchestrations bestow grandeur and a romantic intensity wholly appropriate to the subject matter.

WILLIAMSON, KEVIN (1965–). The experienced horror director **Wes Craven** might have brought the suspense and shocks to the enormously successful *Scream* franchise, but it was screenwriter Kevin Williamson who made the teenage characters credible and likeable. His screenplay for *Scream* (1996)—which he had originally entitled *Scary Movie*—rejuvenated tired **slasher** conventions through giving more space to the interactions between the teenagers, as well as providing a clever whodunnit narrative structure. His subsequent work on *I Know What You Did Last Summer* (1997), *Scream 2* (1997), and *The Faculty* (1998) maintained this focus on teenagers, although the **werewolf** film *Cursed* (2005), which reunited him with Craven, was less successful. His directorial debut, the black **comedy** *Teaching Mrs. Tingle* (1999), was also not well received. He was one of the producers on *Halloween H20: 20 years Later* (1998), *Scream 2* and *Scream 3* (2000) and created and produced the popular teenage **television** drama series *Dawson's Creek* (1998–2003).

WINSTON, STAN (1946–). The **makeup**, special effects and creature designer Stan Winston is best known for his work on **James Cameron**'s *The Terminator* (1984) and *Terminator 2: Judgment Day* (1991) and the **science fiction**/horror/action hybrid *Predator* (1987) as well as for his contribution to *Jurassic Park* (1993). However, he also has a substantial pedigree in horror, where his credits have included *The Bat People* (1974), *Dr. Black, Mr. Hyde* (1976), *Mansion of the Doomed* (1976), **Dracula's Dog** (*Zoltan, Hound of Dracula*) (1978), *The Entity* (1981), *The Hand* (1981), *Dead and Buried* (1981), *Aliens* (1986), *The Monster Squad* (1987), *Leviathan* (1989), *Interview with the Vampire* (1994), *The Island of Dr. Moreau* (1996), *Lake Placid* (1999), *End of Days* (1999), *Darkness Falls* (2003), *Wrong Turn* (2003), and *Constantine* (2005). Winston has acted as producer for some made-for-cable science fiction/horror films—including *Earth vs. the Spider* (2001), *How to Make a Monster* (2001), *The Day the World Ended* (2001), and *She Creature* (2001)—as well as for the **rural horror** *Wrong Turn*. He also directed the superior monster movie *Pumpkinhead* (1989) and the horror-themed Michael Jackson musical short **Ghosts** (1997).

WISE, ROBERT (1914–2005). The American director Robert Wise experienced considerable success with the blockbusting musicals *West Side Story* (1961) and *The Sound of Music* (1965). However, in a busy career that also included thrillers, war dramas, **science fiction**, and historical epics, he also made a few highly effective horror films. It was noted horror producer **Val Lewton** who gave Wise his first opportunity to direct with *The Curse of the Cat People* (1944). Although Wise had to share co-director credit with Gunther von Fritsch, the resulting film was an impressive **ghost** story, and Wise went on to direct another Lewton project, *The Body Snatcher* (1945), a subtle adaptation of a Robert Louis Stevenson story. Both of Wise's later horror films displayed the influence of Lewton in their reliance on suggestion and in their evocative use of sound. *The Haunting* (1963) remains one of the most striking of all cinematic ghost stories and is notable for never showing its audience a ghost. *Audrey Rose* (1977) was an underrated **possession** story that was made in the era of *The Exorcist* (1973) but which avoided a melodramatic blood-and-thunder approach in favor of a quieter treatment of its subject. It was an old-fashioned film in the good sense of that term. *See also* AMER-ICAN HORROR.

WITCHCRAFT. Witches have only appeared sporadically in horror cinema, but those appearances have often been memorable. The Danish pseudo-**documentary** *Häxen* (*Witchcraft Through the Ages*) (1922) was an early witchcraft film, but in the 1930s the most widely seen cinematic witches were the fairytale villains from the Walt Disney animated feature *Snow White and the Seven Dwarves* (1937) and the Judy Garland vehicle *The Wizard of Oz* (1939). By contrast, *Weird Woman* (1944), a campus-based tale of witches, was a tame horror adaptation of Fritz Leiber's novel *Conjure Wife*.

Horror-based witches did not really come into their own until the 1960s. **Mario Bava**'s classic **Italian horror** *La maschera del demonio* (*The Mask of Satan, Revenge of the* **Vampire**, *Black Sunday*) (1960) featured a powerful vampire-witch in the form of **Barbara Steele**, while the **British horror** production *Night of the Eagle* (*Burn, Witch, Burn!*) (1962) was a highly effective second version of Leiber's *Conjure Wife*. Other British witchcraft films included **Don Sharp**'s atmospheric *Witchcraft* (1964), **Hammer**'s staid *The Witches* (1966), and the more exploitative *Virgin Witch* (1970). At about the same time, **Mexican horror** offered the spectacle of masked wrestler **Santo** taking on witches in *Atacan las brujas* (*The Witches Attack*) (1965). The Italian director **Dario Argento** later portrayed some awesomely powerful witches in the ultra-stylish *Suspiria* (1977) and *Inferno* (1980), and Sigourney Weaver delivered a grandstanding performance as a fairytale witch in the revisionary *Snow White: A Tale of Terror* (1997).

In all these cases, the figure of the powerful woman was rendered as monstrous and evil in a manner that could readily be construed as misogynist, although this was often accompanied by a fascination with the witch and her supernatural abilities. A few horror or horror-related films—among them **George Romero**'s *Jack's Wife* (1972), *The Witches of Eastwick* (1987), and the **teenage horror** *The Craft* (1996)—have taken this further through an exploration of the possibilities offered by witchcraft for female bonding and a resistance to male authority.

Michael Reeves' British horror *Witchfinder General* (1968) contained no witches but it did dwell in disturbing detail on the twisted male psychologies of the witch hunters. The German productions *Hexen bis aufs Blut gequält* (*Mark of the Devil*) (1970) and *Hexen geschändet und zu Tode gequält* (*Mark of the Devil 2*) (1973) did something similar, although they were considerably cruder and nastier than Reeves' intelligent work. More recently, a folkloric American witch featured in *The Blair Witch Project* (1999). However, the threat of folkloric witchery in *An American Haunting* (2005)—which was based loosely on the alleged real-life story of the Bell Witch— turned out to be something of a red herring.

Comedy witches have shown up in *I Married a Witch* (1942), *Bell, Book and Candle* (1958), *Hocus Pocus* (1993), and *The Witches* (1990) and the **television** series *Bewitched* (1964–1972) and *Sabrina, the Teenage Witch* (1996–2003).

WOMEN DIRECTORS. Having a separate entry for women directors in a book of this kind might be seen as entailing an unfortunate ghettoisation. However, the fact remains that, to date at least, there are very few women directors who have had a sustained career in the horror genre. To a certain extent, this reflects a broader situation in the film industry where, back in the 1930s and 1940s, very few women got a chance to direct and where even today the majority of directors are male. The question of whether horror itself is an area of culture that is in some way intrinsically masculine, and therefore best suited to male filmmakers, is far from straightforward. As authors and performers, women have made very substantial contributions to the development of horror both in literature and in film, and evidence suggests that women also form an important part of the horror audience.

This entry lists the small number of women who have had the opportunity to direct horror. Some of their films are individually distinguished, but they are also so varied in subject and tone that it is hard to detect any general underlying qualities deriving from the fact that they were all made by women. Most of the female filmmakers involved here seem to have passed through horror in the context of a career that was grounded in other areas of culture, in other genres or on **television**—for instance, Gabrielle Beaumont with *The Godsend* (1980), Kathryn Bigelow with *Near Dark* (1987) and *Blue Steel* (1990), Antonia Bird with *Ravenous* (1999), Claire Denis with *Trouble Every Day* (2001), Mary Harron with *American Psycho* (2000), Amy Jones with *The*

Slumber Party Massacre (1982), Barbara Peters with *Humanoids from the Deep* (1980), and Rachel Talalay with *Freddy's Dead: The Final Nightmare* (1991) and **Ghost in the Machine** (1993). By contrast, Genevieve Joliffe has, to date at least, only directed one film, *Urban Ghost Story* (1998) and Fran Robel Kuzui has directed nothing since *Buffy the* **Vampire** *Slayer* (1992). Stephanie Rothman directed the interesting vampire film *The Velvet Vampire* (1971) and some other exploitation projects but stopped directing in the mid-1970s, while Katt Shea's directorial credits include the vampire film *Dance of the Damned* (1988) and **Carrie** *2: The Rage* (1999), her last cinema release to date. Mary Lambert has had a more sustained career with *Pet Sematary* (1989), *Pet Sematary II* (1992), and *Urban Legends: Bloody Mary* (2005), although the last two of these were not widely released. Roberta Findlay has probably directed more horror films than any other woman—among them the notorious **Snuff** (1976) as well as *Blood Sisters* (1987), *Prime Evil* (1988), and *Lurkers* (1988), although none of these have received any significant critical or **fan** praise.

WOOD, EDWARD D. (1924–1978). It seems unfair that Ed Wood has so often been described as "the worst film director ever," given that there are so many other directors who are just as bad. However, his posthumous claim to fame undoubtedly lies in the sheer awfulness of his films. Some have argued that they are so bad that they magically become enchanting. In actuality, watching his horror titles *Bride of the Monster* (1955), *Night of the Ghouls* (1959), and the infamous *Plan 9 from Outer Space* (1959) is a dispiriting experience, especially so for *Bride of the Monster* and *Plan 9*, both of which feature an aged and visibly ill **Bela Lugosi** in his final roles.

In 1994, **Tim Burton** directed the biopic *Ed Wood*, a fond but romanticized account of the director that featured Johnny Depp as Wood and Martin Landau in an Academy Award-winning performance as Lugosi. *See also* AMERICAN HORROR.

WOODBRIDGE, GEORGE (1907–1973). The burly British actor George Woodbridge appeared in several **Hammer** horror films and was an integral part of their cozy familiarity. He was an innkeeper in *Dracula* (*Horror of Dracula*) (1958) and *Dracula—Prince of Darkness* (1966) (although it was not clear whether it was meant to be the same innkeeper in both films), as well as a bemused policeman in *The Mummy* (1959) and a surly peasant in *The Curse of the Werewolf* (1961). He was also a memorably sadistic janitor in *The Revenge of Frankenstein* (1958), where he mercilessly beats Frankenstein's creation. In 1968—perhaps in homage to his Hammer innkeeping experience—he was cast as a hotelier in Jonathan Miller's now classic **television** adaptation of M. R. James' **ghost** story *Whistle and I'll Come To You.*

His other genre credits include for Hammer *The Reptile* (1966) and for other companies *The Queen of Spades* (1949), *Jack the Ripper* (1958), *The Flesh and the Fiends* (1959), *What a Carve Up* (1962), and *Doomwatch* (1972).

WRAY, FAY (1907–2004). Fay Wray was the first of horror cinema's "Scream Queens." Her most spectacular screams are to be found in **Merian C. Cooper** and **Ernest B. Schoedsack**'s *King Kong* (1933), but she also screamed effectively in *The Most Dangerous Game* (*The Hounds of Zaroff*) (1932), which was directed by **Irving Pichel** and Schoedsack, and in two films for director **Michael Curtiz**, *Doctor X* (1932) and *Mystery of the Wax Museum* (1933), as well as in *The Vampire Bat* (1933); she also featured in the **voodoo** film *Black Moon* (1934). However, as is the case generally with Scream Queens, she was far from being a passive victim. In all of her horror films, Wray might have been victimized by men, and ultimately saved by men as well, but she was also inquisitive, articulate, charismatic and on occasion more than capable of fighting back herself, for example in *Mystery of the Wax Museum* where she manages to smash in the wax mask of her assailant. She did not reside in the horror genre for long. There was a final performance in the British supernatural thriller *The Clairvoyant* (1934), and then she was off into the more wholesome world provided by comedies, musicals and crime thrillers. Yet she still remains an enduring genre icon.

– Y –

YAGHER, KEVIN (1962–). The **makeup** effects specialist Kevin Yagher began his cinematic career working on various instalments of the *Friday the 13th* and *Nightmare on Elm Street* horror cycles. He went on to design the murderous **doll** Chucky for *Child's Play* (1988). Other horror makeup credits have included *Retribution* (1987), *The Hidden* (1987), *The Seventh Sign* (1988), *The Phantom of the Opera* (1989), *Man's Best Friend* (1993), *Dr. Jekyll and Ms. Hyde* (1995), *Bordello of Blood* (1996), *Rumpelstiltskin* (1996), and *The Astronaut's Wife* (1996). Yagher directed *Hellraiser: Bloodline* (1996) but disowned the final version and was billed as "Alan Smithee," the name customarily adopted in such circumstances. He also received a credit for the screen story of **Tim Burton's** *Sleepy Hollow* (1999), a project that at one point he was slated to direct, and worked on the *Tales from the Crypt* (1989–1996) **television** series. More recently, he has focused on makeup effects for non-horror projects such as *Mission Impossible II* (2000) and *Aeon Flux* (2005).

YAMAMOTO, MICHIO (1933–2004). The director Michio Yamamoto had a brief but interesting career in **Japanese horror** with a trilogy of **vampire** films that sought to transpose Western horror conventions into a Japanese context and which also provided an early example of the 1970s tendency of locating vampires in modern-day settings. *Yûreiyashiki no kyôfu: Chi o suu Ningyô* (*The Fear of the Ghost House: Bloodsucking Doll, Night of the Vampire, Legacy of Dracula, The Vampire Doll*) (1970) was a fascinating attempt to psychologize the state of vampirism. By contrast, *Noroi no yakata: Chi o sû me* (*Bloodsucking Eyes, Bloodthirsty Eyes, Lake of Dracula*) (1971) and *Chi o suu bara* (*Bloodsucking Rose, The Bloodthirsy Roses, Evil of Dracula*) (1974) featured more traditional vampire villains and offered a more awkward mix of Western and Japanese elements. Yamamoto also directed the horror film *Akuma ga yondeiru* (*Terror in the Streets*) (1970).

YARBROUGH, JEAN (1900–1975). The director Jean Yarbrough—who is sometimes referred to as Jean Yarborough—made some interesting contributions to 1940s **American horror** cinema. His first genre credit was *The Devil Bat* (1940), a silly but enjoyable low-budget vehicle for **Bela Lugosi** in which bats are trained to attack people wearing a particular brand of aftershave. This was followed by *King of the Zombies* (1941), an indifferent zombie film enlivened by some comic interludes provided by **Mantan Moreland**. *House of Horrors* (1946) and *The Brute Man* (1946) both featured **Rondo Hatton** as "The Creeper." Hatton suffered in real-life from a disfiguring condition, and his casting as a monster was, to put it mildly, in questionable taste. If one can put this aside, Yarbrough's direction of *House of Horrors* is stylish and creates a brooding atmosphere, although *The Brute Man*, which sets out the origins of the Creeper, is less successful in this respect. Yarbrough's other two 1940s horrors both show the influence of horror producer **Val Lewton**. Despite its title, *She-Wolf of London* (1946) is not actually a **werewolf** film but instead a murder mystery in which the female lead believes that she can turn into a wolf. There are clear parallels here with Lewton's *Cat People* (1942), although Yarbrough's film lacks the originality or atmosphere of Lewton's film. Similarly *The Creeper* (1948)—which has nothing to do with Rondo Hatton—plays like a downmarket version of a Lewton shocker. Yarbrough returned to the genre in the 1960s with *Hillbillys in a Haunted House* (1967), which featured horror stalwarts **John Carradine, Lon Chaney Jr.**, and **Basil Rathbone**, although sadly none of them were at their best.

YU, RONNY (1950–). The Hong Kong-based work of Chinese director Ronny Yu often contained supernatural or horror-like elements, with this evident in films such as *Jui gwai chat hung* (*The Trail*) (1981), *Ling qi po ren* (*The Occupant*) (1984), *Meng gui fo tiao qiang* (*Bless This House*) (1988), and the period fantasy drama *Bai fa mo nu zhuan* (*The Bride with White Hair*) (1993) and its **sequel** *Bai fa mo nu zhuan II* (*The Bride with White Hair II*) (1993). Like a number of other Chinese directors and actors, Yu moved to the United States during the 1990s and contributed films to three **American horror** franchises. *Bride of Chucky* (1998), the fourth in the *Child's Play* cycle, and *Freddy vs. Jason* (2003), which brought together the *Nightmare on Elm Street* and *Friday the 13th* cycles, were both slick and violent crowd-pleasers that demonstrated Yu's ability to work within the American horror idiom. Yu has recently returned to Chinese subject matter with the Jet Li martial arts drama *Huo yuan jia* (*Fearless*) (2006). *See also* CHINESE HORROR.

YUZNA, BRIAN (1949–). The first part of Philippines-born Brian Yuzna's career as a prolific writer-director-producer was spent working in the United States on a range of low budget genre films, often in association with director **Stuart Gordon**. Among others, he produced *Re-animator* (1984) and *From Beyond* (1985), Gordon's gory **comedy**/horror adaptations of stories by **H. P. Lovecraft**, as well as *Dolls* (1987), another Gordon horror, *Warlock* (1989), *Infested* (1993), and the Lovecraftian horror **anthology** *Necromonicon* (1994). During this period, he also started directing. His auspicious debut was the **body horror** film *Society* (1989), which combined an astonishing level of **gore** with elements of social critique and some none too subtle humor. This was followed by *Bride of Re-animator* (1990), *Return of the Living Dead III* (1993), a contribution to *Necronomicon*, *The Dentist* (1996), *Progeny* (1998), and *The Dentist 2* (1998), with many of these offering a similar mix of extreme body-related imagery softened by humor. He also found time to co-write and co-produce the family fantasy entertainment *Honey, I Shrunk the Kids* (1989).

In 1999, Yuzna relocated to Spain, where he helped to set up **Fantastic Factory**, a Spanish company producing English-language horror films, some of which were directed by Yuzna himself. These included *Faust* (2001), *Beyond Re-animator* (2003), *Rottweiler* (2004), and *Beneath Still Waters* (2005). None of these have matched the inventiveness or achievement of the best of Yuzna's American work. However, Yuzna has also produced some of the most outstanding Fantastic Factory films, namely Stuart Gordon's stylish Lovecraft adaptation *Dagon* (2001), *Darkness* (2002), and the **werewolf** drama *Romasanta* (2004). See also AMERICAN HORROR; SPANISH HORROR.

– Z –

ZOMBIE, ROB (1965–). Rob Zombie's rock **music** has graced many films, including *Urban Legend* (1998), *Bride of Chucky* (1998), and *End of Days* (1999). He made the transition from musician to director with *House of 1000 Corpses* (2003), a gory example of **rural horror** that, while uneven in tone, demonstrated Zombie's affection for the genre (as does the fact that he changed his name to Rob Zombie from Robert Cummings). His direction of *The Devil's Rejects* (2005), a **sequel** to *House of 1000 Corpses*, was more assured and consequently more disturbing in its depiction of appalling human behavior. Zombie's films are not easy to watch, especially for anyone unused to horror, but they are distinctive and intelligent. In 2007, Zombie released a **remake** of **John Carpenter**'s *Halloween* (1978). *See also* AMERICAN HORROR.

ZOMBIES. The disturbing notion that the dead might return and threaten us has underpinned a range of horror monsters, including **vampires**, the **mummy** and **ghosts**. The zombie represents the most brutish form of this; physically repellent and usually mindless, it offers a spectacle of death unmitigated by the attractiveness or charisma possessed by some other monsters.

The idea of the zombie is derived from **voodoo**-related religious practices, especially those associated with Haiti. It was W. H. Seabrook's best-selling pop-anthropology study *The Magic Island* (1929) that introduced voodoo and the zombie to a wider public, and **Victor Halperin**'s *White Zombie* (1932) was the first film to exploit the book's success. *White Zombie* presented a scenario in which white characters abroad encounter strange native customs and are either overwhelmed by these or—in the case of the film's villain (played by **Bela Lugosi**)—exploit them for nefarious ends. The zombies themselves were in essence slaves, with their climactic assault upon their white master functioning as a coded social rebellion. The racial dimension of this was never far from the surface, but the foreign location helped to disavow any connection with contemporary reality. Other American zombie films of the 1930s and 1940s followed a similar pattern in their emphasis on a white-centered touristic or colonial experience of non-American cultures. The level of achievement ranged from the crude—for example, Halperin's boring *Revolt of the Zombies* (1936), **Jean Yarbrough**'s *King of the Zombies* (1941) and *Revenge of the Zombies* (1943)—to the sophisticated and innovative, notably the **Val Lewton/Jacques Tourneur** production *I Walked with a Zombie* (1943). Despite the quality of Tourneur's film, the zombie remained a minor horror monster throughout this period, relegated in the main to the lower end of the genre.

The 1960s saw a limited upward movement in the zombie's status. This was first hinted at in **Hammer**'s *The Plague of the Zombies* (1966), in which zombies were figured again as voodoo-created slave labor, but where they were also presented as more visceral and aggressive than they had ever been before. However, it was **George Romero**'s seminal **American horror** film *Night of the Living Dead* (1968) that redefined and modernized the zombie, jettisoning its connection with voodoo and foreign lands and relocating it within contemporary American society. Romero also made his zombies cannibalistic, and he spared no detail in depicting their consumption of human flesh. The director went on to make three **sequels** to *Night* and, amidst the taboo-breaking **gore**, explored with great intelligence the social significance of the zombie and the way in which it could be used to comment critically on the state of our world. From Romero's perspective, the zombie became an expression of normality itself, of who we were or could become.

Many of the zombie films produced in the wake of Romero's success were less ambitious in scope. During the 1970s, British filmmakers returned to zombiedom with the remarkably silly *Psychomania* (1972), in which bikers returned from the dead, and one of the episodes in the **Amicus anthology** *Tales from the Crypt* (1972). In the United States, **Bob Clark** offered *Children Shouldn't Play with Dead Things* (1973), and the blaxploitation horror *Sugar Hill* (1974) engaged in a crude way with the racial politics of voodoo and the zombie. Spanish filmmaker **Jorge Grau** directed the grim and graphic *Non si deve profanare il sonno dei morti (The Living Dead at the Manchester Morgue)* (1974), while the stylish Spanish *Blind Dead* cycle, also from the 1970s, featured the Knights Templar rising from their graves in modern Spain.

From the late 1970s onwards, a series of Italian zombie films—including **Lucio Fulci**'s *Zombi 2 (Zombie, Zombie Flesheaters)* (1979) and **Umberto Lenzi**'s *Incubo sulla città contaminata (Nightmare City)* (1980)—took the gore and **cannibalism** onto a yet more graphic level, but they also reduced elements of social critique to a point where they were sometimes hard to detect at all. Other treatments of the zombie since have included **Wes Craven**'s *The Serpent and the Rainbow* (1988), which returned the zombie to its Haitian voodoo context, the **Stephen King** adaptation *Pet Sematary* (1989), and **Michele Soavi**'s *Dellamorte dellamore (Cemetery Man)* (1994), an altogether more poetic, although still gory, rendition of a zombie story. **Comedy** zombies showed up in **Dan O'Bannon**'s *The Return* *of the Living Dead* (1985) and **Peter Jackson**'s *Braindead* (1992). More recently, **Paul Anderson**'s *Resident Evil* (2002) and **Uwe Boll**'s *House of the Dead* (2003) were adaptations of **computer games** that combined Romero-like zombies with frenetic action sequences. Romero's own *Dawn of the Dead* (1978) was remade in 2004 in a version that significantly diminished the original's social commentary. Only Romero's own *Land of the Dead* (2005) continued to take the zombie as something more than a convenient fright device, and it is arguable that, in post-1960 horror cinema at least, it is only Romero who has grasped the full potential of this particular monster. It is certainly the case that major zombie films are very limited in number—with *I Walked with a Zombie*, *Night of the Living Dead* and *Dawn of the Dead* perhaps representing the pinnacle of achievement. The association of the zombie with crude low-budget productions has undoubtedly limited its development as a movie monster.

ZUCCO, GEORGE (1886–1960). The British character actor George Zucco appeared in several British films in the early 1930s—including an adaptation of the H. G. Wells story *The Man Who Could Work Miracles* (1936)—before relocating to the United States. There he worked in a variety of genres but increasingly specialized in sinister roles in crime and horror films. He was Professor Moriarty in *The Adventures of Sherlock Holmes* (1939), returned as another villain in *Sherlock Holmes in Washington* (1943), and also appeared in sinister support in *The Hunchback of Notre Dame* (1939) and *The Cat and the Canary* (1939). He was a villainous high priest in **Universal**'s *The Mummy's Hand* (1940), *The Mummy's Tomb* (1942), and *The Mummy's Ghost* (1944), and played a succession of **mad scientist** roles in *The Monster and the Girl* (1941), *The Mad Monster* (1942), *Dr. Renault's Secret* (1942), *The Mad Ghoul* (1943), and *The Flying Serpent* (1946). The films were of variable quality, but Zucco was a reliable heavy who became an integral part of the 1940s **American horror** scene. Other genre credits include *Dead Men Walk* (1943), *Voodoo Man* (1944), *House of Frankenstein* (1944), *Fog Island* (1945), *Scared to Death* (1947), and the **comedy**-horror *Who Killed Doc Robbin?* (1948).

Bibliography

CONTENTS

INTRODUCTION

The critical literature dealing with the horror film is as varied as the genre itself. Approaches have ranged from the appreciative and devoted to the coolly analytical and the downright hostile. Critics have sought to explain the peculiar pleasures of horror—and indeed this is one of the few popular genres where pleasure has become a crucial issue—and have also explored specific horror cycles and different horror styles, locating both in historical and national contexts.

349

They have probed beneath the surface of apparently straightforward horror narratives to uncover all sorts of unsettling subtexts and transgressive values, and they have also offered up paeans of praise to the distinctive and disturbing visions of particular horror artists.

This critical activity has been characterized by a fluidity that makes it difficult to divide it up into neat categories. However, certain trends are evident, and this was already clear in some of the key early texts of horror criticism. "Early" here means the 1960s and 1970s. The horror film has existed as a distinct generic category since the early 1930s, but there was little sustained critical writing on it for a long time. There were certainly investigations and celebrations by journalists and by fans—not least Forrest J. Ackerman whose magazine *Famous Monsters of Filmland* introduced the genre to younger fans from the late 1950s onwards—but these existed as fragments rather than as something more organized or purposeful. There had also been some writing on various aspects of what would later come to be thought of as horror's pre-history—notably on German Expressionist cinema—but these tended to ignore or downplay the contribution of these films to horror cinema.

It was the absence of any substantial historical survey of horror cinema that made Carlos Clarens' 1967 book *An Illustrated History of the Horror Film* (later republished as *Horror Movies: An Illustrated Survey*) so important. Its obvious intelligence and seriousness helped to elevate the horror genre to a kind of cultural reputability which, for many other critics, it singularly lacked. Equally serious was *A Heritage of Horror: The English Gothic Cinema 1946–1972*, David Pirie's fine 1973 study of a particular national style of horror, which convincingly placed British horror within both its social and its cultural context. Finally, the writings on the genre by British-born, Canadian-based critic Robin Wood that appeared in the 1977 collection *The American Nightmare* explored horror cinema in ideological terms. For Wood, the genre provided a cultural space in which relationships between normative and oppositional values were played out, with this having the potential for both politically progressive and conservative inflections.

The focus of much subsequent historical writing on horror has been on English-speaking horror, especially in its American and British variants. More recently, however, an interest in national cinemas has broadened out to include not just national horror traditions from a wide range of other countries but also the constantly shifting relations between these. One outcome of this "internationalized" approach has been the gradual fragmentation of an earlier synoptic model of horror history that saw the genre's development in terms of a linear movement from one neatly defined cycle of production to another. The more recent work presents instead a complex but arguably more credible picture of both national endeavor and transnational interaction.

Critics and theorists have also—in the manner of Robin Wood—continued to explore what might be termed the representational politics of horror. The main focus here has been the representation of gender, perhaps understandably given that women have often been figured as victims in horror cinema. Here again, there has been a general movement from a simplistic rejection of horror to an engagement with some of its complexities, and particularly the way in which the genre seems to offer a space within which conventional gender identities are thrown into disarray. A good example of this is provided by the changing critical status of the American slasher film of the late 1970s and early 1980s. Initially criticized for its apparent misogyny, this unloved horror format was reinterpreted in Carol Clover's groundbreaking book *Men, Women and Chainsaws* as offering a more convoluted mixture of both sadistic and masochistic impulses, and later critics have developed Clover's ideas not just in relation to the slasher but to other types of horror cinema as well. In comparison, discussions of racial and class difference have been somewhat overshadowed, although impressive work has been done on both these subjects; for example in Rhona J. Berenstein's book *Attack of the Leading Ladies*.

At the same time, the way in which horror films have an effect on their audiences has proved a lively area for critical endeavor. Here, as is the case elsewhere in writings on horror, the psychoanalytical method has been especially influential. The emphasis in much psychoanalytical writing on discovering things that are not immediately obvious can be very alienating for the uninitiated but nevertheless it has proved productive; both Wood and Clover, for example, have drawn extensively on psychoanalytical concepts in their writing. So far as an understanding of horror's effects are concerned, psychoanalytical approaches have sometimes presented horror as a therapeutic experience in which an audience can confront its fears but have also seen the genre as offering subtler, more open-ended engagements with issues to do with identity. By contrast, approaches rooted more in an audience's cognitive abilities have suggested that we are far more conscious of what we are doing when we buy a ticket for a horror film and that the experience is, in certain respects at least, more akin to a rollercoaster ride than it is to a dream or nightmare: Noel Carroll's book *The Philosophy of Horror* remains the clearest and most developed statement of this approach. Critical work that involves actually talking to horror audiences, and in particular considering the activities of horror fans, has helped to develop further this area through giving a sense of how audiences themselves interpret the horror experience in relation to their own lives. It is perhaps a sign of the changing times that critics and theorists writing about horror now frequently acknowledge their own fandom and their own personal commitment to the horror genre.

In the face of such variety, this bibliography is designed to help the reader find the type of critical literature for which he or she is looking. If you prefer American horror, or have a taste for the British or Italian version, or indeed have yet more exotic tastes, go to the National Horror Cinemas section, where you might find that horror is even more international than you thought it was. If you believe instead that the most valuable thing about horror cinema is its directors (and you are certainly not alone in believing that), then head for the section on Personnel where you will find books on such genre luminaries as Dario Argento, John Carpenter, Wes Craven, David Cronenberg, Terence Fisher, and James Whale, along with publications on some filmmakers that you have probably never heard of before, and not just directors either. If vampires, werewolves, and zombies are more your thing (and again you are not alone), then the section dealing with thematic studies of horror will be the one for you, and while there you might find items that are both unexpected but also interesting—for example, Joan Hawkins' fascinating study *Cutting Edge: Art-horror and the Horrific avant-garde* or Isabel Cristina Pinedo's stimulating *Recreational Terror: Women and the Pleasures of Horror Film Viewing*. Reference books are also listed for those of you who require the reassurance of solid facts, and there is also a listing of anthologies that bring together the wide range of critical writings that has been generated in response to the horror film. You could end up reading material here that fascinates you, baffles you, and annoys you (and perhaps all three at once). Your ideas about horror could be challenged and upturned, and your whole view of the genre could be changed forever. Or you could return to the horror films you love secure in the knowledge that they are in fact the best of the lot.

If nothing else, the sheer variety of books and articles listed here suggests a horror genre that is a long way from being formulaic. Critics, historians, and theorists operating from radically different perspectives have all found things in horror that merit discussion and argument. There might not be much of a consensus about what horror actually is or what it does, but there is a shared sense of its capacity for provocation and fascination. Given this, it is perhaps appropriate that this bibliography is so open-ended. There is more than one way into it and more than one way through it. Needless to say, what route you choose is up to you. But beware. As is the case with most horror films, there may be a few surprises along the way.

GENERAL STUDIES

Clarens, Carlos. *An Illustrated History of the Horror Film.* New York: Putnam, 1967.
Gifford, Denis. *A Pictorial History of Horror Movies.* London: Hamlyn, 1973.

Hutchings, Peter. *The Horror Film.* Harlow, England: Pearson, 2004.
Marriott, James. *Horror Films.* London: Virgin Books, 2004.
Marriott, James, and Kim Newman. *Horror: The Complete Guide to the Cinema of Fear.* London: Andre Deutsch, 2006.
Tudor, Andrew. *Monsters and Mad Scientists: A Cultural History of the Horror Film.* Oxford: Blackwell, 1989.
Wells, Paul. *The Horror Genre: From Beelzebub to Blair Witch.* London: Wallflower, 2000.
Worland, Rick. *The Horror Film: An Introduction.* Oxford: Blackwell, 2006.

ANTHOLOGIES OF CRITICISM

Gelder, Ken, ed. *The Horror Reader.* London: Routledge, 2000.
Grant, Barry K., ed. *The Dread of Difference: Gender and the Horror Film.* Austin: University of Texas Press, 1996.
———, ed. *Planks of Reason: Essays on the Horror Film.* Metuchen, N.J.: Scarecrow Press, 1984.
Huss, Roy, and T. J. Ross, ed. *Focus on the Horror Film.* Englewood Cliffs, N.J.: Prentice-Hall, 1972.
Jancovich, Mark, ed. *Horror: The Film Reader.* London: Routledge, 2002.
Newman, Kim, ed. *Science Fiction/Horror Reader: A Sight and Sound Reader.* London: British Film Institute, 2002.
Prince, Stephen, ed. *The Horror Film.* New Jersey: Rutgers University Press, 2004.
Schneider, Steven Jay, ed. *Fear Without Frontiers: Horror Cinema Across the Globe.* Godalming: FAB Press, 2003.
———, ed. *Horror Film and Psychoanalysis: Freud's Worst Nightmare.* Cambridge: Cambridge University Press, 2004.
Schneider, Steven Jay, and Daniel Shaw, eds. *Dark thoughts : philosophic reflections on cinematic horror.* Lanham Md.: Scarecrow Press, 2003.
Schneider, Steven Jay, and Tony Williams, eds. *Horror International.* Detroit, Mich.: Wayne State University Press, 2005.
Silver, Alain, and James Ursini, eds. *Horror Film Reader.* New York: Limelight, 2000.

THEMATIC STUDIES

Arnzen, Michael A. "Who's Laughing Now? The Postmodern Splatter Film." *Journal of Popular Film and Television* 21, no. 4 (1994): 176–188.

Baird, Robert. "The Startle Effect: Implications for Spectator Cognition and Media Theory." *Film Quarterly* 53, no. 3 (2000): 12–24.

Barker, Martin, Ernest Mathijs, and Xavier Mendik. "Menstrual Monsters: The Reception of the Ginger Snaps Cult Horror Franchise." *Film International* 4, no. 3 (2006): 68–77.

Benshoff, Harry. *Monsters in the Closet: Homosexuality and the Horror Film*. Manchester: Manchester University Press, 1997.

Black, Andy. "Crawling Chaos: H. P. Lovecraft in Cinema." 109–122 in *Necronomicon, Book One*, edited by Andy Black. London: Creation Books, 1996.

Boss, Pete. "Vile Bodies and Bad Medicine." *Screen* 27, no. 1 (1986): 14–24.

Briefel, Aviva. "Monster Pains: Masochism, Menstruation, and Identification in the Horror Film." *Film Quarterly* 58, no. 3 (2005): 16–27.

Brophy, Philip. "Horrality—the Textuality of Contemporary Horror Films." *Screen* 27, no. 1 (1986): 2–13.

Bunnell, Charlene. "The Gothic: A Literary Genre's Transition to Film." 79–100 in *Planks of Reason: Essays on the Horror Film*, edited by Barry K. Grant. Metuchen, N.J.: Scarecrow Press, 1984.

Carroll, Noel. *The Philosophy of Horror, or Paradoxes of the Heart*. London: Routledge, 1990.

Chaudhuri, S. "Visit of the body snatchers: alien invasion themes in vampire narratives." *Camera Obscura* 40/41 (1997): 180–99.

Cherry, Bridget. "Refusing to Refuse to Look: Female viewers of the horror film." 187–203 in *Identifying Hollywood's Audiences: Cultural Identity and the Movies*, edited by Melvyn Stokes and Richard Maltby. London: British Film Institute, 1999.

Crane, Jonathan Lake. *Terror and Everyday Life: Singular Moments in the History of the Horror Film*. London: Sage, 1994.

Creed, Barbara. "Dark Desires: Male Masochism in the Horror Film." 118–133 in *Screening the Male: Exploring Masculinities in Hollywood Cinema*, edited by Steve Cohan and Ina Rae Hark. London: Routledge, 1993.

———. *The Monstrous-Feminine: Film, Feminism, Psychoanalysis*. London: Routledge, 1993.

———. *Phallic Panic: Film, Horror and the Primal Uncanny*. Melbourne: Melbourne University Press, 2005.

Dadoun, Roger. "Fetishism and the Horror Film." 39–62 in *Fantasy and the Cinema*, edited by James Donald. London: British Film Institute, 1989.

Derry, Charles. *Dark Dreams: A Psychological History of the Modern Horror Film*. New York: A. S. Barnes, 1977.

Dickstein, Morris. "The Aesthetics of Fright." 65–78 in *Planks of Reason: Essays on the Horror Film*, edited by Barry K. Grant. Metuchen, N.J.: Scarecrow Press, 1984.

Donald, James. "The Fantastic, the Sublime and the Popular: Or, What's at Stake in Vampire Films?" 233–252 in *Fantasy and the Cinema*, edited by James Donald. London: British Film Institute, 1989.

Dyson, Jeremy. *Bright Darkness: The Lost Art of the Supernatural Horror Film*. London: Cassell, 1997.

Evans, Walter. "Monster Movies: A Sexual Theory." 53–64 in *Planks of Reason: Essays on the Horror Film*, edited by Barry K. Grant. Metuchen, N.J.: Scarecrow Press, 1984.

Frayling, Christopher. *Mad, Bad and Dangerous?: The Scientist and the Cinema*. London: Reaktion, 2006.

Freeland, Cynthia. "Feminist Frameworks for Horror Films." 195–214 in *Post-Theory: Reconstructing Film Studies*, edited by David Bordwell and Noel Carroll. Madison: University of Wisconsin Press, 1996.

———. *The Naked and the Undead: Evil and the Appeal of Horror*. Boulder, Colo.: Westview Press, 2000.

———. "Realist Horror." 126–142 in *Philosophy and Film*, edited by Cynthia Freeland and Thomas Wartenberg. New York: Routledge, 1995.

Friedman, Lester D. "'Canyons of Nightmare': The Jewish Horror Film." 126–152 in *Planks of Reason: Essays on the Horror Film*, edited by Barry K. Grant. Metuchen, N.J.: Scarecrow Press, 1984.

Gifford, Denis. *Movie Monsters*. London: Studio Vista, 1969.

Giles, Dennis. "Conditions of Pleasure in Horror Cinema." 38–52 in *Planks of Reason: Essays on the Horror Film*, edited by Barry K. Grant. Metuchen, N.J.: Scarecrow Press, 1984.

Glut, Donald F. *Classic Movie Monsters*. Metuchen, N.J.: Scarecrow Press, 1978.

———. *The Dracula Book*. Metuchen, N.J.: Scarecrow Press, 1975.

———. *The Frankenstein Legend*. Metuchen, N.J.: Scarecrow Press, 1973.

Guerrero, Ed. "AIDS as Monster in Science Fiction and Horror Cinema." *Journal of Popular Film and Television* 18, no. 3 (1990): 86–93.

Hantke, Steffen, ed. *Horror Film: Creating and Marketing Fear*. Jackson: University Press of Mississippi, 2004.

Hawkins, Joan. *Cutting Edge: Art-horror and the Horrific avant-garde*. Minneapolis: University of Minnesota Press, 2000.

Hogan, David. *Dark Romance: Sexuality in the Horror Film*. Jefferson, N.C.: McFarland, 1986.

Hutchings, Peter. "Masculinity and the Horror Film." 84–94 in *You Tarzan: Masculinity, Movies and Men*, edited by Pat Kirkham and Janet Thumim. London: Lawrence and Wishart, 1993.

———. "Tearing Your Soul Apart: Horror's New Monsters." 89–103 in *Modern Gothic: A Reader*, edited by Vic Sage and Allan Lloyd-Smith. Manchester: Manchester University Press, 1996.

Jancovich, Mark. "'A Real Shocker': Authenticity, Genre, and the Struggle for Distinction." *Continuum: Journal of Media and Cultural Studies* 14, no. 1 (2000): 23–35.

Kermode, Mark. "I was a teenage horror fan: or 'How I Learned to Stop Worrying and Love Linda Blair.'" 57–66 in *Ill Effects: The Media/Violence Debate*, edited by Martin Barker and Julian Petley. London: Routledge, 1997.

Kinder, Marsha, and Beverle Houston. "Seeing is Believing: *The Exorcist* and *Don't Look Now.*" *Cinema* 34 (1974): 22–33.

Krzywinska, Tanya. *A Skin For Dancing In: Possession, Witchcraft and Voodoo in Film*. Trowbridge, Wiltshire: Flicks Books, 2000.

Lowenstein, Adam. *Shocking Representation: Historical Trauma, National Cinema, and the Modern Horror Film*. New York: Columbia University Press, 2005.

Mank, Gregory William. *It's Alive! The Classic Cinema Saga of Frankenstein*. New York: A. S. Barnes, 1981.

McCarty, John. *Splatter Movies: Breaking the Last Taboo of the Screen*. New York: St Martin's Press, 1984.

Meikle, Denis. *Jack the Ripper: The Murders and the Movies*. London: Reynolds and Hearn, 2002.

———. *The Ring Companion*. London: Titan Books, 2005.

Modleski, Tania. "The Terror of Pleasure." 155–167 in *Studies in Entertainment: Critical Approaches to Mass Culture*, edited by Tania Modleski. Bloomington: Indiana University Press, 1987.

Newman, Kim. *Nightmare Movies*. London: Bloomsbury, 1988.

Olney, Ian. "The Problem Body Politic, or 'These Hands Have a Mind All Their Own!': Figuring Disability in the Horror Film Adaptations of Renard's *Les mains d'Orlac.*" *Literature Film Quarterly* 34, no. 4 (2007): 294–302.

Pattison, Barrie. *The Seal of Dracula*. London: Lorrimer, 1975.

Pinedo, Isabel Cristina. *Recreational Terror: Women and the Pleasures of Horror Film Viewing*. New York: State University of New York Press, 1997.

Pirie, David. *The Vampire Cinema*. London: Quarto, 1977.

Powell, Anna. *Deleuze and Horror Film*. Edinburgh: Edinburgh University Press, 2005.

Prawer, S. S. *Caligari's Children: The Film as Tale of Terror*. Oxford: Oxford University Press, 1980.

Reed, Joseph. "Subgenres in Horror Pictures: The Pentagram, Faust and Philoctetes." 101–112 in *Planks of Reason: Essays on the Horror Film*, edited by Barry K. Grant. Metuchen, N.J.: Scarecrow Press, 1984.

Rockett, W. H. "The Door Ajar: Structure and Convention in Horror Films that Would Terrify." *Journal of Popular Film and Television* 10, no. 3 (1982): 130–136.

———. "Landscape and Manscape: Reflection and Distortion in Horror Films." *Post Script* 3 (1983): 19–34.

Roth, Lane. "Film, Society and Ideas: *Nosferatu* and *Horror of Dracula*." 245–254 in *Planks of Reason: Essays on the Horror Film*, edited by Barry K. Grant. Metuchen, N.J.: Scarecrow Press, 1984.

Russell, Jamie. *Book of the Dead: The Complete History of Zombie Cinema*. Guildford, Surrey: FAB Press, 2005.

Russell, Sharon. "The Witch in Film: Myth and Reality." 113–125 in *Planks of Reason: Essays on the Horror Film*, edited by Barry K. Grant. Metuchen, N.J.: Scarecrow Press, 1984.

Sanjek, David. "Fans Notes: The Horror Film Fanzine." *Literature Film Quarterly* 18, no. 3 (1990): 150–160.

Schneider, Steven. "Monsters as (Uncanny) Metaphors: Freud, Lakoff, and the Representation of Monstrosity in Cinematic Horror." 167–191 in *Horror Film Reader*, edited by Alain Silver and James Ursini. New York: Limelight, 2000.

———, ed. *100 European Horror Films (BFI Screen Guides)*. London: British Film Instititute, 2007.

Schreck, Nikolas. *The Satanic Screen: An Illustrated Guide to the Devil in Cinema*. London: Creation Books, 2001.

Sconce, Jeffrey. "Spectacles of Death: Identification, Reflexivity, and Contemporary Horror." 103–119 in *Film Theory Goes To The Movies*, edited by Jim Collins, Hilary Radner and Ava Preacher Collins. London: Routledge, 1993.

———. "'Trashing the Academy': Taste, Excess, and an Emerging Politics of Cinematic Style." *Screen* 36, no. 4 (1995): 371–393.

Sharrett, Christopher. "The Horror Film in Neoconservative Culture." 253–276 in *The Dread of Difference: Gender and the Horror Film*, edited by Barry Keith Grant. Austin: University of Texas Press, 1996.

Short, Sue. *Misfit Sisters: Screen Horror as Female Rites of Passage*. London: Palgrave Macmillan, 2006.

Skal, David J. *Screams of Reason: Mad Science and Modern Culture*. New York: W. W. Norton, 1999.

Sobchack, Vivian. "Bringing It All Back Home: Family Economy and Generic Exchange." 143–162 in *The Dread of Difference: Gender and the Horror Film*, edited by Barry Keith Grant. Austin: University of Texas Press, 1996.

Telotte, J. P. "Faith and Idolatry in the Horror Film." *Literature Film Quarterly* 8 (1980): 143–155.

———. "Through a Pumpkin's Eye: The Reflexive Nature of Horror." *Literature Film Quarterly* 10 (1982): 139–149.

Tudor, Andrew. "From Paranoia to Postmodernism: The Horror Movie in Late Modern Society." 105–116 in *Genre and Contemporary Hollywood*, edited by Steve Neale. London: British Film Institute, 202.

———. "Why Horror? The Peculiar Pleasures of a Popular Genre." *Cultural Studies* 11, no. 3 (1997): 443–463.

Twitchell, James. *Dreadful Pleasures: An Anatomy of Modern Horror.* Oxford: Oxford University Press, 1985.

Ursini, James, and Alain Silver. *The Vampire Film.* New York: A. S. Barnes, 1975.

Westfahl, Gary, and George Slusser, eds. *Nursery Realms: Children in the Worlds of Science Fiction, Fantasy, and Horror.* Georgia: University of Georgia Press, 1999.

Williams, Linda. "Film Bodies: Gender, Genre, and Excess." 140–158 in *Film Genre Reader 2*, edited by Barry K. Grant. Austin: University of Texas Press, 1995.

———. "When the Woman Looks." 83–99 in *Revision: Essays in Feminist Film Criticism*, edited by Mary Ann Doane et al. Frederick, Md.: University Publications of America, 1984.

Wood, Robin. "Burying the Undead: The Use and Obsolescence of Count Dracula." 364–378 in *The Dread of Difference: Gender and the Horror Film*, edited by Barry Keith Grant. Austin: University of Texas Press, 1996.

Zimmerman, Bonnie. "Daughters of Darkness: The Lesbian Vampire in Film." 379–387 in *The Dread of Difference: Gender and the Horror Film*, edited by Barry Keith Grant. Austin: University of Texas Press, 1996.

CROSS-MEDIA STUDIES

Aaron, Michele, ed. *The Body's Perilous Pleasures: Dangerous Desires and Contemporary Culture.* Edinburgh: Edinburgh University Press, 1999.

Auerbach, Nina. *Our Vampires Ourselves.* Chicago, Ill.: University of Chicago Press, 1995.

Bann, Stephen, ed. *Frankenstein, Creation and Monstrosity.* London: Reaktion, 1994.

Botting, Fred. *Making Monstrous: Frankenstein, criticism, theory.* Manchester: Manchester University Press, 1991.

Gelder, Ken. *Reading the Vampire.* London: Routledge, 1994.

Halberstam, Judith. *Skin Shows: Gothic Horror and the Technology of Monsters.* Durham, N.C.: Duke University Press, 1995.

Hills, Matt. *The Pleasures of Horror.* London: Continuum, 2005.

Jancovich, Mark. *Horror.* London: Batsford, 1992.

———. *Rational Fears: American horror in the 1950s*. Manchester: Manchester University Press, 1996.

Jones, Daryl. *Horror: A Thematic History in Fiction and Film*. London: Arnold, 2002.

Levine, George, and U. C. Knoepflmacher, eds. *The Endurance of Frankenstein: Essays on Mary Shelley's Novel*. Berkeley and Los Angeles: University of California Press, 1979.

Littau, Karen. "Adaptation, Teleportation and Mutation from Langelaan's to Cronenberg's *The Fly*." 141–155 in *Alien Identities: Exploring Differences in Film and Fiction*, edited by Deborah Cartmell et al. London: Pluto Press, 1999.

Morgan, Jack. *The Biology of Horror: Gothic Literature and Film*. Carbondale: Southern Illinois University Press, 2002.

O'Flinn, Paul. "'Leaving the West and Entering the East': Refiguring the Alien from Stoker to Coppola." 66–86 in *Alien Identities: Exploring Differences in Film and Fiction*, edited by Deborah Cartmell et al. London: Pluto Press, 1999.

———. "Production and Reproduction: The Case of *Frankenstein*." 196–221 in *Popular Fictions: Essays in Literature and History*, edited by P. Humm et al. London: Methuen, 1986.

Punter, David. *The Literature of Terror: Volume 1—The Gothic Tradition, 2nd edition*. London: Longman, 1996.

———. *The Literature of Terror: Volume 2—The Modern Gothic, 2nd edition*. London: Longman, 1996.

Silver, Alain, and James Ursini. *More Things Than Are Dreamt Of: Masterpieces of Supernatural Horror—from Mary Shelley to Stephen King—in Literature and Film*. New York: Limelight, 1994.

Skal, David. *The Monster Show: A Cultural History of Horror*. London: Plexus, 1993.

Waller, Gregory A. *The Living and the Undead: From Stoker's Dracula to Romero's Dawn of the Dead*. Urbana: University of Illinois Press, 1986.

NATIONAL HORROR CINEMAS

Great Britain

Barker, Martin, ed. *The Video Nasties*. London: Pluto Press, 1984.

Boot, Andy. *Fragments of Fear: An Illustrated History of British Horror Films*. London: Creation, 1996.

Chibnall, Steve, and Julian Petley, eds. *British Horror Cinema*. London: Routledge, 2002.

Conrich, Ian. "Traditions of the British Horror Film." 226–232 in *The British Cinema Book, 2nd edition*, edited by Robert Murphy. London: British Film Institute, 2001.

Earnshaw, Tony. *Beating the Devil: The Making of Night of the Demon.* Sheffield: Tomahawk Press, 2005.

Fenton, Harvey, and Dave Flint, eds. *Ten Years of Terror: British Horror Films of the 1970s.* Godalming, Surrey: FAB Press, 2001.

Freeman, Nick. "London Kills Me: The English Metropolis in British Horror Films of the 1970s." 193–210 in *Shocking Cinema of the Seventies*, edited by Xavier Mendik. Hereford: Noir Publishing, 2002.

Hearn, Marcus, and Alan Barnes. *The Hammer Story.* London: Titan, 1997.

Hunt, Leon. *British Low Culture: From Safari Suits to Sexploitation.* London: Routledge, 1998.

Hunter, I. Q. "Hammer Goes East: A Second Glance at *The Legend of the Seven Golden Vampires.*" 138–146 in *Shocking Cinema of the Seventies*, edited by Xavier Mendik. Hereford: Noir Publishing, 2002.

Hutchings, Peter. *Hammer and Beyond: The British Horror Film.* Manchester: Manchester University Press, 1993.

———. *Dracula.* London: I.B. Tauris, 2003.

Kinsey, Wayne. *Hammer Films—The Bray Studio Years.* London: Reynolds and Hearn, 2002.

———. *Hammer Films—The Elstree Studio Years.* Sheffield: Tomahawk Press, 2007.

Lowenstein, Adam. "'Under-the-skin horrors': social realism and classlessness in *Peeping Tom* and the British New Wave." 221–232 in *British Cinema, Past and Present*, edited by Justine Ashby and Andrew Higson. London: Routledge, 2000.

Meikle, Denis. *A History of Horrors: The Rise and Fall of the House of Hammer.* Lanham, Md.: Scarecrow Press, 1996.

Murphy, Robert. *Sixties British Cinema.* London: British Film Institute, 1992.

Petley, Julian. "The Lost Continent." 98–119 in *All Our Yesterdays: 90 Years of British Cinema*, edited by Charles Barr. London: British Film Institute, 1986.

Pirie, David. *A Heritage of Horror: The English Gothic Cinema 1946–1972.* London: Gordon Fraser, 1973.

Porter, Vincent. "The Context of Creativity: Ealing Studios and Hammer Films." 179–207 in *British Cinema History*, edited by Vincent Porter and James Curran. London: Weidenfeld and Nicolson, 1983.

Rigby, Jonathan. *English Gothic: a century of horror cinema.* London: Reynolds and Hearn, 2000.

Smith, Gary A. *Uneasy Dreams: The Golden Age of British Horror Films, 1956–1976.* Jefferson, N.C.: McFarland, 2000.

Wright, Peter. "The British post-*Alien* intrusion film." 138–152 in *British Science Fiction Cinema*, edited by I. Q Hunter. London: Routledge, 1999.

Italy

Del Valle, David. "The cosmic mill of Wolfgang Preiss: Giorgio Ferroni's *Mill of the Stone Women*." 105–110 in *Fear Without Frontiers: Horror Cinema Across The Globe*, edited by Steven Jay Schneider. Godalming, Surrey: FAB Press, 2003.

Erickson, Glenn. "Women on the Verge of a Gothic Breakdown: Sex, Drugs and Corpses in *The Horrible Dr. Hichcock*." 269–280 in *Horror Film Reader*, edited by Alain Silver and James Ursini. New York: Limelight, 2000.

Hunt, Leon. "Burning Oil and Baby Oil: *Bloody Pit of Horror*." 172–180 in *Alternative Europe: Eurotrash and Exploitation Cinema Since 1945*, edited by Ernest Mathijs and Xavier Mendik. London: Wallflower, 2004.

———. "A (Sadistic) Night at the *Opera*: Notes on the Italian Horror Film." 324–335 in *The Horror Reader*, edited by Ken Gelder. London: Routledge, 2000.

Koven, Mikel J. *La Dolce Morte: Vernacular Cinema and the Italian Giallo Film*. Metuchen, N.J.: Scarecrow Press, 2006.

Mendik, Xavier. "Detection and Transgression: The Investigative Drive of the Giallo." 35–54 in *Necronomicon, Book One*, edited by Andy Black. London: Creation Books, 1996.

———. *Tenebre/Tenebrae*. Trowbridge, Wiltshire: Flicks Books, 2000.

Needham, Gary. "Playing with genre: defining the Italian giallo." 135–144 in *Fear without Frontiers: Horror Cinema Across the Globe*, edited by Steven Jay Schneider. Godalming, Surrey: FAB Press, 2003.

Slater, Jay, ed. *Eaten Alive! Italian Cannibal and Zombie Movies*. London: Plexus, 2002.

Tohill, Cathal, and Pete Tombs. *Immoral Tales: Sex and Horror Cinema in Europe 1956–1964*. London: Primitive Press, 1994: 29–39.

Totoro, Donato. "The Italian zombie film: from derivation to invention." 161–173 in *Fear Without Frontiers: Horror Cinema Across The Globe*, edited by Steven Jay Schneider. Godalming, Surrey: FAB Press, 2003.

Spain

Tohill, Cathal, and Pete Tombs. *Immoral Tales: Sex and Horror Cinema in Europe 1956–1964*. London: Primitive Press, 1994: 63–74.

Willis, Andrew. "Spanish horror and the flight from 'art' cinema, 1967–73."
71–83 in *Defining Cult Movies: The cultural politics of oppositional taste*,
edited by Mark Jancovich, Antonio Lazaro Reboll, Julian Stringer and Andy
Willis. Manchester: Manchester University Press, 2003.
———. "From the margins to the mainstream: trends in recent Spanish horror
cinema." 237–250 in *Spanish Popular Cinema*, edited by Antonio Lázaro
Reboll and Andrew Willis. Manchester: Manchester University Press, 2004.
———. "The Spanish Horror Film as Subversive Text: Eloy de la Iglesia's *La
semana del asesino*." 163–179 in *Horror International*, edited by Steven Jay
Schneider, and Tony Williams. Detroit, Mich.: Wayne State University Press,
2005.

United States

Asselle, Giovanna and Behroze Gandhy. "*Dressed to Kill*." *Screen* 23, no. 3–4
(1982): 137–143.
Babington, Bruce. "Twice a Victim: *Carrie* Meets the BFI." *Screen* 24, no. 3
(1983): 4–18.
Benshoff, Harry. "Blaxploitation Horror Films: Generic Reappropriation or
Reinscription." *Cinema Journal* 39, no. 2 (2000): 31–50.
Berenstein, Rhona J. *Attack of the Leading Ladies: Gender, Sexuality, and
Spectatorship in Classic Horror Cinema*. New York: Columbia University
Press, 1996.
———. "Mommie Dearest: *Aliens, Rosemary's Baby*, and Mothering." *Journal
of Popular Culture* 24, no. 2 (1990): 55–73.
Berks, John. "What Alice Does: Looking Otherwise at The *Cat People*." *Cinema Journal* 32, no. 1 (1992): 26–42.
Billson, Anne. *The Thing (BFI Modern Classics)*. London: British Film Institute, 1997.
Bracke, Peter M. *Crystal Lake Memories: The Complete History of Friday the
13th*. London: Titan, 2006.
Briefel, Aviva and Sianne Ngai. "*Candyman*: Urban Space, Fear, and Entitlement." 281–304 in *Horror Film Reader*, edited by Alain Silver and James
Ursini. New York: Limelight, 2000.
Britton, Andrew. "*The Exorcist*." *Movie* 25 (1977/8): 16–20.
Brookover, Linda and Alain Silver. "What Rough Beast? Insect Politics and
The Fly." 237–246 in *Horror Film Reader*, edited by Alain Silver and James
Ursini. New York: Limelight, 2000.
Brottman, Mikita. "Fecal Phantoms: Oral and Anal Tensions in *The Tingler*."
103–117 in *Trash Aesthetics: Popular Culture and its Audience*, edited by

Deborah Cartmell, I. Q. Hunter, Heidi Kaye, and Imelda Whelehan. London: Pluto Press, 2004.

———. "Once Upon A Time In Texas: *The Texas Chainsaw Massacre* As Inverted Fairytale." 7–21 in *Necronomicon, Book One*, edited by Andy Black. London: Creation Books, 1996.

Brunas, Michael, John Brunas, and Tom Weaver. *Universal Horrors: The Studio's Classic Films, 1931–1946.* Jefferson, N.C.: McFarland, 1991.

Bundtzen, Linda K. "Monstrous Mothers: Medusa, Grendel, and now *Alien.*" *Film Quarterly* 40, no. 3 (1987): 11–17.

Carroll, Noel. "*King Kong*: Ape and Essence." 215–244 in *Planks of Reason: Essays on the Horror Film*, edited by Barry K. Grant. Metuchen, N.J.: Scarecrow Press, 1984.

Clover, Carol J. *Men, Women and Chainsaws: Gender in the Modern Horror Film.* London: British Film Institute, 1992.

Conlon, James. "Silencing Lambs and Educating Women." *Post Script* 12, no. 1 (1992): 3–12.

Conrich, Ian. "Before Sound: Universal, Silent Cinema, and the Last of the Horror Spectaculars." 40–47 in *The Horror Film*, edited by Stephen Prince. New Jersey: Rutgers University Press, 2004.

———. "*The Friday the 13th* Films and the Cultural Function of a Modern Grand Guignol." 103–118 in *Cauchemars americains: fantastique et horreur dans le cinema moderne*, edited by Frank Lafond. Lihge: Les Éditions du CEFAL, 2003.

———. "Seducing the Subject: Freddy Krueger, Popular Culture and the *Nightmare on Elm Street* Films." 118–131 in *Trash Aesthetics: Popular Culture and its Audience*, edited by Deborah Cartmell, I. Q. Hunter, Heidi Kaye and Imelda Whelehan. London: Pluto Press, 2004.

Constable, Catherine. "Becoming the Monster's Mother: Morphologies of Identity in the *Alien* series." 173–202 in *Alien Zone II: The Spaces of Science Fiction Cinema*, edited by Annette Kuhn. London: Verso, 1999.

Derry, Charles. "More Dark Dreams: Some Notes on the Recent Horror Film." 162–174 in *American Horrors: Essays on the Modern American Horror Film*, edited by Gregory Waller. Urbana: University of Illinois Press, 1987.

Dika, Vera. "From Dracula—with Love." 388–400 in *The Dread of Difference: Gender and the Horror Film*, edited by Barry Keith Grant. Austin: University of Texas Press, 1996.

———. *Games of Terror: Halloween, Friday the 13th, and the Films of the Stalker Cycle.* London: Associated University Presses, 1990.

Dillard, R. H. W. "*Night of the Living Dead*: It's Not Just Like a Wind That's Passing Through." 14–29 in *American Horrors: Essays on the Modern*

American Horror Film, edited by Gregory Waller. Urbana: University of Illinois Press, 1987.

Doherty, Thomas. "Genre, Gender and the *Aliens* trilogy." 181–199 in *The Dread of Difference: Gender and the Horror Film*, edited by Barry Keith Grant. Austin: University of Texas Press, 1996.

———. *Teenagers and Teenpics: The Juvenilization of American Movies in the 1950s*. Boston: Unwin Hyman, 1988.

Dyer, Richard. *Seven (BFI Modern Classics)*. London: British Film Institute, 1999.

Erb, Cynthia. "Have You Ever Seen the Inside of One of Those Places?: *Psycho*, Foucault, and the Postwar Context of Madness." *Cinema Journal* 45, no. 4 (2006): 45–63.

———. *Tracking King Kong: A Hollywood Icon in World Culture*. Detroit, Mich.: Wayne State University Press, 1998.

Erens, Patricia Brett. "*The Stepfather*: Father as Monster in the Contemporary Horror Film." 352–363 in *The Dread of Difference: Gender and the Horror Film*, edited by Barry Keith Grant. Austin: University of Texas Press, 1996.

Fischer, Lucy. "Birth Trauma: Parturition and Horror in *Rosemary's Baby*." *Cinema Journal* 31, no. 3 (1992): 3–18.

Fischer, Lucy, and Marcia Landy. "*Eyes of Laura Mars*: A Binocular Critique." *Screen* 23, no. 3–4 (1982): 4–19.

Garrett, Gregg. "Objecting to Objectification: Re-viewing the Feminine in *The Silence of the Lambs*." *Journal of Popular Culture* 27, no. 4 (1994): 1–12.

Grant, Barry Keith. "Rich and Strange: The Yuppie Horror Film." *Journal of Film and Video* 48, no. 1–2 (1996): 4–16.

Greenberg, Harvey Roy. "*King Kong*: The Beast in the Boudoir—or 'You Can't Marry That Girl, You're A Gorilla!'" 338–351 in *The Dread of Difference: Gender and the Horror Film*, edited by Barry Keith Grant. Austin: University of Texas Press, 1996.

Grove, David. *Making Friday the 13th: The Legend of Camp Blood*. Godalming, Surrey: FAB Press, 2005.

Harris, Martin. "You can't kill the boogeyman: *Halloween III* and the modern horror franchise." *Journal of Popular Film and Television* 32, no. 3 (2004): 98–109.

Heba, G. "Everyday Nightmares: The Rhetoric of Social Horror in the *Nightmare on Elm Street* Series," *Journal of Popular Film and Television* 23, no. 3 (1995): 106–115.

Heffernan, Kevin. *Ghouls, Gimmicks, and Gold: Horror Films and the American Movie Business, 1953–1968*. Durham, N.C.: Duke University Press, 2004.

Hendershot, Cyndy. "The cold war horror film: taboo and transgression in *The Bad Seed*, *The Fly*, and *Psycho*." *Journal of Popular Film and Television* 29, no. 1 (2001): 20–31.

———. *I Was a Cold War Monster: Horror Films, Eroticism and the Cold War Imagination*. Bowling Green, Ohio: Popular Press, 2001.

Hollinger, Karen. "The Monster as Woman: Two Generations of Cat People." 296–308 in *The Dread of Difference: Gender and the Horror Film*, edited by Barry Keith Grant. Austin: University of Texas Press, 1996.

Hoxter, Julian. "*The Evil Dead*: From Slapstick to Splatshtick." 71–83 in *Necronomicon, Book One*, edited by Andy Black. London: Creation Books, 1996.

Humphries, Reynolds. *The American Horror Film: An Introduction*. Edinburgh: Edinburgh University Press, 2002.

———. *The Hollywood Horror Film, 1931–1941: Madness in a Social Landscape*. Metuchen, N.J.: Scarecrow Press, 2006.

Jenks, Carol. "*The Bride of Frankenstein*: Sexual Polarity and Subjugation." 158–162 in *Necronomicon, Book One*, edited by Andy Black. London: Creation Books, 1996.

Jones, Martin. "Head Cheese: *The Texas Chainsaw Massacre* Beyond Leatherface." 178–192 in *Shocking Cinema of the Seventies*, edited by Xavier Mendik. Hereford: Noir Publishing, 2002.

Jordan, J. J. "Vampire cyborgs and scientific imperialism: a reading of the science-mysticism polemic in *Blade*." *Journal of Popular Film and Television* 27, no. 2 (1999): 4–15.

Kavanagh, James H. "Feminism, Humanism and Science in *Alien*." 73–81 in *Alien Zone: Cultural Theory and Contemporary Science Fiction Cinema*, edited by Annette Kuhn. London: Verso, 1990.

Kawin, Bruce. "*The Funhouse* and *The Howling*." 102–113 in *American Horrors: Essays on the Modern American Horror Film*, edited by Gregory Waller. Urbana: University of Illinois Press, 1987.

———. "The Mummy's Pool." 3–20 in *Planks of Reason: Essays on the Horror Film*, edited by Barry K. Grant. Metuchen, N.J.: Scarecrow Press, 1984.

Keesey, Pam. "*The Haunting* and the Power of Suggestion: Why Robert Wise's Film Continues to 'Deliver the Goods' to Modern Audiences." 305–315 in *Horror Film Reader*, edited by Alain Silver and James Ursini. New York: Limelight, 2000.

Kermode, Mark. *The Exorcist, 2nd edition (BFI Modern Classics)*. London: British Film Institute, 2003.

Linderman, Deborah. "Cinematic Abreaction: Tourneur's Cat People." 73–97 in *Psychoanalysis and Cinema*, edited by E. Ann Kaplan. London: Routledge, 1990.

Lindsey, Shelley Stamp. "Horror, Femininity, and Carrie's Monstrous Puberty." 279–295 in *The Dread of Difference: Gender and the Horror Film*, edited by Barry Keith Grant. Austin: University of Texas Press, 1996.

Lowry, Edward, and Richard deCordova. "Enunciation and the Production of Horror in *White Zombie*." 346–389 in *Planks of Reason: Essays on the Horror Film*, edited by Barry K. Grant. Metuchen, N.J.: Scarecrow Press, 1984.

Magistrale, Tony. *Hollywood's Stephen King*. New York: Palgrave Macmillan, 2003.

Manguel, Alberto. *Bride of Frankenstein (BFI Film Classics)*. London: British Film Institute, 1997.

Medovoi, Leerom. "Theorizing historicity, or the many meanings of *Blacula*." *Screen* 39, no. 1 (1998): 1–21.

Neale, Steve. "*Halloween*: Suspense, Aggression and the Look." *Framework* 14 (1981), 25–29.

———. "Issues of Difference: *Alien* and *Blade Runner*." 213–223 in *Fantasy and the Cinema*, edited by James Donald. London: British Film Institute, 1989.

Newman, Kim. *Cat People (BFI Film Classics)*. London: British Film Institute, 1999.

Newton, Judith. "Feminism and Anxiety in *Alien*." 82–87 in *Alien Zone: Cultural Theory and Contemporary Science Fiction Cinema*, edited by Annette Kuhn. London: Verso, 1990.

Paglia, Camilla. *The Birds (BFI Film Classics)*. London: British Film Institute, 1998.

Paige, L. R. "The transformation of woman: The 'Curse of the Cat Woman' in Val Lewton/Jacques Tourneur's *Cat People*, its sequel, and remake." *Literature Film Quarterly* 25, no. 4 (1997): 291–299.

Paul, William. *Laughing Screaming: Modern Hollywood Horror and Comedy*. New York: Columbia University Press, 1994.

Prince, Stephen. "Dread, Taboo and *The Thing*: Toward a Social Theory of the Horror Film." *Wide Angle* 10, no. 3 (1988): 19–29.

Rathgeb, Douglas. "Bogeyman from the Id: Nightmare and Reality in *Halloween* and *A Nightmare on Elm Street*." *Journal of Popular Film and Television* 19, no. 1 (1991): 36–43.

Rhodes, Gary D., ed. *Horror at the Drive-In: Essays in Popular Americana*. Jefferson, N.C.: McFarland, 2003.

Rigby, Jonathan. *American Gothic: Sixty Years of Horror Cinema*. London: Reynolds and Hearn, 2006.

Rodowick, D. N. "The Enemy Within: The Economy of Violence in *The Hills Have Eyes*." 321–330 in *Planks of Reason: Essays on the Horror Film*, edited by Barry K. Grant. Metuchen, N.J.: Scarecrow Press, 1984.

Sample, Mark. "There Goes the Neighbourhood: The Seventies, the Middle Class and *The Omega Man*." 29–40 in *Shocking Cinema of the Seventies*, edited by Xavier Mendik. Hereford: Noir Publishing, 2002.

Schneider, Stephen. "Kevin Williamson and the Rise of the Neo-Stalker." *Post Script* 19, no. 2 (2000): 73–87.

———. "Possessed by Soul: Generic (Dis) Continuity in the Blaxploitation Horror Film." 106–120 in *Shocking Cinema of the Seventies*, edited by Xavier Mendik. Hereford: Noir Publishing, 2002.

Sharrett, Christopher. "The Idea of Apocalypse in *The Texas Chainsaw Massacre*." 255–276 in *Planks of Reason: Essays on the Horror Film*, edited by Barry K. Grant. Metuchen, N.J.: Scarecrow Press, 1984.

Simpson, Philip L. *Psycho Paths: Tracking the Serial Killer Through Contemporary American Film and Fiction*. Carbondale: Southern Illinois University Press, 2000.

Skal, David. J. *Hollywood Gothic: The Tangled Web of Dracula from Novel to Stage to Screen*. London: Andre Deutsch, 1990.

Sobchack, Vivian. "Revenge of *The Leech Woman*: On the Dread of Aging in a Low Budget Horror Film." 336–345 in *The Horror Reader*, edited by Ken Gelder. London: Routledge, 2000.

Soister, John T. *Of Gods and Monsters: A Critical Guide to Universal Studios' Science Fiction, Horror and Mystery Films, 1929–1939*. Jefferson, N.C.: McFarland, 1999.

Staiger, Janet. "Taboos and Totems: Cultural Meanings of *The Silence of the Lambs*." 142–154 in *Film Theory Goes To The Movies*, edited by Jim Collins, Hilary Radner and Ava Preacher Collins. London: Routledge, 1993.

Tasker, Yvonne. *The Silence of the Lambs (BFI Modern Classics)*. London: British Film Institute, 2002.

Tharp, Julie. "The Transvestite as Monster: Gender Horror in *The Silence of the Lambs* and *Psycho*." *Journal of Popular Film and Television* 19, no. 3 (1991): 106–113.

Thomson, David. *The Alien Quartet*. London: Bloomsbury, 1998.

Tietchen, Todd F. "Samplers and Copycats: The Cultural Implications of the Postmodern Slasher in Contemporary American Film." *Journal of Popular Film and Television* 26, no. 3 (1998): 98–107.

Trencansky, Sarah. "Final Girls and Terrible Youth: Transgression in 1980s Slasher Horror." *Journal of Popular Film and Television* 29, no. 2 (2001).

Turner, George E., and Michael H. Price. *Forgotten horrors: early talkie chillers from Poverty Row*. New York: A. S. Barnes, 1979.

Waller, Gregory, A., ed. *American Horrors: Essays on the Modern American Horror Film*. Urbana: University of Illinois Press, 1987.

Warren, Bill. *The Evil Dead Companion*. London: Titan, 2000.

Wee, Valerie. "Resurrecting and Updating the Teen Slasher: The Case of *Scream.*" *Journal of Popular Film and Television* 34, no. 2 (2006): 50–61.

———. "The *Scream* Trilogy, Hyperpostmodernism, and the Late Nineties Teen Slasher Film." *Journal of Film and Video* 57, no. 3 (2005): 44–61.

Wexman, Virginia Wright. "The Trauma of Infancy in Roman Polanski's *Rosemary's Baby.*" 30–43 in *American Horrors: Essays on the Modern American Horror Film*, edited by Gregory Waller. Urbana: University of Illinois Press, 1987.

White, Patricia. "Female Spectator, Lesbian Spectre: *The Haunting.*" 130–150 in *Women in Film Noir*, 2nd edition, edited by E. Ann Kaplan. London: British Film Institute, 1998.

Williams, Linda. "Discipline and Fun: *Psycho* and Postmodern Cinema." 351–378 in *Reinventing Film Studies*, edited by Christine Gledhill and Linda Williams. London: Edward Arnold, 2000.

Williams, Tony. "Family Horror." *Movie* 27/28 (1981): 117–126.

———. *Hearths of Darkness: The Family in the American Horror Film.* Madison, N.J.: Fairleigh Dickinson University Press, 1996.

———. "Trying to Survive on the Darker Side: 1980s Family Horror." 164–180 in *The Dread of Difference: Gender and the Horror Film*, edited by Barry Keith Grant. Austin: University of Texas Press, 1996.

———. "Is the Devil American? William Dieterle's *The Devil and Daniel Webster.*" 129–150 in *Horror Film Reader*, edited by Alain Silver and James Ursini. New York: Limelight, 2000.

Wood, Robin. *Hollywood from Vietnam to Reagan.* New York: Columbia University Press, 1986.

———. "Neglected Nightmares." 111–128 in *Horror Film Reader*, edited by Alain Silver and James Ursini. New York: Limelight, 2000.

Wood, Robin, and Richard Lippe, eds. *The American Nightmare.* Toronto: Toronto Film Festival, 1979.

Worland, Rick. "OWI meets the monsters: Hollywood horror films and war propaganda, 1942 to 1945." *Cinema Journal* 37 (1997): 47–65.

Young, Elizabeth. "Bods and Monsters: The Return of the Bride of Frankenstein." 225–236 in *The End of Cinema As We Know It: American Film in the Nineties*, edited by Jon Lewis. New York: New York University Press, 2001.

———. "Here Comes the Bride: Wedding Gender and Race in *Bride of Frankenstein.*" 309–337 in *The Dread of Difference: Gender and the Horror Film*, edited by Barry Keith Grant. Austin: University of Texas Press, 1996.

Other

Austin, Guy. "Vampirism, gender wars and the 'Final Girl': French fantasy film in the early seventies." *French Cultural Studies* 7, no. 3 (1996), 321–332.

Halle, Randall. "Unification Horror: Queer Desire and Uncanny Vision." 281–303 in *Light Motives: German Popular Film in Perspective*, edited by Randall Halle and Margaret McCarthy. Detroit: Wayne State University Press, 2003.

Jenks, Carol. "*Daughters of Darkness*: A Lesbian Vampire Art Film." 22–34 in *Necronomicon, Book One*, edited by Andy Black. London: Creation Books, 1996.

Mathijs, Ernest, ed. *The Cinema of the Low Countries*. London: Wallflower, 2004: includes essays on horrors *Daughters of Darkness*, *Man Bites Dog* and *The Vanishing*.

McRoy, Jay, ed. *Japanese Horror Cinema*. Edinburgh: Edinburgh University Press, 2005.

Schneider, Steven Jay. *Fear Without Frontiers: Horror Cinema Across the Globe*. Godalming, Surrey, FAB Press: contains essays on horror films from Austria, Brazil, China, Cuba, France, Germany, India, Indonesia, Japan, Korea, Mexico, the Philippines, Poland, and Turkey.

Schneider, Steven Jay, and Tony Williams, eds. *Horror International*. Detroit, Mich.: Wayne State University Press, 2005: contains essays on horror films from Australia, Belgium, Canada, China, Egypt, Germany, Holland, Ireland, Japan, New Zealand, Romania, Russia, and Thailand.

Tohill, Cathal, and Pete Tombs. *Immoral Tales: Sex and Horror Cinema in Europe 1956–1964*. London: Primitive Press, 1994: 41–52 on German cinema and 53–61 on French cinema.

Tsutsui, William Minoru. *Godzilla on My Mind: Fifty Years of the King of Monsters*. London: Palgrave Macmillan, 2004.

PERSONNEL

Actors

Beck, Calvin Thomas. *Heroes of the Horrors*. New York: Collier Books, 1975.

———. *Scream Queens*. New York: Collier Books, 1978.

Bojarski, Richard, and Kenneth Beals. *The Films of Boris Karloff*. Secaucus, N.J.: Citadel Press, 1974.

Bradley, Doug. *Sacred Monsters: Behind the Mask of the Horror Actor*. London: Titan, 1996.

Campbell, Bruce. *If Chins Could Kill: Confessions of a B Movie Actor*. New York: St. Martin's Press, 2001.

Cushing, Peter. *Past Forgetting: Memoirs of the Hammer Years*. London: Weidenfeld and Nicolson, 1988.

———. *Peter Cushing: An Autobiography*. London: Weidenfeld and Nicolson, 1986.

Gemünden, Gerd. "From 'Mr. M' to 'Mr. Murder': Peter Lorre and the Actor in Exile." 85–107 in *Light Motives: German Popular Film in Perspective*, edited by Randall Halle and Margaret McCarthy. Detroit: Wayne State University Press, 2003.

Jenks, Carol. "The other face of death: Barbara Steele and *La maschera del demonio*." 149–162 in *Popular European Cinema*, edited by Richard Dyer and Ginette Vincendeau. London: Routledge, 1993.

Jensen, Paul M. *Boris Karloff and His Films*. London: Tantivy Press, 1974.

Lee, Christopher. *Tall, Dark and Gruesome: An Autobiography*. London: Granada, 1977.

Mank, Gregory William. *Women in Horror Films, 1930s*. Jefferson, N.C.: McFarland, 1999.

———. *Women in Horror Films, 1940s*. Jefferson, N.C.: McFarland, 1999.

Meikle, Denis. *Vincent Price: The Art of Fear*. London: Reynolds and Hearn, 2006.

Miller, David. *The Peter Cushing Companion*. London: Reynolds and Hearn, 2000.

Richards, Jeffrey. "Tod Slaughter and the Cinema of Excess." 139–159 in *The Unknown 1930s: An Alternative History of the British Cinema, 1929–1939*, edited by Jeffrey Richards. London: I. B. Tauris, 1998.

Rigby, Jonathan. *Christopher Lee: The Authorized Screen History*. London: Reynolds and Hearn, 2003.

Tjersland, Todd. "Cinema of the doomed: the tragic horror of Paul Naschy." 69–80 in *Fear Without Frontiers: Horror Cinema Across the Globe*, edited by Steven Jay Schneider. Godalming, Surrey: FAB Press, 2003.

Underwood, Peter. *Horror Man: The Life of Boris Karloff*. London: Frewin, 1972.

Williams, Lucy Chase. *The Complete Films of Vincent Price*. Secaucus, N.J.: Citadel Press, 1998.

Composers

Huckvale, David. *James Bernard, Composer to Count Dracula: A Critical Biography*. Jefferson, N.C.: McFarland, 2005.

Larson, Randall, D. *Music from the House of Hammer 1950–1980*. Metuchen, N.J.: Scarecrow Press., 1996.

———. *Musique fantastique : a survey of film music in the fantastic cinema*. Metuchen, N.J.: Scarecrow Press, 1985.

Directors

Barcinski, André. "Coffin Joe and José Mojica Marins: strange men for strange times." 27–38 in *Fear Without Frontiers: Horror Cinema Across The Globe*, edited by Steven Jay Schneider. Godalming, Surrey: FAB Press, 2003.

Beard, William. *The Artist as Monster: The Cinema of David Cronenberg.* Toronto: University of Toronto Press, 2001.

Bird, Daniel. "Fascination—Jean Rollin: Cinematic Poet." 62–70 in *Necronomicon, Book One*, edited by Andy Black. London: Creation Books, 1996.

Bissette, Stephen R. "Curtis Harrington and the Underground Roots of the Modern Horror Film." 40–50 in *Underground U.S.A.: Filmmaking Beyond The Hollywood Canon*, edited by Xavier Mendik and Steven Jay Schneider. London: Wallflower, 2002.

Blake, Linnie. "Another One For the Fire: George A. Romero's American Theology of the Flesh." 151–165 in *Shocking Cinema of the Seventies*, edited by Xavier Mendik. Hereford: Noir Publishing, 2002.

———. "Jörg Buttgereit's Nekromantiks: Things To Do In Germany With The Dead." 191–202 in *Alternative Europe: Eurotrash and Exploitation Cinema Since 1945*, edited by Ernest Mathijs and Xavier Mendik. London: Wallflower, 2004.

Bliss, Michael. *Brian De Palma.* Metuchen, N.J.: Scarecrow Press, 1983.

Brottman, Mikita. "Herschell Gordon Lewis: Compulsive Tales and Cannibal Feasts." 154–157 in *Necronomicon, Book One*, edited by Andy Black. London: Creation Books, 1996.

Campbell, Mary B. "Biological Alchemy and the films of David Cronenberg." 307–320 in *Planks of Reason: Essays on the Horror Film*, edited by Barry K. Grant. Metuchen, N.J.: Scarecrow Press, 1984.

Castle, William. *Step Right Up! I'm Gonna Scare the Pants Off America: Memoirs of a B-Movie Mogul.* New York: Pharos Books, 1976.

Castoldi, Gian Luca, Harvey Fenton, and Julian Grainger. *Cannibal Holocaust and the Savage Cinema of Ruggero Deodato.* Godalming, Surrey: FAB Press, 1999.

Chibnall, Steve. *Making Mischief: The Cult Films of Pete Walker.* Guildford, Surrey: FAB Press, 1998.

Conrich, Ian, and David Woods, eds. *The Cinema of John Carpenter: the technique of terror.* London: Wallflower Press, 2004.

Cooper, L. Andrew. "The Indulgence of Critique: Relocating the Sadistic Voyeur in Dario Argento's *Opera*." *Quarterly Review of Film and Video* 22, no. 1 (2005): 63–72.

Corman, Roger. *How I Made a Hundred Movies in Hollywood and Never Lost a Dime.* New York: Random House, 1990.

Crane, Jonathan. "Come On-A My House: The Inescapable Legacy of Wes Craven's *The Last House on the Left*." 166–177 in *Shocking Cinema of the Seventies*, edited by Xavier Mendik. Hereford: Noir Publishing, 2002.

———. "Scraping Bottom: Splatter and the Herschell Gordon Lewis Oeuvre." 150–166 in *The Horror Film*, edited by Stephen Prince. New Jersey: Rutgers University Press, 2004.

Creed, Barbara. "Phallic Panic: Male Hysteria and *Dead Ringers.*" *Screen* 31, no. 2 (1990): 125–146.

Curtis, James. *James Whale.* Metuchen, N.J.: Scarecrow Press, 1982.

Dixon, Wheeler Winston. *The Charm of Evil: The Life and Films of Terence Fisher.* Metuchen, N.J.: Scarecrow Press, 1991.

———. *The Films of Freddie Francis.* Metuchen N.J.: Scarecrow Press, 1991.

Drew, Wayne, ed. *David Cronenberg.* London: British Film Institute, 1984.

Fisher, Terence. "Horror Is My Business." *Films and Filming* 10, no. 10 (July 1964): 8.

Gallant, Chris, ed. *Dark Dreams: The Cinema of Dario Argento.* Godalming, Surrey: FAB Press, 2001.

Gatiss, Mark. *James Whale: A Biography (or The Would-Be Gentleman).* London: Cassell, 1995.

Graham, Allison. "'The Fallen Wonder of the World': Brian De Palma's Horror Films." 129–144 in *American Horrors: Essays on the Modern American Horror Film,* edited by Gregory Waller. Urbana: University of Illinois Press, 1987.

Grant, Barry Keith. "Taking Back the *Night of the Living Dead*: George Romero, Feminism, and the Horror Film." 200–212 in *The Dread of Difference: Gender and the Horror Film,* edited by Barry Keith Grant. Austin: University of Texas Press, 1996.

Grant, Michael. "Fulci's Waste Land: Cinema, Horror, and the Dreams of Modernism." 61–71 in *Unruly Pleasures: The Cult Film and its Critics,* edited by Xavier Mendik and Graeme Harper. Guildford, Surrey: FAB Press, 2000.

———, ed. *The Modern Fantastic: The Films of David Cronenberg.* Trowbridge, Wiltshire: Flicks Books, 2000.

Guins, Ray. "Tortured Looks: Dario Argento and Visual Displeasure." 141–153 in *Necronomicon, Book One,* edited by Andy Black. London: Creation Books, 1996.

Halligan, Benjamin. *Michael Reeves.* Manchester: Manchester University Press, 2003.

Handling, Piers, ed. *The Shape of Rage: The Films of David Cronenberg.* Toronto: General Publishing, 1983.

Hantke, Steffen. "Spectacular optics: the deployment of special effects in David Cronenberg's films." *Film Criticism* 29, no. 2 (2004): 34–52.

Hawkins, Joan. "'No Worse Than You Were Before': Theory, Economy and Power in Abel Ferrara's *The Addiction.*" 13–25 in *Underground U.S.A.: Filmmaking Beyond The Hollywood Canon,* edited by Xavier Mendik and Steven Jay Schneider. London: Wallflower, 2002.

Howarth, Troy. *The Haunted World of Mario Bava.* Godalming, Surrey: FAB Press, 2002.

Hunt, Leon. "*Witchfinder General*: Michael Reeves' Visceral Classic." 123–130 in *Necronomicon: Book 1*, edited by Andy Black. London: Creation Books, 1996.

Hutchings, Peter. "Authorship and British Cinema: The Case of Roy Ward Baker." 179–189 in *British Cinema, Past and Present*, edited by Justine Ashby and Andrew Higson. London: Routledge, 2000.

———. "The Argento effect." 127–141 in *Defining Cult Movies: The cultural politics of oppositional taste*, edited by Mark Jancovich, Antonio Lázaro Reboll, Julian Stringer and Andy Willis. Manchester: Manchester University Press, 2003.

———. *Terence Fisher*. Manchester: Manchester University Press, 2001.

Jermyn, Deborah, and Sean Redmond, eds. *The Cinema of Kathryn Bigelow: Hollywood transgressor*. London: Wallflower, 2003.

Jones, Alan. *Profondo Argento: The Man, The Myths and the Magic*. Godalming, Surrey: FAB Press, 2004.

Kerekes, David. *Sex Murder Art: The Films of Jörg Buttgereit*. London: Critical Vision, 1998.

Knee, Adam. "Gender, Genre, Argento." 213–230 in *The Dread of Difference: Gender and the Horror Film*, edited by Barry Keith Grant. Austin: University of Texas Press, 1996.

Lowenstein, Adam. "Films Without A Face: Shock Horror in the Cinema of Georges Franju." *Cinema Journal* 37, no. 4 (1998): 37–58.

———. "Canadian Horror Made Flesh: Contextualizing David Cronenberg." *Post Script* 18, no. 2 (1999): 37–51.

MacKinnon, Kenneth. *Misogyny in the Movies: The De Palma Question*. Newark: University of Delaware Press, 1990.

Mayer, Geoff. *Roy Ward Baker*. Manchester: Manchester University Press, 2004.

McDonagh, Maitland. *Broken Mirrors, Broken Minds: The Dark Dreams of Dario Argento*. London: Sun Tavern Fields, 1991.

McLarty, Lianne. "Beyond the Veil of the Flesh: Cronenberg and the Disembodiment of Horror." 231–252 in *The Dread of Difference: Gender and the Horror Film*, edited by Barry Keith Grant. Austin: University of Texas Press, 1996.

Mendik, Xavier. "Gouts of Blood: The Colourful Underground Universe of Herschell Gordon Lewis." 188–197 in *Underground U.S.A.: Filmmaking Beyond The Hollywood Canon*, edited by Xavier Mendik and Steven Jay Schneider. London: Wallflower, 2002.

———. "Trans-European Excess: An Interview with Brian Yuzna." 181–190 in *Alternative Europe: Eurotrash and Exploitation Cinema Since 1945*, edited by Ernest Mathijs and Xavier Mendik. London: Wallflower, 2004.

Murray, John B. *The Remarkable Michael Reeves: His Short and Tragic Life.* Baltimore, Md.: Luminary Press, 2004.

Naha, Ed. *The films of Roger Corman.* New York: Arco, 1982.

Norden, Martin F., and Madeleine Cahill. "Violence, Women, and Disability in Tod Browning's *Freaks* and *Devil Doll.*" 151–166 in *Horror Film Reader,* edited by Alain Silver and James Ursini. New York: Limelight, 2000.

Odell, Colin, and Michelle Le Blanc. "Jean Rollin: Le sang d'un poète du cinema." 160–171 in *Alternative Europe: Eurotrash and Exploitation Cinema Since 1945,* edited by Ernest Mathijs and Xavier Mendik. London: Wallflower, 2004.

Orr, John, and Elzbieta Ostrowska, eds. *The Cinema of Roman Polanski: Dark Spaces of the World.* London: Wallflower, 2006.

Perks, Marcelle. "A Very German Post-Mortem: Jörg Buttgereit and co-writer/assistant director Franz Rodenkirchen Speak." 203–215 in *Alternative Europe: Eurotrash and Exploitation Cinema Since 1945,* edited by Ernest Mathijs and Xavier Mendik. London: Wallflower, 2004.

Ringel, Harry. "Terence Fisher: The Human Side." *Cinefantastique* 4, no. 3 (1975): 5–16.

———. "Hammer Horror: The World of Terence Fisher." 35–45 in *Graphic Violence on the Screen,* edited by Thomas R. Atkins. New York: Monarch Press, 1976.

———. "Terence Fisher Underlining." *Cinefantastique,* 4, no. 3 (1975): 19–26.

Robb, Brian J. *Screams and Nightmares: The Films of Wes Craven.* New York: Overlook, 1999.

Robbins, Helen W. "More Human Than I Am Alone: Womb Envy in David Cronenberg's *The Fly* and *Dead Ringers.*" 134–147 in *Screening the Male: Exploring Masculinities in Hollywood Cinema,* edited by Steve Cohan and Ina Rae Hark. London: Routledge, 1993.

Rodley, Chris, ed. *Cronenberg on Cronenberg.* London: Faber, 1992.

Sanjek, David. "Dr. Hobbes's Parasites: Victims, Victimization, and Gender in David Cronenberg's *Shivers.*" *Cinema Journal* 36, no. 1 (1996): 55–74.

———. "The Doll and the Whip: Pathos and Ballyhoo in William Castle's *Homicidal.*" *Quarterly Review of Film and Video* 20, no. 4 (2003): 247–63.

Short, Sue. "'No flesh shall be spared': Richard Stanley's *Hardware.*" 169–180 in *British Science Fiction Cinema,* edited by I. Q Hunter. London: Routledge, 1999.

Silver, Alain, and James Ursini. "Mario Bava: the Illusion of Reality." 95–109 in *Horror Film Reader,* edited by Alain Silver and James Ursini. New York: Limelight, 2000.

Skal, David J., and Elias Savada. *Dark Carnival: The Secret World of Tod Browning.* New York: Anchor Books, 1995.

Szulkin, David. *Wes Craven's Last House on the Left: The Making of a Cult Classic.* Godalming, Surrey: FAB Press, 2000.

Thrower, Stephen. *Beyond Terror: The Films of Lucio Fulci.* Guildford, Surrey: FAB Press, 1999.

Tohill, Cathal, and Pete Tombs. *Immoral Tales: Sex and Horror Cinema in Europe 1956–1964.* London: Primitive Press, 1994: contains chapters on Walerian Borowczyk, Jesus Franco, José Larraz and Jean Rollin.

Welsch, Janice R., and Syndy M. Conger. "The Comic and the Grotesque in James Whale's Frankenstein Films." 290–306 in *Planks of Reason: Essays on the Horror Film,* edited by Barry K. Grant. Metuchen, N.J.: Scarecrow Press, 1984.

Willemen, Paul, and Claire Johnston, eds. *Jacques Tourneur.* Edinburgh: Edinburgh Film Festival, 1975.

Willemen, Paul, David Pirie, David Will, and Lynda Myles, eds. *Roger Corman.* Edinburgh: Edinburgh Film Festival, 1970.

Williams, Tony. *Larry Cohen: The Radical Allegories of an Independent Filmmaker.* Jefferson, N.C.: McFarland, 1997.

———. *The Cinema of George A. Romero: Knight of the Living Dead.* London: Wallflower Press, 2003.

Winter, Douglas. *Clive Barker: The Dark Fantastic.* London: HarperCollins, 2001.

Wood, Robin. "The Shadow World of Jacques Tourneur." *Film Comment* 8, no. 2 (1972): 64–70.

Wu, Harmony, H. "Trading in horror, cult and matricide: Peter Jackson's phenomenal bad taste and New Zealand fantasies of inter/national cinematic success." 84–108 in *Defining Cult Movies: The cultural politics of oppositional taste,* edited by Mark Jancovich, Antonio Lázaro Reboll, Julian Stringer and Andy Willis. Manchester: Manchester University Press, 2003.

Makeup Artists

Sachs, Bruce, and Russell Wall. *Greasepaint and Gore: The Hammer Monsters of Roy Ashton.* Sheffield: Tomahawk Press, 1999.

Savini, Tom. *Grand Illusions: A Learn-By-Example Guide to the Art and Technique of Special Make-Up Effects from the Films of Tom Savini.* Philadelphia, Pa.: Imagine, 1983.

Producers

Hamilton, John. *Beasts in the Cellar: The Exploitation Film Career of Tony Tenser*. Godalming, Surrey: FAB Press, 2005.

Nochimson, M. P. "Val Lewton at RKO: The Social Dimensions of Horror." *Cineaste* 31, no. 4 (2006): 9–17.

Siegel, Joel. *Val Lewton: The Reality of Terror*. London: Secker and Warburg, 1972.

Telotte, J. P. *Dreams of Darkness: Fantasy and the Films of Val Lewton*. Urbana: University of Illinois Press, 1985.

Thompson, John O. "Cat Personae: Lewton, Sequelhood, Superimposition." 85–97 in *Cinema and the Realms of Enchantment*, edited by Duncan Petrie. London: British Film Institute, 1993.

Writers

Murray, Andy. *Into the Unknown: The Fantastic Life of Nigel Kneale*. London: Headpress, 2006.

Sangster, Jimmy. *Do You Want It Good or Tuesday: From Hammer Films to Hollywood—A Life in Movies*. Baltimore, Md.: Midnight Marquee, 1997.

Wells, Paul. "Apocalypse then!: the ultimare monstrosity and strange things on the coast . . . an interview with Nigel Kneale." 48–56 in *British Science Fiction Cinema*, edited by I. Q. Hunter. London: Routledge, 1999.

REFERENCE WORKS

Hardy, Phil, ed. *The Aurum Film Encyclopedia: Horror*. London: Aurum Press, 1985.

Newman, Kim, ed. *The BFI Companion to Horror*. London: British Film Institute, 1996.

Skal, David, J. *V is for Vampire: The A–Z Guide to Everything Undead*. Harmondsworth: Penguin, 1996.

Sullivan, Jack, ed. *The Penguin Encyclopedia of Horror and the Supernatural*. Harmondsworth: Penguin, 1986.

Willis, Donald C. *Horror and Science Fiction Films: A Checklist*. Metuchen, N.J.: Scarecrow Press, 1972.

JOURNAL SPECIAL ISSUES

Journal of Popular Film and Television 27, no. 2 (1999): special issue on Vampires in Film and Television.

Post Script 15, no. 2 (1996): special issue on the films of David Cronenberg.

Post Script 21, no. 3 (2002): special issue on Realist Horror Cinema, Part I—Dimensions of the Real.

Post Script 22, no. 2 (2003): special issue on Realist Horror Cinema, Part II—Serial Killers.

Screen 27, no. 1 (1986): special issue on Body Horror.

About the Author

Peter Hutchings was born in England and obtained a B.A. in film and literature from Warwick University and a Ph.D. from the University of East Anglia. He is currently a reader in film studies at Northumbria University, Newcastle upon Tyne, Great Britain. His doctoral thesis was on the British horror film, and he has continued to undertake research both on British cinema and on the horror film as well as developing broader interests in film genres and transnational cinemas. He is the author of four monographs, *Hammer and Beyond: The British Horror Film* (1993), *Terence Fisher* (2002), *Dracula* (2003), and *The Horror Film* (2004). He also co-edited (with Joanne Hollows and Mark Jancovich) *The Film Studies Reader* (2000) and has contributed essays to numerous books, including *British Science Fiction Cinema* (ed. Ian Hunter, 1999), *British Cinema—Past and Present* (eds. Justine Ashby and Andrew Higson, 2000), *British Horror Cinema* (eds. Steve Chibnall and Julian Petley, 2001), *The British Cinema Book, 2nd edition* (ed. Robert Murphy, 2002), and *Defining Cult Movies: The Cultural Politics of Oppositional Taste* (ed. Julian Stringer et al, 2003). Reference books to which he has contributed include Kim Newman's *The BFI Companion to Horror* (1996), Brian McFarlane's *The Encyclopedia of British Film* (2003), and Robert Murphy's *Directors in British and Irish Film Cinema: A Reference Guide* (2006).

CPSIA information can be obtained at www.ICGtesting.com
Printed in the USA
LVOW091503070212

267540LV00001B/188/P